National Intelligencer
Newspaper Abstracts
1858

Joan M. Dixon

HERITAGE BOOKS
2008

HERITAGE BOOKS
AN IMPRINT OF HERITAGE BOOKS, INC.

Books, CDs, and more—Worldwide

For our listing of thousands of titles see our website
at
www.HeritageBooks.com

Published 2008 by
HERITAGE BOOKS, INC.
Publishing Division
100 Railroad Ave. #104
Westminster, Maryland 21157

Copyright © 2008 Joan M. Dixon

All rights reserved. No part of this book may be reproduced or transmitted in any form or by any means, electronic or mechanical, including photocopying, recording or by any information storage and retrieval system without written permission from the author, except for the inclusion of brief quotations in a review.

International Standard Book Numbers
Paperbound: 978-0-7884-4793-8
Clothbound: 978-0-7884-7577-1

NATIONAL INTELLIGENCER NEWSPAPER
WASHINGTON, D C
1858

TABLE OF CONTENTS

Daily National Intelligencer -Washington, D C, 1858: pg 1

Acts passed at last session of Congress just closed [Jun]: 246-247
American Medical Association: 189

Appointments by the President: See index

Appropriations made by the 35th Congress: 315-318
Army Intelligence: 97; 178; 465-466
Army Orders: 283-288
Army and Navy: 189
Atlantic Cable: 324; 467
Atlantic Telegraph: 321; 333; 340

Balt, Md: Henry Gambrill murdered Policeman Benj Benton: 414

Cadets appointed by the President: 122
Central Railroad disaster-Albany, N Y: 197
Centre Market, 1799, Pres Washington: 407
Colonization Society of Va: 153
Colt, Samuel: 9; 168
Columbia Typographical Society: 11-12
Combats with hostile Indians: 424-425

Commencements: Academy of Visitation-Gtwn: 282; 288-289
                Academy of Visitation-Wash: 291-292
                Columbian College: 194; 273
                Gtwn College: 281
                Mount Holyoke Seminary, Ohio: 291
                St John's College: 322
                St Mary's, Chas Co, Md: 349

Cornerstone of St Patrick's Cathedral, N Y: 332
Court Martial of Capt Seth M Barton: 268
Court Martial of Col E V Sumner: 120
Court Martial of Maj Gen Twiggs: 123; 300

Curiosities: 218
Cuyshoga Historical Society: 402

Death of American Seamen: 427
Death of Judge Adam Beatty: 253
Death of Col Benton: 151
Death of Michael Clear, native of Md: 147
Death of Rev Harry Croswell: 114
Death of Hon Saml Dickson: 187
Death of Mrs Sarah Flinn: 125
Death of Pierre Gentin: 81
Death of Col John F Hamtramck: 190
Death of Mr Lauriston B Hardin: 128
Death of Gen Kenton Harper: 22
Death of Col Robt Monroe Harrison: 253
Death of Rev Hugh Hamilton Holcomb: 49
Death of Cmdor Thos Ap Catesby Jones: 226
Death of Miss Eliza Leslie, authoress: 5
Death of Mrs Eliz Lee: 261
Death of Mrs James Maher: 392
Death of Gen Wm Marks: 156
Death of Gen Chas Fenton Mercer: 186; 277-278
Death of Dr Eliakin Morse: 21
Death of Rev Jacob Norton: 31
Death of Duchess of Orleans: 229
Death of Cmdor Matthew Calbraith Perry: 95-96
Death of Mrs O H Perry: 57
Death of Lt Chas Radziminski [U S Army]: 461
Death of Gen Persifer F Smith: 209
Death of Prof Henry A Washington: 88

Defeat of Col Steptoe: 298
Divorce in England: 79
Divorce of Lucius Bulkley: 182

Fauquier White Sulphur Springs for sale: 4-5
First church, Hartford: 386
First Colony in Va: 109
First white woman in Cincinnati: 369
Funeral of the Queen of Oude [Paris]: 84

Gonzaga College incorporated: See index

Heirs of Walker Reid: 56

Jennens estate: 149
Jury-Washington City: 90; 154; 167; 210; 256; 296; 305; 448-449

Kansas candidates: 28; 34

Ladies Mount Vernon Assoc for the purchase of Mount Vernon: 28; 56; 129; 169; 184; 271; 414; 455

Letters of Gen Washington: 12
Loss of new schnr Prairie Flower: 242
Loss of ship John Milton: 85
Loss of steamship Indian Empire: 443

Maryland Agricultural Society: 254; 348
Methodist Episcopal appointments: 104-106
Murder of the Francis Gouldy family, N Y: 403; 405; 431; 443
Murder of Mrs Lieure: 2

Naval intelligence: 218
Naval Officers: See index

Officers of the: Colorado: 199
                         Congress: 18
                         Fulton: 372
                         Niagara: 365
                         Preble: 394
                         San Jacinto: 341
                         Water Witch: 394
                         Westernport: 394

Ogle, Benj R, shot and killed John Webb, boy: 25; 26; 53; 62; 172; 199

Patents issued: 293-294; 470-471

Queen's message to the President [Atlantic Tel Co]: 333; 334

Railroad disaster, N Y: 301
Redemption of Va Stock: 415-417
Remains of Pres Monroe: 237; 253; 263

Sale of Piney Point, Md: 126
Signers of the Declaration of Independence: 318
Sir Houston S Stewart, Vice Admiral, R N: 217
Special Police Ofcrs, Washington: 230-233

Steamer Col Crossma disaster: 82
Steamer Eliza Battler disaster: 106
Steamer Magnolia disaster: 62
Steamer Pennsylvania disaster: 248
Steamer Sultan disaster: 142
Steamship Austria great disaster: 369-370; 373; 374; 375; 380; 401; 413
Steamship Hammonia disaster: 383
Steamship James Adger disaster: 181
Survivors of the War of 1812: 49; 254

Trial of Devlin brothers for murder of Mr Thos B Berry: 143; 269; 282
Trial of John Essex for the murder of Owen Quigley: 21; 161; 167; 210
Trial of Jas Powers for the murder of Edw A Lutts: 96; 154

Wakefield estate, Va: 184
Washington policemen: 295
Washington City tax sale: 63-75
Washington Corp-nominations by the Mayor: 270-271
West Point Academy members: 297
West Point Cadets, appointments: 122
Will of David Watkinson: 3

Yellow fever death-frig Susquehanna: 160; 165; 168-169; 176; 194; 201
Yellow fever deaths on the ship Sparkling Wave: 326

Index: pg 479

Dedicated to my cousin Edward Jos Neff,
b 1925, Wash, D C; mrd 1958, Pa
Joan Barnes, b 1932, Pa

PREFACE
Daily National Intelligencer Newspaper Abstracts
1858
Joan M Dixon

The National Intelligencer & Washington Advertiser is hereafter the Daily National Intelligencer. It was the first newspaper printed in Washington, D C; Samuel H Smith, the originator. The same was transferred to Jos Gales, jr on Aug 31, 1810; on Nov 1, 1812, the paper was under the firm of Jos Gales, sr, & Wm W Seaton. The Library of Congress has microfilm of the paper from the first issue of Oct 31, 1800 thru Jan 8, 1870, the final paper. The Evening Star Newspaper of Jan 10, 1870 reports: The Intelligencer is discontinued: the proprietor, Mr Alex Delmar, says that having lost several thousand dollars, & being in poor health, he has resolved to discontinue its publication.

Included in the abstracts are advertisements; appointments by the President; Hse o/Rep petitions; passed Acts; legal notices; marriages; deaths; mscl notices; social events; military promotions; court cases; deaths by accident; & maritime information-officers-crews. Items or events which might be a clue as to the location, age or relationship of an individual are copied.

No attempt has been made to correct the spelling. Due to the length of some articles, it was necessary to present only the highlights of same. Chancery and Equity records are copied as written.

The index contains all surnames and *tracts of lands/places*. **Maritime vessels** are found under barge, boat, brig, frig, schn'r, ship, sloop, steamboat, tugboat, yacht or vessel.

ABBREVIATIONS:

AA CO	ANNE ARUNDEL COUNTY
CMDER	COMMANDER
CMDOR	COMMODOR
ELIZ	ELIZABETH
ELIZA	ELIZA
MONTG CO	MONTGOMERY COUNTY
PG CO	PRINCE GEORGE'S CO
WASH, D C	WASHINGTON, DISTRICT OF COLUMBIA

BOOKS IN THE NATIONAL INTELLIGENCER NEWSPAPER SERIES: 1800-1805/1806-1810/1811-1813/1814-1817/1818-1820/1821-1823/1824-1826/1827-1829/1830-1831/1832-1833/1834-1835/1836-1837/1838-1839/1840/1841/1842/1843/1844/1845/1846/1847/ 1848/1849/ 1850/1851/1852/1853/1854/1855/1856/1857/1858. SPECIAL: CIVIL WAR 2 VOLS, 1861-1865

DAILY NATIONAL INTELLIGENCER NEWSPAPER
1858

FRI JAN 1, 1858
Trustee's sale of real estate on the Island, by a decree of the Circuit Court of Wash Co, D C made in the matter of Saml Lee, a lunatic: public auction on Jan 14, 1858, of parts of lots 1 & 2 in square 767, in Wash City, on 3rd st, between I & K sts south. -Peter M Pearson, trustee -Jas C McGuire, auct

The Sec of the Navy on Wed placed the U S steam-frig **Niagara** at the disposal of the Transatlantic Co to assist in a second attempt to lay down the telegraphic cable. It is presumed that the operations will be resumed sometime during the month of June.

Hon Hiram G Runnels, formerly Govn'r of Mississippi, & a Senator elect from Harris Co in the present Legislature of Texas, died at Houston on Dec 16, after a lingering illness of many months.

The Intelligencer recorded the death of Mrs Anna Maria Mason, relict of Gen John Mason, late of Cleremont, Fairfax Co, Va. She died on Nov 29, 1857. She was the daughter of Dr Jas Murray, of Annapolis, Md, & died in her 81st year. She leaves numerous descendants to mourn over her, among whom the distinguished Senator from Va is one. **Analostan Island** was once the patrimonial estate of Gen Mason & then his residence. She died in calmness, as she lived, in the belief of a better world. To live in hearts we loved is not to die.

The European papers report the death at Dresden, on Dec 3, of Christian Rauch, the great German sculptor, at age 80 years. He was born at Waldeck on Jan 1, 1777, of humble parentage, & studied art at Cassel, under an obscure master. He went to Rome & became a favorite pupil of Thorwaldsen.

Mrd: on Dec 29, by Rev Jos Aschwanden, S J, Wm G Pettit to Maria Catharine, daughter of the late Thos O N May, all of Gtwn, D C.

N H journal: a young lady, Helen M Kittredge, died at Nelson, N H; on Dec 16th. She exhibited some symptoms of typhoid fever & drank a remedy known as rum-sweat. Her mother & brother stood near to aid her. The alcohol was too much and her nervous system was completely overpowered, & her whole body was dreadfully burnt.

At Brunswick, Geo, On Dec 24, a difficulty arose between Jacob W Moore & Carey W Styles, in which Moore was killed. Moore was from Glynn Co, & Mr Styles of Brunswick. Moore was shot through the body, & died in about an hour.

Wm Ferguson, postmaster at Mottville, Mich, has been arrested for embezzling letters. It is said that his guilt is beyond question.

Orphans Court of Wash Co, D C. Letters of administration on the personal estate of John L Wirt, late of Wash Co, deceased. –Margaret R Wirt, admx

Circuit Court of Wash Co, D C-in Chancery. John A Bailey, A C Washburn & Ellen M his wife, & Frank Moore & Laura M his wife, against Mary Curtis, Geo Curtis, Susan Edgerton, Robt F Hunter, Curtis Fowler, Stephen B Fowler, Susan H Fowler, Frances D Fowler, Gilbert & Mary his wife, the widow & heirs of Edw Curtis, deceased, & the several children [whose names are unknown] of his brother, Jos W Curtis, deceased, other of the heirs-at-law of said Edw Curtis & David A Ball. In 1850 the cmplnts were the owners of square 571 in Wash City; said Hall was their agent & atty, having charge of the same for them, with authority to sell the same; in Sep, 1850, he represented to the cmplnts that he had sold the same to said Edw Curtis, & they, believing the same to be right, confirmed the same & executed said deed to said Curtis for said square; that they have recently discovered that at the time of said pretended sale to said Curtis it was understood & agreed between him & said Hall that the latter was to be half interested in said square or in the proceeds thereof whenever afterwards resold; that said Laura M Moore was a minor at the time she executed her said deed; that said Edw Curtis hath departed this life, leaving the said dfndnts above named, [except said Hall] his widow, & heirs-at-law, to whom the said agreement between said Hall & their ancestor in relation to the division of said square or the proceeds or profits thereof is well known; that said heirs & said Hall have recently offered said square or their interests therein for sale; & the said bill charges that the said sale of square 571 was a fraud upon them; & the object of the bill is to have the same & the said deeds set aside & declared void, the cmplnts offering to return the purchase money which was paid them & interest thereon & the taxes since paid; & forasmuch as all the dfndnts above named [except said Hall] & the other heirs of said Edw Curtis, unknown to cmplnts, reside out of this District of Columbia, it is ordered that the absent dfndnts appear in the ofc of the Clerk of the said Court, on the first Mon of May, 1858. –Jno A Smith, clerk

MON JAN 4, 1858
Mr John Abel, a clerk in the employ of J B McCreary & Co, Jeanesville, Pa, died on Dec 27, from the bite of a cat 10 weeks before. On Dec 26th he took to his bed, & suffered intense agony. Medical skill proved of no avail.

Shocking tragedy in the neighborhood of Sandy Spring, Montg Co, Md, on Thu last. Geo Lieure, residing near that place with his wife, cut her throat in a fit of desperation & then attempted to commit suicide by cutting his own, inflicting a dreadful wound in the jugular. The woman died immediately, but the man was still alive, though he will probably die. It is said the parties lived very unhappily together.

Orphans Court of Wash Co, D C. Letters of administration on the personal estate of Thos Barnes, late of Wash Co, deceased. –Thos Welsh, adm

Jos E Birch was found not guilty of the murder of Eugene Lanahan

The will of the late David Watkinson, of Hartford, Conn, covers upwards of 100 pages of manuscript. The Hartford Times says the property left by him is estimated at about half a million of dollars. Among the bequest: his nephews & nieces, 30 in number, each $10,000. For the purpose of establishing, in connexion with the Conn Historical Society, a Library of Reference, to be accessible at all seasonable hours & times to all citizens & other residents & visiters in the State of Conn: $100,000. To establish a Juvenile Asylum & Farm School, 10 acres of land, known as the Pavilion property, valued at $40,000 & $20,000 in cash. To the Hartford Hospital: $40,000. For support of indigent orphan children, or the children of indigent parents, in connexion with the Hartford Orphan Asylum & the Female Beneficent Society: $30,000. To establish a Refuse in or near Hartford, where discharged criminals may be advised, assisted, & put in the way of supporting themselves: $5,000. To the Widows' Society of Hartford: $5,000. To the Retreat for the Insane, Hartford: $3,000. To the Wadsworth Atheneum, Hartford: $1,000. To the Young Men's Institute, Hartford: $1,000. To the Dissenting church of Lavenham Co, of Suffolk, England, where his parents lived, one hundred pounds sterling: $500. American Homes Missionary Society: $500. American Board of Com'rs: $500. American Bible Society: $500. American Tract Society: $500. American Sunday School Union: $500.

TUE JAN 5, 1858
House of Reps: 1-Resolved, that Lewis Benedict have permission to withdraw his papers from the files of the Clerk's ofc, for the purpose of filing them in the Indian ofc. 2-Bill for the relief of John N Dobbin, late a purser in the U S navy. 3-Bill to grant bounty land to the ofcrs & soldiers of Capt Jos H Burk's & Wm D Alexander's companies of Merriwether Co volunteers. 4-Bill for the relief of the heirs & legal reps of Pierre Broussard, deceased. 5-Bill for the relief of John W Chevis, of Louisiana. 6-Bill for the relief of Wm Kingsbury, of Ohio. 7-Bill granting to the ofcrs, musicians, & privates of Capt Jos Quigley's company of Ohio militia, in the war of 1812, each 160 acres of land. 8-Bill for the relief of Richd B Alexander, late a major in the first Tenn regt, Mexican war. 9-Bill for the relief of Saml Winn, the only surviving child or Richd Winn, a Revolutionary ofcr. 10-Bill for the relief of Jesse W Page, sr, of the State of Tenn. 11-Bill granting a pension to Mary A M Jones. 12-Bill for the relief of Benj Sayre. 13-Memorial of Capt Henry W Wharton was referred to the Cmte on Military Affairs.

Jas B T Benjamin was accidentally killed at New Haven on Jan 1st. Whilst running with an engine he slipped upon the ice, & in the effort to recover himself the neap of the engine swayed round, which brought the end of a break against Benjamin's back, just above the hip. He died in a few minutes. He was an intelligent & worthy young man.

N Y murders in 1857. The Police Gazette publishes a list of 60 murders which have been committed in N Y since Jan 1, 1857. One execution has taken place, that of the colored man Dorsey. Three persons convicted of capital crimes are now under sentence of death: Michl Cancemi, for the murder of policeman Anderson; Jas Rogers, for the murder of John Swansey; & Jas Shepherd, for arson in the 1st degree.

Senate: 1-Memorial from Nicholas D P Maillard, a citizen of the U S, now residing in Liverpool, England, asking redress for wrong & violence committed against him by a mob in Ireland. [He sets forth that in Apr, 1857, he became the purchaser of a large number of cattle sold at auction in Queen's Co, Ireland, & that when he sent for the cattle, for which he had previously paid, his men were resisted by a violent mob, armed with bludgeons, & that he was unable to procure necessary protection from the Irish authorities.] 2-Memorial from J M Morrill, in behalf of the Bangor City Greys, asking that said company may be allowed bounty land. 3-Memorial from J D Dutton, Jared Smith, John Taylor, & several other citizens of New Sharon, Maine, asking an enactment of a law more effectually to enforce the provision of the Constitution in relation to the recovery of fugitive slaves. 4-Ptn from Mrs Mary Walbach, widow of the late Gen J B Walbach, asking to be placed on the pension roll. 5-Cmte on Private Land Claims: bill to confirm the title of Henry Volcker to a certain tract of land in the Territory of New Mexico. Same cmte: bill for the relief of John R Temple. 6-Bill for the relief of Michl Kinney, late a private on Co I, 8th regt U S army: introduced. 7-Bill for the relief of Manuel Lisa, A Joachim Lisa, & others, to provide for the location of certain informal private land claims. 8-Bill for the relief of Alex'r J Atocha: brief discussion: passed over. 9-Bill for the relief of Geo P Marsh: passed.

John Welch, at Ellenville, N Y, was shockingly & fearfully burnt, a few evenings ago, by the explosion of a lamp he was carrying in his hands.

Mrd: on Dec 28, at the residence of Dr Williamson P Fisher, Chicago, by Rev Dr Butler, B I Semmes, [of the law firm of Hooper, Ayer & Semmes,] to Sallie F Reynolds, of Ky.

Trenton, N J, Jan 4. Jas P Donnelly, who is sentenced to be executed on Jan 8, escaped from Monmouth Co jail last night, but was re-arrested early this morning. [Jan 9th newspaper: Donnelly was hung today at 2 o'clock at Freehold, N J. He made a speech of upwards of 2 hours' duration, & declaring his innocence of the crime. An immense concourse was present. The body of the deceased was taken to N Y by his friends. Dr Cumming administered religious consolation to the dying man.]

Mrd: on Jan 2, by Rev Andrew G Carothers, Danl Murphy to Emily Cavenaugh, both of Wash City.

Fauquier White Sulphur Springs for sale: under deed of trust executed by Thos Green, dated Mar 24, 1854, of record in Fauquier Co, which deed contains the following provisions, to wit: that if default shall be made by the said Thos Green, his heirs, or executors in the payment of the bonds aforesaid, or of any part thereof, then & in that case the said trustee, or the survivor of them, shall or may proceed to sell the whole of said real & personal estate, or so much thereof as they may in their discretion deem sufficient, to pay off & discharge the sum or sums of money then due on account of said default, or to pay off & discharge the whole debt & costs, if the said trustees deem it best to make such entire sale; & the said Thos Green shall have the right to make sale of the whole or of any part of said real or personal property, by & with the consent only of said trustees, given in writing, & upon condition that the proceeds of said sale shall be

applied, under the knowledge & by the consent of the said trustees, in the purchase of other personal property in substitution of that sold, to be held subject to this trust in like manner as the original, or shall be paid over, together with the money for the real estate so sold, to said trustees on account of the said bonds. Subject to these modifications & stipulations, the said B H Shackelford & Isham Keith, or the survivor of them, shall proceed, in the execution of this deed of trust, according to the requirements & directions of the Code of Va upon the subject of trust deed, section 6, title 3, & chapter 117-the undersigned trustees therein mentioned, in pursuance of the terms thereof & for the payment of the sum of $20,000, with interest, after the rate of 6% per annum, from Dec 15, 1853, will, on Feb 26, 1858, offer for sale at public auction, for cash, the springs, hotel bldgs, & also 65 acres of ground attached, including the Mineral Spring, gardens, & out-houses, which 65 acres has been laid off from the residue of the tract by survey recently made by Thos Green. If this sale is not sufficient to pay the aforesaid sum of money & interest, the undersigned will then proceed to sell, at the same time & place & on the same terms, the furniture of said hotel & bldgs & other personal property included in said deed of trust, consisting in part of stock & farming utensils. It this is not sufficient, then the undersigned will proceed to sell that portion of said springs tract of land which lies north of the river, supposed to contain about 300 acres.
–Isham Keith, B H Shackelford, trustees

WED JAN 6, 1858
Miss Eliza Leslie, whose name is verily a household word in American homes, died on Sat last at Gloucester city, N J. She was born in Nov, 1787, & fulfilled the three-score & ten of human life. She was a Philadelphian by birth, but her parents were Scotch, & emigrated to America in 1745. Among her books were "Mrs Washington Potts," "Amelia, or a Young lady's Vicissitudes," & lastly, in 1853, "The Behavior Book." Miss Leslie has a brother living in England, Chas R Leslie, of the Royal Academy; & another brother is Maj Thos J Leslie, U S Army. [*1745 has been scratched over by hand, & this is what it appears to be.]

Hon David Stewart died at his residence in Balt yesterday. He was a prominent member of the Balt bar, & formerly for a brief period a Senator in Congress from Md under Executive appointment.

The U S ship **Saratoga**, Capt Chatard, reported in Hampton Roads on Fri from Greytown, came up on Sat & anchored at the naval anchorage. She has on board the returned filibusters of Walker's army. Lt Edw R Byles, one of Walker's ofcrs, has been arrested on a warrant from the Mayor of this city, issued upon the oath of F B Miller, that he is guilty of a larceny committed while in the employment of Haskins & Heiskill, of Phil, to the amount of $10,000. He is now in prison awaiting a requisition from the Executive of Pa. –Norfolk Herald

Orphans Court of Wash Co, D C. Letters of administration on the personal estate of Kitty E A Gassaway, late of Wash Co, deceased. –Henry A Barron, adm

Senate: 1-Ptn from the heirs of Col Wm Washington, of Gen Wm Moultrie, of Jas Hamilton, & numerous other heirs & reps of Revolutionary ofcrs, urging a settlement of their claims to half-pay: referred. 2-Ptn from Jas A Black, special agent of the State of S C, asking that said State may be refunded certain sums of money expended in the common defence of the U S A. 3-Ptn from W P Wright & other members of Capt Walker's company of infty of the Kansas militia, called out by order of Gov Geary, asking to be allowed bounty land. 4-Ptn from Horace B Sawyer, asking to be allowed the difference between the furlough & leave of absence pay. 5-Ptn from the heirs of Capt Thos Stevens & of Capt Absalom Foot, of the Conn line of troops in the Revolutionary war, asking to be allowed the pension to which their ancestors were entitled. 6-Ptn from Wm Moss, asking compensation for carrying the mail from Wash, Ark, to Clarkesville, Texas. 7-Ptn from the heirs of Noah Warriner, a Revolutionary soldier, asking to be allowed the pension to which he was entitled. 8-Cmte on Foreign Relations: memorial of Nicholas D P Maillard.

The New <u>Conservatory</u> attached to the Pres' Mansion is said to be the largest in the U S, & will contain a variety of native & exotic shrubs & flowering plants. The bldg is in the shape of the letter L. Much is due to the skill & perserverance of Mr John Watt, the principal gardener for some 6 or 7 years past.

Criminal Court-Wash-yesterday. 1-Wm H Mangum was acquitted of a charge of larceny. 2-Isaac Lambert was found guilty of grand larceny in stealing clothing, & sentenced to 6 months' imprisonment. 3-Jas Aldridge was found guilty of petty larceny, & sentenced to 6 months' imprisonment.

Norfolk, Jan 5. Walker's men were discharged from the U S ship **Saratoga** today by orders from Washington. Many of them are wandering about the city in a destitute condition, without money & poorly clad.

Orphans Court of Wash Co, D C. Letters of administration on the personal estate of Kitty E A Gassaway, late of Wash Co, deceased. –Henry A Barron, adm

Circuit Court of Wash Co, D C-in Chancery. Edw M Linthicum vs John C McChesney, Saml McChesney, Louis McChesney, Henry N Myers & Eliza Myers his wife, heirs at law of David McChesney, deceased, & Eliz Long, Anna M Long, Richd Long, & Wm Long, children & heirs at law of Mary Long, deceased, who was one of the heirs of said David McChesney. The bill states that David McChesney, late of said District, deceased, being on Jul 17, 1832, indebted to the cmplnt in the sum of $957.39, on 2 promissory notes, payable one in 8 & the other in 12 months from said date, with interest, in order to secure the payment of said debt, & all other debts he might subsequently contract with & owe to the cmplnt, by his deed, dated the day & year aforesaid, did grant & convey unto Otho M Linthicum, his heirs & assigns, the southern half part of lot 190 in Thos Beall's addition to Gtwn, in said District, with one-half of the coach-house erected on said entire lot, in trust, if said David failed to pay said notes when due, or any other debt he might afterwards owe to the cmplnt, to sell the said premises in the manner & on the terms set forth in said deed, & apply the proceeds of such sale, after satisfying the expenses of said

trust, to the cmplnt's said debt, & any other debt that might be owing from said David to the cmplnt; &, further, from the date of said deed until such sale, or payment of said debts, to rent the said property & apply the proceeds to pay taxes & charges on the said property, & the residue to the debt due the cmplnt. The bill states that said David was at the time of his death indebted to the cmplnt in the further sum of $228.32 for the like sum paid by cmplnt to one David English, at the instance & request of said David McChesney; that said premises have been continuously under rent, but the proceeds were not sufficient to pay the taxes on the premises & keep down the interest on the said notes; that the said original debt of $957.39, & also the subsequent debt of $228.32, are both still owing & unpaid, with an arrear of interest thereon; that said David McChesney died intestate, leaving 5 children, his heirs at law, namely, John C McChesney, Saml McChesney, Louis F McChesney, Eliza Myers, the wife of Henry N Myers, & Mary Long, who has since died, leaving 4 children, her heirs at law, namely, Eliz Long, Anna M Long, Richd Long & Wm Long, all of whom reside in the State of Ky, & beyond the reach of the process of said Court; the said named descendants of the said David McChesney are made dfndnts to said bill. The bill further states that Otho M Linthicum, the trustee, is dead, leaving the trusts therein mentioned unexecuted; that 2 out of 4 of his heirs at law are minors, & are incapable of executing the same. The object of the said bill is to obtain a decree for the appointment of a new trustee in the place of the said Otho M Linthicum, & a sale of the said mortgaged premises, for the payment of the debts aforesaid due to cmplnt, with the arrear of interest thereon. Said absent dfndnts are to appear at the Clerk's ofc on the first Monday of May next.
–Jas J Morsell -Jno A Smith, clerk

THU JAN 7, 1858
Firemen, machinists, & others are informed that the subscriber is manufacturing at his Factory, 33 South Eutaw st, Balt, near the Camden Station, leather hose & belting, & copper rivets. –John H Haskell.

By authority of a deed of trust, regularly executed by Thos H Havenner & Mary Cornelia his wife, recorded in Calhoun Co, Va, I shall, at my auction house, in Wash City, sell at public auction, for cash, the tract of land conveyed to me in said deed, it being a moiety of a tract of 1,000 acres of land in said county & State of Va, on the west fork of Little Kanawha river, it being a moiety of the tract of land conveyed by Norval Wilson & Cornelia S Wilson his wife, to Thos H Havenner & Edmund H Wilson, by deed dated Oct 4, 1852, recorded in Gilmer Co, Va. The title to this land is believed to be indisputable, but, acting as trustee, I shall convey only the title vested in me. –S S Baxter, trustee -Jas C McGuire, auct

Villa Estate for sale: charming residence in the State of N Y, surrounded by about 80 acres of fertile lands. Saratoga, Albany, & Troy are easily accessible by a railroad now partially constructed in the city of Albany. The house can be shut up & left during the winter months in perfect safety. More land can be purchased if desired. Apply to Judge Neale, Alexandria, Va.

Senate: 1-Ptn from Thos G Clinton, of the District of Columbia, urging an increase of the salary of the Pres of the U S; & suggesting that $1,000 from every State & Territory & for the District of Columbia would only be a very reasonable salary for that ofc. 2-Ptn from Robt Carter, Passed Assist Surgeon in the U S Navy, asking the difference of pay between Assist Surgeon & Passed Assist Surgeon from the time at which he was entitled to his examination to the time when actually examined. 3-Ptn from Jos Reynes, asking to be confirmed in his title to certain lands in the State of Louisiana, claimed under a Spanish grant, & to be indemnified for such lands in said grant as may have been sold by the U S. 4-Ptn from Camille St Armant & others, asking that certain entries of lands made by then in Louisiana may be confirmed. 5-Ptn from the widow of Maj Chas H Larnard, late of the U S army, asking to be allowed a pension. 6-Ptn from the 4 children of Polly Colgrere, asking authority to locate or assign a land warrant to which their mother was entitled. 7-Ptn from the widow of Chas S Merchant, late of the army, asking to be allowed a pension. 8-Ptn from Wm G Hansell, Wm H Underwood, & the exec of Saml Rockwell, asking compensation for services in negotiating the treaty of 1835 with the Cherokee Indians. 9-Ptn from Edwin M Chaffee, asking an extension of his patent for preparing India rubber without the use of solvent. 10-Ptn from J W Sullivan, asking indemnity for losses sustained in consequence of the repeated failure of the mail between New Orleans & San Francisco. 11-Cmte on the Post Ofc & Post Roads: memorial of Wm S Mundy, Knox Walker, & others, of the Legislature of Tenn, asking for protection to the overland mail route through the Territory of Arizona: asked to be discharged from the consideration of the ptn & that it be referred to the Cmte on Territories, which was agreed to. 12-Cmte on Military Affairs: asked to be discharged from the consideration of the memorial of Jas Hudgens, of Ga, & that it be referred to the Cmte on Revolutionary Claims; referred to the Cmte on Pensions. Same cmte: asked to be discharged from the consideration of the memorial of the heirs of John Champe, of Lee's legion of cavalry in the Revolutionary war, & that it be referred to the Cmte on Revolutionary Claims, which was agreed to.

On Friday 5 boys were skating on Cedar Swamp Pond, in Milford, Mass, when the ice gave way & they fell into the water. Michl Griffin & John Curtin were drowned.

Mrd: on Jan 5, by Rev B N Brown, Mr Saml Dohnar, of Gtwn, to Miss Clara Cunlberg, of Wash.

Died: on Jan 6, in Wash City, Josephine, 2nd daughter of Michl Sardo, & beloved wife of Alex'r B McFarlan, of Wash City, in her 53rd year. Her illness was protracted. Her funeral is today from her late residence, H & 10th sts. [No time given.]

Died: on Dec 2, in Tunis, Barbary, in her 66th year, after a long & painful illness, Mrs Margaret Heap, widow of the late Dr S D Heap, for many years Consul of the U S for the city & kingdom of Tunis, & sister of the late Cmdor David Porter.

Died: on Jan 6, in Wash City, Alice C, daughter of J C & M McKelden, aged 2 years & 8 months. Her funeral is today at 2½ o'clock, from the residence of her father, 416 F st.

Died: on Jan 4, in Gettysburg, Pa, John B McPherson, in his 69th year. At the time of his decease he was cashier of the Bank of Gettysburg, a post he has held since the organization of the bank in 1815. His health has been feeble for some time, & he sank gradually & peacefully to his rest, leaving a reputation behind him which is a pleasant inheritance to his children. –Adams Sentinel

Wash Corp: 1-Cmte of Claims: bill for the relief of Dr John M Roberts & Dr Thos Miller: passed.

Firemen, machinists, & others are informed that the subscriber is manufacturing at his Factory, 33 South Eutaw st, Balt, near the Camden Station, leather hose & belting, & copper rivets. –John H Haskell.

Orphans Court of Wash Co, D C. Letters of administration de bonis on on the personal estate of Oliver Whittlesey, late of Wash Co, deceased. –Wm A Whittlesey, adm d b n

FRI JAN 8, 1858
Dr Isaac Spangler, an old & much respected citizen of Zanesville, Ohio, was killed instantly at that place on New Year's Day, by the carelessness of some boys in firing a small cannon loaded with slugs. The Doctor was aged about 55 years, & leaves wife & 2 children, besides a large circle of patrons & acquaintances to mourn his loss.

Senate: 1-Memorial from Saml Colt urging upon Congress an extension of his patent for an improvement in fire-arms. [He shows he assigned his original patent in 1836 as the only means of introducing his invention to the public; that he never received any benefit from it for 14 years, but experienced a very heavy loss of time & money; that he did not recover legal rights until 1850, under an extension granted for 7 years.] 2-Ptn from H D B Hennon, a soldier in the late war with Great Britian, setting forth the helpless condition of many of the old soldiers of the war of 1812, & urging upon Congress to grant a pension to himself & all other survivors of that war. 3-Memorial from Jos Hardy & Alton Long, asking that certain rents collected by agents of the U S, for working of mines not the property of the U S, may be returned to them. 4-Memorial from Chas Fairbanks & others, asking an extension of the patent laws. 5-Cmte on Public Lands: asked to be discharged from the consideration of the memorial of Craton W Brant, asking to be allowed bounty land for his services as a mechanic during the war with Mexico; & the memorial of Wm Smith, a teamster, for bounty land, in consideration of services in said war; which was agreed to.

Ninety-five persons died in Providence last year who were 70 years of age & upwards. Patrick Donnelly, a native of Ireland, was the oldest, & he attained the age of 103 years.

Richmond, Va, Jan 7. Wm H Clowes, formerly identified with the pro-slavery men in Kansas, who subsequently served under Walker in Nicaragua, & was afterwards connected with the Memphis Bulletin, committed suicide here last night by means of laudanum.

Criminal Court-Wash-Wed. 1-Wm Ewing was convicted of burglary on the house of Geo W Appleby, & sentenced to 4 years in the penitentiary. 2-Lewis Carr, colored, was convicted of petty larceny, & sentenced to 6 months in jail. 3-Caleb Batson & John Holley, both colored, were convicted of grand larceny, & sentenced each to 2 years in the penitentiary. 4-Geo Gaines, colored, was convicted of grand larceny, & sentenced to 1 year in the penitentiary. 5-Jacob W Powers, convicted of assault & battery with intent to kill at the same affray in which Geo Krouse was concerned as below, & the motion for a new trial of whom the Court overruled, has been sentenced to 3 years in the penitentiary, to take place on Jan 20. 6-Wm Patterson, colored, guilty of petty larceny, & sentenced to 9 months in jail. 7-Archibald McLeese was found not guilty for an assault on police ofcr McHenry. 8-Geo Krouse, some time since convicted of assault & battery with intent to kill one Hilliary at Rupple's tavern, in Gtwn, in Feb last, was sentenced to 5 years in the penitentiary, to take place from & after Jan 14. 9-Benj McGraw, convicted on Dec 4 of riot, was sentenced to 6 months in jail & pay a fine of $20 & costs.

Died: on Jan 6, Charles Soule, child of Edmund F & Margaret A French, aged 4 months & 10 days. His funeral is on Fri at 3 o'clock.

Norfolk, Jan 7. The U S sloop-of-war **Cyane** arrived at the naval anchorage this evening, 27 days from Port au Prince, via Havana. The ofcrs were all well, but 14 of the crew were on the sick list. She brought from Cape Haytien Capt Mayo, of the brig **R W Packer**, who had been imprisoned there, & the remains of Passed Midshipman Brodhead from Port au Prince. No accident or death had occurred on board for 22 months. The **Cyane** left the Spanish squadron at Havana. 300 men had died on board one of the Spanish ships of war of the fever. Considerable fever still existed at Havana. The yellow fever was also raging at Port au Prince, especially among the shipping.

SAT JAN 9, 1858
Talcott Burr, jr, Editor of the Wilmington [N C] Herald, died there on Jan 5, in his 39th year. His contemporaries render him the tribute due to a well spent life, & to the qualities which adorned his social career-filial duty & love, paternal affection & unselfish heart.

To Be Executed. Jas Eldredge, the schoolmaster who murdered Sarah Jane Gould, in Louisville, St Lawrence Co, N Y, in May last, has just been convicted & sentenced to be hung on Feb 11.

Excellent household & kitchen furniture at auction on Jan 14, at the residence of Chas W Pairo, corner of Prospect & Fred'k sts, Gtwn, D C. –Sam C Edes, trustee
-Jas C McGuire, auct

The Govn'r of Pa has issued warrants for the execution of the McKeesport murderers, [Henry Fife & Charlotte Jones,] to take place on Feb 12, 1858; also of Monroe Stewart, [who, by the confession of Charlotte Jones, is exonerated from complicity in the murder,] to take place a fortnight after.

Wm Brown, brother of the Postmaster General, was shot on Sat week, at his residence in Giles Co, Miss, but by whom is unknown. Mr Brown, though wounded in the face & head, is not fatally injured, notwithstanding the assassin took 2 fires at him.

The Columbia Typographical Society having determined to celebrate their 43rd Anniversary, & honor the birthday of Franklin, will give a Ball on Jan 18, 1858, at Odd Fellow' Hall, 7th st. No hats or caps will be allowed in the room. Refreshments will be furnished the Ladies, under the supervision of U H Ridenour, Confectioner. Prosperi's String Band is engaged. The Ball will be opened at 9 o'clock by a Grand Promenade.

Managers at Large:
Jos Gales
Hon W W Seaton
Hon Peter Force
R C Weightman
A O P Nicholson
Hon H King
Jacob Gideon
G W Bowman
S C Stambaugh
A D Banks
W W Moore
Maj J P Heiss
Maj Thos Donoho
Hon W A Harris
C Wendell
John C Rives

Ferd Jefferson
Wm Woodward
Jas F Halliday
C W C Dunnington
Geo S Gideon
W D Wallach
Ben Perley Poore
John Dowling
A B Claxton
Jas English
Wm Towers
Capt L Towers
F McNerhany
Joshua T Taylor
E B Robinson
Capt Jos B Tait

Jos W Davis
Geo W Cochran
C Alexander
Henry Polkinhorn
Theo Barnard
Wm H Moore
Robt Waters
John Trenholm
Martin Buell
Wm Blanchard
John Larcombe
Thos Devaughn
Geo Whittington
Henry Walker
Geo Gregory

Executive Cmte:
Wm R McLean
Chas Schell
Wm L Jones
Wm E Morcoe
P Hefferman

Chas B Hough
Com P Brown
Jesse J Judge
John H Thorn
Thos Rich

H S Bowen
M Caton
Wm M Belt
J C Franzoni

Reception Cmte [White Rosette.]
J P Cogswell
A J Robinson
John Cunningham
H F Barnard
Geo Caton
J C C Whaley
W M C Breggeman
Chas E Orme
John J Johnson
A J Appleby
W S Miles
Robt Penman

B C Wright
Thos Caton
W H Snyder
Jos D Harris
F J Waters
E H Edmonston
Jas Charles
Jas D Chedell
Milton Clarke
Jos Mattingly
Chas J Canfield
Saml Murphy

Jos Hamacher
C E Leves
F Glenroy
C D McPherson
G W Rock
C A Helm
E S Cropley
G A R McNeir
Joel S Brown
G W Hall
John McIntire
F Dorsett

Floor Managers [Red Rosette.]

Wm L Jones	Wm M Belt	Saml P Robertson
F M Detwiler	Chas Schell	Saml E Culverwell

Tickets, admitting a gentleman & ladies, $2; to be obtained of any member of the Executive Cmte, & at the door on the evening of the Ball.

Land Warrant, No 1,353, for 120 acres, issued in the name of Mary Ann Van Ness, was mailed by us on Jul 15, 1857, to A Brawley, register of land ofcr at Stevens' Point, Wisc, the said warrant has not been received by him, & has never been assigned by the warrantee. We have filed a caveat in the General Land Ofc to prevent the issuing of a patent of the same, & will in due time apply to the Pension Ofc for the issuance of a duplicate certificate. –M Snyder & Son, Bankers, Wash, D C

Suit for the recovery of letters of Gen Washington. In the N Y Supreme Court on Jan 4, before Judge Davies. Wilson Eyre & Louisa Lincoln Lear Eyre, his wife, vs Edw Y Higbee & wife. This was an action to recover possession of a large number of letters, written by Gen Washington to Col Tobias Lear, who was Washington's private & military secretary for many years, & a member of his household. This gentleman died intestate at Washington in 1816, leaving a widow, Frances D Lear, & a son, Benj Lincoln Lear, who was his sole heir. This son died in 1832, leaving a will made in ignorance that he would have issue. But his wife gave birth to a daughter after his decease, being his heir at law & one of the plntfs in the suit. The letters remained in possession of Benj Lear from the time of his father's death until his own death, when they, as alleged, were taken possession of by Mrs Higbee, under the following circumstances: The widow of Tobias Lear, shortly before her death, directed Mrs Higbee to take the letters, which were bound in a large volume, & send them to Mrs Mason, mother of Senator Mason, of Va, with a letter expressing the desire of Mrs Lear that they should be held subject to the directions of Mr Richd Rush, of Phil, & that he should use the letters in whatever way he deemed proper, in the way of their publication, & to eventually arrange for their presentation to the State of Va; & also suggested that Senator Mason would be the proper channel through which the presentation should be made. Is is now alleged by the plntf that Mrs Higbee took away the volume & has kept it ever since, without carrying into effect the request of Mrs Lear. In April last Louisa Lincoln Lear Eyre, the posthumous child already referred to as being one of the plntfs, took out letters of administration upon the estate of her grandfather, Tobias Lear, in order to recover these letters. The case came up on court on demurrer, the principal points of which were that the right of Mrs Eyre to letters of administration to the estate of Tobias Lear had expired, 40 years having passed since the death of the intestate, & that the letters are not such property as could be made the subject of this sort of action. The letters were mostly written in 1790 & 1799, & treated of foreign & home politics, appointments to office, & addresses to Congress. Counsel for dfndnts stated that they were willing to present the letters to the State of Va, in accordance with the wishes of Mrs Lear. Decision reversed.

Persons wishing to purchase Sewing Machines, of the undersigned, will apply to Messrs Wall, Stephens & Co, our only agent for Wash & Alexandria. –J M Singer & Co

Nicholas Longworth, the Cincinnati millionaire, best known for his native-American wines, celebrated his 50th anniversary of his marriage on Christmas eve by a splendid golden wedding, at which every person who officiated at his marriage was present save one. The family pastor pronounced an appropriate prayer, & the ring of the golden wedding was placed upon the hand of the bride by the great-grandchild of the loving pair.

MON JAN 11, 1858
At N Y, on Thu, 2 men, Edw Kennedy & Michl Casey, got into an altercation with Special Deputy Sheriff Michl Wogan, when the latter shot both of them. Casey died soon after being shot, & Kennedy is mortally wounded.

Appointments by the Pres: Collectors of the Customs:
Thos Cunningham, Wiscasset, Maine, vice Babson
Jos Berry, Bath, Maine, vice Bodfish
Dudley F Leavitt, Bangor, vice Sewell
John H Kennedy, Waldoborough, vice Wilson
Amos F Parlin, Machias, vice Droman
Arthur W Austin, Boston, vice Peaslee
Moses Macdonald, Portland, vice Carter, jr.

N Y C, Jan 9. Judge Ingraham has granted a stay of proceedings in the case of Jas Rogers, convicted of the murder of John *Swanson. [Oct 4th newspaper: At N Y, on Sat, in the Supreme Court, Jas Rodgers, the boy who murdered John *Swanston, was ordered to be executed on Nov 12 next. The Supreme Court has issued its warrant commanding the sheriff to cause Rodgers to be hanged on Nov 12 next. *Note the 2 spellings.]

Died: on Jan 9, Elizabeth, youngest daughter of Augustus E & Mary Jane Perry, aged 11 months & 21 days.

Died: on Jan 9, in Wash City, after a short but painful illness, B Franklin Walmsley, in his 29th year, a native of Balt, Md, but for the last 3 years a resident of Phil. His funeral is this afternoon at 3 o'clock. May he rest in peace!

Criminal Court-Wash-Sat: 1-Trial of Benj Woods for the murder of a colored man, Saml Brown, in Sept last. Jury returned a verdict of manslaughter. [Jan 13th newspaper: Benj Wood was sentenced to 8 years in the penitentiary.]

Orphans Court of Wash Co, D C. Letters testamentary on the personal estate of Mary A Deigenhart, late of Wash Co, deceased. –John Robinson, exc

$100 reward for runaway negro woman, Daphne Gustis, about 30 years old.
-Wm J Belt, living near Huntingtown, Calvert Co, Md.

TUE JAN 12, 1858
Positive sale of liquors, brandies, wines & cigars at auction, on Jan 18, at the store of Mr J Patterson, 86 4½ st, near Md ave. –Wall & Barnard, aucts

Rev John Knox, D D, senior pastor of the Collegiate Dutch Church of N Y, died in that city on Friday night from the effects of a fall, a day or 2 previous, by which he received a severe injury on his head. He was 68 years old, & had been for many years one of the pastors of the old Collegiate Dutch Church, & was much beloved.

Orphans Court of Wash Co, D C. Letters of administration on the personal estate of Richd G Briscoe, late of Wash Co, deceased. –E C Morgan, adm

Senate: 1-Ptn from Christian Hanen, asking the establishment of an ocean mail route between N Y & Gluckstadt, on the Elbe, via Plymouth & Roterdam, & offering proposals for carrying the mails between those places. 2-Ptn from Jane M McCralh, widow of a quartermaster in the navy, asking compensation for certain services rendered by her husband in the Florida war. 3-Ptn from Wm D Moseley, asking to be released from a contract for furnishing live oak for the bldg of a sloop-of-war assumed by him as surety, but which he is unable to complete. 4-Ptn from Ebenezer Higgins, a soldier in the last war with Great Britain, asking to be placed on the pension roll. 5-Ptn from Benj Ward, a privateersman in the last war with England, asking that pensions may be allowed to all those who were imprisoned at Dartmoor. 6-Ptn from Saml Jas Ignatius Lucus, & others, asking compensation for day services as day watchmen in the Navy Dept. 7-Ptn from Edw P Collum, an assist surgeon in the army, asking remuneration for losses in consequence of shipwreck while traveling under orders. 8-Additional papers in relation to the claim of Jervis M Barker: submitted. 9-Cmte on Indian Affairs: bill for the relief of Wm B Trotter.

Edwin Saunders, a promising young man of about 19 years, son of Geo Saunders, of Orland, Me, while on a gunning excursion with Chas Durham, of the same town, last week, was shot accidentally-they having separated, & mistaking him, in the bushes, for a deer which they were in pursuit of. He lived through the night, but they were unable to get him home before he expired.

Land Warrants lost: application will be made to the Com'r of Pensions for the issues of a duplicate of Land Warrant No 47,206 for 80 acres, issued to John O'Neal, & No 47,207 for 80 acres, issued to Asa O'Neale, under the act of Mar 3, 1855, the same having been lost in being transmitted to Jas G Austin, deceased, late of Wash, D C, & caveats entered against their location. –John S Burrus, Atty for Warrantees, Middletown, N C, Jan 8.

I certify that Wm J Johnson, of Wash Co, brought before me as a stray a light bay mare. –D Rowland, J P Owner is to prove property, pay charges, & take her away. –Wm J Johnson, 5th st, between N & O, Island.

Mrd: on Dec 16, in Omaha City, Nebraska Territory, at the residence of the bride's father, A L King, formerly of Nashville, Tenn, to Miss Gertie Clarke, late of Wash, D C.

Mrd: on Jan 5, at Palmyra, N Y, by Rev Dr Daggett, of Canandaigua, N Y, John Albert Granger, jr, of Canandaigua, to Annie J Townsend, daughter of Edwin D Townsend, of Palmyra.

Died: on Jan 8, at Chicago, Ill, of typhoid fever, in his 28th year, Dr John C Morfit. He was a native of this city, & resided here during the earlier portion of his life.

Died: on Dec 18, at Balt, Md, Elenora C, in her 19th year, 3rd daughter of Jas L Maguire.

WED JAN 13, 1858
Dr Anson Jones, ex-Pres of Texas, committed suicide at Houston on Jan 8, by blowing out his brains. [Jan 16th newspaper: The cause of the act is not stated. He was recently a candidate for the U S Senate, but yielded place to Gen J Pinkney Henderson.]

Convention held by the Veterans of the War of 1812 at Military Hall, N Y, on Jan 8, Col T Hardenbrook, of King Co, was called to the chair. Gentlemen appointed Vice Presidents: Messrs, Porter, Hulsart, Baker, Howard & Williams; Adj Hildreth was appointed sec; Messrs Monell & Ross assistant secs.

The Christian Examiner, Jan 1858, Boston. The bi-monthly periodical has now reached its 205th number, & is at present under the editorial management of Rev F H Hedge, D D, & Rev Edw Everett Hall.

The <u>Mormon</u> agents in England have stopped emigrating from Europe during the pending difficulty, but will probably resume operations as soon as it is decided to what quarter they shall direct their steps.

Senate: 1-Memorial from Henry O Rielly, concerning military highways, or Stockade routes, for protecting travellers & settlers, facilitating mail & telegraphic communication through vast interior territories, & rendering the U S independent of foreign countries for transmitting mails between the Atlantic & Pacific States. 2-Memorial from Jas O Reilly, J J Speed, & Tal P Shaffner, corporators of the St Louis & Salt Lake Telegraph Co, proposing to extend telegraphic communication through Kansas & Nebraska to *Fort Laramie*, before Aug 18 next. 3-Ptn from Virginia Rose & other heirs of Capt Alex'r Rose, an ofcr of the Revolutionary army, asking to be allowed half pay. 4-Ptn from the widow of John Stroop, a Revolutionary soldier, asking to be allowed a pension. 5-Additional papers submitted in the case of the allowance of extra pay to the ofcrs & seamen of the expedition in search of Dr Kane. 6-Ptn from A S H White, asking to be allowed compensation for services an assistant secretary to sign land patents, under an appointment from the Pres of the U S. 7-Cmte on Naval Affairs: asked to be discharged from the consideration of the memorial of Jane Baker, & that it be referred to the Cmte on Pensions: agreed to.

Chief Justice John Duer, Chief Justice of the Superior Court, was visiting at the house of his associate, Judge Woodruff, in 29th st, & while descending the steps fell & fractured his right thigh. He was removed to his own residence near Union Square, & the best surgical aid was procured.

Maggie Hawkins, residing at 68 Crosby st, N Y, a young woman, was burned badly when the camphene lamp she upset exploded. She had to be taken to the hospital.

Sarah Beyner, a native of Reading, Pa, aged 80, while filling a fluid lamp at her residence, the fluid caught fire from another lamp & communicated to her clothes, burning them entirely off from her. She was conveyed to the hospital.

U S Patent Ofc, Wash, Jan 11, 1858. Ptn of Palmer Sumner, of N Y, praying for the extension of a patent granted to him on Apr 25, 1844, for an improvement in metallic laths, for 7 years from the expiration of said patent, which takes place on Apr 25, 1858. –Jas Holt, Com'r of Patents

Orphans Court of Wash Co, D C. In the case of Franklin Little, adm of Peter Little, senior, deceased, the administrator & Court have appointed Feb 2, 1858, for the final settlement of the personal estate of said deceased, of the assets in hand.
-Ed N Roach, Reg/o wills

Mrd: yesterday, at Grace Church, by Rev Alfred Holmead, Mr Geo Cooper, formerly of Wash City, to Miss Angerauer Beard, of PG Co, Md. [Jan 14th newspaper: mrd-on Tue, at Grace Church, by Rev Mr Holmead, Mr Geo Cooper, formerly of Wash City, to Miss Angeroner Beard, of PG Co, Md.]

Died: on Jan 12, in her 84th year, Mrs Rebecca Karrick, formerly of Phil. Her funeral will take place on Wed at 2 o'clock precisely, from the residence of Mr Henry Ingle, on D st, between 2nd & 3rd sts.

Died: on Jan 12, after a brief but severe illness, in his 56th year, Thos B Reily, long a faithful clerk in the Post Ofc Dept. Descended from a distinguished officer of the Md line of the Revolution, he inherited all those traits of a noble character which the officers of that period so pre-eminently possessed. His funeral will take place from his late residence, 555 N J ave, Capitol Hill, on Thu next, at 11 o'clock A M.

THU JAN 14, 1858
The contents of the City Post Ofc, in charge of J G Berret, having been yesterday transferred from its position, facing on 7th st, to the new, spacious, & handsome apartments provided in the Genr'l Post Ofc Extension, & facing F st, our citizens will this morning & henceforth be served from the latter place.

A Mr Holden, who was killed mysteriously at Ann Arbor, Mich, had an insurance on his life for $27,000, which the companies refuse to pay, alleging that he committed suicide for the benefit of his family. A good many men might commit suicide for the benefit of their families even without life insurance. –Prov Journal

Excellent household & kitchen furniture at auction on Jan 19, at the residence of W E G Keen, K st, near 12th st. -Jas C McGuire, auct

Office removed from his residence, No 10, to 279 Pa ave, near 10th st, south side, over Potentini's. –C H Van Patten, Dentist

Senate: 1-Memorial from Ed N Kent, of N Y C, representing that he is the inventor of a useful apparatus for separating gold from foreign substances, the exclusive right of which has been secured to him by letters patent. By use of this invention the savings to the Gov't is about $8,600 per year. For the great saving effected the inventor has received no compensation or reward from the Genr'l Gov't, & asks that the small sum of $20,000 be awarded to him for the perpetual use of his invention in all U S minting establishments. 2-Ptn from Janet H McCall, widow of an ofcr of the Revolutionary army, asking to be allowed a pension & bounty land. 3-Ptn from A P Robinson & others, of the Washington Iron Pavement Co, asking Congress to authorize a contract to be made with them for laying an iron pavement on Pa ave. 4-Ptn from the exec of Danl Randall, asking the payment of a balance of the commission claimed by him for collecting & disbursing money in behalf of the Gov't during the war with Mexico. 5-Ptn from A Van Camp & Virginia P Chapin, asking indemnity for the illegal seizure of their property by the U S Consul at Apia, in the Navigator's Island. 6-Cmte on Military Affairs: asked to be discharged from the consideration of the memorial of John Bronson, & that it be referred to the Cmte of Claims: agreed to. Same cmte: bill for the relief of J G Benton, E B Babbitt, & Jas Longstreet, of the U S army. 7-Cmte of Claims: bill from the Court of Claims for the relief of Jas Beatty's personal reps, reported back the bill without amendment, & recommended its passage. 8-Mr Doolittle introduced a joint resolution directing the Pres of the U S to authorize a medal to be presented to Cmdor Hiram Paulding of the U S Navy, as a testimonial of the high sense entertained by Congress of his gallant & judicious conduct on Dec 8, 1857, in arresting a lawless military expedition set on foot in the U S under the command of Gen Walker, & in preventing the same from carrying on actual war against the feeble & almost defenceless Republic of Nicaragua, with which the U S are at peace. 9-Mr Chandler introduced a bill to authorize & direct the settlement of the accounts of Ross Wilkins, Jas Witherell, & Solomon Sibley.

The Rural Intelligencer, published at Gardiner, Me, calls attention to the present said condition of Hon Parker Shelden, who, but a few years ago, was one of the most prominent business men in that State. He is now in his old age & second childhood, when his bodily mental powers are exhausted, a town pauper; that he has actually been sold as such by a neighboring town to the lowest bidder for his support.

Obit-died: on Nov 6, 1857, in Washington, Ky, John W Henry, M D, in his 50th year. He was born in Lexington, educated at the Univ of Transylvania; & settled in Wash about 1830, where he resided to the hour of his death, pursuing his arduous professional duties with unusual success. He seemed to have inherited the gentleness of his most excellent mother, Robina Jane Lake, daughter of Isabella & Laird Richd Lake, of Shielhill, Scotland. As a husband he was uniformly kind & considerate; as a father he was devoted to his children; & as a brother & son he may have been equaled, but never excelled. In him the church has lost an ornament & the poor a tireless friend. His illness was long & trying.

Pew in St John's Church for sale: Pew No 81, suited for 4 persons, well located. Inquire of C H Middleton, the Sexton of the Church, or address X Y Z through the Post Ofc.

Time Go By Turns: a remarkable poem by Robt Southwell, an English Jesuit, who was born in 1560, & executed at Tyburn in 1595. It is a perfect mosaic of maxims, &, with very slight alteration, would bear cutting up into lines, every one of which would serve as an apothegm. —Charleston Mercury

Died: on Jan 13, Joel Downer, in his 75th year. His funeral is on Jan 15 at 2 o'clock P M, from his late residence on D st, near 13th.

Died: on Jan 12, in her 70th year, Mrs Margaret Delaney, widow of the late Jas Delaney. The deceased was a native of Dublin, Ireland, & for the last 38 years a resident of Wash City. Her funeral will be this afternoon, at 3 o'clock, from her late residence on C st, between 13th & 13½ sts.

Died: on Jan 10, after a few days' illness, Mrs Nancy Talbot, in her 73rd year, late of PG Co, Md.

FRI JAN 15, 1858
Naval. The frig **Congress**, bearing the broad pennant of Flag Ofcr Breese, arrived at Phil yesterday from a cruise. She left the Mediterranean about 47 days since, & passed Gibraltar on Dec 8. The following is a list of her ofcrs: Flag Ofcr, S J Breese; Capt of Fleet, Geo A Magruder; Cmder, Thos T Craven; Lts, Wm May, Saml Marcy, John P Jones, W C B S Porter, L H Newman, Jas Stillude, B P Lozall; Fleet Surgeon, Wm F Patton; Assist Surgeon, D B Conrad; Purser, J A Simple; Chaplain, Mason Noble; Midshipmen, A F Crossman, E P Lull, T McK Buchanan, E Law, A Hopkins, P Porcher; Cmdor's Sec, Jos P Smith; Cmder's Clerk, Henry Emerson; Purser's Clerk, B G Barmeister; Boatswain, G Willmuth; Gunner, Geo Sirian; Carpenter, J Mead; Sailmaker, T C Herbert; Capt of Marines, B E Brooke; 1st Lt of Marines, J R F Tatnall. The crew consists of 425 men.

Appointments by the Pres: 1-Nathan Clifford, of Maine, to be an Assoc Justice of the Supreme Court of the U S, vice Benj R Curtis, resigned. 2-C Bailey Thornbury, Surveyor for the Port of Hickman, Ky, vice F Roulhac, deceased; & Thos W Fleming for the Port of Augusta, Ga.

Rev J J Lehmanowsky died in Clark Co, Ia, on Jan 4. He was a Pole by birth & an ofcr in the Napoleonic wars, but some time after his arrival in this country became a minister in the Lutheran Church.

House of Reps: 1-Memorial of Capt Douglas Otinger, U S revenue service, asking remuneration for his invention of a marine life car. 2-Ptn of Geo Parker, Thos Parker, Wm B Jackson, Noah Walker, & many others, residents of Wash City, to repair Pa ave in a suitable manner.

Edw Snowden, Genr'l Claim & Real Estate Agent: ofc corner of 7th st & Louisiana ave, Wash. [Local ad.]

Senate: 1-Ptn from A H Abrahams, of Charleston, S C, asking that certain duties illegally paid into the custom-house of Charleston may be refunded to him. 2-Ptn from David Gordon, of Miss, complaining of injury which has resulted to himself & others in consequence of the failure of the Sec of the Treasury to execute the act of Congress of Dec, 1854, & asking that the execution of that act may be transferred to the War Dept, with such provisions as will insure enforcement. 3-Ptn from Jas M Hand, in behalf of the heirs of John B Hand, asking that certain moneys paid for the purchase of Choctaw Reservations may be refunded. 4-Ptn from Wm J Walker & others, messengers in the Post Ofc Dept, asking to be allowed the benefit of the joint resolution of 1856 relating to the compensation of laborers in the Executive & Legislative Depts. 5-Ptn from the heirs of Despit St Amand, asking the enactment of a law to place them in a position fairly & legally to maintain their rights of ownership to certain land. 6-Ptn from Jane Stoneham, aged 99 years, widow of Henry Stoneham, a soldier of the Revolution, asking to be allowed a pension. 7-Ptn from Saml Stone & Isaac H Marks, asking compensation for property taken by the Indian agent, under an agreement of arbitration, for Gov't purposes. 8-Cmte on Public Lands: asked to be discharged from the consideration of the ptn of Jos Haynes, & that it be referred to the Cmte on Pensions: agreed to. Same cmte: adverse reports in the following cases: on that of Salmon G Grover; of Polly Colgrove; of Wm P Wright; of Mark P Shepherd, & other members of Capt Saml Walker's company of Kansas militia; of J M Merrill; & of John A Ragan. 9-Cmte on Commerce: bill for the relief of Tench Tilghman. 10-Cmte on Foreign Relations: bill for the relief of Fred'k A Beelen. 11-Bill for the relief of Wm K Jennings & others. [This bill proposes to pay from the Treasury, out of the fund heretofore received from Great Britain under the 1st article of the treaty of Ghent for slaves taken & carried away by the forces of Great Britain during the war of 1812, according to the following rate: to Wm K Jennings & wife, $1,120; to Henry A Wise, $280; to Ann Robinson, $280; to Ed Rudd, for 6 slaves, $1,680; & to Robt Lindsay's representative, $390.] The bill passed.

Mrd: on Jan 13, at the residence of her father, Fairfax Co, Va, by Rev R T Brown, H Wm Throckmorton to Miss Rebecca E Upton.

Died: on Jan 13, Bridget Caton, in her 85th year. Her funeral is this afternoon, at 3 o'clock, from the residence of her son-in-law, Jas King, 435 E st.

Died: on Jan 14, at the Univ of Va, of typhoid fever, John Allen Terrill, son of Wm H Terrill, of Bath Co, Va, in his 18th year.

SAT JAN 16, 1858
Wanted: a teacher capable of teaching all the branches usually taught in a classical school, in the Romney Classical Institute, in Hampshire Co, Va. A married gentleman would be preferred, whose wife would be capable of taking charge of the female dept. Address A W McDonald, jr, Sec to Board of Visiters, Romney, Hampshire Co, Va.

For rent, the large & commodious bldg at 13½ & Pa ave, known as Nailor's Bldg, & lately occupied by C Wendell for the public printing. Possession given on Feb 1. Apply to Allison Nailor or Thompson Nailor, on the premises. –Allison Nailor

Appointments by the Pres, by & with the advice & consent of the Senate:
Francis W Pickens, of S C, to be Envoy Extraordinary & Minister Plenipotentiary of the U S to Russia.
Jas W Borden, of Indiana, to be Com'r of the U S to the Kingdom of Hawaii.
Beverly L Clarke, of Ky, to be Minister Resident to the Republic of Guatemala.
Beverly Tucker, of Va, to be Consul at Liverpool.
Wm Thomson, of NY, to be Consul at Southampton.
John Endlich, of Pa, to be Consul at Basle
C J Fox, of Mich, to be Consul at Aspinwall.
Wm Trevitt, of Ohio, to be Consul at Valparaiso.
Chas F W Glanz, of Pa, to be Consul at Stettin.
Wyman B S Moor, of Maine, to be Consul Genr'l for the British North American Provinces.
Ernest Volger, of Va, to be Consul at Barcelona
Henry W Spencer, of N Y, to be Consul at Paris.
J F Porteous, of S C, to be Consul at Oporto.
Collectors of the Customs:
Wm Littlefield, Newport, Rhode Island, vice Turner.
Jas A Aborn, Providence, vice Bradford.
Naval Officers:
Wm Rider, Newpoet, vice Milton Hall.
Thos J Gardiner, Providence, vice Comstock.
Surveyors:
Francis M Dimond, 2nd, port of Bristol, Rhode Island, vice John Gladding, jr.
Jas Fisher, Pautuxet, vice Smith.
Walter Spencer, East Greenwich, vice Millard.
John B Cary, Hampton, Va, vice Laws, resigned.

Died: New Year's Day, in Wash City, Thos Barnes, aged about 60 years, a native of Ireland, but for many years a resident of Wash City. His funeral will take place on Sunday next from St Patrick's Vault, on G st, near 10th, to which his friends are invited.

Criminal Court-Wash-Wed. 1-John Barret was found not guilty for complicity in the robbing of a horse & buggy. 2-Mary Desmond, found guilty of keeping a disorderly house, & fined $25. Friday: 3-John Fay, Thos Venable, Wm Hurdle, Wm Moore, & Jos Murphy, were put to trial for riot on Nov 28. Jury was out when the Court adjourned. 4-David Westerfield, an ofcr, tried for assault & battery on Anna Vierstein, was acquitted. 5-John Ogden, colored, found guilty of stealing 4 hogs from Bruce Dent: sentenced to 2 years in the penitentiary. 6-Jos Ward, colored, convicted some days ago for mayhem was sentenced to 4 years in the penitentiary. [Jan 19th newspaper: Hurdle, Fay, Venable, & Moore were found guilty. Jos Murphey not guilty. Hurdle was sentenced to 9 months; imprisonment & fined $5; each of the 3 others to 6 months & fined $5 each.] [Jan 20th newspaper: In the list of rioters that of Chas Hurdle was given; it should have been Wm Hurdle.]

We regret to learn that Hon Mr Fenton, of N Y, has been detained from his seat in the House of Rep by illness.

Judgment was rendered on Jan 5 against Gen Wm Walker & his surety, S F Slatter, in the Circuit court of the U S, at New Orleans, for $2,000 on the recognizance of the former to appear to answer for a breach of the neutrality laws, & which recognizance was forfeited by his departure in the ship **Fashion** in Nov.

John Essex, who escaped from custody in Jun, 1856, on the charge of killing Owen Quigley on Pa ave, returned to Wash City. He presented himself at the house of the Deputy Marshal, & was committed to jail. Yesterday he sent for Justice Goddard & made an affidavit, exculpating H T L Wilson from all complicity in his escape. Wilson is now suffering punishment for that crime.

Dr Eliakin Morse, a venerable citizen of Watertown, died there on Sat, at the patriarchal age of 98 years, 10 months & 26 days. In his early years he was a drug merchant in the city of Boston, & was one of the first to dispatch a vessel from this country to Europe upon the close of the Revolutionary war. Dr Morse was a native of that part of Shewsbury now West Boylston, & came to Watertown more than 50 years ago. At one time in his life he owned the only packet, the packet **Galen**, then running between Boston & London. The destruction of a large part of his property at sea by the French gave him a claim on Government, which he prosecuted with great pertinacity during the latter part of his life.

The *Sea View House* at Highlands, N J, in which the barkeeper, Moses, was murdered by the book-keeper, Jas P Donnelly, was together with the cottage occupied by Mrs Jarvis, totally destroyed by fire on Sunday night. The fire was the work of an incendiary. The loss is about $15,000.

Mrd: on Jan 14, at the F st Presbyterian Church, by Rev Dr Harrison, of Alexandria, Va, Auguste E P Petersen, of Copenhagen, Denmark, to Jane Dade, daughter of Nathl Carusi.

Mrd: on Jan 14, by Rev Wm H Chapman, Jas S Harrison to Miss Eliza Jane Rawlings, all of Wash City.

Died: on Jan 15, at Balt, Purser Francis B Stockton, U S Navy, in his 66th year. His funeral will take place at Emanuel Church, Balt, on Jan 18, at 9 o'clock A M.

Died: yesterday, Alice L, wife of Robt H Clements, aged 60. Her funeral is on Sunday, at 3 o'clock P M, from the residence of J E Hilgard, 457 North D st.

MON JAN 18, 1858
The St Louis Republican states that Capt J L Brent, Assist Quartermaster in the U S Army, died at Leavenworth, Kansas, on the Wed preceding. Col Brent was a Virginian by birth, & has been connected with the service for nearly 28 years.

Appointments by the Pres lately confirmed by the Senate:
John Appleton, Assist Sec of State
Richd K Meade, Envoy Extraordinary & Minister Plenipotentiary to Brazil
Wm B Reed, Envoy Extraordinary & Minister Plenipotentiary to China
John Bigler, Envoy Extraordinary & Minister Plenipotentiary to Chili
Henry C Murphy, Minister Resident to the Netherlands
B F Angel, to be Minister of Sweden
Jas Williams, Minister Resident to Constantinople
Wm R Calhoun, Sec of the Legation at Paris

Latest news from the South announce the death of the famous Gen Alvarez, the leader of the revolution of Ayutla, & the first choice for President. The report, however, seems not to have been generally credited.

Orphans Court of Wash Co, D C. Letters of administration on the personal estate of Ann Talbott, late of Wash Co, deceased. –Francis R Davidson, adm

Died: on Jan 13, at his residence in Chamersburg, Pa, Geo Kenton Harper, aged about 79 years. He was the editor & proprietor of that old & popular journal, The Franklin Repository, for nearly 40 years. In the war of 1812 he served as an ofcr of infty in 2 campaigns; first, on the Canada lines, & again in the defence of Balt. On the latter occasion he & Capt Culbertson, with drum & fife & the flag of the Old Blues, raised a company of over 100 men, & had them on the march to the scene of action in a few hours. He survived nearly all his contemporaries, in active life in the community where he lived, & had become from long retirement & age & infirmity almost a stranger where he was once so prominent & respected as universally as he was known.

Died: on Jan 16, in Wash City, Mrs Helen W Hungerford, of King Geo Co, Va, but for the last 27 years a resident of Wash City.

Communicated-died: on Jan 14, in Charlottesville, Va, in his 19th year, John A Terrill, son of Wm H Terrill, of Bath Co. Brought up by a pious mother, he was ever noted not less at college than at home for gentleness of disposition & rectitude of conduct.

TUE JAN 19, 1858
House of Reps: 1-Bill for the relief of the children of Jas Kip, a Revolutionary soldier: referred. 2-Bill for the relief of the heirs of Joshua Leland, a Revolutionary soldier: referred. 3-Bill for the relief of Enoch B Talcott, late collector of customs at Oswego, N Y: referred. 4-Bill to amend an act for the relief of Whitemarsh B Seabrook & others: referred. 5-Bill for the relief of Mrs Louisa Brinker: referred. 6-Bill for the relief of the surviving children of John Neal, deceased: referred. 7-Bill to revise an act entitled-An act for the relief of the heirs or their legal reps of Wm Conway, deceased: referred. 8-Bill for the relief of Mary Thompson, of Summit Co, Ohio: referred. 9-Bill for the relief of Wm D Mann, jr: referred. 10-Bill for the relief of Terence Kirby, of Tenn: referred. 11-Bill for the relief of Lucien R Adams, surviving executor of Jas Adams, deceased: referred.

Senate: 1-Ptn from Douglas Ottinger, of the U S revenue service, asking permission to exhibit before an appropriate cmte his invention of an apparatus for rescuing the passengers & crews of sinking vessels on the open sea. 2-Ptn from Dr M Byrne, a surgeon in the army, asking compensation for certain special services rendered under contract with the commanding ofcr at **Fort Gilleland**, Fla. 3-Ptn from Henry C Flagg, asking to be allowed his portion of the half pay to which his father was entitled for services in the Revolutionary war. 4-Papers in relation to the claims of Danl S Ryan & Henry C Wiley to the reimbursement of an amount paid for certain lands purchased of Gov't, & of which they had been deprived by the claims of certain Indians thereto: referred. 5-Ptn from Geo Frasier, asking compensation for losses occasioned by the Mexican authorities, to be paid from the fund provided by the Mexican treaty. 6-Cmte on the Judiciary: asked to be discharged from the consideration of the memorial of Wm D Elam: which was agreed to. 7-Cmte on Pensions: bill for the relief of Michl Kinney, late a private in the 3rd regt U S infty, reported it back without amendment. 8-Bill for the relief of Wm B Trotter was considered & passed. 9-Cmte on Public Lands: adverse to the passage of the ptn of Polly Colgrove; of John A Ragan; of W P Wright; of Mark Shephard; & J M Morrill.

Trustee's sale of a very extensive assortment of Groceries, Wines, & Liquors on Jan 21, by deed of trust, duly recorded, at the store of Wm M Cripps, on La ave, all the stock in the store, & fixtures. –Richd H Laskey, Atty for Trustees -A Green auct

Bibb, Swann, & Thrift, Attys & Counsellors at Law, Wash City, D C.
-Geo M Bibb, Edw Swann, Robt G Thrift: ofc 26 La ave, near City Hall.

General Orders, No 3. Headquarters of the Army, N Y, Jan 15, 1858. The following named ofcrs will report at **Fort Leavenworth** by Mar 20 next, to join their respective regts & companies: Maj S Eastman, 5th Infty, in quartermaster general's ofc. Capt A Pleasanton, 2nd dragoons, acting assist adj genr'l to Gen Harney. Capt N C Givens, 2nd dragoons, topographical duty in dept of Texas. Capt H Heth, 10th infty, on special duty under orders of the Sec or War. 1st Lt J C Kelton, 6th infty, Military academy.
By command of Brvt Lt Gen Scott. –Irwin McDowell, Assist Adj Gen

Hon Rufus Bullock, of Royalston, Mass, died at his residence in that town on Jan 10th. He was a native of Royalston, & commenced life at the age of one & 20 as a day laborer. He rapidly rose, by industry & skill, to be one of the wealthiest men in Worcester Co. He was a senator for several years & a member of the Constitutional Conventions of 1820 & 1853. He was a large real estate owner, & manufacturer. –Vt Patriot

Died: on Jan 17, in Wash City, Anna, beloved wife of Lewis Johnson, aged about 72 years. Her funeral will take place on Jan 20 at 9½ o'clock A M, from her late residence, 358 G st.

WED JAN 20, 1858
Thos Washington Smith, of Md, charged of having murdered Richd Carter, at the Lawrence Hotel, in Phil, was brought to a close yesterday. The verdict: not guilty.

Senate: 1-Ptn from Moses Olmstead, asking to be allowed arrearages & increase of pension: referred. 2-Ptn from John Caris & other volunteer soldiers of the war of 1812, asking to be allowed pay & rations to the time of discharge: referred. 3-Ptn from Maurice K Simons, asking an increase of pension: referred. 4-Ptn from the heirs of John Forsyth, asking that certain charges erroneously made against said Forsyth in the settlement of his accounts as U S Minister at Madrid may be adjusted & the amount refunded: referred. 5-Ptn from Anastiacio Caxxillo, asking remuneration for losses & inconvenience suffered in consequence of the erection of a lighthouse on a rancho owned by him: referred. 6-Ptn from Thos Jenkins, asking to be allowed arrears of pension: referred. 7-Cmte of Claims: bill for the relief of Jonas P Keller; also a bill for the relief of Elias Hall. 8-Cmte on Naval Affairs: bill for the relief of Dr Chas D Maxwell, a surgeon in the U S Navy. 9-Bill for the relief of Jas Beatty's personal rep: passed. 10-Bill for the relief of Jas G Benton, E B Babbitt, & Jas Longstreet, of the U S army: passed.

House of Reps: 1-Bill for the relief of Stacy Lamphere: referred. 2-Bill for the relief of the widow of Malachi F Randolph: referred. 3-Memorial of Oliver Evans Woods, of Phil, relative to a plan for increasing the efficiency of the delivery branch of the Pacific mail service.

Household & kitchen furniture at auction on Jan 25, by order of the Orphans Court of Wash Co, D C; at the residence of Mary A Deigenhart, deceased, on G st, between 10th & 11th sts. –Johns Robinson, exc -A Green auct

Died: on Jan 18, in his 77th year, Boyd Reilly. His funeral will take place today at 3 o'clock P M, from the residence of his son, 302 West 17th st, between H & I sts.

Obit-died: on Dec 26, at his residence Eastern View, Fauquier Co, Va, Robt Lee Randolph, in his 67th year, was son of the late Col Robt Randolph, of Revolutionary service, from whom he inherited a good name & an ample fortune. In his youth he united himself with the Episcopal Church. To his children he leaves the fullness of that benignant promise unto the descendants of such as love God & keep His commandments. -T T F

Harrisburg, Pa, Jan 19. The new Govn'r of this state, Wm F Packer, was installed into office today in the presence of the Legislature & a large concourse of spectators.

Orphans Court of Wash Co, D C. Letters testamentary on the personal estate of Alfred Cook, late of Wash Co, deceased. –Ann Cook, excx

Orphans Court of Wash Co, D C. Letters testamentary on the personal estate of Sarah Berry, late of PG Co, Md, deceased. –Robt C Brooke, exc

THU JAN 21, 1858
House of Reps: 1-Bill for the relief of Maj Benj Alvord, paymaster of the U S army: referred. 2-Joint resolutions of the State of Texas in relation to the rank of John G Todd, late of the Texas navy: referred.

Wash Corp: 1-The bill of Patrick Scanlon for building the walls of the bridge across Tiber creek, on H st north, was presented: referred to the Cmte on Improvements. 2-Ptn of Mrs E F Simms asking relief from a special tax: referred to the Cmte of Claims.

Died: on Jan 20, in Wash City, Dennis Gallagher, aged 24 years, son of Thos & Sarah Gallagher. His funeral will take place this afternoon at 5 o'clock.

Senate: 1-Ptn from Walter Nexsen, purser's clerk, asking that he may not be required to refund any portion of the pay he has been receiving for several years past: referred. 2-Ptn from Henry Addison & Robt Ould, in behalf of the citizens & corporate authorities of Gtwn, D C, urging the removal of the Long Bridge over the Potomac river at Wash, & the construction of a bridge above Gtwn. 3-Ptn from Eliz Uber, heir-at-law of Eliz Wirt, heir-at-law of the widow of ensign Phillip Wirt, of the Revolutionary army in Pa, asking, as an act of justice, that she may be allowed the pension her mother would have obtained under the act of Jul, 1836, up to the time of her death, had she perfected her claim: referred. 4-Ptn from Geo Walters, heir of Michl Walters, asking to be allowed the pension his father was entitled: referred. 5-Ptn from M C Gritzner, asking compensation for damage sustained due to the non-fulfilment of a contract entered into by him with the Com'r of Patents for preparing & executing descriptions & illustrations of patents. 6-Cmte on Private Land Claims: submitted a special report, with a bill authorizing Mrs Jane Smith to enter certain lands in the State of Alabama. Same cmte: bill for the relief of John Dick, of Fla. 7-Cmte on Private Land Claims, reported a bill to amend an act entitled-An act to authorize a relocation of land warrants Nos 3, 4, & 5, granted by Congress to Gen Lafayette, approved Feb 26, 1845. 8-Cmte on Naval Affairs: bill for the relief of Wilcox Jenkins. 9-Cmte for the District of Columbia: joint resolution for the compensation of R R Richards, late chaplain to the U S Penitentiary, for his salary up to Jun 20, 1857: recommended its passage. 10-Bill to comfirm the title of Henry Volcker to a certain tract of land in New Mexico.

FRI JAN 22, 1858
Ruthless murder, attended by circumstances of more than usual disregard of human life, was committed on Wed in Gtwn. Pupils of the Catholic free school, at 1st st, going home, playing at foot ball along the street, when a negro in sport picked up their ball. One of the boys threw a stone at the negro, which, missing him, struck the porch or front door of Benj R Ogle, painter & glazier, living on 1st st, near Fred'k st. Almost immediately Ogle presented himself at his door, with a loaded musket in hand, & leveled & fired at a little boy named John Webb, then passing with his school-books under his arm. The little fellow was instantly killed, the musket having been loaded with ball, which passed into the boy's head. Ogle was speedily arrested & committed to jail for trial at the Criminal Court. It is said he had been drinking for several days previous to the commission of the savage deed, & had not recovered from its effect at the time. [Feb 25th newspaper: in the

Ogle case, the Jury has been out since Friday last, & stated the improbability of their agreeing on a verdict. The Court then adjourned.]

Senate: 1-The late Senator, Gen Thos J Rusk, committed suicide on Jul 29, 1857, by shooting himself with a rifle. He was born in Pendleton district, S C; did not inherit the advantages of fortune, of family, or of patronage. He was descended from an Irish patriot, who was cast upon our shores in consequence of the troubles of 1791 in Ireland. He removed to the State of Ga & rose rapidly to distinction in his profession-the law. Having connected himself with an estimable lady, he removed with his family to Texas in 1834. In 1835, when the enemy invaded Texas, & took possession of San Antonio, he immediately marched with a force from eastern Texas, & rendered signal assistance to Gen Austin, then in command of the Texan forces. He remained with the army until after the capture of Gen Santa Anna, the imperial ruler of Mexico. He was appointed to the command of the army of Texas. He became a statesman in the highest sense of the term. 2-Ptn from Nancy Hammond, daughter of a Revolutionary ofcr, asking remuneration for the services & sacrifices of her father during the Revolutionary war: referred. 3-Ptn from Randall Pegg, asking to be allowed the difference between the pay he received & that allowed to the other watchmen who were employed at the public bldgs during the time he served at the Patent Ofc: referred. 4-Ptn from Jos Dowd, asking an increase of pension: referred. 5-Ptn from Wm C Pease, a capt in the U S revenue service, asking to be reimbursed an amount of public money lost by him while on deposite in bank, & which he was compelled to pay out of his private funds: referred. 6-Cmte on Public Lands: bill to vest the title to certain land warrants for land in Geo M Gordon. Same cmte: to issue land warrants to Jos Chase, Jas Young, & Alex'r Keef. 7-Cmte on Private Land Claims: bill for the relief of Lawrent Millandon. 8-Bill for the relief of the heirs & legal reps of Olivier Landry, of the State of Louisiana: introduced. 9-Bill introduced to incorporate *Conzaga/Gonzaga College in Wash City, D C. 10-Bill for the relief of Fred'k A Beelen: passed. 11-Bill for the relief of Michl Kinney, late a private in Co I, 8th Regt U S Army: passed. [*Feb 2nd newspaper: correct spelling Gonzaga-not Conzaga.] [*Feb 25th newspaper: splg Gonzago.]

House of Reps: 1-Cmte on Invalid Pensions: bill for the relief of Mary Bainbridge; of Eliz E V Field; of Catharine R Russell; of Stephen Bunnell; of Charlotte Butler; of John M Plummer & Mary R Plummer, minor children of Capt Saml M Plummer; & a bill to increase the pension of John Richmond: severally read & committed. Same cmte: bill for the relief of Saml Goodrich, jr; & also a bill for the relief of Henry Taylor: committed. Same cmte: bill for the relief of Mary Bennett; of Nancy Serena; of Mgt Whitehead; & of Sylvanus Burnham: committed. 2-Mr Danl W Gooch, Rep elect from the 7th district of the State of Mass in place of Mr Banks, resigned, was duly qualified & took his seat on the floor of the House. 3-Cmte on Elections: bill for the relief of Chas J Ingersoll: committed. 4-Cmte on Claims: bill for the relief of Capt Jas Macintosh, U S Navy: committed. Same cmte: bill for the relief of Geo W Biscoe: committed. 5-Cmte on Commerce: adverse report in the case of Edw B Tippett: laid on the table. Same cmte: bill to indemnify Henry Leef & John McKee for the illegal seizure of a certain barque: committed. 6-Cmte on Revolutionary Claims: bill for the relief of the heirs of Alex Stevenson: committed. Same cmte: adverse reports on the ptn of John McCurdy for a pension; & in the case of Alex R Boteler: laid on the table. 7-Cmte on Private Land Claims: bill for the relief of the reps of Wm Smith, deceased, late of Louisiana; of the legal reps or assignees of Jas Lawrence; of the legal reps of Pierre Broussard; & of N C Weems, of Louisiana: committed. Same cmte: to revive an act for the relief of the heirs or their legal reps of Wm Conway, deceased: committed. Same cmte: bill for the relief of Francis Woldecki: committed. Same cmte: Bill for the relief of Regis Loisel, or his legal reps: committed. 8-Cmte on Naval Affairs: bill for the relief of Dr Chas Maxwell, a surgeon in the U S navy: committed. 9-Act to grant a pension to Ansel Wilkinson: passed. Note that followed: The amendment is in the spelling of the name of the pensioner; which should be Asel instead of Ansel. 10-Cmte on Naval Affairs: adverse report in the case of Thos Pember: laid on the table. Same cmte: bill for the relief of Wm Heine, artist in the Japan Expedition: committed. Same cmte: bill for the relief of Eliphalet Brown, jr: committed. 11-Cmte on Foreign Affairs: adverse report in the case of Lewis Lafitte: laid on the table. 12-Cmte on Revolutionary Pensions: adverse reports in the cases of Danl Mandigo, Jos P Iryal, & Jacob Jeho: laid on the table. 13-Cmte on Invalid Pensions: bill for the relief of Mary Bainbridge; of Eliz E V Field; of Catharine R Russell; of Stephen Bunnell; to increase the pension of John Richmond; of Charlotte Butler; of Jos M Plummer & Mary R Plummer, minor children of Capt Saml M Plummer: committed. Same cmte: bill for the relief of Saml Goodrich, jr; of Henry Taylor; of Mary Bennett; of Nancy Serena; of Mgt Whitehead; & of Sylvanus Burnham.

Mr Tho Allibone, late Pres of the Bank of Pa, is a passenger in the ship **America**, & may be expected in Phil in a few days. He had determined to return home to throw much light upon the intricate involved affairs of the institution with which he was connected, & to explain many circumstances which now seem strange, mysterious, & incomprehensible.
–Phil Inquirer

John Frednock, keeper of a porter-house in N Y, & John Hazzard, his bar-tender, were arrested on Monday for passing counterfeit quarter dollars & ten cent pieces. $70 in bogus money was found on their premises.

Mrd: on Jan 20, in Wash City, by Rev J C Granbury, Wm Ferguson, of Pa, to Mary F, eldest daughter of J F Divine, of Va.

Mrd: on Jan 21, in Wash City, by Rev T N Haskell, Jas L Gray, of Texas, to Miss Kae/Kate Clephane, of Wash, D C.

Died: on Jan 20, in Wash City, aged 31 years, Julia Stockton, wife of John Calvert, & daughter of Hon Richd Rush, of Phil

SAT JAN 23, 1858
Sale of stoves, chandeliers, vices, carriage-makers' tools, & carriage bodies: on Jan 27, at the bldg known as Haslup & Weeden's Carriage Factory, C & La ave.
–Wall & Barnard, aucts

House of Reps: 1-Cmte on Revolutionary Claims: bill for the relief of the heirs of John Hopper; also, a bill for the relief of the heirs of John A Hopper: committed. 2-Cmte on Indian Affairs: bill for the relief of the heirs of the late Richd Tarvin: committed. 3-Cmte on Foreign Affairs: adverse report in the case of Jas C Pickett: laid on the table. 4-Cmte on Invalid Pensions: bill for the relief of Zenah Williams: committed. 5-Cmte on Printing: adverse report on the memorial of Wm B Willis & others: laid on the table.

Appointments: the Senate has confirmed the following nominations:
Beverly L Clarke, of Ky, Minister resident to the Republic of Guatemala; also Minister resident to the Republic of Honduras.
F McMullen, Gov'r of Wash Territory.
Abraham Rencher, Govn'r of New Mexico.
Alfred Cumming, Govn'r of Utah.
John Hartnett, Sec of the Territory of Utah.

Justices of the Peace in Wash Co:

Wm Cooper	Wm G Palmer	Patrick McKenna
Chas R Queen	Terence Drury	Franklin Darly
Richd Burgess	Henry G Murray	John R Queen
Richd R Shekell	Geo Mattingly	

Mrs Cassin, of Gtwn, widow of the late Cmdor Cassin, was so severely burnt yesterday, by her clothes taking fire, that her death is anticipated. She was alone at the time of the accident. [Jan 25th newspaper: Mrs Cassin died yesterday after suffering much agony.]

Both branches of the Va Legislature have passed a bill providing for the conveyance to the State of Va of the birthplace of Washington & the home & graves of his progenitors in America. The adoption of this measure may be regarded as a patriotic prelude to the consummation of the noble enterprise in which the Ladies' Mount Vernon Association is engaged. The bill appropriates $5,000 to enclose the places with an iron fence, & to erect substantial tablets to commemorate for the rising generation those notable spots, as required by Lewis W Washington in his offer of conveyance.

The dwlg house of Danl B Morrison, near Martinsurg, Va, was destroyed by fire a few days since. The fire originated by a cat catching fire & running under a bed, & setting fire to some paper.

The two tickets in Kansas. Names of the candidates at the election on Jan 4 in Kansas:

Offices	Democratic	Republican
Govn'r	F J Marshall	Geo W Smith
Lt Govn'r	Wm J Mathias	Wm Y Roberts
Sec of State	W T Spicely	P C Schuyler
Auditor	Blake Little	Joel K Goodin
Treasurer	T J B Cramer	Andrew J Mead
Congress	J B Carr	Mar J Parrott

Household & kitchen furniture at auction Jan 27, at the residence of Wm Nourse, 11th & N sts, by virtue of a deed of trust, duly recorded. –S C Edes, trustee -J C McGuire, auct

The following naval officers, whose positions were changed by the operation of the act of Congress of Feb 28, 1855, have been confirmed by the Senate & restored to the active list of the navy:

Jos Smith, now a capt on the reserved list, to be a capt in the navy from Feb 9, 1837, to take rank as such next after Capt M C Perry.

Uriah P Levy, dropped, to be a capt in the navy from Mar 29, 1844, to take rank as such next after Capt Hiram Paulding.

Jos R Jarvis, now a cmder on the reserved list, to be a capt in the navy from May 24, 1855, to take rank as such next after Capt Chas H Bell.

John S Chauncey, dropped, to be a capt in the navy from Sep 14, 1855, to take rank as such next after Capt Jos D Hull.

Jas Glynn, now a cmder on the reserved list, to be a capt in the navy from Sep 14, 1855, to take rank as such next after Capt Robt B Cunningham.

Robt Ritchie, now a cmder on the reserved list, to be a capt in the navy from Sep 14, 1855, to take rank as such next after Capt John Rudd.

John S Nicholas, now a cmder on the reserved list, to be a capt in the navy from Sep 14, 1855, to take rank as such next after Capt Geo F Pearson.

Calwalader Ringgold, now a cmder on the reserved list, to be a capt in the navy from Apr 2, 1856, to take rank as such next after Capt Hugh Y Purviance.

Isaac S Sterett, now a cmder on the reserved list, to be a capt in the navy from Mar 2, 1857, to take rank as such next after Capt Henry W Morris.

Robt D Thorburn, now a cmder on the reserved list, to be a cmder in the navy from Oct 3, 1850, to take rank as such next after Cmder Wm C Whittle.

Saml Lockwood, now a cmder on the reserved list, to be a cmder in the navy from Oct 18, 1850, to take rank as such next after Cmder Robt D Thorburn.

Wm S Ogden, dropped, to be a cmder in the navy from Apr 22, 1851, to take rank as such next after Cmder Saml Lockwood.

John Calhoun, now a cmder on the reserved list, to be a cmder in the navy from Nov 4, 1852, to take rank as such next after Cmder Robt G Robb.

Murray Mason, now a cmder on the reserved list, to be a cmder in the navy from Feb 25, 1854, to take rank as such next after Cmder Henry K Hoff.

Wm E Hunt, now a lt on the reserved list, to be a cmder in the navy from Aug 22, 1855, to take rank as such next after Cmder John W Livingston.

Matthew F Maury, now a lt on the reserved list, to be a cmder in the navy from Sep 14,1855, to take rank as such next after Cmder Jas F Schenck.

Jas S Palmer, now a lt on the reserved list, to be a cmder in the navy from Sep 14, 1855, to take rank as such next after Cmder S W Godon.

Robt Handy, now a lt on the reserved list, to be a cmder in the navy from Sep 14, 1855, to take rank as such next after Cmder Guert Gansevort.

Henry Walker, now a lt on the reserved list, to be a cmder in the navy from Sep 14, 1855, to take rank as such next after Cmder B M Dove.

Lewis C Sartorri, now a lt on the reserved list, to be a lt in the navy from Sep 8, 1841, to take rank as such next after Lt C B Poindexter.

Fabius Stanly, now a lt on the reserved list, to be a lt in the navy from Sep 8, 1841, to take rank as such next after Lt Edmund Lanier.
John N Maffit, now a lt on the reserved list, to be a lt in the navy from Jun 25, 1843, to take rank as such next after Lt Jas D Johnston.
A Davis Harrell, dropped, to be a lt in the navy from May 17, 1847, to take rank as such next after Lt S D Trenchard.
Alex'r Murray, now a lt on the reserved list, to be a lt in the navy from Aug 12, 1847, to take rank as such next after Lt Jos N Barney.
Thos H Stevens, dropped, to be a lt in the navy from May 10, 1849, to take rank as such next after Lt W C B S Porter.
Van Rensselear Morgan, now a lt on the reserved list, to be a lt in the navy from Oct 26, 1849, to take rank next after Lt Wm E Boudinot.
Abner Read, dropped, to be a lt in the navy from Feb 6, 1854, to take rank as such next after Lt Henry K Stevens.
Geo A Stevens, dropped, to be a lt in the navy from Sep 14, 1855, to take rank as such next after Lt Leonard Paulding.
Augustus McLaughlin, dropped, to be a lt in the navy from Sep 14, 1855, to take rank as such next after Lt Jonathan H Carter.
Wm W Low, now a master in the line of promotion, on the reserved list, to be a lt in the navy from Sep 14, 1855, to take rank as such next after Lt Wm P Buckner.
J Howard March, dropped, to be a lt in the navy from Sep 15, 1855, to take rank as such next after Lt John L Davis.
Jas S Thornton, dropped, to be a lt in the navy from Sep 15, 1855, to take rank as such next after Lt Alex'r A Semmes.
Edmund C Grafton, now a passed midshipman on the reserved list, to be a lt in the navy from Sep 15, 1855, on the active list, to take rank as such next after Lt Jos Fry.
The following dropped officers, placed on the reserved list, have been confirmed:
Saml W Lecompte to be a cmder in the navy from Sep 8, 1841, on furlough pay.
Wm A C Farragut to be a lt in the navy from Dec 9, 1844, on leave-of-absence pay.
Richd W Meade to be a lt in the navy from Dec 20, 1837, on furlough pay.
Thos Brownell to be a lt in the navy from Dec 26, 1843, on furlough pay.
Julius S Bohrer to be a master in the line of promotion in the navy from Mar 1,1 854, on leave-of-absence pay.
Nathl T West to be a passed midshipman in the navy from Aug 10, 1847, on leave-of-absence pay.
The following transfers from the furlough to the leave-of-absence pay of the reserved list have been confirmed:
Capts: Jesse Wilkinson, Thos M Newell, Wm K Latimer, John H Graham, & Wm Inman.
Cmders: Chas T Platt, Henry Bruce, & Chas H Jackson.
Lts: Peter Turner, Gabriel G Williams, Simon B Bissell, John J Glasson, Henry A Steele, Wm Chandler, Jas M Gillis, John P Parker, Edw C Bowers, Augustus S Baldwin, Wm B Whiting, & Mathias C Marin.
Master: R Clarendon Jones. Passed Midshipman: Saml Pearce

Mrd: on Jan 20, by Rev B A Maguire, Benj Smith, of Louisville, Ky, to Miss Kate, daughter of T O'Donnoghue, of Gtwn, D C.

Farm for rent: the farm & residence of the late Washington Berry, situated on the heights north of Washington; contains about 400 acres of land, & a large & handsome brick dwlg house, brick stable, & other necessary outhouses. Application may be made to the subscriber, residing near the premises, or at the City Hall, Wash. –E J Middleton

Seminole Chief Dead. Yah-hah-Toxica, a chief of the Seminole tribe, one of the delegation in transit to Florida, at the instance of the Gov't, to induce Billy Bowlegs to emigrate westward, died in New Orleans on Jan 10. He was overtaken by sickness in the street & died there, chanting his war-song, surrounded by a group of braves.

Death of Rev Jacob Norton, the oldest graduate of Harvard. Rev Norton died at his residence in Billerica, Mass, on Jan 17. He was the son of Saml Norton; was born in Abington, Mass, on Feb 12, 1764, & had attained the great age of 93 years, 11 months & 5 days. He graduated with distinction at Harvard in 1786; ordained over the Congregational Church in Weymouth on Oct 10, 1787, where he continued his pastoral labors for 37 years, until 1824, when he resigned his charge, & a few years afterwards removed to Billerica, where he resided during the remainder of his long life. In 1789 he married Eliz Cranch, the eldest daughter of Hon Richd Cranch, of Braintree, [now Quincy,] sister of the late Judge Wm Cranch, of Wash, D C, & niece of the wife of Pres John Adams. His wife died several years ago. He leaves 2 daughters, 11 grand-children, & 11 great grand-children. Two of his sons, Richd Cranch Norton & Wm Smith Norton, graduated at Harvard College in 1808 & 1812 respectively. Mr Norton retained his mental & physical powers to a remarkable degree until past the age of ninety. For the last year or two he spent most of his time during the day reading, & without glasses, which he never used, with the exception of a short time, & then laid them aside as useless. -Boston Advertiser of the 19th.

Died: on Jan 21, in Wash City, after a lingering illness of 10 months, Mr Notley L Adams, aged 70 years, 6 months & 6 days. He was formerly of Md, but for many years had been a resident of Wash City. He leaves a large family to mourn his loss. His funeral will take place this afternoon at 2 o'clock.

Died: on Jan 20, near Balt, suddenly, Caboline, daughter of the late Enoch Reynolds, in her 46th year. [Caboline as written.]

Died: at the navy yard, Pensacola, in his 34th year, Jas M Woodward, gunner in the U S Navy, & son of Col A Woodward, of Wash City. [No death date given-current item.]

Died: on Wed, at **Tranquillity**, Spalding's Distict, PG Co, Md, Mrs Eliz U Dyer, consort of Horatio Dyer, in her 69th year.

Died: on Jan 22, at the residence of Thos C Donn, in Wash City, Edward, son of John H Baker, of the Md House of Delegates, from Harford Co, aged 18 months, after an illness of a few months.

Brook Hill School, 6 miles north of Charlottesville, Va, will begin the next term on Feb 1, 1858. Address the principal, Chas Minor, M D, Charlottesville, Va.

MON JAN 25, 1858
Zaccheus Robinson, a Revolutionary veteran, aged 93 years, died at Southboro, Mass, on Jan 17. His aged partner still survives, being 85 years.

Orphans Court of Wash Co, D C. In the case of Woodville Latham, adm of Robt Latham, the administrator & Court have appointed Feb 16 next, for the final settlement of the personal estate of said deceased, of the assets in hand. -Ed N Roach, Reg/o wills

The Salem Gaz, in noticing the recent death in that city of Mrs Mary E, widow of Hon Leverett Saltonstall, at age 70 years, says she was one of the few surviving reps of the palmy days of Salem. United in marriage to a son of Salem, who made still more eminent an honored name, she was early called to fill a prominent position in social life, which she adorned by her varied & sterling qualities.

Criminal Court-Wash-Fri: 1-Washington Sullivan, alias Causee, was found guilty of larceny & sentenced to 6 months in jail. 2-On Sat Columbus Murphy, Saml Anderson, Moses Anderson, Baker McDaniel, Oliver Landon, & Wm Major were all found guilty for committing a riot on last Christmas eve across the Anacostia river. [Jan 26th newspaper: C Murphy, S Anderson & M Anderson, each sentenced to 3 weeks in the county jail, & Wm Major was fined $20 & costs. McDaniel & Landon not being in court, bench warrants were issued for their appearance.]

Died: on Jan 23, in Wash City, after a short illness, Geo Washington Burch, in his 20th year. His funeral will be this afternoon at 3½ o'clock, from the residence of his grandmother, corner of 5th & H sts.

Late from Europe: 1-Advices from India announce that Gen Havelock had died of dysentery. 2-Marshal Radetzky, Redschid Pacha, & Rachel, the tragedian, are dead. [Jan 26th newspaper: Gen Havelock died on Nov 25 from dysentery, brought on by exposure & anxiety.] [Jan 28th newspaper: Maj Gen Henry Havelock, C B, was born at Bishopwearmouth in 1795, & educated at the Charter House. In 1813, in consequence of adverse fortune, Ingress Park, his father's property in Kent, was sold to Gov't, & Havelock was entered at the Middle Temple, & was an intimate associate with the late Sir Thos Talfourd. An elder brother had distinguished himself in the Peninsular war & at **Waterloo**, & Henry, yielding to the military propensities of his family endeavored to obtain a commission. A month after Waterloo he was appointed 2nd lt in the Rifle Brig, 95th, where his military training was assisted by Capt [afterward Sir] Harry Smith, the victor of Aliwal. His elder brother, Col Wm Havelock, was killed at Kamnuggur.]

Died: on Jan 23, at **Glen Ross**, Montg Co, Md, Mrs R L Ross, aged 33 years. Her funeral will be on Jan 25 at 11 o'clock A M, from her late residence.

Died: on Jan 23, in Wash City, Albert F, aged 6 months & 6 days, youngest son of Wm & Eliz M Tucker. His funeral will be this afternoon at 2½ o'clock, from the residence of his parents, 351 C st, between 4½ & 6th sts.

Wmsport, Md, Jan 21. W Anderson, Chas Miller, Wm Lewis, & Peter Zarver, convicted with conspiring to commit burglary & larceny, & to manufacture & pass gold & silver coin. Anderson & Miller sentenced to 4 years & 2 months, Lewis to 3 years & 2 months, & Zarver to 1 year & 2 months.

Hartford, Conn, Jan 23. The large 5 story bldg owned by Willis Thrall, occupied by several manufacturers, was totally destroyed by fire last night. Total loss $100,000. The suffers are Willis Thrall, T Kohn, Willis & Wylie, printers, S Andrus & Son, W W House, stereotype plates, A R Johnson, Chas Parker, L Stebbins & Co, & Geo Metcalfe.

TUE JAN 26, 1858
Senate: 1-Ptn from the widow of Silas Halsay, an ofcr of the army who died of disease contracted in service, asking to be allowed a pension: referred. 2-Ptn from Elijah R Huff & others, asking the establishment of a mail route between St Jos', Missouri, & Maysville, in Kansas Territory: referred. 3-Ptn from Maj J L Donaldson, assist quartermaster in the army asking to be released from liability on public money stolen from his possession: referred. 4-Ptn from Thos Phenix, asking to be allowed extra compensation for the time he was employed as a paymaster's clerk in the army: referred. 5-Ptn from Euirice Brake, asking arrears of pension: referred.

Lumber, lumber-wagon, & large scales, at auction: on Jan 27, at the lumber yard of John Purdy, on First st west, all the remaining stock of lumber in the yard. -A Green auct

House of Reps: 1-Memorial of Geo H Howell, U S Navy, praying for relief: presented. 2-Memorial of John Tiers, exec of the estate of Cornelius Tiers, deceased, praying for the payment of a sum of money due said estate: presented. 3-Memorial of Henry S Crabbe, of Phil, praying for relief: presented.

Foreign-India: 1-Col Rooke, 19th regt, died at Calcutta from cholera on Nov 30. 2-Capt Day, of the 64th, is reported killed at Cawnpore.

Southern Chronicle, published at Orange Court-house, Va: We learn that the remains of Mrs Madison were brought from Washington by her nephew, Mr Cutts, on Jan 13, & deposited in the cemetery at Montpelier, near the monument recently placed by the citizens of this county over the grave of her husband. This was in compliance with a wish expressed by Mrs Madison herself.

Criminal Court-Wash-Mon: 1-Robt Bruce acquitted of assault & battery with intent to kill John Chisholm. 2-Chas Hurdle, Jas Slatford, & Jos Goldsmith were found guilty of riot on Nov 24 last. The latter two were remanded, but Hurdle could not be found. A bench warrant was issued for his arrest.

Election shall be held throughout the Territory of Kansas on the first Tue in Mar, A D, 1858, for the election of delegates to form a constitution for the State of Kansas. Delegates to the Convention, passed Feb 19, 1857:
Leavenworth Co: Adam Fisher, S N Latta, & Geo W Purkins
Atchison: Chas F Kob, Caleb May, & J T Hereford
Doniphaan: Thos H McCollock, Isaac Tollman, & Ebenezer Blackiston
Brown: Orville Root, Thos J Drummond, & Wm C Foster
Nemaha: Thos Newton, Royal U Torrey, & C Beurre
Pottawatomie: Robt Wilson, Uriah Cook, & A Jackson Chapman
Marshall: J M Middleton, W S Blackburn, & J E Clardy
Riley: J M Morris, Dr A Hunting, & Geo Montague
Calhoun: Abram Ray, Wm Owens, & Dr Oden
Jefferson: Wm Grisby, Jesse Newell, & I Hollinsworth
Shawnee: A Polly, W S Gaylord, & Elliot Carriger
Coffey: Wm R Saunders, S M Parsons, & H McMahon
Woodson: Chas Cameron & John Woolman
Richardson: Jas Fletcher, S T Ross, & S A Baldwin
Breckinridge: Dr E P Bancroft, E Goddard, & Wm Grimsley
Madison: A D Graham, S C Brown, & Harmon G Elliott
Johnson: Benj Dare, Jos Mathews, & Jas D Allen
Lykins: H H Williams, John Yelton, & Dr W Heiskell
Linn: David Sibbett, E Barnes, & Dr J H Barlow
Bourbon: Dorn & McGee
B B Newton, John Hamilton, & Gov E Ranson.
Douglas: Robt J Nelson, J R Abbot, & Jas Blood
Franklin: Jacob A Marcell, P P Elder, & J A Reid
Anderson: Davis Frankinberger, Dr R Gilpatrick, & W F M Arnu
Allen & Greenwood: J A Coffee, Watson Stewart, & A J Riever
Davis: Jas W Blair, E M Thurston, & Wm B Marshall
Wise: T S Huffacker, E Mosier, & S M Hays
Hunter: E R Zimmerman & Dr Wiebly

Mobile, Jan 25. Gen Walker arrived here yesterday, & today was arrested by an order from New Orleans, but was discharged on habeas corpus. Judge Gale quashed the proceedings.

Miss Rebecca D Briggs, who died suddenly at Manchester, N H, Jan 12, of heart disease, at age 17 years, was not buried until Jan 21, 9 days after death, because the continued life-like appearance of the face, upon which a rosy hue lingered for several days after death, led to a postponement of the funeral ceremonies from a hope that it might prove to be a case of suspended animation only.

Died: on Jan 16, at *Metropolis View*, near Wash City, Fred'k Brooke, youngest son of Dr John E Berry, of PG Co, Md, in his 21st year.

Died: on Jan 16, at the College of St James, Thos Matthews, youngest son of the late Gen John Matthews, of Chas Co, Md, aged 19 years.

Died: on Jan 18, at **Woodbury**, the residence of Dr Wm A Spence, Westmoreland Co, Va, after a protracted & painful illness, Mr Alex'r Spence, in his 67th year. When a young man he was employed as a clerk in the post ofc at Richmond, Va; from thence he removed to Edenton, N C, where he resided until about 1847, when he emigrated to the State of Missouri, where he remained 2 years, & making Wash City his home for a short time, he finally returned to his native county, where his bones now rest. He had the character of a true Virginia gentleman. -H

Ball for the benefit of the St Joseph's Male Orphan Asylum, on Feb 4. Managers:

Jas G Berrett	Richd H Clarke	John F Fills
Wm T Dove	Hudson Taylor	Jos F Brown
John F Coyle	Francis Mohun	R H Laskey
Walter Lenox	John C Fitzpatrick	Wm H Ward
Jas F Haliday	Thos J Fisher	

WED JAN 27, 1858
Administrator's sale of a good work-horse, at auction, on Jan 28, belonging to the estate of the late Thos Barnes. By order of Thos Welsh, adm -A Green auct

On Sat a melancholy accident occurred at the house of Mr John T Grady, Balt, which resulted in the death of one of his children, a bright little boy between 7 & 8 years of age. The parents had gone out, when the child got hold of a double-barreled pistol which was heavily charged. It is supposed he held the muzzle towards his person & attempted to cock it, when the hammer slipped from his hand, causing the cap to explode & the weapon to fire. The report of the pistol was heard by one of the members of the family, who found the boy lying on his face, with life extinct.

A few weeks ago a Spanish gentleman of high connexions, Stephen Despratt, died in London, in a starved condition. He possessed wealth to the amount of $150,000, but was so penurious that he denied himself the common necessaries of life.

John W Tyzack, a brass founder at St Louis, was shot dead a few weeks ago during a fracas with constable Meek.

Wm L Hall & Nelson Cross have been convicted of murder in the first degree in Franklin Co, Mo.

Orphans Court of Wash Co, D C. In the case of Jas McSherry, adm de bonis non, with the will annexed, of Peregrine Warfield, deceased, the administrator & Court have appointed Feb 20 next, for the final settlement of the personal estate of the deceased, of the assets in hand. -Ed N Roach, Reg/o wills

Orphans Court of Wash Co, D C. Letters of administration on the personal estate of Timothy Shannon, late of Wash Co, deceased. –Maria Shannon, admx

Criminal Court-Wash-Yesterday: 1-Jacob Keppell found guilty of stealing a watch & chain: sentenced to 2 years in the penitentiary. 2-Thos Dawson acquitted of resisting an ofcr in the discharge of his duty. 3-Chas Hurdle, Jas Slatford, & Jos Goldsmith were each sentenced to 10 months' imprisonment & a fine of $5.

Mrd: on Jan 26, in the Unitarian Church, by Rev Mr Haley, Mr Jas E Thompson to Miss Virginia Purdy, all of Wash City.

Senate: 1-Ptn from Jane McKean, Catharine E Kean, & Mary A Reynolds, asking Congress to grant them compensation for the services & sacrifices of their parents in the Revolutionary war: referred. 2-Ptn from Geo H Howell, as assist surgeon in the navy, asking to be allowed certain back pay: referred. 3-Ptn from Mary Walsh & other pensioners under the act of Feb, 1853, asking to have their pensions continued: referred. 4-Ptn from F M Gunnell, assist surgeon in the navy, asking compensation for extraordinary expenses incurred in the discharge of his duty in Calif: referred. 5-Ptn from Lts J H Carter, J M Bennett, & R B Lowry, of the navy, asking to be allowed the difference of pay between the grades of masters & lts during the time they served as lts in the East India squadron: referred. 6-Ptn from Reynell Coates, asking compensation for losses sustained & services rendered while connected with the scientific corps of the South Sea Exploring Expedition: referred. 7-Cmte on Military Affairs: bill for the relief of Maj Benj Alvord, Paymaster U S Army. Same cmte: bill for the relief of Susannah T Lea, widow & admx of Jas Magiennan, late of the city of Balt. 8-Cmte of Claims: bills from the Court of Claims for the relief of Jane Smith, of Claremont Co, Ohio; of John Erickson; & of Lucinda Robinson, of Orleans Co, Vt. Same cmte: adverse report on the bill for the relief of Nahum Ward. 9-Cmte on Military Affairs: bill to continue a pension to Christine Barnard, widow of the late Brvt Maj Moses J Barnard, U S army. Same cmte: bill for the relief of Geo A O'Brien. Same cmte: bill from the Court of Claims for the relief of Geo Ashley, adm de bonis non of Saml Holgate, deceased; & recommended its passage. 10-Cmte of Claims: memorial of Pamelia Preswick & other heirs of Wm Wigton, referring all the papers to the Court of Claims: which was agreed to.

Died: on Jan 25, Owen O'Toole, father of the Rev Pastor of St Patrick's Church. For 7 years after coming to this country deceased resided in Balt, when he removed to Wash City a little over 12 months ago. After a long life of unvarying good health, now in his 75th year, in the bosom of his family, he calmly gave up his soul to God. His funeral will take place at 10 o'clock on Thu, from his late residence on 9th st, between F & G, when high mass will be celebrated at St Patrick's Church for the repose of his soul.

Died: on Jan 26, in Wash City, Jas Dixon, a native of Scotland, for the last 32 years a resident of this country, in his 67th year. His funeral will take place on Thu at 2 o'clock, from 418 D st, between 6th & 7th sts.

Died: on Jan 26, in Wash City, Fielder Burch, in his 62nd year. His funeral is this evening, at half-past 2, from his late residence, on 14th st, between E & F sts.

Marshal's sale, by writ of fieri facias: public sale on Feb 20, of part of lot 13 in square 254; seized & levied upon as the property of Wm J Smith, & will be sold to satisfy judicials No 11, to May term, 1858, in favor of Edwin Green.
--J D Hoover, Marshal for D C.

THU JAN 28, 1858
Senate: 1-Ptn from J K Kane & other citizens of Phil urging that a pension may be granted to the widow of Foxall A Parker, late a capt in the navy: referred. 2-Ptn from the excx of Oziel Smith, asking indemnity for property destroyed by the enemy in the war of 1812: referred. 3-Ptn from Frances Ann McCauley, widow of Danl S McCauley, late consul general at Alexandria, Egypt, asking compensation for certain judicial services performed by her husband under the act of Aug, 1818: referred. 4-Ptn from Eliza Gerry S Townsend, asking to be allowed a pension: referred. 5-Ptn from Wm C Fowler & others, asking to be allowed bounty land for services in the last war with Great Britain: referred. 6-Ptn from Jas A Glanding, asking to be allowed a pension for a wound received in the defence of Balt in 1814: referred. 7-Ptn from Henry S Crabbe, first clerk to the Commandant of the navy yard at Phil, asking Congress to cause an error to be corrected in relation to his compensation: referred. 8-Ptn from Jas Suddards, a passed assist surgeon in the navy, asking to be allowed a balance of pay which he alleges to be due: referred. 9-Ptn from John M Chase, for himself & other owners of the barque **Attica**, asking that certain money paid on account of that vessel, under a certain act of Congress, may be refunded: referred.

Another slice of the McDonogh estate gone. The Supreme Court at New Orleans has decided the case of Francis Pena vs the cities of Balt & New Orleans in favor of the plntf, who claimed $100,000 from the estate of the late John McDonogh, who, he claimed, bequeathed him the sum, to be paid in 4 years after his [McDonogh's] death. The Court decided that the document was authentic as it was fully established by 6 witnesses.

The late Rev Chas Avery, of Pittsburg, left an estate valued at $700,000. He bequeathed $100,000 to institutions & churches. His relatives were also handsomely provided for.

More damages against the Great Western Railroad Co: suit of Thos M Benson, plntf, son of the late Mr T Benson, of Port Hope, who was a passenger at the time of the accident & killed. Damages rendered: to the widow Benson $2,000; to the plntf $400; to Richd Benson $1,200; to Miss Benson $800; to Alicia Benson $1,200; to Emma Benson $1,200; & to Fred'k Benson $1,200.

Orphans Court of Wash Co, D C. In the case of John H Strider, adm of Eleanor West, deceased, the administrator & Court have appointed Feb 20 next, for the final settlement of the personal estate of said deceased, of the assets in hand. -Ed N Roach, Reg/o wills

Died: on Jan 27, Mrs Anna W Whitwell, aged 58 years, relict of John G Whitwell, & daughter of the late Capt John Coyle. Her funeral will be this afternoon at 2 o'clock, at the First Presbyterian Church, on 4½ st.

An arrest was made in Wash City by ofcrs Allen & Boss, of Luke Anderson, charged with the murder of Wm Griffin, near Aquia creek, Stafford Co, Va, on Dec 24 last. Anderson is in jail to await a requisition of the Govn'r of Va.

Worthy of Notice. Intending to retire from my present business, I offer a rare opportunity to anyone disposed to take charge of a Hotel conducted on the European style. Water, gas, & all other conveniences are upon the premises. The house is on Pa ave, between 3rd & 4½ sts. Address Wm Rupp, Proprietor.

FRI JAN 29, 1858

Senate: 1-Cmte on Revolutionary Claims: bill for the relief of Eliz Montgomery, heir of Hugh Montgomery. Same cmte: adverse report on the memorial of the heirs of John Champe. 2-Cmte on Commerce: bill for the relief of Simon De Visser & Jose Villarubia, of New Orleans. 3-Ptn from Danl J Browne, of the agricultural division of the Patent Ofc, asking compensation for extra services & an increase of his salary: referred. 4-Ptn from Geo McWeston, Com'r of Maine, asking the reimbursement of certain expenditures incurred by the State, as provided in the treaty of Washington: referred. 5-Ptn from the Copr of Gtwn, D C, asking an appropriation to complete the erection of lamp posts in that town: referred. 6-Ptn from O B Browne, asking indemnity for depredations in Kansas, committed by marauders during the political excitement in that Territory: referred. 7-Cmte on Military Affairs: bill for the relief of Mrs Agatha O'Brien, widow of Brvt Maj J O'Brien, late of the U S army. Same cmte: bill for the relief of Thos Phoenix, jr. Same cmte: adverse report on the memorial of S W Aldrick & others, ofcrs of the Tampico Mounted Rangers. 8-Cmte on Public Lands: bill releasing to the legal reps of John McNeil, deceased, the title of the U S to a certain tract of land.

Messrs Nathl Tyler & O Jennings Wise have purchased an interest in the Richmond Enquirer, & will in future be connected with the editorial dept of that paper.

The famous Chippewa Chief, Hole-in-the-Day, best known for his efforts in arresting the Spirit Lake murderers, was killed in a duel at Crow Wing, Minn, on Jan 12, by Mr Giggy, a citizen of Crow Wing. The cause of the duel was an insult given to Mr Giggy by the Chief while drunk.

On Jan 18, at Whitewater, Wisc, a party of young men inflicted a charivari upon Richd N Pierce & wife, a newly married couple. Pierce became exasperated at the affair & discharged a rifle, instantly killing Wm Hamilton age 21 years. Pierce, who is said to be a peaceable young man, gave himself up to the authorities.

Among the skaters at Northampton, Mass, a few days ago was Rev Dr Allen, aged 72, who exhibited a degree of vigor & agility quite equal to many of the boys.

Criminal Court-Wash-Thu. Mary McFerson was found guilty yesterday of manslaughter in the death of Nancy Buckhanan, on Sep 7 last, by beating her with a chair.

Mrd: on Jan 26, at St Paul's Church, Balt, by Rev Wm E Wyatt, D D, Chas J M Gwynn to Matilda E Johnson, daughter of Hon Reverdy Johnson.

Mrd: on Jan 14, at **Fort Leavenworth**, Kansas Terr, Capt Geo H Steuart, 1st Regt, Cavalry U S Army, to Miss Maria H Kinzie, adopted daughter of Maj D Hunter, U S Army.

Three days from Europe. An unsuccessful attempt had been made to assassinate the Emperor Napoleon. He was fired at on the evening of Jan 14 while entering the opera house. Three explosions from hollow projectiles took place. 60 persons were wounded & 3 killed. The conspirators are Italians. Many persons were arrested. The Emperor remained till the end of the opera, & was afterwards enthusiastically hailed by the people.

SAT JAN 30, 1858
House of Reps: 1-Memorial of Jas A Galligher, praying for relief against his unjust privation of a post ofc contract: referred. 2-Memorial of Hannah Stroop, of Phil, widow of John Stroop, a soldier of the U S army in the war of the Revolution, praying Congress to pass a law to grant her a pension.

Closing out sale at the Grocery Store of Wm M Cripps, by deed of trust: sale on Feb 4 next, at the store on La ave, between 6th & 7th sts: all the fixtures, counters, cases, scales & gas fixtures. –B H Laskey, atty for trustees -A Green auct

Bowling alleys & fixtures at auction, on Feb 1, at the Bowling Saloon recently kept by Mr Wiley, on D st, between 8th & 9th sts. -A Green auct

Mr Lemuel Putnan Grosvernor, who died in Pomfret, Conn, on Jan 19, has bequeathed to the Connecticut Historical Society the sword that was owned & used by Gen Israel Putnam during our Revolutionary struggle.

I have this day bought out the Drug Store, Pa ave & 4½ st, lately kept by W H Gilman, & shall keep on hand a full supply of Drugs, Medicines, Perfumery, Fancy Articles, & Photographic Chemicals. –Danl B Clarke [W H Gilman is retiring from the business & recommends Mr Clark.]

Died: on Jan 28, after a protracted illness of nearly 3 years, Ann Rebecca, in her 40th year, wife of Orlando R Delphy, & daughter of the late Wm Beck, of PG Co, Md.

Died: on Jan 23, at New Orleans, Granville S Oldfield, jr, only son of G S Oldfield, of Balt. But a few brief weeks have gone since Mr Oldfield, in the vigor of health was suddenly attacked by an acute disease. Even the gentle balmy air of the tropics failed their healing influences, & Mr Oldfield died, at New Orleans, on his return from Havana, surrounded by his family & friends. He was connected with the Treasury Dept, a valuable ofcr. -H

Mrd: on Dec 22, at the residence of her father, near Gonzales, Texas, by Rev Mr Jones, of the Episcopal Church, Anne Eliza Atkinson to H Clary Pleasants, of Clinton, Texas, formerly of Goochland Co, Va.

Cincinnati, Jan 28. The steamer **Fanny Fern**, bound to St Louis from Pittsburg, with 400 tons of produce, 15 cabin & 20 deck passengers, exploded her boiler this afternoon 18 miles' below this city. 15 lives are reported to be lost, including Capt Woodward, several deck hands & firemen, & 3 ladies. The boat took fire, burnt to the water's edge, & then sunk. The Ohio & Mississippi train brought up 30 of the passengers, 15 were wounded.

MON FEB 1, 1858
Household & kitchen furniture at auction on: Feb 11, at the dwlg corner of Green & West sts, Gtwn, the entire effects assisgned to us by Alex H Dodge. –H C Matthews, Edw Chapman, trustees -Barnard & Buckey, aucts

In a breach of promise case in Cincinnati, between Mary Jane Cribbet & Wm Mathers, the jury brought in a verdict of $10,000 for the complainant.

Criminal Court-Wash-Fri. 1-Saml Shekells was found guilty on a charge of assault in the same case as that in which Wm Garner participated on Jan 18. 2-Jas Kearny was found guilty of grand larceny, & sentenced to hard labor in the penitentiary for 1 year. 3-Chas Calvert, colored, was found guilty of petty larceny in 2 cases, & sentenced to 6 months' imprisonment in jail in each. 4-Michl McIntire was found guilty of a charge of larceny.

Fire in the first Ward on Sat broke out in one of the two adjoining houses, property of Mr Hook, on Pa ave, between 19th & 20th sts. Property destroyed: drug store & dwlg occupied by Mr C Hines, $1,000 insurance on the bldg, owned by Mr G Johnston, contents uninsured; a frame dwlg & property of Mr Waters, uninsured; Mr Hook's two house, a frame & brick; Mr Saml Duvall's dwlg, insured $2,500, but not enough to cover his loss. No doubt the work of an incendiary.

Mrd: on Jan 24, by Rev Wm H Chapman, Jas L Griffin to Miss Sarah Adeline Losser, all of Wash.

Died: on Jan 31, Mary Ann Hopkins, aged 2 years & 11 months, the only child of W M S & Sarah E Hopkins. She will be buried at 3 o'clock this afternoon, Feb 1st.

Died: on Jan 31, Charles F E, infant son of C F E & Charlotte Richardson. His funeral is today at 3½ o'clock.

TUE FEB 2, 1858
Valuable business stand at auction, on Feb 10, all that property known as Arny's Confectionary, fronting on Bridge st north side, between Wash & Congress sts, 21 feet, running back 276 feet. There is on the lot a first-rate 3 story brick store & dwlg, extensive back bldg, stables, & ice-houses. Sale positive. The title is perfect, & the terms must be complied with by Friday. –Barnard & Buckey, aucts

Senate: 1-Ptn from S W & A A Turner, asking compensation for the transportation of the mail in their steamboats from Cleveland, in Ohio, to Detroit, in Mich: referred. 2-Ptn from Alex'r Hays, late a lt in the army, asking to be relieved from a disability in the settlement of his accounts: referred. 3-Ptn from Eliz A Middleton, asking to be allowed a sum of money expended by her grandfather in the Revolutionary war: referred. 4-Ptn from A M Winn, asking to be reimbursed for moneys paid by him in relieving the sick & burying the dead in Calif, some of whom were emigrants from every State in the Union: referred. 5-Ptn from the widow of Capt H Addison, of the Sea Fencibles, asking to have her pension continued: referred. 6-Ptn from Isaac W Brown, representing that he has invented a new & useful fire-arm, which invention, he alleges, is used in the U S service, & asks an investigation thereof: referred. 7-Cmte of Claims: the case of the heirs & reps of Gastano Carusi, now pending before the Senate, be referred to the Cmte of Claims. Same cmte: bill for relief of Ephraim Hunt. Same cmte, to which was referred the bill from the Court of Claims for the relief of O H Berryman, submitted an adverse report on the same: ordered to be printed. Same cmte: to which was referred the bill from the Court of Claims for the relief of Moses Noble, reported it back without amendment, & recommended its passage. 8-Cmte on the District of Columbia: bill to incorporate **Gonzaga College**, & recommended its passage. 9-Cmte on Pensions: adverse report on the bill for the relief of John McVey. 10-Introduced: bill for the relief of Elijah F Smith, Gilman H Perkins, & Chas F Smith. Also, a bill for the relief of Mrs Jane Turnbull.

Parson Green, of Hempstead, Long Island, is 99 years of age, & was one of the Revolutionary soldiers who formed the hollow square inside of which the Declaration of Independence was read on Jul 4, 1776. After the war he entered the ministry of the Presbyterian Church, & for 60 years preached in Setancut, his salary not exceeding $300 a year. He was complimented with his annual donation party on Thu last.

House of Reps: 1-Ptn of Mary Ann Henry, widow of the late Capt Henry Henry, U S Navy, praying Congress to grant to her a pension.

The partnership heretofore existing between Lewis Johnson & Edw Simms, under the style of the Wash City Saving Bank, having expired, the general banking business will be hereafter conducted by the undersigned under the firm of Lewis Johnson & Co. -Lewis Johnson, David Walker, & L J Davis

Hon Freeborn G Jewett, ex-Judge of the Court of Appeals of N Y, died at Skaneateles, N Y, Jan 26. He served one term in Congress some 26 years ago, & has faithfully filled several offices of profit & honor in his State. At the time of his death he was 68 years old.

At New Haven, on Fri last, the examination of A S Tuckerman, charged with robbing the mails, began before Com'r Ingersoll. On Sat the prisoner waived further examination, & was bound over in the sum of $20,000 to take his trial on the 4th Tue of Feb. The prisoner, not obtaining the bail necessary, was returned to jail. [May 12th newspaper: On Friday the prosecuting atty, asked a verdict of acquittal from the jury. The evidence disclosed some strange processes in the banking business. –Balt Sun, May 8]

Jerome B Kimball was on Fri last elected Atty Genr'l of Rhode Island by the Genr'l Assembly of that State, to fill the vacancy occasioned by the resignation of Chas Hart.

Criminal Court-Wash-Mon: 1-Wm Garner guilty for assault with intent to kill a marine, Otto Sherman: sentenced to 4 years in the penitentiary. 2-Saml Gates was put to trial for a similar offence against Bridget Callahan; but, it appearing to have been accidental as regarded Bridget, he was acquitted. 3-Jas Power, a young man, was arraigned for the murder of Edw A Lutz on Dec 8 last in Marble Alley. His trial will go on for some days- Mr Morgan for defence.

More fires: on Sat the tavern kept by Mr Boarman, on East Capitol st, was totally destroyed. The hotel just north of the Railroad depot, built by the late John Foy, & of late occupied by Mr Lloyd, was totally consumed. The inmates escaped with difficulty.

John Miller, baggage master at Hartford, Conn, for the Providence railroad, has been arrested for robbing the mails. H confesses the crime.

Yale College, Jan 29. The annual Bishop Prize debate [founded by Hon Wm D Bishop,] took place on Jan 20 in the Sinonian Society of Yale College. Question: Ought the U S Gov't use force for the suppression of Mormonism? The umpires were W Hooker, M D, Jos Sheldon, & D C Gilman. Disputants: H A Post, H S Merhant, O A Roberts, W E Park, S H Davis, W E Sims, W H Fuller, E G Holden, W E Foster, J C Tyler, G M Towle, W Chester, T S Wynkoop, E L Gaul, S Shearer, C Eddy, & G E McLaughlin. The 1st Sophomore prize was awarded to Wm E Foster, of New Haven. The 1st Freshman prize to Henry S Merchant, of Nassau, N Y; 2nd prize, E G Holden, of Ohio; 3rd prize, S H Davis, of New London. Wm E Park & Sextus Shearer were meritoriously mentioned.

The Supreme Court of Mass, at its present session, has decreed as null & void from the beginning a marriage consummated some 5 years since, there being 2 children, the result of said marriage, now living. The case is that of Chas Heary Hill, of Billerica, & the allegation is that Emeline W Hill was at the time of her marriage with the said Chas Hill, & from that time to the present has been incapable of becoming a party to a marriage contract by reason of insanity. The question as to the amount & kind of insanity sufficient to disqualify a person from being a party to a valid marriage contract must have been a very nice one to decide, & in it are involved principles of vital importance never before settled by any similar decree from the Supreme Court in this State.
-Worcester Aegis

Letters received in Boston by the steamer **Canada**, dated Angier, Nov 22, report that a very serious mutiny had occurred on board the clipper-ship **Kate Hooper**, Capt Jackson, of Balt, bound from Hong Kong to Havana with a large number of coolies. The coolies for some cause broke out into mutiny, & at one time got possession of the lower deck, & 3 times set the ship on fire. Capt Jackson & his officers, by their determined action, finally overpowered the mutineers & suppressed the flames, but not until they were compelled to shoot some 50 of the ringleaders.

Hartford, Feb 1. John W Seymour, Sec & Treasurer of the Hartford Co Savings Association, left town on Sat, & subsequent to this departure it was ascertained that he was a defaulter to the extent of $100,000 or more. The money was lost in stock & other speculations. Seymour was president of the Mercantile Bank, which does not lose a dollar.

Albany, Feb 1. A verdict has been rendered in the Circuit Court against Dr Townsend, of Sarsaparilla fame, for $104,000 in favor of the heirs of Reuel Clapp. Dr Townsend was bondsman for the Howard trustee estate, & suit was brought to recover $80,000.

The subscriber offers his Farm & residence adjoining in Warrenton, Fauquier Co, Va, for sale: contains 265 acres; the house is entirely new, completed in the fall of 1856, contains 12 rooms, with closets & storerooms. There is a servants' house with 6 good rooms. Both houses are of brick. The stable is 60 x 40 feet. Address Nat Tyler, Warrenton, Va.

WED FEB 3, 1858
House of Reps: 1-Memorial of Jas Suddards, passed assist surgeon U S Navy, praying for relief.

Criminal Court-Wash-Tue: 1-Chas Davis, colored, was found guilty of stealing a watch & chain: sentenced to 16 months in the penitentiary. 2-Henry Dumbar, colored, was found guilty of assault & battery on a white man, J Brown; sentenced to 6 months' imprisonment in jail. 3-Saml Shekells, found guilty of assault on the marine Otto Sherman, was sentenced to 3 months' imprisonment in jail. 4-On motion of the acting District Atty, Clifton Hellen was admitted an atty of this Court.

Senate: 1-Ptn from P S Duvall & Co, asking indemnity for the loss of paper & plates for the second volume of the Japan Expedition, which were destroyed by fire in Phil in Apr, 1856: referred. 2-Ptn from Mary S Taylor & from Anna M E Ring, asking to be allowed bounty land: referred. 3-Cmte for the District of Columbia: bill for the relief of John Scott, Hill W House, & Saml O House. Same cmte: adverse reports on the memorial of the legal reps of Geo Mayo, deceased, & of Wm Moss. 4-Cmte on Pensions: bill for the relief of Wm Allen, of Portland, Maine. Same cmte: adverse report on the ptn of John Wentworth. 5-Cmte on Pensions: adverse report in the case of Elijah Roath. Same cmte: bill for the relief of Jeremiah Pendergrast, of D C. Same cmte: adverse report on the ptns of the heirs of Isaac & Sarah Blauvert, & of Garret A Hopper. 6-Cmte on Public Bldgs & Grounds: asked to be discharged from the consideration of the memorials of Sarah Foy, widow of John Foy, & of Randall Pegg, & that they be severally referred to the Cmte of Claims: which was agreed to. 7-Cmte on Revolutionary Claims: bill for the relief of the heirs of Lt Nathan Weeks, deceased. Same cmte: memorial of Herford Smith, reported a bill for his relief.

Shirley Female Seminary, Urbana, Fred'k Co, Md: institution commences on Feb 1 & closes on Jul 1. Address Geo G Butler, A M, principal.

THU FEB 4, 1858
Household & kitchen furniture at auction on: Feb 8, at the residence of T H Baird, 512 K st, between 4th & 5th sts. -A Green auct

Trustee's sale, by deed of trust from Jesse Reeler, recorded among the land records of Wash Co, D C, in Liber J A S No 117, folios 144: public auction on Feb 25 next, of part of lot 3 in square 558, with a new well-built 3 story brick bldg: at the corner of 3rd & K sts, one square in the rear of the fine dwlgs recently erected by Mr Douglas & others, in a most rapidly improving part of the city. –J H Goddard, jr, trustee -A Green auct

Mr John McChesney, lumber & coal merchant, of Toronto, Canada, died suddenly on Monday in a dentist's chair, after taken chloroform to have his teeth extracted.

House of Reps: 1-Cmte of Ways & Means: bill for the relief of Benj F Hall: committed. Same cmte: adverse report on the ptn of Dr Lewis Feuchtwanger: laid on the table. Same cmte: adverse report on the ptn of A H Abrahams, of Charleston, S C: laid on the table. 2-Cmte of Claims: bill for the relief of A Bandoouin & A DD Roberts: committed. 3-Cmte on the Post Ofc & Post Roads: adverse reports on the ptns of A Bingham: on L J Hillborn; & on Alex'r Hayes: all laid on the table. 4-Cmte on the Judiciary: reported adversely on the House bill for the relief of Jesse W Page, jr, of Tenn: laid on the table. Same cmte: adverse report on the ptn of the heirs of John G Camp: laid on the table. 5-Cmte on Revolutionary Claims: bill for the relief of Nancy D Holkar: committed. Same cmte: adverse report in the case of Nathl Riddick, adm of Richd Taylor: laid on the table. 6-Cmte on Private Land Claims: bill for the relief of John R Temple, of La, which was referred to the Cmte of the Whole. Same cmte: bill for the relief of Pierre Gagnon, of Natchitoches, La; committed. Same cmte: bill to authorize the claimants in right of John Huertes to enter certain lands in Fla: committed. 7-Cmte on Indian Affairs: bill for the relief of the heirs of Mary Jemison, deceased: committed. Same cmte: transmit all papers & correspondence relating to the official conduct of Anson Dart, late superintendent of Indian affairs in Oregon Territory, not heretofore transmitted. 8-Cmte on Military Affairs: bill for the relief of Whitemarsh B Seabrooke & others: passed. Same cmte: bill for the relief of the heirs of John J Bulow, jr, deceased: committed. Same cmte: bill for the relief of Wm Hutchinson: committed. Also, a bill for the relief of Thos Phenix, jr, late paymaser's clerk in the service of the U S: committed. Same cmte: adverse report on the ptn of Maj Bayley's battalion of Illinois volunteers for compensation for services during the Black War: laid on the table. 9-Cmte on Naval Affairs: adverse report on the memorial of Cmdor Thos Ap Catesby Jones; & on the ptn of seamen of the Gulf squadron for extra pay; also, on the ptn of John G Wilkinson: all laid on the table. 10-Cmte on Territories: bill for the relief of Harvey P Hovey: committed. 11-Cmte on Invalid Pensions: adverse report in the case of John Crinian, a soldier in the Rogue river war: laid on the table. Same cmte: bill to increase the pension of Henry K E Read, a citizen of Ky: committed. 12-Resolved, That Cmdor Hiram Paulding, in arresting Wm Walker & his associates, & returning them to the jurisdiction of the U S, acted within the spirit of his orders, & deserves the approbation of his country.

Ex-Govn'r Gaines, of Oregon, whose death was announced by the last arrival, was a native of Va. He served in the war of 1812 at the battle of the Thames & in the war with Mexico. During the latter war he was taken prisoner & confined for several months in the city of Mexico, but finally made his escape & joined the American army. He was frequently a member of the Ky Legislature, & twice elected to Congress from that State. He was appointed Govn'r of Oregon in 1849 by Pres Taylor, & served out his full term.

Hon Jas W Grimes, U S Senator elect from Iowa, in place of Hon Geo W Jones, for 6 years from Mar 4, 1859, has just completed his term of ofc as Govn'r of Iowa. He is a native of N H, & was formerly a Whig, but is now a Republican.

Mr Jos H Bowman, of Roxbury, died on Sunday from the effects of inhaling carbonic acid gas & carbonic oxyde gas, generated from the combustion of coal gas in a patent gas stove. A nephew of the deceased entered his room, having been attracted by a disagreeable odor, & discovered him lying on a sofa, dead. The room was badly ventilated.

Criminal Court-Wash-Wed: 1-Wm A Wroe found guilty of resisting an ofcr in the performance of his duty: sentenced to pay a fine of $10 & costs. 2-Chas Grant, colored, acquitted of larceny. 3-John Magee found guilty of 2 charges of assault on John McBride & his family on Dec 18: sentenced to pay a fine of $8 & costs in each case. 4-Franklin Minor, was, on motion, admitted an atty of this Court.

R W Young, a young man of highly respectable connexions, was arrested on a charge of embezzling drafts, bonds, & money letters, which came into his hands as a clerk in our city post-ofc. He was held to bail for trial at Court in the sum of $6,000.

Senate: 1-Cmte of Claims: memorial of Henry Hubbard for compensation for services as an agent of the U S for the preservation of public property at the harbor of Ashtabula, Ohio: bill for his relief. Same cmte: bill for the relief of David Myerle. 2-Cmte on Naval affairs: adverse reports on the following memorials, to wit: on that of Wm H Kennon, late purser in the navy; on that of Capt John Pope, of the navy; & on that of John Hughes, who served in a privateer during the war of 1812. 3-Cmte on Naval Affairs: bill for the relief of Thos Ap Catesby Jones. 4-Mr Chandler asked the Senate to take up the joint resolution for the compensation for R R Richards, late chaplain to the U S penitentiary, for his salary up to Jun 30, 1857, which was agreed to, & the resolution was passed.

House for sale: Prof D J Capron, of **St John's College**, Annapolis, will soon remove to his new house on the College grounds, & he offers for sale the House in which he now resides. It has a front on West st of 60 feet, & a yard & garden on Cathedral st of 171 feet. It contains 17 rooms. There is also a smoke–house & pump in the yard.

Genealogies of the Families & Descendants of the early settlers of Watertown, Mass, including Waltham & Weston; to which is appended the early history of the town, with illustrations, maps, & notes. By Henry Bond, M D. For sale by Blanchard & Mohun, corner of 11th st & Pa ave, Wash.

FRI FEB 5, 1858
Senate: 1-Ptn from Geo W Flood, a laborer in the Topograpical Bureau, asking compensation for services performed as clerk: referred. 2-Ptn from Edw Ambush & Robt Boston, employed as laborers in the Court of Claims, asking an additional compensation: referred. 3-Ptn from Sarah M Smead, asking an increase of her pension: referred. 4-Cmte on Revolutionary Claims: bill for the relief of Jas Bell, deceased: referred.

Criminal Court-Wash-Thu. 1-Patrick O'Callahan was acquitted of 2 charges of riot & disturbance in the First Ward. 2-John Hopkins was sentenced for riot in Gtwn, of which he was convicted some time since, & fined $8 & costs.

At Norwich, Ct, Widow Ann Randall came to a horrible death by hydrophobia, contracting by putting her hand, with a slight abrasion of the skin of one finger, into a pail of water which she had offered to a cow that had been bitten by a mad dog. The froth from the cow's mouth had become mixed with the water. [No death date given-appears to be a current item.]

House of Reps: 1-Cmte on Revolutionary Pensions: bill for the relief of the heirs of Wm York: committed. 2-Cmte on Invalid Pensions: bill for the relief of Isaac Carpenter; bill for the relief of Leonard Loomis; also, a bill for the relief of Hector St John Beatley: all committed. Same cmte: bill for the relief of Henrietta S Clark; of Thos Alcock; & of Mary W Thompson: all committed. Same cmte: bill for the relief of Timothy L O'Keefee, of Mo: committed. Same cmte: adverse report in the case of Thompson H Crosby: laid on the table. 3-Cmte on Patents: bill extending the patent granted to Wm Crampton for an improvement in figure or fancy power looms for 7 years from Nov 25, 1858: committed. Same cmte: bill for the relief of David Bruce: committed.

Mrd: in Wash City, at the Southern Methodist Church, by Rev Mr Granbury, A T McCallum, of Wilmington, N C, to Miss M C Beck, of Wash City. [No date given-current item.]

Died: on Feb 4, after a lingering & painful illness, Philip Otterback, born at Kunzelsau, in the kingdom of Wurtemburg, Sep 9, 1786, aged 71 years, a resident of Wash for 47 years. His funeral will be on Sun at 2 o'clock P M, at his late residence near the Navy Yard.

Died: on Feb 1, in Wash City, Thomas J Boyne, 2nd son of Thomas J & Cecilia Boyne, aged 3 years.

SAT FEB 6, 1858
Mrs W H Johnson, wife of the representative in the Missouri Legislature from Maries Co, was foully murdered last week by her step-son, who shot her with a pistol. He was arrested & confessed the deed. Mrs Johnson was formerly of Ky, & is respectably connected.

Orphans Court of Wash Co, D C. Letters of administration on the personal estate of Wm Morrow, late of Wash Co, deceased. –Alex Provest, exc

Criminal Court-Wash-Fri: 1-John Hopkins was arrested for having grossly assaulted Rev Mr Combs, of Gtwn. He confessed by his counsel a few days since in submission to the Court. He was sentenced to 3 months' imprisonment in jail.

Hon A C Dodge, American Minister at Madrid, Spain, has transmitted to Hon B F Hallett, of Boston, a copy of the pardon granted by the Queen of Spain, through the Minister of State, to John Campbell, of Boston. This young man, the son of a widow, was one of the crew of the ship **Waverley** at the time of the horrible act by which 200 Chinese Coolies were destroyed in the port of Manilla by the cruelty of the commanding ofcr. The crime having been committed within the Spanish jurisdiction of the Philippine Islands, the master & seamen of the **Waverley** were tried before the legal tribunal there & sentenced to the gallies. Among the prisoners was the young man Campbell, who was sentenced to 3 years' punishment in the chain gang. A year ago his mother applied to Mr Hallett, then U S Atty, who voluntarlily made the proper representation through the State Dept to Mr Dodge, American minister, to intercede with the Queen for the pardon of Campbell, who was in reality not guilty having acted ignorantly under the orders of the captain. –Boston Patriot

A despatch from Paris, dated Jan 16, announced the death of M de Argout, ex-Govn'r of the Bank of France.

MON FEB 8, 1858
Kansas Daily Ledger, published at Leavenworth, up to Jan 29, is partly occupied by depositions, taken by a Board of Com'rs appointed by the Territorial Legislature, showing the manner in which the late elections the Territory were conducted. Jas C Grinter sworn: was at Delaware Agency, Leavenworth Co, Kansas Territory, at the election held there on Jan 4, 1858; Theodore Garrett & Isaac Mundee were Judges; the clerks were Wm Wilson & Jas Findlay; Maj Robinson was there; Mr Garrett lives on the Wyandot lands; & Mr Findlay resides in Westport, Missouri. Isaac Mundee sworn: resides at Delaware Crossing, Kansas Territory, lived there 13 years. John D Henderson sworn: I consider my home in Leavenworth city; I left this place for Shawnee, in Johnson Co, on Jan 3; I saw Col Titus at the polls; Mr Oliver Diefendorf I suppose was the principal com'r. Diefendorf was appointed com'r by John Calhoun. He is a brother-in-law of Mr Calhoun. J H Noteware sworn: Mr Henderson was then under arrest, charged with altering the election returns from Delaware Crossing precinct; Henderson wished me to carry a letter to Calhoun; also requested me to see Gov Denver in his behalf. A B Miller sworn: resides in Leavenworth City, Kansas Territory; lived here since Mar, 1856; he saw Gen John Calhoun at Weston Missouri on Thu of Fri. Judge Cato is the Judge of the district in which Lecompton is situated. Richd Hathaway sworn: resides in Kickapoo precinct, Leavenworth Co, Kansas Territory; have lived there since 1855, & before the precinct was districted; to the best of my knowledge there are between three & four hundred voters in the entire precinct. John L Thompson sworn: resides in Kickapoo; has lived there about 2 years; knows nearly every person I meet who lives there; last May there were 375 voters in the precinct, according to the census taken by Mr Hathaway & my own knowledge. Wm H Elliott sworn: I am sheriff of Leavenworth Co; reside at

Kickapoo; was there at the election on Dec 21, 1857; have lived here nearly 3 years; I knew most of the men at the polls: Thos F Marshall, Thos H Benton, Horace Greely, John P Hale, Jas Buchanan, John C Fremont, J W Denver, Wm H Seward, Edwin Forrest, or Isaac Atchison; more than 6 Calverts over 21, 4 men by the name of Brooks; & J W Martin. Chas F Laiblin sworn: has resided in Kickapoo nearly 3 years. I find 70 names of persons whom I know to be non-residents. Green Arnot resides in Nebraska Territory; J B Black lives in Weston, Mo; J T Elkins, Wm Jacobs, L W Jacks live in Mo; H J Freeland lives in Platte city, Mo; Wm M Gibson lives in Weston, Mo; N Jenkins, Benj Jacobs, Thos F Marshall, Wm J Preston, non-residents; M O Jenkins resides in Weston Mo; John McDaniel resides near Weston, Mo; John Murdock, Robt Murdock, John McDonald, John L Merchant, C D Morris, Wm L Newman live in Platte Co, Mo; Wm Runnalls, Wm L Ross, live in Weston, Mo; Saml Ross, D R Ross live in Mo; Jas Thompson died at Kickapoo on Sep 7 last; Benj Tracy & Robt Tracy both left for Ky in July last, have not been back since; Thos F Tracy is about 13 or 14 years of age, lives in Kickapoo; Geo Wells lives in Mo. I do not know a man by the name of Jones living in the precinct; there are 24 of that name on the list. Do not know but 2 men by the name of Johnston there; I find 14 of that name on the list. I do not believe that one-half of the names on that list are residents of Kansas. John L Thompson sworn: has resided in Kickapoo about 2 years; know that the statements made by C F Laiblin in his affidavit before this board are true. [Mar 5th newspaper: More on the alleged frauds in the elections in Kansas on Dec 21 & Jan 4 last. Comrs' Court: 1-J W Denny, sworn, says he is Acting Govn'r of Kansas Territory. 2-Jas C Grinter sworn: was at Delaware Agency, Leavenworth Co, Kansas Territory, at the election held on Jan 4, 1858. Theodore Garrett & Isaac Mundee were other judges; the clerks of the election were Wm Wilson & Jas Findlay. 3-Isaac Mundee was sworn: resides at Delaware Crossing, Kansas Territory; has lived there 13 years. 4-Benj F Dare & Chas Mayo, com'rs appointed, made solemn oath that they would faithfully discharge the duties imposed upon them as com'rs to take the census for the township of Oxford. –S F Hill, Judge Probate]

Maj Henry D Brevoort died at his residence in Detroit on Sat last. He was connected with the U S service in his youth, having been a lt of marines on the Ohio river, at 1790, in command of a gun-boat. In 1797 he was order to Lake Erie, & took charge of the new war brig **Adams**. During the war of 1812, he was in the battle of Lake Erie, which resulted in the great Perry's victory. High official encomiums were passed upon his gallant conduct. -Advertiser

Rev Geo E Fisher, dismissed by council from the Congregational Church, North at Amherst, Mass, preached a farewell sermon, in which he expressed his opinion with perfect freedom of the opposition which procured his dismission. He said: "It was an opposition conceived in sin, brought forth in iniquity, increased by ignorance, fed by envy, fostered by jealousy, promoted by pride, fanned by disappointed ambition, continued in malice, encouraged by timidity, strengthened by the unexpected yielding of good men, perpetuated in stubbornness, & triumphant in self-will & wickedness."

Hon Fayette Mcmullin, Govn'r of Washington Territory, refers to the able report of his predecessor, Gov Isaac J Stevens, on the Nothern Pacific Railroad, a valuable work.

Trustees of the Upper Marlborough Academy wish to engage a gentleman to take charge as Principal for the ensuing year. –Jas Harper, Pres of the Board of Trustees

I have a note to pay, & in order to meet it will sell Wood & Coal much lower than the usual prices for cash. –H B Riehle, N Y ave, between 13th & 14th sts. P S-2,240 lbs to the ton.

A deaf mute named Benj Rollins, between 50 & 60 years of age, was killed in Marion Co, Alabama, while on his way to Bexar Co, Texas. He had left the public road & was discovered by a young man whom he so frightened by his attempts to talk that he shot & killed him. Over $1,300 in gold & silver was found upon his person. His heirs are advertised for.

Obit-died: on Jun 13, 1857, in the Mission House at Cavalla, near Cape Palmas, west Africa, Rev Hugh Hamilton Holcomb, recently a resident of Wash for many years, aged 32. He was born in Granby, Conn, & educated by his father, Saml C Holcomb, A M, & entered Trinity College, Hartford, Conn, in 1841; entered Union College, Schenectady, in his senior year; graduated with honor in Aug, 1845, at age 20 years. He then resided in Wash for several years, engaged in the study of the law, & in 1852 was admitted to the bar in the District of Columbia. He entered the Theological Seminary, Alexandria, Va, & was ordained deacon by Bishop Meade Jun 29, 1855. On Mar 14, 1856, he sailed for Africa, & landed at Capt Palmas Jun 13, just 1 year before his death. Rev S D Dennison, of N Y, Sec of the Board of Foreign Missions, on Nov 15 last, in Trinity Church, in Tariffville, Conn, preached an impressive sermon commemorative of the virtues & death of Rev Holcomb. Rev Henry H Bates took part in the service.

Criminal Court-Wash-Sat. 1-Benj Robinson, colored, convicted of manslaughter in killing a colored boy named Thos Turner: sentenced to 3 years in the penitentiary. 2-Jos C Lewis, Jos K Lewis, Benj Devaughn, Chas Knowles, Thos Campbell, & Asa Knowles were put to trial for riot on 7th st in Sept last. The evidence failed to prove any riot; the jury found an acquittal.

The Association of the Survivors of the Soldiers of the war of 1812 assembled on Sat to appoint a delegation to represent them in the celebration of Feb 22, at Richmond, Va. The following compose the delegation: Col Wm W Seaton, Pres of the Assoc; Col John S Williams & Gen St John B L Skinner, Vice Presidents; Jas Laurenson, Sec; Jas A Kennedy, Treasurer; Maj Edw Simms, Col Wm P Young, Marshal, F B Lord, Wm Miles, Chas Fletcher, F R Dorsett, Maj Burgess, Col Peter Force, Wm A Bradley, Gen Roger C Weightman, Thos Quantrille, Jacob Gideon, Peter Bergman, & A Baldwin-delegates.

Died: on Feb 6, Michael, aged 9 months, son of John & Agnes McDermott. His funeral will be this evening at 3 o'clock, from his father's residence on D, near 7th st.

TUE FEB 9, 1858
John H Seavers, superintendent of the American Hospital at Staunton, Va, committed suicide at that place on Monday last by taking laudanum. He was formerly manager of the Columbian Hotel at Richmond.

The annual report of the Atty Genr'l contains a table noting the names, ages, & birthplaces of 25 persons, who, according to the report of the Coroner Dannoy, have committed suicide in New Orleans during the year 1857. The youngest of these self-murderers was 12 years of age, Francis Noe, a German. The eldest was Richards, aged 66 years. Four of them were women: Mary Mahon, an Irish women, Mrs Siffrin, a German, Eliza Jessesson, a Virginian, & Helena Silliers, a German.

Danl Chisholm, who lived alone, near Oakland, Allegany Co, Md, was found murdered in his bed on Thur of last week. He was a bachelor & has lived alone for a long time.

Senate: 1-Ptn from the legal reps of John Love, a surgeon's mate in the army of the Revolution, asking a pension: referred. 2-Ptn from the administrator of J W P Lewis, asking the payment of a balance due said Lewis as agent for bldg a light-house on Sand Key, Fla: referred. 3-Ptn from Anna M McKenny, widow of the late Chaplain Wm McKenny, asking to be allowed a pension: referred. 4-Ptn from Louisa Merrill, widow of an ofcr of the army killed in the war with Mexico, asking the renewal of her pension: referred. 5-Ptn from Jas B Thomas, asking to be compensated for certain Indian depredations: referred. 6-Ptn from Geo Clermont & other, citizens of Mass, asking that the public land may be appropriated to the free & exclusive use of actual settlers: referred. 7-Cmte on Private Land Claims: bill for the relief of the heirs & legal reps of Jose de la Maya Arredondo. 8-Cmte of Claims: bill for the relief of Geo Phelps.

Fatal accident on Butte Creek, Oregon, on Dec 2: John Matthews & a young man, Woodson Tucker, went hunting. It appears that Matthews accidentally shot & killed him, supposing he was a bear. Matthews was exonerated of blame. –Oregon Sentinel

Criminal Court-Wash-Mon: 1-Frank Shann was found guilty of assault on Chas H Robinson: sentenced to pay a fine of $5. 2-Wm Johnson, similarly charged, was similarly convicted & sentenced. 3-Geo A Springman was charged with assault & battery on Chas Schunk: fined $10 & costs.

Died: on Sunday, in Gtwn, at the residence of her father, Geo Poe, jr, Mrs Caroline De Bow, wife of J D B De Bow. Her funeral is this afternoon at 4 o'clock. The friends & acquaintances of the two families are invited to attend.

Died: on Feb 8, after a protracted illness, Mrs Mary Gibbs, relict of the late John V Gibbs, in her 68th year. Her funeral will take place from the residence of her son-in-law, Mr J P Keller, 469 13th st, on Feb 10, at half past 12 o'clock.

Died: on Feb 8, Mr Jos Stephenson, sr, aged 81 years. The deceased was a native of Northumberland Co, England, but for the last 33 years a resident of Wash City. His funeral will be on Feb 10 at 2 o'clock P M, from Ryland Chapel.

In pursuance of an order passed by the Circuit Court of PG Co, in the matter of the application of John L Townsend for the benefit of the insolvent laws, the creditors of said John L Townsend previous to his application for the benefit of the Insolvent Laws are notified to file their claims, duly authenticated, with the Clerk of said Court on or before May 1 next. –Danl C Digges, trustee

WED FEB 10, 1858
Large stock of fine imported liquors, wines, & cordials: at public auction: owing to unexpected business arrangements elsewhere, the Messrs Moner & Co, of N Y, will discontinue their agency in Wash City, on Feb 16, at the store 367 Pa ave, opposite the Nat'l Hotel. –Wall & Barnard, aucts

Senate: 1-Ptn from Jeremiah Y Dashiel, a paymaster in the army, asking to be released from responsibility for certain public money lost by the upsetting of a boat in the surf at the mouth of the Indian river, in Fla: referred. 2-Ptn from Jas Hendebert, asking that he may be reimbursed for money advanced to Capt Hudry while engaged in the prosecution of his claims against the U S before Congress: referred. 3-Ptn from Robt A Parkhill & 149 others, of N Y, asking that the public lands may be set apart in farms or lots for the exclusive use of actual settlers: referred. 4-Cmte on Pensions: adverse report on the ptn of Thos Johnson. 5-Cmte on Revolutionary Claims: adverse report on the memorial of Mary D Hayes & R S Fassett, & upon the heirs of the Revolutionary ofcrs of the Continental line.

Hon G S Duncan died at his residence in Clarksburg, Va, on Feb 5; about 68 years of age. He was a man who filled with honor many offices of high public trust.

At Taunton, Mass, Mr Thos Shaw, 35 years old, was poisoned to death by drinking a solution of cyanuret of potash & nitrate of silver, at the house of a friend. He lived only 5 minutes after drinking it.

In the Court of Common Pleas at Cincinnati, on Fri, Jacob Parker was sentenced to imprisonment in the penitentiary for the term of his natural life, for killing a young man named Bennett.

London Times: Marshal Radetzky, who has played so prominent a part in the history of the Austrian Empire during the last 75 years, recently expired at the age of 92. He was born at Trobuitz, in Bohemia, in 1766. He fell & broke his hip & lingered until the morning of the Feb 5th, when he expired. Radetzky was married in 1797 to the Countess Fanny Strassoldo, by whon he had 5 sons & 3 daughters. Of these only 1 son & 1 daughter survive. His son is a staff ofcr in the Austrian service; his daughter is married to Count Wenkheim.

Isaac Tunnell, cashier of the Farmers' Bank at Gtwn, Del, has held that position for 50 years, & is now 91 years old.

Mr Levi J North, the well-known equestrian, now a Chicago millionaire, is a candidate for alderman in that city.

House of Reps: 1-Cmte of Claims: bill for the relief of Benj L McAtee & J L Eastham, of Louisville, Ky: committed. Same cmte: adverse report upon the claim of Addison Farnsworth for property lost during the Mexican war; adverse report in the case of Wm B Barry; & adverse report in the case of Ephraim Shackley: all laid on the table. Same cmte: bill for the relief of Brvt Maj H L Kendrick: committed. 2-Cmte on Commerce: adverse report on the ptn of John B Bayleys for a law to prohibit the importation of liquors: laid on the table. 3-Cmte on the Post Ofc & Post Roads: adverse report on the ptn of J W Sullivan: laid on the table. Same cmte: bill for the relief of John F Cameron: committed. 4-Cmte on the District of Columbia: bill to reimburse to the Corp of Gtwn, in D C, a sum of money advanced towards the construction of the Little Falls bridge: committed. Same cmte: bill to provide for the payment of the claim of J W Nye, assignee of Peter Bruzy, jr, & Hugh Stewart: committed. 4-Cmte on Revolutionary Claims: bill for the relief of Mary E H Van Buskirk: committed. 5-Cmte on Military Affairs: joint resolution for the relief of Gen Sylvester Churchill: committed. 6-Cmte on Invalid Pensions: adverse report on the case of Andrew Longsbough, an applicant for an invalid pension: laid on the table. Same cmte: bill for the relief of Mary Boyle: committed. 7-Memorial of Margaret Watts praying she may be allowed half-pay pension: presented. 8-Memorial of B Clovis Renois, of St Clair Co, Ill, praying for a half-pay pension, or other allowance, to the minor children of Jos Tremble, deceased, who was an invalid pensioner of the U S. 9-Bill to continue the pension heretofore paid to Mary C Hamilton, widow of Capt Fowler Hamilton, late of the U S army: introduced. 10-Bill for the relief of Hannah Stroop: introduced.

The Belair [Md] Aegis states that the 5 year old daughter of Mr Devereux, was shot dead by a small orphan boy near Fork Meeting-house on Monday. Her mother went to the store, & left her child in charge of the little boy until she returned. A loaded gun was left in a corner of the room, which in handling discharged, the contents hitting the little girl.

Orphans Court of Wash Co, D C. Letters of administration de bonis non on the personal estate of Thos Barnes, late of Wash Co, deceased. –Edw Simms, adm de bonis non

The late Jas M Ramsey: the ofc of the First Comptroller of the Treasury Dept held a meeting of the ofcrs & clerks on Feb 6, to express their deep sense of the loss that the public service & themselves have sustained in the demise of their worthy chief clerk, Jas M Ramsey. [No other information.]

Mrd: on Feb 9, in Balt, by Rev Wm H Pitcher, A P Douglas, of Wash, to Miss Laura Virginia Pitcher, of Balt.

Mrd: on Feb 9, in Wash City, by Rev D Ball, at the McKendree Church, Mr Wm W Lester, of Miss, to Miss Eliz J Walker, daughter of Mr J T Walker, of Wash City.

Mrd: on Feb 9, in Wash City, by Rev Mr Ball, at the residence of the bride's mother, Mr John W Anderson, of Balt, to Miss Charlotte L Knight, of Wash.

Criminal Court-Wash-Tue: 1-Geo Smith pleaded guilty to stealing a coat, hat, & umbrella of Mr Wetherall: sentenced to 1 year in the penitentiary. 2-Wm Ferguson, Dink, alias Martin King, & Andrew Kidwell, who have been confined several months in jail on a charge of rioting, were discharged from jail. They are to appear at the next term. 3-Benj Ogle was arraigned on the indictment for the murder of the boy John Webb, in Gtwn, preparatory to his trial, which is set for Tue next, to which day the Court adjourned.

In the matter of Saml Lee, a Lunatic. Peter M Pearson, the trustee, reported the sale of the real estate of the said Saml Lee, consisting of parts of lot 1 & 2 in square 767, to Chas S Whitney for $250; & purchaser complied with the terms of sale. –Jno A Smith, clerk

In Equity. John Hooper & Jas Hooper, vs Abel Bird, Mgt Bird, Chas Bird, Eburn Bird, John H Bird, Susan C Bird, Mgt H Bird, John P West & Ann E West his wife, & Wm H Ward, heirs & adms of Wm Bird, deceased. The parties to the above cause are to appear before me to be heard touching the premises, & the creditors of said Wm Bird to file their claims with me, at City Hall, on Feb 18, at 12 o'clockM. –Walter S Cox, Special Auditor

THU FEB 11, 1858
Household & kitchen furniture at auction on Feb 17, at the residence of M M Hitchcock, No 443 9th st, between F & G sts. -A Green auct

Senate: 1-Cmte on Naval Affairs: bill for the relief of Edw D Reynolds.

Orphans Court of Wash Co, D C. In the case of Edwin C Morgan, exc of Rezin Estep, deceased, the executor & Court have appointed Mar 6 next, for the final settlement of the personal estate of said deceased, of the assets in hand. -Ed N Roach, Reg/o wills

Appointments by the Pres, by & with the advice & consent of the Senate:
Consuls:
Geo Vail, of N J, at Glasgow
John S Daney, of N C, at Dundee
Alex Henderson, of Pa, at Londonderry
H Rives Pollard, of Kansas, at Bangkok
Brooke B Williams, of D C, at Revel
F L Sarmiento, of Pa, at Venice
John D Diomatari, of Ga, at Athens
Stokes L Roberts, of Pa, at Trinidad de Cuba
John B Costa, of Texas, at Nice
Jos Walsh, of Louisiana, at Monterey

Obit-died: Rev Beverly Waugh, the senior Bishop of the Methodist Episcopal Church, died at Balt on Tue last, in his 69th year. He was born in Fairfax Co, Va, in 1789; joined the church in 1805, became a minister in 1808, elevated to the Bishoprick of the Church in 1836. The departed Bishop leaves a wife, 1 daughter, & 3 sons.
+
Rev Bishop Thos A Morris, who has been Bishop next in the order of seniority, will succeed to the rank of senior Bishop, vacated by the death of Bishop Waugh.

Fatal accident in target shooting yesterday, by which the life of drill sgt Wm Webb, well known in the militia corps of this city & elsewhere for his professional skill, has been brought to an untimely close. He & Hunter, the drill sgt of the fort, were in a shooting match, when due to his near-sightedness, he accidentally shot Webb. Webb died later in the hospital of the fort. -Toronto Leader, 5th..

Died: on Feb 9, Mrs Provey Gadsby, widow of the late John Gadsby, aged 73years. Her funeral will be from her late residence, No 1 President's Square, on Thu, at 1 o'clock.

Died: yesterday, in his 8th year, Jackson Morton, youngest son of Hon Jackson Morton, of Fla. His funeral will be this afternoon at 3 o'clock, from the residence of his father, 432 G st.

Patapsco Female Institute, Md: announces the additional bldgs & improvements commenced by them a year ago, are now completed; the new chapel is handsome & most appropriate, for the exclusive use of the inmates of the Institute. Mrs Lincoln Phelps intends to resign her ofc of Principal at the close of the present school year, & Robt H Archer has been elected as her successor. For many years he conducted the School for Young Ladies in the city of Balt. —Chas W Dorsay, Pres; Wm Denny, M D, Sec; T Watkins Ligon, E Hammond, John P Kennedy.

Orphans Court of Wash Co, D C. In the case of Edwin C Morgan, adm of Lewis J Kennedy, deceased, the administrator & Court have appointed Mar 6 next, for the final settlement of the personal estate of said deceased, of the assets in hand.
-Ed N Roach, Reg/o wills

Orphans Court of Wash Co, D C. Letters of administration on the personal estate of Jas Dixon, late of Wash Co, deceased. —Jas Walker, Dorsey's Hotel, adm

FRI FEB 12, 1858
Mrd: on Feb 10, in Wash City, by Rev Raymond Young, Henry M Morris, of N Y, to Eliza, daughter of the late Maj P G Howle, of the U S Marine Corps.

Mrd: on Feb 8, at N Y, by Rev Dr Hawks, Maj Jas G Martin, of the U S Army, to Hetty, daughter of Chas King, Pres of Columbia College.

Died: on Feb 10, in Wash City, of paralysis, Mrs Mary Ann Canfield, in her 63rd year, after a short illness. Her funeral will be today at 2 o'clock P M, from the residence of her son, corner of 11th & I sts.

Died: on Jan 25, at his residence, in Chas Co, Md, Saml C Moran, in his 58th year.

Senate: 1-Ptn from Capt Wm P Paff, of Albany, N Y, asking leave to enlist a rifle regt into the service of the U S to serve during the war in Utah Territory: referred. [He proposes to command the regt, & to have the appointment of his own staff & field ofcrs, subject to the orders of the superior officers of the regular service, & 320 acres of land to each officer & man upon condition of settling there.] 2-Ptn from W W Bassett, late a master in the navy, asking to be allowed the difference between the pay of master & that of lt for the time he acted in that capacity. Ptn from Edson Sherwood & others, of Green Bay, Wisc, asking the confirmation of a title to certain lands claimed by the Domestic & Foreign Missionary Society of the Protestant Episcopal Church in the U S. 3-Ptn from Sarah A Searle & Eliz Pennegar, heirs of a Revolutionary ofcr, asking to be allowed half-pay.

SAT FEB 13, 1858
Capt Wm V Taylor, of the Navy, died at his residence in Newport on Thu, aged 70 years. He was in the battle of Lake Erie & navigated the ship **Lawrence**, Com Perry's flag-ship, into & during the action. His last cruise was in command of the ship **Ohio 74**, on a cruise to the Pacific. Since that time the infirmities of age have gradually overcome him.

Pittsburg, Feb 12. Henry Fife & Charlotte Jones, the McKeesport murderers, were hung at 2 o'clock. Both delivered addresses acknowledging the justice of their sentence & pronouncing Stewart innocent.

House of Reps: 1-Cmte of the Whole-adverse reports from the Court of Claims on the ptns of Fred'k Griffin; Francis Pickard; adm of Pierre Ayott; Geo W Dow & John H Ditmas; Danl Van Winkle; Jos Lorenger; Michl Musy & Andre Galtier; Henry G Carson, adm of Curtis Grubb; Philip Lamoy & others; Ezra T Marnay, adm of Louis Marnay; Henry Miller; Stephen C Hayden; David Noble; E B Chamberlain & others, heirs of Capt Joshua Chamberlain; Eliza Shafer, widow of Jonathan Shafer; Alexander; H Cook; Jas M Thorne; J C Buckles; J H King & others, heirs of Jas Green; T S J Johnson; Llewellyn Jones; Robt S Garnett; Ann W Butler, admx of Gen Richd Butler; Christiana Dener, widow of Geo Fred'k Dener; Stephen C Philips, adm of Jonathan Porter Felt; Ralf Richardson, exc of Mgt B Cameron, daughter of Jas Bell; Nathl Williams; the heirs of Hugh Hughes; Richd L Page, adm of Wm B Page; Robt Roberts; Saml M Puckett; John P McElderry; Louis G Thomas & others; Shepherd Knapp; Wm W Cox; J D Holman, exc of Jesse B Holman; John C Hale; Susan Decatur; H L Thistle; Abel Gay; J Boyd; J K Rogers; Cortland Palmer; Rebecca Heald, widow of Maj Nathan Heald; Benj H Springer; John Etheridge; of Ill Central Railroad Co.

Yesterday the carpenter's shop of Mr Cissel, at Gtwn, was set on fire & consumed with its contents.

The Grand Lodge of Masons of Virginia have adopted a plan of co-operation with the Ladies' Mount Vernon Association in the purchase of **Mount Vernon**. It is by a small but adequate assessment of each Mason in the U S, [one dollar each,] with the single condition that they shall have full liberty to occupy the premises one day in each year. There is stated to be an aggregate of 350,000 members in the U S. The Southern Matron, as Pres of the Ladies' Mount Vernon Association has gratefully accepted the proposition, & a circular on the subject has been sent to each Grand Lodge in the U S from the Grand Lodge of Va.

Mrd: on Feb 4, in Gtwn, by Rev Dr Murray, Mr Richd Davis to Miss Amelia a Claxton, all of Gtwn.

Mrd: on Feb 11, at St Matthew's Church, Wash, D C, by Rev Mr Waldron, Chas De Ronceray to H Rosalie Crosson.

To the heirs of Walker Reid, late of Mason Co, Ky, deceased. You are hereby notified, that, under a decree of the Circuit Court of Fairfax Co, Va, in the case of Reid vs Reid, you are entitled, as heirs & distributees of Jane Reid, late of said county, deceased, to the sum of $595.21, & to one negro girl. Upon proof of heirship the same will be decreed to be paid & delivered to you. The heirs are represented to be: John Reid, son of said Walker, residing in Lafayette Co, Mo; Jos Key, infant son of Mary Key, deceased, late of Mason Co, Ky, who was a daughter of said Walker, & 3 infant children of Charlotte Beatty, deceased, [names unknown,] late of Thibbedeauxville, La, who was another daughter of said Walker Reid. Address me at Fairfax Court-House, Va. –Alfred Moss, Receiver of the Circuit Court of Fairfax Co, Va.

Thos Jefferson's father, Peter Jefferson, is described by Mr Randall as a man of gigantic stature, plain, & averse to display-he was grave, taciturn, slow to make, & not over prompt to accept, advances. He was one of those calmly & almost sternly self-relying men, who lean on none, who desire help from none.
And, he certainly had both muscles & mind which could be trusted. He could simultaneously "headup" [raise from their sides to an upright position] two hogsheads of tobacco, weighing nearly a thousand pounds apiece. He once directed three able-bodied slaves to pull down a ruinous shed by means of a rope. After they had again & again made the effort, he bade them stand aside, seized the rope, & dragged down the structure in an instant. Traditions have come down of his continuing his lines as a surveyor through savage wildernesses after his assistants had given out from famine & fatigue, subsisting on the raw flesh of game, & even of his carrying mules, when other food failed.

Orphans Court of Wash Co, D C. Letters testamentary on the personal estate of Ann R Delphy, late of Wash Co, deceased. –Enoch Burnett, exc

Died: yesterday, in Wash City, Mr Wm Cox, in his 48th year. He was a native of Loudoun Co, Va, but has been for the last 20 years a resident of Wash, & for some years one of its most effective police officers. His funeral will take place on Sunday at 2 o'clock, from his late residence on F st, between 9th & 10th sts, Island.

MON FEB 15, 1858

Foreign Obituary. 1-Fred'k Wm Louis, Grand Duke of Baden, died on Jan 21. He was born on Sep 20, 1829, succeeded as regent in place of his brother Louis, Apr 24, 1852, & was created Grand Duke by patent Sep 5, 1856. His wife is a daughter of the Prince of Prussia, & sister of the husband of the Princess Royal of England. He will be succeeded by his infant son, born in 1857, but probably the Grand Duchess, his widow, will be regent. 2-Wm Spencer Cavendish, 6th Duke of Devonshire, died at Hardwicke Hall, Derbyshire, on Jan 17, aged 68 years. He has been well known as one of the wealthiest of English noblemen, the Lord of Chatsworth & other estates that were fit to be residences for royalty. He died unmarried, & is succeeded by his cousin, Wm Cavendish, Earl of Burlington. 3-On Jan 22, while the preparations for the royal marriage in St James' Palace were going on, the Marchioness of Westmeath, who occupied apartments in the Palace, adjoining the Royal Chapel, where the ceremony was to be performed, died, & the signs of mourning were exhibited at the moment that the nuptial arrangements were making. These death had cast a gloom over the courtly circles in the midst of the wedding festivities.

Ex-Pres Fillmore was married last week at Albany. The bride is the widow of the late Ezekiel C McIntosh, & has for some time occupied the Schuyler Mansion, formerly the residence of Alex'r Hamilton, & subsequently occupied by Col Schuyler. The bride will accompany her husband to Buffalo to reside.

Sugar Estate-the **Houmas plantation**, near Donaldsonville, La, lately owned by Col John S Preston, has been sold to John Burnside, of New Orleans, for one million of dollars.

Obit-died: Rev Dr Saml Gilman, D D, of Charleston, S C, pastor of the Unitarian Church of this city. He died yesterday at the residence of his son-in-law, Rev Chas J Bowen, at Kingston, Mass. He had been in declining health for some weeks. We believe he was in his 68th year, & had been pastor of the Unitarian Church of Archdale st for about 39 years. He was a graduate of Harvard in 1811, & received his first pastoral call in 1819, as successor to Rev Anthony M Forster.

Mrs Perry, the widow of Cmdor O H Perry, died in Newport on Thu, after a brief illness. Since his lamented death in 1820 she has resided in Newport, occupying the venerable mansion purchased by Cmdor Perry at the close of the war of 1812. She had for a neighbor & friend the widow of the gallant Capt Lawrence, of the ship **Chesapeake**, who is still living. On the morning of the day of Mrs Perry's death, & in the same town, died her husband's companion in the battles of Lake Erie. Capt Taylor's death was occasioned by paralysis. He was 78 years of age.

Col Wade Hampton, of S C, died suddenly at his plantation in Mississippi on Feb 10, as we learn by a private dispatch from Columbia.

Mrs Fifield, a young wife, was drowned at Millbridge, Maine, when an ice-boat in which she was sailing ran into an open place on the falls. She was carried under the ice & lost; the rest of the party escaped.

Dr Edwin Price, of Brunswick, Mo, died at his residence there on Jan 24, of erysipelas. The disease first made its appearance on his upper lip, from thence it spread with great rapidity to his brain, causing death in less than 48 hours. He was an old citizen of Missouri, & was universally esteemed as a man of sterling integrity.

Died: on Feb 9, at his residence, in Leesburg, Loudoun Co, Va, Dr Geo Lee, in his 57th year.

S B Martin, an itinerant artist, shot & killed Mr Cunningham, aged 60 years, of Mansfield, La. The difficulty originated in words which passed between the parties while Martin was intoxicated. He was committed to jail.

Rit Rev Alonzo Potter, Bishop of the Episcopal Church in Pa, is said to be in a critical condition at Greensbury, Pa, from an attack of apoplexy on Wed last.

Freeman's Journal: Rev Dr McFarland, has been appointed Roman Catholic Bishop of Hartford, Conn.

Orphans Court of Wash Co, D C. Letters testamentary on the personal estate of Francis B Stockton, late of Wash Co, deceased. –Anna P Stockton, excx

Orphans Court of Wash Co, D C. Letters of administration, with the will annexed, on the personal estate of Thos R Gedney, late of the U S navy, deceased. –Jas L Edwards, Adm, with the will annexed.

Boarding on Capitol Hill: Chas P Russell, 68 East Capitol st, between 2nd & 3rd sts. [Ad]

TUE FEB 16, 1858
Orphans Court of Wash Co, D C. Household & kitchen furniture at auction on: Feb 19, at the late residence of Mrs Cmdor Cassin, deceased, the entire personal effects. –Barnard & Buckey, aucts [No address given.[

Ex-Govn'r Wm Bebb, of Ohio, who now resides near Rockford, Ill, was last fall indicted for shooting at & mortally wounding one of a party of reckless young men who were infesting his residence & annoying his family with a charivari or horning party on the occasion of the marriage of one of Gov Bebb's sons. He was tried for murder last week at Rockford, & triumphantly acquitted. Tom Corwin & Judge Wm Johnston, of Ohio, conducted the defence.

Senate: 1-Memorial from Geo M Weston, Com'r of the State of Maine, asking the reimbursement to that State of the expenses incurred in organizing a regt for the war with Mexico. 2-Ptn from Ambrose Whitlock, asking additional compensation for services as receiver of public money at Terre Haute & Crawfordsville, Ind. 3-Addition papers submitted in relation to the claim of Benj Ward. 4-Ptn from Nathl Hayward, asking an extension of his patent for an improvement in the manufacture of India rubber. 5-Ptn from C J Fox, U S Consul at Aspinwall, in relation to an increase of his salary, & showing pretty clearly by statements in figures the utter inadequacy of the pay. 6-Ptn from Jas W Rea, adm of Jas H Mattocks, deceased, asking compensation for property destroyed by the Indians. 7-Ptn from Walter James, asking compensation for a horse lost while employed in transporting baggage & munitions of war in the last war with Great Britain. 8-Ptn from Danl Whiteness, asking the confirmation of his claim to a certain tract of land at Green Bay, Wisc. The above 7 were all referred. 9-Cmte on Indian Affairs: bill for the relief of the heirs of John B Hand. Same cmte: bill for the relief of W G Hansell, _ H Underwood, & the reps of Saml Rockwell. 10-Cmte on Foreign Relations: bill for the relief of the legal reps of J E Martin. 11-Cmte on the Judiciary: asked to be discharged from the consideration of the act for the relief of Whitemarsh B Seabrook & others, & that it be refered to the Cmte on Military Affairs; which was agreed to. 12-Cmte of Claims: bill for the relief of the heirs at law of the late Abigail Nason, sister & devisee of John Lord.

House of Reps: 1-Ptn & papers in the claim of Sidney S Coudon, of Jonesborough, Ill, praying compensation for services rendered as Assist Surgeon in the Mexican war: presented. 2-Ptn & papers in the claim of John C Rathbun, of Madison Co, Ill, praying a pension for wounds received in the war of 1812 with Great Britain in the line of duty.

Jas E Eldridge was hung at Canton, N Y, on Thu, for the murder by poison of Sarah J Gould, a young widow, to whom he was affianced. He was a school teacher, 21 years of age, & Miss Gould was 24. Jas Toole & Danl Tenbrook, two of the young men engaged in the murder of Teresa Spitzlen at N Y, have plead guilty of manslaughter in the 1st degree, & been sentenced, Toole to 12 years & 3 months imprisonment, & Tenbrook to 10 years & 2 months.

Died: on Feb 15, in Wash City, at the residence of Mr A Green, 400 D st, Mr Geo M Merrett, a printer by profession, & a native of Luzerne Co, Pa. Although a stranger in this city, the deceased commanded the respect & esteem of all with whom he became acquainted. His funeral will be today at 3 o'clock P M, from the above place.

Indianapolis, Feb 15. Policemen Hohl & Castillo were shot by an Irishman while interfering to prevent a disturbance in a drinking saloon on Sat night. Castillo is dead, & Hohl fatally wounded.

WED FEB 17, 1858
Chancery sale of valuable property: by decree of the Circuit Court of Wash Co, D C, made in a cause wherein Jos Libbey is cmplnt & Jas B Phillips & others are dfndnts: public auction on Mar 10 next, of Lots U & V, in the subdivision of lots 1 thru 4, 10,

& 11, in square 452, fronting on Mass ave & 6th st west, with the cottage dwlg thereon. Also, part of lot 1 in square 452. –Wm R Woodward, trustee -A Green auct

Senate: 1-Ptn from Saml H Taylor, asking additional compensation as messenger & laborer in the ofc of the Third Auditor: referred. 2-Ptn from Anthony Casto, a soldier in the last war with England, asking to be allowed a pension: referred. 3-Ptn from Martin Layman, asking permission to enter a quarter section of land on which he had settled & made an improvement in Minnesota, before the Gov't surveys had been made in that territory: referred. 4-Ptn from the surviving partner of Benj & Thos Laurent, asking that certain moneys belonging to that firm, & take by Gen Scott as property of the Gov't of Mexico during the war, may be refunded: referred. 5-Cmte on Military Affairs: bill for the relief of Brvt Maj J L Donaldson, Assist Quartermaster U S army. 6-Cmte on Foreign Relations: bill for the relief of Geo W Lippitt. Same cmte: bill for the relief of Capt Chas G Ridgeley, U S Navy. 7-Cmte on Pensions: bill for the relief of Hannah Stroop, widow of John Stroop, deceased. 8-Cmte on Claims: bill for the relief of Jas Suddards. Same cmte: bill for the relief of Geo H Howell. Same cmte: asked to be discharged from the consideration of the ptn of memorial of Henry S Crabbe, & that it be referred to the Cmte on Naval affairs: which was agreed to. 9-Cmte on Pensions: asked to be discharged from the consideration of the ptn of Richd E Randolph, & that it be referred to the Cmte on Public Lands: which was agreed to.

Orphans Court of Wash Co, D C. Letters of administration on the personal estate of Chas G Ridgely, late of the U S Navy, deceased. –St Geo Croghan, adm

Orphans Court of Wash Co, D C. Letters of administration on the personal estate of Benj Laurent, late of the city of Mexico, deceased. –David Bone, adm

In this place on Sunday last, Mrs Hannah Eisenbise, wife of Maj Danl Eisenbise, was burnt to death when a fluid lamp accidentally fell from the table onto her lap while she was reading the Bible. Her husband hurried to subdue the flames, but to no avail. She lingered in the most excruciating agony until the next morning, when death relieved her of her sufferings. –Lewistown [Pa] Democrat

Chas Albaugh, a young man, was sentenced to 3 years in the penitentiary for mail robberies. He was the son of highly respectable parents at Mount Gilead, & but a fortnight ago was married to a young lady of one of the first families there. He had been employed to carry the mail from Mount Gilead to the railroad.
–Cleveland Herald of Feb 12.

Andrew McNally, a young man, died at the N Y Hospital on Sat, from accidentally drinking a quantity of cyanide of silver. He died about an hour after drinking it.

Died: on Feb 14, Levi H Parish, aged 64 yers. His funeral is on Wed at 2 o'clock, from his late residence on Missouri ave, between 3rd & 4½ sts.

Died: on Feb 15, Mr John C Nevins, of the Dept of State. He graduated at Gtwn College, & has always resided in the District. He was among the most efficient clerks employed in the Census Ofc under Mr Kennedy, where his knowledge of foreign languages & his talents as a statistician rendered his services of great value. Form the Census Ofc he was transferred to the Dept of State. His funeral will be today at 4 o'clock, from his mother's residence, on E st, opposite the Gen Post Ofc.

Died: on Feb 15, of consumption, Minnie, eldest daughter of Maj Jas M McRea. Her funeral is this evening at 4 o'clock, from the residence of her father, 2nd st west, between B & C sts.

For sale: a cottage-house at Ellaville, about half a mile from the Bladensburg depot of the Wash & Balt railroad. Inquire of Chas B Calvert, near Bladensburg, Md.

THU FEB 18, 1858
Distinguished engineer, Mr Thome de Gammond, has published his curious memoir on the practicability of a submarine tunnel between France & England. Mr Thome estimates the total expense at a hundred & seventy million francs-too large for private capital.

Clinton Courier: Wm Phelps, an octogenarian, & one of the oldest residents in Oneida Co, N Y, has taken leave of his many friends there, & started for a new home in Wisconsin; & adds that his late residence & adjoining grounds on Verona st, *Vernon*, has been purchased by Rev John Henry Canoll, late of Albany.

Valuable lot for sale adjoining Brown's Hotel, fronting on Pa ave: by decree of the Circuit Court of Wash Co, D C, in equity, in a cause wherein Celinda J Byng is cmplnt & Jos H Bradley & Virginia Byng et al are dfndnts, passed on Jan 21, 1858: sale on Mar 15 in front of the premises, at public auction, part of the west half of lot 4 in square 491, in Wash City, D C. –Jos H Bradley, jr, trustee -Jas C McGuire, auct

Senate: 1-Ptn from Margaret McGuire, asking that her pension may be continued: referred. 2-Ptn from Marie Genand, sole heir of John Hudry, deceased, asking the reimbursement of money advanced in the years 1814-15 by said Hudry during the defence of New Orleans: referred. 3-Additional evidence presented in the claim of Chas West to a pension. 4-Cmte on Naval Affairs: bill for the relief of Lt Joshua D Todd, U S Navy. Same cmte: bill for the relief of Robt Carter, Passed Assist Surgeon in the U S Navy. Same cmte: adverse report on the claim of Robt Morris for remuneration while in service on board the U S ship **Vandalia**. 5-Cmte of Claims: bill for the relief of Joshua Shaw, of Bordentown, N J.

Died: Feb 16, Mrs Mary Wollard, wife of J F Wollard, in her 36th year. Her funeral will take place today at 3 o'clock P M, from her late residence on D, between 7th & 8th sts.

All persons are warned not to purchase or sell Land Warrant No 50,500 for 160 acres, issued in favor of Jas C Pierce on account of services rendered in the Mexican war, as a caveat has been filed in the Land Ofc & application made for a duplicate warrant.

Wilmington, N C, Feb 17. The river steamer **Magnolia**, hence for Fayetteville, exploded her boiler yesterday at Whitehall, killing 15 or 20 persons. Some of the bodies have been recovered, but many are missing. [Feb 20th newspaper-**Magnolia**: white persons killed: Capt Stedman, cmder of the boat; Dr Fellows, a young gentleman from Phil, said to have been raised in Sampson; Mr Tyson; a female from Wilmington, & boy about 8 years old, neither names known. Colored persons killed: Simon, the cook; Chas, the pilot, & 2 or 3 others, names unknown. A colored man named Carver, or Carter, was mortally wounded. The boat was valued at $10,000. –Wilmington {N C} Journal]

Criminal Court-Wash-Wed. 1-Jury in the trial of Benj Ogle for the murder of John Webb in Gtwn on Jan 10 last: John Laurie, Jas W Coombs, Richd Abbott, Geo W Uttermuhle, Geo Burns, Wm H Baum, Robt Cohen, Thos Milstead, Henry A Clarke, Lewis Wright, Jas Crandell, & Richd Butt. Witnesses: Godfrey M Hunter, also a boy; Walter S Cox, of Gtwn; Mr Wm Slemmer; Thos Ball; & Dr Snyder. Mr Richd H Trunnel testified to arresting Ogle in his house, & finding the gun in the room where he was. When witness entered the room Ogle was sitting down eating. Mr Joshua Bateman testified that the mother of Ogle is crazy, that his father was not very sound, & his aunt hardly compos mentis; that Ogle is drunk three-fourths of his time, or always when he gets liquor; that he talks simple & foolish at times. Sold Ogle, or rather his wife, a house 9 months ago. They had paid for it. Mr Geo Ellis testified that Ogle's aunt acted strangely sometimes. Has seen her once with a rope round her neck. His mother used to walk about late at night. Mr Jacob Riffle had known the parents of Ogle. Though the father not right in his mind & the mother at times deranged. She had once told him that a whole row of houses in Gtwn was hers, but they had been taken from her by fraud. Ogle's uncle was crazy also. Dr Lauck had been Ogle's physician several years. Ogle is a very intemperate man, & almost always under the influence of liquor. Had attended him about 2 months ago for mania a potu. Had never considered him insane except when drinking. Defence closed. [Feb 19th newspaper: Mr Slicer Dennison testified-saw marks of bullet shots on Mr Slemmer's house, & on a tree box, after the shooting. Mr C P Sengstack was Ogle's master, with whom he learned his trade. He lived 6 months with witness. Knew his father & always thought him absent-minded at times. His mother was also very subject to aberrations. When Ogle lived with witness he gave signs of partial mental aberation; he left his employ suddenly & without reason. He is also very near-sighted. Mr Robt Waters, the jailor of the county, testified that during Ogle's being in jail since Jan 20 he had seen no evidences of insanity in him. He was perfectly rational, & behaved well & civilly. Mr Thos Ball had known the prisoner a long time. Never before heard of his being near-sighted, or his sight being bad.]

FRI FEB 19, 1858
The trial of Isaac L Wood, at Genesco, N Y, on an indictment for murdering Rhoda Wood, his brother's wife, by poison, came to a conclusion on Wed. The jury were unable to find a verdict; 11 were for conviction, but the 12th, Mr Moses Long, would not concur, because he had conscientious scruples respecting the death penalty. Wood is under another indictment for the murder of his brother.

York [Pa] Republican: on Tue, in Manchester township, 5 children ventured too far upon the ice on the Codorus, & 3 of them drowned: 2 were sons of Mr Baylor, & the other a son of Mr Philip Lehr. Mr Hubley rescued the 2 other children at the risk of his own life.

Senate: 1-Ptn from Frank Madison, a colored man, who served as waiter in the Florida war, asking to be allowed a pension: referred. 2-Cmte of Claims: bill for the relief of Anthony S Robinson, heir & legal rep of Jno Hamilton Robinson. 3-Cmte on Naval Affairs: 2 bills each for the relief of Thos J Page. 4-Cmte on Public Lands: adverse report on the memorial of John Pickell. Same cmte: adverse report on the ptn of Mary Hopper, widow of John A Hopper.

The Pres has pardoned John Webster, sentenced in June last to 12 months' imprisonment for participation in the riots at the 7th Ward precinct. He was discharged yesterday.

Died: Thu, at his residence, on 9th st, near G st, in his 59th year, John Robt Dorsey, eldest son of the late Judge Walter Dorsey, of Md. Exemplary in his relations of husband, father, son, & brother, the deceased will long be held in affectionate remembrance by those who knew him. His funeral will be from his late residence, this afternoon at 3 o'clock.

N Y, Feb 18. John Brower, an eminent merchant, committed suicide by hanging on Sunday morning.

Martha Wailes, Florian Hitz, & Wm H Stanford, against Benj M Wailes, Stephen C Wailes, Isaac Newton Wailes, Jacob S Black, & Mary Anna Black. The parties above named are notified that on Feb 27 I shall state an account of the personal estate of Isaac H Wailes, deceased, the debts he owed at his death, & inquire if it be necessary to sell part of his real estate in aid of his personal for payment of his debts. Meeting at my ofc in the City Hall, Wash. —W Redin, auditor

City property to be sold for taxes: Collector's Ofc, City Hall, Wash City, Feb 19, 1858. To whom assessed-years due 1856 & 1857.

Allen, Albert G	Arnold, Jos W
Armitage, Benj	Adams, Jas
Abert, Chas	Adams, Jemima & others
Andrew Cornel	Adams, Mgt
Ashford, Craven	Allen, Mary E
Addison, Danl D	Arvine, Richd
Appleby, Geo W	Ayton, Richd
Armstrong, Geo B	Ager, Susan E
Atkinson, Geo	Adams, Saml H
Andrews, Horatio N:	Anderson, Saml J
Adams, Jos	Adams, Thos N
Austin, John	Austin, Wm F
Ager, Jas B	Austin, Wm
Anderson, Jas	Adams, Wm

Arnold, Wm
Ager, Jas B & Wm McLean
Bowman, Alex H
Balmain, Andrew
Brush, Abner
Bennett, Alex'r
Bean, Benj
Butler, Benj
Bayliss, Buckner
Butler, Clement M
Ball, Chas G
Bell, Chas
Bennett, Clement W
Beall, Chas
Boyle, Cornelius & others
Barrett, E B
Bury, Eliza
Bird, Eburn & John H
Bowen, Fielder
Ballinger, Francis
Ball, Francis H
Bailey, Gamahel
Bryant, Geo, [colored]
Bomford, Geo
Barker, Geo
Borgershausen, Geo W
Bowman, Hannah
Berrien, Hobart
Bateman, Henry E
Butler Henry, [colored]
Barry & Holtzman
Brooks, Henry
Brown, Hanson
Ball, Henry W
Ball, Henry W & others
Barker, Jas W
Bright, Jesse D
Bond, John F
Bronaugh, John C
Brown, John D
Brereton, John
Boone, John F
Biglow, Jacob
Boyle, John
Boss, Jas H
Bradley, Jos H

Addison, Anthony, & W Cockrell

Ball, John
Beaseley, Jos
Burche, John C, in trust
Bull, John B-colored
Barry, Julianna
Birch, Jas H
Breckinridge, J
Brady, John
Bryan, John
Butcher, Jas
Baeschlin, John
Beach, Levi
Borreman, Mary Ann
Barker, Murray
Byrne, Moriah
Brown, Marshall [colored]
Bowen, Martha
Brooks, Mary
Bryan, Mary A
Brady, Nathl
Bias, Noah
Brown, Patrick & wife
Briscoe, Palmer
Bell, Patsey
Bridgett, Richd B
Barry, Richd
Bale, Robt
Buchley, Rudolph
Brent, Robt Y
Boarman, Ralph
Briscoe, Richd G
Bowling, Robt
Brown, Robt S
Brown, Robt T
Brooks, Richd
Burns, Richd
Bryan, Sarah E
Bowen, Sayles J
Bagget, Saml J
Brereton, Saml
Burche, S Q A
Burche, Saml
Byington, Saml
Brown, Thos [colored]

Bingey, Thos S
Burley, Thos
Benton, Thos H
Barrett, Thos J
Bicksler, Thos J
Blagden, Thos
Ball, Wm H
Birth, Wm W
Breckenridge, Wm D
Bigley, Wm
Burdett, Walter W
Bates, Wm
Berry, Augustus F, trustee for J F Kidwell
Boen, Anthony, Wm Craig, & P Briscoe,
Brown, Wm, in trust for E Carrico & others
Campbell, Ann
Clements, Aloysius N
Cheshire, Archiblad
Cook Abraham
Clements, Benj H
Chambers, Benj
Choteau, C P
Clements, Chas A
Chubb, Chas St John & J M
Collins, Charlotte & Mary E
Codrington, Camilla
Collar, Chas B
Church, Chas B
Connolly, D A & Eliz
Chapman, Eliz
Curtis, Edw
Chester, Elijah
Costigan, Eliza
Cross, Eli
Craig, Eliza J & Indiana
Casteel, Edmund
Curry, Francis
Campbell, Geo W
Cochran, Geo W
Collins, Geo W
Crown, Geo W
Coombe, Griffith
Clark, H B
Carrico, Jas
Campbell, Jas
Compton, Julia R

Baby, Wm
Bradley, Wm A
Bush, Wm [colored]
Bosse, Wm
Becket, Wm
Beach, Wm
Boone, Wm
Bird, Wm, jr
Bronaugh, Wm J
Baden, J W, T E, E, & W W
Bradley, Wm A & Wm Thompson
Brady, Nathl, in trust for E McGilton

Corse, J D
Collins, Jas F
Colclazer, J F
Cloakey, John E
Cassiday, Isabella
Cope, Jasper
Coombes, Jos J
Connor, Jas
Clarke, Jos S
Cole, John A
Considine, John
Crutchett, Jas
Cannon, John
Crandell, Jas
Clark, John D
Cushley, John
Clarke, Jas T
Costigan, John
Carroll, Jas T
Coombs, Jos J & J Welsh
Chisholm, Lewis
Conington, Michl
Connor, Martin
Cluskey, Michl W
Cavenaugh, Michl
Callahan, Mary
Childs, Mary
Callan, Nicholas
Callan, Peter
Clapdore, Parmelia
Curtis, Patrick

Coumbe, Rachael
Cruit, Richd
Cox, Richd S
Cochran, Robt
Chilton, Saml
Chilton, Saml, in trust
Cassin Stephen
Cloakey, Saml
Clarke, Stephen
Cook, Saml
Corcoran, Thos & W W
Corcoran, Thos
Collins, Thos
Connelly, Thos & John
Connolly, Thos C
Cokendorfer, Thos
Croggan, Thos
Chandler, Walter S
Collins, Wm
Corcoran, Wm W
Campbell, Wm [colored]
Clampitt, Wm H
Clarke, Wm
Coumbe, Wm
Campbell, Wm W
Cocking, Wm
Coke, Wm [colored]
Cranch, Wm G
Costtin, Wm
Cross, Washington
Collins, Wm T
Cabot, Jos Scahoe, John F
Curtis, Thos & others, trustees
Coleman, Henry & E Williams
Clarke, Jos S & R G Briscoe
Chittenden, Henry A & H C Bowen
Caton, Michl, use of Eliz Holland
Callan, Nicholas, in trust for Jan Lynch
Clarke, Richd H, in trust for E Hassler

Collins, Reuben, in trust for Mary A Campbell
Clark, Robt & others, trustee of the Baptist Church
Carbery, Thos & W Jones, in trust for E Miles
Collingsworth, Wm P, in trust. On 4th st the same which was conveyed to A D Collingsworth by John G Adams, by deed dated Nov 23, 1854.
Carlisle, Jas M, Geo S Gideon, & W D Davidge, in trust. Due for 1855, in the name of W H Winder

Dayton, Aaron O
Davis, Alex'r McDonald
Davidson, A B
Dent, Benj
Davis, Charlotte
Dunbar, Betsey & Susan
Dove, Benj M
Dart, C H B
David, Schs B
Dougherty, Cornelius A
Donaghue, Dennis & Patrick
Donaldson, Danl
Dyer, Edw C
Davidson, Eleanor
Dyer, Edw
Douglas, Earl
Dickens, Francis A
Dyer, Geo F
Davis, Geo A
Dove, Geo M
Dent, H H
Densley, Hugh
Douglas, Henry
Dodson, Henry [colored]
Digney, Hugh
Daly, Jas
Dobson, Jos
Dove, Jos
Donelan, Jas B
Dickson, John
Drury, John H
Duvail, John
Dickson, John & Wm King
Dulin, Joshua V
Davis, John F
Dyer, John F
Dyer, John F in trust
Dufief, John L

Dalton, John
Davis J & G W Garrett
Disher, Lewis
Devers, Lewis
Degges, Mgt O
Davidson, Mgt
Donoho, Mary
Dove, Marmaduke
Doll, Maximillian
Daley, Oliver A
Drueken, Phillippine
Donnoghue, Patrick
Duley, Robt W
Dyer, Edw, in trust for Susan Thomas
Diamond, Alex'r, Saml Byington, & Richd Wallach
Eaton, Chas & J M
Ellis, Chas F
Edelin, Chas K
Eckloff, Edw C
Evans, Estwick
Eakle, Elias H
Evans, French S
Edelin, Horace, in trust
Ellis, Henry
Elliot, Jonathan
Espey, Jas
English, John A, & Wm Bayne, trustees
Favier, Agricol
Fatio, America G
Faw, Abraham
Fowler, Abraham
Fales, Barnabas
Fisk, Chas B
Flint, Chas W
Finch, David
Fitzgerald, David
Fox, Gracey Ann
Fields, Geo
Fisher, Henry
Farrell, Harriet
Fowler, Henderson
Faber, John C
Fox, John, & J W Van Hook
Fowler, John L
Freeman, John, jr, & others
Farrar, John

Doyle, R E
Davis, Richd [colored]
Dement, Richd
Donn, Thos C
Davis, Thos B
Donovan, Wm
Durr, Wm
Dewees, Wm
Donelan, Wm C
Downing, Wm B
Davidge, Walter D
Denham, Z W

Elvans, John R
Edelin, Jos
Elliot, Lynde
Edwards, Lewid
English, Patrick, in trust
Emerick, Peter
Ellis, Robt
Easby, Wm
Evans, Wm
Ewing, Wm G & Geo W

Foller, John
French, Jas
Fugitt, Jos
Fenne, J Brooks
Fitzgerald, Jas
Foy, John
Fry, Jos
Fowler, Jas J
Fowler, Jas J, in trust
Follansbee, Jos
Foulkes, John C & wife
Fraser, Jas, jr
Frank, Lewis
Fowke, Lucy B
Ferris, Mgt
Foy, Mary A & Sarah
Forrest, Mary
Fleet, Mgt
Frye, Nathl
Ford, Patty

Flannery, Patrick
Ford, Sarah
Frasier, Simon
Fugitt, Thos M
Fahey, Thos
Forrest, Wm H
Fort, Wm S
Foster, Adams, in trust for Susan Burch & children
Faulkenberger, Chas & Alex'r Wittenauer
Farquhar, E Y, in trust for Jane L Taggart
Gladmon, Addison B
Gibson, Amy
Gladmon, Burgess K
Graves, Banner
Green, Ben E
Grenacker, Caroline
Gaston, Catharine J
Garner, Catharine H
Gallagher, Danl
Gill, David
Gallant, Edw
Goddard, Emma A C
Greenleaf & Elliott
Grindall, Edw
Geddes, Geo
Graham, Geo M, in trust
Gillis, Groenveldt, & others
Griffin, Sarah A
Gonter, Saml M
Gibson, Stephen D
Gregg, Saml
Green, Thos E
Gwinn, Sarah Jane, Susannah M & Francis A
Hyde, Anthony
Hoover, Andrew
Hetzel, A R
Hines, A F
Hamilton, Anna M
Heitmiller, Alfred & Anton
Humphries, Ann M
Herold, Adam G
Hill & Brother
Hollohan, Christopher
Havener, Chas W
Horseman, Geo
Hunt, Henry & B O Tayloe

Faherty, Wm P, in trust
Foster, Wm J
Fraser, Wm
Faulkner, Wm H
Force, Wm Q
Fischer, Harriet & Thos Gunton

Garrett, Geo W
Grammer, G C
Goldsborough, Jno B
Garland, John
Gadsby, John
Goddard, Isaac
Garner, Jas W
Glover, Jane
Goddard, John H
Gardner, Jacob B
Greenleaf, Jas
Gallighan, Jas, & son
Gill, John F
Groff, Michl
Grenan, Patrick
Gallant, Peter

Gray, Thos K
Gadsby, Wm & A Newton
Gordon, Wm
Goddard, Wm C
Gunnell, Wm H

Harkness, Danl S
Homans, Danl
Hall, David A
Hollidge, Eliz
Hubbard, Eleanor
Haw, Eliza F
Howard, Flodoardo
Housam, Fred'k
Hill, Geo
Herrick, Geo R
Harvey, Geo, in trust
Hall, Henry
Hoban, Henry

Harman, John L
Hicks, Josiah
Holtzclau, John M
Hutchinson, Jas
Hurley, John
Henry, Jas
Houston, John H
Howard, John F
Herd, John
Heise, Jos L
Hurley, John
Howard, Jos
Herrity, Jas
Hoffman, John W
Hennessy, John
Henke, Lewis, trustee
Hunt, Montgomery
Hetzel, Mgt J
Houston, Mary F
Hughes, Thos
Holmes, Wm
Haislip, Wm, & others
Howell, W P & J W Morsell
Herbert, Wm W, in trust for Amelia J Irwin
Holtzclaw, T J & R W Bruff
Herty, Jas, Mary Ann, & others
Heath, Geo A [assessed in the name of Wm H Gunnell]
Ingle, Christopher, in trust
Ireland, Susan
Iddins, Saml
Johnson, thos J
Jewell, Wm
Jackson, Alex'r
Johnson, Chas H
Jones, Chs S
Jackson, Chaney
Jeffers, Columbus
Jones, David & B Minon
Johnson, Dearborn
Jones, Emily G
Johnson, Lewis, in trust for M A McGunigle
Kibble, Alex'r
Kaiser, Adam
Kleindenst, Antoine
Kennedy, Christopher
Kiernan, Chas

Hamilton, Mary M
Hawkins, Matilda [colored]
Hoover, Michl
Hannay, Peter
Higgins, Patrick
Hepburn, Peter, jr
Hill, Mary B
Harrison, Richd
Hawley, Reuben
Hyde, Richd
Hutton, Salome R
Harkness, Saml
Hamilton, Sarah
Hyatt, Seth
Harkness, Thos F
Havenner, Thos
Havenner, Thos H
Hurley, Thos
Hickey, Thornton F
Hardy, Wm
Howison, Wm G
Hutchinson, Wm

Ingram, Washington
Ingle, Wm

Jones, Francis Lee & others
James, John S
Joy, John, jr
Jones, Jas
Johnson, John
Jones, Joel W
Johnson, Richd D
Johnson, Saml
Jones, Joel W
Johnson, Jas & others, trustees

Kingman, Eliah
Key, Francis S
Kendrick, Francis J
Keithley, Francis
Keating, Geo

Key, Henry S
Klopfer, Henry A
Key, John Taylor
King, John H
Kelly, Jas
Kurtz, John & others
Kennedy, J C G
King, John F
Kay, Jas
Kedglie, John
Kidwell, John H
Kibbey, John B
Kleindenst, John
Kennelly, Martin
Leggett, Aaron
Lindsay, Adam
Luckett, Alex'r
Lephard, A & A F
Landrick, Ann
Lewis, Alfred J
Longdon, Chas
Linkins, Chas
Lee, D C
Lawrence, De Witt C
Lutzohann, Dorothe
Lacey, Emanuel
Lautner, Geo
Leehy, John
Lare, John G
Larcombe, John
Little, John E
Lewis, Thos J, in trust for C E Lewis
Lockery, Edw, A W Thomas, & W T Hook
Michlin, A H
Matthews, Allan
Macomb, Alex'r
Miller, August
Miller, A W
Milburn, Benedict
McCorkle, Christiana
Mix, Chas E
Myers, Chas
McNamee, Chas
Myers, Chas [colored]
McDonald, Danl
Mitchell, Danl

King, Martin
Kain, Mary
King, Nathan G
Key, Philip
Kurtz, Peter
Knight, Saml M
Kane, Sarah
King, Saml D
Keally, Sarah A
Kelly, Thos
King, Wm
King, Wm F, & others
Kibbey, Wm B
King, Z M P
Lane, Jonathan H
Lewis, John T
Lambell, Kelly H
Lear, Louisa
Lanahan, Michl
Lloyd, Mary E
Leslie, Robt
Leckie, Robt
Lackey, Robt J
Lloyd, R B
Lewis, Saunders
Lunt, Saml
Lundy, Thos
Lloyd, Thos
Law, Thos
Lenox, Walter
Lambert, Wm & Eliza Cissell

Mudd, Dominick
McCarthy, Eugene
Mosher, Eliza M
Milstead, Eliza
McGinness, Eliz
Meigs, Francis C
McCarthy, Florence S
McGlue, G T
McKnight, Geo B
Mitchell, Geo W
Massey, Geo T
Mitchell, Harriet M
Morfitt, Henry M

Maryman, Horatio R
Maryman, Horatio R, in trust
Magruder, Henry [colored]
Mason, Jas M
Mason, Jos
Mitchell, Isaac W
Moore, Jas
Mickum, John T
Meade, Jas H
McKnight, John L
Mulloy, John J
Magill, John W
Melvin, Josiah
Mankin, Jas
Merman, Jane
Morgan, John B
Marlow, John W
McCollum, John J
McGinnis, John, jr
McGuire, Jas C
McLeod, John R
McCalla, John M
Maury, Isabel,
McKelden, J C
McCarthy, John F J C, & Jos
Missimer, John
McCauley, John
McGill, John B
McKeon, John B
Murphy, John D
Milstead, John D, in trust
Mitchell, John [colored]
Morgan, E C, in trust for E O Magruder
Mc Ginnity, Mich L & Thos Williams
Nailor, Allison
Newton, Augustine, in trust
Nourse, Chas H
Noyes, Crosby S
Naylor, Henry, trustee
Naylor, Henry
Nally, Henry
Nairn, Jos W
Naylor, Henry, in trust for Matilda E Smith
Nailor, Dickerson, in trust for Wm C Nailor
O'Neale, Dennis
Oyster, Geo

Maguire, Jas
McGee, John S
Mister, Isaac
Mackall, Leoanrd
Mitchell, Levi
McDowell, Mary B
Mountz, Michl
Mackey, Mary
Mitchell, Martha A
Mitchell, Perry A [colored]
Meister, P A B
Moore, Rhoda
McPiers, Sarah
McMeehan, Sarah A C
Morsell, S T G
McDowell, Sally C P
Mosher, Theorore
McLaughlin, Thos
Morris, Thos
Moseley, Wm H
Maddox, Wm A T
Magruder, Wm B
Morton, Wm
McLean, Wm
Morrow, Wm
Mockabee, Wm
Martin, Wm
Mohun, Wm P
Maxwell, Wm H
McKnew, Z W, in trust
McLean, Wm, & Saml C Wroe
May, Fred'k, & Julia M McRae

Naylor, Joshua S
Nelson, Madison
Norfleet, Thos
Nicholas, Wm S
Nourse, Wm
Norris, Wm G
Naylor, Henry, in trust for E Walls
Nichols, Wm S & W W Corcoran

Owens, Jas
O'Neale, John H

O'Donaghue, Patrick
Osgodby, T W, in trust
Pleasonton, Alfred
Pons, Anthony
Powers, Ann
Patterson, Basil
Pratt, Cary
Pettit, Chas
Phillips, Catharine
Phelps, Chas H
Peter, David
Pancoast, David
Peugh, David L
Peter, Geo
Parker, Geo & Thos
Preinhart, Geo C
Parker, Geo
Peck, H P K
Pratt, Henry, & others
Polk, Jas
Powell, Jas
Porter, John E
Phillips, John H
Pumphrey, John W, in trust
Phillips, Jas B
Pumphrey, Thos B, Jas W, & Francis A
Philips, Richd, in trust for Angelica Davis
Posey, Richmond, in trust for Lucy Duckett
Rothwell, Andrew
Reed, Armistead
Ritchie, Catharine
Rich, David
Ratcliffe, Danl
Ryther, Edwin A
Ritter, Fred'k W
Risque, Ferdinand W
Rithmuller, Henry
Riggs, John M
Rye, John T
Ricar, John P C
Reed, Jas, in trust
Ross, Jemima [colored]
Ridgeway, Jos A
Ruler, Jesse
Ragan, Jas
Rowland, Jas W

O'Donnoghue, Timothy
O'Neale, Wm
Patterson, Jas
Purdy, John
Paul, John
Pumphrey, Jackson
Peters, Mary
Prout, Mary
Prathers, Owen J
Parker, Priscilla
Prindle, Parrot
Patterson, Robt S
Pollard, Richd I
Pleasonton, Stephen
Parker, Selby
Pugh, Saml A
Platt, S H
Pairo, Thos W
Phillips, Thos H
Purcell, Thos
Plumsill, Thos
Pitcher, Thos J
Parker, Wm H
Porter, Wm D
Phillip, Wm H

Ruff, Joanna
Rappetti, John J
Ratrie, Jas
Ray, Josiah
Ricker, Lawrence
Ricker, Lawrence & Mary
Reardon, Michl
Ray, Nicholas B
Rodier, P L
Ryan, Richd J
Richardson, Robt R
Regester, Saml
Redfern, Saml
Ritchie, Thos
Ridgely, Wm G
Redin, Wm
Ruggles, Wm, jr
Rawlings, Washington

Richards, Wm & Thos
Randolph, Wm B
Smith, Ann
Stone, Anna Maria
Smith, Archer B
Simmons, August
Sands, B F
Spiqual, B & W B
Settle, Barbara, & others
Sengstack, Chas P, jr
Steele, Chas
Sherman, Chas
Spence, Christopher
Serrin, Danl
Shoemaker, David L
Slater, Eliz
Sommer, Edw
Simms, Edw
Slater, Eliz
Sarger, Eli J
Schlegal, Ferdinand
Scala, Francis M
Selhausen, F W & P A
Schaubb, Gallus
Sweeny, Geo
Stewart, Geo
Scott, Geo B
Seibel, Geo C
Seuftleben, Gustavus
Sweeny, Hugh B
Sage, Henry
Stone, Henry
Saner, Henry
Sommers, Henry W
Shryock, Henry
Steers, Henry, & Henry C
Steers, Henry C
Schureman, J H A
Smallwood, J B
Smith, John S
Suter, John
Street, John
Sumby, Jas [colored]
Schwartz, Jos
Strange, Jas
Stewart, J E

Riley, Wm R
Robinson, John G & Jas Friend
Simms, Ignatius [colored]
Sharretts, John F
Scrivener, Jas
Steele, Jas R
Shedd, Jas J
Smith, John C
Sears, Jas W
Spaet, John
Scott, Jas W
Springman, John M
Stinchcomb, John H
Smitson, John H
Smith, John Geo
Saur, Louis
Scott, Leonidas
Shephard, Lodowick
Scott, Mary
Scholfield, Mary E
Shields, Mary Ann
Sweeney, Mary
Simms, P H
Sullivan, Patrick
Semmes, Raphael
Schwarze, Robt
Schureman, Sarah A
Sandiford, Saml
Stettinius, Saml
Slade, Stephen M
Sterling, Sherman H
Smitson, Sarah
Summerscale, Thos
Sylvester, Thos
Smith, Thos [colored]
Saint Thos Literary Society
Sibley, Wm J & John B Morgan
Swann, Wm T
Stonestreet, Wm
Smallwood, Wm H [colored]
Steiger, Wm T
Stewart, Wm T
Shuster, Wm M & W H Clagett
Smith, Wm S
Smith, Wm, in trust
Stewart, Wm W

Simms, Wm
Sharretts, John F, & Martha A E
Smith, John L, in trust for Mary Williams & others
Thomas, Augustus — Talbert, Jas
Thruston, Buckner — Taylor, Jos
Thorn, Chlorinda A — Trook, John N
Taylor, Dennis H — Thompson, Michl, in trust
Tilghman, Frisbey — Towle, Nath C
Todsen, Geo P — Tenney, Pompey
Taylor, Geo — Taylor, Robt
Thomas, Hope — Thompson, Robt L & Kate T
Turner, Henry, & others — Travers, Sidney V
Toll, Isaac D — Todd, Seth
Tayloe, John — Trook, Susanna C
Taylor, John — Thompson, St John
Taggart, Jane L — Tucker, Thos
Thompson, Jas — Turner, Thos
Tobin, John — Thumlert, Wm
Tait, Jas A — Todd, Wm B
Throckmorton, John A — Tyler, Wm
Towers, John T, in the name of Martha E Dixon
Tucker, Wm, in trust for Eliza & Mary A Keefer
Thorn, Mary Jane, in trust for M J & W H Thorn
Uttermohler, Geo W — Vinson, H R F
Venable, Chas H — Van Reswick, John
Van Patten, Chas H — Van Ness, John P
Vass, Douglass — Veihmeyer, Jacob
Venable, Ellen
Van Reswick, John, & others, trustees for Greenleaf School Association
Williams, Alpheus S & others — Wheeler, Geo W
Waller, A B — Wilson, Geo
Wilcox, A M — Walters, Geo H
West, Benj O — Wilson, Geo G
Winder, Chas H — Walker, Geo W
Whelan, Catharine Ann — Watterston, Geo
Wallach, Chas S — Wright, Geo
Wiltberger, Chas H — Williams, Hannah O
Watson, Chas C & Edw A — Williams, Harrison
Wilkes, Chas — Wilson, Harriet & Hannah
Williams, Danl — Waters, Henrietta
Welch, David — Webb, Jos W
Waters, David S, jr — Whalen, John
Wilkerson, Edw — Wilson, John
Wheeler, Ephraim — Williams, J & J
Wilson, Fred'k T — Winder, John H
Wood, Ferdinand F — Wood, John

Wheatley, John F
Wise, Jas A
Woods, Jane
Webb, John F
Walker, Jonathan T
Wimsatt, Jos
Wirt, John L
Wise, John H
Williams, Jos
Wheatley, Ignatius
Walsh, Jas
Weed, J C & N S
Wilson, John
Wallace, Israel
Weed, J C & Hannah
Williams, John
Williams, Lemuel
Winder, Lewis H
Whitney, Lewis F
Wheeler, Lucinda
Washington, Mary
Watmough, Mary M
White, Martha R & others
Wood Mary Ann E
Walker, Maria E
Walker, Nathan W
Webb, Wm B, in trust for Mary Mechlin
Walters, Jas, sen, & Thos Walters
Watterston, Geo, in trust for Mary Sweeny
Woodward, C J Maguire, & Chas Miller
Yerby, Albert F & A L, in trust for M S Yerby
Younger, Edw
Young, Noble
Young, Thos
Young, Nicholas, Notley, & Ignatius, & Benj & Sarah E Clagett
Zellers, David

Wagner, Philip F
Waters, Robt A
Warring, Richd M
Williams, Sarah B
Williams, Saml S
Wroe, Saml C
Williams, Thos E
Welsh, Thos
Ward, Ulysses B
Ward, Ulysses
Ward, Wm J
Wallingsford, Washington
White, W G W & Jas L
Willink, Wilhelm
West, Wm H
Wilson, Wm B
Wilson, Wm H
Walker, Wm H
Webb, Wm P
Walworth, Wm B
Wilson, Wm
Walker, Wm B
Weaver, Wm A
Wilson, Wm T
Walker, Wm T

SAT FEB 20, 1858
The late Chevalier Francois Andre Michaux, the distinguished botanist, who, together with his father, traveled throughout the U S, has bequeathed to the American Philosophical Society $14,000, for the special purposes connected with his constant aspirations, the progress of agriculture with reference to the propagation of useful forest trees.

Died: on Feb 18, in Wash City, Mattie Thorburn Morris, wife of Lt Geo W Morris, U S Navy. Her funeral will take place this morning at 11 o'clock, from the residence of Mrs Cmdor Morris, on H st, & Vt ave.

Died: on Feb 19, in Wash City, Geo Turner, in his 37th year. His funeral will take place from the Wash Infirmary this day. [No time given.]

Died: on Feb 18, in Wash City, after a short illness, Catherine, only daughter of John & Eliza Ennis, aged 12 months. Her funeral will be tomorrow, from 263 N Y ave, between 6th & 7th sts. [No time given.]

Appointments by Gov Hicks: Annapolis, Md: Richd D Sellman, of Anne Arundel Co, to be his private sec; John H Alexander, of Balt city, commissioned as agent to the State to procure certain documents pertaining to the colonial history of Md for the State library. The following appointment have been confirmed by the Senate: Sec of State, Jas R Partridge,of Balt city; Judges of Orphans' Courts, [to fill vacancies,] Anne Arundel Co, John H Collison; Queen Anne Co, John C Ruth; Charles Co, Francis K Wills; Howard Co, Jas Billingsley; St Mary's Co, Wm E Cole; Dorchester Co, Algernon Thomas. Justices of the Peace: Caroline Co, Elias Cox; Cecil Co, Jos P Cantwell; Fred'k Co, Peter Young; Howard Co, R C Nicholson; Washington Co, Otho B Castle & Geo S Hawkins; Worcester Co, Elijah S Maddrix. County Com'rs-Kenty Co, Geo B Westcott.

Land Warrant Lost: application will be made to the Com'r of Pensions for the issue of a supplicate of Land Warrant No 47,471, for 160 acres, issued to W W Mann under the act of Mar 3, 1855, the same having been lost & a cavear entered against its location.

Senate: 1-Ptn from Douglas Ottinger, asking compensation for the labor & expense attending his invention of an apparatus for rescuing passengers from sinking vessels in the open sea, called the life surf car: referred. 2-Ptn from J C R Kingland, asking payment for paper for printing ordered by the 33rd & 34th Congresses: referred. 3-Ptn from John Van Sickell & J R Bellerjean, contractors for carrying the mail from N Y to Phil, asking an increase of their compensation: referred. 4-Ptn from Apollo Herold & other citizens of the U S, asking the passage of the homestead bill: referred. 5-Ptn from Jos Irwin & Co, asking indemnity for losses suffered while transporting merchandise to great Salt Lake City, in consequence of certain orders given by Col Johnston, commanding the U S troops in Utah: referred. 5-Additional papers presented in relation to the claim of J E Peay & C Ayliff, contractors on mail route 7,503, to additional compensation: referred. 6-Cmte on Public Lands: bill for the relief of John L Allen & A R Carter. 7-Bills passed-relief of: Tench Tilghman; Jonas P Keller; Elias Hall, of Rutland, Vt; Dr Chas D Maxwell, surgeon in the U S navy; of John Dick, of Fla; of G Danl Whitney; of J Wilcox Jenkins; of Laurent Millaudon; of Geo A O'Brien, & of Maj Benj Alvord, paymaster U S army. Also, to authorize Mrs Jane Smith to enter certain lands in the State of Alabama; & to vest the title to certain warrants for land in Geo M Gordon. A bill for the relief of Dempsey Pittman, approved Aug 16, 1856. Bill for the relief of Susanna T Lea, widow & admx of Jas Maglenen, late of the city of Balt.

Rutland, Vt, Feb 19. The passenger cars & freight train for Burlington were thrown off the track near Clarendon, seriously injuring Mrs Sheldon, of Fairhaven, Vt; Wm Hoskinson, of Healdville; Ephraim Jones, or Reading, Vt; J C Hurd, of Jefferson Co, N Y; & Franklin Maynard, of Cambridge, Mass.

MON FEB 22, 1858
Valuable business stand, corner of 12th & L sts, for sale on Mar 23 next, by deed of trust from A N Clements to Jos H Bradley, jr, recorded in Liber J A S No 103, folios 35 thru 39, of the land records for Wash Co, D C: sale of lot 13 in square 316, with improvements thereon. –Jos H Bradley, jr, trustee -Jas C McGuire, auct

Mr John Washington Farmer, a plumber, residing in N Y, has established a free dining saloon for the benefit of the poor of that city. It has been in successful operation for several months. The number of regulars who present themselves every day is about 600.

Rev Mr Webb, of Campbell Court-House, Va, has received the sad intelligence of the murder of his brother by the rebels in India on Jun 18 last. The information was in a letter from the widow of the unfortunate gentleman. He was inhumanly murdered.

The Jacksonvill [Fla] Republican records the death of Mrs Winnie Lassiter, on Jan 28, aged 130 years. She was a native of N C, & was married in that colony many years before the Revolution.

Rioting & murder on Sat near 2nd st & Mass ave, in front of the Hibernia Club. On the pavement a young man, John Rawlings, was shot dead. Two others were shot, but not severely: Martin [alias Dink] King & Geo W McElfresh. Wm Hussey was committed to jail as being implicated, as were Thos Brown, Michl Kelley, & Fred'k Denny. Jas Ragan, supposed to be one of the principals, was arrested last evening by Ofcrs McHenry & Irving.

John Kearney, the youth who was present at the shooting of Murphy at Mrs Hughes', on 2nd st, about 3 months ago, & whose evidence was deemed so important in the case, was not to be found on the day of the investigation. He was yesterday committed to jail.

Death of a Washingtonian in China. A letter from the U S steamer **San Jacinto**, dated Hong Kong, Dec 14, memtions the death of Jas A Gates, of Wash City, a gunner in the U S navy, & attached to the ship **Portsmouth**. He leaves a wife to mourn his loss. His merits as an ofcr & a man were testified to by a large attendance of the ofcrs & men of the U S squadron at his funeral, who also did not fail, during the weary days of his illness & the struggles of his dying hour, to show unto him every kindness, & to smooth his pathway to the tomb. –States [Feb 24th newspaper: He leaves a devoted wife, an affectionate sister, & a loving brother. He was born in Chas Co, Md, on Nov 27, 1827, & died on board the U S ship **Portsmouth**, at Hong Kong, China, on Dec 13, 1857.]

Orphans Court of Wash Co, D C. Letters of administration on the personal estate of Jas G Austin, late of Wash Co, deceased. –Abram Van Buskirk, adm

For sale: the property where I at present reside; contains about an acre of land; the dwlg is in first-rate order, contains 10 rooms, a deep dry cellar, kitchen, smoke, carriage, pantry, & other out-houses in good repair. Pump of pure water at the door. If desired, will include 10 or 15 acres of first-rate meadow-land. Apply to C C Hyatt, Bladensburg

Mrd: on Feb 16, at the House of Prayer, Newark, N J, by Rev Mr Shackelford, Henry Wm Herbert, of England, to Adela R, daughter of the late Thos Budlong, of Rhode Island.

Mrd: on Feb 16, at Berryville, Clarke Co, Va, by Rev Mr Hooff, Saml J C Moore to Ellen Kownslar, daughter of D Randolph Kownslar, all of the above named place.

Died: yesterday, in Wash City, Lily, infant daughter of Ellwood & Julia A Fisher. Her funeral is today at 4 o'clock, from the residence, corner of C & 3rd sts.

Died: on Feb 20, Florence Edwards, only child of Rev T N Haskell & Annie Edwards Haskell, aged 11 months & 15 days.

St Louis, Feb 18. The Kickapoo correspondent of the Republican says that on Feb 6 a party, headed by Chas Lenhard, burnt the ofc of Mr Boyd, lawyer, & Mr Davis, physician, & destroyed all their property. Messrs Boyd, Davis, Kelly, Laughlin, Lynch, & many others fled to Missouri. Much excitement existed.

St Louis, Feb 21. Fire broke out in the Pacific Hotel, about 3 o'clock this morning; there were in the house about 100 persons, between 40 & 50 of whom are missing. The following are the names of those who it is thus far ascertained are among the killed: Messrs Bruce McKnitt, Burkhardt Wurst, Pane Sterrell, & Mrs Jenney Jones & child, all of this city; Henry Rochester & T Hart Strong, of Rochester, N Y; Mr ___ Johnson, of Chicago; Wm Sanders Taylor, Geo Crane, Miss Jones, & Chas Davis, residences unknown; Wm Cunningham, of the Terre Haute & Alton railroad; Miss Hunter, Mr & Mrs Hubbard, residences unknown. Also, 9 persons who were in one room, & whose names & residences are unknown. The following are seriously injured: Jas F Geary, Reporter of the St Louis "Leader;" Elihu Hayne, of N Y; Jonathan Jones, Mr Towns, Wm Turner, & Mr Sharke, the watchman of the house. The fire originated in the drug store under the hotel. The loss of property is estimated at $50,000. [Feb 23rd newspaper: corrected list of the dead: Henry H Rochester & Thos H Strong, of Rochester; H M Gregg, Chas Davis, Wm Cunningham, Geo A Crane, Evan J Watkins, Mr Johnson, of Mich; Ephraim Doane, of Chicago, & Miss Hunter. Missing & supposed to be dead: Bruce McNutt, Burkhardt Wiest, Paul Sterrell, Wm Taylor, J Wagner, Dr Lord, of Cincinnati. Severely injured: Mr & Mrs Hubbard, of Boston, [the latter fatally,] Elihu Hayes, Wm W Torrence, Mr Sharpe, Mrs Jonathan Jones. The funeral of those not identified will take place on Wed. Other bodies are supposed to be in the ruins.]

TUE FEB 23, 1858
Ignatius F Mudd, Fashionable Tailor, 380 D st, between 7th & 8th sts. [Ad]

Divorce in England: For two centuries & a half the marriage contract in England has been by law indissoluble; but between 1701 & 1752 about 250 divorce bills have been passed by special act of Parliament. This mode of remedy was too expensive for thousands. A commission on the subject was appointed in 1850, which resulted in 1853 in an elaborate report, recommending inter alia the abolition of the anomalous system of legislative divorce & the constitution of a new tribunal empowered in certain cases to dissolve the marriage contract & to enable the parties to contract other marriages. Lord Palmerston determined to carry out the principal recommendations of the commission, & in the short session of 1857 succeeded, against a determined opposition from all quarters, in passing an act to amend the law relating to divorce & matrimonial causes. This tribunal has just commenced its session.

Executrix's sale of saddles, saddlery, saddler's hardward & tools, at auction, Mar 1, of the estate of the late Danl Campbell, deceased, at my auction store, 526 7th st. –Jane Campbell, excx -A Green auct

Yesterday two brothers, Wm & Patrick Farrell, bricklayers, & a companion named Kinsley, were returning from their work on the Island, & called at the tavern on Pa ave, to drink. After coming out they were assaulted by two persons, one of whom was Geo Williams, originally from Balt. The Farrells successfully defended themselves, but not before one of them was severely cut in the back by a bowie knife of Williams. Farrell's wound is said to be dangerous. Williams has been arrested.

Death of Capt Jackson. The ship **Kate Hooper**, of Balt, on board of which vessel it will be recollected a revolt recently took place in the Chinese waters, arrived at Havana on Feb 12, having made the passage from Macao, China, in 116 days. She had on board 650 Coolies, & arrived in charge of Mr Francis Bowen, her first ofcr, Capt Jackson, we regret to learn, having died of fever on Deb 15, when the ship was only 10 days out from the Straits of Lundo; 3 of the ships apprentices had also died. Capt Jackson was well & favorably known as one of the most intrepid & enterprising ship-masters belonging to Balt, & for many years has commanded some of the finest vessels out of our port, & his death will be learned with regret by his many warm personal friends. –Balt Patriot

Mr John Brouwer, formerly Pres of the East River Ins Co, was found dead in his ofc, 72 Wall st, N Y, on Thu, having hung himself on the knob of a safe by his neck-tie. No cause is assigned for the act. Mr Brouwer was well advanced in life, & has long been much respected. His recent business was that of a broker or real estate agent. The point of suspension was not more than 4 feet from the floor.

Notice is given that application will be made to the Com'r of Pensions for a duplicate of Land Warrant No 50, 504, for 160 acres, issued to Jas C Pierce, under the act of Mar 3, 1855, the same being lost & a caveat entered against its location. –Jos C G Kennedy

Mrd: on Feb 22, at the Nat'l Hotel, Wash, by Rev J C Granbury, Mr Jas W Payne to Miss Maria E Jones, both of Charlottesville, Va.

Died: on Feb 20, in Gtwn, D C, of consumption, Abraham, eldest son of the late L P Wingerd.

Died: on Sunday, Ruth Belden, youngest daughter of W B & Caroline M Chace, aged 12 months & 5 days.

Obit-died: on Feb 7, Caroline, wife of J D B De Bow, in her 25th year. Tender, affectionate, devoted in all the relations of wife, mother, daughter, & friend.

Buffalo, Feb 22. Mr Foote, Editor of the Commerical Advertiser, of this city, died here on Sat. He was Minister to Bogota under Pres Harrison, & Minister to Vienna under Pres Fillmore.

Phil, Feb 22. Hon Judge Kane died in this city last evening. [Feb 24th newspaper: Hon John K Kane, the eminent Judge of the U S District Court for the Eastern District of Pa, died on Sunday at his residence in Phil. He had been suffering for some days from a very severe attack of pneumonia, the fatal termination of which has been anticipated by all who attended him. He was the father of the late Dr Kane. He was educated at **Yale College**, & studied law in Phil; admitted to the bar in 1817; in 1845 appointed Atty Gen of the State, which ofc he resigned in 1846, when appointed Judge of the U S District Court. –Phil Bulletin]

WED FEB 24, 1858
Senate: 1-Ptn from Jane Raustead, widow of Jas Raustead, of the Revolutionary army, asking a pension: referred. 2-Ptn from Edw Merritt, an express rider during the war with Mexico, for a pension or other compensation for important services rendered & injuries received while engaged in the service of his country: referred. 3-Additional papers submitted in the case of Richd G Dove, messenger in the Third Auditor's Ofc, asking for compensation allowed by law to those performing the duties of messenger: referred. 4-Cmte of Claims: bill for the relief of Mrs Eliza A Merchant, widow of the late 1st Lt & Brvt Capt Chas G Merchant, of the U S army. Same cmte: bill to provide for the settlement of the accounts of the late Capt John W McCrabb.

House of Reps: 1-Bill for the relief of Wm Howell, of Tenn: referred. 2-Bill granting bounty land to Andrew J Flemming, of Gettysburg, Pa: referred. 3-Joint resolutions to a geological survey by Dr John Evans: referred to the Cmte on Public Lands.

The aged & illustrious Baron Von Humboldt, now in his 90th year, is still fresh in intellectual & conversational powers. He attended a ball given in Berlin on Jan 29, in honor of the royal wedding.

Our community has to mourn the loss of a distinguished citizen in the death of Fred'k A Schley, who died at his residence in Fredericktown, on Feb 5, in his 70th year. Mr Schley pursued & finished his legal studies in the ofc of the venerable Chief Justice Taney, then a practitioner of law in this city, & was admitted to the Bar in 1810. –Fred'ktown Citizen

Wash Corp: 1-Act to refund an excess of license paid by Wm H Lusby: license for a butcher's stall in the Eastern Market: sum of $10.

New Orleans Picayune: Pierre Gentin, a veteran of the war of 1814-15 died this morning at age 69. He had for a year or two past been special ofcr of Lafayette Square, & was at one time a terror to loafers & a joy to the rising generation. Yesterday as he was walking across the square, he suddenly became paralyzed & was conveyed to his residence in a state of utter helplessness. He died in the morning. Mr Gentin was a native of the ancient city of Geneva, & had devoted his early years to the profession of arms. Since 1806 he resided in this city, & during the war of 1814-15 served as a volunteer under Gen Jackson. He has been in numerous duels. After the battle of New Orleans, he received the appointment of custom-house ofcr, & remained in that position for several years. [No death date given-current item.]

Mr Wm Farrell, who was stabbed on Monday by Geo Williams, lies in a very critical condition. His testimony to the facts of the assault was taken yesterday at his place of residence in the First Ward by Justice Donn. [Feb 25th newspaper: Wm Farrell died on Tue night. This will have a more serious complexion to the charge against his assailants.]

Gtwn College: oration delivered before the Philonomosian Society by Jos P Orme, of this District, & the Farewell Address of Washington was read by Paul Bossier, of Louisiana.

Died: on Feb 9, in Bedford Co, Va, at the residence of her husband, Wm Radford, Mrs Eliz Radford, aged 72 years, daughter of Gen Wm Mosley, an ofcr of the Revolution. After a long illness she resigned herself into the hands of her Maker without a complaint or sigh.

Circuit Court of Wash Co, D C-in Chancery. Alex'r H Mechlin against Wm H Carroll & Eliza J his wife, Thos K Handy, John H Handy, & Maria L Crutcher, & Edw Breathett, heirs at law of the late John H Eaton, & Mgt Eaton, his admx. The bill: the late John H Eaton purchased on May 17, 1854, of the cmplnt, lot 21 in square 127, in Wash City, for $3,427, & paid one third thereof or thereabouts, & was to have given his two notes in equal sums, payable at 6 & 12 months from said day, with interest, to be satisfactorily secured; but he departed this life after the expiration of the said period, without having given said notes or paid the said residue of the said purchase money & interest or any part thereof. That he died leaving a will, by which he gave all his property to his widow, the said Mgt Eaton, & who hath obtained letters testamentary on his estate, & possessed herself of personal property of the said John H Eaton sufficient to pay the said residue of said purchase money & interest. That the heirs at law known to the cmplnt, as far as he can ascertain them, are the above named, & he may have left out others who are unknown to the cmplnt, all of whom reside out of D C. That the said residue of said purchase money & interest has not been paid. The object of the said bill is to obtain a specific execution of the said contract for the purchase of said lot, & payment of the residue of the purchase money & interest. All are to appear in this Court in person or by solicitor, on or before the first Monday in July. -Jno A Smith, clerk

Orphans Court of Wash Co, D C. Letters of administration on the personal estate of Jacob Fellins, late of the State of Md, deceased. –John W Mead, adm

Orphans Court of Wash Co, D C. Letters of administration, with the will annexed, on the personal estate of Maria Brown, late of Wash Co, deceased. –Mary M Brown, admx w a

THU FEB 25, 1858
St Louis Democrat: the loss of Mr E L Cheever, of this city, who was with his wife, among the passengers on the ill-fated steamer **Col Crossma**. Mrs Cheever & her husband were sitting in the ladies' cabin, when he decided to go forward & note the progress of the boat. Within a few seconds she heard the explosion of the boiler, & rushed forward, but was stopped by a gentleman who told her that her husband was safe, but was assisting those who had been hurt. She returned to the cabin. Soon after her husband was brought to her side covered with blood, with a deep cut upon his head, over the ear, & other severe wounds. He stated he was severely but not dangerously hurt. She dressed his wounds, & scarcely able to walk, he went back to assist others. Shortly after returning to assist in bearng the body of Capt Converse, who had been mortally hurt by the explosion, Mrs Cheever heard the cry of fire. Her husband came to be at her side, & he remarked that they were in danger of being lost. After the crew had departed with the yawl, Mr Cheever procured a plank, which he proposed to his wife they should use, until they could get other assistance. Capt Cheever saw his brother & wife, & called to them to desist, as the plank would not keep them both up. He told his brother to jump himself with the plank, & he would get something else for his wife. Mr Cheever threw himself overboard with the plank, & that is the last his wife saw of him. He was unable to retain his hold upon the plank, being exhausted by the loss of blood. Mrs Cheever saw Capt G D Taylor, with a child in his arms, swimming towards her, on a door. He held the door for her & talked afternately to his little daughter & Mrs Cheever, & his kind words had much to do in preserving her strength. After floating some 2 or 3 miles downstream, Mr Taylor called loudly to those on shore for help. They were miraculously saved. Mrs Cheever did not ascertain the death of her husband for some time afterwards.

The theatre at Richmond was crowded on Tue for the presentation of Washington's cane to Hon Edw Everett, & of his spy glass to Hon Wm L Yancy. Mr Everett delivered his eulogy on Washington, which was listened to with rapt attention. -Whig

The funeral of the venerable Jesse Anthony was attended from the North Second st Methodist Church at Troy on Fri. At the end of the discourse an old gentleman, Rev Saml Howe, of Lansinburgh, a member of the Troy Conference, rose near the pulpit & said a few words, concluding with: "I am seventy-eight years old; my feet are near those of brother Anthony; & I shall soon join him." The congregation was dismissed, a portion of them following thr corpse to the grave. Mr Howe entered the basement, where, seating himself in a rocking chair, he almost immediately expired. The cause of death was disease of the heart, quickened by the excitement of the occason. –Troy Whigg

Mrd: on Feb 23, by Rev Dr Cummins, Dr C P Culver, of Georgia, to Miss Louisa E, eldest daughter of W M Morrison, of Wash City.

The Hamburg ship **Howard**, Capt Walter, from Hamburg, arrived at the port of N Y on Monday, after a passage of 96 days, the voyage being a stormy one from beginning to end. She left Hamburg Nov 17, with 286 passengers, 37 of whom died on the passage from a sickness resembling cholera, & from weakness occasioned by shortness of provisions & water, the latter being dealt out in very small quantitites for the past 42 days, & most of it being made from steam from salt water.

Senate: 1-Ptn from Franklin Kellsey, asking that an appropriation be made for bldg, equipping, & testing a steamboat on a scientific model invented by him: referred. 2-Ptn from Alex'r B & D R Hagner, guardians of the infant children of the late Maj J R Hagner, of the U S army, asking that said children may be allowed a pension: referred. 3-Ptn from Henry Cordier & 54 other citizens of the U S, asking that the public lands may be granted only to actual settlers & in limited quantities: referred. 4-Memorial & joint resolution, in behalf of J B Thomas & his family, who were sufferers by Indian depredations: referred. 5-Cmte of Claims: asked to be discharged from the consideration of the memorial of David Gordon: referred to the Cmte on Indian Affairs. Same cmte: bill for the relief of Eleazer Williams. 6-Cmte on Military Affairs: bill from the House of Reps for the relief of Whitemarsh B Seabrook & others, asked its immediate consideration: considered & passed.

Died: on Feb 15, at her residence in Hoboken, N J, Mrs Mary S Chilton, relict of the late Geo Chilton, of N Y, & mother of R S Chilton, of Wash City.

Died: on Feb 24, Henry D, infant son of Danl & Eliz Robertson. Suffer little children to come unto me, & forbid them not, for of such is the Kingdom of Heaven.

Troy, Feb 24. The percussion-cap manufactory belonging to Chas H Kellogg was destroyed by explosion of fulminating powders. One man was killed & another injured. [Feb 27th newspaper: Mr Geo Baker, the foreman, was killed. Two of his sons were injured, though not dangerously.]

Circuit Court of Wash Co, D C-in Equity. Stephen Whitney et al vs A Day et al. Cornelia W Haven filed her ptn in said cause, praying to be allowed & paid the dividend on her 4 shares on a certificate of stock in the Galveston Bay & Texas Land Co, issued to her in her then name of Cornelia W Griswold; & it appearing by her said ptn that the said certificate of the said petitioner has been lost or mislaid, it is by the court ordered that a notice be published, warning all persons who may claim any interest in said certificate of stock adverse to the petitioner, or produce the same & prove their right thereto, on or before Mar 25 next. –Jno A Smith, clerk

Circuit Court of Wash Co, D C-in Chancery. Thos Redin vs John Ratrie et al. Trustee reports that he sold part of lot 1 in square 881, in Wash City, which belonged to Jas Ratrie at the time of his death, at public auction to Matthew Tremble for the sum of $710, & the purchaser has complied with the terms of the sale. –Jno A Smith, clerk

Orphans Court of Wash Co, D C. In the case of Isaac Beers, adm of John B Floyd, deceased, the administrator & Court have appointed Mar 20 next, for the final settlement of the personal estate of said deceased, with the assets in hand. -Ed N Roach, Reg/o wills

Orphans Court of Wash Co, D C. In the case of Anthony Buchly, adm of Ann E Marselas, deceased, the administrator & Court have appointed Mar 20 next for the final settlement of the personal estate of said deceased, with the assets in hand. -Ed N Roach, Reg/o wills

FRI FEB 26, 1858
Trustee's sale: by deed of trust from Ann Smith, dated Sep 15, 1855, recorded in Liber J A S No 105, folios 448-451, of the land records for Wash Co, D C: public auction on Mar 31, of lot 8 in square 73, with a small frame bldg; on K st, near the Circle, 57 feet. -F W Jones, trustee -Jas C McGuire, auct

Senate: 1-Ptn from Capt Robt A Wainwright, of the ordnance corps, asking the reimbursement of certain public money which was stolen from him in Boston while commandant of the arsenal, & for which he had accounted to the Gov't: referred. 2-Ptn from J & J R Porter, asking remuneration for losses sustained while transporting merchandise to Great Salt Lake City, in consequence of the orders given by the cmder of the U S troops in the Territory of Utah. 3-Cmte on Commerce: bill for the relief of the owner of the barque **Attica**, of Portland, Maine. 4-Cmte on Public Lands: asked to be discharged from the consideration of the papers relating to the claim of B E Edwards, & that they be referred to the Cmte on Private Land Claims: agreed to. 5-Cmte of Claims: memorial of Anthony S Robinson, submitted a report to accompany a bill previously reported.

The funeral of the Queen of Oude, who recently died in Paris, was a rare spectacle for the pageant-loving population of that great metropolis. The coffin, almost square & covered with white silk, was drawn by 6 milk white led horses. On each side walked persons of the late Queen's suite, clad in velvet silk robes, with pointed caps or bonnets on their heads. Two domestics following, in strange, motley garments, after whom walked the son of the deceased in a blue mantle of ample dimensions, who on his head "the semblance of a kingly crown did wear,' a strong ornament. Behind came a complete throng of Indians, enveloped in gorgeous silks & cashmeres of every hue. Previous to the interment, the ceremony of embalming the body was performed by the Queen's attendants in the court-yard of the hotel where they lodged. No incisions were made, but aromatic substances & perfumes were copiously introduced throught the mouth, ears, & nostrils, & the corpse was profusely annointed with odoriferous oils & essences. It was then wrapped in bands of fine muslin & covered with a cloth of gold, while fires were kept constantly burning all around it until it was removed.

For sale or rent: a Market Farm, convenient to Wash, adjoining Tennally-town, formerly owned by Dr Benj F Bohrer, & then by Robt Bowie; contains 92 acres of good land, with a small dwlg, stable, & orchards. Apply to Barnard & Buckey, Gtwn, or to R W Barnard, of Wall & Barnard.

The ship **John Milton**, whose loss at Montauk Point, Long Island, during the snow storm of Fri & Sat last, has been before announced, was a fine clipper ship of 1,444 tones, built in 1854, & cost, ready for sea, upwards of $100,000. She was owned in New Bedford, principally by Edw M Robinson, & was valued at about $65,000, which together with the freight money, is partly covered by insurance. Letter written Feb 22, 1858, tells of the loss of the vessel & no possibility of the safety of any of her crew, unless perchance some one of her boats might have left her & picked up by some vessel. No trace has turned up except her long boat & 2 light surf boats. The remainder of the ship was found on the shore one complete mass of ruin. Mr Stratton, who lives with half-mile of the scene of the disaster is quite positive that the ship could not have struck until that morning. Eleven of the unfortunate crew were found, & probably the next tide will bring in more.

St Louis Republican of Sunday: Yesterday the *Pacific Hotel*, corner of 7th & Poplar sts, was entirely consumed by fire. The origin of the disaster is not known. It is thought the flames broke out in the rear of the drug store of Dumont Jones. There were about 100 persons sleeping in the hotel; whe the entire bldg was enveloped in the raging element; the staircases in front & behind were gone, or so nearly so that an attempt to escape by these means would be only rushing into the arms of death. Of those who endeavored to save their lives, was Mrs Hubbard-injured; Mr Hubbard-in a dangerous condition; Miss H Hunter, who jumped from the 2nd floor, was a corpse before she reached the Sister's Hospital. Jas F Geary, local reporter of the Leader, of this city, attempted to escape with his wife & child. He fell to the cellar & is since dead. Mr Sharpe, night clerk at the hotel, was awfully burnt & considerably disfigured. Elihu Hayes, a stranger from Wisconsin, was much injured, with little or no hope of his recovery. T Hart Strong, a lawyer of this city, jumped from the second story, & died a little later. At King's Hotel we found the family of Dr White, whose escape was miraculous. He jumped to the ground & encouraged his wife, 3 children, & nurse to follow. They had a few skin-deep wounds. The hotel was completed in Jan, 1857, being owned by Geo B Field, who estimated its value at $20,000. It was originally leased to Danl W Strader; he subsequently opened the place in June, when Jacob Lyons entered into partnership with him. The bldg was 3 stories high. Mr Thos M Barker, of the Jefferson [Mo] Examiner, occupied room #21, & said he saw Mr Rochester break a window to get air. Mr Rochester fell backward, & I saw him no more. Mr Barker, along with Mr Torrence & Mr Strong, got on the roof of a small bldg. Strong fell & died in about 20 minutes. Torrence jumped & was considerably injured. Those who died inside of the hotel felt none of the pain of burns, as they died doubtless of suffocation before the flames reached them. About 20 are ascertained to be dead up to the evening of Feb 23, 5 from injuries received in jumping, & the remainder from burning. [Feb 27th newspaper: Chas L Taylor, alias Sanders, has been arrested on the charge of setting fire to the *Pacific Hotel*, & of murdering Ephraim Doane, one of the inmates. Dr Strader, the landlord, & Chas Waldrup, the watchman, have also been arrested. It is supposed to be one of the most atrocious & diabolical acts ever committed.]

Mrd: on Feb 23, by Rev Wm H Chapman, Enoch L McDaniel to Miss Ann Maria Duvall, all of Wash City.

Died: on Feb 25, Amelia Susan, infant daughter of Jas R & Caroline McAlister, aged 4 months. Her funeral is this evening at 3 o'clock.

Rev J T Headly has resumed his labors as an author, & is now engaged in the preparation of a life of Gen Havelock, which, from the full private documents in his possession, not accessible to others, promises to be of unusual interest. -Exchange

SAT FEB 27, 1858
Cincinnati Gaz: terrific explosion of gas in the Methodist church in that city on Feb 19. Mrs Mgt Hock had entered the church but a short time previous with her daughter Charlotte, a young woman, & her son, Wm Henry, some 12 or 14 years of age. Mrs Hock was taken from the ruins in a helpless & painful condition; she has since died. Her son's injuries are severe, & his recovery is extremely doubtful. Mrs Mary Hamill suffered a crushed right foot, & will probably have to suffer amputation of the foot. Rev Danl Kinney, Pres of the Ohio Conference, with Rev Mr White, the pastor of the church, had reached within 4 or 5 feet of the door, & were blown across 6th st. They were both badly bruised. Mr F D Williams, who was in the entry, was badly hurt, & also V Williams, a young man. Mrs Hummel & son, also in the entry, were both hurt. Mr Reese & Mr C Meads, who were trying to discover where the gas was escaping, got off with some severe burns & bruises.

We regret to record the death of Dr Thos M Foote, editor of the Buffalo Commercial Advertiser, which occurred on Sat. Dr Foote was appointed Charge to New Granada in 1849 by Gen Taylor, & Minister to Austria by Pres Fillmore. Since his return from Europe his health has been poor, & some 2 or 3 years ago he disposed of his interest in his paper, with a view to retirement, but circumstances occurred which induced him to resume it. His age was not far from 50. -N Y Times

Napoleon's new decree constituting the Empress Regent at once, on the regular accession of the Prince Imperial, with a council of regency, was joyfully hailed by the Senate. -Journal of Commerce

Antoine Krepple, convicted of murder, was hung at New Orleans on Friday of last week. The execution was private, within the walls of the jail, & only about 20 persons were allowed to be present.

$200 reward for runaway negro boy Jim, aged about 21 years, not very dark. –John H Bayne, residing in PG Co, Md.

One of our most worthy & respectable citizens, Mr Saml Peach, met with a fatal accident. On Thu he was walking on the track of the Orange & Alexandria railroad, about a mile from town, near the Cameron Run crossing, when he was overtaken by the train of cars coming in. He was not seen by the engineer, & before the train could be stopped or Mr Peach make his escape, he was struck by the cow-catcher of the locomotive & thrown violently off the track. He died about 15 minutes later, & never spoke. –Alexandria Gaz

Yesterday at half past noon the colored woman, Jenny, recently convicted of murder, was executed at the county jail in Alexandria.

Mrd: on Feb 25, in Wash City, by Rev G W Samson, Mr Wm S Smith to Annie Eilbeck Browne, both of Va.

Died: on Feb 26, at Gtwn, D C, in his 61st year, Silvanus G Deeth, formerly of New Brunswick, N J. His funeral is tomorrow, Sunday, at 3 o'clock P M, from his late residence, corner of Prospect & Fred'k sts.

Died: on Feb 26, in Wash City, of measles, Harvey Roberts, son of John W & Eliza Glover, aged 9 months & 4 weeks. His funeral will be at 3 o'clock P M on Sunday, at the residence of his parents, 537 11th st.

MON MAR 1, 1858
From Calif: 1-On Feb 21 John McKay, Jas Cupples, & Jas McDonald were drowned by the capsizing of a boat in the Sacramento river above Colusi. 2-Jan 25th an affray occurred near Stockton, in which a man named Glenn shot 2 brothers, Francis & Robt Brubacker. Robt was killed instantly, & Francis expired on Feb 25. 3-On Jan 23 a shooting affray occurred at Snelling's Ranch, Merced Co, between E P Barclay, Wm Stevens, & Jas Wilcox, friends of one Edwards, who killed Snelling some 8 or 10 days previous, & Chas F Bloodworth, Dr J W Goodin, & Benj White, friends of Snelling. Some 30 shots were fired, & Barclay, Stevens, & Goodin were killed. 4-On Jan 28 Jas McQuade was garroted in Stockton. 5-Jan 18th Wm Frank, a Russian by birth, committed suicide at Tomales Bay by shooting himself. 6-Jas C Coger & a cousin, says the Nevada Journal, were killed a few days since by the falling of a tree on a cabin, near Forest City, Sierra Co. Another cousin was severely though not mortally injured at the same time. 7-Jas Wallace was killed at Moore's Flat recently while picking out an old blast, by the powder exploding. He left a wife & 7 children, who reside at Mineral Point, Wisc. 8-Francis Acosta, who was found guilty of murder in the 2nd degree in the District Court of Placer Co for the killing of Philip Geary, was sentenced Jan 27th to 10 years in the penitentiary. 9-At San Francisco, Jan 20, Adolph F Branda, a native of Va, employed in the store of Macondray & Co, as book-keeper, commited suicide by taking syrychnine. 10-On Jan 26, Chas O'Connell, a native of Ireland, committed suicide by taking strychnine. 11-On Jan 27, John Monteban, an Englishman, who, 4 years ago, came down from the mines with $40,000, but latterly had become a vagrant, committed suicide on Jan 29. 12-Feb 1, a man named Voorhees, formerly of Marysville, committed suicide in this city. He was a native of Ohio, where it is said he has relatives. 13-On Feb 2, Otto Frank, a native of Prussia, aged 22 years. Committed suicide by taking prussic acid. 14-A large amount of land has been finally confirmed to the <u>Catholic Church</u>. These are the old mission bldgs, with their lots, gardens, & cemeteries, at San Diego & San Luis Rey, San Fernando, San Juan Capistrano, San Gabriel, San Buenaventura, Santa Barbara, Santa Inez, La Parissima, San Luis Obispo, Sam Miguel, San Antonio, La Soledad, Carmel, San Juan Baptista, Santa Clara, San Jose, San Francisco, San Rafael, & Sonora. Besides these church houses & lots there is a ranch of 20,000 acres in Santa Barbara Co, & another of 4,438 acres in San Luis Obispo Co.

Bailiff's sale of household & kitchen furniture at auction Mar 5, at the residence of Jas H Boss, on Mass ave, at 4th st west. -Solomon Goddard, bailiff -A Green auct

At Phil, on Fri, Timothy McCartny got in a altercation with John Gross, & whilst directing a severe blow at him, he missed, fell forward, & struck his head against the hinge of a cellar door; from the effect of which he died after a brief interval of suffering.

The question is often asked, "who is Cmdor Paulding?" Paulding entered the navy in 1811, & served on Lake Erie & Lake Champlain; was on board the ship **Ticonderoga** in the battle of Sep 11, 1814,-on Lake Champlain, & Paulding fired his guns during the attack with the flash of a pistol, [there being no locks then in use on our cannon. He served in the squadron of Cmdor Decatur, & served on board the frig **Constellation** in the Algerine war; he served in the frig **Macedonian**, then on board the ship **Independence**, then the brig **Prometheus**, & again out on a 3 years' cruise in the Pacific on board the frig **Macedonian**. He continued to serve his country & I find nothing on the records derogatory to his official conduct or private character. -H

Wm Cousins, arrested in Canada last week for murdering his nephew, hung himself to a bed-post at a hotel where he was stopping in custody of 2 constables.

We regret to learn that Prof Henry A Washington, of Wmsburg, Va, met with an unfortunate accident at his lodgings, in this city, yesterday, by which his life was brought to a premature end. Whilst handling an air gun, it was by some accident discharged, the ball taking effect in his head, & causing his death in about 2 hours. The deceased had been a sojourner in this city for the last 4 months under medical treatment, & had made preparations to return to Va this morning. He was recently Prof of History in Wm & Mary College, of Va, & was the editor of the last edition of the Jefferson Papers. His age was only 36 years.

The shop of Mr Munck, gunsmith, on 6th st, south of Pa ave, was broken into on Sat & a number of valuable firearms were stolen. Mr Munck offers a reward of $50.

A deed of violence was committed yesterday at Bell's toll-gate on 7th st, in Wash Co, by Cross & Martin, from Wash, on a man named Augustus Norton. He was struck down by one with 2 blows of a slung shot & then badly cut by the other with a knife. The assailants then speedily decamped in a buggy they had with them. It is supposed that the assault grew out of a grudge.

Orphans Court of Wash Co, D C. Letters of administration on the personal estate of Thos Lamb, late of Wash Co, deceased. –Wm Poulton, adm

Died: on Feb 28, Mrs Catharine B Tyler, aged 70 years, relict of the late Chas Tyler, of Indiana. Her funeral is this day at 4 o'clock, from her late residence on K st, between 12th & 13th sts.

Died: on Feb 27, at **Kalorama**, Louisa, wife of Arthur Bruse Lansing, & daughter of the late Thos Lovett, of N Y.

Died: on Feb 23, Albert Lawrence, infant son of A M & Robt Pywell, aged 7 months.

Died: on Feb 27, Willie H Scheel, son of John & Susan Scheel, aged 3 years & 10 days. "Our Willie is transplanted." His funeral is on Monday at 2 o'clock, near 22nd st, Pa ave.

Died: on Feb 28, John Independence, son of John H & Fanny Tretler, aged 7 months & 24 days. His funeral is this evening at 3 o'clock, from the residence of his parents, 310 8th st, between L & M sts.

Died: on Feb 13, at **Rockland**, Loudoun Co, Va, Eliza Southgate, wife of Armistead T M Rust, & dghtr of Hon Jno W Lawrence, of N Y, in her 29th year. She leaves her loving husband & 3 small children, & a large circle of relatives & friends to mourn her loss.

TUE MAR 2, 1858
Chas Haskins has this day associated with him Mr Chas A Alexander, Architect, & the business will be conducted under the name of Haskins & Alexander. Ofc: Pa ave, between 10th & 11th sts, Wash, D C.

Information wanted of Mr Stephen Sharp or Mrs Mary Ann Sharp, [late of the town of Romsey, Hampshire, England.] Mrs Sharp's maiden name was Mary Ann Cross. They emigrated to America in 1824. Her niece, Eliza Cross, is anxious to obtain tidings of them. When last heard of they were in the State of Michigan. Any information respecting them will be thankfully received by their nephew. –Richd Mason, care of Maclear & Co, 16 King st, Toronto, C W, Feb 17, 1858.

For sale: a tract of land containing 170 acres at **Bayly's X Roads**, 6½ miles s w of Washington. Inquire of F H Smith, reporter at the House of Reps, or of J H Cleveland, on the premises.

Senate: 1-Hon J Pinckney Henderson, chosen by the Legislature of Texas a Senator from that State, to fill the vacancy occasioned by the death of Hon Thos J Rusk, for the term ending Mar 3, 1863, oath was administered, Mr Henderson took his seat. 2-Ptn from Jas H Frost & Eliza A Johnson, legal reps of J A Frost, of the South Sea Exploring Expedition, asked to be allowed extra pay: referred. 3-Ptn from the heirs of Christoval & Mignel De Armas, asking confirmation of certain land titles: referred. 4-Ptn from Jno C F Saloman & Geo W Morris, asking that measures may be taken to test certain improvements in the construction & fitting up of sailing-vessels & steamers, by which the perils of oceanic navigation will to a very great extent be obviated: referred. 5-Cmte on Commerce: adverse report on the register or enrollment to the vessel **James McIndoe**, now owned by Thos Coatsworth, of Buffalo, N Y. 6-Cmte on Pensions: adverse report on the ptn of Jos Dowd. 7-Cmte on Naval Affairs: bill for the relief of Otway H Berryman; also a bill for the relief of Wm D Mosely. 9-Cmte of Claims: bill for the relief of Mary Petery.

A 3 story bldg at Broadway & Bleecker st, N Y, took fire on Sat & 3 men who slept in the 3rd story were burnt to death: Hugh O'Brien, John Reiley, & Michl Maddin. The first two first were young men, & Maddin was over 60 years old. None of them had families.

Germond Crandell has bought out the store & business lately conducted by Mr E K Lundy, 128 Bridge st, Gtwn, & respectfully solicits the continued support of Mr Lundy's customers & the public in general. He offers for sale School Books, Stationery, Periodicals, & Hardware. [E K Lundy recommends his successor, Mr Crandell.]

Joshua Mellen, of Wayland, father of Chief Justice Mellen, of the Court of Common Pleas, Massachusetts, died there on Monday night, at the advanced age of 94 years.

Criminal Court-Wash: March term: Grand Jury:

Thos Carbery, Foreman	Wm Stone, sr	Geo A Rohrer
Stephen P Franklin	Geo Mattingly	Wm Wilson
Richd R Crawford	Geo McCerry	Peter H Hooe
Thos Donoho	Geo Lowry	Adolphus H Pickrell
John M Brodhead	Augustus E Perry	John L Kidwell
Robt Beale	Benj J Semmes	Geo W Beall
Nicholas Callan	Leonidas Coyle	Saml Pumphrey
Dr Thos Miller	Elijah Edmonson	Joshua Pierce

Petit Jury:

Wm Cooper	Wash Wellingsford	Edwin Knowles
Christopher Gill	Wm E Spalding	Martin P King
Danl Barry	John B Turton	Benedict Hutchins
Albert Hurdle	Wm H Perkins	Serephim Masi
Thos Galligan	Geo D Spencer	Thos Baker
Rich Butt	Thos Proby	Theodore Meade
Thos D Larner	John T Baker	Jeremiah Smith
Joshua Hilton	John H Trunnell	Jas Rhodes
Thos Bartly	Wm Slater	Thos Riggles
Geo S Noyes	Wm H Gilman	Peter Hepburn

The duties of the District Attorney have been resumed by Philip Barton Key, in person, his health having considerably improved.

Henry Martin, one of the young men concerned in the assault on Augustus Norton on Sunday, was arrested on Sunday night & committed to jail to await a further examination.

Mrd: on Feb 24, at Petersville, Md, Mr Jas Owner, of Wash, to Miss Mary E Stuck, of the former place.

The funeral of Mrs Lansing at **Kalorama** will be on Wed, at 1 o'clock. The remains will be conveyed to Rock Creek Church.

WED MAR 3, 1858
Senate: 1-Ptn from Francis D Pons, in behalf of himself & late partners in trade, asking to be permitted to take & file testimony in support of his claims for losses in Florida during the years 1812-13, & that the judge of the northern district of that State may be authorized to receive & adjudicate the same: referred. 2-Ptn from the heirs at law of S Girard & others, asking the confirmation of their titles to certain lands in the State of Louisiana: referred. 3-Ptn from Wm A Vaughn, John Smith, Wm D Little, & Nathl Dennett, jr, asking that compensation may be made to them for the time they were employed as inspectors at the port of Portsmouth, N H: referred. 4-Ptn from Robt Hale on the subject of his new war-rocket, asking compensation for the improvement in that style of missile & the stand on which it is fixed: referred. 5-Cmte on Foreign Relations: asked to be discharged from the consideration of the memorial of Geo Frasier asking remuneration for losses sustained due to the seizure of his property & imprisonment by the Mexican authorities in 1840, & that it be referred to the Cmte of Claims: which was agreed to. 6-Cmte on Private Land Claims: bill for the relief of the heirs & legal reps of Olivier Landry, of Louisiana, submitted a report in favor of the passage of the bill. 7-Cmte on Indian Affairs: bill for the relief of Anson Dart. 8-Cmte on Private Land Claims: bill to confirm Wm Marvin title to lands in East Florida. Same cmte: adverse report on the memorial of Thos Henderson. 9-Cmte of Claims: adverse report on the memorial of Moses Devine. 10-Bill for the relief of S W Holladay & others: referred.

House of Reps: 1-Memorial of F A Reitz, Fred'k Weichel, & 1,100 others on the freedom of the public lands: referred.

Nat'l Medical College: 36th annual course of lectures closed. Commencement this evening: Dr Binney, Pres of Binney Columbia College will confer degrees upon:
Robt S Bernard, of Va
Isaac R Jones, of Mo
Robt W Hales, of Ohio
Wm E Waters, of D C
Cyrus Bacon, of Mich
Henry Waldron, of N Y
J W Lackey, of La
B C Cooke, of N C
Selden W Crow, of Ohio
C Miller, of D C
The Dean of the Medical Faculty, Prof I I Waring, M D, will deliver the valedictory address. The Faculty consists of:
Prof: Th Miller, M D, Prof of Anatomy
Prof W P Johnston, M D, Prof of Obstetrics
Prof J Riley, M D, Prof of Materia Medica
Prof J F May, M D, prof of Surgery
Prof G Tyler, M D, Prof of Practice of Medicine
Prof I I Waring, M D, Prof of Physiology
Prof E G Hilgard, Ph D, Prof of Chemistry
Prof W A Bradley, M D, Demonstrator of Anatomy

Mrd: on Feb 11, at New Orleans, Philip F Dandridge, of Va, to Mrs Bliss, widow of the late Col Bliss, U S Army, & daughter of the late Pres Taylor.

Mrd: on Feb 21, at the residence of the bride's father, by Rev D Ball, Mr Jas E Waugh to Miss S Victoria McKelden, both of Wash.

THU MAR 4, 1858
Household & kitchen furniture at auction on: Mar 8, at the residence of John F Burgin, 236 F st, between 13th & 14th sts. -A Green auct

In looking over our Calif files we find that Lt Beale, with 14 camels, arrived at Los Angeles on Jan 8. The appearance of these uncouth animals created great excitement among the people. Most of them are well broken to the saddle & are very gentle. All the camels belong to the one hump species, except one, which is a cross between the one & two hump kinds.

Senate: 1-Ptn from R C Smith, adm of Arthur Middleton, asking to be allowed the outfit of charge d'affaires, the duties of which office were discharged by said Middleton while secretary of legation at Madrid, from Dec 2, 1836 until the arrival of Mr Eaton in Apr, 1837: referred. 2-Ptn from John Mason & others, heirs of Jeremiah Gilman, an ofcr of the army of the Revolution, asked to be allowed half-pay: referred.

Mr Wm D Massey was on Tue elected Mayor of our neighboring city of Alexandria, & Mr S J McCormick Auditor.

Died: on Mar 2, in Wash City, of congestion of the lungs, Capt Jos B Tate, in his 40th year. He was a native of Wash City, & was for some years employed in the ofc of the Intelligencer. He subsequently established the Evening Star newspaper, of which he has been ever since the financial manager, though he soon disposed of his proprietary interest in it to its present owner. As a husband, father, son, & friend, his death will leave a void in many hearts. His end was calm & peaceful. His funeral will take place on Fri at 2 o'clock, from his late residence on M st, one door east of 10th st.

Died: on Tue, Anne, wife of Rev Chas E Pleasants. Her funeral service will be at her late residence, 529 H st, between 6th & 7th sts, this afternoon at 4 o'clock.

Died: at **Cassilis**, near Charlestown, Jefferson, Co, Va, Andrew Kennedy, in his 61st year. [No death date given-current item.]

Died: on Mar 2, suddenly, at **Clover Dale**, the residence of Peirce Shoemaker, Kate, third daughter of the late Geo & Charlotte Templeman. Her funeral will be this morning at 10 o'clock from Trinity Church, Gtwn.

Pocket-book found. Owner to describe same & pay for this ad. Apply to Peter Conlan, Grocer, G & 3rd sts.

N Y, Mar 3. Freeman Hunt, editor of the Merchant's Magazine, died here this morning. [Mar 5th newspaper: Mr Hunt's death occurred after a brief illness from inflammation of the brain, at his residence in President st, near Clinton st, Brooklyn. –N Y Com Adv]

FRI MAR 5, 1858
Orphans Court of Wash Co, D C. In the case of Chas Brown, adm of Rubin Brown, deceased, the administrator & Court have appointed Mar 23 next, for the final settlement of the personal estate, of the assets in hand. -Ed N Roach, Reg/o wills

Died: on Mar 1, at the residence of her father-in-law, in Wash City, Gertrude Allis, wife of Wm A Browning.

Died: on Mar 3, in Gtwn, D C, Fanny Wyatt, infant daughter of Caroline & Robt P Dodge.

N Y, Mar 4. Cmdor Perry died here this morning.

Senate: 1-Ptn from Ebenezer Ricker, asking to be allowed a pension on account of a wound received while in the military service in Florida: referred. 2-Ptn from Jeremiah Pendergrast, asking to be allowed the difference between the pay he received as a watchman of the Patent Ofc & that allowed to other watchmen: referred. 3-Cmte on Commerce: asked to be discharged from the consideration of the papers referred relating to C J Fox, U S Consul at Aspinwall, & that it be referred to the Cmte on Foreign Relations. Same cmte: asked to be discharged from the consideration of the ptn of of memorial of John C F Salamon & Geo W Morris, & that it be referred to the Cmte on Naval Affairs. 4-Cmte of Claims: bill from the Court of Claims on Dec 10, 1857, for the relief of Channer T Scaife, adm of Gilbert Stalker, reported it back without amendment. 5-Bill for the relief of Com Thos Ap Catesy Jones had twice passed the Senate at former sessions, & Mr Mason expressed the hope that the Senate would take it up & dispose of it: motion being agreed to. Mr Stuart opposed the bill on the ground that the relief contemplated by the bill was beyond the power of the Constitution & the authority of Congress to grant. Mr Mason argued at length in favor of the power of Congress to grant the relief, & complimented Cmdor Jones for his gallant service during the struggle at New Orleans. Further debate was cut short.

SAT MAR 6, 1858
House of Reps: 1-Cmte on Commerce: bill for the relief of Isaac S Smith, of Syracuse, N Y: committed. Same cmte: adverse report on the ptn of Anne Dudley, keeper of the Lighthouse at St Marks, Fla: laid on the table. 2-Cmte on Public Lands: bill recognizing the assignment of land warrant No 35,956, issued to John Davis, as valid: committed. 3-Cmte of Claims: adverse report in the case of Coale & Burr & the heirs of Michl Johnson: laid on the table. Same cmte: bill from the Court of Claims for the relief of Jas Smith, of Clermont Co, Ohio, with a recommendation that it do not pass: referred to the Cmte of the Whole & ordered to be printed. 4-Cmte of Claims: adverse report on the following bills: of Lucinda Robinson, of Orleans Co, Vt; of Hannah Weaver, of Wayne Co, Pa; of Ann Clark, of Madison Co, Tenn; of Mary Burt, of Sciota, Ohio; of Esther Stevens, of Van Buren, Mich; of Mercy Armstrong, of Gloucester, Rhode Island; of Nancy Madison, of Fairfield, Ohio; of Anne Parrott, of Clinton, Ohio; of Mgt Taylor, of Putnam, Tenn; of Lavina Tepton, of White Co, Tenn; of Lucretia Wilcox, of Wayne Co,

Mich; of Mary Robbins, of Westmoreland, Pa; of Tempy Connolly, of Johnson, Ky; of Rosamond Robinson, of Belknap, N H; of Jane Martin, of Harrison, Va; of Melinda Durkee, of Ga; of Sarah Weed, of Albany, N Y; of Mary Peirce, of Cortland, N Y; of Sarah Eaton, of Worcester, Mass; of Temperance Lydia Clapp, of Wash, N Y; of Eliz Morgan, of Rensellaer, N Y; of Phebe Polly, of Otsego, N Y; of Nancy Ittig, of Herkimer, N Y; of Mary Ann Hooper, of Va; of Almira Reniff, of Pa; of Sarah Loomis, of New London, Conn; & of Mary Grant, of S C: referred to the Cmte of the Whole. Same cmte: adverse report on the memorial of Horace S Campbell: laid on the table. Same cmte: bill for the relief of Ben Sayre: committed. 5-Cmte on the Post Ofc & Post Roads: adverse report on the ptn of Geo W Hopkins; on the ptn of Wm Moss; & on the ptn of A M Pettingall: all laid on the table. Bill for the relief of John B Roper: committed. 6-Cmte on the District of Columbia: bill for the relief of J W Nye, paying him $3,482.44, for improvements made upon the public grounds: committed. 7-Cmte on Revolutionary Claims: bill for the relief of the heirs of Rev Jas Craig, deceased: committed. Same cmte: bill for the relief of Wm Watkins: committed. Same cmte: bill to allow the legal reps of Saml Jones 5 years' full pay in lieu of half-pay for life: committed. Same cmte: bill for the relief of the heirs of Lt Bartlett Hinds: committed. 8-Cmte on Private Land Claims: bill for the relief of the legal reps of Marie Malines: committed. Same cmte: bill for the relief of Cyrenius Glass: committed. 9-Cmte on Indian Affairs: adverse report on the ptn of W K Greenwood; & on John Francis & others: both laid on the table. 10-Cmte on Indian Affairs: bill for the relief of Geo Chowpening & Eliz Woodward, widow of Absalom Woodward, deceased, & the children of the said Eliz Woodward: committed. Same cmte: bill for the relief of Messrs Dent, Vantine & Co, for provisions furnished to Indians in Calif during the years 1851 & 52: committed.. Same cmte: adverse report in the case of Cecil Compare, for leave to sell her Kansas half-breed lands: laid on the table. 11-Cmte on Military Affairs: adverse report on the ptn of Capt Wm P Paff for leave to enlist a rifle regt into the service of the U S: laid on the table. Same cmte: bill for the relief of Richd B Alexander; & relief of Maj Jas N Dashiell, paymaster in the U S army: both committed. Same cmte: bill for the relief of Simeon Stedman; & of Susannah Redman: both committed. Same cmte: adverse reports in the case of Jonas P Levy, & in the case of John G Clayton for a horse lost in the service of Gov't: laid on the table. Same cmte: bill for the relief of Hiram Paulding: committed. [The bill provides for the payment of his expenses in entertaining officers & other visitors to the frig **St Lawrence**, at Southampton, England, not to exceed $968.92. Also, $2,694 for entertaining Gov't officers at Bremerhaven & Stockholm in 1849 & 1850.] Mr Winslow, of N C, from the same cmte: bill for the relief of John M Brooke: committed. 12-Cmte on Foreign Affairs: bill for the relief of Francis Denaise: committed. Same cmte: adverse report in the case of Chas L Deman, U S Consul at Acapulco, Mexico: laid on the table. 13-Cmte on Invalid Pensions: bill providing an increase of pension to Peter Van Buskirk, of Wash City, D C: committed. Same cmte: bill for the relief of John Harris, of Warren Co, Ky: committed. 14-Cmte on Revolutionary Pensions: adverse report in the case of Jemima Daman, widow of Jedediah Daman, asking for a pension for his services in the Revolutionary war: laid on the table. 15-Cmte on Invalid Pension: bill for the relief of John Campbell; bill granting a pension to Mary Blattenberger; relief of Capt Stanton Shoals; & relief of Nancy Magill, of Ohio: committed. Same cmte adverse reports on the ptns of Mary Thompson; of John Ketchum; of John K Tucker; on the application of Saml Hamilton: laid on the table. Same cmte: bill for the relief of Wm Sutton; & of Jos Webb: Committed. 16-Cmte on Patents: bill for the relief of Edwin M Chaffee: committed. 17-Cmte on Printing: ptns of Jas B Steadman, printer to the House, & S M Knapps, lithographer: referred to the Cmte of Ways & Means. 18-Cmte of Claims: ptn of Arnold Harris, adm of Robt Armstrong, laid aside with a recommendation that it be concurred in. Same cmte: adverse reports on the ptn of Jas Thompson, surviving partner of C M Strader & Co; & on the ptn of Nathl Williams: recommended that they be referred to the Cmte of Claims. 19-Bills laid aside to be reported favorably to the House: bills for the relief of John Hamilton; of Thos Smithers; of the heirs of Alex'r Stevenson; of the reps of Wm Smith, deceased, late of Louisiana; of the legal reps or assignees of Jas Lawrence; of N C Weems, of Louisiana; of Francis Wlodecki; of Dr Chas B Maxwell, a surgeon in the U S navy; & for the benefit of the captors of the British brig **Caledonia** in the war of 1812. 20-Bill for the relief of John Hamilton taken up.

Letter from Oxford, Ohio, to the Presbyterian of the West: Rev Seth Howell, in a fit of deep, protracted melancholy, committed suicide by hanging, in his own house, Feb 18.

In consequence of my health I shall be absent from Wash City during the months of March & April. The business will be conducted by my clerk Mr Geo Bogan.
–Saml H Young, 9th st, between D & E sts.

Cmdor Matthew Calbraith Perry died on Thu, at his residence in N Y C, age 63 years. He was born in South Kingston, on Narragansett Bay, Rhode Island; his mother was Sarah Alexander; his father was Christopher Raymond Perry, who became an ofcr of the infant marine of the U S in 1798. His elder brother was Oliver H Perry, the hero of the battle of Lake Erie. The first of the Perry family in this country emigrated to Massachusetts from Devonshire, England, about the middle of the 17th century. Matthew C Perry entered the U S Navy as a midshipman on Jan 16, 1809, when he joined the schnr **Revenge**, from which he was soon after transferred to the frig **President**. In Nov, 1813, ordered to the frig **United States**; in Apr, 1814, back to the **President**; end of 1814 ordered to the brig **Chippewa**; transferred to the Navy Yard at Brooklyn with the rank of lt; in Aug 1819, ordered to the ship **Cyane**, which was sent to the Coast of Africa to aid the Colonization Society in its attempt to found a settlement of free blacks upon the Island of Sherbro, near Sierra Leone. The mortality became so great that it became evident no colony could be planted there, & Lt Perry selected Mesurado Cape as a more suitable locality for a town. He fixed the first settlement in Libera. In May, 1821, he was put in command of the schnr **Shark**; again attached to the Brooklyn navy yard until 1824; ordered to the ship **North Carolina**, of 96 guns, under command of Cmdor John Rogers- served as 1st lt & capt of the fleet. Promoted to the rank of Cmder & took charge of the recruiting at Boston, until 1830; took command of the corvette **Concord**, in which he conveyed John Randolph as U S Minister to Petersburgh, & then cruised 3 years in the Mediterranean. Once more at the Brooklyn navy yard as superintendent of a school of gun practice & in the organization of a steam naval service. In 1838 Capt Perry was sent to Europe to visit the dock yards & light houses; was appointed to the chief command of the Brooklyn navy yard for 2 years, when, at his own request, he was appointed to the command of the African squadron; in 1846 he sailed in command to Cmdor Conner, to the Gulf of Mexico, & assumed the chief command in time to direct the naval bombardment of Vera Cruz. The most distinguished service was the expedition to Japan, which sailed from the U S on Nov 24, 1852, & in command of which Cmdor Perry negotiated the treaty with Japan signed on Mar 31, 1854. The disease which caused Cmdor Perry's death was gout in the stomach. He had complained of feeling poorly for several days past, but was not considered in danger until the hour of his death. We believe he leaves & widow & 6 children, 3 sons & 3 daughters. One of the sons is now consul at Hong Kong. Of the daughters, two are married [Mrs John Hone & Mrs August Belmont] & one remains single. The wife of Rev Dr Vinton, of Trinity Church, is a niece of Cmdor Matthew C Perry, & a daughter of Cmdor Oliver H Perry. The deceased had served at sea 25 years, & on shore more than 17 years, & had only been unemployed about 6 years during the whole time since his entrance in the navy. –N Y Com Adv

Criminal Court-Wash-Thu. 1-Patrick Walsh was found guilty of larceny: sentenced to 9 months in the county jail. 2-Jacob Seymour, colored, guilty of assault: sentenced to 9 months in jail. Yesterday: 3-Thos Connolly, about 17, found guilty for assault & battery with intent to kill Henry Brooks with a knife: sentenced to 3 years in the penitentiary. 4-Danl Smith, late a justice of the peace for Wash Co, was brought into Court under an attachment for contempt, & having been adjudged a material witness in the case of Jas Powers for the murder of E A Lutts, &, in default of giving bail in $500 for his appearance to testify, was committed to jail. [Jun 18th newspaper: Jas Powers will suffer execution today. For precaution sake a force of 20 marines has been granted by the President to the Marshal to be present in the yard. The execution will be private.] [Jun 19th newspaper: respite of Jas Powers by the Pres of the U S. He is now to be executed on Jun 26, 1858.] [Jun 28th newspaper: Jas Powers was executed on Sat last. He had been left with his spiritual friend, Rev Mr O'Toole, when he received the announcement. Upon the scaffold, holding each end of a rosary in his hand, he said several prayers, & impressed a warm kiss upon the crucifix. Rev O'Toole administered final absolution. Jas Powers was about 5 feet 9 inches high, of light complexion & flaxen hair, well formed, of rather mild expression of countenance, not yet in his 20th year. In the course of the morning he was visited by his widowed mother & his sisters & brothers. In parting with his brother John, James urged upon him as his last request the abandonment of intemperate habits. Mr Walter Lenox stood with his friend on the scaffold. The body of the deceased was conveyed to his friends in Balt for interment.]

Mrd: on Mar 4, by Rev Dr Murray, Mr Robt P Luckett to Miss Catharine A Claxton, daughter of R W Claxton.

Died: on Mar 3, Robert Wilson, son of S W & Kate E Owen.

MON MAR 8, 1858
On Sat last two children named McCauley, aged 4 & 6 years, drowned at Mavin's Dam, a few miles from Leesburg, Va. They fell through the ice while playing on it.. An older sister & the mother of the children rushed to their rescue, but they also went under, & with much difficulty were saved from the same fate as the helpless little ones.

Died: on Mar 6, in Wash City, Mrs Mary Brown, consort of Wm Brown, deceased, in her 61st year. She died as she lived, a devout Christian. Her funeral will be this afternoon at 3 o'clock, from her late residence on 20th st, between E & F sts.

Army Intelligence: by direction of the President orders have been issued from the War Dept convening a general court martial at Carlisle Barracks, on Mar 10, for the trial of Col Edwin V Sumner, 1st regt of cavalry. The court will be composed of:
Brvt Maj Gen Thos S Jesup, quartermaster genr'l
Brvt Maj Gen John E Wool
Brvt Maj Gen Persifer F Smith
Brvt Brig Gen S Churchill, inspector genr'l
Col Jos K F Mansfield, inspector genr'l
Col Jos Plympton, 1st infty
Brvt Col Justin Dimick, 2nd artl
Brvt Col Jos P Taylor, subsistence dept
Col Henry R Craig, ordnance dept
Lt Col Geo B Crittenden, mounted rifles
Maj John F Lee, judge advocate

Appointments by the President, by & with the advice & consent of the Senate:
Registers of Land Ofcs:
E O F Hastings, of Marysville, Calif, vice Chas S Fairfax, resigned
Re-appointed:
Oliver Basham, at Clarksville, Ark
Wm J Owen, at Champagnole, Ark
H J Johnson, at Wash, Ark
L B Cunningham at Fayettsville, Ark
Wm W Lewis, at Batesville, Ark
W H Graves, at Springfield, Mo
Mark L Means, at Warsaw, Mo
John B Cloutier, at Natchitoches
Louis Palms, at New Orleans
Louis G Pyles, at Newnansville, Fla
Receivers of Public Money-reappointed:
Jas C Tappan, at Helena, Ark
W T Sargent, at Champagnole, Ark
C B Mitchell, at Wash, Ark
J L Dickson, at Fayetteville, Ark
T J Bishop, at Springfield, Mo
N B Holden, at Warsaw, Mo
H W Palfrey, at New Orleans
J B McClendon, at Greensburg, La
A L Woodward, at Tallahassee, vice Bond, deceased.

Died: on Mar 6, of pneumonia, in his 6th year, Richard Wallach, youngest son of Catherine & C W Boteler, jr. His funeral is this day at 1 o'clock, from his father's residence, 365 D st, between 9th & 10th sts.

Died: on Mar 6, in Gtwn, D C, Mrs Anna Tenney, in her 76th year. Her funeral will take place from the residence of her daughters, on Beal st, this afternoon, at 3 o'clock.

Died: on Mar 5, in N Y, Margaretta E, wife of Lt J R M Mullany, U S Navy.

For rent: a 3 story house, No 23 A st south, between N J ave & 1st st east on Capitol Hill. Possession given on Mar 16. Apply to Wm Wheatley, next door.

We have just taken the well-known stand of Wm Emmert, at which we intend carrying on the Confectionary business in all its branches. –Atz & Brother, Bridge st, Gtwn.

St Joseph's Orphan Asylum of Wash City. Board of Trustees: Rev T J O'Toole, Pres; Gregor Ennis, Vice Pres; H B Sweeny, Treasurer; W H Ward, Sec; Very Rev Dr Byrne, R H Clarke, Nicholas Callan, Thos Foran, & J S Harvey. The present Lady Managers: Mrs S Redfern, Pres; Mrs Madelaine Goddard, Treas; Mrs Williams, Sec; Mrs T Berry, Miss E Brooks, Mrs John F Coyle, Mrs J C Fitzpatrick, Miss Emily Mason, Mrs McLaughlin, Mrs F Mohun, & Mrs Stourton. The most Rev Archbishop of Balt, under whose advice they first sought their charter, the Trustees made arrangements with the Very Rev E Sorin, Superior of the <u>Order of the Holy Cross</u>, to place St Joseph's in charge of Sisters of that Order, giving into their hands the entire internal management & discipline of the house, with full control over the education & religious training of its inmates. The mother-house of this Order is at Notre Dame de Lac, St Joseph's Co, Indiana, where they have a large & flourishing community. There are 18 orphans in this temporary asylum. –Board of Trustees, T J O'Toole, Pres

Richmond, Mar 7, John Warrock, printer to the State Senate, died last night. He was probably the oldest printer in the South, & an estimable citizen.

TUE MAR 9, 1858
Excellent household & kitchen furniture at auction on Mar 16, at the residence of Mrs Hamilton, 529 H st, between 6th & 7th sts. -Jas C McGuire, auct

N Y: The burial of Cmdor Perry was one of the most imposing scenes of the past year. It was largely attended by people of all ranks & conditions, beside the distinguished officials, state & National. The religious services were conducted by Rev Drs Hawks, Vinton, Higbee, & Montgomery, & the beautiful Episcopalian service for the dead was never more effectively given, accompanied with music of the highest order.

The Shepherdstown Register announces the death, on Mar 4, of Col Edw Lucas, Paymaster at the Harper's Ferry Armory. The deceased was an ofcr of the war of 1812, had been a member of the Va Legislature & of Congress, & was a gentleman of fine qualities of head & heart.

The Martinsburg [Va] papers announce the death of Maj Lewis Burwell Willis, a gallant ofcr of the regular army in the war of 1812. He died in his 80th year. [No death date given-current item.]

Died: on Mar 7, in Fairfax Co, Va, at *Vaucluse*, the residence of her late husband, the late Lord Thos Fairfax, Mrs Margaret Fairfax, in her 76th year. She was a remarkable woman in all the relations of life.

Birth: on Mar 8, at 13th st, Mrs W Hope, of a son.

Senate: 1-Memorial from Pollard Webb, offering to sell to the U S **Meridian Hill**, as a summer residence for the Pres of the U S: referred. 2-Ptn from Wm R Brownlee, a soldier of the war of 1812, asking a pension: referred. 3-Ptn from T W Yonley & others, citizens of Missouri, asking to be protected in their location by certain lands in the Plattsburg district of that State: referred. 4-Ptn from Caleb Sherman, asking to be relieved from liability for public money received by him as collector of customs for the district of Paso del Norte, Texas, & stolen from him while in his custody: referred. 5-Ptn from Jas Bawden, asking that a patent may be issued to him for certain lands embraced in the Light-House reservation of Eagle Harbor, Lake Superior, upon which was made valuable improvements: referred. 6-Additional papers submitted in support of the claim of the <u>Bangor City Greys</u> to bounty lands for their services: referred. 7-Ptn from Richd W Clarke, asking additional compensation for extra services while a messenger in the Pension ofc: referred. 8-Ptn from R D Hills & others, asking the erection of a lighthouse at the mouth of Kewannee river, Wisc. 9-Ptn from Jas Foster, J Craig, & others, asking for a mail route from Oregon, Missouri, to White Cloud, Kansas; from White Cloud to Marysville; from **Fort Des Moines**, Iowa, to **Fort Riley**, & from White Clous to Iowa Point: referred. 10-Ptn from Wm Cruikshank & others, asking permission to prosecute their claims to a certain tract of land in Calif before the U S district court for the northern district of Calif: referred. 11-Cmte on Private Land Claims: bill for the relief of Anna M E Ring & sisters, Louis M Ring, Cordelia E Ring, & Sarah J De Lannoy, & asked its immediate consideration: bill passed. Same cmte: bill to confirm the title of Benj E Edwards to a certain tract of land in the Territory of New Mexico. 12-Cmte of Claims: bill for the relief of A W McPherson. 13-Cmte on the Judiciary: bill to authorize & direct the settlement of the accounts of Ross Wilkins, reported it without amendment. 14-Bill for the relief of Mary Peters: passed. 15-Bill to continue a pension to Christian Barnard, widow of the late Brvt Maj Moses P Barnard, U S Army: passed. 16-Bill for the relief of Eliz Montgomery, heir of Hugh Montgomery was brought up.

House of Reps: 1-Bill for the relief of John Hamilton: passed. 2-Resolved: that the Cmte on the Judiciary employ a stenographer whilst engaged in the investigation of the official conduct of Hon John C Watrous, late district judge of the U S Court for the eastern district of Texas.

Died: on Mar 6, of rheumatic fever, Clark Rider, in his 25th year. His funeral will be this evening, at 2 o'clock, from his late residence No 494 C st, & 13th st.

Died: very suddenly, at Fitzgerald's, Pa ave, Calvin J Crocker, only son of Hon Ira Crocker, of Portland, Maine. He was a member of the advance party of exploring engineers of the South Pass wagon-road expedition, & a man of most daring & resolute character. His old comrades were with him during his short illness & at his death.
[No death date given-current item.]

Died: on Feb 19, in Castroville, Medina Co, Texas, Geo A Stevens, aged 37 years, recently a resident of this city.

Obit-died: Gertrude Allis Browning, the only & idolized child of doting parents, the beloved & devoted wife of but 9 months' duration, she died far distant from those beloved parents who knew not the loss they had sustained until summoned to see her a corpse in the house of those whom she had come amongst as a daughter & a sister. [No death date given; no other information.]

Trustee's sale of *Summer Hill*, containing 150 acres, on the Wash & Alexandria Turnpike road; with a frame dwlg, stables, servants' house, & all necessary out-bldgs. Maj Tochman, residing on the premises, will show them to any one desiring to purchase. -I Louis Kinzer, trustee

Orphans Court of Wash Co, D C. Letters testamentary on the personal estate of Philip Otterback, late of Wash Co, deceased. –Sarah Otterback, excx

WED MAR 10, 1858
Senate: 1-Ptn from F M Lander, asking compensation for a reconnaissance made by him of a railroad route from Puget's Sound to the South Pass: referred. 2-Ptn from Jas McCutcheon, an invalid pensioner, asking an increase of his pension. 3-Cmte on Finance: bill for the relief of Edw N Kent. 4-Cmte of Claims: bill for the relief of Rufus Dwinel. 4-Bill for the relief of John Hamilton: referred to the Cmte on Military Affairs.

Cmdor Matthew C Perry, who died on Mar 4, was buried on Sat in the church-yard attached to St Mark's Church, in N Y C.

Private Instruction. The services of Mr J E Kittredge, of Yale Univ, may be secured as private instructor in Greek, Latin, or the various branches of Mathematics. Rugby House, 14th & K st, from 10 A M, or after 4 P M.

The English papers state that Col Thos Allsop, charged with complicity in the late attempt on the life of Emperor Louis Napoleon, had escaped to America about the time of the sailing of the steamer **America**. The Metropolitan Police Com'rs of London have issued a description & a reward of L200 for the apprehension of the accused. He is said to be concealed in N Y.

Fire on Feb 23 at Newburn, N C, destroyed 5 bldges, 2 of which belonged to the estate of Capt Outten, & another occupied by Mr Thos J Marshall. Mr Marshall saved himself by jumping from an upper-story window. His wife was also saved, having escaped by the stairway, but the child she had in her arms was so badly burnt that it soon died. Two other children, one in his 5th & the other in his 3rd year, perished in the flames.

The Cincinnati Gaz states that a bill has passed the Senate of that State prohibiting the intermarriage of <u>first cousins</u>.

Died: on Mar 8, after a short illness, John Dougherty, aged 48 years. His funeral is this afternoon at 2 o'clock, from his late residence on G st, between 1st & 2nd sts.

Died: on Mar 9, after a protracted illness, Mr Walter Stewart, a much respected citizen of Wash, aged 70 years. His funeral will take place tomorrow afternoon at 3 o'clock, from his late residence, 461 12th st, between G & H sts.

Died: on Mar 9, Maj Jas N Barker, aged 76 years. His funeral will be on Thu at 3½ o'clock, from his late residence, corner of Pa ave & 6th st.

Criminal Court-Wash-Tue: 1-John Cunningham, about 17, was found guilty for assault & battery with intent to kill a colored boy, Henry Lemmon: sentenced to 3 years in the penitentiary, to commence on Monday. He also was tried & found guilty on a similar charge of willfully assaulting & shooting at Mr Nathan Burnham, & without the smallest provocation. Cunningham was sentenced on this conviction to 5 years in the penitentiary, to commence after the expiration of the former sentence. 2-The same prisoner, with Wm Hutton & John Welsh, were tried for riot & assault; the first was acquitted, & the latter two convicted, but a motion for a new trial was granted by the Court. 3-Jas Mellville, a marine, was convicted of petty larceny, & sentenced to 3 months in the county jail. 4-Edgar Patterson was acquitted for petty larceny.

<u>Appointments by the President, by & with the advice & consent of the Senate:</u>
Collector of the Customs:
Re-appointed:
Jesse Sharpe, district of Delaware
G T Wright, Tappahannock, Va
Lucien D Starke, Camden, N C
Edmund Wright, Edenton, N C
Oliver S Dewey, Ocracoke, N C
Wm F Colcock, Charleston
Thaddeus Sanford, Mobile
Jos Sierra, Pensacola
John P Baldwin, Key West
Hamilton Stuart, district of Texas, Texas
Robt Parks, Cuyahoga, Ohio
W S Pomeroy, Fairfield, Conn
John S Parker, Cherrystone, Va
H F Hancock, Wash, N C
Julius A Baratte, St Mary's, Ga
Collector of Customs:
Wm S Jackson, Vienna, Md, vice Smith
John Thompson Mason, Balt, vice Thomas
John T Hammond, Annapolis, vice Sands
Tench Tilghman, Oxford, Md, vice Willis, deceased
H C Matthews, Gtwn, D C, vice White
Timothy Rives, Petersburg, Va, vice Banks, resigned
John Hunter, Natchez, vice J W McDonald
Thos Ledwith, St John's, Fla, vice Dell, deceased
Geo S Paterson, Sandusky, Ohio, vice Jones

Dennis Coghlin, Miami, Ohio, vice Riley
Geo P Eddy, Niagara, vice Hotchkiss
Orville Robinson, Oswego, vice Talcott
Warren Bryant, Buffalo, vice Hudson
Wm H Curtis, Yorktown, Va, vice Brittingham, resigned
B F Washington, San Francisco, vice Latham, resigned.
Surveyors of the Customs:
Re-appointed:
J R Thompson, at Town Creek, Md
W H Brown, at Llewellensburg, Md
Grodon Forbes, at Yeocomico, Va
Andrew J Pannell, at Wheeling
W B Flanner, Wilmington, N C
Myer Jacobs, Charleston
Wm Hayden, Hartford, Conn
Wm A Quynn, Nottingham, Md
Wm Shands, City Point, Va
Wm N Mitchell, Windosr, N C
Chas Fagot, Ponchartrain
Joshua H Davis, La Vaca, Texas
Wm A Linn, St Louis, Mo
Surveyors of the Customs:
Washington Finley, Balt, vice Wharton
A J Denby, Norfolk, vice Dawley, deceased
T P Bagwell, Accomac, Va, vice Melvin, resigned
Zachary Herndon, Valasco, vice Rudder, deceased
H T Hulbet, Memphis, vice Ballard, deceased
Appraisers of Merchandise: Beale H Richardson, Balt, vice Poultney
David C Springer, Balt, vice Gosnell
John W Baughman, of Md, as appraiser general, vice Pouder
Naval Officers: Wm N Peden, Wilmington, N C: reappointed
Chas G Greene, Boston: reappointed
C C Robinson, Norfolk: reappointed
Levi K Bowen, Balt, vice Kettlewell

Trustee's sale of valuable farm in Montg Co, Md: at the request of Mrs Rebecca Winn, & by deed of trust executed by Jas Donnelly & wife, dated Aug 13, 1855, recorded in Liber J G H, No 5, folios 282 thru 284, one of the land records of the Circuit Court for Montg Co, Md, [made to secure a certain debt therein named due to Mrs Rebecca Winn,] public sale on Apr 12 next, of ***Williamsborough***, in said county. Part of the boundaries include the dividing line between John Offutt & Mortimer Offutt; to a stone now planted & shown by Mr John Offutt, as the end of the last line of Wm & Jas. Contains 398½ acres of land, more or less, [it being the same land which was conveyed by the said Rebecca Winn to the said Jas Donnelly,] with all improvements, privileges, hereditaments to the same belonging to in any manner appertaining. –B F Middleton, trustee

THU MAR 11, 1858
Senate: 1-Ptn from John Drout, asking that his pension may commence from the date of his discharge from the army: referred. 2-Ptn from John A & Hiram A Pitts, asking the renewal & extension of their patent for certain useful improvements in a machine for threshing & clearing grain: referred. 3-Ptn from W P Cook, Jas A Lucas, M E Bradley, & 940 other citizens of southern New Mexico, asking a separate Territorial organization of southern New Mexico, from Texas to the Colorado of the west, under the name of Arizona: referred. 4-Ptn from John Brest, asking an increase of pension: referred. 5-Ptn from Jos H Wheat, a clerk in the Post Ofc Dept, asking to be allowed a certain amount of salary of which he alleges he was deprived without justice by the late Postmaster Genr'l. 6-Cmte on Private Land Claims: to which was referred the memorial of Danl Whitney, submitted a report, accompanied by a bill for the confirmation of a certain land claim in favor of Pierre Grignon or his legal reps. 7-Cmte on Military Affairs: asked to be discharged from the consideration of the memorial of Horace E Dimmick, asking an appropriation to test his improvement of the rifled cannon for throwing solid shot & shells: which was agreed to. Same cmte: adverse report on the memorial of Alex'r Hays, asking to be relieved from disability in the settlement of his accounts. Same cmte: asked to be discharged from the consideration of the claims of Nannie Denman & Ann E T Partridge, & that they be referred to the Cmte on Pensions: which was agreed to. Same cmte: discharged from the consideration of the bill for the relief of Robt Dickson, of the Ky volunteers, & it was referred to the Cmte on Pensions.

A letter from Rome of Mar 12. Another prince of the church, Cardinal Louis Gazeli, died yesterday, after a very short illness. He was at the head of the Order of Deacons. His death tends to confirm an idea, generally entertained here, & from which the cardinals themselves are not exempt, that those high dignitaries generally die off by threes.

Baron Krudener, formerly for several years the Russian Envoy to the U S, has just died, aged 70 years.

The Pres of the U S has appointed the following cadets at large for the year 1858:
1-Geo McKee, of Ky, whose father was killed in battle at Buena Vista, leading his regt in the final conflict.
2-Saml M Mansfield, son of Col Mansfield, who was distinguished for gallant services at **Fort Brown**, at Monterey, where he was severely wounded, & at Buena Vista.
3-Singleton Van Buren, son of Col A Van Buren, late of the army, distinguished in the battles of Cerro Gordo, Contreras, & Churubusco.
4-Wm S Beebe, who was the adopted son of his uncle, Capt Casey, during his life-an intelligent, zealous, & highly meritorious officer, who died in the service in Florida.
5-Geo N Bomford, son of Brvt Lt Col Bomford, of the army, distinguished for gallant conduct in the battle of Contreras & Churubusco, with the storming party at the battle of Molino del Rey, & at the battle of Chapultepec.
6-Wm H Betts, son of Lt Betts, distinguished & wounded in action at **Fort Drane**, Florida, from the effects of which he died.
7-Chas R Suter, son of Assist Surgeon Suter, formerly of the army, who was distinguished in the battle of Contreras, & died soon after in the city of Mexico.

8-Wm Bartlett, son of Prof Bartlett, a zealous, accomplished, & highly valuable officer of the Military Academy, who has contributed as much to the efficiency of the institution as any officer connected with it.
9-Roland S Mackenzie, son of the late Capt Mackenzie, of the navy, who died in the service.
10-John R Blocker, brother of Sgt Wm Butler Blocker, who, from the wounds of his superiors, was in command of his company at the battle of Gareta Belen, & was killed at the head of his company; cousin of Col P M Butler, who was killed at the head of his regt at Churubusco; of Whitfield G Brooks, who died of wounds received at the same time & place; & of Richd Watson, who, after being twice wounded, was shot down in the storming party at Chapultepec.

The two State tickets of Indiana are composed as follows:

	Democrat	Republicans
Sec of State	Danl McClure	Wm A Peel
Auditor	John W Dodd	Albert Lange
Treasurer	N F Cunningham	John H Harper
Super't of Instruc'n	Saml L Rugg	John Young
Atty Gen	J E McDonald	Wm T Otto
S C Judges	Saml E Perkins	H P Biddle
	Andrew Davison	A W Hendricks
	Jas M Hanna	Simon Yandes
	Jas L Worden	W D Griswold

Franklin Philp intends to open his new book store on Sat next. New Bookstore, 332 Penn ave, between 9th & 10th sts.

Methodist Episcopal Appointments: Balt M E Conference. The cmte on obituaries reported on the deaths of Rev Job Guest, Rev J J Leatherbury, & the late venerated Bishop Waugh. The appointment of preachers for the ensuing year were announced:
Balt District-Wm Hamilton Presiding Elder.
Balt: City Station: N J B Morgan, B F Brooke, Wm T D Clemm, E F Busey, W V Tudor; Charles st, R L Dashiell; Hanover st, J R Effinger; City Mission, J M Clark; Fayette st, W Hirst, B P Brown; Franklin st, M Goheen; Union Square, ThoS Sewall; South Balt, John Thrush, J W Bull, sup; Columbia st, Fielder Israel; Seamen's Bethel, W H Laney; Sharp st & John Wesley: Jas Sewall; Asbury & Orchard st, W Prettyman.
Balt circuit: T H W Monroe, W M Showalter, J L Gibbons, sup, A J Myers, sup; Summerfield, T A Morgan, W H Holliday; Patuxent, F S Cassiday, one to be supplied; Severn, J L Gilbert, J H Perry, J Turner, sup; South River, J C Dice; Annapolis, W Krebs; West River, T Myers, J M Green; Calvert, J W Lambeth, A B Dally, T B Chew, sup; Patapsco, J M Grandin; Patapsco circuit, T McGee, L W Berry, C A Reul, sup.
Md Colonization Society, P D Lipscomb, agent, member of Fayette st quarterly conference. Md State Bible Society, J Bear, agent; Dickinson College, Chas Collins, Pres; both members of City Station quarterly conference. Dickinson Seminary, John Wilson, teacher; member of Fayette st quarterly conference. Morgantown Female Seminary, Va, A S Hank, principal, member of Fayette st quarterly conference.

Potomac District-John Lanahan, Presiding Elder
Alexandria, B N Brown, R R S Hough, A Griffith, sup; Gtwn, W B Edwards, W R White, sup; West Gtwn & Tenallytown, W F Speake.
Washington-Foundry, B H Nadal; Wesley Chapel, I F Morgan; Waugh Chapel, Theodore M Carson; McKendree Chapel, Dabney Ball; East Washington, W H Chapman; Ebenezer, to be supplied; Ryland Chapel, S Rodgers; Gorsuch Chapel, Henry N Sipes; Union Chapel, J N Coombs, W O Lumsden, sup; Fletcher & Providence, H C McDaniel, M A Turner, sup; Asbury & Mount Zion, J W Hoover.
Fairfax, J W Tongue, Saml Dickson; Stafford, W Gwynn Coe, one to be supplied, H Leber, sup; Fredericksburg, J A McCauley; St Mary's, B H Smith, R R Murphy, J Bunting, sup; Bladensburg, W H Wilson, J A Williams; Woodville, John H Ryland; Charles, C G Linthicum, F Ward; Rockville, S Register, T B McFalls, B Barry, sup; Friendship, Isaac Collins; Montgomery, S Cornelius; Mount Vernon, H McNemar.
Metropolitan Collegiate Institute for Young Ladies, J N Hank professor, member of Foundry quarterly conference.

Winchester District-Wm G Eggleston, Presiding Elder
Winchester, S B Blake; Winchester circuit, S McMullin, one to be supplied; Jefferson, N Wilson, Geo V Leech; Berryville, J W Start, J T Trome; Shannondale, to be supplied; Martinsburgh, J Landstreet; Berkeley, F H Richey, C L Torryson; Berkeley Springs, T T Wysong, one to be supplied; Capon, Edw F Hetrick; Wardersville, S H Griffith, one to be supplied; Springfield, W Champion, one to be supplied; Shepherdstown, J H March, one to be supplied; Harper's Ferry & Bolivar, J S Deale; Hillsborough, W S Baird, J M Littell, S S Roszel, sup; Leesburgh, E D Owen; Rehoboth, J T Eakin; East Loudoun, R M Lipscomb, T E Carson; West Loudoun, J H Waugh, S V Leech; Warrenton, David Thomas, Wm Badgeley.

Rockingham District-E R Veitch, Presiding Elder.
Staunton, Geo G Brooke; Augusta, O P Wingman, Benj Frampton; Rockingham, Jas N Davis, F A Mercer; Rushville, to be supplied; East Rockingham, John W Wolff, A Y Graham; Woodstock, John W Kelley; Front Royal, J N Eakin, W Rippetoe; Luray, E L Kuglo; Lost River, C Parkison; South Branch, C B Young, J W Cornelius; New Creek, Henry Hoffman; Moorefield, T Hildebrand, S H Cummings; Franklin, R Smith, J F Beane.
Wesleyan Female Institute, Benj Arbogost, principal, member of Staunton quarterly conference.

Roanoke District-John S Martin, Presiding Elder.
Salem, Jas E Armstrong, one to be supplied; Christiansburgh, Isaac Gibson, Geo R Jefferson; Jacksonville, J W Ewans; Fincastle, D W Arnold, W R Stringer; Lexington circuit, H A Gaver, J H Wolf; Lexington Station, J R Wheeler; Rockbridge, Jas Beatty, one to be supplied; West Rockbridge, to be supplied; Churchville, F C Tebbs, W G Ferguson; Newcastle & Newport, J J Engle.

Lewisburg District-E P Phelps, Presiding Elder.
Lewisburg, H C Westwood; White Sulphur & White Sulphur circuit, J H M Lemon & J E Wasson; Frankford, J P Etchison & J L Snyder; Greenbrier, P S Sixeas, one to be supplied; Blue Sulphur, A W Wilson; Monroe, J J Sargent; Union, J F Liggett & A P Bowds; Sweet Springs, Johnsey Leaf; Covington, A Burhman & J F Chittum; Bath Alum, J F Graham; Warm Strpings, P B Smith; Highland, Saul B Dally; Monterey, L D Nixon;

Crab Bottom, M L Hawley; Greenbank, C C Cronin; Little Levels, J L Gardner, one to be supplied.
Transferred:
J Banks, E Welty, J T Phelps, & J Forrest, transferred to the East Balt Conference; J Montgomery transferred to the Peoria Conference; J Poisal transferred to the N Y Conference; W S Edwards transferred to Minnesota Conference.

Drug Store for sale, the stock, fixtures, & good will of a Drug store on Pa ave; an old & well established stand. –R H Laskey, Atty at Law, 36 Louisiana ave.

Trustee's sale of valuable real estate: by decree passed on Nov 6, 1857, by the Circuit Court for PG Co, sitting as a Court of Equity, in a cause wherein Mgt S A Cumming, next friend to Edmund B Cumming & others, is cmplnt, & Edmund B Cumming & others are dfndnts, the undersigned, as trustee, will expose at public sale on Dec 10, all that valuable real estate in said county, which was heretofore conveyed to Hon Thos U Cumming [now deceased & intestate] by Martin Buel & Lucy Ann, his wife, in fee simple, containing 162½ acres, more or less. The country road to Washington by way of 7th & North Capitol sts is a boundary on one side; it is within 2 miles of Soldiers' Home; adjoins the property of the late Stephen Markwood, the Messrs Wingerd, Diggs, Clarke, & others. The dwlg-house & out-houses on this estate are large & commodious, & in excellent order. –Danl C Digges, trustee, Upper Marlboro, Md.

On Mar 1, as the steamer **Eliza Battle**, Capt S G Stone, was coming down the Tombigbee river, on her way to Mobile, at a point about 45 miles below Demopolis, when discovered to be on fire in the after part. All on board were driven to the forward part of the boat, where they remained until the scorching flames drove them into the water. Some clung to bales of cotton & others on tree limbs, for several hours, until rescued after daylight. The night was bitterly cold, & of those who perished it is more than probable a majority were frozen to death. Persons ascertained to have been lost: Mrs B Cromwell & child, frozen, Sumter Co; Mrs H G Turner & child, frozen, Wash Co; Mr W T Smith, frozen, Greene Co; Mr Caradine, frozen, Chickasaw Co; Mr Willis, frozen, Chickasaw Co; Mr Augustus Jones, frozen, Columbus, Miss; Mr Martin, frozen, Ky; Mr John Powell, bar keeper, frozen, Eliza Battle; Dr S W Clanton, frozen, Warsaw, Ala; a young man, unknown, frozen, Fairfield, Ala; Rev Mr Newman, frozen, from Louisville, Ky; M A Galloway, never seen, Gainesville, Ala. Three white deck hands, never seen; P Kirkland, died after getting ashore, Greene Co, Ala. Dr S H Jones, never seen, Greene Co, Ala. Mrs Cromwell & child died from cold in her husband's arms in a tree. Fourteen of the crew, mostly colored, were also lost.

Trustee's sale of valuable real estate: by decree passed on Nov 6, 1857, by the Circuit Court for PG Co, in Equity, in a cause wherein Mgt S A Cumming, next friend to

Mrd: on Mar 10, in Wash City, at the residence of the bride's father, by Rev Septimus Tustin, D D, Jas F Shunk, son of the late Govn'r Francis R Shunk, of Pa, to Miss Rebekah, daughter of Hon Jeremiah S Black, Atty Gen of the U S.

Died: on Mar 6, in the city of Balt, Jos Benson, in his 95th year. He was born in Talbot Co, Md, on Mar 11, 1763, & during the Revolution, from 1779 to 1783, he was actively engaged in the defence of his native State. At an early age Mr Benson learned to place his faith in Him who is never trusted in vain. His end was as serene as his life had been consistent.

Died: yesterday, in Wash City, Cornelius Wendell, aged 9½ months, son of John & Catharine S Larcombe. His funeral is at 3 o'clock this afternoon.

New Haven, Mar 10. Rev Nathl W T Dwight, Professor in Yale College, died this morning, aged 71 years. [Mar 13th newspaper: N Y: It was Rev Nathl W Taylor, D D, Dwight Prof of Didactic Theology in Yale College, & not Prof Dwight, who died on Mar 10, at New Haven, Conn.]

To Machinist. I have purchased of Wm P Wood & Saml DeVaughan, the entire right of their Scrowl, or Jig Saw & Sawing Machines, as secured to them by letters patent & assignments & re-issued, referred to in the deed of assignments of Mar 4, & recorded in the Patent Ofc. Persons wishing to purchase Machines & Rights will please address the undersigned, assignee of Wm P Wood & Saml DeVaughan. –S DeVaughan, Wash, D C

Circuit Court of Wash Co, D C–in Equity. Buckner Bayliss vs Chas H Winder, Wm H Winder, & others. At Oct term, 1855, John H McBlair obtained a judgment against Chas H Winder for $548.22, with interest from Jul 1, 1854, & costs, which is still unsatisfied. It further shows that by a deed dated Mar 14, 1855, said Chas H Winder conveyed lots 9 & 10, in square 178, lot 16, in Davidson's subdivision of square 169, part of lot 19 in said square, & part of lot 1, in square 170, in Wash City, to W D Davidge in trust to secure a debt of $4,500 to Wm H Winder. It calls upon the dfndnts to show whether anything, &, if so, & how much, of said debt remains due; & it seeks to subject Chas H Winder's equity of redemption in this & other property described in the bill, & also incumbered the sale for the payment of the judgment. It futher states that the dfndnt Wm H Winder, is a non-resident of this District. Non-resident dfndnt is to appear in person, or by solicitor, on or before the first Monday of Aug next. –Jno A Smith, clerk

FRI MAY 12, 1858
The undersigned, residents near or frequent travellers upon the Wash & Rockville Turnpike, would state that we have been gratified with the generous outlay upon said road for several years past, & are pleased with its present good condition. We petition Congress to make an appropriation to make this road free.

E Lindsly	Chas R Knowles	David Miller
B L Porter	R B Normant	John Saul
W G W White	Jas M Taylor	John Wineberger
J C Lewis	Wm Cammack	Wm B Beall
Jas L White	Wm Horner	Thos Fitman
Eleazer Knowles	J W Horner	
J Knowles Lewis	Jno P Dickinson	

Trustee's sale of valuable house & lot in Gtwn: by deed of trust from Geo Rhodes, jr, & wife, dated Mar 2, 1857, recorded in Liber J A S No 129, folios 409, of the land records of Wash Co, D C: public auction on Apr 2, near the Market-house, in Gtwn, D C, part of lot 36, in the original plan of Gtwn; with brick dwlg & other improvements thereon. -Wm R Woodward, trustee -Edw S Wright, auct

Fire last evening broke out in a small shop occupied by a shoemaker on 12th st, between H & I sts. It communicated to a stable belonging to Mr Geo Stewart, which was destroyed. The horses were removed in good time. The fire then consumed the dwlg occupied by Mr Franklin Myers.

Book-binding: Messrs Goff & Thomas, s e corner of 8th & D sts, Wash. [Ad]

St Patrick's Day Dinner: on Mar 17, in Munder's saloon. Tickets may be had of Chas Klotz, or of Messrs John F Ennis, John F Coyle, Wm Forsyth, John Dowling, Francis McNerhany, Wm R Grubb, Andrew Carroll, Martin Renahan, Thos Donoho, John Savage, or any member of the Cmte of Arrangements. –Wm Forsyth, chairman

Senate: 1-Memorial from the Legislature of Wisconsin in behalf of the claim of John Shaw for compensation for his services as a spy & scout in the war of 1812, & compensation for losses sustained in furnishing supplies for the Missouri & Illinois mounted rangers during that war. Also, a memorial from Mr Shaw, asking compensation for furnishing 6 companies of rangers on the Mississippi with provision, ammunition, etc, during the last war with Great Britain: referred. 2-Ptn from Alex'r C Good, in behalf of his wife, heir & co-heirs of John Swan, of Balt, asking indemnity for French spoliations prior to 1800: referred. 3-Five memorials, all numerously signed by the most influential citizens of Phil, urging that the proposals of Thos Rainey for conveying the mails from Phil to Brazil, touching at Savannah & certain ports in the West Indies, may be accepted: referred. 4-The papers in the case of Mrs A P Derrick, widow of Wm S Derrick, late chief clerk in the Dept of State, were taken from the files & referred to the Cmte of Claims. 5-The papers in the case of Theresa Dardenne were taken from the files & referred to the Cmte of Claims. 6-The papers in relation to the claim of the heirs of Jas Purvis were taken from the files & referred to the Cmte on Revolutionary Claims.

The comrades & friends of the late Ensign Jos C Peck, of the Pres' Mounted Guard, have given testimony of the warm & deep esteem in which they held their deceased comrade & friend by the preparation of a white marble tombstone of large size, inscribed in a style of superior taste & workmanship by Mr Thos Gagliardi, a member of the corps.

Died: on Mar 11, Chas Draine, in his 62nd year, a native of county Antrim, Ireland, but for the last 36 years a resident of Wash City, leaving a wife & 6 children. His funeral is on Sat at 10½ o'clock, from his late residence, 390 10th st.

Died: on Mar 11, Catharine H, infant daughter of Wm & Virginia McCauley, aged 4 months. Her funeral will take place today, at 1 o'clock, at her father's residence, 221 Va ave, Island.

Carlisle, Mar 11. The Court Martial in the case of Col Sumner was opened today. The accused was arraigned on 2 charges: 1-Prejudice of good order & military discipline; & 2-Violation of an article of war in sending a challenge. Sumner pleads not guilty. The prosecution rests upon the correspondence. Col F Lee, for the defence, testifies to the use of insulting language by Gen Harney towards Col Sumner during the trial at **Fort Leavenworth**. Col Sumner is defended by Hon F Watts.

In Equity-No 1359. Smith Petit against Anne G S McKinstry, Calister Ann & Wm McKinstry, & Wm B Webb, adm, widow & heirs of Wm McKinstry. The parties above named are to meet in my office on Mar 26. I shall state an account of the personal estate of the said Wm McKinstry, deceased, of the debts he owed at his death, & inquire whether it is necessary to sell any part of his real estate in aid of the personal for payment of his debts. –W Redin, auditor

Criminal Court-Wash-Thu: 1-John Mortimer was convicted of assault & battery, & fined $3. 2-Wm Brown, for assault at a fire at the N Y Yard, was found guilty, & fined $10. 3-Lucien Pipsico, colored, for an assault on his wife, fined $4.

SAT MAR 13, 1858
Records of the London Co for the <u>First Colony</u> in Virginia: found in the Feb Historical Magazine. The records of the Commercial Companies in England for the colonization of America constitute the Genesis & Exodus of our English-American history. Passing Cabot's patent of Mar 5, 1496, Gilbert's of Jun 11, 1578, & intermediate documents. We come to the incorporation, Apr 10, 1606, of certain adventurers for colonizing that part of America commonly called Virginia. They were divided into 2 companies, one of which, the London company, had the southern portion of the territory. This corp kept a record of its transactions till its virtual suppression by proclamation, Jul 15, 1624. Jas Stuart's darling project of a Spanish match for his son Chas was then on foot, & he was persuaded by Gondomar, the unscrupulous but faithful Minister of Spain, to destroy this great commercial company, in order to conciliate the Spanish Court & secure the coveted marriage. The most active of these adventurers was Nicholas Ferrar, a London merchant, associated with Sir Thos & Sir Hugh Middleton, in the commerce of both the East & West Indies. Sir Walter Raleigh, Sir John Hawkins, Sir Francis Drake, Sir Edwin Sandys, & their compeers were frequent guests at his table. His third son, Nicholas, born Feb 23, 1592, was the friend of Geo Herbert, specially remembered in Izaak Walton's life of the poet. Izaak mentions two other names in this memoir interesting to New England readers. One is Dr Arthur Lake, Bishop of Bath & Wells, the friend of John White, of Dorchester, illustrious men, named by Hugh Peters as the two who occasioned, yea founded that work, of colonizing Massachusetts. The good Bishop died May 4, 1626. The other one referred to is Mr Herbert Thorndike, Fellow of Trinity College, Prebendary of Westminister, & one of the editors of the Polyglot Bible. His brother, Mr John Thorndike, an early settler of the Massachusetts Colony, was one of the founders of

Ipswich, & the ancestor of a worthy New England family. Mr Thorndike died in England, & the graves of the Church Prebendary & his Puritan brother are side by side in Wetminister Abbey. But to return to Nicholas Ferrar, jr. After several years of travel on the Continent among the learned he returned to England in 1618, & died Dec 2, 1637. About 1654 materials for a memoir of this gentlemen were prepared by his brother, Mr John Ferrar, who had been deputy Gov'r of Virginia Co for some 3 years. These, with materials from other sources, were edited & published by Rev Dr Peter Peckard, of Magdalen College, Cambridge, in 1790. Here we leave the memoirs of Ferrar, & turn to Virginia for further information about these natal records of a State, rather of a nation. Stith, the excellent historian of Virginia, writing in 1747, hands down to us the following account of them, which he had received many years ago in conversation with Col Byrd & Sir John Randolph. Col Byrd's father being in England in 1667, at the time of the death of the Duke of Southampton, purchased these records of that nobleman's executors for sixty guineas. Each page is subscribed by Edw Collingwood, the Company's Sec; thus, Com Collingwood, which is, as I take it, Compared, Collingwood. There is a testification at the end of each volume. At the end of the first, under under the hands of Edw Waterhouse & Edw Collingwood, Secs of the two Companies for Virginia & the Somer-Islands, that they had compared that with the original court book & found it to be a true & perfect copy of the same, except the omission of one court & part of another. The second volume is signed by said Sec Collingwood & Thos Collet, of the Middle Temple, gentleman, testifying the same thing, except in a few immaterial points, where were wanted some original papers. These volumes contain the Companys' proceeding for a little above 5 years, viz: from Apr 28, 1619, to Jun 7, 1624, including the whole time of Sir Edwin Sandy's & the Earl of Southampton's administration. Stith was a grandson of Wm Randolph, of Henrico Co, whose brother, Isham Randolph, had grandsons, Thos Jefferson & Jas Pleasants. –J W T [Richd Randolph, of Hanover, Va, informs me that there is a series of early manuscript volumes in Richmond of an important historical character.]

Connecticut: the two State tickets in Connecticut, to be voted on Apr 1 next are

	Democrats	Republicans
Govn'r	Jas T Pratt	W A Buckingham
Lt Govn'r	John Cotton Smith	Julius Catlin
Treasurer	Danl B Warner	Lucius J Hendee
Secretary	E Williams, jr	John Boyd
Comptroller	Poleg C Childs	Wm A Buell

The St Louis Leader has changed hands. Mr Chas L Hunt has disposed of his interest therein, Mr W A Seay retires from his editorial connexion therewith, & Mr Edw Wm Johnston, a political writer of known & eminent ability, becomes its future proprietor & publisher.

A large tobacco house & cow house, belonging to Mr Jas Mullikin, in the forest of PG Co, with their contents, were entirely destroyed by fire on Fri last. The lost is estimated at $4,000. No insurance. The fire originated from a pipe carried to the bldg by a negro woman.

Senate: 1-Ptn from A B Davis & other highly respectable citizens of Montg Co, Md, engaged in agriculture & in the transportation of country produce to Wash City, feel deeply the disadvantages under which they labor in not being on an equality with farmers & traders residing in other parts of the vicinity of the Capitol, for whom the liberality of Congress has provided free roads & free bridges, & ask that the District plank road may be free: referred. 2-Ptn from Webster B Steele, a soldier of the war of 1812, asking to be allowed a pension: referred. 3-Cmte on Private Land Claims: bill for the relief of Manuel Leisa, Joachim Leisa, & others, to provide for the location of certain private land claims, reported back with an amendment. 4-Cmte on Military Affairs: bill for the relief of John Hamilton, & asked its immediate consideration. 5-Cmte on Public Lands: bill for the relief of Ashton S H White. Same cmte: bill for the relief of Jas Rawden, of Mich, asking that the Sec of the Interior be authorized to issue a patent to him for certain lands at Eagle, Lake Superior.

<u>Historical Sketches of North Carolina</u> from 1834 to 1851, by John H Wheeler. Price $2. For sale by Taylor & Maury, Booksellers, near 9th st.

House of Reps: 1-Cmte on Commerce: bill for the payment of extra compensation to Enoch B Talcott, for his services & expenses in recovering Gov't funds embezzled by Jacob Richardson: committed. Same cmte: adverse repot in the case of A A Millard: laid on the table. 2-Cmte of Claims: adverse report on the ptn of Jas Young: laid on the table. Bill for the relief of Nahum Ward: committed. Bill for the relief of Eli Q Gough: committed. 3-Cmte on Revolutionary Claims: bill for the relief of the heirs of Capt Saml Miller: committed. Same cmte: bill for the relief of the heirs of Wm Edmondston: committed. 4-Cmte on Private Land Claims: bill for the relief of Rawson Minard, father of Theodore Minard, deceased: committed. Bill for the relief of Abel M Butler: committed. Bill for the relief of Saml Little & for other purposes: committed. 5-Cmte on Foreign Affairs: bill for the relief of Duncan Robertson: passed. [The bill refunds to Mr Robertson, the Norwegian Consul, $749.92, paid by him at the Gosport Navy Yard for repairs to the barque **Ellen**, which rescued a part of the passengers of the wrecked steamship **Central America**.] Same cmte: bill for the relief of John P Brown: committed. Same cmte: bill for the relief of Wm Rich: committed. 6-Cmte on Invalid Pensions: bill for the relief of Mrs Mary Ann Henry: committed. Bill granting an invalid pension to Henry Miller: committed. Bill granting a pension to Mrs Mary A M Jones: committed. Bill for the relief of Mary P Dusenbery: committed. Bill granting a pension to Jeremiah Wright: committed. Bill for the relief of John Duncan: committed. Same cmte: asked to be discharged from the consideration of the case of John McGinniss: which was granted.

A heart-rending accident on Monday last, at the residence of Mrs Brown, near Jackson, in the parish of East Feliciana. Lawrence Brown, about 21, his cousin, Mary J East, & other members of the family were in the parlor engaged in conversation, when a boy entered to inform Lawrence that there was a flock of robins in a tree near-by. As Lawrence attempted to uncock his gun, the hammer slipped, & came down with sufficient force to explode the cap, & the whole charge entered the left temple of Miss Mary J East, causing instant death. –Bayou Sara [La] Times, 27th ult

Died: Mar 11, in Wash City, Frank Moreno, eldest son of Hon S R Mallory, of Florida, aged 11 years. His funeral will take place from the Nat'l Hotel at 11 o'clock today. [Mar 16th newspaper: A crowd of distinguished persons assembled on Sat in the parlors of the Nat'l for the funeral of Francis Moreno Mallory, son of the Senator from Fla. Beautiful & intelligent by 11 years, he was buried with the rites of the Catholic Church. Descended by his mother from one of the old Spanish Catholic families of Fla, he had been baptized in that communion.]

A Choctaw newspaper mentions the resignation of Alfred Wade, Govn'r of the Choctaw Nation. The reason is continued ill-health. Hon Tandy Walker, pres of the Senate, succeeds to the ofc of Govn'r for the expiration of the term of Govn'r Wade-such being a provision of the Choctaw constitution. He had held the chief excutive office of the nation for 20 years, without interruption.

The <u>Old Gas Works</u> lot for sale, being lot 7 in square 382, corner of Louisiana ave & 10th st: 10, 400 square feet of ground, with a front on Louisiana ave of 109 feet, on 10th st, 69 feet, & on Canal st 100 feet. Inquire at the ofc of the Gas Light Co of J F Brown, Sec in charge.

MON MAR 15, 1858
Grand closing out sale for Messrs Vito Viti & Sons: on Mar 16, at Crouch's Academy of Music, Pa ave & 11th st, the residue of their beautiful goods of Marble Statuary; Garden Statuary, Bronze, Alabaster Vases, & Urns. -Jas C McGuire, auct

Orphans Court of Wash Co, D C. Letters testamentary on the personal estate of Provey Gadsby, late of Wash Co, deceased. –W Gadsby, exec

Circuit Court of Wash Co, D C-in Equity, No 1,329. Chas W Pairo, against Chas H Winder, Wm H Winder, & others. At Oct term, 1855, the cmplnt recovered 3 judgments against said Chas H Winder, two for $41.36 each, & the third for $41.87, with interest on all from Nov 22, 1852, & costs, which are still unsatisfied; on Mar 14, 1855, said Chas H Winder conveyed lots 9 & 10 in square 170, lot 16 in Davidson's subdivision of square 169, part of lot 19 in said square, & part of lot 1 in square 170, all in Wash City, to a trustee, to secure $4,500 to W H Winder; & the object is to discover whether any thing, & if so how much, remains due of said debt, [charging the whole to have been paid,] & to subject the equitable estate of said Chas H Winder in said premises to sale for the satisfaction of said judgments. It appears that W H Winder does not reside in this District, & he is warned to appear in this Court, in person or by solicitor, on or before the first Mon in Aug next. –Jno A Smith, clerk

Attempted murder. On Friday night last, Louis Jones, son of the late G H Jones, was fired upon by 2 men, who continued in pursuit of him from 13th & N Y ave to his home, between 9th & 10th st, on Pa ave. Mr Jones is believed to have no enemies; robbery was possibly the motive for the incident.

Circuit Court of Wash Co, D C-in Equity. Chas Hoemiller, against Chas H Winder, Wm H Winder, & others. At the Oct term, 1855, the cmplnt recovered a judgement against Chas H Winder for $197.46, with interest thereon & costs, which is still unsatisfied; on Mar 14, 1855, said Chas H Winder conveyed lots 9 & 10 in square 170, lot 16 in Davidson's subdivision of square 169, part of lot 19 in said square, & part of lot 1 in square 170, all in Wash City, to a trustee, to secure $4,500 to W H Winder; & the object is to discover whether any thing, & if so how much, remains due of said debt, [charging the whole to have been paid,] & to subject the equitable estate of said Chas H Winder in said premises to sale for the satisfaction of said judgments. It appears that W H Winder does not reside in this District, & he is warned to appear in this Court, in person or by solicitor, on or before the first Mon in Aug next. –Jno A Smith, clerk

Senate: 1-Ptn from Cynthia Corey, widow of Saml Corey, asking a pension on account of the services of her late husband during the war of 1812: referred. 2-Ptn from D Meriwether, asking that an appropriation may be made for his salary as superintendnt of Indian affairs in the Territory of New Mexico, from Jul 27, 1854, to Apr 30, 1857: referred. 3-Ptn from Arnold Harris & S F Butterworth, sureties of Wm G Kendall, late postmaster at New Orleans, asking to be released from the payment of judgment against them, on the ground that an intemperate clerk in the Post Ofc Dept, since dismissed, had, in the first instance, rendered the account against said Kendall $5,365 & a fraction less than was really due the Gov't: referred. 4-Ptn from Chas Knap, asking that the Sec of the Treasury be authorized to make such change in existing contracts with him for furnishing iron for the custom-house at New Orleans as to him may seem reasonable, so that the memorialist may receive a fair compensation for materials furnished & services performed: referred. 5-Ptn from Geo Chorpenning, asking remuneration for losses sustained by himself & Absalom Woodward by Indian depredations while carrying the mails from Calif to Salt Lake city under contracts with the Post Ofc Dept: referred. 6-Cmte of Claims: bill for the relief of J Hardy & Alton Long, asking the return of rent collected y U S agents for the working of mines not the property of the U S. 7-Bill for the relief of Dr Chas D Maxwell, a surgeon in the U S navy, & the bill for the relief of the captors of the British brig **Caledonia**, in the war of 1812: referred to the Cmte on Naval Affairs. 8-Bill for the relief of the legal reps or assignees of Jas Lawrence & for the relief of N C Weems, of Louisiana, & for the relief of Francis Wlodecki: referred to the Cmte on Private Land Claims. 9-Bill for the relief of the heirs of Alex'r Stevenson: referred to the Cmte on Revolutionary Claims. 10-Bill to increase the pension of John Richmond & for the relief of John Smithes: referred to the Cmte on Pensions. 11-Cmte of Claims: bill for the relief of the heirs at law of the late Abigal Nason, sister & devsee of John Lord, deceased: passed. 12-Bill to authorize & direct the settlement of the accounts of Ross Wilkins, Jas Wetherell, & Solomon Sibley, reported from the Cmte on the Judiciary: recommended that it pass.

Died: on Mar 12, in New Orleans, of typhoid fever, Mrs Susan Brown, daughter of the late Townshend & Rachel J Waugh, formerly of Wash City.

Died: on Mar 2, at St Paul, Minn, James Corcoran, only child of C N & S C Thorn, aged 8 months.

Died: on Sunday, Duncan Stewart, son of Franklin Steele, of Minnesota, aged 1 year. His funeral will take place on Mar 16 at 11 o'clock, from 322 K st, Franklin Square.

Died: on Mar 12, at Annapolis, Mr Absalom Ridgely, junior editor & proprietor of the Annapolis Republican, in his 31st year. At the time of his death he was secretary & treasurer of the Annapolis & Elkridge Railroad Co, & treasurer of the Corp of Annapolis. He was for several years a resident of Wash City.

TUE MAR 16, 1858
Rev Francis P McFarland was on Sunday consecrated as the Catholic Bishop of the Diocese of Hartford, comprising the States of Connecticut & Rhode Island. Archbishop Hughes presided, assisted by 7 bishops & a great number of priests.

Trustee's sale of valuable Country Garden Land: by deed of trust from Michl Byrnes, dated Nov 16, 1855, recorded in Liber J A S No 117, folios 216, of the land records for Wash Co, D C: public sale on Apr 15 next, of the south half of lot 13, in the plat of resurvey made by Lewis Carbery, & formerly known as *Bayley's Purchase*, containing 26 acres & 14 perches, more or less. The tract is about a mile beyond Benning's bridge, on the road to Marlboro. –Richd H Clarke, Danl Ratclif, trustees -A Green auct

Administrators sale of the personal effects [watch & chain, lot of dentists' tools, wearing apparel, & pistols,] of the late Thos Lamb, on Mar 20, at the Auction Rooms of J C McGuire. –Wm Poulton, adm -Jas C McGuire, auct

Rev Harry Croswell, D D, died on Sat at his residence at New Haven, Conn. But a few hours have passed away since our announcement of the death of Rev Dr Taylor, of the same city. Dr Taylor was 72 & Rev Dr Croswell had reached his 82nd year. Dr Croswell was in the 44th year of his ministry, & has been rector of the Protestant Episcopal Church, [Trinity,] New Haven, for 43 years. When he retired from the press he became the rector of St James' Church in Albany, & thence was called to Trinity Church, New Haven, where he continued down to the time of his death. –N Y Com Adv

On Fri, John Birch, an Englishman, about 45 years of age, was instantly killed by the bursting of a large grindstone, in the establishment of Messrs Brown & Tetley, Wood st. -Pittsburg Dispatch

Miss Barnard, a daughter of Geo M Barnard, a merchant of Boston, residing on Beacon st, lost her life there on Sat by her clothes taking fire from a grate where cannel coal was burning. She was 21 years of age.

Circuit Court of Wash Co, D C-in Chancery. Agnes M Easby, against Horatio N Easby, John W Easby, Henry King & wife, W R King & wife, & Cecelia J Hyde. Wm B Webb & Richd H Clarke have sold to John W Easby lot 13 in square 1,028, for $200.44; & the purchaser has complied with the terms of the sale. –Jno A Smith, clerk

House of Reps: 1-Memorial of Dr Robt K Smith, for confirmation of title to certain land in New Orleans: presented.

Senate: 1-Ptn from Charlotte Taylor, now residing in the State of Conn, only surviving child of the late Wm Scarbrough, of Savannah, Ga, an enterprising man, of great mechanical genius. She states that her father constructed, in 1818 & 1819, with his own means & those of every friend he could enlist, the first steamer that ever crossed the Atlantic, The steamer **Savannah**, of Savannah, Stephen Rogers, of New London, Conn, commanding her; that her voyage was entirely successful. She asks that Congress will consider the great sacrifices made by her father in accomplishing so great a work, which literally ruined & improverished him, & asks some pecuniary acknowlegement may be made her: referred. 2-Ptn from Dr R F Mason, of the U S navy, asking to be allowed the difference of pay between assist surgeon & passed-assist surgeon from the date at which he passed his examination & the date at which he was actually entitled to it: referred. 3-Ptn from Ebenezer Watson, asking an increase of his pension: referred. 4-The papers on file in relation to the claim of Thos W Ward were referred to the Cmte on Commerce. 5-The papers on file in relation to the claim of the heirs of John W Pray were referred to the Cmte on Revolutionary Claims. 6-Cmte on Military Affairs: bill for the relief of Maj Jeremiah Y Dashiell, paymaster in the U S army. 7-Cmte on Indian Affairs: on the memorial of David Gordon: joint resolution devolving upon the Sec of War the execution of the Act supplemental to an act therein mentioned, approved Dec 22, 1854.

Mrd: on Mar 14, by Rev F S Evans, Mr John Francis Doone to Miss Eliz Barnes.

Died: on Mar 13, Owen McGee, in his 44th year. His funeral will take place this afternoon at 3 o'clock, from his residence at 4th st & Md ave, east Capitol Hill.

Died: on Mar 15, of congestion of the brain, Jas A, infant son of John & Rosina M Saul, aged 7 months & 21 days.

Circuit Court of Wash Co, D C-in Chancery, No 1,066. Agnes M Easby vs John W Easby, Horatio N Easby, Henry King & wife, W R Smith & wife, & Cecelia J Hyde. Horatio N Easby, John W Easby, & Agnes M Easby, excs of the last will & testament of Wm Easby, deceased, reported to the Court that they have, in conformity with the supplemental decrees passed in the above cause on Dec 31, 1856, sold to H W Hamilton & ___ Clarke, lot 14 in square 559, for $366.25; to ___ Howard, who has assigned his purchase to S M Golden, parts of square 907, for $287.50; that, having no bid for square 983, they sold the same at private sale to Wm H Philip for $1,100; & the purchasers have complied with the terms of sale. –Jno A Smith, clerk

WED MAR 17, 1858
Senate: bill for the relief of Jas Bawden: passed.

Died: on Mar 16, Matilda Bayne, beloved daughter of Wm H & Mary Arnold, aged 2 years & 7 months. Her funeral is this afternoon at 2 o'clock, from their residence, 601 8th st, Navy Yard.

Died: on Mar 16, in Wash City, Mollie Blanche, youngest daughter of Eliza & John W Glover, aged 2 years, 2 months & 16 days. Her funeral is Thu at 3 o'clock, from the residence of her parents, 537 11th st.

House of Reps: 1-Bill introduced for the relief of Slade Colloway: referred. 2-Bill introduced for the relief of John A H Shepherd & Walter K Caldwell, of Pike Co, Mo: referred. 3-Bill for the relief of John R Nourse: referred. 4-Bill for the relief of Chas H Mason: referred. 5-Bill for the relief of Monroe D Downs: referred. 6-Bill for the relief of John Hastings, collector of the port of Pittsburg: referred. 7-Cmte on Private Land Claims: inquire into the expediency of granting to Job Stafford, of the State of N Y, who was a soldier of the war of 1812, 160 acres of land in consideration of his having been engaged in an action with the enemy & totally disabled by a cannon ball: referred. 8-Ptn presented of Wm R Ashton, adm of Dr Ben Chapin, deceased, late a surgeon in the navy of the Revolution, asking 7 years' half pay: referred.

We learn from reliable quarter that the court martial upon Col Sumner, at Carlisle Barracks, recently, was the acquittal of Col Sumner upon both the charges preferred against him. Col Sumner leaves Carlisle this morning for Watertown, N Y, where he will meet his family. He is under orders for Utah, & will leave **Fort Leavenworth** with his regt on May 10. -N Y Times of yesterday

Chillon Castle Manor Farm at Public Auction: exec's of the last will & testament of the late Wm Easby, will sell on Apr 10, his farm lying partially in Wash Co, D C, & PG Co, Md, containing in all 62 acres, more or less. –Horatio N Easby, John W Easby, Agnes M Easby, excs -Jas C McGuire, auct

Executor's sale of improved & unimproved real estate. Exec's of the last will & testament of Wm Easby, deceased, by decree of the Circuit Court of Wash Co, D C-in Chancery, passed in a cause, No 1,066, wherein Agnes M Easby is cmplnt, seeking an admeasurement of dower & other relief in equity, & Horatio N Easby & John W Easby, Henry King & Marian his wife, Cecilia J Hyde, Wm R Smith & Wilhelmina his wife, are dfndnts: auction on Apr 8, of:
Lot 9 in square 20   Lots 3 & 4 in square 143
Lot 2 in square 59   Lot 6 in square 57
Lot 2 in square 44   Lot 6 in square 104
Lots 2 thru 5 in square 61, lying between Water st & the C & O Canal.
Lots 6 thru 8 in square 63, improved by 3 small frame houses
Lots 9 thru 11 in square 63, with valuable lime-kilns, known as the **Hamburg Lime-kilns**.
–Horatio N Easby, John W Easby, Agnes M Easby, excs -Jas C McGuire, auct
[Sep 21st newspaper: this sale is repeated in the newspaper of Sep 21, with an auction date of Oct 13, 2004.]

Mrs M A Knight, 447 Pa ave, near 3rd st, has vacant 2 elegantly furnished bedrooms on the first floor.

On Tue fire broke out in the blacksmith's shop of Mr Betzar, on Water st, Gtwn. It spread to the shop of Mr Hachtel, which was also consumed.

Chancery sale of valuable real estate on E st north, between 12th & 13th sts west: by decree of the Circuit Court of Wash Co, D C, sitting as a Court of Equity, duly passed on Jan 29, 1858, in a certain cause, wherein Alpheus S Williams et al are cmplnts, & Saml Wise et al dfndnts. Public auction on Apr 12 of part of lot 4 in square 290, in Wash City, D C. –Wm J Stone, trustee -J C McGuire, auct

Capt John Young, of Poplar Island, met with his death on Mar 6. Easton [Md] Gaz: Capt Young, with his son-in-law, was crawling down through some bushes to shoot ducks, when some bushes came in contact with the lock of the gun in the hands of the latter, causing the gun to go off, the contents of which killed the Capt instantly.

Circuit Court of Wash Co, D C. Van Bibber vs Van Bibber. The trustee reported he has sold the interest of the parties to this suit in Lot 2 in square 2, to Andrew Hoover, for $400; lot 9 in square 846, to Chas Nelson, for $67; lots 10 thru 12 in square 846, to Francis S Walsh, for $223; lots 7 thru 10 in square 1,043, to David Rawlings, for $414; lot 26 in square 1,043, to Wm Morris, for $100; & the purchasers have complied with the terms of the sale. –John A Smith, clerk

Orphans Court of Wash Co, D C. In the case of Jane H Scott & John H Semmes, adms of John D Scott, deceased, the admins & Court have appointed Apr 6, for the final settlement of the personal estate of said deceased, of the assets in hand.
-Ed N Roach, Reg/o wills

THU MAR 18, 1858
Public auction of the effects of the Variety Store of J Handley, on 7th st, between G & H sts, on Mar 19. -A Green auct

Household & kitchen furniture at auction on: Mar 24, at the residence of Rev F S Evans. -A Green auct

Obit-died: on Mar 2, in Lancaster Co, Pa, after a short illness, in his 73rd year, Hon Jeremiah Brown. He was a member of the State Legislature, a member of the Convention that formed the extant consitution of the State, a Rep of the Lancaster district in the 27th & 28th Congresses, & he was one of the first associate judges elected by the people. -R

Died: on Mar 16, Chas F P Cummins, in his 26th year. His funeral will be this afternoon, at 3½ o'clock, from his residence, 218 north I st.

N Y, Mar 17. In consequence of the dense fog last night the magnificent steamer **Empire State**, from Fall river, run on Mattinicock Point & was totally wrecked. Fortunately no lives were lost, & a portion of the freight was saved by the Stonington boat.

Senate: 1-Ptn from Jas H Birch, asking to be protected in his location of lands therein mentioned: referred. 2-Ptn from Eliza E Ogden, asking an equitable allowance or percentage on certain disbursements made by her late husband, Maj Edw A Ogden, for the suppression of Indian hostilities while acting as Assist Quartermaster in the U S Army: referred. 3-Ptn from Lawrence Kearny, Capt U S Navy, asking compensation for certain expenses incurred & services rendered: referred. 4-Paper submitted in support of the claim of Catharine Keller to a pension for the services of her husband, Conrad Keller, in the Revolution: referred. 5-On motion by Mr Kennedy, the heirs of Cmdor Joshua Barney obtained leave to withdraw their memorial & papers. 6-Cmte on Revolutionary Claims: bill for the relief of Susannah Hayne Pinckney, sole heir of Capt Richd Shurbrick. Same cmte: adverse report on the claims of the heirs of Col Saml Hammond, of Jane M Kean, Mary A Reynolds, & Catharine E Kean, & of Sarah Smith Stafford. Same cmte: bill for the relief of the legal reps of Chas Porterfield, deceased. 7-Cmte on Naval Affairs: asked to be discharged from the consideration of the memorial of Douglass Ottinger, & that it be referred to the Cmte on Commerce: which was agreed to.

Household & kitchen furniture at auction on: Mar 25, at the residence of Col Chas Thomas, on N Y ave, between 9th & 10th sts. -J C McGuire, auct

Trustee's sale of highly improved & valuable real estate: on Apr 5, by deed of trust dated Jul 5, 1855, recorded in Liber J A S No 84, folios 232 thru 134, of the land records for Wash Co, D C: public auction of *Flint's Hotel*, being part of lot 6 in square 254, in Wash City, fronting 37 feet 3 inches on north E st, between 13th & 14th sts west, running back 159 feet to a 30 foot alley, together with a well built 3 story brick dwlg house, with large back bldgs, finished in the most superior manner, with marble mantels.
–Wm P Williams, trustee -Jas C McGuire, auct

Mr Savage, of Dougherty Co, recently died, leaving a will which devised his property to his wife, but in the event of her marriage to go to his children, thus cutting off the wife without a shilling. Mr Morgan, the counsel for the widow, argued that this provision in the will, being in restraint of marriage, was contrary to the policy of our law & illegal; but the Court held that a man had a right to leave his property to his wife during her widowhood & cut her off if she married, & that the Savage will was legal. The Georgia judges are not quite so gallant as their brothers in the Keystone State, who, if we remember right, some time since came to a directly opposite conclusion on a similar state of facts.

FRI MAR 19, 1858
Trustee's sale of highly improved & valuable real estate: on Apr 24, by deed of trust, dated Oct 18, 1854, recorded in Liber J A S No 87, folios 67 thru 71, of the land records of Wash City, D C: public auction, the premises, formerly owned & occupied by Wm H Faulkner, being lot 25, in square A, near the line of Michl McCarty, with 4 story brick dwlg-house & back bldgs, finished in superior manner. –M Thompson, trustee
-A Green auct

Senate: 1-Ptn from B F Simms & Arthur Barbaria, inventors of an electro-magnetic fog bell which insures continuous ringing in places on the coast difficult of access, asking a small appropriation to test its practicability & utility: referred. 2-Additional evidence submitted in support of the claim of S W & A A Turner: referred. 3-Ptn from Ann L Rogers, wife of John A Rogers, asking compensation for his services as examiner of the land offices in the States of Alabama & Mississippi: referred. 4-Letter of T J Bowen, on the files of the Senate, in relation to the exploration of the river Niger, in Africa, be referred to the Cmte on Commerce. 5-Cmte of Claims: bill for the relief of John Hastings, collector of the port of Pittsburgh. 6-Adverse report on the memorial of Sarah Stafford & that it be committed to the Cmte on Revolutionary Claims.

House of Reps: 1-Memorial of Gen Horatio Hubble, of Phil, the original projector of the transatlantic telegraph, in relation thereto, presented.

I have for sale 25,000 of the most new & celebrated Roses known in Europe & America; & ornamental trees & shrubs. –A Jardin, Florist & Nurseryman, Conn ave & M st.

Household & kitchen furniture at auction on: Mar 23, at the residence of the late Maj Jas N Barker, 6th & Pa ave. –C W Boteler, auct

Trustee's sale of small farm above Gtwn, being part of a tract of land called **Alliance**: by deed of trust dated Nov 7, 1855, recorded in Liber J A S No 107, folios 348 thru 351, of the land records for Wash Co, D C: containing & laid out for 10 acres, 3 roods, & 11 perches of land, more or less; together with all the improvements, which are good. -Francis Mohun, Wm H Ward, trustees -Wall & Barnard, aucts

Very extensive sale of superior Rosewood 7 octave Chickering Piano Forte, elegant city made Cabinst Furniture, handsome gilt frame mirrors, rich silk & damask curtains, & velvet & Brussels carpet: on Mar 29, the effects of the **Ebbitt House**, on F st, between 13th & 14th sts. -Jas C McGuire, auct

Mrd: on Mar 18, at St Matthew's Church, by Rev Mr Walron, Col Saml Strider, of Jefferson Co, Va, to Miss Eliza Carrico, of Wash City.

The first Delegation of Orientalists at Wash, 8 years ago. The Hungarian delegation to this city in 1850, consisting of old Govn'r Ujehazy, Gen Pragey, Prof L R Breisach, Maj Damburghy, Dr Chas Kraitsir, & Count Vase. Of this delegation 3 became citizens of the U S & are still living in this their adopted country, & the other 3 are now dead. Geo Pragey died as a fillibuster Gen, second to Gen Lopez on the battle-field of Las Pasas, Cuba. Maj Damburghy died, after his return from Austrialia, in Paris. Count Vase returned to Austria, & it is said to have died in Vienna. Govn'r Ujehazy lost his wife & some of his children in the West, & lives as a farmer, with the rest of his family, at San Antonio, Texas. Dr Chas Kraitsir wrote & published, 3 years ago, a valuable book for philologists, on the nature of languages. Prof L R Breisach introduced, 5 years ago, an important invention from Germany, of which his brother was alleged to be one of the inventors, the now well-known & used wood-gas.

The Court-Martial of Col E V Sumner. War Dept, Adj Gen's Ofc, Wash, Mar 16, 1858. Charge I-Conduct to the prejudice of good order & military discipline. Specification: In this, that he, the said Sumner, did, at Syracuse, N Y, on Jan 18, 1858, attempt to make a personal affair with said Harney out of an official matter-that is to say, the answer made by said Harney to a general court-martial which inquired of him in regard to his prejudice or bias against said Sumner. Charge II-Sending a challenge to another officer to fight a duel, in violation of the 25th of the articles of war. Specification-In this, that he, the said Sumner, did, at Wash, D C, on Feb 15, 1858, on account of said answer by said Harney to said court-martial, send a challenge to said Harney to fight a duel, in words as follows: Wash, Feb 15, 1858. Sir: As more than 24 hours have passed since my note to you of yesterday, I have a right to presume that you do not intend to answer it. I have, therefore, to invite you to leave this city with me tomorrow morning, to go to any place you may designate. I send this note privately, to avoid committing any friend as long as possible. An early answer is requested. I am, with due respect, E V Sumner, Col 1st Cavalry. [To Brvt Brig Gen W S Harney, Col 2nd Dragoons.] Charge III-Upbraiding another officer for refusing a challenge, in violation of the 28th of the articles of war. Specification-In this, that he, the said Sumner, did, at Wash, D C, on Feb 16, 1858, upbraid the said Harney for refusing to fight a duel, in words as follows: Wash, Feb 16, 1858. Sir: I received with great surprise your note of last evening, & have only to say to you that a man who could insult a brother officer, from an official covert, & afterwards refuse to apologise, or to give him that satisfaction which he had a right to demand, is utterly unworthy of any further notice from me. I am, E V Sumner, Col 1st Cavalry. [To Brvt Brig Gen W S Harney, Col 2nd Dragoons.] P S: This correspondence will be sent to every member of the court. E V S To which charges & specifications the accused pleaded not guilty. The Court, after maturely considering the evidence, find the accused, Col Edwin V Sumner, 1st Cavalry, as follows: Charge I; Charge II; & Charge III: Specification, not guilty & not guilty of the charge.
+
War Dept, Mar 15, 1858. There is no dispute as to the facts in this case. The Dept disapproves the finding of the court: that Gen Harney's answer to the court-martial at **Fort Leavenworth** was not an official matter; & that Col Sumner's letter of Feb 15 is not a challenge to a duel. 1-Gen Harney admitted he never had any or very little respect for Col Sumner as a soldier. 2-Col Sumner's note of Feb 15 is a challenge within the meaning of the article of war. –John B Floyd, Sec of War. III-The Gen Court Martial, of which Brvt Maj Thos S Jesup is president, is dissolved. IV-Col Edwin V Sumner, 1st cavalry, is released from arrest, & will join his regt in Kansas. By order of the Sec of War, S Cooper, Adj Gen

Meeting of the Stockholders of the Chesapeake & Ohio Canal Co met yesterday at City Hall, Jas A Magruder, of Gtwn, in the chair. Elected for the ensuing 2 years, viz: Pres: Lawrence J Brengle, of Fred'k City, Md. Directors: Danl C Bruce, of Frostburg; David W McCleary, of Cumberland; F Dorsey Herbert, of Hagerstown; John S Bowles, Clearspring; H Franklin Viers, of Rockville; Jas A Magruder, of Gtwn.

SAT MAR 20, 1858
On Sat, Rembrandt Peale, of Phil, will exhibit in the Smithsonian Lecture room a collection of the portraits of Washington, viz: Rembrandt Peale's sr, taken in 1772; Houdon's, taken in 1785; Trumbulls, taken in 1790; Stewart's, taken in 1796; also his own invaluable portrait, taken under the most favorable circumstances, in 1795. In addition to these, he will exhibit at the same time the portrait of Lady Washington, taken by himself in 1795. Himself is the only living artist for whom Washington sat.

The barn of Mr Thos P Remington, of Lancaster road, near Phil, was destroyed by fire several nights ago, together with a number of valuable stock.

Mr Saml Coe, of Piscataway district, PG Co, lost his dwlg house & most of its contents by fire week before last.

The dwlg & store-house belonging to Richd A Harwood, in Anne Arundel Co, Md, were consumed by fire on Sunday last. Mr Harwood was absent, & there was no person residing on the premises. It is supposed to be the work of an incendiary.

The copartnership under the firm of Colley & Sears was dissolved by mutual consent on Mar 15. Sears disposed of his interest to Colley, the latter will settle the business of the late firm. –J W Colley, Jas W Sears

The late John Avery Parker, a successful merchant of New Bedford, was at one time warned to leave Westport, Mass, under the old law or custom of warning strangers who were likely to become a public charge. He died worth $1,800,000.

Senate: 1-Ptn from Geo L Browne & Wm Curry, merchants at Key West, asking to be allowed a portion of the moneys paid on certain coal landed from a submerged wrecked vessel: referred. 2-Cmte on Naval Affairs: memorial of Lt Fabius Stanley, U S Navy, asking extra pay as executive officer at the navy yard at San Francisco in 1854-5, submitted a report, with a bill for his relief. 3-Cmte of Claims: bill for the relief of Jos C G Kennedy, asking to be indemnified for damage done to his bldgs while they were used by the Gov't. 4-Bill for the relief of Dr Chas D Maxwell, a surgeon in the U S navy, passed.

The clergyman who died suddenly on Mar 4 while riding in his buggy, near Rockingham, N C, was Rev David Dernelle, a faithful & zealous agent of the American Bible Society.

Died: Caroline Rebecca, youngest daughter of Abner H & Mary A Young, aged 17 years. Her funeral will be on Sunday at 3 o'clock, from the residence of her parents, 439 I st. [No death date given.]

Died: on Mar 2, in Middleburg, Julia Heiskell, wife of Rev O A Kinsolving, & daughter of Rev Chas P Krauth, D C. She has been a bright & devoted member of the Episcopal Church since the early age of 14 years.

Died: on Monday last, at the residence of ex-Govn'r Graham, Hillsboro, N C, Mrs Eliz Washington, in her 79th year.

Appointment of Cadets at the U S Military Academy at West Point, to fill vacancies from the several States, according to their representation in Congress:
Maine: Jared A Smith, O A Blanchard
Mass: Geo Burroughs, John H Calef, C C Chaffee, W B Chapman
Conn: Jas D Webb
N Y: F J James, John Egan, J R Reed, T Y Kinne, H C Dodge, A M Murray
N J: W C Barnard
Pa: C W Smith, J H Porter, Jas Riddle
Md: R E Noonan, J F Stone
Va: J P Cox, T G Dearing, R S Dinney
N C: C H Barron, W C Cannady, David R Adams, G W Clayton
S C: Jas Hamilton, H S Farley
Ga: J B Johnson, J S Blount, J A Alexander, E C Arnold, J A West
Ky: G M Ewing
Tenn: A Paine, T B Smith, E McE Ross, Frank Mancy
Ohio: H B Denny, V Coonrod, Morris Shaff, F B Hamilton, Asa Boiles, H S Wetmore
La: H Gilly, A Selby
Ind: J W Shrewsbury, Isaac Helm, J P Drake, W F Spurgin, J A Krebs
Ill: Jos W Vanie
Miss: R A Higgason
Ala: O J Semmes, J N McNab, Edw Nicholson
Mo: Jos Crane, J F Templeton
Fla: Stephen A Moreno
Iowa: R B Merritt
Calif: W A Marye
Kansas Territory: G W Smith
Nebraska: H C Wharton
The Cadets appointed are under orders to report in person at West Point between the 1st & 20th of June next.

The Md Conference of the Methodist Protestant Church, at its late session in Phil, stationed the Ministers for the ensuing conference year, according to the usuage of the Church: 1-Rev Dr F Swentzel returns to the Ninth st station. 2-Rev J R Nichols to the Navy Yard or East Washington Mission. 3-Rev John Roberts to Alexandria. 4-Rev J J Murray, D C, transferred to Phil. 5-Rev David Wilson occupies the station at Gtwn.

MON MAR 22, 1858
Farm for sale-beautiful residence & farm containing 416 acres, on the 7th st road, about 8 miles from Wash; the dwlg is an elegant family residence, new & supplied with all modern improvements, such as baths, water closet, hot & cold water in bedrooms, range & pump in kitchen, conservatory, & furnace. Address W Batchelor, Cottage Post Ofc, Montg Co, Md.

It is reported that a court-martial has been ordered to assemble at Newport, Ky, for the trial of Maj Gen Twiggs, who is accused of making remarks censuring the War Dept for its strictures upon his official course. [Mar 23rd newspaper: The court-martial will assemble on Apr 28, for the trial of Brvt Maj Gen David E Twiggs. The court will be composed of the following officers: Brvt Maj Gen T S Jesup, Quartermaster Gen; Brvt Maj Gen J E Wool; Brvt Maj Gen Persifer F Smith; Brvt Brig Gen Sylvester Churchill, Inspector Gen; Brvt Brig Gen W S Harney, Col 2nd Dragoons; Col J R F Mansfield, Inspector Gen; Col Jos Plympton, 1st Infty; Brvt Col John L Gardener, Lt Col 1st Artl; Brvt Col R E Lee, Lt Col 2nd Cavalry; Col Thos T Fauntleroy, 1st Dragoons; Col Henry K Craig, Ordnance Dept; Col Chas Thomas, Assist Quartermaster Gen; Lt Col G B Crittenden, Mounted Riflemen.]

The statue of Beatrice Cenci was executed by our countrywoman, Miss Harriet Hosmer. She is the daughter of a physician residing near Boston, & for the purpose of prosecuting her talents she set out for Italy, accompanied by her father, about 4 years since, taking with her a certificate for anatomical studies at the College of St Louis, & some daguerreotypes of a fancy bust modeled in marble by herself. The story of Beatrice Cenci will be found in Sismondi's History of the Italian republics. Her history was most unhappy; condemned to death, she yet entertained hopes of a pardon; & when the priest went in to announce to her that she was to die in the morning, he found her peacefully & calmly asleep in her miserable cell. The work is intended for the public library at St Louis, & may be seen at the exhibition room of Mr Franklin Philp, 322 Pa ave.

Mrd: on Mar 4, by Rev Chas Mann, Geo Brewer, of Balt, to Lucy H, daughter of the late Thos T Tabb, of Toddsbury, Gloucester Co, Va.

Shipowners & Underwriters. Mr Jos Humphries has lately patented a Floating Anchor or Drag, which is hereby offered for sale. Address him at the Navy Yard Hill, Wash, D C.

Notice: Certificates of stock issued by the Corp of Wash, No 271, dated Jul 8, 1856, & No 367, dated Feb 11, 1858, having been lost or stolen, the subscriber gives notice that a renewal thereof will be requested. –Harriet Donohoo

Miss Lizzie Petit will read Shakespeare's Play of Much Ado about Nothing, at the Philharmonic Hall, Pa ave, on Mar 22, at 8 o'clock. Admission $1.

Choice garden & flower seed for sale: John Saul, 396 7th st, corner of H st, Wash. [Ad]

Orphans Court of Wash Co, D C. Letters of administration on the personal estate of Granville S Oldfield, jr, late of Wash Co, deceased. –Virginia S Oldfield, admx

TUE MAR 23, 1858
Senate: 1-Memorial of Andrew Glassell, asking compensation for services as Assist U S District Atty for the northern district of Calif, in 1856: referred to the Cmte on the Judiciary.

House of Reps: 1-On Feb 15 last, this House, by its resolution, did commit John W Wolcott to the common jail of the District of Columbia, for an infringement of the privileges of the House in refusing satisfactorily to answer certain questions put to him by order of the House, & is still held in custody under the said order. The Court has determined that said Wolcott cannot be tried in said presentment as long as this House holds him in custody; therefore, he will be released from jail & delivered over to the Marshal of said District of Columbia, or other person authorized to receive him. He had said that his wife was extremely indisposed; a messenger to Boston learned that there was no indisposition in his family. Matter postponed.

Proposals will be received at St Patrick's Church, in Wash City, up to Fri next. Mar 26, for the bldg of a stone wall & the erection thereon of an iron railing along the road front of the new Catholic cemetery on the Bladensburg road, opposie what is known as the Spring Tavern.

On Sat last Robt Schmidt, of Theresa, Dodge Co, shot down, in the street of that place, Harriet Seidler, a young lady of about 20 years. The parties were engaged to be married about 1 year ago, & Schmidt had come over from St Paul, Van Buren, Co, Mich, where he has resided about a year, to fulfill the engagement, but the parents of the young lady objected to the marriage, in consequence of which it was arranged between the lovers that Schmidt should first shoot the young lady & then shoot himself. He failed to shoot himself on account of the loss of the cap on his gun. He then ran & threw himself into the river, but was rescued by persons who saw him. He is now arrested & awaits a trial. The young lady expired on Sunday. She had her senses up to the last, & charged her parents with being responsible for the awful deed, & acquitted her lover of all blame. The parties, as their names indicate, were Germans. –Milwaukee News of the 16th.

Obit-died: on Mar 9, Maj Jas N Barker, in his 76th year. Maj Barker was a son of John Barker, mayor & sheriff of Phil in the olden time. Maj Barker served his country gallantly as capt on the Canada frontier in 1812, & some years subsequently was elected Mayor of the city. He was Collector of the port of Phil from 1829 to 1838, when he was transferred to Wash by Mr Van Buren as First Comptroller of the Treasury, & has, with a short intermission, been connected with the Treasury Dept ever since. He was a gentleman of fine literary taste, an earnest & energetic writer. He was the author of the successful drama of Marmion, the tragedy of Superstition, the comedy of Smiles & Tears, & other smaller matters. -Pennsylvanian

Norfolk, Mar 22. A large portion of the business section of Eliz City, N C, was destroyed by fire this morning. Among the stores burnt are those of N A Cohen, White & Laverty, W B Burgess, T D Knot, B T Miller, J C Grandy, Wm Shannon, H Culpepper, B Sprewell, W H Clark, C M Laferty, & others. The loss of property is said to be immense. The Marine Hospital is also in ruins. N A Cohen has been arrested on suspicion of having feloniously caused the fire.

Died: on Mar 15, in Chartiers township, near Pittsburg, Pa, Mrs Sarah Flinn, consort of Wm Flinn, aged 78 years & 9 months. She was the daughter of David Sample, of Westmoreland Co, atty at law, in which profession he occupied a very eminent position in his day. Mr Sample, owing to the dangers to which his family was exposed from the frequent incursions of the Indians, especially in his absence from home attending to official duties, removed them, for a short time, to Cumberland Co. It was in this county, near Big Spring, that Mrs Flinn was born. During the closing scene of her earthly pilgrimage she was severely afflicted, but her confidence in God, through Christ, was unfailing. She left a disconsolate husband & 3 children, a son, who resides in Wash City, & 2 daughters to mourn her death. Her remains were followed, the day after her death, to their resting place, where they will repose until the resurrection. –Pittsburg Gazette

Extensive & valuable property for sale: by decree of the Circuit Court of Wash Co, D C, made in the cause of the U S vs Schwartz, Livingston, et al, No 1,065, equity: public auction on Apr 14, of the whole of squares 468, 469, 470, 498, & lots 82 thru 84, in the subdivision of square 465, on the Island. –Walter S Cox, trustee -Jas C McGuire, auct

The Cecil Whig says the old Presbyterian Church at the Head of Christiana, Md, was burnt to the ground on Sunday week, the fire catching between the ceiling & roof while the stoves were being lighted in the morning. It was erected in 1750. Preliminary steps have been taken towards rebuilding it. It has been for some time past under the pastoral charge of Rev Mr Vallandigham; & standing on the tongue of land lying between Md & Delaware, theoretically belonging to Pa. It drew its congregation from the 3 States.

WED MAR 24, 1858
Senate: 1-Ptn from Lydia Weeks, asking to be allowed the pension her husband was entitled to at the time of his death: referred. 2-The papers relating to the cliam of the heirs at law of Gen Henry Miller: referred to the Cmte on Revolutionary Claims.

About 8 years ago Martha French, of Pembroke, N H, became insane, & has continued so up to the present time. She received medical treatment at home, but received no benefit therefrom, & was removed to the asylum at Concord. After remaining there some time without improvement, she was taken to her mother's house at Pembroke & confined in her room. In Apr, 1856, she escaped, & her bonnet was found upon the bank of the river, & this was the only trace they could find of her. Last spring, the New England Farmer copied a notice from a Va paper that a maniac woman had been committed to jail in Hanover Co, Va; that she belonged to Mass, had worked in the Lowell Mills, & had been in the Insane Asylum at Concord twice. Her name was not given. Some one acquainted with Miss French sent the paper to her mother & sister at Pembroke. The sister wrote to the jailor & learned that she had been transferred to the Wmsburg hospital. Dr Simpson, of Lowell, who had been acquainted with her, visited her at the hospital, & recognized her at first sight. She said he used to doctor me; he was Dr Simpson. Her mind later wandered most strangely, & he thought best to let her remain there. Nothing would be charged for her board there until the room was wanted by patients belonging to the State. -Lowell Courier

Died: on Mar 17, at the residence of her brother, Mr John Saunders, in Montg Co, Md, Mrs Mary Jane Peck, in her 35th year, wife of Clement A Peck, formerly of Loudoun Co, Va. As a wife, a sister, & a friend she was all that could be desired. Early in life she embraced the Methodist Episcopal Church.

Trustee's sale of *Piney Point*: embracing about 225 acres of land; with extensive bldgs; public auction on May 6 next; by deed of trust from Wm W Dix & wife to the subscribers, recorded in Liber J T B No 2, folios 176 thru 178, of the land records of St Mary's Co, Md: being all that tract in said county called *Suter's Fancy*, being the same that was patented to Henry Suter, jr, by the State of Md, on Apr 23, 1825, & which patent is recorded in the Land Patent Ofc of the Western Shore of Md in Liber J B, No F, folio 372. -Jno C C Hamilton, Jos H Bradley, jr, trustees

Mrd: on Mar 18, by Rev Mr Waldron, Col Saml Strider, of Jefferson Co, Va, to Miss Eliza Jane, only daughter of Mr Jas Carrico, of Wash City.

THU MAR 25, 1858
Sale by order of the Orphans Court of Wash Co, D C, of the personal effects of Jas Dixon, deceased: on Mar 27, at the auction store of A Green, 526 7th st, all the furniture & personal effects of the deceased. –Jas Walker, exc -A Green auct

Senate: 1-Ptn from John J Rink, architect & engineer, asking Congress to purchase the right to use certain improvements made by him in the construction of submarine masonry: referred. 2-Ptn from J G Heaton asking to be allowed pay & bounty land for services in the war of 1812: referred. 3-Ptn from P O Beebe, asking the patronage of Congress to aid him in publishing an analysis of American law: referred. 4-Ptn from Wm B Whiting, U S Navy, asking an amendment of the pension & bounty land laws: referred. 5-Ptn from Findley Patterson, asking to be allowed payment for work done in Kansas under a contract with the Govn'r of that Territory, & indemnity for losses sustained in consequence of the suspension of the same: referred. 6-Cmte of Claims: adverse report on the claim of Mary B Renner for property destroyed during the war of 1812. 7-Cmte on Military Affairs: asked to be discharged from the consideration of the memorial of J W Browne, asking Congress to purchase his patents for the manufacture of fire-arms: which was agreed to. Same cmte: adverse report on the memorial of Wm J Russel, asking indemnity for property destroyed in consequence of being occupied by U S troops. Same cmte: adverse report in the case of Capt McClelland's company of Florida volunteers. 8-Cmte of Claims: bill for the relief of Jos C G Kennedy. 9-Cmte on Naval Affairs: adverse report on the memorial of Martin Hubbard for indemnity for the loss of a vessel by collision with the U S steamer **Engineer**. 10-Cmte of Claims: adverse report on the memorial of Capt Wainright for reimbursement of a sum of money stolen from him in Boston, while acting as commandant of the arsenal at Watertown, Mass. 11-Mr Mason introduced a joint resolution authorizing Lt Wm N Jeffers to accept a sword of honor from her Majesty the Queen of Spain: passed.

Died: yesterday, after a very severe illness, Mrs Julia A Leehe, wife of Henry Leehe. Her funeral is this afternoon, at 3½ o'clock, from the residence of her husband, on 6th st, at H.

Orphans Court of Wash Co, D C. In the case of Geo W Uttermuhle, adm of Jacob Hunsberger, deceased, the administrator & Court appointed Apr 17 next, for the settlement of the personal estate of the deceased, of the assets in hand. –Ed N Roach, Reg/o wills

Trustee's sale: by deed of trust from Wainright Preston & wife to us, dated Jul 6, 1854, recorded in Liber J A S No 81, of the land records for Wash Co, D C: public auction on May 1 next, part of lot 2 in square 553, fronting on First st west, in Wash City, D C, with improvements thereon. –E C Morgan, H B Sweeny, trustees

Died: on Wed, Mrs Mary Simonds, in her 71st year, in full confidence of a blessed immortality. Her funeral is this afternoon at 4 o'clock, at the residence of her son-in-law, corner of 4th & K sts, Navy Yard.

Died: on Mar 18, in Zanesville, Ohio, Mr Moses Moorehead, in his 81st year.

On Sat lat a girl named Ellen Callahan hired herself as a house-servant in the family of Mr Kellogg, living on Pa ave, near 21st st. On Monday, proving perfectly useless as a servant, she was discharged. Mrs Kellogg later discovered that several of the family silver spoons were missing. They were found by Squire Drury, who had a warrant, in her trunk, at a dwlg near 22nd st. She was arrested & committed for trial at Court.

FRI MAR 26, 1858
N McDonald & G C Grammer [Notary Public] Attys & Counsellors at Law, No 15 north Second st, St Louis. [Ad]

N Y C: A man named Finley & his wife have been brought back by the police from ***Ellicott's Mills***, where they were traced, after having kidnapped & offered for sale in Washington a free colored girl of N Y.

Trustee's sale of furniture, crockery, & glassware, at public auction, on Apr 1, at the store of Wm Dowling, on Bridge st, Gtwn, all the stock & trade & effects of the said Dowling. -Thos J Fisher, trustee -Jas C McGuire, auct

Senate: 1-Ptn from Cmder Chas H Jackson, of the navy, stating that he had been placed on the furlough list by the Naval Board & subsequently restored to leave of absence pay, & asking that the arrears of pay may be paid him: referred. 2-Ptn from Robt K Smith, asking confirmation to his title to a certain tract of land lying within the Bastrop grant: referred. 3-Additional evidence submitted in relation to the claim of Anson Dart: referred. 4-Cmte on Military Affairs: adverse report on the memorial of the members of Capt Campbell's company of volunteers in the war of 1812. 5-Mr Hamlin asked the Senate to indulge him by taking up a bill on the private calendar for the relief of Wm Allen, of Portland, Maine: read a third time & passed.

Mrd: on Feb 2, at Memphis, Missouri, by Rev Mr Clanton, Mr Zephaniah Prather, of PG Co, to Miss Eliza Jane Watson, of Memphis Scotland Co, Missouri.

The Pacific Christian Advocate, printed at Portland, Oregon, Feb 6, reports that great excitement has been caused in Pierce & Thurston Counties, Washington Territory, by the non-execution of the Indian chief Leschi, who was convicted of the murder of Mr J B Moses, in Nov, 1856, & sentenced to be hanged on Jan 22, 1858. On the day appointed for the execution the sheriff was arrested on a warrant issued by the U S Com'r, charging him with the crime of selling liquor to Indians, & during the process, the period named in the death warrant for the execution expired & Leschi was not hanged. The acts of the sheriff of Pierce Co, the U S Com'r, & the atty of the Indian chief Leschi, are denounced as also dishonest, disreputable, & infamous.

It was with painful surprise that we read yesterday in a city paper the announcement of the sudden decease of Mr Lauriston B Hardin, for many years a faithful officer in the Navy Dept, & a most estimable gentleman. He was the Registering Clerk & Disbursing Clerk of the Navy Dept. He was at his post yesterday, & was out last evening visiting some friends. He returned home & retired in apparent usual health. He experienced some unusual sensations, & started to return to the room of Capt Adams, in the same house, but his affection became so violent as to completely prostrate his system, & he fell in the passage. Dr Whelan was called but all efforts to relieve him were unavailing, & he died in about 10 minutes. The deceased had been occupying the same position in the Navy Dept since May 1, 1831, having received his first appointment from Govn'r Branch, then Sec of the Navy, during Andrew Jackson's first Administration. He was originally from N C, where he has a large circle of relatives still residing. He was a widower at the time of his death, of about 55 years of age, & leaves 3 children. He had held the same prominent public position for 27 years. –Evening Star
+
Died: on Wed, in Wash City, suddenly, Lauriston B Hardin, a native of the State of North Carolina, & for many years the Register of the Navy Dept, aged about 55 years. His funeral will take place on Sat at 12 o'clock M, from St Paul's Episcopal Church, Alexandria/

A jury of the Circuit Court of Frederick Co, Md, has, after a trial lasting 3 days, awarded the sum of $10,000 damages & costs in favor of Rev Moses A Stewart & wife, & against Danl Gaver, who, it was charged, uttered certain scandalous & defamatory words against Mr Stewart.

Died: on Mar 24, Emily, daughter of Wm G & Sophia Ridgely. Her funeral will be this afternoon at half past 3 o'clock, from her father's residence, 76 First st, Gtwn.

Died: on Mar 25, in his 10th year, Robert, only son of Robert & Marinda V Cochran.

Fredericksburg, Mar 25. Jesse Crockett, who was yesterday convicted of the murder of Wm Griffin, at Aquia Creek, on Christmas eve last, has been sentenced to be hung on Apr 30th next.

SAT MAR 27, 1858
Wm Tucker, Merchant Tailor: 426 Pa ave, between 4½ & 6th sts. [Ad]

Both Houses of the Va Legislature have passed a bill amending the act incorporating the **Mount Vernon Ladies' Association**, of which the following is a part:

2-It shall be lawful for the said **Mount Vernon Ladies' Association** of the Union to purchase, hold, & improve 200 acres of *Mount Vernon*, including the late mansion, as well as the tomb of Geo Washington, together with the garden, grounds & wharf, & landing, now constructed on the Potomac river; & to this end they may receive from the owner & proprietor of the said land a deed in fee simple, & shall have & exercise full power over the use & management of the same, as they may by bye-laws & rules declare; provided, however, that the said **Mount Vernon Ladies Association** of the union shall not have power to alien the said land, or any part thereof, nor to create a charge thereon, or to lease the same, without the consent of the Genr'l Assembly of Va first had & obtained.

3-The capital stock of the said **Mount Vernon Ladies' Association** of the Union shall not, including the 200 acres of land aforesaid, exceed the sum of $5,000. The said association, in contracting with the proprietor of *Mount Vernon* for the purchase of the same, may covenant with him so as to reserve to him the right to inter the remains of such persons, whose remains are in the vault at *Mount Vernon*, as are not now interred, & to place the said vault in such a secure & permanent condition as he shall see fit, & to enclose the same so as not to include more than half acre of land; & the said vault, the remains in & around it, & the enclosure shall never be removed nor disturbed; now shall any other person hereafter ever be interred or entombed within the said vault or enclosure.

4-The said property herein authorized to be purchased by the said **Mount Vernon Ladies' Association** of the Union shall be forever held by it sacred to the Father of his Country; &, if from any cause the said association shall cease to exist, the property owned by the said association shall revert to the Commonwealth of Va, sacred to the purposes for which it was originally purchased. It is understood that Mr Washington will now consent to sell *Mount Vernon* to the association.

St John's College, Annapolis, Md: summer term will commence on Apr 12 next.
-Rev C K Nelson, Principal

A piece of machinery, very free from complexity & occupying no appreciable space, has been put up by Mr Saml Gardiner, jr, on the floor of the U S Senate, for the purpose of producing instantaneous ignition of the gas lights in the great chandelier overhead.

House of Reps: 1-Cmte of Claims: bills for the relief of Ferdiannd Coxe & Peter Parker: committed. Bill for the relief of the assignees of Hugh Glover: committed. Same cmte: bill for the relief of Jos C G Kennedy: committed. Same cmte: bills for the relief of Wm F Wagner & for the relief of Jos Hardy & Alton Long: committed. Adverse report on the ptn of Alex'r Turner: laid on the table. Same cmte: bill for the relief of Enoch B Talcott, late collector of customs at Oswego, N Y: committed. Same cmte: bill for the relief of Saml A Fairchilds: committed. Adverse reports in the cases of Maj E H Fitzgerald & Wm H Young: laid on the table. Joint resolution for the relief of Hall Neilson: committed. Senate bill for the relief of Elias Hall, of Rutland, Vt: committed. 2-Cmte on Commerce: bills for the relief of Shade Galloway; & relief of D O Dickinson: committed.

3-Cmte on Public Lands: bill authorizing Mrs Jane Smith to enter certain lands in Ala: committed. 4-Cmte on the Post Ofc & Post Roads: adverse report in the case of Wm M Dillard: laid on the table. 5-Cmte on Revolutionary Claims: bill for the relief of the heirs of Nehemiah Stokely: committed. Bill for the relief of the administrator of Lt Thos Williams: committed. Same cmte: adverse reports on ptns of the heirs of Joshua Olgner/Olgner, Benj Harrison, Augustine Willett, & J P Harrison: laid on the table. Same cmte: bill for the relief of the heirs of Nathl Heard: committed. 6-Cmte on Private Lands Claims: bill for the relief of the heirs or legal reps of Francois Guillary: committed. Same cmte: bill for the relief of the legal reps of Jean Baptiste Devidrine: committed. Senate bills for the relief of Laurent Millaudon, for the relief of John Dick, of Fla, & for the relief of Anna M E King, Louisa M King, Cordelia E King, & Sarah I De Lannoy: severally committed. 7-Cmte on Invalid Pensions: bill granting an invalid pension to Beniah Wright, of N Y: committed. Adverse reports in the cases of Reuben Apperson, of Va, Jas Fuller, of Tenn, & Jos Drake, of Indiana: laid on the table. Same cmte: bill granting an invalid pension to John Lee, of the State of Maine; also, a bill for the relief of Elmira White, widow of Capt Thos R White; also, a bill granting an invalid pension to Jas Fugate, of Mo: committed. Same cmte: bill for the relief of Michl Kinney, late a private in the U S Army: committed. Same cmte: bill for the relief of Cornelius H Latham: committed. 8-Cmte on Patents: bill for the relief of Edw N Kent: committed. 9-Cmte on Foreign Affairs: adverse report in the case of Stephen H Weems: laid on the table. Bill for the relief of John H Wheeler, late U S Minister at Nicaragua: committed. Same cmte: adverse report in the case of Francisco Lopez Urriga: laid on the table. Same cmte: joint resolution in favor of Michel Papreniza: committed. Adverse report in the case of Thos L L Brent: laid on the table. 10-Cmte on Military Affairs: adverse report in the case of John H Thompson: referred to the Cmte of the Whole. Bill for the relief of Dr Thos Antisell: committed. Same cmte: adverse report in the case of Jas Armstrong: laid on the table. Same cmte: bill for the relief of Jas G Bennett, E B Babbit, & Jas Langstreet, of the U S army: committed. Senate bill to continue a pension to Christine Barnard, widow of the late Brvt Maj Moses Barnard, U S Army: committed. Senate bill for the relief of Susanna T Lea, widow of Jas Maglenen, late of Balt: committed. 11-Cmte on Naval Affairs: bill for the relief of Robt W Cushman, formerly an acting purser in the U S Navy: committed. 12-Cmte on the Judiciary: adverse report on the claim of R T Birdette, assignee of Thos H Duvall: laid on the table. 13-Cmte on Indian Affairs: bill for the relief of Wm B Trother: committed. 14-Cmte on Revolutionary Pensions: bill for the relief of Micajah Brooks: committed. Same cmte: adverse report in the cases of Thos Moody & Rebecca Halsey: laid on the table. 15-Cmte on Invalid Pensions: bill granting an invalid pension to Brvt Maj John Jones, of Tenn: committed. Bill for the relief of Kennedy O'Brien: committed. Same cmte: bill for the relief of Eveline Porter, widow of the late Cmdor David Porter, of the U S navy: committed. Bill granting an invalid pension to Silas Stevens, of Va: committed.

Mr Bartholomew Nason, 73 years of age, while attending a prayer-meeting at Hallowell, on Tue, fell dead in his seat; probably from disease of the heart. He expired immediately. He occupied a high position among the leading citizens of the State.

Mrd: on Mar 25, in Wash City, by Rev Wm H Chapman, Mr John V Smith to Miss Maria E Thompson, all of Wash City.

The friends of the late L B Hardin request us to state that those desirous of being present at his funeral, which takes place at St Paul's Episcopal Church, Alexandria, today, at 12 o'clock, can procure passage to Alexandria in the steamer **George Page**, which leaves the foot of 7th st at 11 o'clock. The officers of the Navy are requested to attend the funeral in undress uniform

MON MAR 29, 1858
Augusta [Geo] Chronicle of Mar 24. The Sandersville Georgian had an account of the trial & conviction of a man for the murder of his slave, at the late term of the Superior Court for Wash Co. Green Martin, charged with murder, came up for trial on Sat last. Green Martin & Godfrey Martin, his son, on May 9, 1857, beat a negro boy, Alfred, aged about 13 years, until he was discovered to be dead. The material witnesses on the part of the State were 3 daughters of Green Martin, 21, 19, & 16, & a little boy by the name of Bedfood, who was hired by Martin. Dr Tucker, the physician, examined the body; Mr Orr, was the coroner; & both were sworn. The counsel for the State were Atty-Gen McClaws, Col Jas S Hook, & F E Tebeau. For the defence, Iverson L Harris, of Milledgeville, E S Langmade, & Evans & Harman, of the local bar. The jury returned with a verdict of guilty. A motion for a new trial is now pending.

Calif: 1-An avalanche occurred near Poor Man's creek, in Plumas Co, on Feb 17, in which Mr Wilson & a little son of Mr Gentry were killed. A number of other persons were wounded. 2-David C Butler, whose true name is said to be Mason C Bolin, was hanged, in accordance with law, at Nevada, on Feb 26, for the murder of Mr Moffatt. 3-Dr Chas Emile Birce, a Frenchman, committed suicide, by taking opium, at Benicia, on Feb 23. He was a stranger, & the cause of his fatal determination remains unknown. 4-On Feb 21, at Grass Valley, Nevada Co, Michl Brenan, an educated & intelligent Irishman, who has been acting as the Pres of the Mount Hope Mining Company, on that day poisoned his wife & his 3 children with prussic acid, & then committed suicide by the same agency. Mr Brenan had been unfortunate in his mining enterprise, & had involved himself in debt to the amount of $100,000. Mrs Brenan had no knowledge of the intention of her husband. She was poisoned first, followed by the children. Brenan was a graduate of Trinity College, Dublin. He had been in this State about a year, & has been connected with the N Y press. He left letters disposing of his effects.

Capt A W Reynolds has been confirmed by the Senate as a quartermaster in the army, a post to which he was recently nominated by the Pres. Capt Reynolds is thus restored to the position he lost some 2 years ago. -Union

Jas E Thompson & Ed M Hamilton have associated themselves under the name & firm of Thompson & Hamilton, & will continue the Grocery & Liquor business at the old stand, 393 Pa ave.

Appollo Hall for sale: apply to Alex'r Provest, exc

Mrd: on Mar 25, by Rev Mr Friend, at **Prospect Hill**, Caroline Co, Va, Chas Herndon, of Fredericksbrug, to Lucy W, daughter of Bazil Gordon.

Mrd: on Mar 4, at **Shannondale Farm**, near Brownsville, Texas, by Rev Wm Passmore, Chaplain of the U S Army, Lt Loomis L Langdon, 1st Artl, to Kattie, daughter of Col Wm Moffett, of Ky.

Died: on Mar 27, Gertrude, wife of Wm H West, of the Treasury Dept, & daughter of the late Hugh Minor, of Va, in her 39th year.

TUE MAR 30, 1858

Senate: 1-Ptn from Lt David D Porter, U S navy, asking the settlement of his accounts upon principles of equity for certain secret services performed by him in the island of San Domingo under an order of the Sec of the Navy: referred. 2-Ptn from Alex'r Copeland, for confirmation of his title to certain lands in Sonora Co, Calif: referred. 3-Ptn from Cassandra S Witherell, asking that a land warrant may be issued to the heirs-at-law of her late father, Maj Gen Hugh Brady: referred. 4-Ptn from Beverly Diggs, late an ofcr in the revenue service, asking relief in consideration of his having been without cause dismissed the service: referred. 5-Ptn from the widow of Capt Jos Smoot, late of the navy, asking a pension: referred. 6-Ptn from A G Allen, late Navy Agent at Wash, D C, asking to be allowed additional compensation for disbursements to officers & others entitled by law to extra pay: referred. 7-Ptn from Hannah Thompson, asking that her pension may be continued: referred. 8-Cmte of Claims: asked to be discharged from the consideration of the memorial of J W Sullivan, asking indemnification for losses caused by repeated failures of the mails between New Orleans & San Francisco, & from the memorial of A L & Geo Pennock, & that they be referred to the Cmte on the Post Ofc & Post Roads: which was agreed to. Same cmte: asked that the memorial of Findlay Patterson, asking payment for work on the Capitol of Kansas at Lecompton, under a contract with the Govn'r, & for losses sustained in suspending his contract, asked that it be referred to the Cmte of Claims: which was agreed to. 9-Cmte on Indian Affairs: memorial of D Merriweather for an appropriation for his salary as superintendent of Indian Affairs in new Mexico, submitted a report, concluding with a resolution that the prayer of the petitioner ought not to be granted. 10-Bill for the relief of Brvt Brig Gen Jas Bankhead, late of the U S army: referred to the Cmte on Military Affairs. 11-Bill for the relief of Brvt Maj Jas D Donaldson, assist quartermaster of the U S army: passed. 12-Bill for the relief of Maj Jeremiah Y Dashiell, paymaster in the U S army; & after having been advocated & explained by Mr Johnson it was read a third time & passed. 13-Bill for the relief of Com Ridgely: postponed.

Estrays, a small red steer; also, a small red cow, with a bell. Inquire of John Burrows, **Grassland**, about 2 miles northwest of Gtwn, D C.

Private sale of a nearly new carriage & double harness, with a pair of very sprightly bay horses. The owner has no further use for them. Inquire at the Columbian Stabler, 8th st, between D & E sts. –Keleher & Pywell

$250 reward for information which shall lead to the apprehension & conviction of the person or persons who attempted to assassinate Isaac Entwisle & Reeve Lewis at the n e corner of Capitol Square on the night of Mar 27. The reward will be paid on the certificate of the District Atty, after conviction, upon application at the Bank of Wash.

Mr Junius M Baylor, the eldest son of Col Geo Baylor, of Staunton, Va, was so mangled by being caught in the large wheel at his father's mill, near that place, on Thu last, as to cause his death in a few hours.

Died: on Mar 29, in Wash City, Tuck-A-Lix-Tah, or "The man that has many horses;" son of Cha-hicks-staca-nashuro, or "The white-man chief" who was noted as a brave of the Pawnee tribe of Indians. The deceased was with a number of his tribe in Wash City, upon business with the Gov't, in charge of Maj W W Dennison. The acting Com'r of Indian Affairs, with his characteristic kindness, directed every attention to his comfort during his illness. His remains will be interred in the *Congressional Cemetery*. They will be taken from the hotel of Mr Maher today at 12 o'clock.

Died: on Mar 29, in Wash City, Ashmun D Luckett, son of Legrand I Luckett, in his 20th year. His funeral will be this afternoon, at 3 o'clock, from the residence of his mother, 583 north L st.

Died: at *Woodlands*, Montgomery Co, Md, Mrs Ellen M Maher, aged 75 years. Requiescat in pace! [No death date given-current item.]

Died: on Mar 18, in Norfolk, of a lingering illness, Roberta Slemons, aged 2 years & 4 months, only child of Robert S & Maggie Flagg, of Martinsburg, Va.

Burlington, Iowa, Mar 29. T B Cumming, Sec & Acting Govn'r of Nebraska, died on Mar 28.

Z C Cochran, M A, Principal Coatesville Academy, Chester Co, Pa, who has been for the last 4 years & still as Principal of a large & flourishing Institution for the education of both sexes, near Phil city, has in view going to the South, if he can learn of an eligible location for the permanent establishment of a Seminary similar to that of which he now has charge. Satisfactory references given.

WED MAR 31, 1858
House of Reps: 1-Mr Whiteley, of Delaware, on leave, introduced a bill to continue the pension of Mrs Olivia W Cannon, widow of Jos S Cannon, deceased, late a midshipman in the U S navy: referred to the Cmte on Invalid Pensions.

Appointments for District offices were yesterday confirmed by the Senate:
For Marshal of the District, Wm Selden   For Postmaster of Wash, Wm P Jones
For District Atty, P B Key   For Navy Agent, Wm Flinn

Senate: 1-Memorial of Jas Myer was taken from the files & referred to the Cmte of Claims. 2-It was ordered that Thos Quantrill have leave to withdraw his memorial & papers. 3-It was ordered that the heirs of Col Wm Bond & Col Wm Douglas have leave to withdraw their memorials & papers. 4-The memorial papers of the heirs of Col Isaac Shelby were taken from the files & referred to the Cmte on Revolutionary Claims. 5-Cmte on Private Land Claims: bill for the relief of S W Haliday & others, reported it back directing the Atty Gen to make careful examination of the nature & validity of the title conveyed to the U S by the city of San Francisco, Dec, 1852. Same cmte: adverse report on the memorial of Cassandra S Witherell, heir of Maj Hugh Brady. 6-Cmte of Claims: memorial of Isaac Swain, submitted a report referring all the papers in the case to the Court of Claims: which was agreed to. Same cmte: asked to be discharged from the consideration of the memorial of Randall Pegg, asking the same wages as other watchmen in the Executive Dept, & that it be referred to the Cmte on Patents. 7-Cmte on Pensions: adverse reports on the ptns of Jno S Develin & of Wm R Broombee.

Geo H Lamb, a hotel keeper at Mendota, La Salle Co, Ill, has been arrested on suspicion of having murdered his first wife, Sarah Stafford, formerly of Maine, & to whom he was married in Nov. It appears she left her father's house in company with him in Dec, he pretending that he intended taking her on a visit to Memphis. In a short time he returned alone, & informed his father-in-law that his wife had died in Memphis. His story was believed until Christmas day, when he again married. Inquiry made in Memphis found that his wife had never reached there. Lamb was then arrested, & it said has since confessed that he took her in a small boat on the Mississippi & held her head under water until she was dead. Lamb is a native of N Y & 35 years of age.

$300 reward for my man Frank, about 36 years old, color dark brown. –B E Harrison, La Grange, near Thoroughfare, Prince Wm Co, Va.

Riot in Balt on Thu night: arrested were-Geo Peacock, John Cooper, Thos Henry, Thos Everett, John Thurlow, & Wm Snyder. Another attempt at murder was made last night on Pratt st, when a young man named Worthington received 3 balls & fell in the street. He has since died.

Hon Philemon B Hopper, the circuit judge of the 4th judicial district of Md, died at his residence, in Centreville, on Sunday, after a protracted illness. He was highly esteemed for his unblemished character. –Balt Sun

Wm Carey Jones, late special agent of the U S to Central America, returned to Wash City last evening. We learn that he is in good health.

Three days from Europe: Orsini & Pierri were guillotined on Mar 18, but Rudio was respited by the Emperor, & his sentence commuted into penal servitude for life.

THU APR 1, 1858
Female Academy, I st, between 18th & 19th sts. The institution will resume on Apr 5. -E E Janney, Principal

Camels in Calif. Lt Beale & about 14 camels stalked into town last Fri week, & gave our streets quite an oriental aspect. These camels under Lt Beale are all grown & serviceable, & most of them are well broken to the saddle, & are very gentle. All belong to the one-hump species except one, which is a cross between the one & the two humped kinds.

A man with 8 wives. A crowd flocked to the preliminary hearing at Phil. On Mar 25, Anna Thompson, married him as Wm H Boytington, at Trenton, N J, on Oct 5, 1853. Prudence Arlshton, married him as Jas R Williams, at Phil, Aug 19, 1857. These women produced their marriage certificates. The scoundrel obtained $800 from first named, & then deserted her; he got $261 from the other woman & then ran away from her. There are said to be six other women who married him & received the same treatment. He is described as being a man of full 250 pounds, portly, but well made.

John Kahler, aged 23 years, died at Phil from an attack of hydrophobia. He was bitten by a dog about 9 weeks since, but no bad symptoms appeared until Thu, when he discovered that he could not swallow any coffee. He expired yesterday after suffering great agony.

The London Watchman records that Rev John Hickling, 93 years of age, & having been 70 years a preacher, on Feb 2, delivered a discourse of an hour & twenty minutes on Early Methodism. There was no deficiency of voice, memory, or mental power.

The copartnership under the firm of Todd & Co is dissolved by mutual consent. Wm B Todd retires from the concern. The business will be conducted at the same place by Jas Y Davis. –Wm B Todd, Jas Y Davis

Senate: 1-Cmte of Claims: adverse report on the memorial of the legal reps of Seth Belknap, claiming payment due from Farrow & Harris for erecting a fortification on Dauphin Island. 2-Cmte on the Judiciary: bill for the relief of Andrew Glassell: passed. 3-Cmte on Military Affairs: bill for the relief of Mrs Harriet O Read, excx of the late Brvt Col A C W Fanning, of the U S army. Same cmte: bill for the relief of Ed Ingersoll. 4-Cmte on Foreign Relations: bill for the relief of Frances Ann McCauley. 5-Cmte on Naval Affairs: bill for the relief of R W Meade. Same cmte: asked to be discharged from the consideration of the ptn of memorial of citizens of Phil asking that a pension be granted to the widow of Capt Foxall Parker, U S navy, & of Ann E Smoot, widow of Capt Smoot, for a pension, & that they were referred to the Cmte on Pensions: which was agreed to. Same cmte: adverse reports on the following memorials: on that of Wm Reynolds, asking the amount of $100 for stockings stolen from the storeship **Fredonia** while he was acting purser; also, on the memorial of J H Carter, J W Bennett, & R B Lowry, lts in the navy, asking to be allowed the difference of pay between the grades of master & lts during the time they served as lts in the East India squadron; also, on that of W W Bassett, making a like request. 6-Bill for the relief of Jeremiah Moore: referred to the Cmte on Commerce.

Baxter & Henderson, Attys-at-Law, have associated themselves for the Practice of Law in the Circuit Court of Wash Co, D C. –Sidney S Baxter, Richd H Henderson

The Directors of the Chesapeake & Ohio Canal Co met yesterday in full Board, L J Brengle, Pres. The Board proceeded to the election of subordinate officers, as follows: John G Stone, of Clearspring district, Gen Superintendent & Engineer of the Canal; Horace Benton, Superintendent Gtwn division; Silas Browning, Superintendent Monocacy division; Levin Benton, Superintendent Antietam division; A K Stake, Superintendent Wmsport division; Lewis G Stanhope, Superintendent Hancock division; Lloyd Lowe, Superintendent Cumberland division; I Mc Henry Hollingsworth, Collector at Gtwn, Clement A Peck, assist; Jno A Rickard, Collector at Wmsport; Henry Wells, Collector at Hancock; John H Shaw, Collector at Cumberland.

The effects & good-will of Allen's Restaurant, 7th & E sts, will be offered at public auction on Apr 6. -A Green auct

Orphans Court of Wash Co, D C. In the case of Levi T Walker, adm of Nathl M Walker, deceased, the administrator & Court have appointed Apr 24 next, for the final settlement of the personal estate of the deceased, of the assets in hand. -Ed N Roach, Reg/o wills

Wash City Patrol: 5 citizens appointed from each Ward; the Mayor is requested to clothe such persons with proper legal authority to act in maintaining peace & order. Cmte appointed in each ward:
1st Ward: Dr Storrow, Fielder R Dorsett, Jas Kelley, J W Easby, Jos Gawler
2nd Ward: W H Digges, Saml Lewis, Jas Pilling, W H Clampitt, Geo Jillard
3rd Ward: J A M Duncanson, Dr Antisell, Dr Borrows, Theo Sheckel, J Y Bryant
4th Ward: F Mohun, J H Bradley, jr, W P Browning, S Bacon, Geo H Varnell
5th Ward: Jas Coleman, Dr Busey, Edw G Handy, B F Beers, John F Tucker
6th Ward: Jas Gordon, John McCathran, J W Thompson, Wm Gaddis, A W Miller
7th Ward: Dr J D Stewart, W E Richards, Jas Birch, Wm Wise, Jackson Pumphrey

Mrd: on Mar 30, in Balt, by Rev Thos G Myers, Wm G Phillips, of Wash City, to Miss Mary Catharine, eldest daughter of Mr Geo S Pumphrey, of Balt Co.

Mrd: on Mar 30, by Rev Thos G Myers, David Wiber, of Wash City, to Miss Anna Niles, eldest daughter of Mr Henry N Locke, of Balt.

Died: on Mar 27, at **Woodlands**, Montg Co, Md, the residence of her brother-in-law, Col F C Clopper, Mrs E M Maher, in her 75th year. Mrs Maher was a native of Phil; a woman of superior mind & of boundless charity. A large circle of friends, as well as her immediate family, will mourn her loss. She died in peace, in full communion with that Holy Church to which she was faithfully & devoutly attached.

FRI APR 2, 1858
A likely young Negro woman, aged 19 years, the property of a lady in PG Co, Md, a slave for life, will be sold unrestricted. Inquire of Chafin & Bro, 422 7th st, Wash, or Dr Heiskel, of PG Co, Md.

Mrd: on Mar 30, by Rev F Swentzell, Chas Edmonston, of Wash City, to Miss Mary E Cammack, near the same place.

Shocking murder at Portsmouth, N H, on Sunday last: Mr Danl H Spinney & his wife had taken tea at the house of Nelson N Downing, who is a cousin to Mrs Spinney. A dispute led to a personal collision between the two men, in which Downing, who had been drinking, was the aggressor. Spinney & his wife left the house amid threats of Downing that he would shoot them. Downing followed them to their house when he fired & killed Mrs Spinney, & shot through the arm of Mr Spinney. He is about 40 years old, has a wife & 6 children, & a peaceful man when not under the influence of liquor. Mr Spinney is a man of respectability & a peaceful citizen.

Senate: 1-Court of Claims: adverse opinions on the following claims, viz: on that of Jos Ratcliffe, of Oliver Dubois, of Arthur Edwards, John Owen, & Ira Davis; of Dennis Cronan, of A O P Nicholson, of the heirs of Lewis Ansart, & of Joshua I Guppey, trustee for the settlers & occupants of Portage city. Also, the opinion of the Court on the claim of Jos Clymer, referring it back to the consideration of Congress. All of which cases were referred to the Cmte of Claims. 2-Ptn from Henry Kellogg, asking to be indemnified for losses sustained in consequence of the failure of Congress to make appropriations for the continuation of the Wash Aqueduct. 3-Ptn from the citizens of Wash, D C, urging an examination & settlement of the claims of J W Nye for furnishing horses & carryalls for the House of Reps; for macadamising Pa ave, & for improving a public square in Wash City. 4-Cmte on Public Lands: asked to be discharged from the consideration of the memorial of Robt K Smith, asking confirmation of a title to land in the Bastrop grant, & that it be referred to the Cmte on Private Land Claims: which was agreed to. 5-Cmte of Claims: adverse report on the memorial of Anna Mathieson, which relates to indemnity for property destroyed where her husband was murdered by the Indians, & to be discharged from the further consideration of so much of the same as relates to confirming the title to land on which her husband had settled to the Cmte on Public Lands: which was agreed to. Same cmte: adverse report on the claim of the heirs of Jabez B Rooker. 6-Bill for the relief of Jane Turnbull: referred to the Cmte on Pensions. 7-Bill for the relief of the legal reps of Danl Hay, deceased: referred to the Cmte on Pensions.

House of Reps: 1-Joint resolution authorizing Lt Wm N Jeffard to accept a sword of honor from the Queen of Spain was passed. 2-Cmte of Claims: bill for the relief of Jas Romp: committed.

A company of Sappers & Miners, 64 in number, under the command of Capt Duane & Lt Alexander, left West Point on Wed for Utah. They were taken to Newburgh in the steamboat **West Point**, & were to proceed, by way of the Erie railroad, westward at 7 o'clock. The company is in most excellent discipline, & consists of picked men, who have been for a year past under the training & instruction of Lt Alexander, one of the most accomplished & promising engineer officers in the service. –N Y Post

Sale of stock of groceries at auction: on Apr 5, at the store of Wm A Lerpeux, Pa ave & 12th sts. —Wall & Barnard, aucts

Charleston Courier of Mar 26. Obit-died: on Mar 25, Mr Jonathan Bryan, at the patriarchal age of 83 years. Mr Bryan was born in Phil, in Oct, 1774, & removed to this city in 1790, when 16 years of age. He was a son of Hon Geo Bryan, a distinguished patriot & worthy of the Revolution, who in 1778 was elected Pres of the Supreme Executive Council of Pa, & in 1780 a Judge of the Supreme Court of that State, & who, in 1765, had been a member of the first Colonial Congress in America. Mr Jonathan Bryan married a daughter of the late venerable Danl Latham, [long known among us as one of the few Quaker denomination in our city,] & embarked in mercantile pursuits, to which he devoted himself until near the close of his protracted life. He was above all a Christian, at once sincerely pious & of a truly catholic spirit. As late as Wed night he was conversing with his family, in apparent health, & yesterday, with scarce an hour's notice to the members of his family, the lamp of life went out, peacefully & quietly, & the spirit of the aged pilgrim returned to God who gave it.

Two brothers-in-law, John McLaughlin & Dennis O'Connell, quarreled over a game of cards at the apts of the latter, 143 Mulberry st, N Y, on Tue, when McLaughlin inflicted a fatal blow upon the head of O'Connell. The assailant was arrested.

SAT APR 3, 1858
Senate: 1-Ptn from T H Hyatt, U S consul at Amoy, China, asking compensation for judicial services under the act of Congress of August, 1848: referred. 2-Papers in relation to the claim of Levi Johnson & Mary Buckfield to bounty land: referred. 3-Ordered that the papers of John B & Thos Johnson, on the files of the Senate, be referred to the Cmte of Claims. 4-Ordered that Mrs Emma A Wood have leave to withdraw her memorial & papers. 5-Cmte of Claims: asked to be discharged from the further consideration of the memorial of Chas Knap, & that is be referred to the Cmte on Commerce: agreed to. Same cmte: asked to be discharged from the consideration of the memorial of Jno W Phillips, & that he have leave to withdraw his papers: agreed to. 6-Bill for the relief of Saml C Phagin & others: referred to the Cmte on the Judiciary.

Promotions in the Navy, by & with the advice & consent of the Senate. John G Walker, John G Mitchell, Francis M Ramsay, Richd W Meade, jr, Marshal C Campbell, Robt Boyd, jr, Calvin F Thomas, & Chas C Carpenter, have been nominated by the Pres to be lts in the navy from Jan 23, 1858, to fill existing vacancies. Also, Andrew J McCartney, to be a lt from Feb 18, 1858, vice Lt Garret V Denniston.

Robt J Griffin, who was arrested at Paris, Ky, a few days ago, & confined in the Bourbon Co jail, to await trail on a charge of having been engaged in setting fire to barns in that vicinity, was taken out of jail on Monday morning, by a mob, & hung by the neck until he was dead.

Mrd: on Apr 1, at the McKendree Parsonage, by Rev D Ball, Mr Thos S Devaughan to Miss Ann E Moreland.

Ex-Govn'r John S Peters, of Conn, died at Hebron on Thu. He was a member of the Assembly as Senator or Rep for several years, & Lt Govn'r from 1827 to 1831, when he succeeded Gideon Tomlinson as Govn'r, holding the office 2 years. In 1833 he was defeated by Henry W Edwards, & he has not since appeared in political life except as Presidential elector. We have not heard his age, but he must have been over 80 at the time of his death. –Hartford Press of Mar 31.

Letters have been received at the War Dept, from Lt J C Ives, commanding the Colorado expedition, dated Feb 10. The steamer had reached the Mojave villages. All the party were well, & no accident whatever had occurred.

Died: on Mar 29, at *Fair View*, PG Co, Md, Rosalie Eugenia, infant daughter of Oden & Alice Bowie, aged 3 weeks & 1 day.

On Thu an arrest was made by officers McHenry & Irvin, of a man whose real name appears to be Chas Augustus Hamlin, but who has been using a couple of aliases, on suspicion of connexion with the robbery of the gunsmith's shop of Mr C H Munck, on 6th st, some weeks ago. He has been employed on the work of the Capitol extension as a blacksmith, but was discharged about a week ago.

Crime in Phil, from the Phil Evening Journal of Thu. Residents of the rural districts adjoining Phil are much agitated on account of the fearful increase in the number of incendiary attempts upon their property. Dwlgs at Chestnut Hill robbed on Fri last: the residence of St Geo T Campbell, Ambrose White, Mr Hildeburn, John Piper, Rev R Owen, Dr Smith, & E S Sanford; & on Monday the residence of Mr Cowperthwait, at Rising Sun. Incendiary fires in March: the barn of Mr Womrath, at Frankford-adjacent mansion was barely saved from ruin. The barn of Mr Ford, at Olney, was burnt soon after. The barn of Mr Remington, on the Lancaster turnpike, with 50 head of cattle perished in the flames. The barn of Jas Deveraux, near Fox Chase, on the Oxford plank road, was burnt down on Sunday last. The barn of Geo Weiss, at Byberry, was utterly destroyed, with all its contents. The barn of Geo W Smick, on the Ridge road, near the 7 mile stone, was burnt on Tuesday night.

Mrs Levely announces that her house, 1,216 Chestnut st, Phil, still remains open for the reception of Boarders.

Dissolution of the business carried on in the name of J T Hopkins & Co, by mutual consent, & will hereafter be carried on in the name of J & G W Hopkins, as heretofore. -Jno Hopkins, G W Hopkins

MON APR 5, 1858
Mrd: in Princeton, Mass, by Rev Ebenezer Mirick, Mr Wm H Mirick, of Wash City, to Miss Emily A, eldest daughter of Mr Saml Griffin, of Princeton. [No marriage date given-current item.]

Trustee's sale of a tract of land & house & lot at auction: on Apr 28, by authority of a decree of the Circuit Court of Wash Co, D C, wherein John Costigan is cmplnt, & the heirs in law of the estate of Thos Perkins, deceased, are dfndnts: sale of a tract of land in Wash Co, called the *Ridge*, containing 27 acres, 2 roods & 4 perches, more or less; adjoining the lands of Thos Jenkins. Also, a house & 2 lots of ground, in Uniontown, near the Anacostia Bridge, by the Navy Yard, with a good 2 story frame dwlg house, nearly new, & a small store house. –John Costigan, trustee -A Green auct

Criminal Court-Wash-Thu. 1-Richd Walker, Jno W Hillary, John Walker, Hilleary Hutchins, & Wm Dorsey, found guilty of riot in Gtwn on Mar 3. 2-Fred'k Gussell, about 17 years of age, guilty of the larceny of articles of jewelry & clothing from David Brenten: sentenced to 1 years' imprisonment. 3-On Sat the Pres of the U S granted a pardon to John M Meeks, who has been suffering a sentence of 10 years' imprisonment & hard labor in our penitentiay, rendered by the district court of Western Md in Oct, 1852, for robbing the U S mail.

Died: on Mar 29, at Sandy Spring, Md, after a short illness of pneumonia, Jos Gilpin, in his 78th year. Not many have lived to so advanced an age with fewer enemies, for he was universally esteemed wherever known.

Richd Holmes, of Cape May Co, N J, has probably saved more human lives at risk, than any other in the nation. He has for many years acted as the agent of the N Y & Phil insurance companies & underwriters there, & had great experience of the perils of that coast, & in saving ships, crews, & cargoes when thrown among the terrible breakers so fatal to everything that is at their mercy. A few years ago Mr Holmes was lithe, active, with a heart as big as a bushel, in a slender frame of no more than 130 pounds. His hand & heart are as sound as ever, but his frame is but a wreck, made so by paralysis, brought on by exposure to severe cold.

TUE APR 6, 1858
Senate: 1-Ptn from Henry King & others, asking a patent for the manufacture of Russia sheet iron: referred. 2-Ptn from Giles S Isham, asking a grant of land in the proposed Territory of Arizona for the purpose of establishing a colony of industrious farmers, mechanics, & artisans: referred. 3-Ptn from Saml Gardiner, jr, asking that Congress will purchase his patent for lighting gas, & claiming for the uses to which his invention may be applied the making of signal lights: referred. 4-Cmte on Pensions: adverse report on the claim of Thos R Carman for an invalid pension. Same cmte: asked to be discharged from the consideration of the ptn of Sarah W Halsey, & that she have leave to withdraw her papers: agreed to. 5-Cmte on Revolutionary Claims: adverse report on the claim of Lucretia Bell, heir of Jane Van Dean & widow of Abraham Van Buskirk. 6-Cmte on Private Land Claims: bill for the relief of N C Weems, of Louisiana, & recommended its passage. 7-Comte on Post Offices & Post Roads: adverse report on the memorial of John M Hinton. Same cmte: memorial of Arnold Harris & S F Butterworth, sureties of a paymaster at New Orleans, submitted a report, with a bill for their relief. 8-Cmte on Public Lands: bill for the relief of Martin Layman.

Watches, silverware, jewelry, tools & fixtures of a Jewelry Store at auction: on Apr 9, at the store of W H Forrest, on 7th st, between I & K sts, his entire stock. –A Green auct

We learn that Mr Jos Stratton & Mrs Kendall were married last evening in Union Hall, Athol, by Rev Mr Burt. This was the second marriage of the bridegroom, who is 78 years of age-the third of the bride, whose age is 74 years. The officiating clergyman has reached the venerable age of 92 years. Many citizens were present. –Boston Journal

Edw Dolan, Merchant Tailor, Sign of the Golden Fleece, corner of 14th & Pa ave. [Ad]

Criminal Court-Wash-Mon. 1-Danl Stewart found guilty of assault & battery on Jacob Shaeffer. Not being personally in court he could not be sentenced. 2-The Gtwn parties, found guilty on Sat of assaults on John Frizzle & others, were fined by the Court.

Died: on Apr 5, in Wash City, Judge Benj O Ridgate, formerly of Balt, but for some years past a resident of Wash City. His funeral will be on Wed at half past 4 o'clock, at his late residence, 197 west F st.

Died: on Apr 2, at his residence, in Calvert Co, Md, Capt Wm J Belt, in his 65th year.

Died: yesterday, Richd G Hyatt, formerly of PG Co, in his 33rd year. Mr Hyatt's illness was protracted & painful. His funeral services will take place in the E st Baptist Church on Wed next, at 4 o'clock.

Valuable real estate in Alexandria & Fairfax Counties, Va, for sale: with a view to the settlement of the estate & education of her children, will sell at private sale the following Farms, formerly in possession of & owned by the late Richd M Scott, of Fairfax Co, Va: **Bush Hill**, Fairfax Co, containing 540 acres, more or less. This property is well known as the residence of the late Mr Scott; a very beautiful place, a 2 story brick dwlg-house containing 12 rooms; & numerous outbldgs. A farm in Alexandria Co, known as **Waterloo**, containing 100 acres; with a small log house, corn-house & stable. It adjoins the lands of the late Gen Hunter, now the residence of Bushrod Hunter. Please to call on Peter E Hoffman, Exchange Bank, Alexandria; Rich Smith, Bank fo the Metropolis; J S Gunnell, 397 20th st, Wash, or the subscriber, at **Bush Hill**, near Alexandria.
-Virginia Scott

WED APR 7, 1858
Constable's sale of the furniture of the large boarding house of Mrs Lane, on F st, between 12th & 13th sts. By order of Robt Hughes, bailiff -Wall & Barnard, aucts

Trustee's sale: by deed of trust from Danl Williams to me, dated Jun 6, 1857, recorded in Liber J A S No 135, folios 238, of the land records of Wash Co: public auction on Apr 21, of part of lot 1 in square 559, improved by a dwlg house. –W B Webb, trustee
-C W Boteler, auct

The steamer **Sultan**, Capt Phil E Hannum, left St Louis for New Orleans about dark on Apr 1, having on board passengers & near 1,000 tons of cargo. On Friday flames were discovered issuing from the watchman's locker, which soon enveloped the whole boat. Known to be lost: Jas Poage, Albert Poage, & Mrs Julis Poage, Lagrange Mo. Mrs F A Cheatham, Baton Rouge, La; S B Woolfolk, Scottville, Ill; Henry Ely, St Louis; Capt D D Moore, St Louis; Jos Blackburn, St Louis; barkeeper, name unknown; Dennis Callaghan, St Louis; Patrick Donnell, cabin boy; 2 other cabin boys, names unknown; the barber, 3 firemen, & 4 deck passengers. Boat & freight are one mass of cinders. Most had jumped overboard. –St Louis Republican

Joshua Brown, American, was elected Mayor of the city of Annapolis on Monday, by a vote of 220 against 188 for John Walton, his Democratic competitor.

Household & kitchen furniture at auction on on Apr 12, at the Furniture Store of Geo A Davis, in the old Union Bldg, on E st, between 13th & 14th sts. -Jas C McGuire, auct

Sale by trustees in chancery of valuable real estate. By decree of the Circuit Court of Wash Co, D C, supplemental to the decree heretofore passed by said Court, in a cause, [No 1,066] wherein Agnes M Easby is cmplnt, & Horatio N Easby, John W Easby, Wm R Smith & Wilhelmina M, his wife, Henry King & Marian E his wife, & Cecilia J Hyde are dfndnts: auction on May 4 next of:

Lots 4 & 26 in square 5
Part of lot 2 in square 11
Part of lot 2 in square 12
Lot 7 in square 61
Lot 3 in square 88
Lot 6 in square 55
Lot 3 in square 89
Lots 1 & 6 in square 57
Part of lot 4 in square 730
On May 6: lot 1 thru 8 & 12 in square 925

Lot 9 in square 708
Lot 20 in square 743
Lots 6 & 13 in square 1,028
Lot 7 in square 1,031
Lot 5 in square 1,034
Lot 20 in square 702
Lots 5 & 6 in square 1,121
Lot 8 in square 1,122
On May 5: lot 8 in square 631

-Wm B Webb, Richd H Clarke, Jos H Bradley, jr, trustees -Jas C McGuire, auct

Editor turned Shepherd. Geo W Kendall, one of the proprietors of the New Orleans Picayune, owns large estates in Texas. He writes to a friend in Boston that 3 days a week he passes at his rancho with his family, where he has some 3,000 sheep.

Alex'r Marshall killed Warren Sutton, sr, at **Fort Gaines**, Tenn, on Mar 28, in front of Wardlaw's Hotel. Sutton walked up to Marshall on the street & fired at him. Marshall shot him in the shoulder & stabbed him 4 times with a bowie-knife. He gave himself up, & has given bond in $10,000 for his appearance.

At Balt, early yesterday, the notorious Archibald McAleese, with several others, attempted to force an entrance into a groggery on Holliday st, kept by a man named Levy, when McAleese was shot in the head by Levy, & died at noon.

Senate: 1-Memorial from Amos Kendall, a supplement to the memorial of the Magnetic & Union Telegraph Company: referred. 2-Ptn from Wm M Varnum, agent of the State of Georgia, asking that the proper accounting ofcrs of the Treasury be authorized to ascertain & pay the amount due that State for money advanced in the suppression of the Indian hostilities: referred.

Yesterday Mr Thos B Berry, printer, of Balt, with a friend, called at the house of Messrs John & Jas P Devlin, on Pa ave, Capitol Hill. He had gone to get a change of clothing, his wife having been a Miss Devlin. An altercation arose between Berry & his 2 brothers-in-law. Mrs Devlin, their mother, asked the gentleman outside to use his efforts to compose the strife. Berry retreated by the back door, but was overtaken & stabbed by Jas P Devlin, with a bowie knife several times to the heart. He died very shortly after. Mr John Devlin is a lawyer & a member of the Washington bar. The brothers were committed to jail for further examination.

Criminal Court-Wash-Tue: 1-Wm Bradly acquitted on the charge of larceny in stealing a money purse from Miss Lydia S English. Jas Davis, charged with the same crime, was acquitted. 2-Ellen Callahan found not guilty of stealing silver ware from Mr Henry Kellogg. 3-Andrew Kidwell was found guilty for a violent & unprovoked assault on a colored man 94 years of age, named Wm Washington: sentenced to 6 months' imprisonment & to continue in jail till the costs are paid. 4-John Alworth, charged with assaulting & beating his wife, submitted his case, & under appeal by her to the Court was sentenced to 2 weeks in jail.

Alex'r Eggleston, one of the parties implicated in the disturbances at the June election of last year, & who escaped at the time of the trials, was arrested yesterday, & lodged in jail.

Ofcr Jos M Carrico, whose fears prevented him from the discharge of his duty in making known the assassins that so wantonly assailed Messrs Lewis & Entwisle on Sat night week, has been dismissed from his post.

Died: on Good Friday, in Christ Church, Gtwn, D C, suddenly, of disease of the heart, Mrs Mary Ann Davidson, wife of John Davidson, in her 65th year.

Died: on Apr 5, of chronic croup, Leash Ward, eldest daughter of J R & Anna Thompson, aged 2 years, 11 months & 11 days. Her funeral will be from 406 7th st, between G & H sts. [No date for the funeral.]

Watertown, N Y, Apr 6. The dwlg of Danl Comstock, in Leroy, was burnt on Sunday, & himself & 4 children perished.

THU APR 8, 1858
Excellent household & kitchen furniture at auction on Apr 13, at the Hotel of G D'Ivernois, on Pa ave, between 17th & 18th sts. —Chas S Wallach, trustee
-Jas C McGuire, auct

Senate: 1-Ptn from Rev A G Carothers & other citizens of Wash, asking that the public reservation in the city opposite the Assembly's Church may be enclosed: referred. 2-Ptn from Jno Gardiner & associates, asking that the Postmaster Genr'l be authorized to contract for carrying the mails between the U S & Brazil: referred. 3-Additional papers in support of the claim of Wm Reynolds: referred. 4-Cmte on Revolutionary Claims: bill for the relief of the heirs of Capt Alex'r Rose. Same cmte: adverse reports on the memorials: of Catharine Kellar, widow of Conrad Kellar; of Jas Purvis' heirs; of John W Pray, heir of John Pray; & of John Mason, heir of Jeremiah Gilman. 5-Cmte on Pensions: bill for the relief of John Brest, a soldier in the war of 1812. Same cmte: adverse reports on the following ptns: of Alex'r Hagner & Danl R Hagner, guardians of the minor children of the late Maj Hagner, Paymaster U S army; on that of Chas West, for increase of pension; of Nannie Denman, widow of Lt F J Denman; & on that of Jos Paul. 6-Cmte on Pensions: asked to be discharged from the consideration of the ptn of Jos G Heaton, & that it be referred to the Cmte of Claims: agreed to. Same cmte: asked to be discharged from the consideration of the memorial of certain citizens in behalf of the widow of Faxal A Parker, which was agreed to; from that of Chas Bruckner, adm of Wm White: which was agreed to. 7-Joint resolution for the benefit of the nearest male heir of the late Maj Gen Towson, U S army: referred to the Cmte on Naval Affairs. 8-Bill for the relief of Henry G Carson: referred to the Cmte of Claims. 9-Resolved, that there be printed in pamphlet form, for the use of the Senate, 10,000 copies of the addresses made by members of the Senate & House of Rept: upon the occasions of the deaths of Hon A P Butler, of S C; Hon Jas Bell, of N H; & Hon Thos J Rusk, of Texas, late Senators of the U S, & that the printer prepare in similar manner to the eulogies on the life of Hon John M Clayton.

The Senate on Mar 25 confirmed the appointment of Dr Wm V H Brown as principal clerk of public lands in the Gen Land Ofc.

Annual State election in Rhode Island yesterday. The Providence Journal says that the opposition to the present State officers is merely nominal, & predicts their re-election:

Elisha Dyer, Gov'r
Thos G Turner, Lt Govn'r
John R Bartlett, Sec of State
Jerome B Kimball, Atty Gen
Saml A Parker, Gen Treasurer

Wash Corp: 1-Ptn from Thos Lowns for the remission of a fine: referred to the Cmte of Claims. 2-Claims of Thos Motley for a design & plan for a bridge at H st: referred to the delegation from the 4th Ward.

Hon Saml A Adams, a member of the Senate of Mass, died on Monday. He was suffering from rheumatism, for which aconite had been prescribed as a lotion, & of this he swallowed 3 teaspoonfuls, which ended his life in 2 hours. Aconite is a deadly poison, except in the small quantities in which it is prescribed by homoeopathic physicians. His first feeling, immediately after taking the dose, was a numbness of the lower limbs, followed by severe attacks of pain. He was much respected as an energetic & a upright man. His health had been good up to the rheumatic attack.

Mount Vernon: the Richmond Enquirer of Sat announces that the transfer of *Mount Vernon* to the **Ladies' Mount Vernon Asociation** is now a fixed fact. The following is Mr Washington's reply to a letter from a Southern Matron:" *Mount Vernon*, Mar 19, 1858. Madam: Your letter of Mar 12th has been received, in which you inform me that the bill providing for the purchase of *Mount Vernon* by Virginia has been defeated in the House of Delegates, & in the name & on behalf of the *Mount Vernon Association* you renew your offer to purchase this place. Heretofore I have only been willing to dispose of *Mount Vernon* to the United States or to Virginia, as I believe that in the hands of one or the other it would be better protected & preserved than in the possession of any individual or associaition. The events of the past seven years, however, seem to indicate that neither Virginia nor the United States wish to acquire the place. Under these circumstances, & believing that, after the two highest Powers in our country, the women of the land will be the safest-as they will certainly be the purest-guardians of a national shrine, I am willing so far to comply with your request as to await for a reasonably limited period of time the propositions you wish to make to me on behalf of the association over which you preside. And I assure you that unless these proposals are inconsistent with what I believe to be my duties upon the occasion, I shall be inclined to give them the most favorable consideration. With assurances of the highest respect, I have the honor to be, your obedient servant, John A Washington. [Jul 1st newspaper: the Gov't of the association is well aware that the sum contracted for, as the price of the estate, is greatly beyond its value as a piece of property. It is sufficient to state that it could not be obtained on any other terms. The proprietor has been offered that & even larger sums by parties who wished to acquire the property for pecuniary speculation, & he considered that he had performed his duty to the public by refusing to sell it for any such purpose. It will require a large sum to repair the mansion house, & to restore it with the garden & grounds as nearly as possible to the condition in which they were left by the Great Proprietor.]

Orphans Court of Wash Co, D C. Letters of administration on the personal estate of John R Dorsey, late of Wash Co, deceased. –Mary C Dorsey, admx

Dr J K Mitchell, Grand Master of the Grand Lodge of Freemasons in Pa, died in Phil on Sunday last. He was born in Shepherdstown, Va, on May 12, 1798, & was educated in Scotland. His scientific, literary, political, & miscellaneous productions are of a high order of excellence. As a physician he stood among the most eminent of the profession; as a writer he was brilliant & profound; as a citizen he was justly honored & admired.

Delegates elected in the several wards on Tue to the Anti-Know-Nothing Convention, which is to meet on Apr 15:

W W Davis	John F Ennis	Jas F Devin
Andrew Carrol	Geo E Jillard	Edw Simms
Saml Stover	L F Clark	F W Birch
Wm Grebble	P Gallant	J F Coyle
Wm Fletcher	Wm Sibrey	J Reese
Nicholas Vedder	Dr Borrows	W P Mohun
Geo W Stewart	Chas P Wannall	John J Mulloy

W F Price	J B Brandt	Peter Hepburn, sr
Geo Oyster	Thos Altemus	John T Cassell
J McGran	Richd Brooks	Jas E Johnson
M Duffy	Valentine Conner	H A Clarke
F McNerhany	E M Clarke	

Criminal Court-Wash-Wed: 1-Jas Murtage found guilty for assault & battery: fined $20. 2-Chas Dolman, alias Ellman, found guilty of stealing 2 pistols, 2 swords, & a clock, the property of Dr Maynard: sentenced to 2 years in the penitentiary. 3-Virginia Burch & Sarah Thomas were tried & the latter convicted of keeping a disorderly house, the former was acquitted, Sarah was sent one month to jail. 4-Jas Walters was found guilty of malicious mischief in cruelly abusing & putting out the eye of a mare, the property of Mr G Vanderken, of Gtwn: sentenced to 3 months' imprisonment & fined $10, to be paid before being released from jail.

Mrd: on Apr 7, by Rev F Swentzell, Jas S Topham to Ann Maria M White, all of Wash City.

Mrd: on Apr 6, in Wash City, by Rev B F Bittinger, Jas P Spies, of Brooklyn, to Miss Catharine, daughter of the late Christopher Corley, of N Y.

Died: on Apr 7, Jas Handley, in his 53rd year. His funeral will take place from his late residence on Apr 7, between G & H sts, at 2 o'clock.

Died: on Apt 7, after a protracted illness, Mary Hannah, wife of Robt V Laskey, & 2nd daughter of the late Jas C White, in her 30th year. Her funeral will take place from the residence of her mother, Mrs White, 474 9th st, on Apr 9, at 3½ o'clock P M.

Died: on Apr 7, Richd Shaw, a native of Wash City, in his 45th year, after a brief but painful illness. His funeral will take place at the residence of his brother, Wm Simmons, on M st, 428, this day, Apr 8, at 4 o'clock.

Life of Gen Sir Henry Havelock, by Rev Wm Brock, with fine portrait, 75 cents. Every inch a solidier & every inch a Christian. –Wm Ballantyne, 498 7th st.

FRI APR 9, 1858
Murder on Long Island. The body of Wm C McKee, a well known & highly respectable citizen of this city, was found on Sat last floating on Jamaica Bay, & identified by the deceased's brother-in-law, Wm King, the Port Warden. He was found to have received a gun shot in the forehead. Robbery was undoubtedly the cause of the act, as his coat & valuable, with $20, which he had placed in his pantaloons pockets, were gone. Of course nobody knows anything about it. –Journal of Commerce

Stock of Boots & Shoes, Good Will, Fixtures, & Lease at public auction: on Apr 12, at Mr T G Ford's Boot & Shoe Store, Pa ave, between 12th & 13th sts. -Jas C McGuire, auct

Senate: 1-Ptn from David D Porter, urging the payment of the claim of his father, Cmdor David Porter, against the Mexican Gov't, for services rendered in the navy of that country, out of the Mexican indemnity fund or otherwise: referred. 2-Ptn from Lt Wm Nelson, of the U S navy, asking that an allowance may be made in the adjustment of his accounts for certain moneys lost on account of being made purser of the ship he commanded, & also naval storekeeper of the Pacific squadron. 3-Cmte of Claims: memorial of Geo M Weston, com'r of the State of Maine, submitted a special report, with a bill to provide for quieting certain land titles in the late disputed territory, in the State of Maine, & for other purposes. 4-Cmte on Patents: asked to be discharged from the consideration of the memorial of Isaac W Brown, & that it be referred to the Cmte on Military Affairs: agreed to. 5-Cmte on Military Affairs: bill for the relief of Chas McCormick, assist surgeon in the U S navy.

Affidavit of Mr Grinter. I, Jas C Grinter, aged 31 years, of Delaware Crossing, Leavenworth Co, Kansas Territory, on oath depose & say, that a voting precinct was established at Delaware Crossing for the election appointed for Jan 4, 1858. The judges of that election for that precinct were Theodore F Garrett, Isaac Munday, & myself. Wm Wilson & Jas Findlay were clerks of said election; John D Henderson was in waiting to take the poll-book & ballot-box to Leavenworth city. Theodore F Garret has no family; he formerly lived with his mother. He has been absent from the Territory 2 weeks. Isaac Munday has since died. –Jas C Grinter [Sworn before Chas S Glick, Notary Public for Leavenworth Co, K T.]

Dr B Rhett offers his professional services to the inhabitants of Wash. Residence, west side of 11th st, 3 doors north of E st.

Michl Clear, a native of Queen Anne's Co, Md, died at Greenwich, Conn. In 1810 he was a sailor before the mast, but during the war of 1812 he was captain of the foretop on board the U S ship **Constitution**. He aided at the taking of the British frig **Guerriere**, under Cmdor Hull; at the taking of the British frig **Java**, under Cmdor Bainbridge; & at the taking of the ships **Cyane & Levant**, under Cmdor Stewart. He subsequently returned to the merchant service, where he continued for many years, when he re-entered the U S service, on the sloop-of-war **Erie**, & subsequently on the frig **Congress**. His last position was that of a sailing master at the Brooklyn Navy Yard, to which he was appointed in 1839 as a reward for his faithful services.

Columbus [Ga] Sun of Mar 30: Mrs Daniel, wife of Mr J H Daniel, of that city, & daughter of Hon Alfred Iverson, was very seriously, but it is hoped not fatally, burnt on Thu last at Griffin. In the act of dressing in time to leave for Columbus by the early train her dress took fire while stooping before the fire to tie the shoes of her little child. Without raising an alarm, she at once pulled off some of the bed covering & enveloped herself in it, & then fell on the floor, thus extinguishing the flames, but not until most of her clothing had been burnt off of her & herself badly burnt.

Richmond, Va, Apr 8. A contract was formally entered into on Apr 6 by the **Ladies of the Mount Vernon Association** for the purchase of the Washington estate.

On Fri last, Rev T B Hudson, Professor of Mathematics in Oberlin College, Ohio, was run over by 2 trains of cars at Olmstead, & crushed literally to pieces. The cars started suddenly, & in attempting to get on board he fell under the wheels, & though not killed, was so disabled as to be unable tomove himself from his dangerous position. Shortly after a train on the Cleveland & Toledo road came along, & the engineer saw him made a motion with his hand, but it was too late to stop the train.

Difficulty between Hon Jacob Thompson, Sec of the Interior, & Mr Peter Besancon, of Louisiana, formerly a clerk in the Pension Ofc, occurred yesterday. Besancon was questioning the accuracy of some report alluded to be the Sec, & the Sec replied that he wished to be troubled with no further communication on the subject. Mr Besancon struck the Sec with his fist & placed his hand in his pocket to draw his revolver, when Mr Thompson threw him on the floor. Mr Thompson was taken to the Infirmary for surgical treatment.

Criminal Court-Wash-Thu. 1-Geo Delhi, alias Dutch George, was acquitted of keeping a disorderly house at N Y ae & 7th st. 2-Hugh Sloan was found guilty of assault & battery & fined $5 & costs. 3-Danl Stewart was found guilty of assault & fined $10 & costs.

Augusta, Apr 8. Joel Crawford, formerly a member of Congress from Gerogia, & a gallant officer in the Indians wars of the South, died on Monday in Early Co, aged 75.

Balt, Apr 8. Supposed murder: the body of a man named Benj Jones, aged 49, belonging to Balt, was found floating in the dock today with marks of violence, indicating that he had been murdered. The deceased had some money, & a few weeks since he left here, as was understood, for Texas. It is supposed he was robbed & then murdered. Verdict not rendered.

SAT APR 10, 1858
Richmond Whig: We are happy to announce that on Apr 6, in the presence of the 2 parties, & the counsel of the Association & the proprietor of **Mount Vernon**, a contract was formally entered into before a notary, between John A Washington, & the Regent of the Association, for the purchase of the home & grave of Washington by the Association. The particulars will be given in a few days.

The Newark [Del] tragedy. Saml M Harrington, jr, T B Giles, & I H Weaver, who were arrested on the charge of being accessory to the death of J Edw Roach, who was killed in the recent affray at the college at Newark, Dela, had an exmination on Mon & Tue. The result was the discharge of Harrington & Giles. Young Weaver, however, was remanded to prison to await his trial. [May 27th newspaper: Isaac H Weaver was acquitted in the killing of young Roach at Delaware College.]

Fire in Wmsport, Md, on Wed, consumed Higgins & Fulmer's stores & dwlg houses, together with a frame bldg of Mr Robt Faries. One store was occupied as a confectionery & bakery, & the other as a general dry-goods store. The loss is supposed to exceed $20,000.

Criminal Court-Wash-Fri. 1-Louisa Parker, colored, was convicted of an assault & battery on her own infant child, with intent to kill it, & sentenced to 2 years in the penitentiary. 2-John Wilson was found guilty of petty larceny in stealing some children's clothing: sentenced to 8 months in jail. 3-Chas Hassened was found guilty of burglary on the house of Philip Phillips, with intent to steal therefrom. Sentenced to 3 years in the penitentiary.

Mrd: on Apr 8, by Rev John C Smith, Mr T Connell, formerly of Montg Co, Md, to Miss Jane E Williams, of Wash City.

Mrd: on Apr 6, by Rev Fr Dougherty, Mr Covington Beall, of Fred'k Co, Md, to Miss Eliz E Fenwick, of the District of Columbia.

Mrd: on Apr 7, at **Mount Wellington**, by Rev R T Brown, Mr Alex'r Innis, of Rapides Parish, La, to Miss Virginia Lemoine, 2nd daughter of late Moreau Lemoine, Fairfax Co, Va.

Died: on Apr 9, Francis Whittlesey, son of Alpheus L Edwards, in his 4th year. His funeral is today at 3 o'clock, at the residence of his father, corner of 8th & K sts north.

For sale on reasonable terms: 100 acres of valuable land in Wash Co, D C; adjoins the farms of Geo Livingston, Capt Wankowiz, & Mr Geo Talbot. Apply to Horace Edelin, 38 Louisiana ave.

Marietta, Apr 7. The 70th anniversary of the settlement of Ohio was celebrated here today, & Hon Thos Ewing delivered the address. He is the only survivor of the party of 47 persons who arrived here in 1787. Speeches were made by Geo Goddard & others.

Paper Hangings, cornices, & window shades: 240 Pa ave: John Alexander.

The Jennens estate. The property is said to be under litigation; to want heirs; to be about to revert to the Crown; to amount to forty or fifty millions sterling; to consist of untold gold in chests in the Bank of England for security, & the baronial estate of *Acton Place*. Wm Jennens, of *Acton Place*, near Long Melford, County Suffolk, & Grosvenor Square, was born in 1700, & baptized in Sep, 1701, when King Wm III stood as his godfather. He was the son of Robt Jennens, aid-de-camp to the great Duke of Marlborough, & grandson of Humphrey Jennens, of Erdington Hall, County Warwick. He was in his youth page to Geo I, & during the long period of his life remained a bachelor. He died at his residence in Grosvenor Square on Jul 19, 1798, leaving no will, but an unsigned bequest to one John Bacon, who would have been the residuary legatee had not Mr Jennens, as his servant state, forgotten his spectacles on going to his solicitor's to sign the testametntary instrument, which he finally neglected to sign altogether. He was considered the richest private individual in England. On Jul 29, 10 days after his decease, his body was interred in the family vault at Acton Church, with much funeral pomp, &, in compliance with his instructions, an inscription was put on the monument in the church giving the lineage of the family & an account of *Acton Hall*. The family genealogy, as it is to be found in the Townsend Collection in the Herald's College, will show the heirship to the immense estate, both personal & real. John Jennens, of Birmingham, left a son, Humphrey Jennens, of Erding & Nether Whitacre, in the county of Warwick. Humphrey by Mary, daughter of John Milward, of Snitterton, county Derby, had issue, Chas Jennens, eldest son, from whom descends Earl Howe & Robt Jennens, the father of Wm Jennens, of *Acton Place*. Also, 2 daughters, Esther, who married Wm Hanmer, & Ann, who married Sir Clement Fisher, Bart, of Packington. From Esther descended Wm Lygon, afterwards Earl Beauchamp; & from Ann descended Lady Mary Finch, who married Wm Viscount Andover. As the will of Mr Jennens, without signature, could not convey his estate, letters of administration, with the will annexed, were immediately granted to Wm Lygon, & Hon Mary Viscountess Dowager Andover, the cousins german once removed, & next of kin of the deceased. As next of kin the personality was shared between these parties, while the real estate descended to the testator's heir-at-law, Geo Augustus Wm Curzon, infant grandson of Earl Howe, & from him to the present Earl Howe. In Sep, 1798, the effects of Wm Jennens, at Acton Place, were advertised for a week in the Times over the signatures of the administrators & the heirs at law, & at the close of the month an auction was held at Acton Hall of the furniture, library, pictures, old china, & other moveables of the mansion. *Acton Hall* had been formerly the seat of the Daniels, & sold by them to Robt Jennens, who began to rebuild it, which, though a fine structure, was never completely finished. The bldg contained 54 apartments, & was richly adorned with fine tapestry, which was torn from the walls & sold at the auction with the other furniture. The walls were decorated with some fine paintings by Snyders, of animals, fruit pieces, etc, & in one room was shown a bed, the furniture of which was said to have been lined with the shirts of King Wm III, the godfather of Wm Jennens. Not withstanding the regular descent of the property, a bill was filed in chancery in 1810, by several persons of the name of Jennens, & Lord Beauchamp was cited to bring the administration into court. The Jennens party denied the interest of Lord Beauchamp & Lady Andover, asserting themselves to be cousins german thrice removed; but did not set forth their own interest as paramount to that of Lord Beauchamp, the surviving administrator. The administration had been in undisturbed possession for 12 years, & as the Jennens party had no interest to set forth, they instituted no further suit, & that has been the extent of the litigation in respect of the property. Lord Howe, having another seat, did not reside at *Acton Place*, & the hall fell into decay. The course became overgrown with grass & weeds, & in 1825 Lord Howe offered the estate for sale, & ordered the hall to be demolished. As late as 1852 the English journals gave publicity to statements to the effect that one John Martin, of Maldon, had fallen heir to the Jennens property. The story arose from the fact that a gentleman of that name, quite advanced in years, who had fancied himself the rightful heir, was called to London to sign some instrument, & thinking that by his signature he had secured the estate he gave it out to the journals. But it was immediately contradicted, as have been similar statements made subsequently, & not withstanding the statutes of limitation many persons still indulge the pleasing fancy that they are NEXT OF KIN.

MON APR 12, 1858
On Fri last the 2 negroes, Alex'r Anderson & Henry Richards, convicted of the murder of Mrs Garber & Mrs Ream, expiated their crime on the gallows, at Lancaster, Pa.

Hon Thos Hart Benton, of Missouri, died on Apr 10, in his 77th year, having been born on Mar 14, 1782. His malady was cancer in the intestines, a painful disease, which had wasted him for 2 or 3 months. It is a courious circumstance that the youngest & the oldest of the family should have died within a few hours of each other under the same roof. An nfant grandson of Col Benton, the child of Mr Wm Carey Jones, died in the house of his grandfather yesterday morning, & the nurseling & the grandsire now lie side by side in death on the same bier. The remains of both will be placed in the railroad cars this afternoon on their way to St Louis for interment.

Appointments by the Pres, by & with the advice & consent of the Senate:
Collector of Customs: Jesse J Simkins, Norfolk, Va, vice Sawyer.
Surveyors of the Customs:
Chas Shelton, New Haven, Conn; reappointed.
Walter Havens, Greenport, N Y; reappointed.
Sidney S Norton, Port Jefferson, N Y; reappointed.
Thos B Atkinson, Camden, N J, vice Mickle.
W H Richardson, Snow Hill, vice Parker, deceased.
Champe B Thornton, Port Royal, Va; reappointed.
G W Merchant, Dumfires, Va; reappointed.
Registers of Land Offices:
Saml Plumber at Faribault, Minn; reappointed.
W A Caruthers at Sauk Rapids, Minn; reappointed.
G A Clitherall at Otter Tail, Minn; reappointed.
Chas G Wagner at Stillwater, Minn; reappointed.
Receivers of Public Money:
John D Evans at Forest City, Minn
B F Tillotson at Fairbault, Minn; reappointed.
S L Hays at Sauk Rapids, Minn; reappointed.

Mr Wm D Brown died at Nashville, Tenn, a few days since, in consequence of swallowing, during sleep, a piece of gold plate & 3 artificial teeth, which he had forgotten to remove on retiring to bed.

The N Y Journal of Fashion is a large quarto periodical, issued monthly, & edited by Miss Marie Louis Hawkins & Fannie Lucelle, both of whom are now in the city, at the Nat'l Hotel, & will be happy to receive subscriptions, or personal calls after 4½ P M. The Journal is $3 per annum. Single copies can be had of the usual news-venders.

A correspondent of the N Y Times gives an account of the burning of a whole family in a house, in LeRoy, near Watertown, N Y, on Apr 4. Mr Comstock, the owner & occupant of the house, was a farmer, & he & his 4 daughters, the oldest only 10 years of age, were sleeping in one bed room. Their bodies were found in different places as they doubtless rushed out with their father in the darkness, but were blinded by the smoke & flames. Mrs Comstock was absent at the time, having been in Auburn for 2 months past under medical treatment. A letter from her was received at the post ofc the morning after the calamity, telling them she would be coming home next week. Signed-A M C.

Excellent & nearly new household & kitchen furniture at auction on: Apr 16, at the late residence of J W Weeks, deceased, on Indiana ave, between 1st & 2nd sts. –A Green auct

The funeral of Col Benton will be performed today at 2 o'clock, at the late residence of Col Benton, on C st. Immediately after, the remains of Col Benton, & those of his grandson, just deceased, will be conveyed to the railroad depot for their removal to St Louis, to be interred in the family burial place. Pass-bearers of the deceased Senatro:

Gen Jesup, U S Army
Gen Saml Houston, of Texas
Gov Floyd, of Va
W W Seaton, of Wash

Hon Jas B Clay, of Ky
W H Appleton, of N Y
Jacob Hall, of Missouri
John C Rives, of Wash

Criminal Court-Wash-Sat: 1-Jos Bulgar, colored, was convicted of stealing 108 half dollars & a revolver from Frederic Dawes. 2-Henry Martin was found not guilty for an assault & battery with intent to kill Augustus Norton, near the 7th st road, on Feb 28 last. 3-Fanny Neale, colored, was found guilty for cruelly beating & maltreating a colored child 8 years of age.

Died: on Apr 11, at the late residence of his grandfather, in Wash City, McDowell Jones, youngest child [in his 16th month] of Wm Cary Jones & Mrs Eliza Benton Jones. His funeral services will be performed at the residence on C st at 2 o'clock today.

Orphans Court of Wash Co, D C. Letters of administration on the personal estate of Richd G Hyatt, late of Wash Co, deceased. –Jas Laurenson, R T McLaine, adms

TUE APR 13, 1858
Senate: 1-Ptn from Wm Wheelright, asking that measures may be taken for the establishment of additional communication with the South American States by mail steamers: referred. 2-Additional evidence in the case of A G Allen, late Navy Agent at Wash City: referred. 3-Soldiers' Home: Geo Mason & others of the Military asylum in Wash, asking that an allowance be made to them for their support, instead of subjecting them to the alternative of remaining inmates of the said asylum. 4-Cmte on Patents: memorial of Bancroft Woodcock, submitted an adverse report on the same: agreed to. Same cmte: adverse report on the memorial of John A & Hiram Pitts, & that they have leave to withdraw their papers: agreed to. 5-Cmte on Naval Affairs: bill for the relief of F M Gunnell, passed assist surgeon in the navy: agreed to. Same cmte: adverse reports on the memorials of Saml James, Ignatius Lucas, Chas Tilley, & Thos S Burgey: agreed to. 6-Cmte on Claims: adverse reports upon the memorial of Ambrose Whitlock & of Rinaldo Johnson: agreed to. 7-Papers of the heirs of Gen Stephen Maylan, deceased, be referred to the Cmte on Revolutionary Claims.

Great sale by order of Chancery Court of real estate on the Island: in the cause of the U S vs Schwartz, Livingston, et al, of the whole of squares 468, 469, 470, & 498, & lots 82 thru 84, in subdivision of square No 465. –W S Cox, trustee -J C McGuire, auct

The funeral of the deceased Ex-Senator Benton was performed yesterday, at his late residence. The services were conducted by Rev Mr Hall, of the Protestant Episcopal Church, & Rev B Sunderland, of the Presbyterian Church. The body was conveyed, by the pall bearers & a large procession, to the railroad station, together with the remains of his deceased grand-child, & there deposited on a car to be taken to St Louis, in charge of Wm Carey Jones & Richd T Jacob, sons-in-law of Col Benton.
+
Col Benton names as his executors, & also as trustees of his daughters, his sons-in-law, Wm Carey Jones, John Chas Fremont, & Richd Taylor Jacob, & his friends Montgomery Blair & Philips Lee. The entire remaining library is bequeathed to Mr Jones, who thus becomes the literary legatee. The fourth son-in-law, than whom neither of them is more respected-M Boileau, is not named as one of the executors, on account probably of his remote permanent residence, he being Consul-General of France at Calcutta.

Colonization Society of Va: ofcrs of the Society for 1858. <u>Pres:</u> John Rutherford
<u>Vice Presidents:</u>

Govn'r Wise	Judge Caskie
W H Macfarland	Judge Tyler
Judge Moncure	Wyndham Robertson
Jas C Bruce	John H Cocke
Alex Stuart	

<u>Managers:</u>

P V Daniel, jr	Dr Palmer
P R Grattan	Dr Parker
John O Steger	Jas Dunlop
John Howard	W H Haxall
Jas Thomas, jr	J P Taylor
Dr w H Gwathmey	John M Patton, jr
G W Randolph	Philip Price
M Gretter	Nicholas Mills
R Whitfield	Fleming Jones
Saml Putney	

<u>Sec:</u> Fred'k Bransford; <u>Treasurer:</u> Thos H Ellis; <u>Gen Superintendent</u>: Rev P Slaughter
<u>Agent for Emigrants:</u> Rev W H Starr

Brvt Col Chas A May, major 2nd dragoons, is ordered to report at Carlisle barracks, Pa, for the purpose of conducting the recruits at that station to their respective regts in Utah.

A young man named Andrew Kyle, a printer, was drowned on Sunday in Gtwn. He was walking on the edge of the canal & fell in by accident. He had an excellent character & was much respected by a numerous acquaintance.

Died: on Apr 11, in Wash City, George Washington, infant son of Jas F & Eliza Gibson, aged 9 months. His funeral will take place this afternoon at 4 o'clock, from 334 18th st, between I & K sts.

Died: on Mar 27, at his residence, near Fredericksburg, Va, Capt Geo Hamilton, in his 85th year. A kind & provident father, a mild master, & true friend, an obliging neighbor, many will feel his loss. He had served in the war of 1812, winning the cordial respect of his fellow officers. Several times a member of the Legislature, he was long a useful magistrate & influential citizen.

Criminal Court-Wash-Mon: The trial of Jas Powers for the murder of Edw A Lutts on Dec 7 last-the following jury was chosen:

Thos Riggles	Washington Wallingsford
Thos Proby	Wm H Perkins
John H Trunnel	Alfred Hurdle
Wm Cooper	Joshua Hilton
Jeremiah Smith	Richd Butt
Theodore Meade	Thos D Larner

Witnesses: John Adamson; Mr Danl Smith. Court adjourned, the prosecution not having closed its testimony. [Apr 14th newspaper: first witness-John Carr, brother-in-law of the deceased. Eugene Lanahan; Wm P Smith; Mr John Wade; Michl Gormley; John Powers-brother of the prisoner; John Shotwell, J J Kelly; John McEwen; Mrs Mary Ellen Grady; & Wm Riley, all testified. The Court adjourned.] [Apr 15th newspaper: on Apr 14th the jury returned with a verdict of guilty.] [Apr 19th newspaper: Jas Powers, convicted of the murder of Edw A Lutts, was sentenced to death. His brother, John Powers, appeared more touched by the situation than by the prisoner himself.] [Jun 11th newspaper: John Powers stands sentenced to suffer the last penalty of the law & be executed on Jun 18.]

N Y, Apr 12. 1-Thos R Whitney, formerly member of Congress from Wash City, died today. 2-A Paris letter reports the death of Gen Thomas, Assist Sec of State under the last Administration. The cause was typhoid fever.

WED APR 14, 1858
Senate: 1-Ptn from Lt Jno C Carter, U S Navy, asking that a declaratory act may be passed by which he can receive the sum of $955.36 due him, & which is detained by the accounting officers of the Treasury, owing to some alleged ambiguity in the word of the law passed for his relief Feb 13, 1855: referred. 2-Ptn from Jonathan M Burnett, auditor of the State of Va, asking the payment of a judgment recovered against that State by the administrator of Jas Holmes, deceased, for the commutation of said Holmes as paymaster in the army of the Revolution: referred. 3-Ptn from Jason Smith & others, asking to be allowed pensions for military services in the war of 1812: referred. 4-Ptn from Lt E Carrington Bowers, who was placed on furlough & afterwards transferred to leave service, asking to be allowed the difference of pay between those positions: referred. 5-Ptn from W Brenton Boggs, a purser in the North Pacific Exploring Expedition, asking to be allowed additional pay: referred. 6-Ptn from Jas T Wild & other heirs of Danl Wild, asking indemnity for French spoliations prior to 1800: referred. 7-Ptn from Israel Moses, asking that an improved ambulance which he has invented for the safe & easy transportation of the sick & wounded may be adopted in the army: referred. 8-Cmte on Foreign Relation: bill for the relief of Townshend Harris, asking compensation for diplomatic services in negotiating a treaty with Siam. 9-Cmte on Private Land Claims:

referred the memorial of Agnes Slack & the heirs of de Repentigny, submitted a report, with a bill authorizing the courts to adjudicate the claim of the legal reps of the Sieur de Bonne & Charles de Repentigny to certain lands in the Saut Sainte Marie, in the State of Michigan. Same cmte: adverse report on the ptn of J W Morse. 10-Cmte on Military Affairs: act for the relief of Adam D Stewart, & of Alex'r Randall, exc of Danl Randall. 11-Cmte on Revolutionary Claims: adverse reports on the following cases: in that of Nancy Hammond, daughter of Capt Jas Dennison; in that of Eliz A Middleton, heir of Capt Belair Posey; in that of Martha Brown, widow of Silas Brown; & in the case of Catharine Lydia McLeod, heir of Ebenezer Markham. 12-Cmte of Claims: adverse report on the memorial of Richd G Dove, for increased compensation for duties performed as assistant messenger in the Third Auditor's ofc. 13-Cmte on Pensions: bill for the relief of Anthony Caslo, a soldier of the war of 1812. Same cmte: adverse reports in the cases of Dr Adam Hayes, a surgeon in the war of 1812; & upon that of citizens of Michigan for the extension of Thos Fitzgerald's pension to his children. 14-Bill for the relief of John L Allen & Asa R Carter: passed. 15-Bill to settle the accounts of Luther Jewett, late collector of the district of Portland & Falmouth, in Maine: passed. 16-Bill for the relief of Fabius Stanly: passed. 17-Bill for the relief of Jos Hardy & Alton Long: postponed.

The <u>Stuyvesant Pear Tree</u>, which stands on the corner of Third ave & 13th st, N Y, is again in bud. It was planted in 1547, 211 years ago.

Obit-died: on Apr 4, at **Gay Mont**, Caroline Co, Va, John H Bernard, aged 67. His death, though sudden, was not unexpected. His constitution, always delicate, after resisting repeated attacks, at last gave way, & he was numbered with the dead. He was ever a devoted husband, a kind & affectionate father. He left no enemies, but warm friends.

Died: yesterday, in Wash City, of typhoid fever, Sue, 2nd daughter of Geo Savage, in her 18th year. Her funeral services are tomorrow at 10 o'clock at St Patrick's Church.

From Calif: N Y, Apr 13. In Oregon Lt Allen, who was reported to have perished in the snow, had arrived at Portland, having been abandoned by all his party except one.

THU APR 15, 1858
Calif-San Francisco Chronicle of Mar 20. 1-On Feb 22 S H Stevens, lately from Brighton, Mass, was drowned in Eel river. 2-Thos Waterman was accidentally shot at Benicia on Mar 8. 3-Robt Canon, of Ohio, was killed in El Dorado Co on Mar 9 by the falling of a bank of earth. 4-Mrs Oden & 4 children, with Miss Burns, were burnt to death in a house near San Juan, Monterey Co, on Mar 13. 5-Mr Benjamin & his son were murdered by Indians on Mar 5, on the head waters of Payne's Creek, in the northern part of this State. 6-John Murphy was drowned in San Joaquin river, near Stockton, on Mar 16. 7-Danl Sutter was killed by a Chileno in Centreville, Nevada Co, on Mar 8. 8-The Supreme Court of this State has rendered a decision adverse to the interests of J C Fremont, in the matter of his right to the gold taken from his land in Mariposa Co.

J W Gray, editor of the Cleveland Plaindealer, lost the sight of one eye on Friday last from the explosion of a percussion cap which his little son was firing from a toy gun.

Robt *Pullen, alias Robt Walker, & Wm J Somerville, indicted for entering the U S Customhouse at Richmond, on Oct 12, 1857, & stealing $20,688 in coin from the safe, were arraigned for trial on Monday in the Circuit Court. [Apr 16th newspaper: Somerville was found guilty & sentenced to the penitentiary for 3 years. *Pollen, an accomplice in the robbery, was on Monday sentenced to 8 years' imprisonment in the penitentiary.] *Two spellings for the name Pullen/Pollen.

Obit-died: Gen Wm Marks, who was a member of the Pa Legislature as early as 1810, & for 6 years Pres of the Senate of Pa, died on Sat last. In 1827 he was elected to the U S Senate & served a term of 6 years. He was contemporary with Webster, Calhoun, Van Buren, Benton, Berrien, Hayne & others of the great men of that day; & he died about the same hour & at nearly the same age as Col Benton, with whom he served for 6 years on the Cmte on Military Affairs, & between whom, although different politically, there always existed the closest personal friendship. -Ledger

Senate: 1-Cmte on Indian Afairs: claims of R D Rowland & of Jas M Crook, submitted a report, with a bill for the relief of the heirs or legal reps of Richd D Rowland, deceased. 2-Cmte on Naval Affairs: bill for the benefit of the captors of the British brig **Caledonia**, in the war of 1812, & recommended its passage. 3-Cmte on the Judiciary: bill for the relief of Wm Cruikshank, J S Black, Calhoun Bonham, & Fred'k A Sawyer, of San Francisco. 4-Cmte on the District of Columbia: bill for the relief of Michl Nash. 5-Cmte on Military Affairs: asked to be discharged from the consideration of the memorial of Alex'r Mill, & that it be referred to the Cmte of Claims.

J Addison Thomas, whose death in Paris was mentioned, graduated at West Point in 1834. He left the army & entered the practice of law in N Y C; was appointed a com'r to adjust claims between American citizens & the English gov't under Pres Pierce, & afterwards became Assist Sec of State under Gov Marcy. He went abroad less than a year ago with his family, & has resided in Paris, where his children are being educated. -N Y Post

Last week a young man, Lewis W Reaherd, employed as a clerk in the Brownsville, Pa, post ofc, was arrested for purloining a letter from the mail, & lodged in the county jail for trial. He was caught by a decoy letter & has acknowledged his guilt.

For sale, a pair of stylish Bay Horses. Apply at my stables, on 12th st, near K. -Wm Shields

Mrd: on Apr 8, at the McKendree Parsonage, by Rev D Ball, Mr John Knowles to Mrs Martha Middleton.

Mrd: on Apr 13, at McKendree Chuch, by Rev Mr Ball, Mr Isaac Talks to Miss Mary A Hollidge.

Mrd: on Apr 14, by Rev John C Smith, Francis H Smith to Miss Anna E, daughter of Cyrus Birge, all of Wash City.

Died: on Apr 14, Thomas Johnston, youngest son of Moses & Mary W Kelly, aged 3 years & 4 months. His funeral will take place this afternoon, at a quarter past 4 o'clock, from the residence of his parents, 372 Fourth st, between E & F sts.

N Y, Apr 14. The ship **John Gilpin**, from Honolulu for New Bedford, was lost off Cape Horn, & the crew & passengers, numbering 15, were saved by the British ship **Herefordshire**, 5 of whom were transferred to the ship **Sunny South**, which has arrived at N Y. They were Mrs Wood & 2 children, & Messrs Sherwood & Ford.

FRI APR 16, 1858
N Y C, Apr 14, 1858. Inequality in the terms of punishment awarded to malefactors is sometimes very striking. Michl Wogan is sentenced to 4 years' imprisonment for killing Michl Cassidy, because he meant to kill somebody else, whilst John Meroney is sentenced to 20 years for killing Henry Hamilton.

Melancholy Event. On Sat last Mr Ira Wells & his father, Peterson Wells, an esteemed resident of this county, were about to start out in pursuit of wild turkeys, when young Wells' gun discharged & the entire contents entered through his mouth up to the brain. The unfotunate youth never spoke afterwards. –Petersburg [Va] Democrat, from Dinwiddie Court-house.

Senate: 1-Ptn from the children of Stephen Krebs, a citizen of the Choctaw tribe of Indians, asking to be allowed other land in lieu of that to which they were entitled under the treaty of 1830 with the Choctaw Indians: referred. 2-Ptn from J W Sullivan, asking remuneration for losses sustained by the repeated failure of the mails between New Orleans & San Francisco: referred. 3-Ptn from T B Miller, asking to be allowed a pension on account of injuries received while a teamster in the army: referred. 4-Ptn from the widow of Jacob G Wingard, asking to be paid for the services of her late husband in the ofc of the First Comptroller: referred. 5-Cmte on Public Lands: bill for the relief of Francis Wlodecki: recommended its passage. Same cmte: bill for the relief of the legal reps or assignees of Jas Lawrence, & recommended its passage: was passed. 6-Cmte on Private Land Claims: bill configuring to Alex'r Copeland the title to 480 acres of land in Sonora Co, Calif. 7-Bill introduced for the relief of Edw Ingersoll was recommitted to the Cmte on Military Affairs. 8-Bills for the relief of Cmder Thos J Page, U S navy, & for the relief of Thos J Page, & they were severally passed. 9-Bills passed- relief of Mrs Agatha O'Brien, widow of Brvt Maj J P J O'Brien, lateof the U S army. Relief of Thos Phenix, jr. Relief of John Scott Hill, W House, & Saml O House. Bill to authorize the Sec of the Interior to issue land warrants to Jos Chase, Jas Young, & Alex'r Keef. 10-Cmte of Claims: bill for the relief of the heirs of Wm Kirby: passed. Bill for the relief of Dinah Minis: committed. Same cmte: bill for the relief of Dr Ferdinand O Miller: committed. 11-Cmte on Commerce: bill for the relief of the owners of the barque **Attica**, of Portland, Maine: passed. 12-Bill for the relief of Alonzo & Elbridge S Colbly: committed.

Sale of **Haddock's Hill Farm** by trustees in Chancery: by decree of the Circuit Court of Wash Co, D C, supplemental to a decree heretofore passed in a cause, No 1,066, in said Court, wherein Agnes M Easby is cmplnt, & Horatio N Easby, John W Easby, Wm R Smith & Wilhelmina M his wife, & Henry King & Marion E his wife, & Cecilia J Hyde, are dfndnts. Auction on May 8, of part of **Haddock Hills**, in Wash City, containing 46 acres, 1 rood & 7½ perches. –Wm B Webb, Richd H Clarke, Jos H Bradley, jr, trustees -Jas C McGuire, auct

Anti-Know-Nothing Convention to nominate a candidate for the Moyoralty of Wash City for the 2 years ensuing Jun 1 next met last evening: F McNerhany, Chairman; W P Mohun & J B Brandt, Sec & Assist Sec. Delegates:

W W Davis	W F Divine	M Duffy
Andrew Carroll	Dr Borrows	F McNerhany
Saml Stover	C P Wannall	J B Brandt
Wm Grebble	Edw Simms	T Altemus
Wm Fletcher	F W Birch	Richd Brooks
N Vedder	Dr Houston	V Conner
A B Stoughton	J Reese	E M Clark
John F Ennis	W P Mohun	Peter Hepburn, sr
Geo E Jillard	John J Mulloy	Jas E Johnson
L F Clark	W F Price	J T Cassell
P Gallant	G Oyster	H A Clarke
Wm Sibrey	J McGran	

Mrd: on Apr 10, in Wash City, by Rev Stephen P Hill, Chas H Morse to Eliz Wyman, all of Wash.

Died: on Apr 14, in Wash City, after an illness of 4 months, Mrs Sarah E Lewis, aged 41 years, wife of Reeve Lewis, formerly of Alexandria, Va. Her funeral is this afternoon at 2 o'clock, from her late residence, 289 B st south, near N J ave, Capitol Hill. [Jun 26th newspaper: the funeral of Reeve Lewis, master armorer at the arsenal, will take place this morning at 10 o'clock. His wife died on Apr 15, about 18 days after her husband was so wantonly & fatally wounded.]

Died: on Mar 25, at **Mount Vernon Arsenal**, near Mobile, Ala, Mary Emily Brereton, aged 23 years, youngest daughter of the late Dr J A Brereton, of the Army.

New Orleans, Apr 14. The boiler of the steamer **Falls City** exploded today as the boat was leaving the pier. Seven or eight persons were killed & others were injured. Mr John Simonds was among the wounded.

Fine farm for sale: known as the **Union Lands**, Sullivan Co, Tenn: 800 acres, more or less; with 2 comfortable farm houses & out houses. A plot of the estate may be seen by applying to the agent, Wm S Holiday, Broker, No 2 Todd's Marble Bldg, Wash, D C.

SAT APR 17, 1858
Prof Harvey, of Madison Univ, N Y, baptized on Apr 7 Saml Santhara, a native of Japan. He is a young man, who has been for some time supported by friends in N Y in a course of study, & is the only survivor of a Japanese crew who were wrecked on the Northern Pacific. It is in contemplation to make him a missionary to his own people.

Senate: 1-Ptn from Berlinna S Hutchinson, widow of a volunteer in Capt Nelson's company of Georgia mounted volunteers in the Mexican war, asking to be allowed a pension: referred. 2-Ptn from Geo Stealey, asking compensation for services & expenses while on a mission to the Indian tribes in the northern part of Calif under authority of the Indian commissioners in 1850-51: referred. 3-Cmte of Claims: bill for the relief of Geo W Floor. Same cmte: bill for the relief of Aaron Haight Palmer. 4-Cmte on Pensions: bill for the relief of G Alonzo Breast. 5-Cmte on Indian Affairs: bill for the relief of Anson Dart, reported it back with amendments. 6-**Bills passed-relief of**:

Saml V Niles
Edw D Reynolds
Geo W Lippitt
Eleazer Williams
John Robb
Edw N Kent
Otway N Berryman
Ashton S H White
Livingston, Kincaid & Co
Michl Nash, of D C
T Hart Hyatt
N C Weems, of La
Legal reps of J I Martin
Heirs of Alex'r Stevens
Chas T Scaife, adm of Gilbert Stalker
Heirs of John Brest, a soldier in the war of 1812
F M Gunnell, passed assist surgeon in the navy
Hannah Stroop, widow of John Stroop, deceased
Noah Smith, late a private in the U S army
Heirs or legal reps of Richd D Rowland, deceased, & others
Manuel Leisa, Joachim Leisa, & others: provide for location of certain private land claims
Mrs Harriet O Reed, excx of the late Brvt Col A C W Fanning, of the U S army
Heirs & legal reps of Olivier Landry, of the State of Louisiana
Mrs Eliza A Merchant, widow of the late 1st Lt & Brvt Capt Chas G Merchant, U S army
Settlement of the accounts of the late Capt John W McCrabb
Confirm to Wm Marvin title to certain lands in East Florida
Confirmation of a certain land claim in favor of Pierre Grignon, or his legal reps
Explanatory act approved Aug 18, 1856, entitled-an act for the relief of Adam D Steuart & of Alex'r Randall, exc of Danl Randall

Sale pursuant to the provisions of 2 deeds of trust executed by Jas Williams & wife to the subscriber, dated Jun 21, 1853 & one dated Jan 28, 1854, of the land records of Wash Co, D C, in Liber J A S No 75, folios 109 thru 113: sale of all the title & estate of said Williams & wife in part of No 1 in square 166, at the intersection of 7th st & Pa ave, with a large brick bldg thereon. –Silas H Hill, J B H Smith, trustee -A Green auct

Geo W Stovall, convicted at New Orleans of the murder of Mary Durand, was executed on Apr 9, all efforts to induce the Govn'r to commute the sentence having failed. Stovall made a speech from the scaffold, acknowledging his guilt.

House of Reps: 1-Court of Claims: adverse reports on the ptns of Augustine Demers & others, adms of Francis Chaudonet; of Joshua R Jewett, heir of Jos Jewett; of Robt C Thompson, adm of Wm Thompson; of Ellen Martin, heir at law of Francis Martin; of Francis Nadeau, heir of Basil Nadeau. 2-Adverse reports with the recommendation that they be referred to appropriate cmtes: ptns of Robt Harrison, of Abraham King, adm of John Mandeville; of Abraham R Woolley, of Thos Phenix, jr, of David Myerle. 3-Bill for the relief of Richd H Weightman, [elected a U S Senator from Mexico] was laid aside with the recommendation that it do not pass. 4-Bill for the relief of Geo W Biscoe & for the relief of Capt Jas McIntosh, U S navy, were laid aside to be reported to the House. 5-Ptn of Joshua R Jewett: referred to the Cmte of Claims. 6-Bill for the relief of Cassius M Clay was passed.

The U S steam frig **Susquehanna**, Capt Joshua R Sands, arrived at N Y on Thu from Nicaragua, via Port Royal, Jamaica, where 6 officers & 57 men were landed, sick with yellow fever. She has had 155 cases in all, & 17 deaths are known. She is now detained at quarantine below N Y. The following are the names of those who died:
Mar 20: Littleton Boyer, Capt's after-guard, at Greytown
Mar 23: John Hodnott, ships' steward, at Greytown
Mar 24: Wm J Fougeray, boy, at Greytown
Mar 25: Fred'k Tonndorf, marine, at sea
Apr 3: Cpl Burns, Marine Corps, at sea
Apr 4: *Lt Henry W Queen, marine corps, at sea
Apr 4: Jas Robinson, seaman, at sea
Apr 5: Geo Geyger, fireman, at sea
Apr 5: C H Conway, hospital steward, at sea
Apr 6: Thos Moran, marine, at sea
Apr 6 & 8: Thos C Howe, seaman at Port Royal
        J W J Jones, Landsman, at Port Royal[Remains committed to the deep.]
        Jas Flynn, boy, at Port Royal
        O Balestier, bandmaster, at Port Royal
Apr 11: Jas Read, sailmaker's mate, at sea
Apr 15: Jas Price, seaman, at sea
The **Susquehanna** has been absent about 2 years, during which time she has visited the Mediterranean, taken part in the Atlantic telegraph expedition, & latterly been stationed on the coast of Central America. While lying in the harbor of Greytown, on the 19th ult, the yellow fever broke out among her crew. Surgeon Pinkney, from his attention to the sick, was seized with fever, but his place was filled by Dr Maccoun, who has had much experience in this disease. This is a list of the English medical officers in charge of the sick at Port Royal, Jamaica: Chas R Kinnear, Deputy Inspector; Dr Burke, Staff Surgeon & Storekeeper; Jas Sarsfield Borry, Assist Surgeon; Mr Lewis, Assist Surgeon.
*Lt Queen: Remains committed to the deep. He on several occasions distinguished himself before the enemy during the Mexican war.

The body of Geo W Durfee, of Gloucester, R I, was found suspended to a tree near Slatersville, R I, on Apr 2. A gold watch, $10 in money, & $300 in notes were found in his pocket. He had been employed in Burrillville during the winter, & was last seen alive 7 weeks ago.

D W D Cameron, said to be the owner of considerable real estate & other property in N Y, has occupied for the past 5 years apartments the upper part of No 69 Fulton st. The entire furniture in the whole of the spacious rooms was a single cot, 2 rickty chairs, & a plain pine table. Being unmarried, he has lived the life of a bachelor recluse. On Sunday he was found lying on his cot in an enfeebled state from starvation & died that day.

A large amount of valuable jewels & jewelry have been stolen between Nov last & the present time from Miss M C Williams, at Arlington House, in Alexandria Co. The property has only been missed within a day or two.

Criminal Court-Wash-Fri: 1-Ann Bell, Mary Wakelin, & Rebecca Tillman, were found not guilty for riot on Mar 8 last. 2-If the witnesses living at a distance can be brought on in time, the case of John Essex for the murder of Owen Quigley will be tried next week.

An act of pure wanton ferocity was committed yesterday near the Railroad depot. John White, about 26, recently discharged from shipboard, ran up to 2 wayfarers, Martin Duncan & Mich McNulty, with a large jack-knife & cut Duncan's clothing & inflicted a bad wound on the left side of the lower abdomen of McNulty. He was arrested by ofcrs Nash & Harrover & committed to prison in default of $1,000 bail. The wounded man was also committed to prison as a witness.

On Sunday last the wife of Mr John Logan, of Bloomingdale, N J, met with a very sudden death. Mr Logan left the house for a few moments, & on his return found her standing on the outside of the house with her head in the window, & the sash resting on the back of her neck. She was dead.

Lt De Mercy, of the French army, belonging by birth to a noble family, & son-in-law of the Marchioness de Chatelier, has been condemned to be shot for the assassination of a brother officer, a lt in the same regt. He invited the lt to his room & then killed him with his sabre. His defence was that he killed him in a duel fought without witnesses.

Two men, Louis Hectig & Geo Thompson have been arrested in Wash City for participation in the shameless proceeding at the railroad depot in Alexandria, on Apr 4, whereby a colored girl was shot in the mouth. There is strong evidence that Hectig fired the pistol by which the girl was wounded.

Died: on Apr 15, after a short & painful illness, John A M Duncanson, in his 55th year, one of our most worthy & esteemed fellow citizens & a native of Wash. His funeral will take place on Sunday, at 3 o'clock, from his late residence, 478 H st, between 9th & 10th.

St Louis, Apr 16. Yesterday the remains of Col Benton were exposed in state in Mercantile Library Hall; at least 25,000 persons visited. The final rites of sepulture took place this morning. The streets were densely crowded with thousands of spectators. [Apr 19th newspaper: the funeral rites of Col Benton, at St Louis, were on Friday last. The remains were taken from the hall of the Mercantile Library to the Second Presbyterian Church, where the service was performed by Rev Mr Cowan, assisted by Rev Dr Anderson & Rev Mr Brooks. The body was placed in the hearse & was followed to the **Bellefonte Cemetery** by a most imposing procession. The body of McDowell Jones, a grand-child of Mr Benton, was conveyed to the tomb at the same time.]

N Y, Apr 16. 1-A London letter states that on Apr 1 Geo Peabody paid all his indebtedness to the Bank of England, thereby releasing all his securities held by that establishment. 2-A duel occurred at Paris between Mr Calhoun, Sec of the American Legation, & Mr Breevort, of N Y. Shots were once exchanged, when, owing to an informality in the arrangements, the seconds interfered.

MON APR 19, 1858
Trustee's sale of house & lot, by virtue of a deed of trust from Enoch Ambush, dated Aug 4, 1855, recorded in Liber J A S No 102, folios 226, among the land records of Wash Co, D C: public auction on May 22, of lot 33 in square 388, with a good frame dwlg house & premises. –Richd H Clarke, Erasmus J Middlton, trustee -Jas C McGuire, auct

Trustee's sale of house & lot, by 2 several deeds of trust from Wm Bigley, deceased, & wife, dated Jan 14, 1853, & Jun 10, 1854, recorded in Liber J A S No 51 folios 203, & Liber J A S No 78, folios 216, among the land records for Wash Co, D C: public auction on Mar 24, 1858, of part of lot 1 in square 397, with a good framed dwlg house & premises. –Richd H Clarke, Erasmus J Middleton, trustee -Jas C McGuire, auct

The death of John Greig, of Canandaigua, N Y, caused a vacancy in the Board of Regents of the N Y Univ, which has been filled by the appointment of Wm Cullen Bryant, editor of the N Y Evening Post.

Gen Wm Millburn died at St Louis on Apr 12. He was an Englishman by birth, but had resided for over 30 years in Va & the West. He was formerly Surveyor Genr'l of Ill & Mo, & sheriff of St Louis Co.

The steam frig **Wabash** is now preparing for the Mediterranean squadron at the navy yard, Brooklyn, N Y. The following are her officers: Flag Ofcr, E A F Lavallette; Capt, Saml Barron; Lts, C R P Rogers, Silas Bent, Thos G Corbin, Watson Smith, John H Bassett, E W Henry, & John Taylor Wood; Surgeon of the Fleet, Wm Johnson; Passed Assist Surgeon, J Rudenstein; Assist Surgeon, J S Kitchen; Chief Engineer, B F Garvin; 1st Assist Mate, N P Patterson & M Fletcher; 2nd Assists, E W Manning & J B Kimball; 3rd Assists, J W Thompson, G B N Tower, M H English, & J H Butler.

Senate: 1-Additional papers submitted in relation to the claims of J C Irwin & Co & J & R H Porter: referred. 2-Papers relative to the claims of Benj Page & Henry E Page, heirs of Benj Page, for indemnity for spoliations by the French prior to 1800: referred. 3-Ptn from the heirs of Robt & John Montgomery, asking indemnity for spoliations by the French prior to 1800: referred. 4-Ptn from Thos G Clinton, suggesting changes in the present patent laws: referred. 5-Cmte on Commerce: bill for the relief of Chas Knapp.

House of Reps: 1-Cmte on Commerce: adverse report on the ptn of Alfred Ludlan & others, of Gloucester, Mass, for compensation for the loss of a schooner: laid on the table. 2-Bill for the relief of Isaac Body & Saml Fanning: committed. 3-Cmte on the Post Ofc & Post Roads: adverse report in the case of R F M Mann, of Ga: laid on the table. Bill for the relief of the legal reps of Robt H Morris, late postmaster in N Y C: committed. Joint resolution for the relief of Henry Orndorf, of Ohio: committed. Bill for the relief of Saml W Turner & Alvin A Turner: committed. Same cmte: bill for the relief of John Deamit: committed. Same cmte: bill for the relief of Stuckley & Rogers; & of Wm Doty & others: both committed. Adverse report in the case of Jas M Harris, of Fla: laid on the table. Bill for the relief of J W Hilton, of Ill, committed. 4-Cmte on the Judiciary: adverse report in the case of Saml M Prickett: laid on the table. Same cmte: adverse in the case of Wm A Forward, assignee of Jos S Saucher: laid on the table. 5-Cmte on Revolutionary Claims: bills for the relief of the reps of Henry King, deceased, & for the relief of the Presbyterian Church at Princeton, N J: committed. Same cmte: adverse on the ptn of the heirs of Saml Russell: laid on the table. Same cmte: bill for the relief of the heirs of Maj John Ripley: committed. Same cmte: bills for the relief of the heirs of Benj Wilson, & for the relief of the heirs of Dr Benj Chapin, deceased, late a surgeon in the navy of the Revolution: committed. Same cmte: adverse report in the cases of Wm B Goodwin, Obadiah Hardesty, Wm Rickman, & John McDowell: laid on the table. Same Cmte: bill for the relief of the legal reps of Capt David Noble, deceased: committed. 6-Cmte on Private Land Claims: bill for the relief of Job Stafford, of the State of N Y; relief of Eliz M Brier, only surviving child & heir of Col Archibald Loughry, deceased: both committed. 7-Cmte on Indian Affairs: bill for the relief of the heirs of John B Hand: committed. Same cmte: adverse report in the case of Thos G Asbury; & adverse report in the case of Jesse Morrison: both laid on the table. Same cmte: bill for the relief of M M Marmaduke & others: committed. 8-Cmte on Military Affairs: bill for the relief of Maj Jeremiah Y Dashiel, paymaster of the U S army, [granting him $2,515 for money lost by him in crossing a river in Florida on the way to pay troops;] which was passed. Bill for the relief of Brvt Maj Jas L Donaldson, assist quartermaster U S army: committed. Same cmte: bill for the relief of the adm of Horatio Boultbee, deceased: committed. Adverse report in the case of Angeline C Bowman, widow of Capt F L Bowman, deceased: laid on the table. Same cmte: adverse report on the bill for the relief of Maj Benj Alvord, paymaster U S army: laid on the table. Same cmte: adverse report in the case of Benj D Hyam: laid on the table. Same cmte: bill for the relief of Wm B Dodd: committed. Bill for the relief of Eleazer Williams, sole heir of Mary Ann Williams & Thos Williams, deceased: committed. [The bill directs that $11,000 be paid to the Rev Eleazer Williams for services rendered & losses incurred by his father, Thos Williams, in the war of 1812; also, that he be allowed an annual pension of $219, from May 1, 1855, to the close of his life.] Adverse report on the ptn of F W Lander: laid on the table. Same cmte: adverse report in the case of Lt J C McFerran: laid on the table. Ptn of Geo C Gebhardt & 89 others, citizens of Iowa, to be permitted to raise 2,000 volunteers for Utah: laid on the table. 9-Cmte on Naval Affairs: bill for the relief of the legal reps of Wm B Draper; for the relief of Dr Geo H Howell; & for the relief of Nehemiah S Draper & Wm Draper, heirs of Mary Draper, deceased: all committed. 10-Cmte on Invalid Pensions: adverse reports in the cases of Nicholas Fooks, Geo W Whittier, John Pangburn, Robt W Cauth, & Lucinda E Cureton: laid on the table. Bills for the relief of Elijah Close, of Tenn, granting invalid pensions to Wm Howell, of Tenn, to Conrad Schroeder, to Alex'r S Bean, of Pa, & for the relief of Michl A Deavenport, of Ill: committed. Bill for the relief of Wm Allen, of Portland, Maine: committed. Adverse report on the bill for the relief of the widow of Malachi F Randolph: laid on the table. Same cmte: bill to continue the pensions heretofore paid to Mary C Hamilton, widow of Capt Fowler Hamilton, late of the U S army: committed. Same cmte: bills for the relief of Wm Bullock; increasing the pension of A W Bayard, of Bellefonte, Pa; for the relief of Wright Force; & for the relief of Wyatt Griffith: committed. Adverse reports in the cases of Francis Carver, Geo D Dillon, of Pa, Geo Wever, Robt Jones, of Ky, Avery Stoddard, Nathl Dickinson, jr, Wm Long, Bartholomew C Renois, guardian of children of Jos Tremble, John Bonner, of Louisiana, & R L Gainness, of Tenn: laid on the table. Same cmte: bills for the relief of Robinson Gammon, of Frederich Smith, of Phineas G Pearson, of Judith Nott, & of John C Rathbun: committed. Adverse reports in the cases of Voucher Bonzinska & Ephraim Sharp: laid on the table. Same cmte: bills for the relief of Stephen Fellows, John Perry, of Ill, Ebenezer Hitchcock, Shove Chase, of N Y, & Allen Smith: committed. Adverse reports in the cases of C M Reeves, Alex'r Jones, Wm Johnson, Danl Morse, Mary M Carr, Jas P Bullock, Danl S Chapman, Richd W Stockton, Wm Israel, Pliny Story, Oliver Main, & Terrence Kirby: laid on the table. Same cmte: bill for the relief of David Watson: committed.

Orphans Court of Wash Co, D C. Letters of administration on the personal estate of Lauriston B Harden, late of Wash Co, deceased. –Geo D Fowle, Wm P Johnston, adms

Criminal Court-Wash-Sat: 1-John B Frizel found not guilty for larceny of a cow, the property of Mr Robt Beale. 2-Alex'r Eggleston was found not guilty for an assault & battery with intent to kill, at the 2nd Ward election. [Apr 28th newspaper: Alex'r Eggleston found guilty: sentenced to 3 months in jail for resisting the ofcr who apprehended him, & 3 years in jail & a fine of $20 for the assault on Wm Crampton.]

Mrd: on Apr 15, by Rev Wm H Chapman, Chas H Wilson to Miss Mgt Ann Scott, all of Wash City.

Died: on Apr 18, after a long & painful illness, Sarah Ellen, the eldest daughter of Richd Pettit, of Gtwn, & wife of Jno Alexander, of Wash City, in her 31st year. Her funeral will be on Apr 19, at 4 o'clock, from the residence of her mother-in-law, 531 12th st south, to proceed to Trinity Church, Gtwn, D C.

Died: on Apr 18, in Wash City, after a long & severe illness, Miss Catharine Hays, in her 16th year. Her funeral will take place on Apr 19 at 4 o'clock, from the residence of her mother, on 6th st east.

Died: on Apr 18, at his residence, on B & 8th sts, Island, Wm H Williams, aged 56 years & 2 days. His funeral will take place this afternoon at 3 o'clock.

TUE APR 20, 1858
Senate: 1-Ptn from Geo W Weston, Com'r of the State of Maine, urging an appropriation for the payment of an account of said State against the U S: referred. 2-Ptn from Thos Crown, asking damages in consequence of the arbitrary annulment of a contract by Capt _ence to furnish bricks for the fortifications at Oak Island: referred. 3-Ptn from Danl B Hibbard, asking an appropriation for the payment of his account for carrying the U S mail on special contract with the paymaster at St Johns, Michigan: referred. 4-Ptn from Jonas P Levy in relation to claims against the Republic of Mexico, & urging the interposition of Congress: referred. 5-Cmte on Foreign Relations: bill for the relief of Jeremiah Pendergast. Same cmte: bill for the relief of Randall Pegg.

The steam frig **Susquehanna**: among those landed sick of yellow fever at Port Royal from the **Susquehanna** were the following ofcrs: J C Howell, 2nd Lt; A Henderson, 2nd Assist Engineer; J A Grier, 3rd Assist Engineer; Wm H Cushman, 3rd Assist Engineer; Henry King, 3rd Assist Engineer; J J Lynne, Purser's Clerk.

Judge Eccleston, to whom Govn'r Hicks of Md tendered the Judgeship of the Judicial District, made vacant by the death of Judge Hopper, has declined the appointment. Judge Eccleston will remain on the bench of the Court of Appeals.

Scarlet fever is said to be very prevalent in Montg Co, Md. The Rockville Sentinel states that recently W G Robertson lost 2 children from it, Rev Mr Register one, & Mr Bowman has had all of his [7 in number] swept off.

Criminal Court-Wash-Mon: 1-Van Loman Johnson was put to trial on a charge of riot at the funeral of a child on Nov 8 last. Verdict, guilty. At the close of the trial Johnson was not to be found, & his bond was accordingly forfeited.

Died: on Apr 18, Miss Ann McMechen. Her funeral is this afternoon at 3 o'clock, from the residence of C F Lowrey, 313 6th st.

Died: on Apr 19, in Wash City, Chas Scrivner, in his 47th year, formerly of King Geo Co, Va, but for the last 20 years a resident of the District. His funeral is this afternoon at 4 o'clock, from his late residence, on M st, between 6th & 7th sts.

Died: on Apr 13, in Wayne Co, N C, of typhoid fever. Dr Marshall P Howard, formerly of Montg Co, Md.

Orphans Court of Wash Co, D C. Letters of administration on the personal estate of Richd Shaw, late of Wash Co, deceased. —Wm R Simmons, adm

WED APR 21, 1858
Court of Common Pleas of N Y C the following singular case was tried: Jane C Warner et al against Nathl H Wolfe, to recover damages for death of Wm H Warner, husband of plntf, killed, on passing along the sidewalk, by snow & ice thrown from the top of the house of Mr Wolfe, in 5th ave, while clearing it off. Verdict for the plntf, $3,500.

N Y, Apr 19. N Y correspondent of the Post: Our neighbor, Mr R Storrs Willis, of the N Y Musical World, has been unexpedtedly & sadly bereaved. His wife, young, amiable, & talented has been suddenly called away, leaving a family of 3 children, the youngest of whom is but a few days old. Her devoted husband is left desolate.

Senate: 1-Memorial from S Gilbert & others, asking that a grant of land may be made to aid in the construction of a ship canal round the Falls of Niagara: referred.

Lamentable accident occurred on the Parkersburg branch of the Balt & Ohio railroad on Fri night last: the engine was thrown off the track when it hit a horse. It fell into the river 30 feet below. Three men lost their lives: the engine man, C Hildebrandt; the fireman, W Clinton; a man who was learning the grades as a fireman, Henry Harvey. They were killed by the fall or by drowning. —Balt Patriot

Died: yesterday, Mrs Mary Daniel, wife of Mr J H Daniel, in her 28th year. Her funeral will take place from her late residence on 5th st, between G & H sts, this day at 4 o'clock.

THU APR 22, 1858
Senate: 1-Ptn from Robt F Gills, a soldier of the war of 1812: referred. 2-Papers in the case of Adam Sener for a pension: referred. 3-Ptn from the legal reps of Wm Bond & the legal reps of Wm Douglas, of the Revolutionary army, asking to be allowed interest on the half-pay paid under the act of Jun, 1834: referred. 4-Ptn from John H Merrick, asking payment for services rendered & expenses incurred as sheriff to a court established by the Alcalde in San Francisco in 1849, & to be indemnified for money expended in the relief of support of sick & disabled seamen: referred. 5-Cmte on Public Lands: asked to be discharged from the consideration of the case of Thos Maddin, & that leave be granted to withdraw the papers: agreed to. 6-Cmte on Naval Affairs: bill for the relief of A G Allen. Same cmte: bill for the relief of Duncan Robertson, reported it back without amendment, & asked its immediate consideration, which was agreed to.

Mrd: on Apr 15, at the residence of the bride's father, in Wash City, by Rev Bishop Pierce, D M Dubose of Memphis, Tenn, to Miss Sallie Toombs, only daughter of Hon R Toombs.

Mrd: on Apr 8, by Rev J G Henning, Dr Geo W Bowlen to Miss Felitia Edmonia Candler, all of Montg Co, Md.

Mrd: on Apr 14, at **Malvern**, near Alexandria, by Rt Rev Bishop Meade, Rev Richd R Mason to Nannie Van Dyke, youngest daughter of Rt Rev Bishop Johns, of Va.

Died: on Apr 20, in the vicinity of Wash City, at the residence of her son, Clark Mills, Mrs Juliana French, of Taylor, Courtlandt Co, N Y, in her 78th year. Her remains will be taken by her son to her former home in N Y. The friends of this venerable lady & those of Mr Mills are invited to attend at his house on Friday, at 12 o'clock.

Died: on Arp 14, at the residence of his mother, in St Mary's Co, Md, John L Spalding, late of Phil, in his 45th year.

Died: on Apr 21, Eliza, daughter of Jas F & Eliza Gibson, aged 5 years & 5 months. Her funeral will take place today at 4 o'clock, from their residence, 334 18th st, between I & K sts.

Criminal Court-Wash-Wed. 1-Trial of John Essex for the murder of Owen Quigley on Jun 2, 1856. Jury: Jas Rhodes, Benedict Hutchings, Thos Riggles, Jeremiah Smith, Alfred Hurdle, Thos Baker, John T Baker, Edwin Knowles, Geo D Spencer, Jas Towles, Jas W Barker, & Robt Cohen. The prisoner is defended by Jos H Bradley & Robt Ould. Witnesses: Dr Johnson Eliot; Dr Noble Young; Mr Hamilton D Metcalf; Dr Jas Fines, of Fauquier Co, Va; Mr Chas F Wood; & Andrew Sessford. Court adjourned. [Apr 23rd newspaper: witnesses: Chas H Payne; Jos Lawton; Danl McCarty, one of the companions of Essex at the time; Mark Mankin, of Alexandria; & Jas O Naylor. Court adjourned.]

Public sale of valuable land in upper Fauquier: by 2 deeds of trust executed by Jas Rogers & wife, the first to Richards Payne, dated Oct 13, 1855, & the second to R E Scott & John Spilman, dated Sep 24, 1858, recorded in the clerk's ofc of the county court of Fauquier Co, Va. Public auction on Jun 22, 1858, of a tract of land containing 866 acres of land, in said county, on the waters of Carter's run. Improvements consist of an elegant mansion & all necessary out-bldgs. –Richd Payne, R C Scott, Jno A Spilman

The Senate has confirmed Hon John Cadwallader as Judge of the eastern district court for Pa, vice Judge Kane, deceased; also, Mr Morton, of Nebraska, as Sec of that Territory.

Official information has been received at the Navy Dept of the death of Capt Benj Page. He died at N Y on Apr 16. Capt Page at the time of his death was on the retired list. He was born in England, entered the service Dec 17, 1810, & attained the rank of captain in 1811. He had seen 18 years' service, & was last at sea in 1850.

FRI APR 23, 1858
On Apr 14 Edgar Castine was shot dead in New Hanover Co, N C, by his brother-in-law, Noah Lanier. The land of the latter had been sold for debt & the former purchased it. On preparing to plant his crop Lanier approached him & shot him & his horse dead on the spot & then escaped. Castine was induced to purchase the land in consequence of having paid considerable security money for Lanier.

Senate: 1-Ptn from the widow of the late Brvt Brig Gen Chas Gratiot, setting forth that her husband was unjustly dismissed from the service of the U S, & asking to be allowed the amount of his pay, subsistence, & emoluments as colonel & chief of engineers of the army from the day of his dismission to that of his death: referred. 2-Ptn from Geo A Wheelock for himself & other heirs of Jos Villere, asking the reference of their claim to the Cmte of Claims. 3-Cmte on Private Land Claims: asked to be discharged from the consideration of the memorials of Hugh Ferguson & Jane Roble: which was agreed to. 4-Joint resolution to refer the claim of Jos Valliere to the Court of Claims; which was referred to the Cmte on Private Land Claims.

In the Genr'l Post Ofc for the last quarter of the year, there were found 2,472 <u>dead letters</u> which contained money amounting to $13,457. In one year 9,271 letters were discovered, covering $51,285; nine-tenths of which have been restored to its owner.

Col Saml Colt, in coming the other day from New Havent to Hartford, left his portmonnaie, containing memorianda, some of his cards, & a one hundred dollar Treasury note, on his seat in the cars. A poor man employed on the train found it & immediately sent it to him. The Colonel ascertained his name, & promptly sent him one of his most elegant pistols in a handsome case. –Springfield Republican

Mr ___ Jacobs, age 21 years, died very suddenly on Sat. He had been troubled with a sore throat, & a boil had been formed internally in his throat. It burst on Fri, &, as Dr Beresford declared, in breaking, it carried away a portion of the covering of the carotid artery, so as to leave the remaining protection to the artery thin & weak. On Sat the artery burst & he bled to death. –Hartford Times

Fatal Carelessness. 1-Harry Coomes & Albert Converse, 2 lads of Longmeadow, Mass, were playing with a gun on Sunday, when Coomes' was shot. He died almost instantly. 2-On Mon Geo Eddy, of East Middleboro, Mass, went to the field where a lad, Jeffrey Taylor was at work, to get him to go on a hunting excursion. In setting down his gun it went off its contents killing Taylor, instantly.

<u>Yellow fever patients left at Port Royal, Jamaica</u>, by the U S frig **Susquehanna**:

Edw Bolles	Saml Givizandi	Jacob Bootz
Dennis McCarthy	Jos Mickens	Thos Nugent
Wm Galena	Jas Cassey	Peter Clement
MattheW Henry	Albert Welder	Saml A Blocking
Wm M Blandin	Wm Myers	Jas Shanon
John Reardon	Wm H Hall	Patrick Daily
Thos Mohan	Tulley L Priest	John Collins
Jas R Webb	J W Wasson	Patrick Burke
Patrick Garvin	J Sullivan	G W Simpson
John Quick	John King	Antonio Lancetta
Jos Nesbitt	John Dole	Peter Hesse
John Manning	Hy Quito	Wm Crossman
R J Allen	Danl O'Brien	John H Thompson

Seraphino Bandico	Austin Newell	Peter Rampono
Jas O'Brien	Chas Jones	Freeman Luce
John H Baker	Robt Jackson	Isaac Branson
John Butler	Francis Carr	Robt Blake
Augustus Riedt	John Brewer	Alex'r Lamb
Geo S Smith	D M Lyons	Antonio Freitas
John Sullivan	Geo M Young	Timothy Brenan
Gustavus Jacobs	Robt Newton	Jas Buckley
Francis Gonzales	Geo Hughes	

Died: on Apr 17, in Wash City, Eliz B Dahlgren, aged 17 years, daughter of Capt John Dahlgren, U S Navy; & rarely has our society lost one so admirably fitted for its ornament, or who, at her age, has left so many attached friends to cherish her memory.

SAT APR 24, 1858
Senate: 1-Ptn from Chas Gramp, asking that his pension may be made to commence from the time of his disability: referred. 2-Cmte of Claims: bill for the relief of Bernard M Byrne; relief of Jas Maccaboy; & for the relief of C Edw Habiteht, adm of J W P Lewis. 2-Bill for relief of W Smith, deceased, late of Louisiana. 3-Bill for the relief of the heirs & legal reps of Pierre Broussard, deceased. 4-Act for the relief of the heirs, or their legal reps, of Wm Conway, deceased. 5-Bill for the relief of Regis Loisel, or his legal reps.

Right of a Father. Geo S Hamilton died at Pittsburg, Pa, leaving a widow, Margaretta, & 3 children aged 9, 11, & 13 years. As her husband was a Protestant & the wife a Catholic, he appointed guardians for the children by will, & directed them to be brought up in the Protestant faith. The children were placed at a Protestant school, but the mother applied for a writ of habeas corpus to recover them. The will was sustained, & the mother has to go without her children.

Mount Vernon. John A Washington, owner of **Mount Vernon**, has contracted to convey to the **Ladies' Mount Vernon Association**, on their compliance with the following terms: The payment of $200,000 for 200 acres of land, including the mansion & landing place, &, above all the tomb. $18,000 to be paid on closing the contract, & the remainder of the sum, in four bonds, payable in yearly instalments, with the permission, after payment of the first bond, to pay to Mr Washington any amount of the balance due in sums of not less than $5,000, which sums will be credited to the association, in this manner lessening the interest. The title to the estate & possession to be given on payment of the principal & interest, & the privilege also granted of obtaining possession, on 30 days' notice, at any time the association may be ready to furnish the entire purchase money.

Mr Vorhees, the water rent collector of Cincinnati, a defaulter, is a young man who had always exercised prudence in the management of his business. Eight months ago he found his way into a gambling house & could not withstand the temptation to run on to utter ruin. He started out with between $8,000 to $10,000, & lost it all.

Near San Juan, Calif, on Mar 13, the house of Mr Oden was consumed by fire, together with his wife, 4 children, & a female visiter. Mr Oden was absent from home at the time of the occurrence. The house was a small one story frame bldg, & the inmates prevented from making their escape by the incendiaries. Suspicion attached to a Spaniard who was formerly employed on the place, but had been ordered off by Mr Oden.

Died: on Apr 23, Thomas James, the youngest son of the late Thomas & Ellen C Collins, aged 13 years, 3 months & 23 days. His funeral is tomorrow at 3 P M from the City Hall.

Mrd: on Apr 22, in Wash City, by Rev Dr Harold, Mr Wm Towers to Miss Sarah Hood.

Mrd: on Apr 22, in Wash City, by Rev C A Harold, J K Pitzer, of Roanoke Co, Va, to Lucretia Hart, eldest daughter of the late Wm S Derrick, of Wash.

Died: on Feb 10, at Assumption, Paraguay, Wm C Ouseley, only remaining son of Sir Wm Gore Ouseley, K C B, her Britannic Majesty's Envoy Extraordinary & Minister Plenipotentiary on a special mission to Central America.

Died: on Apr 23, in Wash City, at his residence on H st, near 17th, Jacob Hilbus, aged 71 years & 3 months. The deceased was born in Westphalia, Germany, on Jan 31, 1787; emigrated to this country when a child; was an active participant in the stirring events of 1812, & a soldier in the war of that period, & for 50 years a resident of Wash City. None knew him but to love him, None named him but to praise. His funeral will be on Sunday afternoon at 3 o'clock, from his late residence.

Died: on Apr 13, at his residence, Wayne Co, N C, Dr Marshall P Howard, a native of Brookville, Montg Co, Md.

Died: on Apr 22, in Wash City, of scarlet fever, William Newton Pettit, aged 7 years, 7 months & 15 days, second son of Chas W & Gertrude Pettit. His funeral is this afternoon at 3½ o'clock, from the residence of his parents, 398 Mass ave, between 9th & 10th sts.

MON APR 26, 1858
Household & kitchen furniture at auction on Apr 30, at the residence of J N McIntyre, 375 Mass ave, between 9th & 10th sts: all his household effects. -Jas C McGuire, auct

Senate: 1-Ptn from R T Walton & other heirs of Jehu Walton, asking that the assignment issued in the name of said Jehu Walton may be legalized: referred. 2-Ptn from Ed D Tippet, asking an appropriation to test his cold water steam engine: referred. 3-Ptn from Thos Waits, asking to be allowed arrear of pension: referred. 4-Ptn from Jas C Jewett, ship-master & merchant of N Y C, asking that the U S Gov't will take steps to recover from the Gov't of Peru the losses sustained in consequence of that Gov't failing to comply with the terms of the agreement in relation to the Lobos Islands: referred. 5-Cmte of Claims: bill for the relief of Miles Devine.

The disease of which Col Benton died was Cancer of the Rectum. In the affection itself there was nothing peculiar, as it is a complaint not uncommon to an advanced period of life. Although I had occasionally visited Col Benton for more than 3 years prior to his decease, it was not until Sep, 1857, that my attention was especially called to the disease of which he died. In Feb, 1856, I performed on him an operation for Hydrocele, [a common complaint, & one relieved by a very simple operation,] & to which he alluded when you were standing by his bedside, the day before his death, when he remarked that he had been also treated by me for a disease similar to that which had afflicted the historian Gibbon, & which he requested me to note in my report of his case. I communicated the hopelessness of his case, & he received it with perfect calmness & resignation. –Jno Fred May [To Wm Carey Jones: Wash, Apr 13, 1858.]

Mr Berry Boon, of Leake Co, Miss, was killed a few days since by an accidental shot from his gun while turkey hunting.

A young girl, 15 years of age, daughter of Mr John H Chace, of Providence, was badly burnt on Sat night by the falling of a burning fluid lamp.

A child of Mr Jerod, 4 years of age, living in Norfolk Co, Va, was poisoned some days since by sucking the flower of the yellow jasmine. He died in an hour. The parents would not have known the cause of the sudden death of their child but for a playmate who said it had been sucking the flower, a deadly poison.

Book: The Life of Geo Stephenson, Railway Engineer, by Saml Smiles. From the fourth London edition: $1.25. Ran Away to Sea, an autiobiography by Capt Mayne Reid, 75 cents. Just published & for sale at Philp's New Bookstore, Pa ave, between 9th & 10th sts.

Ira Stout, who, with his sister, Mrs Littles, was indicted for the murder of the husband of the latter has been tried, convicted, & sentenced to be hung on Jun 18 next. Ira Stout slew Chas W Littles on the river bank, & threw his body over the precipice & into the river. Mrs Littles was present, & was implicated with her brother. Mrs Littles has yet to be tried.

Marie Ann Crispin & Jean Baptiste Distorges have been found guilty of murder at Montreal, & sentenced to be hung on Jun 25.

Several years ago Peter Remington was robbed on the Sound steamer **Perry** of a satchel containing $40,000 belonging to the Newport banks. The robbery remained a mystery, but it has lately been discovered that it was committed by Jew Mike, an English thief, & his associates.

Jos A Wood, who had his leg broken in Quebec 27 years ago, in S C 10 years go, in N H 2 years ago, & on Apr 10, in Worcester, he slipped & broke it a 4th time. He concluded to have it cut off and had the amputation performed. –Boston Post

Mrs Empy, in Rochester, not having heard from her husband for 5 years, & giving him up for dead, recently married Dr Thos Robie. Soon after the marriage the original husband returned from Calif, & becoming indignant when he discovered that his ex-spouse had come into possession of a considerable fortune, sued her for bigamy. Dr Robie is a respectable physician, 50 years of age. Husbands Nos 1 & 2 are now at swords' points, & the courts are settling the difficulty.

U S Patent Ofc, Wash, Apr 23, 1858. Ptn of Chas W Brown, of Boston, Mass, praying for the extension of a patent granted to him on Aug 14, 1844, for an improvement in tonguing & grooving machines, for 7 years from the expiration of said patent, which takes place on Aug 14, 1858. –Jos Holt, Com'r of Patents

Orphans Court of Wash Co, D C. In the case of Sarah Foy, excx of John Foy, the executrix & Court have appointed May 15 next, for the final settlement of the personal estate of said deceased, of the assets in hand. -Ed N Roach, Reg/o wills

Orphans Court of Wash Co, D C. Letters of administration on the personal estate of Wm H Williams, late of Wash Co, deceased. –Violet A Williams, admx

Orphans Court of Wash Co, D C. Letters of administration on the personal estate of Jas Handley, late of Wash Co, deceased. –Jos F Hodgson, Wm Flaherty, adms

Jas Dean is reported to have died of a legacy at St Louis. He had the misfortune recently to receive a fortune from a deceased relative in England, & lived so fast that he used up himself & the fortune in a few months, leaving his family destitute.

Mrs Kline obtained a divorce from her husband, in the court of Sandusky Co, Ohio, on the ground that he had become a convert to spiritualism & was very crabbed in his family. The court decreed her alimony to the amount of $3,000.

Criminal Court-Wash-Sat. 1-Frances Penny, colored was found guilty of assault & battery with intent to kill a white woman: sentenced to 3 years in the penitentiary. 2-The second trial of Benj Ogle for the murder of the child of John Webb, in Gtwn, is set for today. 3-The jury in the case of John Essex retired to make up a verdict.

Mrd: on Apr 12, at the First Presbyterian Church, in Natchez, by Rev Jos B Stratton, D D, Levin R Marshall, jr, to Miss Charlotte Dunbar, 2nd daughter of the late Dr Wm Dunbar.

Died: on Apr 21, at his residence, in Calvert Co, Md, Capt Wm J Belt, in his 65th year, for many years a ofcr of the U S Navy. He was appointed a Midshipman by Mr Madison, then Pres of the U S, Sep11, 1811; served through the war of 1812, was twice taken prisoner-the last time taken he was carried to the Cape of Good Hope, where he remained 2 years; from thence to England, sailded from England for the U S in the ship **Cartell** Sep 4, 1815. He afterwards served his country faithfully for many years. His last cruise was in command of the ship **Marion**. No man had more friends nor fewer enemies.

Died: on Apr 11, in Charleston, S C, Dr Francis C Fitzhugh, of King Geo Co, Va, in his 57th year, leaving 2 small children to mourn their loss. He had gone to Florida, thence to Cuba, in order to recruit his health. He commenced life in 1824 as a practitioner of medicine, in his native county, united by the closest ties to many families.

Died: on Apr 24, in Wash City, Ann Elizabeth, daughter of Jas S Holland, aged 12 years. Her funeral will be this afternoon at 4 o'clock, from her father's residence, on 9th st, between H & I sts.

TUE APR 27, 1858
Sale of negro girl Alice, about 13 years old, a slave for life. She will be sold to the highest bidder, for cash, in current funds. By order of the Orphans Court of Wash Co, D C. Public auction, at the auction rooms of A Green. –John H Strider, adm of Eleanor West, deceased. -A Green, auct

Gov Hicks, of Md, appointed Richd B Carmichael, of Queen Anne's Co, a Judge of the judicial circuit composed of the counties of Kent, Queen Anne's, Caroline, & Talbot, made vacant by the death of Judge Hopper.

Senate: 1-Ptn from A Davis Harrell, a lt in the navy, who was placed on the retired list & subsequently transferred to the active list, asking indemnity for money expended in defending himself before the navy board, & rendering an account for fees of counsel, attys, printing, traveling, & other extraordinary expenses: referred. 2-Ptn from John W Wheeler, late U S Minister to Nicaragua, asking remuneration for services, losses, & expenses incident to the mission: referred. 3-Ptn from Thos Jones & others, of Clermont Co, Ohio, asking bounty land for services performed in 1812: referred. 4-Ptn from Madison Sunster, asking compensation for provisions, blankets, etc, furnished the Indians of Dacotah at Traverse des Sioux, in Minnesota Territory: referred. 5-Cmte on pensions: bill for the relief of Webster S Steele; relief of Jas A Glanding; & relief of Thos Smithers. 6-Cmte of Claims: bill for the relief of Franklin Peale.

The U S iron steamer **Water Witch** will be sold, on Jun 1 next, at the U S Navy Yard, Wash, at 12 o'clock M, the Hull of the iron steamer. The vessel was built in Washington Yard in 1844; length on deck 130 feet 6 inches, breadth 21 feet 2 inches, hold 10 feet, & the draft of water as she now floats is 3 feet 3 inches. The estimated weight of the iron is from 70 to 80 tons. The terms are cash. –Wm Flinn, Navy Agent

Col John M Hamtramck died at his residence in Shepherdstown, Va, on Wed last. He was a graduate of West Point, served for some years in the regular army, & during the Mexican war was appointed to command the Virginia regt.

A son of Mr R McAllister, a resident of the First Ward, was attacked by hydrophobia on Tue night. The lad was bitten by a dog about 9 months since. –Phil Press

Wm T Ingraham, of the commercial house of Wm O Price & Co, of Augusta, Ga, committed suicide on Sunday with a pistol, from some cause unknown. He was a native of Albany, N Y.

W M Booker, who was shot in an affray with B H Palmer, at Springfield, about 2 weeks ago, died on Sat last. Palmer was killed at the time. The quarrel arose from rival claims to the command of a volunteer company for Utah.

On Thu last an old man, without friends or money, died at the house of a colored woman at Evansville, Indiana. His name was ascertained to be Dr John Pocock Holmes, a member of the College of Surgeons, London, & formerly in the employ of the Hudson Bay Company, the friend of Capt Parry, the Arctic navigator, & the associate of many of the first people of England. He was also the author of several valuable inventions.

Criminal Court-Wash-Sat. 1-Alex'r Eggleston was found not guilty for assault & battery with intent to kill John Toomey.

Died: on Apr 25, at *Woodbourne*, the residence of her aunt, Mrs Caroline E Sanders, Mrs Emily R Marshall, aged 23 years & 6 days, wife of Chas Marshall, of Balt, & 2nd daughter of Col T P Andrews, U S Army. Her funeral will take place from *Woodbourne*, to Rock Creek Church, today at 1 o'clock P M.

Died: on Apr 26, of pulmonary consumption, Capt Walter Warder, aged 53 years. His funeral will be from his late residence, 354 5th st, between H & I, Apr 28 at 10 o'clock.

WED APR 28, 1858
Household & kitchen furniture at auction on: May 4, at the residence of Com Barron, on G st north, between 14th & 15th sts. -Jas C McGuire, auct

Senate: 1-Ptn from R J Todd, setting forth that the citizens of N Y, Brooklyn, & Wmsburg are so located as to be now considered one city, & asking that the price of postage between them may be reduced: referred. 2-Ptn from Jos Brobst, asking payment of certain continental scrip received by his father in payment for Revolutionary services, with interest thereon: referred. 3-Cmte on Pensions: bill for the relief of Saml Wooster. Same cmte: act granting a pension to Ansel Wilkinson, & recommended its passage. 4-Cmte on Naval Affairs: bill for the relief of David D Porter. 5-Cmte on Private Land Claims: act for the relief of the heirs, or their legal reps, of Wm Conway, deceased. Also, relief of the heirs & legal reps of Pierre Brousard, deceased; of Regis Loisel or his legal reps; & of the reps of Wm Smith, deceased, late of Louisiana. 6-Joint resolution for the benefit of the widow of Cmder Wm Lewis Herndon, U S navy. That Congress entertain a high sense of the devotion to duty, the coolness, courage, & conduct of Cmder Wm Lewis Herndon, U S Navy, in command of the steamer **Central America**, at sea, during the prevalence of a hurricane on Sep 12, 1857; & that the widow of the said Wm Lewis Herndon be entitled to receive, out of any money in the Treasury not otherwise appropriated, a sum equal to 3 years' full sea-service pay of a commander in the navy.

The new dwlg of Alex'r Griffith, in Caroline Co, Md, was, with his furniture, consumed by fire on Apr 10. The dwlg on the farm of A Godwin, & occupied by Thos Diggins, in Caroline Co, was also recently consumed with nearly all its contents. No insurance on either house.

Hygeia Hotel, Old Point Comfort, Va: Jos Segar, Proprietor. The establishment will be open on Jun 1. [Ad]

Orphans Court of Wash Co, D C. Letters of administration on the personal estate of Geo R Griswold, late of the U S Navy, deceased. –Z Chandler, adm

Mrd: on Apr 27, at Mount Calvary Church, Balt, by Rev Thos Richey, Rev Wm Chauncy Langdon, of Phil, to Miss H Agnes Courtney, daughter of E S Courtney, of the former city.

Chancery sale: Philip T Berry & John S Berry vs John Lee. By decree of the Circuit Court of Wash Co, D C, passed in the above cause, dated Nov 9, 1854, & made absolute on May 3, 1855, the subscriber will sell at public auction on Mar 20 next, lots 24 thru 27, on the west side of Montg st; lots 32 & 33 on the west side of Green st; lot 43 & 6 feet on the north side of lot 44, making one lot of 46 feet, on the east side of Green st; lot 11, 101, fronting 40 feet each on the east side of Green st: all in Lee, Deakins, & Cazenove's addition to Gtwn, D C. –Henry King, trustee -Barnard & Buckey, aucts

Fire on Monday discovered in the rear part of a house owned by Geo E Kirk, & occupied by Stephen Brown as a cigar store, on 7th st, near Md ave. The wind was quite high & the following bldgs on 7th st were destroyed: a frame bldg owned by Mr Hughes, occupied by Mr Kagy, liquor refiner; Mr Bailey, harness maker; Mr Tucker, shoe maker; stationery & variety store of J E Baker; Mr Frahluk's clothing store, & Mr S Brown's cigar store. A brick grocery store & dwlg owned by Mr Holmead, now in the West, was occupied by Mr J Purcell. Also, the blacksmith shop of Mr Cornwell; & the wheelwright shop owned by Mr Greenwell. –States

Died: on Apr 26, after a few days' illness, George Washington, son of Mrs Ann E & the late Edw W Davies, aged nearly 5 years.

THU APR 29, 1858
Valuable real estate in PG Co, Md, for sale: the subscriber offers one of his farms, **Beach Hill**, containing 145 1/4th acres; with a commodious dwlg & some very good out bldgs. The farm is not a mile from the Episcopalian, Methodist, & Catholic churches, nor from a primary school. Thos Grimes or Basil Baden, all living near the farm, will show the same. –Gustavus Finotti, care of Thos Grimes, Wash City.

Fancy & Staple Dry Goods: 373 & 375 [recently occupied by Mr C F Perrie] 7th st at I. -R Brice Hall

Household & kitchen furniture, & small stock of groceries at auction on May 3, at the residence & store of Mrs Rumpff, corner of 6th & E sts, Island. -Jas C McGuire, auct

Senate: 1-Cmte on Military Affairs: adverse report on the memorial of Isaac W Brown. Same cmte: asked to be discharged from the consideration of the memorial of Dr A S Wright, asking indemnity for losses occasioned by his expulsion from Mexico, & that it be referred to the Cmte on Foreign Relations: agreed to. 2-Cmte on Pensions: bill for the relief of Catharine Jacobs, widow of Francis Jacobs, a waiter in the military household of Gen Washington, & recommended its passage. 3-Cmte of Claims: adverse report on the memorial of O H Browne; on the memorial of Wm L S Dearing; & on the memorial of Jas Henderbert. 4-Resolved that there be paid to Hon Willis A Groman, Govn'r of Minnesota Territory, $820, as compensation for his service as com'r to investigate the alleged frauds of Alex'r Ramsay, late Superintendent of Indians for the Northern Superintendency, & for reimbursement of his necessary expenses incurred therein.

For rent: the dwlg house of Mr Ellet, 288 H st, between 17th & 18th sts. Apply to Francis de Haes Janvier. N W corner of F & 6th sts.

Cmdor Joshua Sands, U S Naval Cmder of the steam frig **Susquehanna**, has obtained temporary leave of absence. He reached his home, at Stratford, Conn, on Apr 24, where he was welcomed by the young men of the village. The Cmdor is very popular at home.

Died: on Apr 23, at Montpelier, Orange Co, Va, in her 11th year, Mary Agnes, daughter of Chas & Mary Jane Pairo, of Gtwn.

FRI APR 30, 1858
Splendid rosewood 7 octave piano forte, elegant French plate mirrors, rich silver plated ward, household & kitchen furniture at auction on May 6, at the residence of W Henry Palmer, F st, between 13th & 14th sts. -Jas C McGuire, auct

Chancery sale of valuable property, by decree of the Circuit Court of Wash Co, D C, in the cause of Arman Jardin et al against A Favier's heirs & adm, I will offer at public auction, on May 26, on the premises, subdivision D, in square 119, fronting 24 feet 1 inch on 19th st west, between H st & Pa ave, with a 2 story dwlg house.
--W S Coxe, trustee -Jas C McGuire, auct

Brvt Maj Zeilin, U S Marine Corps, has received orders to report on board the frig **Wabash** on May 15, as the commanding Marine ofcr of the Mediterranean squadron. A M Pomeroy, boatswain; John Cook, gunner; John Rainbow, carpenter; Jacob Stephens, sail-maker: also ordered to the **Wabash**. Geo W Elliott, carpenter, & W S L Brayton, sail-maker, have been ordered to the U S frig **Macedonian**.

Richd Ten Broeck, the owner of American horses in England, has gone to Europe again, intending to follow up the English turfmen until he conquers them. Charleston, a favorite South Carolina racer, has left for England in a steamer.

Senate: 1-Ptn from Geo T Parry, urging that the Sec of the Navy be authorized to purchase his patent for an instrument, the object of which is to abolish the friction attending the thrust of propellers, the Gov't having been using the same for the last 3 years in the U S frigs **Niagara, Wabash, & Minnesota**: referred. 2-Ptn from Jas Harrington, asking the establishment of an addition land district in the State of Iowa: referred. 3-Additional papers submitted in relation to the claim of Capt John Pickell: referred. 4-Ptn from citizens of Iowa, asking that a license may be granted to Lewis A Thomas for the establishment of a ferry across the Missouri river, within the limits of the proposed Territory of Dahcota: referred. 5-Cmte on Commerce: bill for the relief of Jeremiah Moors, with a special report. 6-Cmte on Naval affairs: bill for the relief of Henry Etting; & for the relief of the legal reps of John A Frost, deceased. 7-Cmte on Pensions: adverse report on the ptn of Wm Blake. Same cmte: asked to be discharged from the consideration of the papers in relation to the claim of Levi Johnson, & that they be referred to the Cmte on Public Lands: agreed to. Same cmte: discharged from the consideration of the ptn of Wm Roddy. 8-Bill for the relief of Randal Pegg was recommitted to the Cmte on Patents & the Patent Ofc. 9-Bill to incorporate *Gonzaga College*, in Wash City returned from the House with an amendment: passed.

Mrd: on Apr 27, by Rev Wm H Chapman, Mr Alex'r W Eaton to Miss Catharine V Teachem, all of Wash City.

Died: on Apr 29, in Wash City, suddenly, in his 66th year, Peter Hepburn, sen. His funeral will take place on May 1 at 2 o'clock. His male friends are particularly requested to attend.

SAT MAY 1, 1858
All household & kitchen furniture at auction on May 6, at the residence of W Henry Palmer, F st, between 13th & 14th sts. -Jas C McGuire, auct

Jules Gerard, the great lion killer, has just left Paris on a lion hunting excursion with a company of Russian noblemen. They are going to the mountains of Africa.

Two of the distinguished men of the medical world of Paris have died recently. M Chomel, the physician of Louis Philippe, & since his death, of the Orleans family. It was he that refused the oath to the Empire, & was thus excluded from the faculty of Medicine of Paris, of which he was one of the brightest ornaments. Baron Boyer died suddenly from an invagination of the intestines, Mr Chomel from an internal cancer.

For rent: a 3 story brick house, with basement, on Second st, Gtwn, the late residence of M de Bodisco, containing 16 or 17 rooms. The house & lot are large & in complete order, having all the necessary out bldgs & baths. It is one of the most commodious in Gtwn, & well arranged for comfort & elegance. -Brooke B Williams, Gtwn

Now in store a beautiful assortment of rich Berege & Organdie Robes. -J W Colley, 523 7th st, 3 doors north of Pa ave.

Senate: 1-Ptn from Thos W Jordan, late Capt's clerk on the the U S ship **Fredonia**, asking to be allowed the difference between his pay as capt's clerk & that of purser during the period he acted as purser: referred. 2-Cmte on Pensions: bill for the relief of Jas Smith, for injuries received while a soldier in the army. 3-Cmte of Claims: bill for the relief of Capt Jas Mc McIntosh, of the regular army, reported it back without amendment, & asked its immediate consideration, on the ground that Mr Mc McIntosh has been kept out of his claim by an erroneous decision of one of the Auditors of the Treasury obstinately persisted in. Bill was passed.

Notice: on May 26, 1856, I mailed in the post ofc in Shelby, N C, in a registered letter, No 38, the following land warrant: 80 acres issued to Catharine Rudasel, widow of John Rudasel, deceased, under act of Congress Mar 3, 1855, no 34,566, directed to Springs, Oak & Co, Phil, Pa. This land warrant having been lost or feloniously taken from the mail, I shall apply to the Com'r of Pensions for a duplicate of said warrant. –Jos Carroll

Army Intelligence: Movement at once of the 6th regt of infty, & the company of sappers & miners, towards Utah. This command is to take the Bridger Pass route, & to construct a wagon road from the pass to **Camp Scott**, the present headquarters of Col Johnston. Lt Francis T Bryan, topographical engineer, accompanies the command, he having passed over the route. The force assigned to the command of Maj Gen Smith, for the Utah expedition, consists of the following companies & regts.
Light Co B, 4th regt of artl commanded by Capt John W Phelps.
Light Co M, 2nd regt of artl, commanded by Brvt Maj Henry J Hunt.
Light Co A, 2nd regt of artl, commanded by Brvt Maj John P Reynolds.
Company of sappers & miners, commanded by Lt Jas C Duane.
1st regt of cavalry, commanded by Col Edwin V Sumner.
2nd regt of dragoons, commanded by Lt Col P St G Cooke.
5th regt of infty, commanded by Brvt Col Carlos A Waite.
6th regt of infty, commanded by Lt Col Geo Andrews.
7th regt of infty, commanded by Lt Col Pitcairn Morrison.
10th regt of infty, commanded by Col Edmund B Alexander.
The 4th regt of artl, commanded by Col Monroe, & now in the district of the Platte, will be added to the above forces. –St Louis Democrat

Hon David McComas has been elected Judge of the district composed of the counties of Kanawha, Jackson, Roane, Mason, Putnam, Cabell, & Wayne, in Va, to fill the vacancy caused by the resignation of Judge Summers.

Notice to the creditors of Geo S Townshend. In pursuance of an order passed by the Circuit Court for PG Co, Md, on Feb 1, 1858, in the matter of the application of Geo S Townshend for the benefit of the insolvent laws of this state, the creditors of the said Geo S Townshend, previous to his application for the benefit of the insolvent laws, are hereby notified to file their claims, duly authenticated, with the Clerk of the said court, on or before Jul 1 next. –Saml H Berry, trustee

Valuable estate for sale: *Sudley*, lying in the counties of Fairfax & Loudoun, in Va, containing 1,072 acres of land; with a good dwlg house, smoke-house, dairy, ice house, & all the necessary out-houses. –Thos J Turner, Upper Marlborough, PG Co, Md.

Criminal Court-Wash-Fri. The prosecution in the case of Benj Ogle, for the murder of John Webb, in Gtwn, produced several new witnesses in rebuttal of the evidence offered by the defence to show that the prisoner is not a man of sound mind. Mr Mortimer Garrett testified. Mrs Ann Harrison, the prisoner's mother-in-law, testified that on the day of the shooting Ogle was at her house, that he left it about an hour before it took place; remarked strangeness in his conduct that day, & spoke of it; believed he was crazy or deranged that day. Asking to see his wife, who was up stairs, he went to the basement instead. He took no notice of his child, which was very strange for him. Geo Ellis testified to seeing prisoner's aunt attempt to hang herself. John Clements, is the husband of the aunt referred to by Geo Ellis. Has been married to her 37 years, & never saw any sign of insanity in her. Never heard of her alleged attempt to hang herself. They had 12 children; none of them insane; would like the jury to see some of them. Officer R H Trunnell testified to the worth & respectability of Mrs Clemens; never heard of her being insane. Had been brought up with the prisoner, & never saw any insanity about him. John H Trunnell testified similarly to previous witness. Never heard of Mrs Clements attempting to hang herself. Wm H Godey worked with the prisoner since he was a child; never saw any unsoundess of mind in him. Geo W Godey, similarly testified. Francis Hutchings had known all the prisoner's family. Never heard of his being crazy, or his father or grand-father. They were sometimes worsted with drinking. Dr Semmes & Jailer Waters testified to Ogle's rationality since being in jail, & Dr Snyder & Ofcr Trunnell testified to his sanity & soberness on the day of the fatal act. Mr Maury made the opening address to the jury, & was followed by Mr Radcliffe for the defence. Mr Norris will conclude for the defence tomorrow, & Mr Key for the prosecution. [May 3rd newspaper: the jury returned with a verdict of manslaughter.] [May 4th newspaper: Benj Ogle said that the witness, Mr John Clements, had perjured himself. Ogle was sentenced to 8 years' hard labor in the District penitentiary, a term which the Judge said he regretted was the longest the law admitted of. The prisoner was taken back to the jail, & soon after to the penitentiary, his wife accompanying him.]

Died: on Apr 29, in Wash City, of consumption, Jas R McAlister, formerly of St Louis, Mo, aged 33 years. He was for nearly 14 years, a clerk in the office of the 6th Auditor of the Treasury, a position to which he was appointed soon after completing his college course. During the last 5 years, until prevented by his last illness, he was absent but one day from his desk. He was devoted to his family. His funeral will be this afternoon at 4 o'clock, from his late residence, No 4 4½ st.

Died: on Apr 8, in Smithfield, Isle of Wight Co, Va, of pulmonary consumption, Mrs Victoria Buford, wife of R D Buford, & daughter of Willis Wilson, of Smithfield. How brief have been the days of her wedded life! Two short years ago she was a belove bride, in robust appearance. The fatal disease caused her husband to remove her from the home of her adoption to her father's house, with the fond hope that a more genial clime might stay the destroyer's hand.

Died: on Apr 30, of scarlet fever, Fannie A Jones, the adopted daughter of Wm E & Catharine A Stubbs, in her 5th year. Her funeral will be on May 2 at 4 o'clock, from the residence of her parents, 492 E st.

MON MAY 3, 1858
Hon J J Gilchrist, Presiding Judge of the U S Court of Claims, died in this city on Thu last, at the residence of her friend, Dr Whelan, the Chief of the Bureau of Medicine & Surgery. He was a profound lawyer; a citizen of N H; & upon the establishment of the Court of Claims by Congress, was appointed by Pres Pierce one of the judges. He was about 49 years old. His remains were taken on Fri to his native State. –States

Wm Mundar was hung at Wilkesbarre, Pa, on Fri last for having murdered Geo Mathews in Dec last.

Orphans Court of Wash Co, D C. Letters of administration on the personal estate of Henry W Queen, late of the U S Marines, deceased. –Abby E Queen, admx

Orphans Court of Wash Co, D C. In the case of John Taylor, exc of Benj Taylor, deceased, the Court & administrator have appointed May 25 next for the settlement of the personal estate of said deceased, with the assets in hand. -Ed N Roach, Reg/o wills

The Santa Fe Gaz: Mr Gorman, book-keeper in the store of Mr Owens, committed a brutal assault upon a man named Francisco, in the employ of Beck & Johnson. Mr Beck, who was standing outside the store, drew a knife also. Gorman died from a knife wound in the abdomen from Mr Beck. Mr Beck suffered intensely from a wound to the hand, & Friday his life was totally despaired of.

Orphans Court of Wash Co, D C. Letters of administration on the personal estate of Ann McMechen, late of Wash Co, deceased. –Jas F Haliday, adm

New Haven, Conn, Apr 30. The trial of Wm S Tuckerman for mail robbery at various times in Nov last, & which commenced in this city on Apr 27, came to an unexpected termination by one of the counsel for the prisoner notifying the Court that he had concluded to consent to a verdict on the part of the jury of guilty on all four of the charges contained in the indictment. Such was the positive nature of the proof elicited. [May 6th newspaper: Tuckerman, the mail robber, was sentenced to be imprisoned & kept at hard labor, in the Stare prison, for 21 years. The prisoner shook convulsively.]
[May 7th newspaper: trial of Wm S Tuckerman: sentenced to 21 years imprisonment; so ends the career of one of the smartest of Boston boys, who belonged to a good family, was well brought up, had the advantages of our excellent schools, & when quite young obtained the responsible place of treasurer of the Eastern Railroad. Here he turned out to be an embezzler & defaulter to a large amount. –Boston Post]

Mrd: on Apr 29, at the National Observatory, by Rev Geo D Cummins, S Wellford Corbin, of Caroline Co, Va, to Nannie Fontaine, daughter of Cmder M F Maury, U S Navy.

Died: on Apr 25, in Wash City, Mr John T Brown, in his 34th year.

Charleston, May 2. The steamship **James Adger**, from N Y for Charleston, on Fri night, burst her steam-chimney, badly scalding Jos Pollock the engineer, & 4 firemen, 3 of whom have since died. Mr Pollock is under medical treatment. [May 6th newspaper: Mr E K Kent, 2nd engineer, escaped without injury. Lawrence Wallace, a fireman, died in 6 hours & was buried at sea. Jeremiah Bridgwood & Peter Reilly, firemen, died; the first in 20 & the other in 40 hours afterwards. They were buried at Charleston. The deceased all hailed from N Y & leave families. The chief engineer, Mr Jos Pollock, was taken to a private residence & put under the care of Dr Peter Porcher. He is dreadfully scalded in the face, neck & arms, but it is believed that he will recover. –Charleston Courier]

TUE MAY 4, 1858
Senate: 1-Cmte on Pensions: adverse report on the ptn of Jas McCutcheon, asking an increase of his pension. 2-Cmte of Claims: bill for the relief of Saml H Taylor, a messenger in the Third Auditor's ofc, granting him $540. 3-Cmte on Public Lands: bill for the relief of the <u>Hungarian settlers</u> upon certain tracts of land in Iowa hitherto reserved from sale by order of the Pres, dated Jan 22, 1855, reported back the same & recommended its passage.

The Ninth Provincial Council of Balt assembled at the Cathedral in Balt on Sunday. The following were Bishops in attendance:
Most Rev Archbishop Kenrick, of Balt.
Rt Rev Dr O'Connor, Bishop of Pittsburg
Rt Rev Dr McGill, Bishop of Richmond
Rt Rev Dr Neuman, Bishop of Phil
Rt Rev Dr Young, Bishop of Erie, Pa
Rt Rev Dr Barry, Bishop of Savannah
Rt Rev Dr Lynch, Bishop of Charleston
Rt Rev Dr Verot, Bishop of Florida
The Rt Rev Bishop Whelan, of Wheeling, being in Europe, was absent. The Mitred Abbot Weummer, of the Benedictine Convent of Latrobe, Pa, occupied a seat with the Bishops. The Very Rev H B Coskery was assistant priest at the pontifical mass.

Circuit Court of Wash Co, D C-in Chancery, No 1,226. The trustee reports that on Jan 12, 1858, he sold all that part of lot 1 in square 881, in Wash City, which belonged to Jas Ratrie at the time of his death, pursuant to the provision of the decree passed in said cause, to Mathew Trimble for $710, & the purchaser had complied with the terms of sale. -Jno A Smith, clerk

Thos J Turner, of Freeport, Ill, having obtained a divorce from his wife, has settled $3,000 upon her.

The reinforcements going out to Utah, under Gen Smith, consist of 3 light batteries of artl, commanded by Capts Barry, Hunt, & Reynolds; 12 companies of cavalry, commanded by Col E V Sumner; 10 companies of foot artl, commanded by Brvt Col John Munroe; 8 companies of 6th infty, commanded by Lt Col Geo Andrews; 10 companies of 7th infty, commanded by Lt Col Pitcairn Morrison; a detachment of sappers & miners; a detachment of ordnance men-an aggregate of 252 officers & 5,445 men.

In Trenton, N J, on Apr 22, Jos Clayton, aged 107 years & 3 months, died. He enjoyed good health up to a few days before his death. He was an active young man of 25 years of age at the time of the Declaration of Independence, & passed through all the stormy trials that attended the birth & struggles for life of this republic.

Lucius Bulkley, a lawyer of N Y, desirous to be rid of his wife, adopted a singular & temporarily successful maneuver to obtain a divorce. His wife was about to visit her mother in Sacramento, Calif, with, so far as appears, her husband's full consent. As she was about to start he placed or caused to be placed in her hands a tin box, closed, covered with paper & sealed, purporting to be a present for her mother with a note for herself. When at sea the wife opened the box & ascertained its contents to be legal documents summoning her to answer a complaint file in Saratoga Co in 20 days. On arriving at Aspinwall she made an effort to return, but was unsuccessful, & went on to Calif, residing there until Jan, 1857. During her absence her husband had obtained a decree of divorce. On returning she took measures to have this reversed. The husband made a proposition to her that if she would raise $5,000 she should have the custody of her child, & another, that if she would give him $1,400 he would procure & destroy the record of divorce. Neither was accepted, & a suit was brought. Justice Potter decided the manner of serving the papers upon her as she was about to leave the State was a practical denial of the legal right of the dfndnt, who was entitled to time to make a defence to the cmplnt, & that in this cunningly devised stratagem the husband was guilty of most deliberate falsehood, if not legal perjury, & is at least guilty of moral if not legal subordination of perjury. Of course the decree & all the proceeding under which it was obtained were set aside.

Rev Dr Kendall, who is in his 86th year, preached in the Unitarian Church at Plymouth on Fast Day. He has been settled there 58 years.

Died: on May 1, in Wash City, James Forbes, only surviving child of James F & Eliza Gibson, aged 3 years & 9 months.

The Roman Catholics have selected a beautiful square on 14th st, intersected by Vt & Mass aves, purchased by Hon Caleb Cushing, late Atty Gen, & presented to St Andrews' Mission, on which a free Church is to be erected.

WED MAY 5, 1858
Gold medal awarded by his Imperial Royal Highness, Ferdinand Maximillian, Archduke of Austria, to Capt Mathew F Maury, U S Navy, as a testimonial of his respect for that officer's scientific services to the interest of navigation. [Letter dated Apr 30, 1858.]

Senate: 1-Mr Walter Dixon, an American citizen residing at Jaffa, in Palestine. Letter from Mr Walter Dixon, aged 58, of Groton, Mass; of Mrs Sarah Dixon, wife of Walter Dixon, aged 58, of Dunstable, Mass; & of Mary Steinbeck, aged 24, wife of Fred'k Steinbeck, daughter of the above parties; & of Caroline S Dixon, aged 11 years. Horrid outrages perpetrated upon this family, viz, the murder of the son-in-law, the violation of the mother & daughter, & the robbery of the house. J Warren Gorham, the U S Consul at Jerusalem, wrote a letter to the Consul Gen of the U S at Constantinpole. The Prussian Counsul & myself have offered a reward of one thousand piastres for information which may lead to the detection & conviction of the offenders. Mr Appleton, the Assist Sec of State, writes to the U S Consul at Jerusalem, Apr 16, 1858, in which he tells him that the Dept has learned with much regret of the outrages upon unoffending individuals, citizens of the U S residing in Palestine, & has been notified of the arrest & punishment of the offending parties, & fully approved of the course provided. 2-Ptn from Anton L C Portman, asking compensation for his services as interpreter of the Japan Expedition: referred. 3-Ptn from Mary Jane Maltby, widow of Lt West, of the army, asking to be allowed a pension: referred. 4-Cmte on the Judiciary: adverse reports on the memorial of: Francis D Pons; & the memorial of the Legislature of Missouri in relation to the claim of Jarvis M Barker. 5-Cmte on Pensions; adverse report on the ptns of Jas Baldwin & of Harrison Sargent. Same cmte: bill for the relief of John B Mills. Same cmte: adverse reports on the ptns of Thos Watts, of Chas Grampp, & of Adam Sener. 6-Cmte on Private Land Claims: bill for the relief of the reps of Wm Smith, deceased, late of Louisiana, & for the relief of the heirs & legal reps of Pierre Brousard, deceased, & recommended their passage. Same cmte: bill for the relief of Mrs Ambrose Brou, of the parish of St Chas, La; for the final adjustment of private land claims in Fla, La, Ark, & Mo, & for other purposes. 7-Act for the relief of Geo Chorpenning, jr, approved Mar 3, 1857, referred to the Cmte on the Post Ofc & Post Roads.

House of Reps: 1-Cmte on Private Land Claims: bill for the relief of the legal reps of John McDonough, deceased, late of Louisiana: committed. Adverse report on the case of John W Chevis; & on the bill for the relief of Danl Whiting: laid on the table. 2-Cmte on Military Affairs: Act to revive an act for the relief of Dempsey Pittman: committed. Same cmte: adverse in the case of Prof Homer Anderson, of Garrettsville, N Y: laid on the table. Same cmte: adverse in the cases of Rice M Brown & Alex'r Hays: laid on the table. Same cmte: discharged from the consideration of the case of Jane Turnbull. 3-Cmte on Naval Affairs: bill for the relief of Benj Wakefield: committed. Adverse in the case of V Hall; & adverse in the case of H R Coates: laid on the table. Bill for the relief of Wilcox Jenkins, deceased, & for the relief of Fabius Stanley: committed.

Capt Marsh, who was in command of the steamer **Ocean Spray** at the time she was destroyed by fire, & also the 2nd engineer & the mate of the steamer, have been arrested & are undergoing an examination at St Louis on a charge of manslaughter, preferred against them by the U S Marshal of that district. When the **Ocean Spray** took fire she was engaged in racing another steamer.

In 1856 Col Lewis W Washington presented the State of Va, on certain conditions, the ground comprising the birth-place of Geo Washington & the graves of the Washington family, on the *Wakefield estate* in Westmoreland Co, Va. This estate was sold in 1813, by Col Geo C Washington, [who derived it from his father Wm Augustine Washington,] of John Gray, of Stafford Co, reserving 60 feet square of the ground around the birth-place, & 20 feet square around the vault. Col Lewis W Washington [son & heir-at-law of Col Geo C Washington] presented these reservations to the mother State of Va, in perpetuity, on condition solely that the State require the said places to be permanently enclosed with an iron fence based on stone foundations, together with suitable & modest [though substantial] tablets, to commemorate to the rising generations these notable spots. Gov'r Wise accepted the donation, & addressed a message to the Legislature asking an appropriation to comply with the conditions, which request, after some delay, was granted & the sum of $5,000 appropriated for the purposes mentioned. In fulfillment of the objects for which the appropriation was made, Govn'r Wise visited Westmoreland Co on Apr 27, for the purpose of surveying the ground on which it is proposed to erect this memorial to the Pater Patrie. The birth place is now marked by the debris of a crumbling chimney, & is overgrown by a thicket of fig-trees, among which lies a marble tablet, now broken in three pieces, & bearing the inscription, "Here, on the 11th of February, 1732, George Washington was born." This slab was placed there in June, 1815, by G W P Custis. About a mile from this spot lies the burial ground & vault, in which are interred the remains of the father, grandfather, & great grandfather of Washington. We learn that it is proposed suitably to enclose these consecrated localities, & to attach to them a porter's lodge, in which shall be installed a custodian of the grounds, as well as guide for the visitors who may make a pilgrimage to this Mecca of American patriotism. [May 6th newspaper: Govn'r Wise, during his recent visit to Westmoreland Co, completed the negotiations for the transfer to the State of the birth-spot of Washington, & the burial place of the Washington family. Mr Wilson, the proprietor of the *Wakefield estate*, consents to give up an acre of ground, comprising the site of the house in which Washington was born, & the old chimney standing there. This area will be enclosed with an iron fence, & an appropriate monument erected on the spot. The negotiation includes the right of way across the plantation, to the road & to the vault; & this latter place is also to be enclosed & improved. –Richmond Dispatch]

An appeal for **Mount Vernon**. Orators, Statesmen, the noble brotherhood of Masons, Odd Fellows, Patriots, one & all, have come promptly to the aid of woman!. And ye, women of the North & of the South, of the East & of the West, will ye not rally to the work? Will ye not vie one with another which will give most & do most, that we may, on the twenty-second of Feb, 1859, claim & take possession of the Home & Grave of him who loved us all, & thus make his birthday the birthday also of Republican gratitude, justice, & fraternal love. –Ann Pamelia Cunningham, Regent **Mount Vernon Ladies' Association**

Criminal Court-Wash-Tue. 1-Eight Germans from Balt were put on trial, charged with abuse & maltreatment of a German woman, Vicoria Fugleman, on Apr 14, between Wash & Bladensburg. West B Rooker was assigned by the Court for their defence. The jury found 5 guilty and 3 were acquitted. Chas Hoffman [who had exhibited a knife] was sentenced to 15 years' hard labor in the penitentiary, & John Sitzer, David Franck, Wm Schmidt, & Hermann Julius to 12 years each.

The following gentlemen were appointed by the Pres of the U S last Monday as members of the Levy Court for Wash Co, D C:

Lewis Carbery	Wm J Palmer	Henry Haw
Saml Drury	Joshua Pierce	Richd R Crawford
Geo W Riggs	H Loughborough	Henry Naylor
Jas A Kennedy	Robt White	

For sale: handsome residence on the Heights of Gtwn: presently occupied by Chas W Pairo. The dwlg house is large & roomy, having a front of 95 feet, with the wings, heated by a furnace, lighted with gas, & contains bath fixtures for hot & cold water, a large cistern, kitchen range; & out-houses. Possession can be given immediately. Apply to Saml C Edes, trustee, at Pairo & Nourse's Banking House, opposite Treasury Dept.

THU MAY 6, 1858
House of Reps: 1-Cmte on Foreign Affairs: bill for the relief of E Geo Squier, of N Y: committed. Same cmte: adverse report in the case of Wm G Moorhead: laid on the table. Same cmte: Sec of the Treasury to furnish the House with copies of the papers on file in his Dept in relation to the claim of John H Wheeler, late Minister to Nicaragua, for losses charged to have been sustained by him by discounts upon drafts for his salary, together with the grounds upon which said claim was disallowed by the Treasury Dept.
2-Resolved, that the capture of Wm Walker on the coast of Nicaragua by Cmdor Paulding was without authority of law.

Mr Alex'r Henry was elected Mayor of the city of Phil on Tue last by a majority of some 3,500 votes. He was supported as the People's candidate, in opposition to Mr Richd Vaux, the present Democratic incumbent.

Very extensive sale of superior Rosewood 7 octave Chickering Piano Forte, excellent household & kitchen furniture at auction on: May 17, by deed of trust from J H Freeman, dated Nov 4, 1857, recorded in Liber J A S, No 146, folios 152, all the furniture & effects of the Ebbet House, on F st, between 13th & 14th sts. -Ferdinand Moulton, W A Case, trustees -Jas C McGuire, auct

Col Schouler, in the Ohio State Journal of Apr 17, announces that his connexion with that paper is dissolved. He returns to Boston, where he will resume the pursuits of his profession as a journalist in connexion with the Bee newspaper.

Mr Josiah Turner, of Lisbon, Maine, dropped down dead on Apr 25, while walking into the meeting-house. He appeared to be well, but all of a sudden his arms were thrown up, & he fell & expired instantly.

Senate: 1-Ptn from R S Simpson, assist surgeon in the army, setting forth that he had rendered professional services in the marine hospital at Key West from Oct 1 to Dec 25, 1856, & asking for such compensation as may be deemed just: referred. 2-Ptn from W A Buckingham, Wolcott Huntington, & other citizens of New London, Conn, urging Congress to make a grant of land to each State in the Union for the purpose of endowing an industrial university for a liberal & practical education being exended to the working classes in their pursuits & professions in life: referred. 3-Cmte on Pensions: adverse reports on the ptns of Frances Cato, widow of Burwell Cato, & of Edw Merritt. 4-Cmte of Claims: adverse report on the memorial of Danl J Browne, asking compensation for extra service & an increase of his salary for the management of the agricultural division of the Patent Ofc. Same cmte: asked to be discharged from the consideration of the report of the Court of Claims adverse to the claim of Jonas P Levy, & that it be referred to the Cmte on Foreign Relations: which was agreed to. 5-Joint resolution for the benefit of the widow of Cmder Wm Lewis Herndon, U S Navy, was taken up. Mr Slidell felt compelled to vote against the passage of the resolution. He would be willing to go one year's pay, but to grant 3 years' full pay to a widow who already enjoyed a pension amounting to some $7,500 he could not consent. Passage was decided in the affirmative: yeas-32; nays-8.

Trustee's sale of highly improved property & real estate; by deed of trust dated Oct 18, 1854, recorded in Liber J A S No 87, folios 67 thru 72, of the land records of Wash City, D C, I shall sell, in front of the premises, formerly owned & occupied by Wm H Faulkner, lot 25 in square A, adoining the line of Michl McCarty, with 4 story brick dwlg house, with back bldgs. –M Thompson, trustee -A Green auct

Gen Chas Fenton Mercer, formerly for many years a distinguished Rep in Congress from the State of Va, died on May 4 at Howard, Fairfax Co, Va, aged 80 years. His funeral will take place this morning at 10 o'clock, at the Theological Seminary, near Alexandria. [May 7th newspaper: obit-died: on May 4, at Howard, near Alexandria, Gen Chas Fenton Mercer, after a protracted illness, in his 80th year. He was for several years a prominent member of the Legislature of Va, afterwards, for a long period, represented the Loudoun district in Congress. He was an ardent advocate of internal improvements, & particularly of the Chesapeake & Ohio Canal, which work was mainly carried through by his constant exertions in its behalf. He was a friend of peace, a true patriot, & a lover of his country. Since his retirement from public life he has passed his days in travel & study, & returned to spend his last hours in the district he once represented, & among those whom he had served faithfully & constantly. –Alexandria Gaz]

J J Poindexter, of Va, having provided by will that his negroes should be allowed to choose between freedom & slavery, the heirs contested the legality of the provision, & were sustained by the Court of Appeals, Judge Daniel deciding that although a master enter into the forms of an agreement with his slave to manumit him, & the slave proceed fully to perform all required of him in the agreement, he is without remedy in case the master refuse to comply with his part of the agreement, & that a slave cannot take anything under a divise or will except his freedon. It follows, therefore, that a slave cannot exercise an election with regard to his manumission.

Hon Saml Dickson, a Rep in the last Congress from the State of N Y, died at his residence in New Scotland, near Albany, on May 3, in his 51st year. [May 7th newspaper: Dr Saml Dickson, Rep of this district in the last Congress, died at his residence at New Scotland on May 3. His death was the result of spinal injuries received while at Wash, towards the close of the last session. While sitting in his room, engaged in writing, he rose to reach a book, & in leaning over the table unknowingly pushed his chair backward. Upon attempting to resume his seat he fell to the floor. His wife, who was present, laughed at the mishap as a joke, but Dr Dickson did not rise, & said " are you not going to help me up?" She immediately went to his assistance, & found that he had hurt his back very badly. The next day Dr Dickson took his seat in the House, but was compelled to leave & was confined to his room for a week. He returned to his duty. In the autumn he could not refrain from taking an active part in the political canvass, & through riding some distance in a wagon he irritated the injured spine & was soon confined to his bed. For the past 3 months he has been unable to walk, & 3 or 4 weeks since it became evident that his days were numbered. –Albany Statesman]

Died: on May 1, in Newbern, N C, Jas G Stanley, in his 75th year, carrying to the grave the tears, love, & veneration of a distressed family. Though Clerk of Craven Co Court 51 years, & living in times of change. He commanded universal homage & respect. -F

Roanoke river land for sale: on May 20, the **Level estate**, containing 1,000 acres; about 4 miles from the depot at Halifax, N C. Refer to Messrs Sands & Worthington, Balt. -H G Burgwyn

Part of **Wollaston's manor** for sale: containing about 200 acres; situated at the mouth of Cuckhold's creek, on the Potomac river, Chas Co, Md, with new bldgs & out houses. Apply to Dr F M Lancaster, Tompkinsville Post Ofc, Chas Co, Md.

Circuit Court of D C-in Equity, No1,226. Thos Redden against John Ratrie & Jas C Haviland. On May 28 next, I shall state the trustee's account of the proceeds of the lots sold by Chas Walter, trustee, the amount due to J C Haviland on the mortage made to him, & the distribution of the residue. –W Redin, auditor

FRI MAY 7, 1858

Jos Dane died at his residence in Kennebunk, Maine, on Sat. From 1820 to 1828 he represented the York district in Congress, was subsequently in the Legislature as a member of the House for 6 years, & was a member of the Senate in 1829. He was chosen a member of the Executive Council of Mass in 1817, & to a similar station in Maine in 1841, but he declined both offices. He was a nephew of Nathan Dane, of Beverly, whose name is associated with the ordinance of 1787. He graduated at Harvard in 1799, & settled in Kennebunk early in the present century. –Boston Post

It has been ascertained that Cutting & Tuttle, both firemen, were the only 2 persons killed outright at the Federal st fire, in Boston, on Sunday. Mr Reardon & Mr Moran are at the hospital, & may possibly recover. The loss incurred by the fire will reach $250,000, the greater part of which is insured in Boston.

Senate: 1-Ptn from McKean Buchanan, a purser in the navy, asking that remuneration may be made to him for losses sustained in consequence of illegal & unusual orders of his commanding ofcr: referred. 2-Ptn from Dorcas Hall, widow of Simeon Reno, a sgt in the army of the Revolution, asking that she may be allowed a pension & bounty land: referred. 3-Ptn from Joshua B Bartlett, asking to be reimbursed for certain expenditures made by him as Com'r of the U S under the treaty of Guadalupe Hidalgo for running & marking the boundary line between the U S & Mexico: referred. 4-Papers in the case of T L Lisharoon, to locate certain warrants on any public land belonging to the U S: submitted & referred. 5-Ptn from residents near the Northwestern Lakes, asking an appropriation to test Prof Ballot's rule in relation to storms: referred. 6-Ptn from the legal reps of Jas Johnson, asking the confirmation of their title to certain land: referred. 7-Cmte on Commerce: adverse report on the memorial of Douglas Ottinger, of the U S revenue service, respecting an invention for the rescue of crews & passengers of sinking vessels. 8-Cmte on the Post Ofc & Post Roads: adverse reports on the memorial of John Frink, asking a remission of the fines imposed on him under a contract with the Post Ofc Dept, & on that of S Van Sickell & other post-route agents for increase of compensation. 9-Bill for the relief of Thos L Disharoon: referred to the Cmte on Private Land Claims. 10-Bill for the relief of Rufus Dwinell: passed. 11-Bill for the relief of Keep, Bard & Co, J Caulfield, & Jos Landis & Co: referred to the Cmte on the Judiciary.

Dr Saml H Dickson, of Charleston, S C, has been elected to the Professorship of Theory & Practice in the Jefferson College, Phil, vice the late Prof John K Mitchell.

The following visiters to the Military Academy at West Point in 1858 have been appointed by the Sec of War, from the States & districts entitled to be represented:
Rhode Island, 2nd district, Francis J Dickman
Delaware, State at large, Andrew C Gray
Arkansas, 2nd district, Hon Albert Pike
Virginia, 3rd district, P Henry Aylett
South Carolina, 1st district, C W Dudley
Tenn: 3rd district, Geo W Rowles
Ky, 2nd dist, Thos C McCrary
Indiana, 3rd district, Hon John W Davis
Illinois, 3rd district, Hon Robt E Goodell
Mich, 3rd district, Jas L Glen
Missouri, 6th district, Jas A Scott
Texas, 2nd district, Gen Jas W Speight
Calif, State at large, J L Brent
Note-Visiters from N H & Vt & N J are yet to be appointed.

The Catholic Provincial Council of the province under the charge of Most Rev Archbishop John B Purcell, of Cincinnati, convened at the Cathedral in that city on Sunday. Bishops Purcell, Lefevre, Spalding, Barraga-of Saut Ste Marie, Carrell, & Luers were present. The opening discourse was delivered by Rt Rev M J Spalding, D D, Bishop of Louisville. The Bishop of St Pallais presided at the P M vespers.

Army & Navy. Changes of stations of ofcrs have been ordered by the Sec of War: Capt Gorgan, ordnance dept, will be relieved from duty at Watervliet arsenal, N Y, & proceed to Charleston, S C, to assume the duties of commanding ofcr of the Charleston arsenal. Capt Kingsury, ordnance dept, will repair to Richdmond, Va, & report to the Colonel of Ordnance for foundry service at that place. Surgeon Chas McCormick, medical dept, is assigned to duty in the dept of the Pacific. He will repair to San Francisco, & report accordingly to the Dept Cmder. Cmdor Smith, Capt Ingraham, & Naval Constructor Lenthall have been constituted by the Sec of the Navy a Board of Com'rs, in accordance with a resolution of the Senate, for the purpose of examining into the merits of a newly invented life-preserving steamboat, by Messrs Morris & Solomon, of Balt. Cmder Wm W Hunter, U S Navy, has been ordered to the command of the receiving ship **Alleghany**, at Balt.

Present at the Eleventh Annual Convention of the American Medical Association. Chair was taken by Pres Lindsly;

Dr R Foster, of Tenn
Dr Grant
Dr Eve
Dr Heywood
Dr Rogers, of N Y
Dr Kemp, of Balt
Dr J F Jenkins, of N Y
Dr AtLee, of Pa
Dr Grafton Tyler
Dr Palmer
Dr Bolton
Dr Cox, of Md
Dr Edwards
Dr Parker, of Va
Dr Wilcox, of Conn
Dr Batchelor, of N Y
Dr Jewell
Dr Wood, of Phil
Dr Sayre, of N Y
Dr Bohrer
Dr Sutton, of Ky
Dr Hyam, of Ohio
Dr Smith, of N J
Dr Humphries
Dr Phelps
Dr Arnold
Dr Hayne, of Va
Dr Morgan, of D C
Dr Atkinson, of Va

Reports read of Dr S M Bemiss, of Ky; of Dr E Andrews, of Ill; of Dr H F Campbell, of Ga; of Dr Mark Stevenson, of N Y; & of J M Sims, of N Y.

Public laws & our political system. In a recent case Thos H Baird, son & heir of Surgeon Baird, to whom was granted & paid 5 years' full pay, without interest, by an act of Congress of Jun, 1836, as commutation for half pay, & this was relied upon by the U S as a final settlement of the half pay claim; but the court in that case say "that upon any principles known to the law this position is wholly untenable. It is easy enough to declare ex cathedra that it was was a final settlement. If it were a case between individuals no one would dream of applying such a term to it." The Court of Claims therefore reported a bill for the relief of Thos H Baird for the amount of the half-pay, with the interest, deducting only the amount of commutation actually paid him in specie instead of worthless certificates. This bill was passed by both Houses, & the money paid at the Treasury.

Theatre. The ascending star now at the Theatre is Miss Avonia Jones, a charming actress & young & beautiful lady, a native of Washington.

Henry Queen offers for sale about 90 acres of a most valuable gardening or farming land, divided into 5 sections, being a part of the tract on which Col Brooks resides, fronting on the back of Bladensburg Road, adjoining the farms of Messrs E Tucker, McCaeny, & N L Queen. Apply to E J Middleton, City Hall, Wash, or at his residence near the premises.

Mrd: on May 6, by Rev Andrew G Carothers, Mr Tobias Robey to Miss Lucy Ann Klock, both of Fairfax Co, Va.

Mrd: on May 6, at the Presbyterian Church, Gtwn, D C, by Rev J Bocock, D D, Lt Thos Wilson, U S Army, to Miss Henrietta W, daughter of B F Rittenhouse, of former place.

Died: on May 5, in Wash City, Margaret, relict of the late Marmaduke Dove, in her 73rd year. Her funeral will be this afternoon at 3 o'clock, from the residence of Dr G M Dove, 472 south I st, Navy Yard.

Died: on May 2, at Ellicott's Mills, Mrs Ann Thorn, in her 73rd year.

Richd Lorman Ross offers for sale his very valuable farm in Montg Co, Md, on the Turnpike Road leading from Wash to Rockville, 7 miles fromWash, containing about 300 acres of land; with a large dwlg house & necessary out-bldgs. If desired a family of servants & all the stock & farming utensils will be sold with the farm. Apply by letter to him at the Cottage Post Ofc, Montg Co, Md; or to E J Middleton, City Hall, Wash.

Obit-died: on Apr 21, at Shepherdstown, Va, in his 61st year, Col John F Hamtramck, a highly respected citizen of the town [for several years its Mayor] & a justice of the peace for the county. Col H was a son of Gen Hamtramck, of the Revolutionary army, who was also prominent as a compatriot of Gen Harmar in his sanguinary contest with the Indians. The deceased was born at **Fort Wayne**, Ind, whilst a battle with the Indians was raging. He was in service with Gen Zachary Taylor, then a capt, on the Indian frontier. He graduated with distinction at West Point, was an ofcr of the U S army, & for several years an Indian agent. His funeral was attended by several of his brother ofcrs & by many of the men whom he had at different times commanded-the largest funeral ever seen in the county.

Boston, May 4. The body of Patrick Reardon was found this morning in the ruins of the fire which occurred in this city on Sunday. Three bodies have now been recovered.

SAT MAY 8, 1858
Auction sale of 33 beautiful **Villa Lots**, on May 19. These lots adjoin **Uniontown**, on the south side of Eastern Branch or Anacostia river, near the Navy Yard Bridge. The undersigned are now making handsome improvements on 2 of these sites for their own residences. –Fox & Van Hook -A Green auct

Funeral of the late Senator Evans: on May 8, at the late residence of the deceased, No 6 Louisiana ave, at 10 o'clock. Pall Bearers: Mr Fitzpatrick, Mr Mason, Mr Collamer, Mr Crittenden, Mr Allen, Mr Fessenden. The family & friends of the deceased will follow. [May 10th newspaper: Senate: announcement of the death of Hon Joshiah J Evans, who died most unexpectedly on May 6, of disease of the heart. He was in the Senate during the entire session of that day. Mr Evans was born in S C; earliest graduate of her then infant college-class of 1808; educated to the bar. He was born on Nov 27, 1786, & was 71 years of age. He had a fond family & ample fortune]

Appointments by the Pres, by & with the advice & consent of the Senate.
Edw G Loring, of Mass, to be Judge of the Court of Claims, vice John J Gilchrist, deceased.
Geo W Belden, of Ohio, to be Atty of the U S for the northern district of Ohio.
Matthew Johnson, of Ohio, to be U S Marshal for the northern district of Ohio.
Collectors & Surveyors:
John Boston, Collector of the Customs for the district of Savannah, Ga, his former commission having expired.
Jas E Godfrey, to be Surveyor of the Customs for the district of Savannah, Ga, his late commission having expired.
John P C Mather, to be Collector of the Customs for the district of New London, Conn.
John R Redman, to be Collector of the Customs for the district of Penobscot, Maine.
Wm B Dameron, to be Surveyor of Customs of the district of San Francisco, Calif.
Registers & Receivers:
Edwin T L Blake, of Fla, to be Register at Tallahassee, Fla.
Wm T Galloway, of Wisc, to be Register at Eau Claire, Wisc.
Noel Byron Boyden, of Wisc, to be Receiver at Eau Claire, Wisc
Saml Ryan, of Wisc, to be Receiver at Menasha, Wisc, vice Benj H Moores, resigned.
Jas D Raymert, of Wisc, to be Receiver at Hudson, Wisc.

Archibald McIntyre, aged 86, died at Albany on May 5. He was comptroller during the bitter contest between Tompkins & Clinton, & took sides with Clinton. He subsequently amassed a fortune as lottery manager in the firm of Yates & McIntyre.

The American Association for the Advancement of Science, lately in session at Balt, adjourned on Tue last. Gentlemen chosen officers for the ensuing year:
Pres: Prof Stephen Alexander, of Princeton, N J.
Vice Pres: Prof Edw Hitchcock, of Amherst, Mass.
Gen Sec: Prof Chauvenet, of Annapolis, Md.
Permanent Sec: Prof Jos Lovering, of Cambridge, Mass.
Treasurer: Dr A L Elwyn, of Phil, Penn.
Among the variety of papers read were by:
Prof Stephen Alexander
Prof Jos Henry
Lt E B Hunt
Prof Arnold Guyot
Mr Jos Saxton
Dr J H Gibbon
Prof John LeConte
Prof A D Bache
Dr J L Hayes

Mr Shillinglaw, of Hamilton, Canada, mistook arsenic for carbonate of soda, drank the fatal draught, & died before medical assistance arrived.

House of Reps: 1-Ptn of Elbert F Sevier, in behalf of himself & others, heirs & reps of Henry Conway, deceased, capt of infty in the Va Continental line, praying for his arrearage of pay & rations: was presented.

Laws of the U S: Public No 11. An Act to incorporate *Gonzaga College*, in Wash City, D C. Be it enacted by the Senate & House of Reps of the U S of America in Congress assembled, that Burcard Villiger, Chas H Stonestreet, Danl Lynch, Edw X Hand, & Chas Jenkins, & their successors be & they are hereby made a body politic & corporate forever, by the name of the Pres & Directors of *Gonzaga College*, for the purposes of charity & education; & by that name may sue & be sued, prosecute & defend; may have & use a common seal, & the same alter & renew at pleasure; may adopt rules, regulations, & by-law, not repugnant to the Constitution & laws of the U S, for property conducting the affairs of said corporation; may take, receive, purchase, & hold estate, real, personal, & mixed, not exceeding in value the sum of $200,000 at any one time, & may manage & dispose of the same at pleasure, & apply the same, or the proceeds of the sales thereof, to the uses & purposes of said corporation, according to the rules & regulations which now are or may hereafter be established. Sec 2: That the said corporation shall have the power & faculty to confer & confirm upon such pupils in the institution, or others, who, by their proficiency in learning or other meritorious distinctions, they shall think entitled to them, such degrees in the liberal arts & sciences as are usually granted in colleges. Sec 3: That the president & directors of Gtwn College by & they are hereby authorized & empowered to convey to the said president & directors of *Gonzaga College* & their successors forever, who are hereby authorized & empowered to receive the same, such lands & property, & such estate, real, personal, or mixed, as the said president & directors of Gtwn College may receive, or may have received, for the use or benefit of said president & directors of *Gonzaga College*. Sec 4: That nothing in this act shall be so construed as to authorize this said corporation to issue any note, token, device, scrip, or other evidence of debt, to be used as a currency. Sec 5: That each of the corporators in said corporation shall be held liable, in his individual capacity, for all the debts & liabilities of said corporation, however contracted or incurred, to be recovered by suit, as other debs or liabilities, before any court of competent jurisdiction. Sec 6: That Congress may at any time hereafter, alter, amend, or repeal the foregoing act. Approved, May 4, 1858.

Senate: 1-Mr Mason presented the credentials of Hon Thos L Clingman, appointed a Senator by the Govn'r of the State of N C to fill the vacancy occasioned by the resignation of Hon Asa Biggs of his seat in the Senate of the U S. The oath prescribed by law was administered & Mr Clingman took his seat.

I offer my present residence in Charlestown, Jefferson Co, Va, for sale. The house is commodious & in a thorough state of repair, with all necessary accommodations for servants & other bldgs. The view is unsurpassed. –Ann J Burnett, Charlestown

Circuit Court of D C-in Chancery. Celinda J Byng vs Virginia Byng, et al. The trustee reported he sold the west half of lot 4 in square 460, in Wash City, to Matthew W Galt & Wm Galt, for $23,300, & the purchasers have complied with the terms of sale. -John A Smith, clerk

In Chancery of N J. In the matter of escheat of lands of Jacob Wortman, deceased, situated in the township of Chester, Morris Co, N J. By writ of escheat issued out of said Court, directed to Wm H Anderson, Sheriff of Chester Co, an inquisition was taken before him at the Court-house at Morristown, in said county, on Apr 10, 1858, pursuant to the act in such case made & provided, whereby & by there turn whereof, signed by the said sheriff & the jurors therein mentioned, it appears that the said Jacob Wortman, at the time of his death, was seized of an equal undivided one-third part of the 3 several tracts of land & premises hereinafter particularly described. The first lot is in the township of Chester, Morris Co, N J [near Peter Wortman's line] containing 201 acres. The second lot is in the same township, being a corner to lands formerly of Hugh Runyon, containing 249 acres. The third lot, in the same township, beinging at a small stone heap in a fence of Jacob Emans, then to Jacob Emans line, to Shangles' line, containing 150 acres. Jacob Wortman had an estate of inheritance in fee simple in & to the equal undivided one-third part of the said lands, tenements, & hereditaments. That the said Jacob Wortman died in May 1842; he made no devise of the said lands, tenements, or hereditaments, or any of them; he did not leave any heirs, & the clear yearly value of the one-third part of the tracts of land at the time of his death is the sum of $200. All persons claiming any interest in the lands are to appear within 20 days after Nov 16 next. Dated Trenton, N J, May 3, 1858. –Wm L Dayton, Atty Gen of N J.

Mrd: on May 6, at Christ Church, Gtwn, by Rev Dr Norwood, Richd H Jones, of Cumberland, Md, to Miss Mary Robinson, eldest daughter of Wm Hunter, Chief Clerk of the Dept of State.

Criminal Court-Wash-Wed. 1-John White found not guilty of an assault with intent to kill Michl McNulty. 2-John Hughes guilty of grand larceny, having stolen $73 in money from Patrick Hand: sentenced to 2 years in the penitentiary.

MON MAY 10, 1858
The Pension Ofc has information from one of its special agents of the arrest in Vt, of J C Buswell, Ebenezer Bickford, R D Waters, & one Wallace, charged with obtaining bounty land warrants on false & forged papers, knowing them to be of that character.

Detroit paper:Geo W Brazie, a young man who has until recently been at student at the Univ at Ann Arbor, Mich, died last week. A band of students conceived the plan of giving him a mock initiation into a sham society, & beer & whisky were provided for the occasion. Brazie drank freely & became intoxicated, & the unfortunate man died before a physician could arrive. His death was by intemperance.

Mrd: on May 5, in Otsego Co, N Y, by Rev Horace Norton, Thos Moore, of Fairfax Co, Va, to Hannah H, youngest daughter of the late J W Morris, of the former place.

Died: on May 8, Mrs Susan M Sothoron, wife of Jno R Sothoron.

Columbian College exercises were held on Friday last at the Smithsonian Institution.
Addresses by:

Chas W Hassler, of Wash, D C
John H Wright, Nansemond Co, Va
Trezvant Harrison, Sussex Co, Va
T Major Freeman, Frankfort, Ky
John T Griffin, Nansemond Co, Va

Robt K Carter, Fred'k Co, Va
Saml R White, Bedford Co, Va
Jos F Deans, Norfolk Co, Va
Wm S Wright, Nansemond Co, Va
John H Wright, Nansemond Co, Va

TUE MAY 11, 1858
Senate: 1-Ptn from Danl F Tiemann, Mayor of N Y, & the Mayors of Brooklyn & of Jersey City, & of the harbor commissioners, a cmte appointed to inquire into the plans & drawing laid down by recommendation of the Superintendent of the Coast Survey, Prof Bache, Senators Seward & King, for the better arrangement of the draining of those cities, & for the improvement of their sanitary conditions by preventing the soil of each city from flowing into the rivers, by forming parallel stone wharfs along the water-front of each city, as may be devised: referred. 2-Ptn from Deborah Burlingham, daughter of an officer of the Revolutionary army, for a pension: referred. 3-Ptn from Frances H Robinson, Ellen Carter, John Harry, Chas Dodge, & other residents on the *Heights of Gtwn, D C*, asking that said Heights may be set apart from the corporate limits of said town, upon the ground that they are so far removd from the business part of the town as to have no benefit from its regulations, or have the slightest protection to property or person through its police: referred. 4-Ptn from Aebel Hildreth, asking an appropriation to enable him to set up & attach to the bell at Whitehead a simple apparatus for keeping up a continual alarm by the rise & fall of the tides: referred. 5-Ptn from H R Schoolcraft, asking compensation for the collection of the facts & materials embodied in the history, statistics, condition, & prospects of the Indian tribes, prepared & published by him: referred. 6-Cmte of Claims: bill for the relief of Mrs Ann P Derrick, widow of W S Derrick, deceased. Same cmte: bill for the relief of Richd W Clarke, for additional compensation for services performed in the Pension Ofc. Same cmte: asked to be discharged from the consideration of the memorial of Walter James, asking compensation for a horse lost whilst employed in transporting munitions of war in 1812: which was agreed to. 7-Bill for the relief of Jeremiah Moore: referred to the Court of Claims.

Purser Rittenhouse has presented to Mr Fred'k H Rose, Assist Surgeon in the British Navy, the gold medal struck for him by order of the sailors of the U S steamship **Susquehanna**, in testimony of their grateful appreciation of his heroic services to the victims of the yellow fever on board that vessel.

A letter from the Seminole Agency, west of Arkansas, to the *Fort Smith Times* says that the Creeks have killed the notorious Indian, Yobi, whohas murdered so many persons in the last few months. They shot him 3 times.

John R Francisco, aged about 15, accidentally hung himself in a shed attached to his father's barn. The father was nearly frantic with grief on finding his son dead.

House of Reps: 1-Bill to continue the pension of Catherine M Horner: referred to the Cmte on Invalid Pensions.

Loefner, the Cincinnati murderer, whose sentence has been commuted to imprisonment for life, is greatly dissatisfied at the change.

John Gregory, for murder, has been sentenced to be hung on May 21 at Halifax, N C.

Chancery sale of valuable real estate: by decree of the Circuit Court of D C, in Equity, for Wash Co, made in the cause wherein Jas Burdine & wife are cmplnts, & Geo Sheckell, Mary Ann Sheckell, & Rosaline V Sheckell are dfndnts. The subscriber will sell at public auction, on Jun 4 next, lot 6 in square 576, with improvements. The lot is on the south side of Md ave, opposite the Govn't green-houses, containing 12,160 square feet of ground, more or less, fronting 125 to 130 feet on Md ave: with an extensive boarding house. –Jno A Linton, trustee -C W Boteler, auct

The Board of Visiters of **Wm & Mary College**, Va, have elected Robt J Morrison, of Richmond city, to fill the vacancy in the professorship of history, vice John A Washington, deceased.

Criminal Court-Wash-Mon. The case of Geo Creager, alias Williams, who was arraigned for the murder of Wm Farrell on Feb 22, was postponed, the defence not ready with their witnesses. [May 12th newspaper: The jury returned a verdict of manslaughter.] [May 14th newspaper: W Farrell sentenced to 8 years' confinement & hard labor in the penitentiary.]

Mrd: on May 9, by Rev Wm H Chapman, Mr Wm H McFarland to Miss Mary Julia May, all of Wash City.

Died: on May 9, in Montg Co, Md, suddenly, Charlotte L Thompson, wife of Jos Thompson, & fourth daughter of the late Fred'k D Tschiffely, of Wash City. Her funeral will be at **Oak Hill Cemetery** this afternoon, at 4 o'clock, without further notice.

Died: on May 7, of consumption, Wm L Todd, formerly of Florence, Ala, for some time a clerk in the Dept of Interior.

Portland Manor for sale on Jun 10, the tract of highly improved land, of which Jas Kent died seized, containing 593 acres. This land will be sold free of all encumbrances, either in the whole or to suit purchasers. –T Blake Kent

Orphans Court of Wash Co, D C. Letters of administration on the personal estate of Peter Hepburn, late of Wash Co, deceased. –David Hepburn, adm

WED MAY 12, 1858

Senate: 1-Ptn from Wm Fleming & others, of the marine artl, who served in the war of 1812, asking to be allowed pensions for said service: referred. 2-Ptn from E T Peyton, asking to be compensated for performing the duties of Sec of Legation in Chili: referred. 3-Ptn from J G Dennison, asking a mail route from Toledo, Iowa, to Decatur, in the Territory of Nebraska: referred. 4-Ptn from Noah H Phelps, remonstrating against the passage of the House bill confirming the title of a certain tract of land to the heirs of Pierre Brouchard: referred. 5-Ptn from Henry M Fleury, asking the passage of a law to authorize him to prosecute against the U S his claim to a certain tract of land: referred. 6-Ptn from Capt R B Cunningham, asking that the pay of ofcrs of the navy may be increased: referred. 7-Ptn from Mrs Jane Turnbull, widow of Col W Turnbull, of the U S Topographical Engineers, asking to be allowed a pension: referred. 8-Cmte of Claims: bill for the relief of Stephen R Rowan, asking to be discharged from liability incurred as receiver of public moneys in consequence of a robbery. Same cmte: bill for the relief of P G Duval & Co, asking indemnity for paper & plates for the second volume of the Japan Expedition destroyed by fire, submitted a special report. 9-Cmte on Foreign Relations: bill for the relief of L C Portman, asking compensation for services as interpreter of the Japan Expedition. 10-Cmte on Pensions: asked to be discharged from the consideration of the bill to continue the pension heretofore granted to Catharine M Hamer, & numerous ptns asking for a continutation of pensions, on the ground that the cases were provided for in a general bill: which was agreed to. Same cmte: bill for the relief of Catharine Dickerson. Same cmte: bill for the relief of Capt John Pickrell, late a lt in the U S army. Same cmte: adverse report on the ptn of Jos Haynes; & on the claim of Rachel Morey. 11-Cmte on Private Land Claims: act for the relief of the heirs or their legal reps of Wm Conway, deceased: recommended its passage.

The Methodist Episcopal Church South: Genr'l Conference at Nashville, on May 1. Rev Joshua Soule, D D, the senior Bishop, presided. Rev T O Summers, D D, was elected Sec. Bishop Soule is now in the 60th year of his ministry, having entered the travelling connexion Jan, 1799. He was ordained in 1824, & has exercised his functions 34 years. Since his ordination the following Bishops have passed away: Mckendree, Geo Emory, Roberts, Hedding, Bascom, Capers, & Waugh.

Federal Court at Staunton: May 4, Hon John Brockenbrough presiding. 1-Young Stewart, of Highland, charged with aiding & assisting Saml Blewitt with robbing the mail on the route from Franklin to Millborough, in May, 1857. The case was prosecuted by F B Miller, U S Atty, & defended by H W Sheffey: verdict of the jury-not guilty. 2-Mr Siegmond Hope for destroying letters not addressed to himself at a post ofc in the Valley, & not containing anything of value: jury returned a verdict of not guilty. 3-Next case was that of Saml Blewitt, a youth of 16 or 18 years of age: guilty. –Staunton [Va] Vindicator

A breach of promise case was tried at Paducah, Ky, on Thu, between Miss Smith, of Cairo, & Mr John Allard, of Paducah, which resulted in a verdict of $2,000 damages for the lady.

Chancery sale of valuable real estate & large quantity of brick, known as the Nat'l Theatre. By decree of the Circuit Court of Wash Co, D C, between Jas A Lenman & John T Lenman as cmplnts, & Wm H Winder & others as dfndnts: public sale on Jun 8, on the premises, the whole of lot 4, part of lot 3, in square 254, not heretofore conveyed to Allison Nailor. The whole property, fronting 88 feet 10½ inches on E st north, between 13th & 14th sts, with a depth of 159 feet. Also, at the same time, all the brick contained in the burnt walls of the old Nat'l Theatre on said lots. –Chas S Wallach, Walter D Davidge, trustees -Jas C McGuire, auct

House of Reps: 1-Memorial of John Frikard, of the city of Phil, praying Congress to afford him remuneration for losses of stock in trade sustained by him in behalf of the Gov't of the U S during the war in Florida in 1838-39: presented. 2-Memorial of Capt Wm Fleming & others, volunteers of the Marine Artl, Delaware flotilla, engaged in the war of 1812-15, praying that they may be remunerated for actual service rendered in said war: presented. 3-Memorial of Wm B Whiting, a lt in the U S navy, praying Congress to pass an act amendatory of the act granting bounty land to certain soldiers, their widows & minors, approved Mar 3, 1835, & the act amendatory, approved May 14, 1856, so that their provisions may extend to children who were not minors n Mar 3, 1855, & also praying that pensions may be granted to the orphans of such soldiers who are not minors, with a cetain proviso: presented.

Thos G Broughton, the worthy editor of the Norfolk [Va] Herald, celebrated the 50th anniversary of his marriage on Friday. Children & grandchildren were present, & an interesting address was delivered by Rev Dr Armstrong. The worthy couple are now 71 years of age.

Albany, May 11. Disaster this morning on the Central railroad, near Whitesborough. The Cincinnati Express train was behind time at Whitesborough, &, coming in at a high rate of speed, met the Utica accommodation train on the bridge over the Sauquoit Creek. The bridge gave way precipitating the cars into the creek. Amongst the dead are A Moore, of Rising Sun, Indiana; two children of Abraham Mack, of Cincinnati; & a child of Karl Hover, of St Louis. Over 40 persons were injured, some fatally. [May 13th newspaper: The following are the dead up to this time: A Moore, of Rising Sun, Ind; Danl S Brayton, of Phelps, Ontario Co, N Y; 2 children of Abraham Mack, of Cincinnati, one a girl aged 12 years, & the other a boy aged 6; John Fitzgerald, of N Y; Wm H Sharpe, a colored preacher; Chas Bettman, of Cincinnati, aged 12 years.]

THU MAY 13, 1858
Household & kitchen furniture & valuable library at public auction on May 24, by deed of mortgage from Alfred Holmead & wife to Sweeny, Rittenhouse & Co, dated Jun 21, 1855, recorded in Liber J A S No 99, folios 305, of the land records for Wash Co, D C: given in lieu of acceptances of J J Frisby, of Norfolk, Va, on which the said Holmead was endorser, the undersigned, by order of the mortgagees, & their assigns, at 173 South B st, opposite the Smithsonian Institute, daily, until all is disposed of, an excellent assortment of furniture. –Clarke & Smith, Attys -A Green auct

Senate: 1-The abstract of title & accompanying papers, enclosed by Mr P Della Torre, were referred to the Atty Gen for his opinion as to their sufficiency to convey a title to the U S. The opinion of that ofcr that the papers did not convey a perfect title has, with the papers, been returned to Mr Della Torre. The papers were referred to the Cmte on Military Affairs. 2-Ptn from Jos Vance, a soldier of the war of 1812, asking to be allowed a pension. 3-Cmte on Military Affirs: bill for the relief of Thos Laurent, surviving partner of the firm of Benj & Thos Laurent. Same cmte: bill for the relief of Assist-Surgeon Edw P Vollum, of the U S Army. 4-Cmte on Finance: bill for the relief of Caleb Sherman. 5-Cmte on Pensions: bill for the relief of Abner Merrill, of the State of Maine. 6-Resolved that the settlers of *Fort Crawford Reservation*, in the State of Iowa, allege that they have been defrauded by Henry M Rice, as agent of the Hon John B Floyd, Sec of War, in the sale of their claims as settlers on said reservation: that the Sec of War instructed Henry M Rice to sell to the settlers on said reservations their claims at $1,25 per acre; that said Rice required said settlers to pay for their claims as the rate of $1.50 per acre, & receipted to them on the payment of said $1.50 per acre for but $1.25 per acre, & refused to receipt to them for the remaining .25 per acre received of them by him. In sundry cases in which settlers applied to said Rice for leave to enter their said claims he referred them to his clerk, who charged them fees varying from ten to eighty dollars each, in addition to the $1.50 pe acre for leave to purchase their said claims; that these fees were charged & received by the said Rice corruptly, & said sellers believe, through the interpositon of his clerk. A cmte to be appointed to investigate the allegations of fraud & extortion made against Henry M Rice: lies over under the rules.

House of Reps: 1-Cmte on MilitaryAffairs: bill to refund to Jas Douglass, Govn'r of Vancouver's Island, $7,000, advanced by him to suppy the volunteers of Wash Territory with clothing & equipage during the late Indian war in that Territory: committed.

Jas Collier, brother of John A Collier, has just had a long lawsuit decided in his favor. Mr Collier was appointed Collector of Customs to Calif. After leaving ofc the Gov't claimed that Mr Collier was a defaulter to the amount of $791,000. The Gov't sued Mr Collier. The verdict resulted in his favor. The case was appealed. Finally on Monday, the Court decided that the Gov't owed Mr Collier $8,000. Quite a difference.
–Penn Inquirer

Wash Corp: Wm D Serrin confirmed for police constable in the first district, in place of David Lucas, resigned.

The death of Jessie Barber, aged 4 years & 9 months, is announced in the Chicago papers. This little girl was the last surviving member of the family of Jabez Barber, of Chicago, who, with his wife & daughter, perished in the Collins steamer **Pacific**, in 1856. At the time of his death his property was estimated at about $250,000, & has since increased in value to $400,000. By his will the entire property fell to the infant Jessie. The nearest of kin are Mary Ann, Harriet, Lucy Barber, of Birmingham, England, & Eliza Bell, of Simcoe, Canada East.

Correct list of the officers of the U S steam frig **Colorado**, expected to leave Hampton Roads on Tue, as the flag ship of the Home Squadron: Flag-ofcr, Jas Mc McIntosh, Cmder-in-Chief; Capt, Wm H Gardner; 1st Lt & Exec Ofcr, Edmund Lanier; 2nd do, Thos H Stevens; 3rd do, Geo H Cooper; 4th do, Abner Read; 5th do, Wm L Powell; 6th do, Saml Magaw, [Flag;] 7th do, Beverley Kennon; Master, Aeneas Armstrong; Fleet Surgeon, Edw Gilchrist; Purser, Edw C Doran; Passed Assist Surgeon, Arthur M Lynch; Assist Surgeon, Alex'r M Vedder; Chaplain, Nathl Frost; Marine Ofcrs, Capt Josiah Watson, 2nd Lt, Philip H W Fontaine; Chief Engineer, Eldridge Lawton; Cmdor's Sec, Wm C Zantzinger; Passed Midshipmen, Edw P Lull, Alex'r F Crosman; Midshipmen, Augustus P Cooke, Thos H Eastman, Geo M Blodgett; Capt's Clerk, E St Clair Clarke; Purser's Clerk, Richd W Byrd; Boatswain, John McKinley; Gunner, John Owins; Carpenter, Francis M Cecil; Sailmaker, Wm Bennett; First Assist Engineers, Francis Dade, Thos A Shock; Second Assist Engineers, John W Moore, Alex'r Greer; 3rd Assist Engineers, Chas H Levy, Franklin K Hain, John Purdy, jr, Philip Inch.

Mrd: May 11, in Wash City, at the Church of the Epiphany, by Rev Dr Hall, Hon Silas M Burroughs, of N Y, to Miss Charlotte S, youngest daughter of S Brintnall, formerly of Watertown, N Y.

Mrd: May 9, at the Chapel of St Andrews, by Rev Jas A Harrold, Mr Jos Miller to Mrs Henrietta Williams, of Wash.

Died: on May 12, in Wash City, Mrs Sarah Hutchinson. Her funeral is today at 4 o'clock, from her late residence on G st, between 8th & 9th sts.

This is to give notice that I have filed in the Gen Land Ofc a caveat to arrest the fraudulent entry or patenting of Bounty Land Warrant No 26,203, for 160 acres of land issued to Evan Jones on Apr 7, 1854, the said warrant never having been received by me or my agent, Jonathan Clarke, of Humboldt, Calif, to whom it appears to have been mailed in Apr, 1854. –Evan Jones, by Jno Johnson, his atty.

Military Warrant No 8,902, for 150 2/3 acres, was issued on Jan 22, 1811, to Theodore S Garnett, one of the heirs of Chas C Taliaferro, deceased, who was one of the devisees of Alex'r Dick, in consideration of the said Alex'r Dick's service in the State line of Va, from Feb, 1776, to the end of the war. The original has been lost & an order of court issued for its renewal. The Register of the Land Ofc in Richmond, Va, has issued a duplicate, & application will be made to the land ofc in Wash City for scrip for the same in due time. –Theodore S Garnett, Caroline Co, Va

Wanted, by a respectable young woman, a situation to do chamber work & plain sewing. The best references can be given. Apply at Mr P Cassady's, next door to Mr G Lowry, Water st, Gtwn.

Fan's of all kind, just received. Travelling bags & baskets. Articles suitable for presents, at McLaughlin's, Penn ave, between 8th & 9th sts. [Ad]

FRI MAY 14, 1858
Court Martial of Maj Gen David E Twiggs, U S Army, on Mar 19, 1858, at Newport Barracks, Ky. Spec 1-In that he, the said Twiggs, commanding the Dept of Texas, having received War Dept Special Orders, No 128, of 1857, did, at San Antonio, on Oct 29, 1857, in contempt of orders, appoint a court of inquiry to examine matters adjudged & decided in said orders. Spec 2-In that he, the said Twiggs, did, at San Antonio, on Dec 14, 1856, in contempt of the Pres' orders aforesaid, publish orders to the troops under his command, confirming a report of said court of inquiry, contradicting a decision pronounced in the Pres' orders aforesaid. Spec 3-In that he, the said Twiggs, having received from the War Dept, in a letter dated Jan 16, 1858, instructions in regard to the breaches of discipline set out in the specifications aforesaid, with orders to publish said instructions to the Dept of Texas, he, the said Twiggs, did, at San Antonio, Texas, on Feb 8, 1858, in contempt of the obedience & submission due to the said decision of the Pres, accompany the publication to the troops under his command with a commentary on the instructions designed to contradict & refute them, & denouncing them as a "poison," & appealing from the order of the Pres to the troops under his command. To which charge & specifications the accused pleaded not guilty. Findings of the Court, as follows:
1st specification: guilty, except the word contempt
2nd specification: guilty, except the word contempt
3rd specification: guilty, & guilty of the charge
Sentence: to be reprimanded by the Pres of the U S.
War Dept, May 10, 1858. The verdict of the Court martial is approved, but, in consideration of his distinguished services, & of the unanimous recommendation of the court, the sentence was remitted. –John B Floyd, Sec of War
III: The Genr'l Court-martial of which Brvt Maj Thos S Jesup is President is dissolved.
IV: Brvt Maj Gen David E Twiggs will resume his sword & the command of the Dept of Texas. By order of the Sec of War. S Cooper, Adj Gen

Sale on Monday next at the marble yard of Mr Jos W Kelly, on E st, next to the burnt Theatre, a lot of Marble, Marble Tomb-stones, Monuments, Head & Foot stones. -Wall & Barnard, aucts

Senate: 1-Ptn from Georgiana M Lewis, widow of Armstrong Irvine Lewis, late a lt in the Texas navy, asking to be allowed the 5 years' pay granted to the surviving ofcrs of that navy. This lady thinks she is entitiled, under the act of Congress of Mar, 1857, to the 5 years'pay granted to the surviving ofcrs of the Texas navy, as her husband survived more than 7 years after the period of annexation: referred. 2-Ptn from John E Caldwell, contractor for carrying the mail from New Orleans to Vicksburg, asking that the Postmaster Gen be authorized to adjust & settle his claim on principles of equity & justice: referred. 3-Cmte of Claims: adverse to the claim of Louis F Tasistro, urging compensation for services rendered in examining the materials for a new volume of the American archives under & by the direction of the Sec of State. 4-Cmte on Military Affairs: asked to be discharged from the consideration of the memoir of Capt J J Cram, & that it be returned to the War Dept.

N Y C: 1-Henry Dwight, a banker of this city, has been arrested on 6 warrants for alleged embezzlement from the funds of the Chicago, Alton, & St Louis railroad to the amount of a million of dollars, & for perjury. 2-A servant girl in the family of Mr A Taylor, 344 Canal st, was dangerously burnt on Mon by the explosion of a camphene lamp.

Medical Corps of the Navy: the following assistant surgeons passed a satisfactory examination: John M Brown, H C Caldwell, & John L Taylor. The following were approved as candidates for admission into the service, & will be appointed as vacancies occur: 1-J C Bortolette, Pa; 2-T W Leach, N H; 3-M P Christian, Va; 4-J J Magee, Pa; 5-B F Gibbs, N J; 6-J O Burnett, Pa; 7-W M King, Pa.

The British screw-steamship **Saladin**, Capt Middleton, arrived at N Y on Wed in 10 days from Kingston, Jamaica. She is bound to Liverpool, & put into that port to land 61 of the crew & ofcrs belonging to the U S steam frig **Susquehanna**, who, being sick with yellow fever, were sent ashore from that vessel at Kingston. On Apr 17 the men were all discharged from the hospital cured, & by the 20th all the ofcrs were discharged. List of those who died at Kingston: J J Lyne, purser's clerk; Edw Bolles, seaman; Wm Galena, cooper; Jas Flynn, boy; C Balestieri, band-master; Jacob Booth, marine; Robt Hodge & Mat Henry, firemen; Peter Simpson, seaman; Jas Buckley, seaman; Austin Fewill, seaman; Jas Stinman, seaman; Alex Lamb, seaman; Thos C Howe, seaman; D McCarty, seaman; J W Napon, master's mate; J W J Jones, seaman; Pat Burke, C H Antonio, Larcetta, boy; Francis Gonzales, seaman; Francis Carr, seaman; Freeman Luce, quartermaster. The following ofcrs arrived in the **Saladin**: Lt J C Howell, Alex'r Henderson, 2nd assist engineer; Glendy King, assist engineer; John Grier, do; M Cushman, do.

Public sale on May 18, in front of Dorsey & Cook's Livery & Sale Stables, on 8th st, between D & E sts, 11 superior Northern-bred Horses. –Jas C McGuire, auct

Trustee's sale of lot 1 in square 257, on Ohio ave & 13½ st, near the Canal. By deed of trust from Jos Wimsatt, dated Oct 31, 1850, recorded in Liber J A S No 17, folios 495: sale with improvements & appurtenances thereto belonging. –Anthony Hyde, Thos B Suter, trustees -A Green auct

The preliminary examination in the case of Waldro Marsh, capt; Danl R Davis, mate; W S Spargo, engineer, of the steamer **Ocean Spray**, [recently burnt at St Louis,] on a charge of neglect of duty, by cause of which the boat was burnt, has just terminated, & they have been held to answer. The capt was bound over in the sum of $4,000 for his appearance at the U S Circuit Court for Missouri District, at its fall term, 1858, & the engineer & mate in the sum of $2,000 each.

Two children of Martin Kalar, of Oshkosh, Wisc, a boy of 10 & a girl of 13 years, ventured upon a small scow sailing near the shore, when a gales came up & drifted them out into the lake. On Sunday they were found in the bottom of the boat frozen to death.

Capt Chas R Webb, of Stamford, Conn, who with the aid of a green boy who had never before been to sea, navigated the yacht **Charter Oak**, 22 feet long, from N Y to Liverpool, is now bldg a yacht 44 feet keel & 16 feet beam, with which he intends to vist the Isle of Wight, St Petersburgh, & some French ports, to let the crowned heads of Europe see what a Yankee can do.

The employees of the Wash Navy Yard, desirous of showing their appreciation of the worth of the ofcr & the kindness of the gentleman to Cmdor E A F Lavallette, on his retirement from the command of the Wash Navy Yard, presented him with a handsome silver pitcher, goblets, & salver, the elegant & artistic work of Messrs M W Galt & Bro, of Wash City. A delegation chosen from the different depts. of the yard to carry out the object constituted a cmte made up as follows, viz: Messrs W P S Sanger, F McNerhany, Thos Champion, T Van Reswick, Z M Offutt, A Woodward, M E Bright, B B Curran, Jas Tucker, Jos Padgett, John F Tucker, Thos Altemus, W C Hoofnagel, W W Browning, Jno Holroydy, Wm Boyd, J R McCathhran, Jas Philipps, Jos Walsh, Andrew French, G W Offutt, Jno W Richardson, A Leonard, Jos Humphreys, N Lewis, & Jno M Thornton.

Mrd: on Thu, by Rev John C Smith, Mr Saml Brereton to Mrs Sarah Ann Goodman, all of Wash City.

Died: on Thu, after a brief illness, Mrs Ellen Reeves, consort of Randolph B Reeves. Her funeral will be this morning at 10 o'clock, from the dwlg, 446 7th st.

Public sale: to millers & factors. **Greenfield Mills**, Houses & Lands, & a large & valuable personal property at public sale. The Real & personal estate of Meredith Davis: sale on May 19, 1858, on the premises, at **Greenfield Mills**, a 2 story dwlg, 2 tenements, ofc, stabling, corn houses & sheds, cooper's shop, millright's shop & blacksmith's shop, & 20 acres of fertile land; adjacent to **Carrollton Manor**, on one side, & the most fertile part of Loudoun Co, Va, on the other side.. The machinery for the most part is new. Also, will be sold on the same day, a productive farm, containing 140 acres of land, more or less. Two comfortable dwlg houses, with lots attached, near each other, adjoining the farm, will be for sale on the same day. –Jas L Davis, B A Cunningham, trustees

SAT MAY 15, 1858
Calif: The case of the slave Archy Lee was finally disposed on on Apr 14 by the opinion delivered by Com'r Geo Pen Johnston, in the U S Circuit Court, setting him at liberty, & constituting him a free man. The announcement gave general satisfaction.

Mrd: on May 13, in the Presbyterian Church, at Fred'k City, Md, by Rev Septimus Tustin, D D, John Reed, jr, to Miss Mary A, daughter of the late John A Marmaduke, both of Shepherdstown, Va.

I have this day disposed of my Wood & Coal Yard on 9th st, between D & E sts, to Mr John I Underwood. I anticipate to remove from the city & it is absolutely necessary that all bills should be settled without delay. –F L Moore

Senate: 1-Ptn from John A Smith, Clerk of the Circuit Court & Criminal Court of D C, asking the passage of an act for settling his accounts, so that he may be charged only with the fees which he has received, or might by due diligence have received: referred. 2-Ptn from Virginia Waldron, widow of the late Brvt Maj Nathl S Waldron, of the U S Marine Corps, asking that she may be allowed a pension: referred. 3-Ptn from Capt Chas Wilkes, U S navy, asking compensation for damage to his property on North Capitol st, Wash City, by the alteration of the grade of that street: referred. 4-Ptn from Mrs A M Roblas Y Robaldo, widow of Francisco Robaldo, late of Santa Fe, asking to be paid for certain property destroyed by American troops in Mexico by order of their commanding ofcr. [The lady states that her husband left Santa Fe to go to Wash to obtain redress for his losses, but hearing of the tardiness of Gov't in the settlement of claims, & ignorant of the mode of procedure, unacquainted with the English language, & despairing of prompt payment, he in a moment of despondency terminated his life by his own hand at or near St Louis, Mo.] 5-Cmte of Claims: bill for the relief of Mrs Ann L Rogers, wife & assignee of John A Rogers. 6-Cmte on Finance: bill for the relief of Elijah F Smith, Gilman H Perkins, & Chas S Smith. 7-Cmte on Pensions: adverse reports in the ptn of Rachel Posey; & also in the claim of Francis Hutimack for a pension. 8-Bills passed-relief of John Ericsson; relief of Eliz Montgomery, heir of Hugh Montgomery; & for the relief of Simon de Visser & Jose Villarubia, of New Orleans. 9-Bill for the relief of Geo Ashley, adm de bonis non of Saml Holgate, deceased, which had received the sanction of the Court of Claims, was rejected on a call of yeas 17, nays 20.

Private sale of valuable real estate in Fred'k Co, Md: *Areadia*, on the country road leading to Buckeystown, containing 350 acres. The mansion house is large & beautifully arranged; & there are numerous out bldgs. The Balt & Ohio railroad runs through this farm, & a station house is within half a mile of the dwlg. –M Keefer, Fred'k City, Md

House of Reps: 1-Bills passed-relief of: Munroe P Downing; of Rebecca M Baldwin, of Va; of Isaac Maclure & other settlers upon the public lands in the State of Wisconsin. 2-Cmte of the Whole: bill to be reported favorably to the House-relief of: Mary Bainbridge; of Eliz E V Field; of Stephen Bunnell; of Nancy Serena; of Mgt Whitehead; of John R Temple, of La; of Pierre Gagnon, of Natchitoches, La; of Wm Hutchinson; of Isaac Carpenter; of Leonard Loomis; of Thos Alcock; of Mary W Thompson; of Benj L McAtee & I N Eastham, of Louisville, Ky; of Brvt Maj H L Kendrick; legal reps of Marie Malines; of Richd B Alexander; of Simeon Stedman; of Susannah Redman, widow of Lloyd Redman; & of B W Palmer & others. Pension to Henry E Read, a citizen of Ky, & for other purposes. Bill recognizing the assignment on land warrant No 35, 956, issued to John Davis, as valid, with an amendment. 3-Reports from the Court of Claims with a recommendation that they be concurred in: adverse report on the ptn of N & B Goddard, excs of Nathl Goddard; adverse report upon the ptn of Chas D Arfwedson; adverse report upon the ptn of Benj Cozzens, trustee; & adverse report upon the ptn of Jacob Bigelow, adm of Francis Cazeau. 4-Bill for the relief of Maj J Y Dashiell, paymaster in the U S army, with a recommendation that it do not pass.

MON MAY 17, 1858

Household & kitchen furniture at auction on May 21, at the residence of Marcus Bull, in Franklin Row, K st, between 12th & 13th sts. -Jas C McGuire, auct

Orphans Court of Wash Co, D C. Letters of administration on the personal estate of John Homberger, late of Wash Co, deceased. –Chas Walter, adm

Death of the Bishop of Arkansas & Texas. This Rt Rev Prelate, Geo Washington Freeman, D D, died at Little Rock, Ark, on Apr 29, aged about 68. He was a native of Sandwich, Mass; was formerly Rector of the Episcopal Church in Raleigh, N C; for many years & subsequently at Newcastle, Dela, from which position he was called to the Episcopate as Bishop of the Southwestern Diocese.

Senate: 1-Mr Gwin presented a joint resolution of the Legislature of Calif in favor of the interposition of the Genr'l Gov't for the release of J M Ainsa, an American citizen held in captivity at Sonora, Mexico. Ainsa is the brother-in-law of Col Crabb, who, with his brave associates, was massacred in Sonora through the instrumentality of the very men who invited & advised the expedition, the history of which bloody tragedy was still unwritten. 2-Court of Claims: in favor of the claim of Richd Fitzpatrick: referred to the Cmte of Claims. 3-Memorial from citizens of Wash City, praying a donation of land or an appropiation of money for the permanent endowment of the **Columbian College**, in the District of Columbia. 4-Ptn from Taliaferro P Shaffner, of Ky, asking Congress to amend the act approved Mar 3, 1857, to expedite telegraphic communication for the uses of the Gov't in its foreign intercourse. 5-Ptn from Wm Merrihew, an ofcr of the army in the Mexican war, praying additional pay as such. 6-Ptn from R H Miller & Sons, praying that the duties paid by them on certain earthenware imported by them & destroyed by fire in transition from New Orleans to St Louis may be refunded. 7-Cmte of Military Affairs: bill to provide for the payment of certain Calif claims, & a joint resolution in favor of the printing of the reportsof Maj Mordecai & Maj Belafield, who were sent to the Crimea in 1855 to collect information in relation to military affairs. 8-Cmte of Claims: ptn of Hezekiah Miller, & reported a joint resolution for the relief of John Grayson. 9-Cmte of Claims: bill for the relief of Mrs Eliza E Ogden.

House of Reps: 1-Cmte of the Whole-bills read a third time & passed-relief of: Mary Bainbridge; Eliz E V Field; of Stephen Bunnell; of Nancy Serena; of Mgt Whitehead; of John R Temple, of La; of Pierre Gagnon, of Natchitoches, La; of Wm Hutchinson; of Isaac Carpenter of Leonard Loomis; of Thos Alcock; of Mary W Thompson; of Benj L McAtee & I N Eastham, of Louisville, Ky; of Brvt Maj H L Kendrick; of John F Cannon; of Gen Sylvester Churchill; of Marie Malines; of Richd B Alexander; of Simeon Stedman; of Susannah Redman, widow of Lloyd Redman; & of B W Palmer & others. Also, an increase in the pension of Henry E Read a citizen of Ky, & for other purposes. Assignment on land warrant No 35,956, issued to John Davis, as valid with an amendment. 2-Court of Claims: adverse report on the ptns: of Chas D Arfwedson, Benj Cozzens, trustee; & Jacob Bigelow, adm of Francis Cazeau. Also, upon the ptn of N & B Goddard, excs of Nathl Goddard, was referred to the Cmte of Claims.

The eminent Dr Robt Hark, Emeritus Prof of Chemistry in the Univ of Penn, died at Phil on Sat last of pneumonia, in his 78th year.

A D Young, of Flatbush, Ky, sued Laban Letton for $10,000 damages on account of the wife of the latter slandering Young's wife. The jury gave him $10,000.

Mrd: on May 13, by Rev B F Bittinger, Mr Chas Washington Langly to Miss Hannah Eliz Hendley, all of Wash City.

Died: on Sunday, Mrs Virginia Auld, the beloved wife of Edw Auld, of Wash City. Her funeral is on Monday at 4½ o'clock.

Chas Kendle & Wm B Gregory, two well known sporting men, got into a fight in Cincinnati on Sunday, when the latter was beaten so badly that he shortly after died. Kendle was arrested & committed to prison.

Harry Parker, late a clerk in the post ofc at Hudson, Wisc, was arrested for stealing a moneyed letter, mailed at Warren, Ohio, to a citizen of Hudson.

Commodious & handsome residence on F, between 13th & 14th sts, at Private Sale: owned & recently occupied by Maj M M Clarke: a 3 story brick dwlg house, with extensive 3 story back bldgs. The house is furnished throughout with all the modern improvements. -Jas C McGuire, auct

TUE MAY 18, 1858
Senate: 1-Cmte of Claims: general bill for the relief of Letitia Humphreys & of Robt Harrison. 2-Cmte on Naval Affairs: asked to be discharged from the consideration of the memorial of Virginia Waldron, & that it be referred to the Cmte on Pensions: which was agreed to. 3-Cmte of Claims: Bill for the relief of Estudillo de Arguello, widow of Santiago E Arguello. 4-Cmte of Claims: bill for the relief of Anthony W Bayard; & bill for the relief of Geo J Knight. 5-Cmte on Pensions: ptns of Sarah A Watson, widow of Col Watson, killed at Monterey, for a renewal of her pension, & of Anna Addison, widow of Capt Addison, asking continuance of her pension from the time it expires, reported that the cmte thought theses ptns ought to be granted, but as a general bill had been reported on the subject he would ask that these ptns lie on the table: which was agreed to. Same cmte: adverse reports on the following ptns: of Lydia Weeks, asking the amount of pension her husband would have been entitled to had he not been stricken from the pension rolls; on that of Ebenezer Watson for an increase of his pension; on that of Jos Morroles, a soldier of the war of 1812, to be allowed a pension; & on that of John Drout, asking to have his pension commence from the date of his discharge from the army.

Wholesale stock of groceries at auction on May 23, at the warehouse of Messrs Getty & Williams, corner of Water & High sts, Gtwn, the remainder of their stock.
-Barnard & Buckey, aucts, Gtwn

House of Reps: 1-Darius Truesdale, of the State of N Y, is appointed Doorkeeper of the House of Reps for the remainder of the 35th Congress.

Summer Boarding House of *Valley View*, near the summit of the Blue Ridge, will be open Jun 1. Price of board for gentlemen or ladies will be $8 per week; children & servants half price, & families on reasonable terms. Mrs Elivira S Fisher, at Linden, Fauquier Co, Va.

For sale: a desirable farm in Montg Co, Md, containing 800 acres of land, with a fine frame dwlg; a brick stable, barn, ice house & corn house. The Overseer now living on the farm will show it. For further information apply to Mrs Geo C Washington, Rockville, Md.

Three valuable farms for sale: the farm on which the subscriber resides, 5 miles from Gtwn, containing 220 acres of land, with good improvements. Also, his farm on the east side of the above, containing 130 acres of improved land with a fine frame house of 8 rooms. Also, the farm belonging to my son, adjoining the above land, containing 185 acres of improved land. Refer to Bradley & Son, Wash, & O Z Muncaster, Gtwn. –G M Watkins

Coroner's inquest was yesterday held on the body of Ellen Murphy, wife of Cornelius Murphy, who was found dead yesterday in a small dwlg on K st, near 4th. It at first was supposed that she came to her death by violence, & her husband was committed to jail, on suspicion. It was found that Cornelius was in no way implicated. Danl Haraday, with whom the woman [in the absence of her husband, who keeps steadily at his work on the Wash aqueduct] appears to have been on terms of close intimacy, involving frequent fierce quarrels. The woman died from excessive intemperance to which she was addicted. Haraday could not be found yesterday, but when he is will be subjected to examination.

Died: on May 17, in her 19th year, Emma Serena Noyes, daughter of Thos L Noyes, of Wash City. Her funeral will be on May 20 at 10 o'clock, from the residence of her father, 672 H st.

Died: on May 17, after a brief illness, Amy Florence, only child of E K & Kate P Reynolds, aged 9 months. Her funeral will be this afternoon at 4 o'clock, at 286 Va ave, [Island.]

Died: on May 12, in Apponaug, Rhode Island, suddenly, Mrs Anna, wife of Hon Wm D Brayton, Rep from the 2nd Congressional district in that State.

WED MAY 19, 1858
Household & kitchen furniture at auction on May 21, by order of the Orphans Court of Wash Co, D C; at the late residence of Jas Handly, deceased, 408 7th st, between G & H sts. -Jos Hodgson, W Flaherty, trustees -A Green auct

Rev Dudley A Tyng, of Phil, Rev Wm Silsbee, of Northampton, Mass, & Rev Jas Freeman Clark, of Jamaica Plains, Mass, have shared equally in the reward offered by a citizen of Springfield, about a year ago, for the best series of newspaper articles on the importance of having good men at the head of all civil & corporate bodies. The first of the successful competitors had died.

The New American Cyclopedia, Vol II, ["Araktsheef" to "Beale."] N Y, D Appleton & Co: Washington, Jos Shillington. In its Biographical Dept are lives of St Augustine, St Basil, Bacon, Audubon, Arista, Cmdor Bainbridge, Prof Bailey, the Barbour Family of Va, Lord Ashburton & others. Sketches of distinguished living characters, such as Avezzana, Atchison, Govn'r Banks, Badger, Barringer, of N C, Geo Bancroft, Rev Dr Bachman of S C, Joshua Bates, Bates of Missouri, Jacob Barker, Rev Dr Bangs, Hon Henry Barnard, Rev Leonard Bacon, & many others.

Mr H W Herbert, known by his writings as "Frank Forester," committed suicide on Monday, at his room in the Steven's House, Broadway, N Y. He had been depressed in spirits, owing to his separation from his wife, to whom he had but a short time been married. What caused the separation is not known, further than that some woman had made mischief between them, as is alleged in a letter from the deceased. On Monday he sent for his friend, Mr Anthon, & told him he intended to commit suicide. He first thought of committing the act over the grave of his first wife, in the cemetery at Newark, but altered his intention. Later, Mr Anthon retired for a moment in the adjoining room, when he heard the discharge of a pistol. Herbert died in a few minutes of hemorrhage. He left letters addressed to the press, to the Coroner, & to Mr Anthon. Mr Herbert was born in London, England, Apr 7, 1807, the eldest son of the very reverend Wm Herbert, Dean of Manchester. He was sent to Eton at age 13 & graduated at Caius College, Cambridge, in 1829. He arrived in this country in Dec, 1831. He published many books. -N Y Com Adv

Senate: 1-Ptn from J H Langly & others, citizens of Illinois, urging the recognition of their pre-emption claims to lands in the late military reservation of Rock Island, Ill: referred. 2-Ptn from Michl Nourse, asking compensation for certain services performed by direction of the First Comptroller of the Treasury: referred. 3-Ptn from Hiram McCullough, asking to be released from his suretyship on the contract of S A West & G McCullough for the delivery of stone at the Gosport navy yard: referred. 4-Cmte on the Post Ofc & Post Roads: adverse report on the memorial of John Wightman. Same cmte: asked to be discharged from the consideration of the joint resolution explanatory of the act of Mar, 1857, for the relief of Geo Charpenning, jr, & from the presentment of the grand jury of the U S for the northern district of Florida, & that they be referred to the Cmte on the Judiciary: which was agreed to. Same cmte: asked to be discharged from the consideration of the papers relative to the adoption of Oliver Evan Wood's plan for the delivery of letters in Calif: agreed to. 5-Cmte on Indian Affairs: bill for the relief of Madison Sweetser. Same cmte: asked to be discharged from the consideration of the memorial of the children of Stephen Krebs, a citizen of the Choctaw tribe of Indiana: agreed to. 6-Cmte on Printing, reported in favor of printing the memorial of Taliaferro P Schaffer, without the map: which was agreed to.

Cumberland White Pine & White Oak Lumber for sale. –John T Woodside, Cumberland, Md.

Before Judge Sutherland, Edw Ayres, age 14 years, applied by petition to have a guardian appointed to prosecute a suit for divorce from his, the petitioner's, not the guardian's, wife. The Judge inquired how old the lady dfndnt might be, & was informed she was 16. The Judge then signed the paper, & granted the prayer of the petition, appointing Jas Hosford such guardian. –N Y Com Adv

On Monday a party of 15 persons started from Cincinnati to N Y to take the next steamer for Europe. Three of the party went by the way of Washington & the balance by Buffalo. The Gazette says the latter consisted of Abraham Mack, his wife, & 6 children; Mr Bettman & his son, Chas, aged about 12 years; Abraham Morris & Wm Stachel. The gentlemen are merchants. Three of the party were killed in the railroad catastrophe near Utica; a daughter of Mr Mack, aged 12, & a son age 6 years. Mr Bettman's son was also killed, & Mr Bettman was badly wounded. A girl going to Europe with the family of Mr Mack was so injured that her brother in Cincinnati was telegraphed to come on immediately if he wished to see his sister.

Three children of Mr Frank Hopewell, of Cotland, Indiana, were burnt to death last week. The mother tried to rescue the children, but in vain. Only one child was saved. As nearly a thousand dollars in gold, which was laid between the beds where the children slept, was missing, it is supposed that the house was set on fire.

On Sat, as 2 lads were gunning in the woods west of Pittsfield, Mass, one of them, Chas Y Swift, was accidentally shot by the explosion of the percussion cap. He lingered until Monday. He was 16 years old, & was the son of Chas H Swift, a commission merchant of Sacramento, Calif.

Mrd: on May 12, by Rev Wm H Chapman, Mr Chas R Jones to Miss Eliz A Owens, all of Wash City.

Mrd: on May 13, by Rev Wm H Chapman, Mr Robt H Cross to Miss Martha R Carter, all of Wash City.

Died: on May 15, Mrs Eliza Crompston, in her 82nd year, daughter of the late Rev Saml Magaw, D D, of the Protestant Episcopal Church.

Died: on May 16, at Huntingdon, Fairfax Co, Va, Mr Isaac G Hutton, in his 67th year, formerly of Wash, & for the last 30 years a resident of Va.

Died: on May 17, in Wash City, in her 26th year, Miss Mary Jane Morgan, after a severe illness. Her funeral is this morning at 10 o'clock, from the residence of her parents, on H st, between 12th & 13th sts.

Chicago, May 18. A fire this morning destroyed some bldgs of little value, & burnt to death 9 persons. Lost are Harrison Barger, wife, & 3 children; Wm Reilly, Mrs Johnson & son. The fire is supposed to have been the work of an incendiary.

Robt Beale will apply to the Corp of Washington for a duplicate of a certificate of tax sale of lot 5 & improvements, in square north of 743, sold on May 22, 1857, to the name of Richd Barry, & bought by the advertiser, as said certificate had been mislaid or lost. –Robt Beale

THU MAY 20, 1858
Chancery sale of real estate & improvements: by decree passed May 17, 1858, by the Circuit Court of Wash Co, D C, in a cause No 1312, pending in said court between F H Newman et al cmplnts, & Ed W Newman et al dfndnts: public auction, on the premises, the north half of lot 26 in square 254, on the west side of 13th st, near Pa ave, with the large & handsome 4 story brick dwlg house on the same. Also, lot 5 in square 243, & lot 8 in square 288, with improvements on said lots. –J B H Smith, trustee -A Green auct

Thos J Lee, of Md, late a captain in the Corps of U S Topographical Enginers, has been appointed by the Govn'r commissioner on the part of Md to retrace & mark the boundry lines between the States of Md & Va.

Trustee's sale of valuable business stand: by deed of trust from Wm T Hook to the subscriber, dated Jun 9, 1854, recorded in the land records of Wash Co, D C: public auction on May 31, of the west part of lot 5 in square 378, in Wash City, fronting 23 feet & a ½ inch on north D st, running back 187 feet & 10½ inches to the public alley, improved with an extensive Coachmaking Establishment, consisting of Brick Bldgs, front & back. –H C Spalding, trustee -C W Boteler, auct

Excellent household & kitchen furniture at auction on: May 26, at the residence of Chas Haskins, 240 I st, between 18th & 19th sts. -Jas C McGuire, auct

Gen Persifer F Smith died on May 16 at Leavenworth. He had been recently assigned to the command of the military dept of which Utah forms a part, & was on his way to discharge the important trust confided to him. Gen Smith was highly distinguished in the Mexican war, & was in most of the severe battles under Gen Scott in the Valley of Mexico, first as cmder of a rifle regt, & frequently in charge of a brigade. He was twice brevetted for gallant & meritorious conduct. He had been eminent as a lawyer in New Orleans, & was first called into military service at the suggestion of Gen Taylor. No man of his rank in the Army better deserved the confidence of the Gov't & country than Gen Smith. [May 20th newspaper: St Louis, May 19. The remains of Gen Smith were to leave Leavenworth for the East on Wed. Gen Harney succeeds to the command of the expedition.]

Mrd: on May 18, in Wash City, at the Tenth St Baptist Church, by Rev S P Hill, H Clay Stewart to Miss Eliz S Barker, all of Wash City.

Senate: 1-Ptn from Chas M Perry, asking compensation for services as a clerk in the ofc of the Treasurer of the U S: referred. 2-Ptn from R C Jones, a master in the navy, placed on the furlough list, & subsequently transferred to leave of absence pay, asking to be allowed the difference between that of the furlough & reserved list: referred. 3-Ptn from Wm B Herrick, a surgeon in the army during the war with Mexico, asking to be allowed a pension: referred. 4-Cmte on Foreign Affairs: adverse report on the claim of Saml Bromberg. 5-Cmte on Military Affairs: to which was referred the memorial of Geo M Weston, Com'r of the State of Maine, submitted a special report, accompanied by a bill to provide for expenses incurred by that State in organizing a regt of volunteers for the Mexican war. Same cmte: bill for the relief of Brvt Maj H L Kendrick, & recommended its passage. Same cmte: claim of J M Pomares to be referred to the Cmte of Claims. 6-Cmte on Pensions: bill to increase the pension of John Richmond: recommended its passage. Same cmte: adverse reports on the ptns of Cynthia Coney, asking a pension for the services of her husband in the war of 1812, & on that of Mary Eliz Lamard, widow of Maj Chas H Barnard, for a pension. 7-Cmte on the Judiciary: bill for the relief of Jos Bard & Co, J Caulfield, & Jos Landis & Co, to be referred to the Cmte on the Post Ofc & Post Roads. Same cmte: refer the act for the relief of Geo Chorpenning to the Cmte on the Post Ofc & Post Roads. 8-Cmte on Private Land Claims: bill for the relief of the legal reps of Marie Malines; of Pierre Gagnon, of Natchitoches, La, & for the relief of Regis Loisel, or his legal reps, reported them back without amendment. Same cmte: bill for the relief of Thos L Disharoon, & recommended its passage.

Three killed. Railroad catastrophe in Indiana, on Friday night, when the train was precipitated into a creek, the bridge having been undermined by the rapid & rising current, of the recent floods. Jas W Irwin, conductor was killed when a splinter entered his skull. Mr Jacob Beitinger was cut almost entirely in two. Mr Patrick Maloney, the fireman, was killed instantly.

Criminal Court-Wash-Wed. 1-Trial of John Essex, charged with the murder of Owen Quigley on Jun 3, 1856: selected jury: Josiah L Venable, John H Peake, Harrison Taylor, Job W Angus, David Shoemaker, Henry B Hoffman, Abel H Lee, Benj Summy, Levi Zell, Aaron A Kagy, Alexis Queen, & John E Chappel. Witnesses for prosecution: Dr Noble Young, Dr Johnson Eliot, Chas H Payne, J W Finks, Chas F Wood, Andrew Sessford, & John O'Dwyer. Witnesses for defence: Danl McCarty, Mark Mankin, Dr Jas C Hall, John H Goddard, Jas J Randolph, Jas G Naylor, & Geo W Appleby. The evidence of Appleby was ruled out as not a part of the *res gestse*. Court adjourned. [May 21, 1858: Criminal Court-yesterday John Essex was found not guilty. He was discharged.]

Died: on Tue last, in Wash City, Emily, infant daughter of Edw H & Emily Fuller.

Died: on May 16, in Fredericksburg, Va, Mrs Hannah Rudd, the venerable mother of Capt John Rudd, U S Navy, in her 81st year.

FRI MAY 21, 1858
Senate: 1-Ptn from P J Hickey, asking for the payment of the sum stipulated to be paid him by the U S by virtue of an agreemen made between said parties, & for the payment of damages & losses occasioned by breach of contract on the part of the U S: referred. 2-Ptn from Clark Mills, asking an amendment of the act authorizing the erection of an equestrian statue of Washington, stating losses suffered by fire, & that it will require $6,000 to complete the statue: referred. 3-Cmte on Pensions: bill for the relief of the legal reps of Danl Hay, deceased, recommending its passage. 4-Cmte on Naval Affairs: joint resolution for the relief of Lt John C Carter, U S Navy. 5-Cmte on Pensions: bill granting a pension to Jos Vance. Same cmte: asked to be discharged from the consideration of the ptn of Eliphalet Lyman: same referred to the Cmte on Public Lands. 6-Cmte on Military Affairs: bill for the relief of the heirs or legal reps of John Hurdy. 7-Cmte on Public Lands: recommended the passage of the House bill recognizing the assignment of land warrant No 35, 956, issued to John Davis, as valid. 8-Cmte on Foreign Relations: bill for the relief of the heirs & legal reps of the late John Forsyth. 9-Cmte on Private Land Claims: bill to authorize the claimants in right of John Huertas to enter certain lands in Florida. 10-Bill for the relief of Myra Clark Gaines: referred to the Cmte on Pensions. 11-Bill for the relief of Anthony Caslo, a soldier of the war of 1812: passed. 12-Bills passed-relief: of J Hosford Smith; of Jeremiah Pendergast, of D C; Jennett H McCall; of Geo Phelps; of Wm D Moseley; & of Joshua Shaw: all passed. 13-Bill to confirm the title of Benj E Edwards to a certain tract of land in the Territory of New Mexico: passed. 14-Bill for the relief of Jos Hardy & Alton Long: passed. 15-Bill for the relief of Frances Ann McCauley: passed. 16-Joint resolution authorizing the Sec of the Navy to pay the ofcrs & seamen of the expedition in search of Dr Kane the same rate of pay that was allowed to the ofcrs & seamen of the expedition under Lt De Haven.

House of Reps: 1-Bill for the relief of Dr Geo G Smith, late postmaster at Atlanta, Ga: referred to the Cmte on the Post Ofc & Post Roads. 2-Joint resolution introduced authorizing Cmder M F Maury to accept the gold medal awarded to him by the Emperor of Austria: referred to the Cmte on Naval Affairs.

A violent tornado passed over the lower part of PG Co, Md, on Sat last, & extended through a portion of Chas Co, Md. The steamer **Planter**, Capt Weems, encountered the gale at Truman's Point, on the Patuxent, & suffered considerable damage, & loss of life. One colored man belonging to the boat fell overboard, never to be seen again. Another of the crew was also drowned. [No names given.] The farm of Mr Geo W Morton, near Aquasco, had every outhouse on the place demolished. –Marlboro Gaz

Died: on May 20, in Gtwn, Mrs Rachel Jackson, widow of the late Jos Jackson, in her 76th year. Her funeral is this afternoon at half past four o'clock.

The ship **Ostervald**, Capt Jarvis, from New Orleans for Liverpool, was burnt at sea on May 7, about 250 miles from the Balize. The Bremen ship **Carl** was in company with the **Ostervald** at the time, & took on board the crew, the specie, & the sailor's clothing.

The trial of Isaac L Wood for the murder of his brother's wife at Dansville, Livingston Co, in June, 1855, was ended on Sat in the conviction of the prisoner. David I Wood was an esteemed citizen of Dansville; his wife was equally esteemed. Isaac L Wood came from N J to Dansville a few years since in quite indigent circumstances, & his brother aided him to purchase a lot of land. On Jun 10, 1855, during the absence of Mrs Wood at the East, David I was taken suddenly ill & died in a few days. Mrs Wood returned home, & was appointed admx of her husband's estate in connexion with another brother. A few days elapsed when Mrs Wood & her children were attacked with similar symptoms attending her husband's death. The children recovered, but she died. Isaac L Wood became the guardian of the children & administrator of his brother's estate. The books of David I were mutilated & made to bear false witness in his favor, &, coincident with these discoveries, papers of arsenic were found about the premises of his late brother. The bodies of the murdered husband & wife were exhumed, & large quantities of arsenic were found in their stomachs. While the sentence of death was being pronounced Wood was convulsed with grief, & said he was entirely innocent of the charge.

Laws of the U S: Public No 21. Act to authorize the Vestry of Washington Parish to take & enclose parts of streets in Wash City for the purpose of extending the ***Washington Cemetery***, & for other purposes. To enclose & use forever those parts of 18th & 19th sts east which lie between the north side of G st south & the north side of Water st; & also those parts of south G & south H sts which lie between 17th & 20th sts east, for the purpose of enlarging the ***Washington Cemetery***. Provided that the said vestry shall not sell for any purpose whatever any of the aforesaid parts of streets, but the U S shall retain & hold such parts thereof as may be laid out for burial purposes for the interment of members of Congress or such officers of the Gov't as may die in Wash. That no canal, railroad, street, or alley shall ever be laid out or opened into or through the ***Washington Cemetery***, except such avenues or walks as may be laid out by the vestry of Washington parish, for the use & purposes of the said cemetery. That the ***Washington Cemetery*** shall be forever free from taxation. Approved May 18, 1858.

Col Arthur P Hayne, recently appointed by Gov Allston U S Senator from S C, to fill the vacancy occasioned by the death of Judge Evans, is a brother of the distinguished Robt Y Hayne, famous for his celebrated contest with Danl Webster, 30 years ago. Col Hayne is a native & resident of Charleston, & is now about 68 years of age. –Richmond Enquirer

SAT MAY 22, 1858
Executor's sale of excellent furniture & household effects, May 27, at the residence of the late Capt B Tate, M st, near 10th, all the effects. –John Mills, exc -Jas C McGuire, auct

By 2 deed of trust to the subscriber, one from Robt Brown, recorded in Liber J A S No 119, folios 474, 475; & one from Saml J Datcher, recorded in Liber J A S No 119, folios 471: public auction on Jun 7, of the north half of lot 13 in square 616, standing in the name of said Robt Brown, & the south half of lot 13 in square 616, standing in the name of said Saml J Datcher, each portion of said lot containing 3,750 square feet of ground. -H C Spalding, trustee -Jas C McGuire, auct

The U S brig **Dolphin** is now at Boston, preparing for the Home Squadron. List of her ofcrs: Lt Commanding, J N Maffit; 1st Lt, J N Bradford; 2nd Lt, E P Williams; 3rd Lt, C C Carpenter; Passed Assist Surgeon, J M Brown.

Accidents: A little child, Eliz Thompson, choked to death in N Y, Mon, eating peanuts. Wm Rooker, a printer, accidentally shot himself dead, at Richmond, Va, while taking a pistol from his trunk. S B Pierce, late Mayor of Shieldsboro, Miss, was shot by his gun going off at half cock, while out on a deer hunt. Mich & John Milia, brothers, 12 & 14 years old, perished at Waukegan, Ill, a few days since, by sinking into a slough in a swamp. The Cleveland schnr **Traveler** capsized off Pint au Peiee, on Lake Erie, Tue last, & Mrs Draper, wife of one the seamen, & 2 brothers Gates, of Buffalo, drowned.

Iowa City was, on Tue last, the scene of a mob & horrid murder. Reporter: two men, Wilkinson & Phillips had a personal animosity between them. On Mon Phillips' barn was burnt, & his partisans suspected Wilkinson of setting it on fire. They went to the house of Wilkinson, tore him from his wife & children, bound his hands behind his back, & cast him headlong into the Iowa river & drowned him. Over 30 citizens of Iowa City were concerned in this horrible act. Eleven of them have been arrested at the latest date.

A German, Henry Winch, at Newark, N J, was accidentally shot & killed at a target firing on Tuesday. He was engaged in watching the target, & had been warned several times to be careful, as the party were shooting with Swiss rifles with hair triggers.

Senate: 1-Additional papers in relation to the claim of Jas Collier, late collector of the customs of Upper Calif, to certain money due him under a decision of the U S Supreme Court: presented. 2-Ptn from John H Newell, asking to be allowed a pension: referred. 3-Cmte on Pensions: asked to be discharged from the consideration of the bill for the relief of Eliz E V Field. Same cmte: bill for the relief of Leonard Loomis, & recommended its passage. 4-Cmte on Public Lands: bill for the relief of Monroe D Downs; relief of Rebecca M Bowden, of PG Co, Va; & relief of Isaac Drew & other settlers, upon the public lands in the State of Wisconsin. 5-Cmte on Pensions: asked to be discharged from the consideration of the ptn of Wm Fleming: referred to the Cmte on Public Lands. Same cmte: bill for the relief of Myra Clark Gaines: recommended its passage. 6-Cmte on the Post Ofc & Post Roads: adverse report on the memorial of Noah Miller. 7-Cmte of Claims: bill for the relief of Richd Fitzpatrick: recommended its passage. 8-Cmte on Foreign Relations: adverse report on the memorial of Saml Bromberg. 9-Cmte on Patents: bill for the relief of Edson Fessenden, conservator of Wm Crompton. 10-Cmte of Claims: asked to be discharged from the consideration of the bill for the relief of Richd B Alexander: referred to the Cmte on Military Affairs.
11-Following bills passed: relief-of the legal reps of Chas Porterfield, deceased; of Jos C G Kennedy; of Martin Layman; of Chas McCormick, assist surgeon in the U S army; of Townsend Harris; of Geo W Flood; of G Alonzo Breast; of Aaron H Palmer; of Anson Dart; of Chas Knap; of Jeremiah Pendergast; of Albert G Allen; of Bernard M Byrne; of Jas Maccaboy; of C Edw Habicht, adm of J W P Lewis; of Webster S Steele; of Jas A Glanding; of Thos Smithers; of Franklin Peale; of David D Porter; of legal reps of John A Frost, deceased; of Jas Smith; of Saml H Taylor; of M C Gritzner; of John B Miller; of

the reps of Wm Smith, deceased, late of Louisiana; of the heirs & legal reps of Pierre Broussard, deceased; of Mrs Ambroise Bron, of the parish of St Chas,La; of R W Clarke; of the heirs & their legal reps of Wm Conway, deceased; of John Pickrell, late a lt in the U S army; of Stephen R Rowan; of P S Duvall & Co; of Anton L C Portman; of Edw Ingersoll; of Abner Merrill, of the State of Maine; of Assist Surgeon Edw P Vollum, U S Army; of Caleb Sherman; of Ann L Rogers; of John Grayson; of Mrs Eliza E Ogden. 12-Relief of Wm Cruickshank, J S Pollack, Calhoun Benham, & Fred'k A Sawyer, of San Francisco: passed. 13-Pension to Ansel Wilkinson, approved Aug 13, 1856: passed. 14-Relief of Elijah F Smith, Gilman H Perkins, & Chas F Smith: passed. 15-Bills passed-relief: of Geo J Knight; of Madison Sweeter; of Brvt Maj H L Kendrick; of Regis Loisel or his legal reps; of Pierre Guinon, of Natchitoches, La; of Marie Malines; of the legal reps of Danl Hay, deceased; of the heirs or legal reps of John Hudry; of the legal reps of John Forsyth; & of Richd B Alexander. 16-Bill to increase the pension of John H Richmond: passed.

The Baldwin Brothers have removed their Steam Factory to First & D sts, where they will be pleased to see their patrons. Sawing & planing of every description.

Having determined, in consequence of declining health, to retire from the charge of the Alexandria Boarding School after the present term & remove to my farm in Montg Co, Md, I offer for sale my Boarding School property & private residence for sale. The school has been for many years constantly full. My residence was built 3 years ago in the most substantial manner. The school lot is about 95 feet in front, & extends entirely through the square from Washington to Columbia sts. Possession given on Aug 8 next. Apply to Robt H Miller, or to the subscriber, Benj Hallowell, Alexandria, Va.

MON MAY 24, 1858
Fire on May 18th in a 2 story tenement on South Wells st, consumed the bldg & persons were burnt & their charred bodies dug from the ruins. They were Mrs Riley, a boy, the son of Mrs Mgt Malone, woman unknown, Wm Riley, Frenchman unknown, Mgt Malone, a boy about 5 years old, a girl about 5 & one about 3 years old, & another unknown. A drunken man was found after the fire buried in the rubbish, uninjured. -Chicago Journal, May 18

Appointments by the Pres, by & with the advice & consent of the Senate:
Geo W Morgan, of Ohio, Minister resident of the U S in Portugal.
Jas M Buchanan, of Md, Minister resident of the U S in Denmark.
T H Dunn, of Mississippi, Consul Gen at Havana
Felix E Forests, of N Y, Consul of Genoa
Alex'r Debbes, of Louisiana, Consul at Marseilles
A G Blakey, of Missouri, Consul at Campeachy
L H Hatfield, of N Y, Consul at Bombay
F Cyrus, of N Y, Consul at Gottenburg
Aug Canfield, of N J, Consul at Candia

Senate: 1-Ptn from O Bowne, in behalf of the com'rs for the removal of the quarantine station of the State of N Y, asking that the value of the property of the U S at present quarantine station may be applied to furnish such accommodations as the Sec of the Treas shall deem necessary for revenue purposes at the new quarantine site: referred. 2-Ptn from Noah Gammon, asking that the money paid by him on the entry of land to which he did not obtain a title may be refunded: referred. 3-Additional papers relating to the claim of Dr Jas A Mott for medical services to sick & wounded soldiers in the war of 1812: referred. 4-Ptn from Wm Nicholson, asking that the children of Marvel Nicholson, deceased, may be allowed to locate or assign a land warrant granted to her: referred. 5-Ptn from E B Bishop, asking an appropriation to test the utility of certain improvements in dredging machines patented by him: referred. 6-Ptn from M Fleury & others, asking the confirmation of a certain land title: referred. 7-Ptn from Lt Wm B Whiting, of the navy, asking an appropriation to make experiments with fire-arms & materials to resist projectiles from fire-arms: referred. 8-Ptn from Henry Addison & Robt Ould, in behalf of the corporate authorities of Gtwn, D C, asking an appropriation for removing obstructions to the channel of the Potomac river caused by the Long Bridge: referred. 9-Cmte on Pensions: asked to be discharged from the consideration of the ptn of Maurice K Simons: which was agreed to. 10-Cmte on the Post Ofc & Post Roads: asked to be discharged from the consideration of the bill for the relief of Keep, Bard & Co, J Caulfield & Jos Landis & Co, & that it be referred to the Cmte on Commerce: which was agreed to. 11-Cmte of Claims: Bill for the relief of Wm Mooney: passed. 12-Cmte of Claims: adverse on the memorial of Anastacia Caxxillo. 13-Bill for the relief of Edson Fessenden, conservator of Wm Crompton, was taken up for consideration. It proposes to extend a patent, the inventor having been insane for several years past, & therefore unable to derive the ordinary benefit from his invention: passed.

The practice ship **Preble** went into commission on Thu, & sailed from Norfolk for Annapolis. Her Officers: Cmder, Thos T Craven; Lt Monroe; Passed Assist Surgeon, R Carter; Purser, Howard; Graves, Gunner. The **Preble** has a crew of 51 men all told.

House of Reps: 1-Ptn of Eliz Webster, widow of Isaac Goodsel, a soldier of the Revolution, praying Congress to grant her a pension: referred.

On May 15, some of the citizens of Auburn, Ohio, attacked the house of bad repute of Mrs Abbey & her 2 daughters, knocking in the doors & windows, & breaking up the furniture. Mr Tyrus Canfield, one of the assailants, was shot in the abdomen, & was taken home about 15 minutes afterwards to die in the presence of his wife. Mr Abbey's father-in-law, Jeremiah Abbey, a man named Condit, & another named Blood, who were in the house attacked, were afterwards arrested. Mr Canfield seems to think he had the right to abate the nuisance of Mrs Abbey's house. He leaves his wife & children.

Criminal Court-Wash-Sat. Van Loman Johnson, a young man convicted of assailing a funeral procession, which took place on a Sunday afternoon last winter, in its passage from a house on I st, near 5th, by the Northern Liberties market-house, to the Catholic burial ground on 14th st, was sentenced to 2 years' imprisonment in the county jail & fined $20.

Richd Willing, one of the oldest reps of one of the most distinguished families in Phil, died yesterday, at his residence, 3rd & York court. He was in his 83rd year. Mr Willing was a son of Thos Willing, former Pres of the old U S Bank. He was born at the old family mansion, [demolished a year or two ago,] at 3rd & Willing's alley, on Dec 25, 1775. Mr Willing inherited great wealth, never engaged actively in business, though in his younger days he made several voyages to India & to Europe as supercargo of vessels belonging to the firm of Willing & Francis. He was married in 1804 to Eliza, daughter of Thos Lloyd Moore. Four daughters & one son survive him. One of the daughters is married to John Ridgeway, & resides in Paris. The son has been abroad, but is expected home by every arrival. A niece of his was the wife of the late Lord Ashburton. Mr Willing enjoyed good health until quite recently, having been seriously ill since April.

Household & kitchen furniture at auction on May 24, at the residence of D E Lawrence, on Pa ave, 2 doors east of Jackson Hall. –Jas C McGuire, auct

At the Board of Regents of the Smithsonian Institution on May 19, 1858, the Sec announced the death of Dr Robt Hare, of Phil, the first honorary member of the Institution. He was late Prof of Chemistry in the Univ of Pa. We offer to the bereaved family of Dr Hare our sincere condolences in their loss.

TUE MAY 25, 1858
House & lot in Gtwn at public sale, by deed in trust from Catherine Norman, dated May 19, 1857, recorded in Liber J A S No 134, folios 266: public sale on Jun 7 next, on the premises, part of lot 104 in Beall's addition to Gtwn, fronting 40 feet on Beall st, between Montgomery & Green sts, running back with that width the depth of said lot, with a frame dwlg-house thereon. –Chas S Wallach, trustee -Jas C McGuire, auct

One argument in the British Parliament in favor of letting men marry their deceased wives' sisters was, that by doing so a man had only one mother-in-law instead of two.

On Thu, as Mr Lewis Lampson, of Scriba, was rolling his meadow in that town, & standing on the frame in front of the roller, driving his team, he by some accident fell forward & got so entangled that the heavy roller was drawn over his body, crushing him to death on the instant. He was a highly respected inhabitant of that town, aged 51 years. –Oswego Times

Trustee's sale of valuable property: by deed of trust, dated Feb 4, 1856, recorded in Liber J A S, No 110, folios 335, of the land records of Wash Co, D C: public auction on Jun 11 next, those pieces or parcels of ground called **Pasture & Gleanings**,& **Little Gleanings**, estimated to contain about 100 acres, more or less. Located about 2½ miles of the Eastern Branch bridge, & adjoins the farms of Mr Geo Livingston, Capt Wankowiz, & Mr Geo Talbot. –Horace Edelin, trustee -A Green auct

On Sat the tonnage engine No 79, coming east with a train upon the Balt & Ohio railroad, ran off the track 2 miles from Mannington Station. The engineman, Jas Caskey, & the fireman, Isaac Phillips, were both killed.

The commendable action of the Va Legislature relative to the removal of the remains of one of the illustrious sons of the Old Dominion from their resting place in N Y C has brought to public notice, in the Churchman, the fact that Jas Monroe had one of the most imposing funeral pageants ever witnessed in N Y C, yet, still his body was depostited in a borrowed grave, & to this day the 5th Pres of the U S has no tomb of his own, but is resting in a vault upon which there is an assessment of many years' standing.

Senate: 1-Ptn from P M Collins, asking compensation for commercial researches in Northern Asia & exploration of the Amoor river, in Asia: referred. 2-Ptn from Thos Motley, asking permission to lay a railroad track across certain avenues in Wash City, a portion of which he proposes to put down as an experiment & at his own expense: referred. 3-Ptn from Geo T Durham, asking compensation for his services as a clerk in the Indian bureau: referred. 4-Ptn from Richd H Long, asking permission to locate upon the reserves on St Andrew's bay, in Florida, certain pre-emption claims held by him: referred. 5-Cmte on the Library: asked to be discharged from the consideration of the memorial of E B Livingston: which was granted. 6-Cmte on Naval Affairs: adverse report on the memorial for the benefit of the nearest male heirs of the late Maj Gen Towson, U S Army, deceased. Same cmte: adverse reports on the memorials of: Sarah Brashears; of Georgiana M Lewis; & of Thos C Jordan. 7-Cmte on the Post Ofc & Post Roads: bill for the relief of John F Cannon: recommended its passage. 8-Cmte on Indian Affairs: bill for the relief of Geo Stealey. 9-Bill introduced for the relief of John P Figh & John H Gindart: referred to the Cmte of Claims.

Sir Houston S Stewart, Vice Admiral R N: provided ready & generous aid to our countrymen on board of one of our nat'l ships while in a foreign port & suffering from yellow fever. He is one of 3 brothers of Sir Michl Shaw Stewart, of Greenock & Blockhall, Scotland. His eldest brother, Sir Nicholson Shaw Stewart, succeeded to the estates on the death of his father; his other brother, Patrick Maxwell Shaw Stewart, was a member of the Scotish bar, & stook very high in his profession. The family seat is **Ardgowan**, in the lower ward of Renfrewshire, in the parish of Inverkip, about 6 miles s w from Greenock; the family have been in possession of their estates for centuries. Sir Houston is the uncle of the present member of Parliament for Renfrewshire, Sir Michl Robt Shaw Stewart, who is now in possession of the estates above mentioned, & who is married to a daughter of Earl Grosvenor, a highly respected old English family. He is also the uncle of the young lady, Miss Shaw Stewart, who so nobly seconded the good mission of Miss Nighingale to the hospitals during the Crimean war. The Shaw Stewart family are known for their Christian kindness & charity. Sir Houston cannot be otherwise than brave as well as kind & benevolent, being of one of the greatest families of Scotland, his original ancestor being Sir John Stewart, of Blockhall, a natural son of King Robert III, of Scotland, the great grandson of the celebrated hero, King Robt Bruce, of Bannockburn memory, a name that is dear to the lovers of freedom in every land. Sir Houston was at the storming & taking of St Jean D'Acre, in 1840. Sir Houston, I think, is over 60 years of age, & was very good looking the last time the writer had the pleasure of seeing him; he is about 5 feet 6 inches high, with very broad shoulders, a handsome face, & very bright blue eyes. His estate in the upper ward of Rendrewshire is known as **Mearus**. -Corlick, Wash, May 8, 1858

$10 reward for strayed or stolen from the subscriber, a medium sized white & brown cow, about 6 years old, near calving. –Chas Tilley, 74 Missouri ave

MAY 26, 1858
N Y C, May 24. 1-At noon today a royal salute was fired from the Cunard steamship **Persia** in honor of the anniversary of Queen Victoria's birthday. She was born on May 24, 1819, & is 39 yers of age. The date of her accession to the throne was Jun 20, 1837. 2-Purser Sinclair, who died on May 22, was the first person appointed as Chief of the Bureau of Provisions & Clothing, & had served his country almost half a century.
+
Purser Wm Sinclair, of the navy, died in N Y C on May 22. Since the death of Purser Todd he stood 3rd on the register in the corps to which he belonged. He was a native of Mass, & entered the service from Georgia in 1809 as a midshipman. He was appointed a purser Mar 26, 1814. The pursers in N Y C resolved to attend the funeral ceremonies in a body as chief mourners.

On Fri Dennis Sullivan was executed in the hall of the jail in Oswego, N Y, for the murder of Joshua Hibbard. Sullivan read a paper declaring his innocence. On the same day Wm Williams was executed at Harrisburg, Pa, for the murder of D Hendricks. He made a confession. His execution was witnessed by a large concourse of people.

Curiosities of Literature & History. Who nominated Geo Washington in the 2nd Continental Congress as Cmder-in-Chief, the reply would probably be based on the authority of our 2 recent historians, Irving & Bancroft. Irving, on page 453, Vol I, says Mr Johnson, of Md, rose & nominated Washington for the station of Cmder-in-Chief. The election was by ballot, & was unanimous. Bancroft, in his last volume, page 393, says Thomas, of Md, nominated Geo Washington, &, as he had been brought forward at the particular request of the people in New England, he was elected by ballot unanimously. Which one of the two really did nominate Washington? -Philosaletheia [Jun 3rd newspaper: A writer in the Nat'l Intell says that Washington Irving, in his Life of Washington, page 453, vol 1, claims for Johnson, as having nominated Washington. By a typographical oversight the name of Johnson was omitted after the Christian name, Thomas, in Mr Bancroft's work. It should have read, "Thomas Johnson, of Md."] [Jun 12th newspaper: There was no Thomas, either from Md or any other colony, in the Congress of 1776; see the Journal; also, American Almanac, 1834, pg 98; & Sparks's Washington, pg 420. It was Thos Johnson, of Md, who made the nomination.]

Naval Intelligence. 1-The following ofcrs have been ordered to report on board the U S steamer **Arctic**, now at NY, preparing to join the home squadron, Cmder H J Hartstene, 1st Lt J R Mulloy, 2nd Lt J H Rochelle, 3rd Lt E P McCrea, Passed Assist Surgeon Edw Hudson, 1st Assist Engineer A C Stimers, 3rd Assist Engineer J S Albert, 3rd Assist Engineer F E Brown. 2-Cmder Rodger will be sent with the steamer **Water Witch** to join the home squadron. 3-Capt Dahlgren, now in command of the ship **Plymouth** has volunteered his services to join the home squadron for the protection of our commerce in the West Indies & the Gulf of Mexico. Capt Dahlgren's new 11 inch shellguns would be dangerous to trifle with. We understand that Capt Dahlgren's offer will be accepted.

We are cognizant of no claim now pending before Congress that appeals more strongly to our sense of justice & our sympathy than that of David Myerle, for losses & sacrifices suffered by him in demonstrating the practicability of water rotting American hemp. He has succeeded in rendering our country independent of a foreign market for an abundant supply of that important staple. We trust that this session of Congress will not pass without having awarded to him the merited & long delayed relief which the bill now pending proposes to give to a man who may be justly viewed as a public benefactor.

Purser Wm Sinclair, of the navy, died in N Y C on May 22. Since the death of Purser Todd he stood 3rd on the register in the corps to which he belonged. He was a native of Mass, & entered the service from Georgia in 1809 as a midshipman. He was appointed a purser Mar 26, 18184. The pursers in N Y C resolved to attend the funeral ceremonies in a body as chief mourners.

Phil, May 25. During the return of the German Lafayette Rifles from a celebration on Lemon Hill last evening a police ofcr was struck by a soldier with his sword. Riot ensued and Frank Wendell, Chas Brenner, privates, were wounded, & it is supposed fatally.

Senate: 1-Ptn from John Leach, a resident of Wash City, asking to have the benefit of the act of Jun, 1832, granting pensions to the soldiers of the Revolution, extended to him, he being now 95 years of age, & knows no one living who is cognizant of the fact of his enlistment & services: referred. 2-Cmte on Pensions: ptns of Mathew Flansburg, a soldier of the Revolution, & of Mary Jane Malthy, widow of Lt Jas West, asking pensions, submitted an adverse report in each case. Same cmte: bill for the relief of Mgt Whitehead, & recommended its passage. Same cmte: bill for the relief of Nancy Serena: passed. 3-Cmte of Claims: bill for the relief of Miles Judson, surety on the official bond of the late Purser Andrew Crosby. Same cmte: adverse on the memorial of Jos G Heaton. 4-Bill passed for the relief of Miles Devine. 5-Bill for the relief of Thos L Disharoon: passed.

THU MAY 27, 1858

A young man named Geo W Taylor, formerly of Phil, & who lately married a young wife in Franklin Co, Mo, blew out his brains with a revolver at a boarding house in St Louis. He left a slip of paper: My dear wife, I have wronged you. Forgive & pray for me. I am a villain, & deserve to die. May God have mercy upon my soul.

Louisville Courier of Apr 28. The trial of Hardesty for the shooting of Grubb at Burlington, Boone Co, Ky. A sister of Hardesty was seduced by Grubb, & Hardesty told the seducer he gave him 6 months in which to marry the girl or be killed. The time expired & Grubb did not marry the girl. Hardesty met him & on sight shot him. The judgment pronounced by Judge Nutall upon the verdict of not guilty by the jury in behalf of Hardesty: Young man, if I had been wronged as you have been, I would have spent every dollar I had on earth, etc, & then starved upon the track of the villain, but I would have had his blood. Go hence without delay. You are acquitted.

Senate: 1-Ptn from A G Sloo, asking the intervention of the Senate to favor a contract with him for transporting the mails from the Atlantic to the Pacific by the Isthmus of Tehuatepec, giving details of his grant from Mexico: referred. 2-Resolution of the Corp of Gtwn, D C, protesting against the passage of any bill or joint resolution for receding any portion of Gtwn to Wash Co: referred. 3-Ptn from Stephen Shiinn, asking payment for materials furnished & money advanced to Saml Colt in aid of his experiment with the submarine battery in 1843 & 1844: referred. 4-Ptn from Rezin Orme, asking compensation for his services as a clerk in the 2nd Auditor's ofc: referred. 5-Ptn from Chas T Platt & H B Sawyer, in behalf of those ofcrs who were transferred from the furlough to the leave of absence pay, asking to be allowed the difference of pay between those grades to the time they were so transferred: referred. 6-Ptn from H De Groot, asking indemnity for losses sustained under his contract with Capt Meigs for furnishing brick for the Washington aqueduct, in consequence of the Gov't having failed to provide the means for carrying on the work: referred. 7-Cmte on Pensions: adverse report on the following ptns: Andrew Chapman, Eliz Ubes, Dolly Lineden, Mgt Smith & Linda Sexton, Cynthia Bishop, Jas Hudgins, Geo Waters, Thos Stevens, & Chas T Bruckner. 8-Cmte on Military Affairs: asked to be discharged from the consideration of the memorial of Ann Gratiot, widow of the late Col Chas Gratiot, & that it be referred to the Cmte on the Judiciary: agreed to. Same cmte: reported in favor of engraving the map of the explorations of Lt Warren in Nebraska Territory. 9-Resolved, that $321 be paid to N C Towle for his mileage & expenses in visiting Arostook Co, Maine, under a resolution of the Senate of Aug 18, 1856.

On May 16 Albert Pike, about 12 years old, a son of a distinguished gentleman of that name, was drowned in the Arkansas at Little Rock. His death is lamented by all.

Two boys at Lawrence stole a jug of rum & became terribly intoxicated. Maurice Roach, a very bright & promising lad, died from the effects of the liquor.

The subscriber offers for sale a most eligible residence in PG Co, Md, 5 miles from Wash, within 5 minutes walk of the celebrated *Spa Spring* at Bladensburg: contains about 4 acres, with a pump of excellent water in the yard. Inquire of the agent at the Bladensburg Depot. –Levi Nally

Mrd: on May 25, at the Church of the Epiphany, by Rev Chas H Hall, Henry Baldwin, jr, to Miss Lizzie O Hammond.

FRI MAY 28, 1858
The steamer **Water Witch** sailed from this city yesterday morning to join our squadron in the Gulf of Mexico. Ofcrs: Cmder, John Rodgers; Lts, H K Stevens, G P Welsh, Clark H Wells, Austin Pendergrast; Passed Assist Surgeon, Wm D Harrison; Acting Boatswain, John A Brisco; 1st Assist Engineer, W C Wheeler; 3rd Assists, B B H Wharton, Z K Rind, & B E Chassaing.

Orphans Court of Wash Co, D C. Letters of administration on the personal estate of Thos P Boswell, late of Wash Co, deceased. –Lucy A Boswell, admx

Senate: 1-Ptn from Eliz Spear, widow of Thos Williams, killed in battle, asking to be allowed a pension: referred. 2-Cmte on Commerce: adverse reports on the memorial of E B Bishop; also, on the memorial of Wm A Vaughan, John Smith, Wm D Little, & Nathan Dennet. 3-Cmte on Pensions: bill for the relief of Ebenezer Ricker. 4-Cmte on Territories: reported adversely on the memorial of citizens of Iowa relative to granting a license to Lewis A Thomas to establish a ferry across the Missouri river, & of Giles S Isham, asking a grant of land in Arizona on condition of taking settlers there. 5-Cmte on Naval Affairs: bill for the relief of B W Palmer & others. 6-Cmte of Claims: asked to be discharged from the consideration of the report of the Court of Claims in the case of Jacob Bigelow, adm of Francis Cazeau, & that it be referred to the Cmte of Claims: agreed to. 7-Cmte to Audit & Control the Contingent Expenses of the States: asked to be discharged from the consideration of the resolution to pay Willis A Gorman for his services in investigating alleged frauds of a superintendent of Indian affairs, & that it be referred to the Cmte on Inidan Affairs: agreed to. 8-Cmte on Naval Affairs: adverse report on the claim of Elbridge Lawton.

Mrd: on May 25, in Wash City, by Rev Wm H Chapman, Mr Geo H Simonds to Miss Catharine C Peippert, all of Wash.

Mrd: on May 27, at St Dominick's Church, by Rev Henry Young, Edw M Bowling, of PG Co, Md, to Mary Martina, 4th daughter of Geo Mattingly, of Wash City.

Died: yesterday, in Wash City, after a protracted illness, Mr Jas H Richardson, in his 36th year. His funeral will take place on Sunday at 3 o'clock, from his late residence in 6th st, between M & N sts.

Died: on May 26, of consumption, Miss Jane Mary Thompson, in her 24th year, 2nd daughter of Wm Thompson, of Wash City. Her funeral will take place next Sat at 3 o'clock P M, from her late residence, 2nd st, between B & C sts.

Died: on May 2, at his residence in Grand Chateau, Thos S Hardy, sr, aged 65 years, formerly of PG Co, Md. Peace to his ashes, respect & veneration to his name.
-Marlboro Gaz

SAT MAY 29, 1858
Extensive assortment of liquors, groceries, & store fixtures at auction, on Jun 2, at the Grocery & Liquor Store of J T Kilmon, 1st st & Pa ave. -A Green auct

Senate: 1-The papers in relation to the claim of John W Geary for the reimbursement of money expended while Govn'r of the Territory of Kansas: referred. 2-Ptn from Jonas P Levy, for himself & others engaged in the Pedrigal mines, in Mexico, asking that the Pres be authorized to compel the Mexican Gov't to liquidate their claims: referred. 3-Ptn from Hosea Thom & others, asking a grant of land on Green river, in Utah, for the purpose of settlement: referred. 4-Cmte on Indian Affairs: reported back the resolution to compensate Willis A Gorman for certain services, with an amendment. 5-Bill for the relief of Mark W Izard: referred to the Cmte on Indian Affairs.

Among the passengers that left N Y for England on Wed in the steamer **City of Baltimore** was Mrs Cookman, the widow of Rev G G Cookman, who perished in the steamer **President**. Mrs Cookman is accompanied by her son, John Emory, & daughter, Mary Barton. Two sons of Mrs Cookman are now stationed preachers of the Methodist Episcopal Church in the city of Phil.

Died: on May 27, in Wash City, of dropsy, arising from scarlet fever, Inez Adelaide, youngest daughter of Adelaide & Saml Carusi, aged 10 years.

Died: on May 23, at his residence in Campbell Co, Va, Judge Fleming Saunders, in his 80th year.

Circuit Court of Wash Co, D C-in Equity-No 1,381. John Curtis against Rose Knox, admx, & Wm Knox, heir at law of Jas Knox. The parties named, & creditors of Jas Knox, are to meet at my ofc in the City Hall, Wash, on Jun 7 next, at 11 o'clock. I shall state an account of the personal & real estate of said Jas Knox. –W Redin, auditor

At about 11 o'clock on the night of May 19 Abram P Phillips, formerly a special police officer, & more recently Capt of the Parish Prison, was waylaid at Canal & Basin sts by a party of unknown men, & was there assassinated. He received 3 pistol shot wounds & no less than 16 stab wounds. The guilty parties have so far escaped detection.

Letters received in Wash City yesterday from the American squadron on the African station bringing the intelligence of the death of one of its gallant young ofcrs, Lt Theodorick Lee Walker. He died at sea on Mar 17, & his remains were interred with the honors of war at Porto Praya, Cape Verde Islands, on Apr 5. Lt Walker was the son of the late Saml P Walker, of this city, where a numerous circle of relatives & friends lament his early death. [May 31st newspaper: U S ship **Dale**, Porto Praya, Apr 15, 1858. Official report from Cmder Wm McBlair, of the sloop-of-war **Dale**, confirms the intelligence of the recent death on board of that ship of Lt T Lee Walker, late executive of this ship. The immediate cause of his death was chronic inflammation of the liver, no doubt hastened by confinement to a small ship without exercise for so long a period. The **Dale**, with the exception of 17 days, had been constantly cruising for 10 months on a coast where the sun during the day & malaria at night rendered exposure for exercise fatal. Lt T Lee Walker was buried at Porto Praya with appropriate honors on Apr 12. Letter to Hon J Toucey, Sec of the Navy, Wash.]

Election Notice. Office **Oak Hill Cemetery** Company, Gtwn, May 29, 1858. The holders of Lots in the **Oak Hill Cemetery** containing three hundred feet & upwards are notified to attend a meeting, to be held at the Cemetery on Jun 7, 1858, at 5 o'clock, to elect four Trustee's to manage the affairs of the Company for the ensuing year. –Henry King, Sec

Mrd: on May 27, at Christ's Church, Wash City, by Rev Wm H Chapman, B Frank Morsell to Mrs Jane McDuell, daughter of the late Wm Morrow, all of Wash.

Mrd: on May 25, in Gtwn, D C, by Rev Mr Edwards, Mr Jos A Hutchinson, of Loudoun Co, Va, to Mrs S E Walker, of Gtwn, D C.

House of Reps: 1-Cmte of Claims: reported favorably on the following bills, which were committed: relief-of Wm H Russell; of Joshua Shaw, of Bordentown, N J; & of Catharine A W Reynolds. 2-Bills laid aside to be reported favorably to the House: relief-of Capt Stanton Sholes; of Nancy Magill, of Ohio; of Wm Sutton; of Jos Webb; of Eli W Goff; of Roswell Minard, father of Theodore Minard, deceased; of John Duncan; of D O Dickinson; of the legal reps of Jean Baptiste Devidrine; of Laurent Millaudon; of John Dick, of Florida. Relief of Anna M E Ring, Louisa M Ring, Cordelia E Ring, & Sarah J De Lannby. Relief of Wm B Trotter; of Jas G Benton, E B Babbitt, & Jas Langstreet, of the U S Army. Continue a pension to Christine Barnard, widow of the late Brvt Maj Moses J Barnard, U S Army. Grant a pension to Mary A M Jones. Relief of Susanna T Lea, widow & admx of Jas Maglenen, late of the city of Balt. Relief of Dr Thos Antisell; of Robt W Cushman, formerly an acting purser in the U S navy; of Michl Papprenitza; of Micajah Brooks; of Kennedy O'Brien; of Evelina Porter, widow of the late Cmdor David Porter, of the U S navy. Granting an invalid penstion to Silas Stevens, of Va; of Beriah Wright, of N Y; of John Lee, of the State of Maine; & to Jas Fugate, of Missouri. Relief of Michl Kinney, late a private in Co I, 8th regt U S Army. Relief of Cornelius F Latham; of Jas Rumph; of Wm Turvin, deceased; of Ferdinand O Miller; of Dinah Minis; of Alonzo & Elbridge G Colby; of Isaac Body & Saml Fleming; of Henry Orndorff; of John Dearmit; of Stuckey & Rogers; of Wm Doty & others; of the legal reps of Henry King, deceased; of Saml W & Alvin A Turner; of Job Stafford, of the State of N Y; of John B Hand; of Eliz McBrier, surviving child & heir of Col Archibald Loughry, deceased. Relief of Brvt Maj Jas L Donaldson, assist quartermaster U S army. Relief of Horatio Boultbee; of Dr Geo H Howell; of Nehemiah S Draper & Wm Holden, heirs-at-law of Mary Draper, deceased; of Elijah Close, of Tenn; of Michl A Davenport, of Ill; of Wm Allen, of Portland, Maine; of Wm Bullock; & of Wright Fore. Grant an invalid pension to Wm Howell, of Tenn; to Conrad Schroeder; & to Alex'r S Bean, of Pa. Continue the pension heretofore paid to Mary C Hamilton, widow of Capt Fowler Hamilton, late of the U S army. Increasing the pension of Anthony Walton Bayard, of Bellefonte, Pa. Relief of Wyatt Griffith; of Francis Carver; of Robinson Gammon; of Fred'k Smith; of Phineas G Pearson; of Judith Nott; of John C Rathbun; of Stephen Fellows; of John Perry, of Ill; of Ebenezer Hitchcock; of Shore Chase, of N Y; of Allen Smith; of David Watson; of the legal reps of John McDonough, deceased, late of Louisiana. Relief of Benj Wakefield; of J Wilcox Jenkins; of Fabius Stanley; of Gardner & Vincent & others; of Lt Loomis L Langdon; of David McClure, adm of Jos McClure, deceased; of Lewis W Broadwell; of Thos Hasam & B S Brewster; of Geo A O'Brien; of Rufus Dwinel; of Jonas P Keller; of Robt A Davidge; & of Douglass Ottinger. Explanatory of an act entitled "An act for the relief of Dempsey Pittman," approved Aug 16, 1856.

MON MAY 31, 1858
Small farm for a gentleman's country residence or for a market farm, at auction, on Jun 7, on the premises, the beautiful small country place, belonging to Geo W McLean, on old Gtwn & Alexandria road, adjoining the property of Jas Roach; contains 32 acres, a new cottage-built dwlg, new stables, new fencing, & young orchard. –Wall & Barnard, aucts

Calif: 1-Sonora Guadalupe Romero died in the valley of the Santa Ana, Los Angeles Co, on Apr 18, at the age of 115 years.

House of Reps: 1-Cmte on Elections: Wm W Kingsbury allowed to retain his seat as delegate from Minnesota. 2-Bill to increase the pension of A W Bayard, of Bellefonte, Pa, [which had been so amended as to reduce instead of increasing his pension,] was rejected. 3-Cmte of the Whole: bill for the relief of Rufus Dwinel: passed. Same cmte: bill granting an invalid pension to Jas Fugate, of Missouri, ayes 90, noes not counted. Same cmte: bill for the relief of Eliz McBrier. 4-Bills passed-relief: of Caleb Shurman, collector of customs at Paso del Norte, Texas; of Elijah F Smith, Gilman H Perkins, & Chas F Smith; of John Mason; of Stephen R Rowan. 5-Joint resolution authorizing Cmder M F Maury to accept the gold medal from the Emperor of Austria: passed. 6-Bill committed: relief of John Sawyer, a soldier of the Revolution, 103 years of age. 7-Bills passed-relief: of Wm Heine, artist in the Japan expedition; of Saml Goodrich, jr; of Sylvanus Burnham; of the heirs of Richd Tarvin; of Zina Williams; of A Baudoin, & A D Roberts; of Thos Phenix, jr, of Augustus J Kuhn; of Timothy L O'Keefe; of David Bruce; of Mary Boyle; & of John B Roper. 8-Bill to allow the legal reps of Same Jones 5 years' full pay in lieu of half pay for life: passed. 9-Bill for the relief of Mgt Van Buskirk, heir of Thos Van Buskirk, late of N J, was also reported favorably, but was rejected-years 17, nays 108. 10-Cmte on Revolutionary Claims: bill for the relief of Nancy D Holkar was reported upon adversely. 11-Bill for the relief of Benj F Hall was laid on the table. 12-Cmte on Foreign Affairs: adverse report on ptn of claimants of the brig **General Armstrong**.

Mrd: on May 27, at St Dominick's Church, in Wash City, by Rev Raymond Young, Edw M Bowling, of PG Co, Md, to Mary Martini, 5th daughter of Geo Mattingly, of Wash City.

Edw S Bartholomew, an American sculptor, died in Naples of an ulcerated sore throat on May 1. He was a native of Colchester, Conn, & from 1845 to 1848 had charge of the Wadsworth Gallery in Hartford. Some years ago he went abroad to better his health & to study his art in Italy, & is represented to have been one of the most promising of the young sculptors.

The English papers chronicle the marriage, at Cheltenham, of Rt Hon Stephen R Lushington, formerly Govn'r of Bombay, & one of her Majesty's Privy Counsellors, for 20 years chairman of cmtes in the House of Commons, son-in-law of the late Gen Lord Harris, of Belmont, the hero of Seringapatam, & grand uncle to the present lord. The bridge was a young good looking lady, a little out of her teens, & the bridegroom, who was brisk & frisky in manner, & juvenile in attire, has passed the allotted period of three score & ten by fifteen years. Born in the year of grace 1773, he was in his 85th year. This matrimonial escapade has given rise to a good deal of comment, as the gentleman is connected with several of the first families in Kent, & the lady upon whom he has conferred the honors of mistress of Norton Court formerly filled a domestic office in the household.

Died: on May 27, at Morven, Fauquier Co, Va, in his 6th year, Thomas Marshall, 3rd child of John & Anna Mason Ambler.

Senate: 1-Cmte of Claims: adverse report on the ptn of Geo W Bluford. Same cmte: asked to be discharged from the consideration of the bill for the relief of Henry G Carson: agreed to. 2-Cmte of Claims: asked to be discharged from the consideration of the bills for the relief of Wm Huthenson; & of Simeon Steadman; & that they be referred to the Cmte on Military Affairs: agreed to. Same cmte: asked to be discharged from the consideration of the adverse report of the Court of Claims in the case of Arthur Edwards, J Owen, & J Davis, & that is be referred to the Cmte on the Post Ofc & the Post Roads: agreed to. Same cmte: bill for the relief of Susanah Redman, widow of Lloyd Redman, & recommended its passage. 3-Cmte of Claims: bill for the relief of Capt John B Montgomery. Same cmte: bill for the relief of Geo W Biscoe, & recommended its passage. 4-Ordered that the memorial of Georgiana M Lewis, widow of Armstrong J Lewis, be recommitted to the Cmte on Naval Affairs. 5-Ordered that the bill granting a sword to the nearest male relative of the late Brvt Brig Gen Towson be recommitted to the Cmte on Naval Affairs. 6-Bill for the relief of Mrs Ann Smith, widow of the late Brvt Brig Gen Persifor F Smith, was refered to the Cmte on Pensions.

St Louis, May 29. Maj Benj Walker, Paymaster U S Army, died at his residence in this city at a late hour last night. He was buried with military honors at Jefferson Barracks this afternoon. Maj Walker was born in Vt & entered the service in Jul, 1819. He was commissioned as Paymaster with the rank of Major in Dec, 1839.

TUE JUN 1, 1858
Senate: 1-Cmte of Claims: bill for the relief of Benj L McAte & J N Eastham, of Louisville, Ky, & recommended its passage. 2-Cmte on Military Affairs: act for the relief of Richd B Alexander; & relief of Simeon Stedman: recommended their passage. 3-Cmte on Public Lands: adverse reports on the following memorials: of Thos Jones, of Clermont Co, Ohio; of Lemuel Wooster; of Mary Jane Taylor; of Eliphalet Lyman; of Wm Flemming, & of Henrietta Carroll. 4-Cmte of Pensions: adverse report on the bill for the relief of Mrs Jane Turnbull. 5-Cmte on Naval Affaris: asked to be discharged from the consideration of the bill for the relief of Nehemiah S Draper & Wm Holden, & that it be referred to the Cmte on Pensions: agreed to. Same cmte: bill for the relief of Benj Wakefield & of Robt W Cushman: recommended their passage. 6-Cmte on the Public Lands: act for the relief of Job Stafford, of the State of N Y; act for the relief of Eliz McBrier, heir of Col Archibald Loughry, deceased; & act for the relief of Saml Body & Saml Fleming: recommended their passage. 7-Cmte on Pensions: adverse reports on the ptns of Thos Jenkins; of Jos Plummer; & of Frank Madison. 8-Cmte on Military Affairs: to inquire into applying to the present or future army of the U S the priming apparatus invented by Jesse S Butterfield, of Phil.

Lake George. The new & beautiful steamer **Minnehaha**, Capt Jas Gale, will commence her regular trips on Jun 1 from Caldwell to Toconderoga, connecting with the steamers on Lake Champlain. The *Fort Wm Henry Hotel*, Caldwell, Lake George, was opened for the reception of guests on May 15. –Danl Gale

Cmdor Thos Ap Catesby Jones, of the U S Navy, died at *Sharon*, his residence in Fairfax Co, Va, on May 30, after a long & painful sickness. He was in his 69th year of his age, & the 53rd in the service of his country. He was born at *Hickory Hill*, Westmoreland Co, Va, Apr 24, 1790, & was the 2nd son of Maj Catesby Jones, who served with distinction in the Revolution. His parents, dying while he was very young, he went to live with his uncle, Meriwether Jones, at Richmond, by whom he was sent to school. He entered the navy as a Midshipman, under an appointment by Mr Jefferson, on Nov 22, 1805, & in Jun, 1807, immediately after the ship **Leopard**'s attack on the ship **Chesapeake**, he was called into active service at Norfolk, where he received his first professional lessons from Hull & Decatur, under whose command he remained until ordered to the South. **Sharon** became a model farm, & with wife, children, & friends, a home of domestic enjoyment & the seat of generous hospitality.
+

Died: on May 30, at *Sharon*, Fairfax Co, Va, Cmdor Thos Ap Catesby Jones, U S Navy, in his 69th year. His funeral will be on Jun 2 at 12 P M, at Lewensville, near his late residence.

John Mardis was arrested on Sunday for abusing an old man. He was today examined & committed for trial in court.

Mrd: on May 30, by Rev John C Smith, Mr Geo W Field to Miss Sallie E M Delphy, both of Alexandria, Va.

Mrd: on May 25, by Rev Wm E Eppes, at the residence of the bride's father, Mr L P Holladay to Miss Lettie B, daughter of Col Robt Gamble, of Tallahassee, Florida.

The copartnership of Haskins & Alexander, Architects, is this day dissolved by mutual consent. Wash, Jun 1, 1858.

WED JUN 2, 1858
Household & kitchen furniture at auction on Jun 8, at the residence of J B Oliver, 457 11th st, between F & G sts north. -A Green auct

The barge **G W P Custis** at auction on Jun 8, at Page's wharf: 125 feet long & 16 feet beam. –Quincy L Page -Jas C McGuire, auct

Trustee's sale of a valuable Market Farm & other real estate, on Jun 21, next, by decree of the Circuit Court of Wash Co, D C, public auction of that Market Farm owned & occupied for the past twelve years by the late Ninian Beall, lying near Tenallytown, partly in said county, & partly in Montg Co, Md. The farm contains between 52 & 53 acres of land, with a nearly new 2 story frame dwlg, with back bldg, a cottage for a gardner or overseer, barn, stables, & other necessary outbldgs. On Jun 24, will be offered at public sale on the premises, 2 houses & lots on Bridge st, Gtwn, D C, on the south side of Bridge st, between High & Potomac sts. Also, all the interest in part of lot 115, & part of lot 116, fronting 62 feet on Green st & 120 feet on Beall st. Mr A E Beall will show the farm. –Geo W Beall, trustee -Barnard & Buckey, aucts

Orphans Court of Wash Co, D C. Letters of administration on the personal estate of John A M Duncanson, late of Wash Co, deceased. –Martha D Duncanson, admx

On Jun 22 next I shall sell my late residence on the corner of N J ave & C st south, comprising lots 3, & 6 thru 9, in square 692, fronting on N J ave 162 feet 9 inches, on C st 206 feet 11 inches, with a comfortable dwlg containing 11 rooms. Also, will be offered the larger portion of square 828, near **Kendall Green**, fronting 105 feet 1 inch on M st north, running back along 5th st east 276 feet 5 inches to Boundary st.
-Wm F Phillips -Jas C McGuire, auct

Senate: 1-Ptn from R F Hunter, a lt in the army, asking to be allowed a credit on his account for certain public money stolen while in his custody: referred. 2-Ptn from Saml G Hensley, asking Congress to recall his papers from the Court of Claims & to make an appropriation to pay him for cattle purchased of him by O M Wozencraft, Com'r & Indian agent of the U S to fulfill the stipulations of Indian treaties: referred. 3-Papers in relation to the claim of Capt Wm H Payne's company of mounted volunteers for services during the Seminole war: referred. 4-Papers in relation to the claim of Israel D Andrews, late agent of the U S, in reference to the reciprocity treaty with Great Britain: referred. 5-Cmte on the Post Ofc & Post Roads: bills passed-relief of John Dearmit; of Stuckey & Rogers; & of Henry Orndorf. 6-Cmte on Revolutionary Claims: bill for the relief of the reps of Henry King, deceased, & recommended its passage. 7-Cmte on Private Land Claims: recommend passage of the bill for the relief of: Roswell Minard, father of Theodore Minard, deceased; for the relief of the legal reps of Jean Baptiste Devidrein; for relief of the legal reps of John McDonough, deceased, late of Louisiana. 8-Cmte on Pensions: recommend passage of the bill granting an invalid pension to Jas Fugate, of Missouri; granting an invalid pension to Conrad Schroeder; & granting an invalid pension to Alex'r S Bean, of Pa. Bill for the relief of Stephen Fellows; of Elijah Cloze, of Tenn; of Micajah Brooks; of Jos Welban; & of Capt Stanton Sholes. 9-Cmte of Claims: bill for the relief of Dr Geo H Howell, recommended its passage. 10-Cmte on Naval Affairs: bill for the relief of Wm Heine, artist in Japan expedition, recommended its passage. 11-Cmte on Pensions: bill to increase the pension of Henry E Reed, a citizen of Ky: recommended its passage. Same cmte: granting a pension Mary A M Jones. Relief of: Michl A Davenport, of Ill; of Francis Carver; of Robinson Gammon; of Fred'k Smith; of David Wilson; of Wright Fore; & of Beriah Wright. Also, to continue the pension heretofore paid to Mary C Hamilton, widow of Capt Fowler, late of the U S army. 12-Cmte on Public Lands: asked to be discharged from the consideration of the memorials of J H Birch & of T D W Gouley & others.

About 7 years since Sinclair Young, a citizen of Harrison Co, Ind, was killed by Wm Marsh, in an affray at Corydon, in that State. Marsh was tried & acquitted. On Wed last, at Brandenburg, Ky, Marsh's son was sitting in front of Ashcraft's tavern, & Stanley Young, a son of the deceased, took deliberate aim with a revolver, & shot Marsh through the head. Marsh fell dead in his tracks. Stanley Young made his escape on his horse.

Orphans Court of Wash Co, D C. Letters of administration on the personal estate of Josephine H Blagrove, late of Fred'k Co, Md, deceased. –Wm B R Williss, Harriet Williss, adms

Orphans Court of Wash Co, D C. In the case of Jas Fitzpatrick, adm of Patrick Fitzpatrick, deceased, the Court & administrator have appointed Jun 26, for the settlement of the personal estate of the deceased, of the assets in hand.
-Ed N Roach, Reg/o wills

THU JUN 3, 1858
The wife of the late H W Herbert was in Indiana, preparing to obtain a divorce from him under the accommodating laws of that State when he killed himself because of her. All the necessary steps to secure a divorce had been taken. It was the knowledge of this fact that probably determined the fatal resolution of the suicide.

Senate: 1-Ptn from Claude Samory, asking the confirmation of certain land titles: referred. 2-Ptn from Ferdinand Coxe, late Sec of Legation at Brazil, asking compensation for services rendered as charge d'affaires at that Court: referred. 3-Cmte of Claims: bill for the relief of John R B Bartlett. 4-Cmte on Military Affairs: bill for the relief of Wm Hutchinson, reported that it ought not pass. 5-Cmte on the Post Ofc & Post Roads: bill for the relief of Lewis W Broadwell, & recommended its passage. Same cmte: bill for the relief of John Ferguson, & recommended its passage. 6-Cmte of Claims-recommended the passage of-act for the relief: of Wm Tarvin; of A Baudowin & A D Robert; of Jos Rumph; of Dr Ferdinand O Miller; of Dinah Minis; of Lt Loomis L Langdon; of the adm of David McClure, Jos McClure; & of Robt A Davidge. Same cmte:asked to be discharged from the consideration of the following bills-for the relief: of Dr Thos Antisell; & the adm of Horatio Boultbee, deceased; & that they be referred to the Cmte on Military Affairs. And that the bill for the relief of Alonzo & Elbridge G Colby be referred to the Cmte on Commerce: agreed to. The cmte was discharged from the further consideration of the bill for the relief of Geo Mayo, deceased. 7-Bill for the relief of Jas Collier: referred to the Cmte of Claims. 8-Act for the relief of Stephen R Rowan: passed.

Mrs Taylor's Boarding House, 411 3rd st, is recommended to both married & single gentlemen & ladies. Mrs Taylor is an exemplary member of the Methodist Church, plain but neat in her dress, the first up & the last to bed. Her son-in-law, Mr Colley, a highly respectable merchant on 7th st, & her intelligent daughter, Mrs Colley, reside with the family, & assist their mother. Capt Bestor, the gentlemanly Cashier of the Patriotic Bank of Wash, has for many years been an inmate in her family, under all its changes.

Hon Wm A Duer, LL D, died on Monday at the residence of his son-in-law, A G King, in this city. The deceased was born in 1780, & was in his 78th year. Like his distinguished brother, Hon John Duer, of the Superior Court, who survives him, Hon Wm A Duer has filled many distinguished public positions in this State. –N Y Com Adv

For sale: my farm, **Locust Grove**, at private sale, containing 106 acres; adjoins the farms of Mrs McDaniel, also the farm lately owned by Mr Willard. It is about 2½ miles from the Centre Market. The improvements consist of a good Frame House, nearly new, of 9 rooms, with all the necessary out-houses. Address me through the post ofc, or apply to me on the farm. –Mary C Fenwick

Died: on Jun 2, suddenly, Miss Eliz Gunton, eldest sister of Dr Wm Gunton, of Wash City. In consequence of repairing in progress at the residence of her brother, the funeral will take place from the house of her sister, Mrs Harriet Fischer, on C st, near 4½ st, this afternoon, at 4 o'clock.

Died: on Jun 1, in Wash City, Mrs Emily V, wife of J Dawson James.

House of Reps: 1-Bill granting an invalid pension to John Holland, of Arkansas: passed. 2-Resolution for the benefit of the widow of Cmder Wm Lewis Herndon, late of the U S navy: passed. 3-Bill for the relief of the heirs & legal reps of Richd B Roland, deceased: passed.

Orphans Court of Wash Co, D C. In the case of Dennis Burns, adm of Dennis Hardy, deceased, the Court & administrator have appointed Jun 22 next, for the final settlement of the personal estate of the deceased, on Jun 22 next, of the assets in hand.
-Ed N Roach, Reg/o wills

Three days from Europe. The Duchess of Orleans died at her residence, near London, after a brief illness, on May 18, aged 49 years.

FRI JUN 4, 1858
Book: The History & Antiquities of the city of St Augustine, Florida; by Geo R Fairbanks. N Y, C B Norton Washington, F Philp [Ad]

A great invention has been patented by Wm D Wright, called the Thief Alarm, which will put a stop to all burglars. It may be obtained of Jas McGrann & Co, who are the sole agents for the District; & for sale at Dr Swartz's Drug Store, between 3rd & 4½ sts, Pa ave, & also at 232 Pa ave, corner of 13th st, & 291 B st, in the rear of Adams & Co's express ofc. The invention can be obtained for a small sum.

Mrd: on May 20, by Rev Mr Ball, Mr Wm H Boose, of Wash, to Miss Mgt A Determan, of Balt, Md.

Mrd: on Jun 1, by Rev Father Boyle, Hiram Richey to Miss Maria Louisa Newton, all of Wash City.

Died: on Jun 2, after a short & painful illness, Sarah Ella, youngest daughter of David & Christiana Hines, aged 6 years, 3 months & 22 days. Her funeral is this afternoon at 3½ o'clock, from the residence of her parents, Pa ave & 20th st.

Senate: 1-Cmte on Naval Affairs: bill for the relief of Geo M Lewis: passed. Same cmte: asked to be discharged from the consideration of the memorial of Robt Morris: agreed to. 2-Cmte on Commerce: bills for the relief of Alonzo & Elbridge G Colley; of Thos Hassam & B S Brewster; & of Gardner & Vincent. Also, bill for the relief of Thos W Ward, U S Consul at Panama. Same cmte: adverse reports on the memorial of G G Powell & others, for an examination of a plan for bridging the East river at N Y; & on the memorial of J Horsford Smith, asking additional allowance during the time he was U S Consul at Beirut, in Syria. 3-Cmte of Claims: bills for the relief of Jane J Wingard; & of Jas Myer. Same cmte: adverse reports on the memorials of Ebenezer Ballard & Rishworth Jordan; of Michl Nourse; & of Chas Vinson. 4-Cmte on Military Affairs: bill for the relief of Dr Thos Antisell: recommended its passage. Same cmte: asked to be discharged from the consideration of the memorial of Robt Hale: agreed to. Same cmte: bill for the relief of R F Blocker, E J Gurley, & J F Davis. 5-Cmte on the Post Ofc & Post roads: bill for the relief of S W & A A Turner: passed. 6-Cmte on Patents: bill for the relief of David Bruce. 7-Bill for the relief of Anthony S Robinson, heir & legal rep of John Hamilton Robinson, deceased, was considered in the Cmte of the Whole.

The Mayor has appointed the following persons special police ofcrs, to act on Monday next, in accordance with power vested in him. To attend at the Polls:

Thos B Entwisle	Edw Edwards	B Random
Henry Burch	Richd Earl	Jno T Rye
Jacob Frank	Jno Bury	S H Sherman
Jas H Hazle	Wm Brown	W W Hough
John Keller	W T Barr	Jas Donaldson
J C Fearson	Saml T McPherson	R B Bridgett
Jno Wilson	Geo W Chism	Henry Birch
Jas Sibley	Saml E Douglass	Danl Ratcliff
Chas Swasser	Jas W Irwin	John B Williamson
Robt Martin	Alfred Gawler	Jos L Savage
John Rheem	Barton Hackney	Jos S Norwood
J E Rawlings	Danl Myers	Wm M Fisher
Jos Linkins	F N Holtzman	Geo Harvey
Geo W Hopkins	Jas Biggs	C A Sengstack
Geo W Emmerson	Solomon Stover	Geo T Stewart
W W Davis	Saml Tinkler	Lemuel Henry
Jno B Harrison	T S Herbert	Thos Wall
Wm Herbert	Geo W Scaggs	Lewis Poole
Wm N Keefe	John H Caldwell	C L Coltman
Jno N Craig	Geo W Dyer	A N Clements
Saml Spalding	Andrew Carroll	T S Donoho
Robt Paine	Robt Earn, sen	Thos Edmonston
Wm Walker	Solomon Fowle	J A Klopfer
A H Mechlin	Wm Fletcher, jr	Geo Turnburke
A M Caldwell	Peter Goodyear	Francis R May
T P Morgan	Danl Linkins	Wm H Clampitt
Saml C Mickum	John McDermott	Michl R Coombs

S S Lovejoy
L F Clark
Nicholas Vedder
Richd Reeder
Columbus Denham
Richd Downer
Geo Leitz
Wm L Bailey
Walter Lenox
Barrow Frere
P J Newman
Jos Reese
Lawrence Murphy
Jas Belt
A Voss
Henry Kaiser
Geo Waters
Andrew S Joyce
C Finkman
John B Medley
Thos Byrne
Jno H Sessford
Jeremiah Twomey
Wm E Spalding
Nichola Callan
Jno F Ennis
W P Drury
R E Doyle
Thos Grady
Jas W Baggett
Thos Burch
Thos McLaughlin
Saml Handy
Chas Lyons
Andrew Hancock
Wm Pettibone
Wm Wisenborne
C Jesse Burch
Chas Lemmon
Jos Burch
Geo Burns
John I Garner
Wm Miles
Nathl Wells
Chas Stewart
Thos H Langley

Theodore Sheckles
Saml Hoover
John Simms
John Smith
John F Carter
Henry Lansdale
Jos Lyons
Jas Ward
Saml P Robertson
Howard Taylor
Dr John J Dyer
Thos Lewis
Thos H Kelleher
Milton Ward
John Adamson
Philip McAlear
David C Davis
Wm T Hook
Chas Brown
J S Rowles
Geo Savage
E L Keese
W W Cox
Wm Stewart
Wm A Waugh
Dr F B Culver
J S Hollingshead
Jas Towles
John McNerhany
Horatio N Steele
John Ross
Danl Shehan
W H Simington
Saml McPherson
Benj Burns
Henry N Johnson
Jeremiah Matlock
John Davidson
Geo Bradley
L A Gobright
John Laurie
Chas T Ball
Francis W Darden
Andrew D Melcher
C Edmonson
Ja Stewart

Saml A Rainey
Jos Peck
Job B Augus
Jedediah Gidding
Thos Creaser
Andrew Small
A Rothwell
J H Goddard
E E O'Brien
Fred'k Shaffer
Hugh B Sweeny
John Kelly
Wm O'Neal
Emanuel Caton
Jas English
Jas Fletcher
A L Newton
Thos Stone
Wm T Joy
A R Allen
John W Hodgson
Francis Hutchins
E M Chapin
Thos Duffy
Chas Kreamer
Jas Allen
Thos C Donn
Patrick English
Thos W Burch
Alex'r Hume
Oliver Burkhead
Jacob Shaffer
John H Noyes
Geo D Spencer
B Ferguson
John E Neal
Philip R Fendall
Saml Bacon
Noble Thomas
Jas C McGuire
Jas Scarf
Henry Burney
Wm Flaherty
Thos J Galt
B F Middleton
Henry Burney

- John Miles
- Saml Stettinius
- Nicholas Galt
- Jas Welsh
- John F Webb
- H Nater
- John Fitzpatrick
- Cornelius Wendell
- Nicholas Wolf
- Edw Semmes
- Marshall Brown
- Jas Roach
- Wm H Harrover
- Geo Noyes
- Leonard Harbaugh
- Thos Young
- Geo Courtney
- Nicholas German
- Cornelius Boyle
- Wm H Grund
- Jas Lusby
- Saml Hardon
- E F French
- Dr John B Brodhead
- John P Ingle
- Thos H Parsons
- W L Bestor
- Jos Hedrick
- Wm F Price
- Chas McNamee
- B B French
- Edmund Barry
- Capt J F Tucker
- B B Curran
- Jos Z Williams
- Saml K Phillips
- Dr Geo McCoy
- John N Barker
- H C Purdy
- Capt Jas A Tate
- Alex'r Dodge
- E O Castell
- John W Mead
- M Maceron
- Robt Barr
- Jos T Mitchell
- Saml Johnson
- Dennis Callahan
- Jacob Fleishell
- Hanson Brown
- Jacob Hess
- B Frank Beers
- Henry Bowen
- Danl Cronin
- John McLaughlin
- Wm P Patterson
- Saml Entwisle
- John B McGill
- John Peabody
- Jas Martin
- Thos H Robinson
- Jas Maceron
- Hugh Dougherty
- Jas Reilly
- John Roney
- Wm E Tucker
- Saml Galt
- Thos M Fugitt
- Thos O Pryor
- John T Moss
- J J Mulloy
- Wm Bean
- John Forrest
- M P King
- John A Hunnicutt
- Isaac Beers
- E D Reynolds
- John Atchison
- Philip Hutchinson
- Wm Scott
- Wm H Burdine
- Thos McDonald
- John B Knott
- Chas Nelson
- Danl Whaling
- Geo W Offutt
- Henry Konig
- Jas W Irwin
- Zach Offutt
- Lewis Marceron
- Andrew Hofnagle
- Jas McFarland
- John Gray
- Jas Lynch
- Thos Luxen
- Geo H Morgan
- A J Norton
- Jas M Freeburger
- Wm H Keilholtz
- John M Thornton
- Thos D Coursey
- Thos Winfield
- Henry Chisholm
- Danl Mullen
- Wm L Cook
- Philip Pyles
- Geo Padgett
- John H Barr
- Jas R Wood
- Thos Champion, sr
- Jas T Bradley
- John Browers
- John Simmons
- Michl Connor
- Wm Mooney
- Jas R Gates
- Thos Griffith
- Edw Short
- Wm Coombs
- Wm H Rose
- Geo W Johnson
- John King
- Isaac Ball
- Geo H Smith
- Jas A French
- John T Smith
- Geo Thompson
- Francis Thompson
- Adam Wright
- John Graham
- A G Davis
- Francis Jenkins
- Jilson J Dove
- Chas Miller, jr
- John McNamee
- Stephen McNamee
- Jos Marceron
- Andrew Ferguson

A Smedley	Thos Geary	Wm E Stewart
J Mansfield	Theodore Wheeler	David Neitzy
Jas Taylor	David Hepburn	Geo Ragan
Thos Lomax	Chas C Mills	Jas H Burch
Jno Landy	Henry M Knight	Peter Hepburn, jr
Fletcher Purcell	Wm Cammack, jr	Wm Cumberland
Richd Evans	Wm Bright	Douglas Sears
Wm Wise	Wm McElfresh	Solomon Beard
John Dudley	Danl F Mockabee	Chas Hulseman
Frank Guess	Wm G Flood	Robt Gill
John Lewis	Wm Cooper	Jno T Bradley
A Dean	Geo E Kirk	Jno R Harbaugh
E S Allen	Jno Tucker	John Sheets
John Wise	E F Carlin	G Cameron
Geo Tatsapaugh	D B Clark	John P Murphy
Geo Adams	John Pettibone	Henry C Hepburn
Jos Kidwell	John H Taylor	Gwin Harris
Alford Carpenter	Nathl Beach	R J Graham
Geo Mattingly	D B Clark	Isaac Mister
Benj D Harrison	Jno W Martin	
Washington Wallingsford		

Commissions & badges will be furnished each member of the special police at the polls on Monday morning. –Wm B Magruder, Mayor

SAT JUN 5, 1858
Household & kitchen furniture at auction on Jun 10, at the residence of W H Brereton, on 7th, between I & K sts. -A Green auct

Handsome bldg lot on Capitol Hill at auction on Jun 11, in front of the premises, lot B, being part of Jas Crutchett's subdivision of lot 7, in square 755, having a front of 18 feet on north E st. -A Green auct

Hon J Pinckney Henderson, one of the Senators in Congress from the State of Texas, who was detained at home by illness until late in the session, & after his arrival in Washington was able to give his attendance in the Senate but a short time, when illness again confined him to his bed. He expired at his lodgings in Washington City yesterday. He was a native of North Carolina, but was an early settler in Texas. [Jun 7th newspaper: The funeral of Hon J Pinckney Henderson took place yesterday, at the late residence of the deceased, 12th st, at 1 o'clock P M, at which time the corpse was removed to the Senate Chamber where Divine service was performed.]

Andrew Gross, a colored man, was killed by lightning yesterday, whilst at work in Mr Hopkins' brick-yard, in the First Ward, Wash City.

An inquest was held in New Orleans on May 28 on the body of Jas Dowling, aged 40 years, who, it appeared died from the effects of drink. He took 16 glasses of gin, won the bet that he could do it, & laid down & died.

Hon John Woodworth, one of the patriarchs of Albany, who was verging upon his 90th year, expired, after a few weeks' illness, on Tue. He had resided in Albany nearly half a century; established himself at Troy in the practice of law more than 60 years ago; member of Assembly in 1802; & an Elector of Pres & V Pres in 1800. In Mar, 1819, he was appointed by Gov Clinton a Judge of the Supreme Court, in the place of the late Chief Justice Spencer, whose constitutional term of service then expired, & remained on the bench till 1823, when, though in full vigor of mind & body, it was assumed that he had reached the period in life when the Constitution interposed a disqualification. The Judge resisted this assumption, & a suit is now pending to recover some 3 years' salary, of which he claims to have been unconstitutionally deprived, being but 57 instead of 60 years of age when removed.

Hon Wm Chappell, a member of the Wisconsin Senate, received $10,000 of the La Crosse & Milwaukee Railroad bribe 2 years ago, & was active in corrupting his legislative associates. The Senate, at its recent session, voted 21 to 6 that he was guilty, & 18 to 9 that he was unworthy a seat in the body. He, however, retained his seat.

The Duchess of Orleans, widow of the eldest son of Louis Philippe, & mother of the Count of Paris & the Duke de Chartres, the former of whom was heir apparent to the throne of France under the late dynasty, died rather suddenly, at her residence at Richmond, England, on May 18. The deceased Duchess, Helene Louise Eliz d'Orleans, was the youngest daughter of Fred'k Louis, hereditary Grand Duke of Mecklenburg Schwerin, & was born on Jan 24, 1814. She was brought up in the Protestant faith, & reluctantly exchanged her pious courts of life for the prospect of a union with the Prince Royal of France. She was married to the Duke of Orleans on Jul 13, 1837, & bore him 2 sons, the first born Aug 24, 1838, & the second Nov 9, 1840. The death of her husband in Jul, 1842, by a fall from his carriage, affected her with profound melancholy, & she devoted herself to the education of her sons. Following the fortunes of her family, she left France on the overthrow of the Orleans dynasty.

Rev Jos Barlow, a Presbyterian clergyman, lost his life at Franklin, Pa, on Sat night. He was aroused by the cry of fire, & opening the kitchen door, where it originated, he probably inhaled a portion of the flame, as he immediately sank down & scarcely showed a sign of life afterwards. His wife & dghts attempted in vain to save him. To save themselves they were compelled to leave him to be consumed where he lay.

The oldest woman in Michigan, Mrs Vilette, of La Salle, Munroe Co, was buried on Wed in the Catholic burying ground. She was 112 years of age, & had lived in that region the better part of a century. Her husband-the third or fourth one-is still living, aged 70 years. She made her will in the latter part of the last century, & has outlived all the persons to whom she had bequeathed property.

The Randolph [N Y] Reporter states that Gov Blacksnake, the celebrated Indian Chief, is still living, & resides about 6 miles from that place, on the Allegheny Reservation. An ambrotype of the distinguished old warrior has recently been taken by Mr Clark, who informs the Reporter that the Govn'r is 116 years of age; but it is understood that his exact age was not known by any one, not even himself. He is probably the oldest person living. He was a favorite of Gen Washington during the Revolutionary war, & has now a beautiful silver medal which was presented to him by Washington. One of his wonderful feats, as a bearer of dispatches in the Revolutionary war, was to run from the Reservation where he now lives to Buffalo & back in one day, a distance of 69 miles each way.

Died: on May 22, at N Y, Wm Sinclair, of the U S Navy, aged 69 years. He entered the navy as a midshipman in 1809. At his death, Mr Sinclair was one of the oldest pursers in the navy, & had been in service nearly 50 years.

Senate: 1-Ptn from Geo B Bacon, asking to be allowed the difference of pay between that of capt's clerk & purser during the time he acted in the latter capacity on board the U S sloop-of-war **Portsmouth**: referred. 2-Ptn from J W Cummins, for himself & others temporarily employed under authority of law, asking that the provisions of the act of Apr, 1854, may be extended to them: referred. 3-Cmte on Military Affairs: adverse report on the memorial of R H Hunter. 4-Senate bills passed-relief: of Wm Money; of Miles Judson, surety on the official bond of the late Purser Arthur D Crosby; of Geo Stealey; of Willis A Gorman; of Ebenezer Ricker; of Capt John B Montgomery. Also, to authorize the Sec of the Interior to issue a land warrant to Russell Fitch, of Ohio. 5-House bills passed-relief: of Alex R Honey; of Susannah Redman, widow of Lloyd Redman; of Geo W Biscoe; of Benj L McAtee, & I N Eastham, of Louisville, Ky; of Simeon Stedman; of Richd B Alexander; of Genr'l Sylvester Churchill; of Robt W Cushman, formerly an acting purser in the U S navy; of Benj Wakefield; of Isaac Body & Saml Fleming; of Job Stafford, of the State of N Y; of Eliz McBrier, only surviving child & heir of Col Archibald Loughry, deceased; of Capt Stanton Sholes; of Jos Webb; of Micajah Brookes; of Elijah Close, of Tenn; Wyatt Griffith; of Stephen Fellows; of Michl A Davenport, of Ill; of Wm Heine, artist in the Japan expedition; of Henry Orndorf; of Stuckey & Rogers; of Dr Geo H Howell; of Roswell Minard, father of Theodore Minard, deceased; of the legal reps of John McDonogh, deceased, late of Louisiana; of legal reps of Jean Baptiste Devidrine; of the heirs of Wm Turvin, deceased; of Jas Rumph; of Dr Ferdinand O Miller; of Lt Loomis L Langdon; of David McClure, adm of Jos McClure, deceased; of Lewis W Broadwell; of Shove Chase, of N Y; of Alonzo & Elbridge G Colby; of Gardner & Vincent & others; of Thos Hasam & B S Brewster; of Thos U Ward, late U S Consul at Panama; of Dr Thos Antisell; of David Bruce; of Jas Myer; & of Jas J Wingen. Also, granting an invalid pension to Conrad Schroeder; invalid pension to Alex'r S Bean, of Pa; granting a pension to Jas Fugate, of Missouri; granting a pension to Henry E Read, a citizen of Ky, & for other purposes; granting a pension to Mary A M Jones: passed. Also, issue a land warrant to Benj Ward: passed.

Jordan's W S Springs, Fred'k Co, Va, 5 miles from Winchester. –Dr R M Jordan & Bro

House of Reps: 1-Private bills laid aside to be reported favorably to the House-relief: of John Harris, of Ky; of John Campbell; & of Wm Rich. Also, granting a pension to Jeremiah Wright. 2-Bill for the relief of Nahum Ward was laid on the table. 3-Bill for the relief of Mrs Harriet O Read, excx of the late Brvt Col Fanning: passed. 4-Bills for the relief of Ferdinand Coxe; & relief of Peter Parker: passed. 5-Bill for the relief of Brvt Maj John Jones, of Tenn, was concurred in. 6-Bill for the relief of Keep, Bard & Co, J Caulfield, & Jos Landis: passed. 7-Bill for the relief of the legal reps of G B Horner, deceased, was taken from the private calendar. 8-Bill for the relief of John Sawyer, a soldier of the Revolution, aged 108 years: passed. 9-Bill granting a invalid pension to Henry Miller: passed. 10-Bill for the relief of Mary B Dusenbury: passed. 11-Bill for the relief of Edwin M Chaffee, pending.

Roscoe, Ill, Jun 4. A culvert in this place was swept away last evening, destroying the house of Rev Horatio Ilsey & drowning Mrs Ilsey & 8 children. [Jun 10th newspaper: The children ranged from infancy to 17 years of age. The family were in their beds, when they were swept into the raging torrent. The father alone escaped. Other houses were damaged.]

MON JUN 7, 1858
Tornado on Mon at the village of Ellison, Ill. Among the dead are Mr John Hand, his son, about 10 years old, & a babe, the latter of whom is supposed to have been drowned. The whole family appear to have been whirled, with the fragments of their dwlg, quite up into the air. Mr Hand was carried about 15 roods, wounded in the side, & survived until the next morning. Mrs Hand had her infant in her arms when she struck the ground, but concussion compelled her to let go. Her dead infant drifted to the shore. Another family named McWilliams suffered terribly. Miss Mary Ann McWilliams, about 22, her sister, Harriet, aged about 16, & her brother, Thomas, about 14, are among the dead, & the poor old mother, 80 years of age, the only remaining member of the family, except some older children who were living at a distance. W E Thompson, his wife, & child, Mrs Brazleton & her 2 children, a son & daughter, Martin Wentworth, Levina Lacey, Hiram John & child & 2 others, names unknown, make up the list of those instantly killed. The stores of Saml Johnson & Jos Knowles were destroyed.

Mr Nicholas Ten Broeck, an estimable bachelor citizen of Greenport, N Y, while in his pig-pen, was shot & killed by his nephew, who had been out shooting at crows, & carelessly fired his revolver at a knot-hole in the pen.

Mr Eben B Jones, one of the paymasters upon the Worcester railroad, on the yacht **Surprise**, on a fishing excursion, to prevent sea-sickness, drank a quantity of ether. He was found in the cabin, in strong convulsions, & expired before he reached Rainsford Island. –Boston Advertiser, 4th

On Thu last Mr Abraham LeFevre, a respectable citizen of Hayfield township, was killed by a bull belonging to a butcher in Conneautville. He was horned & mangled. It was 2 hours before the body could be taken away from the bull. –Meadville Journal

H Barber, a young man, in Clarksburg, Md, while running a race with a young companion, attempted to make his horse leap over a cow lying in the road. The cow raising up, pitched the horse over, killing Barber instantly.

Mrd: on May 25, at the residence of the bride's father, by Rev Geo D Cummins, Dr Thos F Maury to Georgie A, eldest daughter of Geo Parker.

Mrd: on Jun 2, in Richmond, by Rev Mr Minnigerode, Dr Levin S Joynes to Miss Susan V, daughter of Dr Robt Archer.

Appointments by the Pres, by & with the advice & consent of the Senate.
Calvin L Sayre, of Alabama, 2nd Lt in the Marine Corps, vice Butterfield, resigned.
Jas D Murray, of Minnesota, Purser in the Navy.
Geo w Clarke, of Arkansas, Purser in the Navy.
Wm H Wilcox, of Conn, Prof of Mathematics in the Navy, vice Flye, resigned.
Saml V Hunter, of Ky, Purser in the Navy.

TUE JUN 8, 1858
Senate: 1-Bill for the relief of Jas Tilton: referred to the Cmte on Public Lands. 2-Cmte on Pensions: bill for the relief of John Campbell. 3-Cmte on Pensions: bill for the relief of Augustus J Kuhn: recommended its passage. Same cmte: bill granting a pension to Thos Allcock, of Rochester, N Y, reported it back with an amendment.

Howell Hopkins, for many years a prominent member of the Phil Bar, died at his residence in that city on Friday last.

The remains of Pres Monroe: meeting on Thu to take into consideration the propriety of acting in concert, on the coming Jul 4th, [the anniversary of Pres Monroe's death,] with the City Councils & the Va Legislature, in removing the remains from their present resting place in this city, to the city of Richmond, Va, where it is proposed to erect a suitable monument over them. Maj *Hills, U S A, chairman, Mr Price, sec. Cmte: Maj Hill, W H Price, Dr Dennis, Michl Hart, Wm Bell, Jas T Soutter, Dr Banks, Robt Blow, C J Leigh, J F Shepard, Gen Wheat, J T Slassel, J A Patterson, A S Sullivan, & D C Peters. Maj & Hall gave some interesting reminiscences of Jas Monroe, whom he had seen, after which the meeting adjourned. –N Y Sun [*Hills/Hill/Hall-copied as written.]

Local Matters-election yesterday. A crowd of about 60 men caused a disturbance in the 4th Ward. Aquilla R Allen, acting special policeman, tried to disperse them. He shot his revolver & retreated to the City Hall. One shot struck a young man, Richd *Hurlahy, in the right breast. Henry Burns & R H Galt, special policemen, arrived to assist Allen. Three young men, *Hurlahy, Galt, & Tretler were taken to the Infirmary for wounds that they received. Tretler went home to his father's after his wound was dressed. Votes for Mayor: J O Berrett: 3,688; R Wallach: 3,117. [Jun 9th newspaper: Richd *Hurlihy was shot by Ofcr Aquila Allen in self defense. Justice Donn ordered his discharge.]
*Two spellings of Hurlahy/Hurlihy.

Comrs' sale of valuable land in Alexandria Co, Va: by decree of the Circuit Court of Alexandria Co, rendered at its May term, 1858, in the case of Swann, etc, vs Dempsey & others: public auction on Jul 10, of a tract of land in said county, containing about 260 acres, being the property on which Dr R B Alexander resided, & which he died seized. Also, a tract of land, of about 37½ acres, adjoining the above tract, with the Factory bldg & water power thereon. —F L Smith, L B Taylor, I Louis Kinzer, Comrs of sale

Mrd: on Jun 2, by Rev Mr Prout, Dr Thos C Price to Nellie M, youngest daughter of the late Dr Bennett Dyson, all of Chas Co, Md.

Died: on May 30, in Boston, Hon Jeremiah O'Brien, aged 80 years, formerly & for several years a member of Congress from Maine.

Died: on May 27, in Brooklyn, N Y, James M Waterbury, youngest son of Richd W & Clara Forsyth Meade. Remains to be deposited in the vault of his grand-sire, St Mary's Church, Phil.

Died: on Jun 5, at Columbus, Ga, Virginia Hargraves, wife of Mr Geo Hargraves, of that city, & daughter of the late Hon John Forsyth.

WED JUN 9, 1858
Cmder Robt D Thorburn has received orders to take command of the U S sloop of war **Saratoga**, fitting out with all possible dispatch at the Norfolk yard.

Senate: 1-Ptn from Thos F Folk, asking to be allowed an increase of pension: referred. 2-Ptn from Francis Huthman, asking compensation for losses sustained in consequence of alleged illegal proceedings of the Collector of Customs at the port of San Francisco: referred. 3-Ptn from Thos Allen & others, of St Louis, asking that certain land offices in Missouri may be closed under authority of law & consolidated in the city of St Louis: referred. 4-Cmte on Foreign Relations: bill for the relief of Michl Pappreniza & bill for the relief of Wm Rich: recommended their passage. Same cmte: bill for the relief of Ferdinand Coxe; & a bill for the relief of John H Wheeler. 5-Cmte of Claims: bill for the relief of J P Pomares. Same cmte: bill for the relief of Ferdinand Coxe. Same cmte: memorial of Michl Hanson be withdrawn from the Court of Claims & referred to the Cmte on Pensions, & that the memorial of Jno P Figh & Jno H Gindrat be referred to the Court of Claims: agreed to. Same cmte: claim of Peter N Paillet, asking indemnity for losses sustained during the war with Mexico, be referred to the Court of Claims. 6-Cmte on Private Land claims: asked to be discharged from the consideration of the bills to confirm the title to a certain tract of land in the State of Missouri to the heirs of Thos Maddin, deceased; joint resolution to refer the claim of Jos Valliere, deceased, to the Court of Claims; & adverse report on the memorial of Wm Sawyer & John H Phelps. 7-Cmte on Pensions: bill for the relief of John Holland, of Arkansas, & recommended its passage. 8-Cmte on Indian Affairs: bill for the relief of H R Schoolcraft. 8-Cmte on the Post Ofc & Post Roads: bill for the relief of Danl B Hibbard. 9-Bill for the relief of Anthony W Bayard: passed.

The undersigned jewelers have agreed to close their stores, from this day to Oct 1 next, at 7 o'clock in the evening. –M W Galt & Bro, H Semken, Saml Lewis

Anthony Buchly, Practical Undertaker in all its branches: 303 Pa ave, between 9th & 10th sts. No efforts spared to give satisfaction in all cases. Orders attended to at all hours. Residence on the premies. Ready made coffins always on hand.

Mayor's Ofc, Jun 8, 1858, Washington. Persons elected to the Board of Aldermen & Board of Common Council:
Aldermen:Wm T Dove; Thos J Fisher; Jos F Brown; Wm W Moore; C W C Dunnington; Aaron W Miller; & Peter M Pearson.

Common Council:

John B Turton	Lambert Tree	Thompson Van Reswick
Southey S Parker	Christopher S O'Hare	Geo A Bohrer
Chas Abert	Stephen D Castleman	Franklin Ober
Wm Orme	Elijah Edmonston	John Russell
Grafton Powell	Wm P Mohun	Thos E Lloyd
Chas S Jones	Wm A Mulloy	Chas Wilson
Wm G Palmer	Wm F Wallace	Thos Milsted

Died: on Jun 8, Mary E Jirdinston, wife of Jas A N Jirdinston, in her 23rd year. Her funeral is this afternoon at 4 o'clock, from her late residence, 6th st, between G & H sts.

THU JUN 10, 1858
House of Reps: 1-Bill for the relief of Benj Sayre: passed.

Mr R B Rhett, jr, is now the sole proprietor & editor of the Charleston Mercury. Mr John Heart, who had held these relations for 11 years past, announces his withdrawal.

On Jun 12, on the premises, I will sell at auction my country residence, lying near Tenally Town road, adjoining the lands of Mr Murdoch & Mr Borrows, 2 miles above Gtwn. It contains 11 acres of productive garden land. The cottage is plain but comfortable. Also a tenant's house, with other necessary out-bldgs. –John A Somervill -Wall & Barnard, aucts

Died: on Wed, in Gtwn, suddenly, Mr Henry F English, in his 41st year. His funeral is this afternoon at 5 o'clock, from his late residence, 115 Gay st.

Fort Leavenworth, Jun 5. Affray at Lawrence between Gen Lane & Mr Jenkins. It appears that both of them were living upon a contested claim. Jenkins, with 4 friends, all well armed, cut down Lane's fence & proceeded towards the well. Lane warned them not to advance or he would shoot. They disregarded the threats, & Lane fired, killing Jenkins instantly. Lane was shot in the leg, inflicting a wound. He was arrested. Jenkins was held in high estimation, & his death is deeply deplored.

Information wanted of Edw Clinton, who was in or near Phoenix, Oswego, N Y, when last heard from. Any information sent to the care of J N Wheat, Genr'l Post Ofc, Wash, D C, will be thankfully received & all cost paid by his sister, Ellen Clinton.

Circuit Court of Wash Co, D C A Jardin et al vs A Favier's heirs at al. The trustee reported that he has sold to A Jardin subdivision D of Favier's lots in square 119, for $1,500, & that he has complied with the terms of sale. –Jno A Smith, clerk

FRI JUN 11, 1858
Appointments by the Pres, by with the advice & consent of the Senate:
Collectors of the Customs:
Jason M Terbell, Sag Harbor, N Y
Pliny M Bromley, Genesee, N Y
Theophilus Peuguet, Cape Vincent, N Y
Henry J Ashmore, Burlington, N J
Amos Robins, Perth Amboy, N J
Jos B Baker, Phil
John Brawley, Presque Isle, Pa
Moritz Schoeffler, Milwaukee, Wis
Re-appointed:
Eben W Allen, Nantucket
Phineas W Leland, Fall River
Wm Bartoll, Marblehead
Sylvanus B Phinney, Barnstable
Jas Blood, Newburyport
E D Winner, Great Egg Harbor
Stephen Willits, Little Egg Harbor
W S Bowen, Bridgetown, N J
Edw S Hough, Alexandria
Darwin M Stapp, Saluria, Texas
John Adair, Oregon
Naval Officers:
John Ryan, Salem & Beverly, Mass
Nicholas Brown, Newburyport: reappointed
Chambers McKibben, Phil
Surveyors of Customs:
S J Anderson, Portland & Falmouth, Maine
Jas Nichols, port of Eastport, Maine
Josiah H Hadley, Portsmouth, N H
Ebenezer Dodge, Salem & Beverly, Mass
Wm P Dolliver, Gloucester, Mass
Emanuel B Hart, N Y
John Hamilton, jr, Phil
Jas A Gibson, Pittsburg, Pa
Walter N Haldeman, Louisville, Ky
Benj L Dorsey, Alton, Ill, vice John Fitch

Re-appointed:
Saml Porter, port of Beverly, Mass
John Ingalls, Marblehead, Mass
Danl L Willcomb, Ipswich
W C Barker, Providence, R I
S Maxwell, Warren & Barrington
Elisha Atkins, Newport, R I
Asa Gray, Tiverton, R I
Edw Ingraham, Saybrook, Ct
Clarke Elliott, Middletown, Ct
R Edmonds, Carter's Creek, Va
Appraisers of Merchandise:
Chas V Hagner, of Pa, appraiser general
Saml Pleasants, appraiser at Phil
Geo R Berrell, appraiser at Phil
Registers of Land Ofcs:
John O Henning, at Hudson, Wisc
Wm E Keefer, at Springfield, Ill
Jesse Braden, at Chariton, Iowa, vice Baker, resigned
E L T Blake, Tallahassee, Florida
G L Curry, Oregon City, vice Wilcox, resigned
J W Whitfield, Kickapoo, Kansas: re-appointed
Receivers of Public Money:
A G Herndon, at Springfield, Ill
Oscar A Stevens, at Mackinac, Mich
Danl Woodson, at Kickapoo, Kansas: re-appointed

Senate: 1-Memorial from Henry L Goodwin, a citizen of Calif, setting forth that the answer of the Postmaster Genr'l of May 13, touching the violations of law by the postmaster at San Francisco, is evasive, & intends to deceive the Senate, whether so intended or not. 2-Cmte on Naval Affairs: bill for the relief of Saml A West, Geo McCullough, Hiram McCullough, & Chas Pendergrast. Same cmte: adverse report on the memorials of Geo T Parry; & of Reywell Coates. 3-Cmte of Claims: adverse report on the memorial of Charlotte Taylor. Same cmte: asked to be discharged from the consideration of the memorial of John H Merrill, & that it be referred to the Court of Claims: agreed to. Same cmte: adverse report on the claim of Jas A Mott; & adverse on the memorial of Chas Kohler. Same cmte: bill for the relief of John R Nourse. 4-Cmte on Pensions: bill for the relief of Wm S Bradford: passed. 5-Bill for the relief of David Myerle: passed.

Four days from Europe. 1-John O'Connell, son of the late Danl O'Connell, & one of the principal repeal agitators, is dead. 2-The funeral of the late Duchess of Orleans took place at Weybridge, Surry, on May 22, her remains being deposited in the same vault as those of Louis Philippe.

The new schnr **Prairie Flower**, of Salem, left that port for Boston on Tue with nearly 50 passengers. As the boat was proceeding up Broad Sound a thunder storm prevailed, & she was struck by a squall & immediately capsized. The pilot boat **Friend** was near & rescued some of the passengers. The **Prairie Flower** sunk immediately. Persons who lost their lives: Wm Henry Russell, age 21, a clerk in Salem; Osgood Sanborn, 30 years old, lately chief clerk in the Salem post ofc; Danl Fitz, 23, ship-joiner; ___ Donaldson, 20, son of Alex Donaldson; ___ Clark, 20, son of John Clark; Wm Newcomb, 20, son of Caleb Newcomb; & John R Smith, about 14 years of age.

House of Reps: 1-Cmte on Revolutionary Claims: bill for the relief of the heirs of John Paulding, David Williams, Isaac Van Wert, & John Van Camp: committed.

Mrs Parker, mother of the late editor of the Ohio Register was actually frightened to death a few days since. She was on the steamer **Florida**, ascending the Missouri, & before arriving at Kansas city the cry of "fire" was raised. It was a false alarm, but it caused a palpitation of the heart in Mrs Parker, & she died in a few hours.

Saml Harris, one of the oldest & most esteemed citizens of Balt, died at his residence in that city on Sunday last, at the advanced age of 84 years.

Petersburg, Jun 10. Bayliss, the kidnapper, was tried to day by the Circuit Court, & sentenced by Judge Nash to the penitentiary for 40 years, being 8 years on each indictment. He was defended by able counsel. Simpkins, who was arrested with Bayliss, is to be tried tomorrow.

Francis Willner, 365 N Y ave: New Paper-hanging & Upholstery Store. [Ad]

Circuit Court of Wash Co, D C. U S vs Schwartz, Livingston, et al. The trustee reported that he has sold lot 82 in square 465 to J G Smith, for $28.40; lots 83 & 84 in same square to Geo B Smith, for $56.80; lots 1, 33 & 34 in square 468, & lot 10 in square 469 to Simeon Mead, for $174.96; lots 2 thru 7, 19, & 31 & 32 in square 468 to Edw Swann, for $880.95; lot 8 in square 468, lots 25 thru 29 in square 469, lots 12, 23 & 24 in square 498 to Richd Barry, for $996.82; lot 18 in square 468 to Michl Briel for $106.75; lot 9 thru 12, 16 & 17 in square 468 to Robt Beale, for $640.50; lots 20 thru 24 in square 468, lots 3 thru 11, 13 thru 15, 17 thru 19, 25 thru 31, & 32 in square 498 to Buckner Bayliss, for $3.653.10; lot 29 in square 468 to W M McCutchen, for $35.50; lot 13 in square 468 to Alex Adams, for $30.50; lot 15 in square 468 to Jno T Lewis, for $30.50; lot 1, 32 thru 34 in square 469 to S Byington, for $253.85; lots 2 thru 4 in square 469 to D Sands, for $419.58; lots 5 thru 7, 9, 11 thru 24 in square 469, for $1,706.98; lot 30 in square 469 to A Archer, for $99.13; lot 31 in square 469 to J H Granger, for $30.50; all of square 47_ to Geo Mattingly, for $2,127.28; lot 1 in square 498 to J C Wilson, for $378.90; lots 40 thru 42 in square 498 to Chas Allen, for $882.81; lots 33 thru 38 in square 498 to S Pumphrey, for $1,403.11; lot 39 in square 498 to A Smiley, for $234.37; lot 2 in square 498, & lot 8 in square 469 to A B Claxton, for $253.69; lots 20 thru 22 in square 498 to Patrick Culican, for $419.91; & lot 16 in square 498 to John M Wilson, for $140.62; & that the purchasers have complied with the terms of the sale. –Jno A Smith, clerk

Circuit Court of Wash Co, D C. H P Van Bibber vs Fred'k & Mary P Van Bibber. The trustee reported that he has sold the interest of the parties to the cause in lot 8 in square 846 to John A Willett, for $75, & lot 13 in the same square to Adams & al, trustees, for $82, & that they have complied with the terms of sale. –John A Smith, clerk

SAT JUN 12, 1858
At the Commencement of the Univ of Va in July, Mr Jos Hodgson, jr, of Fluvanna, will deliver the Valedictory Oration before the Jefferson Society, & Mr L Southgate, of Norfolk, the Oration before the Washington Society.

At Marietta, Ohio, repose the remains of almost all those noble men who planted New England civilization at the mouth of the Muskingum. Among the monuments will be found that of: "Commodore Whipple, who fired the first gun of the Revolution upon the ocean." Cmdor Whipple, standing upon the deck of an American vessel of war, applied the torch to that cannon which first announced upon the mountain wave the decrees of the Continental Congress. Few persons speak of Whipple now; long years have passed since he was laid in the beautiful grave-yard at Marietta; but there will ever be some to remember him & the gallant barque which dared, in the face of the whole British navy, to ride the highest waves of the Atlantic, with no other banner at her masthead than that which had been baptized in the blood of Bunker Hill & Lexington. –Cincinnati Inquirer

Senate: 1-Cmte on Naval Affairs: joint resolution for the benefit of the nearest male heir of the late Maj Gen Towson, U S Army: passed. 2-Cmte on the Post Ofc & Post Roads: bill for the relief of the trustees of A G Sloo, contractor. 3-Cmte on Pensions: bill for the relief of Mary Walbach, widow of the late Brvt Brig Gen John B Walbach, U S Army. 4-Cmte on Military Affairs: bill for the relief of Geo B Bacon, late acting purser of the sloop-of-war **Portsmouth**, accompanied with a special report. 5-Cmte on the Judiciary: bill for the relief of Gottliet Scheerer, with an amendment. 6-Cmte on Patents: bill for the relief of Randall Pegg, accompanied by a special report. 7-Cmte on Indian Affairs: asked to be discharged from the consideration of the memorial of Saml Stone & Isaac H Marks, asking compensation for property taken under an agreement of arbitration for Gov't purposes: agreed to.

House of Reps: 1-Cmte on the Judiciary: adverse report in the case of Carney & Ramsey: laid on the table. 2-Bill to increase the pension of Peter Van Buskirk, of Wash, D C: passed. 3-Bill for the relief of Jennett H McCall, only child of Capt Jas McCall, of the Revolutionary war: passed. 4-Bill for the relief of Albert G Allen: passed. 5-Cmte on Invalid Pensions: bill granting an invalid pension to Wm Randall: passed.

Land at auction in Balt Co, on Jun 22. I will sell my Farm in said county, adjoining *Hayfields*, residence of John Merryman, Pres Md Agricultural Society, the properties of Mrs Webster & the late Saml Worthington, & near Cockeysville, where the N C railroad crosses the York turnpike. The bldgs are suited for summer residences. Terms liberal. -Chas McLean, Cockeysville P O, Balt Co, Md.

Circuit Court of Wash Co, D C-in Chancery. John R Woods against Richd C Briscoe, Walter C Briscoe, Theodore H Briscoe, et al, heirs at law of Richd G Briscoe & others. The bill of revivor in this case states that the cmplnt had filed in this court his bill of cmplnt against Richd G Briscoe & others, setting forth, among other things, that at the Oct term, 1852, of said court, he obtained a judgment against said Briscoe & Jos L Clark for $573.36, with interest from Mar 19, 1848, & cost, which is still unpaid, on which an execution was issued & returned nulla bona; that Brisoce & Clark had no property upon which it could be levied, but that Briscoe had a large real estate which he had conveyed away, so that cmplnt is hindered, delayed, & defeated in the recovery of said debt; that by certain deeds, recited in the said bill, he had conveyed his property in parcels to various co-defendants to secure the sums stated in said deed to the several other co-defendants, all which deeds, save the one to Thos Pursell, were not real but fictitious, & if real the said debts had been paid or materially reduced; that the cmplnt, though with others secured in said deed to said Pursell, had no remedy, as said Briscoe refused his assent to a sale, which assent, according to the terms of the deed, was necessary; that the cmplnt asked to be permitted & offered to redeem the various defendants secured in said deeds, & then prayed for relief; that the defendants residing in the county were all summoned, & those non-resident had been by an order of publication, duly published, warned to appear by a certain day, which had passed, & none had so appeared & answered, & the cmplnt was entitled to & was to obtain his final decree in the cause, when the said Richd G Briscoe departed this life intestate, leaving 5 children, among whom were the above named defendants; that the suit as to him, said Richd G Briscoe, hath abated, but that cmplnt is entitled to & ask to have the same revived against the said heirs & the adms of said Briscoe; that Richd G Briscoe left no personal estate, &, if any, not enough to pay said debt; that he left other debts to a large amount, & the complnt prays a sale of all the real estate of said Briscoe, which is absolutely necessary for the payment of his debt & the debts of such other creditors as shall come in & claim the benefit thereof, & for other relief; & it appearing to the satifaction of the court that the several dfndnts above named do not reside in this District, but in parts beyond, it is ordered, on motion of Wm R Woodward, counsel for the cmplnt, that notice be given that the non-resident defendants are to appear in this court on or before the third Monday of Oct next.
--Jno A Smith, clerk

Mrd: on May 20, in San Antonio, Texas, Lt Geo Bell, U S Army, to Isabella, daughter of Hugh McCormick, of Wash City.

Mrd: on Jun 10, by Rev John Robb, Mr Jas L Hutchinson to Miss S Emma Leake, all of Wash.

I offer my farm Airley, in Fauquier Co, Va, for sale: adjacent to Catlett's Station, 38 miles from Alexandria; contains 1,466 acres of land; the improvements consist of a new commodious dwlg, with the usual out-bldgs. Refer to my atty, Rice W Payne, at Warrenton, Va. -C J Stovin, P O Catlett's Station, Fauquier Co, Va.

Private sale of a valuable Farm, in Montg Co, Md, 3 miles s e of Darnestown, 6 miles from Rockville: contains 368 acres; with a comfortable 2 story log dwlg house, & other necessary out-bldgs. Apply on the premises to the subscriber, Wm M Hardesty

MON JUN 14, 1858
Senate: 1-Bill for the relief of Mary A M Jones. 2-Bill for the relief of Myra Clark Gaines. 3-Cmte on Pensions: adverse report on the bill for the relief of Mary Bennett. 4-Bill for the relief of Nancy Magill, of Ohio: passed. 5-Bills granting invalid pensions to Wm Howell, of Tenn, & Wm Randolph; & the bills for the relief of Jos Webb & John Holland, of Arkansas: passed.

Appointments by the Pres, by & with the advice & consent of the Senate.
S E Fabens, of Mass, Consul at Cayenne.
Gilbert S Miner, of Va, Consul at Amapola, Honduras.
Wm Bliss, of Penn, Consul at Puerto Cabello
R D Merrill, of N Y, Consul at Sydney
J P O"Sullivan, of Calif, Consul at Singapore
J B Hayne, of Georgia, Consul at Turks Island
Alex M Jackson, of Miss, secretary of New Mexico

Capt Smith, of the schnr **Sheppard A Mount**, at Phil, from St Barts, reports that on May 20 he came on deck at 8:30 A M & found that his son, age 14, was missing. He was not found on board & must be overboard. The vessel put about & beat back over the course she had sailed, & not until 12 o'clock was the boy discovered & picked up. He was swimming manfully, & had diverted himself of most of his clothing. He alleged that he could have sustained himself for 2 or 3 hours longer.

On Jun 5, 8 men left Bruce mine for the Saut in a small sailboat. They were struck by a squall & capsized, & 5 drowned. One of the men who was drowned was Jas Lord, & the other were strangers, names unknown. –Chicago Journal

Superior Rosewood piano forte & household & kitchen furniture at auction on: on Jun 17, at the residence of P M Pyfer, 357 I st, in Caroline Terrace, between 13th & 14th sts. The house is for rent. -Jas C McGuire, auct

By decree of the Circuit Court of Wash Co, D C, in chancery, I shall sell at public auction on Jul 6 next, at the premises, lots 1, 2, 28, 29, & 30, in square 166, with a 2 story brick house & other improvements thereon. On the next evening I shall sell lot 2 in square 685. This property belonged to the late Edw Fitzgerald, Purser U S N, & it may be ranked among the best in Wash. Lots at the corner of 18th & I sts cannot be surpassed for beauty of situation by any place in the city. –Thos Carbery, trustee -Jas C McGuire, auct

From Panama. Wm L Walters, of the engineer corps of the U S Navy, died on board the U S steam frig **Merrimack** on May 27, of congestive fever, & his remains were interred in the American burying ground at Flamenco Island. Mr Walters was 24 years old, a native of Springfield, Ill, & was on his first trip in the service.

On Tue, as 2 daughters of ex-Lt Govn'r Hawley, of Stamford, were setting near a lamp filled with burning fluid, it exploded & both were immediately enveloped in flames. Miss Adelaide Hawley lived but 30 hours after this terrible event. The eldest daughter escaped with slight injuries. –N Y Com

Rev D C Van Norman, A M, [late Principal of Rutger's Female Institute,] reopens his Institute for Young Ladies, at 79 East 14th st, near Union Square, N Y, on Sep 13 next.

Valuable Farm at auction in Alexandria Co, Va, on Jun 25, on the premises. The tract of land contains 82 acres, more or less, & belonged to the late John Donaldson. Improvements consist of a good stone dwlg, & adjoins the land of the late Andrew Hoover. Deed given & a deed of trust taken. –John T Donaldson, adm, Gtwn

Birth: in Cheshire, England, the wife of C G Baylor, U S Consul at Manchester, of a son. [No date given-current item.]

Died: on Jun 7, at her residence in Wash City, Rachel Beall, in her 67th year, daughter of the late Danl Beall, of Montg Co, Md.

Died: on Jun 12, Mary Regina, youngest daughter of Paulus & Parthenia Thyson, aged 8 months & 21 days. Her funeral is this afternoon at 4 o'clock, from her parents' residence, 7th st, between H & I sts.

Information wanted: the heirs of Thos Southcomb & also the heirs of Richd Gerson will hear of something to their advantage by addressing Thos S Page, Frankfort, Ky.

TUE JUN 15, 1858
The following is a list of Acts passed at the session of Congress just closed. 1-Joint resolution for the relief of Gen Sylvester Churchill; relief of Henry Orndorf; resolution authorizing Cmder M F Maury to accept a gold medal awarded to him by the Emperor of Austria; resolution authorizing Lt Wm N Jeffers to accept a sword of honor from her Majesty the Queen of Spain; resolution for the benefit of the widow of Cmder Wm Lewis Herndon, U S Navy; relief of John Grayson; & a resolution to correct an error in the act for the relief of Stephen R Rowan, approved Jun 1, 1858. 2-Private Acts-relief: of John Hamilton; of Thos Smithers; of Whitemarsh B Seabrook & others; of the heirs, or their legal reps, of Wm Conway, deceased; of Geo W Biscoe; of the heirs of Alex'r Stevenson; of the reps of Wm Smith, deceased, late of Louisiana; of the legal reps or assignees of Jas Lawrence; of the heirs & legal reps of Pierre Broussard, deceased; of N C Weems, of Louisiana; of Francis Wlodecki; of Regis Loisel or his legal reps; of Dr Chas D Maxwell, a surgeon in the U S Navy; of Wm Heine, artist in the Japan expedition; of Nancy Serena; of Richd Tarvin; of Pierre Gagnon, of Natchitoches, La; of Oliver P Hoovey; of Isaac Carpenter; of David Bruce; of Brvt Maj H S Kendrick; of John B Roper; of the legal reps of Marine Malines; of Richd B Alexander; of Simeon Sledman; of Susannah Redman, widow of Lloyd Redman; of Capt Stanton Sholes; of Jos Webb; of Duncan Robertson; of D O Dickinson; of the legal reps of Jean Baptiste Devidine; of Robt W Cushman, formerly an acting purser in the U S navy; of Cornelius H Latham; of Jas Rumph; of

Ferdinand O Miller; of Alonzo & Elbridge G Colby; of Isaac Body & Saml Fleming; of John Dearmit; of Stuckey & Rogers; of S W & A A Turner; of Job Stafford, of the State of N Y; of Eliz McBrier, only surviving child & heirs of Col Archibald Loughrey, deceased; of Elijah Close, of Tenn; of Michl A Davenport, of Ill; of Wyatt Griffith; of Judith Nott; of Stephen Fellows; of Shove Chase, of N Y; of the legal reps of John McDonogh, deceased, late of Louisiana; of Benj Wakifield; of Gardner & Vincent & others; of Lt Loomis L Langdon; of David McClure, adm of Jos McClure, deceased; of Lewis W Broadwell; of Thos Hasam & B S Brewster; of Isaac Drew & other settlers upon the public land in the State of Wisconsin; of Wm S Bradford; of John Sawyer, a soldier of the war of the Revolution; of Michl Kinny, late a private in Co I, 8th Regt U S Army; of John R Temple, of Louisiana; of Wm B Trotter; of Jas G Burton, E B Babbitt, & Jas Longstreet, of the U S Army; of Jonas P Keller; of John Dick, of Florida; of J Wilcox Jenkins; of Laurent Millaudon; of Geo A O'Brien; of Dempsey Pittman, approved Agu 16, 1856; of Susanna T Lea, widow & admx of Jas Maglenen, late of the city of Balt, deceased; of Thos Phenix, jr; of Elijah F Smith, Gilman H Perkins, & Chas F Smith; of Wm Allen, of Portland, Maine; of the heirs of John B Hand; of Brvt Maj Jas L Donaldson, assist quartermaster U S Army; of the owners of the barque **Attica**, of Portland, Maine; of Anna M E Ring, Louisa M Ring, Cordelia E Ring, & Sarah J De Lanney; of Rufus Dwinel; of Maj Jeremiah Y Dashiell, paymaster in the U S Army; of Fabius Stanly; of Mrs Harreit O Read, excx of the late Brvt Col A C W Fanning, of the U S army; of the legal reps of Danl Hay, deceased; of the heirs & legal reps of Richd D Rowland, deceased, & others; of the Hungarian settlers upon certain tracts of land in Iowa, hitherto reserved from sale by order of the Pres, dated Jan 22, 1855; of Keep, Bard & Co, J Canfield, & Jos Landis & Co; of Stephen R Rowan; of Caleb Sherman; of Jennett H McCall, only child of Capt Jas McCall, of the Revolutionary war; of Albert G Allen; of Georgiana M Lewis; of Nancy Magill, of Ohio; & of Sherlock & Shirley. 3-Private Acts granting a pension to: John Richmond-an increase of pension; Henry E Read, a citizen of Ky, & for other purposes, an increase of pension; invalid pension to Brvt Maj John Jones, of Tenn; invalid pension to Jas Fugate, of Missouri; invalid pension to Alex'r S Bean, of Penn; continue the pension heretofore paid to Mary C Hamilton, widow of Capt Fowler Hamilton, late of the U S army; continue a pension to Christine Barnard, widow of the late Brvt Maj Moses J Barnard, U S army; invalid pension to John Holland, of Arkansas; invalid pension to Wm Randolph; invalid pension to Wm Howell, of Tenn; & a pension to Mary A M Jones. 4-To incorporate **Gonzaga College**, in Wash City, D C.

On Fri, at the trial of Cancemi, in N Y, for the murder of policeman Anderson, one of the counsel for the defence, & a juryman now sitting in the case, Fred'k Muller, offered an essential witness, the rag picker, Mathias South, $3,000 to leave the country & go to Calif, so as not to be able to give evidence against the prisoner. [Dec 16th newspaper: On his 4th trial he was convicted of manslaughter in the 1st degree. The lowest punishment is 10 years' in the State Prison, while the extreme is imprisonment for life.]

House of Reps: 1-Memorial of Richd Imlay, praying for an extension of his patent for an improvement in the mode of supporting the bodies of railroad cars & carriages.

A design of the monument to the gallant youth, Stewart Holland, has been hung up in the rotundo of the Capitol. It represents him as firing the cannon at the time of the ship **Arctic**'s going down into the ocean. One of the last public acts of Pres Pierce was to fix a location for it. –Balt Clipper

Obit-died: on Jun 2, in Wash City, suddenly, of apoplexy, at the residence of her brother, Dr Wm Gunton, Miss Eliz Gunton, a native of England, & a member of one of the oldest & most esteemed families of Washington. She was during the whole period of her life in Washington a constant attendant on the ordinances of religion, at the First Presbyterian Church. We buried her in the family ground in the *Congressional Cemetery*, where now she sleeps among the kindred of her love.

Mrd: on Jun 9, in Wash City, at St John's Church, by Rev Christopher Wyatt, Augustus F Rodgers, U S Coast Survey, to Serena Livingston, daughter of the late Col Geo Crogham, U S army.

Mrd: on Jun 1, in Leonardtown, Md, by Rev Mr Warner, G Fred Maddox to Susan Ruth, daughter of Benj G Harris.

Died: on Jun 13, Mrs Eliz B Reid, wife of Jas Reid, of Lochgiphead, Scotland, but for some time past a resident of Wash City. Her funeral will be this afternoon at 4:39 o'clock, from her late residence, 183 N Y ave.

Memphis, Jun 14. The steamer **Pennsylvania**, about 70 miles below this place, exploded her boiler on Sunday & burnt to the water's edge. There were 350 passengers on board, 100 of whom are supposed to be killed or missing. Among the lost are known to be, of New Orleans: Fr Delcross, Mrs Mitts & dght, Foster Hurst; N & J Bautschen, & Dennis Corcoran. Of Texas: Jos O Pilan, & H B Nichols. Of St Louis: Mrs Fulton. Of N Y: E Gleason. Of Miss: Mr Sackers. Of Louisville: Mr Lenter, John Luckhorn, Jas Bowles, Jas Burns, & Wm Woodford. Also, an English gentleman from Cuba, & Lewis J Black, E Generous, & Francis Dorris, 2nd engineer. Among the passengers who escaped were Isaac P Tice, of Balt, & H A Snead, of Va.

WED JUN 16, 1858
Mr Chas E Mix has been appointed Com'r of Indian Affairs, vice Mr Denver, resigned.

Orphans Court of Wash Co, D C. Letters testamentary on the personal estate of Jos H O'Brien, late of Wash Co, deceased. –J Jos Repetti, Peter Taltavuol, excs

Mrd: on Jun 9, at Christ Church, South Amboy, N J, by Rev Chas S Lattle, Rev Lewis S Baker to Mary Rachel, eldest daughter of Cmdor Conover, U S Navy.

Lord Lyndhurst completed, on May 21, his 86th year in excellent health. He is the oldest member of the House of Peers with the exception of Lord Sinclair, who will complete his 90th year if he lives to Jul 30th next, & the Marquis Bristol & Viscount St Vincent, who were born in 1769 & 1767, respectively.

In Chancery. Eburn Bird, Wm T Doniphan, & others, cmplnts, vs Amelia T Young, Danl Lee, Sarah Lee, Mary Baily, Oscar Baily, Victoria Terrett, Gibson Terrett, Mary E Young, Elewees Smith, Clement Young, & Julia Young, dfndnts. The object of the suit is to procure good & proper deeds for certain real estate mentioned in the bill sold the cmplnts, the deeds given at the time not being satisfactory. The bill states that the said cmplnts purchased a portion of said real estate, & refers to certain deeds executed by J C Hunter, trustee, Henry N Young, Amelia T Young, & others, in favor of said cmplnts; that the said property was originally a portion of the estate of Benj Young, deceased; that the said property was duly divided, under a commission issuing out of the Circuit Court of D C, amongst the heirs at law of said Young; that the said square was sub-divided for the purpose of partition by com'rs; that the property so purchased by cmplnts was assigned under said commission to said Henry N Young & Notley Young, heirs of said Benj Young; that cmplnts are the true & bona fide holders of said property; but that the deeds in question are not correct by reason of the omission of the word sub-division; that the omission in question was the result of mistake; that cmplnts have improved said property; that the said Henry N Young & Notley Young have departed this life, leaving said dfndnts their respective heirs; & that said dfndnts are non-residents. Absent dfndnts are to appear in person or by solicitor, on or before the first Monday of Nov next.
–Jno A Smith, clerk

The U S practice ship **Preble**, off Annapolis, Md, will probably leave about Jun 20th for the coast of France. List of her officers: Cmder, Thos T Craven; 1st Lt, Robt D Minor; 2nd Lt, Jas I Waddell; Master, Chas H Cushman; Lt, Chas W Flussar; Surgeon, Robt Carter; Boatswain, Henry P Grace; Gunner, Jos Swift; Purser, J K Harwood. The crew consists of 52 seamen, 15 marines, & 90 midshipmen.

Circuit Court of Wash Co, D C-in Chancery. Sally Scaggs & Sarah Ann Scaggs his wife, & others, against John & Francis Brady, et al. Cmplnts filed their bill in this court against Mary Brady & Nathl B Fugitt, setting forth that Nathl Brady, late of PG Co, Md, died seized of certain lots in Wash City, D C, & certain slaves in PG Co, by his will devised all his estate, save a lot given to his slaves, made free by his will, after payment of debts to the cmplnts & said Nathl B Fugitt, a minor, as tenants in common, subject to the life estate of his widow, the said Mary Brady, [who renounced the will & claimed her legal rights as such widow;] that the slaves were sold for the payment of the debts, & the cmplnts prayed a sale of all the said lots in Wash City & a division of the proceeds thereof between cmplnts & Nathl B Fugitt as beneficial to all the parties entitled, & for further relief; that said property was sold under a decree of the court, & the cause referred to the auditor to state the trustee's account & the distribution of the fund, when it was suggested that the above named defendants, heirs at law of said Nathl Brady, should have been made parties; & the object of this amended bill [amongst others] is to make all the heirs at law of said Nathl Brady parties in said cause; & it appearing to the satisfaction of the court, that said non-resident defendants are to appear in this court on or before the first day of next term, being the 3rd Mon of Oct next. –Jno A Smith, clerk

Humboldt writes to Geo Ticknor, of Boston, that his physical strength is slowly declining, but that he still works, chiefly at night, & can stand for an hour without fatigue. He is in his 89th year. The fifth volume of Cosmos is going through the press.

Application will be made to the Com'r of Pensions for renewal by duplicate of Land Warrant No 46,861, for 160 acres, war of 1812, act of Mar 3, 1855, issued Nov 3, 1856, in the name of Rebecca Hamilton, late widow of Walter R Biscoe, duly assigned to the undersigned, which was mailed at or near Wash City, or or about Apr 15, 1857, directed to Wm Williams, **Fort Dodge**, Iowa, which said land warrant never came to hand. A caveat having been filed in the Gen Land Ofc to prevent the issue of a patent, all persons are cautioned against purchasing the same. –Chas E Pleasants

THU JUN 17, 1858
Col Harrison, the American Consul at Kingston, died May 24, & his remains were interred on May 25, at the Parish Church of St Andrews.

Foreign appointments confirmed by the Senate yesterday:
Jos A Wright, of Indiana, Minister Plenipotentiary to Prussia.
John P Stockton, of N J, Minister resident at Rome, vice Cass, resigned.
Jos R Chandler, of Pa, Minister Resident at Naples, vice Owen, resigned.
E Y Fair, of Alabama, Minister Resident at Belgium.
Cotton Smith, Minister Resident at Bolivia.
Wm R Buckalew, of Pa, Minister Resident at Ecuador.
B C Yancey, of Georgia, Minister Resident at the Argentine Confederation.

Sale at auction, by decree of the Circuit Court of D C, pronounced in a cause wherein Francis Wheatley, survivor of Nathl Walker, is cmplnt, & Henry Holt & others are dfndnts, being No 1,085 in Equity, the subscriber, as trustee, will expose to sale at auction, on Jul 19, the following property in Wash Co, known as **Jackson Hill**, being part of **Pretty Prospect**, containing 13 acres of land & upwards; beginning at the end of the 20th line of the tract of land conveyed to John Q Adams, being part of the same tract; to intersect the 20th line of the conveyance from Jonathan Shoemaker to Roger Johnson; being the tract of land conveyed to Henry Holt by Ashton Alexander on Dec 21,1 844. Also, that lot or piece of ground in Wash Co, being part of a larger division of a tract of land called **Mount Pleasant**, which, in the division of the real estate of Robt Peter, deceased, fell to the share of David Peter; near part of the tract so allotted to David Peter, being also the beginning of a tract called **Plain Dealing**, which stone is marked No 30; laid out & believed to contain 13 acres & 23 perches of land, clear of the county road leading from Gtwn to Rock Creek Church, being the same piece of land as was conveyed to said Henry Holt by Robt S Wharton, in Sep, 1848, with the improvements on each of the said pieces of land. –Wm R Woodward, trustee -A Green auct

A student of the Alabama Univ, E L Nabers, from Pickens, was killed a few days ago by another student, whose name is Herring, & who hails from Mississippi. The students had been in the habit of teasing Herring, & when Nabers struck him with a stick, Nabers instantly shot him through the heart. The examing court discharged Herring.

Chancery Sale: by decrees of the Circuit Court of D C & of the Circuit Court of PG Co, Md, passed in a cause wherein Thos Sewell & others are cmplnts, & the widow, heirs at law, & administrators of John Brereton, deceased, are defendants, I will sell at auction, on Jul 14 next, on the premises, that beautiful parcel of land part of the tract called **Granby**, near Bladensburg, about 6 miles from Wash City, containing 185 acres or thereabouts, being the northern part of **Granby**, with the dwlg-house & improvements thereon. -W Redin, trustee -A Green auct

On Jun 8, at Feltville, N J, Anna H Guest & Ellen McCaffrey, employed in the factory, each about 16, went into the upper lake to bathe & both were drowned. They both were good swimmers, but were insensible to their danger.

Valuable real estate for sale: under the authority conferred on me by decree of the Circuit Court of Montg Co, Md, in equity, I will sell the real estate of Thos Hunter, late of said county, deceased, called **Windsor**, containing 400 acres of land, more or less, with a commodious dwlg; also, all the necessary out-bldgs for a farm of this size. This Farm is on the west side of the road leading from Wash to Fredericktown, 1½ miles from Rockville. Apply near Rockville, Montg Co, Md. –S S S Hunter, trustee

Rev Geo Marsden, of the Wesleyan Church, died at Manchester, Eng, on May 15, in his 80th year of his age, & the 66th year of his ministry. Twenty-five years ago, he came to the U S as the rep of the Wesleyan Church of Great Britain to the Methodist Gen Conf.

Mrd: on Jun 9, at Grace Church, Balt, by Rev Dr Cox, Lt Richmond Aulick, U S Navy, to Miss Mary Ogston, of that city.

Mrd: on May 25, at **Glen-Welby**, Fauquier Co, Va, [the residence of the bride's father,] by Rev John D Blackwell, Mr Robt Taylor Scott to Miss Fannie S, the eldest daughter of Richd H Carter.

Mrd: on Jun 2, at Cincinnati, by Rev Dr C M Butler, John A Robinson, of N Y, to Lucy, daughter of Hon Wm Key Bond, of Cincinnati.

Died: on Jun 16, after a long & painful illness, Mrs Sarah Jane Gibson, wife of Francis J Gibson, in her 25th year. Her funeral is this afternoon at 4 o'clock, from the residence of her parents on 10th st, near Md ave.

Died: on Jun 16, in Wash City, Susan Elizabeth, youngest child of Teresa A & Wm E Morcoe, aged 10 months. Her funeral is this evening at 4 o'clock.

FRI JUN 18, 1858
The U S sloop-of-war **Portsmouth**, A H Foote, cmder, arrived at Portsmouth, N H, on Jun 13 from Java, having been on voyage 79 days. She brings home Mr Geo W Reed, recently of the Legation of China. The cmder reports 14 deaths; 9 from diseases peculiar to the Eastern climates, & 5 from wounds received in the attack on the barrier forts at Canton. During her cruise she accomplished a distance of 50,000 miles.

Mr John Walter, M P for the borough of Nottingham, is principal proprietor of the London Times newspaper, holding 19 shares out of 24; Mr John Delane, the editor, has 1 share; Mrs Carden, mother of Sir Robt Carden, the present Lord Mayor of London, has 3.

Henry R Selden, the present Lt Govn'r of the State of N Y declines the use of his name as a candidate for the ofc of Govn'r, a position to which many of his Republican friends were disposed to elevate him. The small pay attached to the office is not sufficient to entice an eminent lawyer from his regular pursuits.

Appointments by the Pres, by & with the advice & consent of the Senate.
Collectors of Customs:
Wait Wadsworth, Plymouth, Mass, vice Bates, jr.
Aug Jenkins, Portsmouth, N H, vice Clement.
Augustus Schell, N Y, vice Redfield.
Elton F Strother, Chicago, vice Fry.
Surveyors of the Custons:
Thos Benneson, Quincy, Ill, reappointed.
Danl Wann, Galena, Ill, reappointed.
T J Sherlock, Cincinnati, vice McLean.
Philip H Rosson, Shreveport, La.
Registers of Land Offices:
Hugh Brawley, at Steven's Point, Wisc.
John R Bennet, at Chatfield, Minn
John J Lowry, at Boonville, Mo.
Receivers of Public Money:
J H McKenny, at Chatfield, reappointed.
E E Buckner, at Booneville, Mo, reappointed.
Postmasters:
Jas J Farran, at Cincinnati
Benj Harrison, at Cleveland, Ohio
Wm D Holt, at Covington, Ky
Geo W Porter, at Harrisburg, Penn
A Buckhart, at Sing Sing, N Y

Savannah Republican-letter from Thomasville, Ga. Fatal explosion. The bursting of a boiler at the steam mill, on Jun 8, in the outskirts of town, killed the proprietor of the mill, Mr John Stephens, a highly esteemed citizen.

Mrd: on Jun 7, in St Paul's Church, Edenton, N C, by Rev Saml I Johnston, Jas C Johnston, jr, to Kate H, daughter of Dr Wm C Warren.

Died: on Sunday last, at the residence of her son-in-law, Mr Smets, near the Episcopal Seminary, Mrs Ann Douglas Macrae, relict of Capt Allan Macrae, deceased, & daughter of the late Capt Wm H Terrett, of Fairfax Co, Va, in about her 60th year.

Orphans Court of Wash Co, D C. In the case of Mary A Arnold, admx of Saml Arnold, deceased, the Court & administratrix have appointed Jul 10 next, for the final settlement of the personal estate of the deceased, with the assets in hand. -Ed N Roach, Reg/o wills

Died: on Jun 9, in Brooklyn, Mrs Mary W Thompson, relict of the late Lt Col Alex R Thompson, in her 68th year. Her husband, Lt Col Alex R Thompson, of the 6th regt U S Infty, fell at the head of his troops in the battle of Okeechobee, Florida, being then 2nd in command to Col Taylor, afterwards Pres Taylor. His remains were deposited at West Point, N Y, where hers now rest beside him. She died shortly after a paralytic attack, surrounded by her friends, in full possession of her reason, & an unwavering faith in the Redeemer, whom she had long believed in & honored.

SAT JUN 19, 1858
The removal of Pres Monroe's remains from N Y C to Va will be in the steamer which will leave that port on Jul 3 next. The Scott Life Guard & a detachment of the 8th regt, Col Lyons, have offered their services as a military escort, but it is determined, we believe, to accept the services of the 7th regt, Nat'l Guard, Col Duryee.

Household & kitchen furniture at auction on Jun 22, at the residence of Capt R B Cunningham, U S N, 457 13th st, between E & F sts. –C W Boteler, auct

The recent death Col Robt Monroe Harrison, Consul of the U S at Kingston, Jamaica, was announced. He was a cousin of the late Pres of that name, & was born in Va in 1768. He was appointed to the navy by Washington, & the date of commission was the same as that of Cmdor Rodgers. He was the associate of Truxton, & resigned his commission during Pres Jefferson's administration. He then went to Russia & participated in the battle of Borodino. In Sweden he married a ward of Count Fersien, Swedish Minister of State, afterward stoned to death by the populace of Stockholm. When the war of 1812 broke out he immediately offered his services to his government, & on his way home was carried a prisoner to Cowe, England. He then went to St Thomas, & there found a commission as Consul for that place waiting for him. He has been U S Consul for the Island of Jamaica for the last 27 years. His son, Richd Adams Harrison, has acted for several years for his father, & is talented, speaks several languages, & is highly esteemed.

In the U S Circuit Court at Portland, on Sat, Judge Clifford sentenced Geo W Young, of Augusta, the mail robber, to 15 years in the State prison.

Obit-died: the Maysville [Ky] Eagle announces the death of Judge Adam Beatty, who died at his residence in that city on Jun 9, in his 82nd year. He was a native of Md, born in 1777, in the midst of the Revolution, of a family distinguished for zeal in the cause of the country, an older brother, a captain in the service, falling gloriously at the head of his company in the terribly disastrous battle of Camden. Judge Beatty studied law with Mr Clay, at Lexington, who, although but a month or two older, was already eminent in his profession. On completion of his legal studies he established himself at Washington, then the seat of Mason Co, & at once entered upon a long, distinguished, & useful career.

Mrd: on Jun 16, at Newcastle, Delaware, by Rev Dr Spotswood, Wm C Spruance to Maria Louisa, daughter of the officiating Clergyman.

The Grand Gold Medal of the U S Agricultural Society was yesterday presented to C H McCormick, of Chicago, for the best Reaping Machine exhibited at the nat'l field trial of harvest implements at Syracuse last summer. The design was drawn by Hammat Billings, of Boston, the die was engraved by Francis Mitchel, of Boston, & the medal was struck at the U S Mint in Phil. On the face is Ceres, [Goddess of the Earth, Patroness of Agriculture,] seated upon a throne.

MON JUN 21, 1858
The Dowager Countess of Effingham, at the age of 80, has recently married a Scripture reader at Brighton, aged 30. The Countess possesses a very large yearly income, & her son is one of the peers of England.

Appointments by the Pres. by & with the advice & consent of the Senate.
Fred'k Dodge, of Nebraska, Indian Agent in Utah.
Chas H Mix, of Minn, agent for the Winebago agency, vice Fletcher.
John C Hays, Surveyor Genr'l for Utah.
Jas Tilton, of Wash Territory, re-appointed Surveyor Genr'l.
Ira Munson, register of the land ofc at San Francisco, vice W W Gift.

Sidney Webster has been appointed to be a Com'r of the U S for Massachusetts in place of Judge Loring, recently selected to fill the vacancy in the Court of Claims occasioned by the death of Judge Gilchrist.

The St Helena Herald of Mar 4 contains an ordinance of the Govn'r granting to the Emperor of the French & his heirs in perpetuity the lands forming the sites of *Longwood* & the tomb of Napoleon I. The lands in *Napoleon's Vale*, where the tomb is situated, comprise about 23 acres, while those of *Longwood* comprise about 3. They recently belonged to private owners, & have been purchased by the Crown for the purpose of the present transfer at a cost of L1,600 for the tomb & L3,500 for the house.

Platte [Missouri] Argus of Jun 10. On Sat a man by the name of Branham, & his young wife, Mary Branham, were in much distress when Hugh Wilson broke into their locked back door, jerked Branham out of bed & dragged him to the garden. The wife flew to her husband's assistance with a club, &, by a dint of well-directed blows, made of Wilson the most horrible corpse one could well look on. The Justices agree that the homicide committed by Mary Branham on High Wilson was justifiable, & she is discharged from custody.

Mrd: on Jun 15, in Wash City, by Rev G W Samson, Mr Jacob Currier to Isabella Damron, both of Nelson Co, Va.

Meeting of the Old Survivors of the War of 1812 was held on Fri last at the City Hall. The following re-elections were made: Col W W Seaton, Pres; Col Jno S Williams, 1st V Pres; Gen J St John Skinner, 2nd V Pres; Capt Jas A Kennedy, Treasurer; Jas Lawrenson, Sec; Col Wm P Young, Marshal; Dr Wm Jones, Surgeon. Executive Cmte: Maj Edw Semmes & Peter Bergman.

On Thu night last, or early on Fri morning, a poor old soldier named Thos Lyons committed suicide by hanging himself on a tree in front of the Military Asylum. He had belonged to the Asylum, but becoming addicted to intemperance was dismissed. At the time of his suicide his restoration to the Asylum was under consideration.

St Andrew's Free Church, [Protestant Episcopal,] propose to give a festive entertainment on Jun 24 at **Meridian Hill**, a beautiful spot on Boundary st, west of 14th. An Address will be delivered by Rev Chas H Hall, of the Church of the Epiphany, on the life of St John the Baptist. Prof F Nicholls Crouch, assisted by his class of vocalists, will execute a rich & tasteful programme of musicial exercises. Mon Pillar's brass band will enliven the entertainment. A police force wil attend to preserve order. –T S Donoho, R B Ironsides, A W Huges, S L Gouverneur, jr, Cmte of Arrangements.

Orphans Court of Wash Co, D C. In the case of Augusta Rosenthal, excx of Chas G E Rosenthal, deceased, the executrix & Court have appointed Jul 20th next for the distribution of the personal estate of said deceased, of the assets in hand. -Ed N Roach, Reg/o wills

U S Patent Ofc, Wash, Jun 18, 1858. Ptn of Francis P Hurd, adm of Jos Hurd, deceased, of South Reading, Mass, praying for the extension of a patent granted to said Jos Hurd for an improvement in cleansing sugar, for 7 years from the expiration of said patent, which takes place on Oct 3, 1858. –Jos Holt, Com'r of Patents

TUE JUN 22, 1858
Real estate sales-Wash: lot 1 in square 257, on Ohio ave & 13½ st, was sold at 26 cents per square foot. Lot 14 in square 290, 28 feet on F st, between 12th & 13th sts, was purchased by A B Stroughton, at $1 per square foot. A lot 50 feet front, adjoining the north side of Secretary's Cass's residence, on Vt ave, has been bought for $1 a square foot by Hon Reverdy Johnson, who is erecting thereon a large & handsome dwlg-house.

The St Joseph [Mo] Journal of Jun 14 gives an account of an extraordinary trip across the Western Plains by Mr Jas E Bromley, the conductor of the mail line. He made the trip from **Fort Bridger** to St Joseph in 16 days, traveling some days as much as 85 hours, & averaging 65 miles per day over the entire route.

Miss Sarah Paul, an interesting young lady, a teacher, was burnt to death in Oglethorpe, Ga, by the explosion of a fluid lamp.

The wholesale grocery store of Messrs Coldes, Ewe, & Co, at Milwauke, Wisc, fell down on Wed last & Mr C W Ewe was killed; Louis Ewe considerably hurt; Emil Weiskirch, another partner, considerably hurt, & Henry Theine was so bady hurt that he is not expected to live. The accident is attributed to the bad manner in which the bldg was constructed.

Died: on Jun 21, after a lingering & painful illness, Nicholas A Randall, aged 56 years. His funeral will be from his late residence on I st, near 10th, today at 10 o'clock A M.

Died: on Jun 19, near Wash, after a brief illness, Margaret Frances, youngest child of Jas & Margaret Selden.

Portsmouth [Ohio] Journal of Jun 4. Robt McAuley went from Lucasville, Scioto Co, Ohio, about 6 years ago to Calif, leaving a family behind. During his absence they have been receiving letters from him, & only a short time ago they received a letter from him in which he stated that he was sick & it was his intention to return home. During last week a gentleman presented himself at Piketown, Ohio, representing himself as Mr Robt McAuley, & said he was out of money & was not able to walk home. A citizen took the sick man to his supposed family. His wife utterly refused to recognize him. He related circumstances to convince his wife & friends that he was no imposter. The family & brothers still refuse to acknowledge him. He knows all his old neighbors & every thing about their history. Some of the neighbors say it is he, but others deny it. [Jun 26th newspaper: the man McAuley, who claimed to be Robt H McAuley, of Portsmouth, Ohio, has at last been proven to be a Wm McAuley, & a horse thief of Cincinnati.]

Criminal Court-Wash-Mon: Grand Jury:

W W Seaton-Foreman	John Pettibone	Jos C G Kennedy
Michl Shanks	Wm R Riley	Bushrod W Reed
Wm A Bradley	Hamilton Loughborough	Pierce Shoemaker
C L Coltman	Ed M Linthicum	Geo Parker
Wm F Bayly	Philip T Berry	Robt Beall
Edw Simms	Jos N Fearson	Eleazer Lindsley
Peter F Bacon	Robt S Patterson	
Benj B French	Aaron W Miller	
Jonathan Prout	Henry Haw	

Petit Jury:

Jas Y Davis	Saml Lewis	Jas Crutchett
Francis Mohun	Jas H Sheckell	Alex M Smith
Christopher Cammack	Danl G Ridgeley	Zadock Williams
Jas F Scott	Adam Geddes	Richd Darnes
Edwin Green	Columbus Alexander	Jas A Bruns
Terence Drury	John T Bradley	Thos Orme
Zadock D Gilman	John W Martin	A F Offutt
A F Kimmell	Henry C Purdy	John H Smoot
Jos W Nairn	John Shaw	John E Neale
Z M P King	John W Ott	Thos H Miles

Stribling Springs, the mountain retreat, in Augusta Co, Va, will be under the management of Mr Peter H Woodward, formerly at Jackson's river & Healing Springs. -Chesley Kinney, proprietor

N Y Commercial Advertiser. Patrick Lally & Geo Megahey, indicted for the murder of Geo Simonson in N Y, were found guilty of manslaughter. Lally received 5 years in the State prison. He, however, threatened to take the life of the officer who testified against him when he came out. Megahey was sent to prison for 2 years.

Desirable residence & land for sale: in accordance with the will of the late Geo Hamilton, deceased, I offer the Farm on which he resided, called **Forest Hill**, in Spotsylvania, Va. The farm consists of 2 tracts-**Forrest Hill**, which has all the improvements, containing about 743 acres; the other, a short distance from the first, containing 200 acres. Mr Stevens, the overseer, will show the premises. –Geo Hamilton, jr, exc of Geo Hamilton, deceased. Brandy Station P O, Culpeper Co, Va.

Trustee's sale, by decree of the Circuit Court for Howard Co, Md: public sale at Clarkesville, in said county, on Jul 16, the Hotel at Clarkesville, with the dwlg hosue, store house, farm & outbldgs belonging to the estate of the late Jas Clarke, thereto attached. The farm contains about 80 acres. Also, the farm on which Jas Clarke resided at the time of his death, containing about 170 acres of land; with a comfortable dwlg & outbldgs; adjoins the land of John O'Donnell & Wm Clarke. Also, the farm belonging to said Jas Clarke's estate adjoining the lands of Basil Johnson & others.
–Wm H G Dorsey, trustee

Circuit Court of Wash Co, D C: Jos Libbey vs Jas B Phillips et al. The trustee reported that he has sold lot S, in subdivision of lots 1 thru 4, 10 & 11, in square 452, to Edw F Queen, for $664.75; lot T in same subdivision & square, to Jas H Smith, for $588.60; & Lots U & V, in the same subdivision & square, with improvements, to Edw Owen, for $2,130; & part of lot 1 in square 453, being 16 feet front on H st north by 85 feet deep, west of & adjoining the east 16 feet of said lot, to Jos Hodgson, [who has assigned his purchase to Douglase Moore,] for $584.80; & that the purchasers have complied with the terms of the sale. –Jno A Smith, clerk

Two weeks ago Mr Thos Marron, son of Mr Marron, Third Assist Postmaster Genr'l, had his leg crushed in the machinery on the ocean steamer **North Star**, of which vessel he was an engineer. On his arrival at N Y amputation became necessary. His father went to N Y, but writes now that his son is recovering slowly, & he himself will return Jun 21.

Blakistone's Pavilion in St Mary's Co, Md, the "Pilgrim County of the State," on the Potomac river, near Blakistone's Island, will be open on Jul 1. –R J Marshall, proprietor

In the First District Court of New Orleans, the other day, Chas Tighe was put on trial on a charge of killing John Sullivan. The Atty Genr'l found the testimony to be inconclusive & quashed the indictment. One of the jurors clapped, for which indecorum Judge Hunt committed him to prison for 3 hours for contempt of court.

WED JUN 23, 1858
On Jun 8, Mr Louis Baehr, while on his way to the Scott House, Pittsburg, was knocked down by Jas McKee, an individual not unknown to the police. Mr Baehr died on Fri. He was an employ of Wm Gaeble & Co, piano manufacturers, of Balt, & was engaged as a traveling agent to dispose of the pianos.

Trustee's sale of the furniture & effects of the <u>Maryland Hotel</u>, near the north gate of the Capitol gate, on Jun 29. –Jas C McGuire, auct

A few days ago the schnr **Keziah**, Capt Wm B Baylis, of Brandywine, Del, was overhauled by a steamer & taken into Norfolk on suspicion of having fugitive slaves secreted on board, & 5 negroes were discovered among the cargo. The case was submitted to trial. Bayliss was convicted. By the law of Va the vessel is confiscated, & the captain & mate compelled to pay a fine of $500, & be sent to the penitentiary, on each indictment, for a term of not less than 3 nor more than 10 years.

On Monday, the vicinity of N Y C was visited by a tornado, accompanied with heavy rain, thunder, lightning & hail. During the gale the American Flint Glass Companys' works, at Hunter's Point, were blown down, burying 25 operatives in the ruins. All were recused alive, except Bernard Slane & Thos Gill, who were killed. The Church of the Good Shepherd of N Y C, [Rev Ralph Hoyt's,] which was nearly completed, was razed to its foundation. –Times

N Y C. 1-Rev Dr Jesse T Peck, formerly Pres of Carlisle College, & an eloquent Methodist preacher, whose services at the Foundry Chapel, Wash, will be long remembered, sailed today for Calif. He intends to make that region his future field of ministerial labor. 2-Two imposing ceremonials have just taken place: the solemn coronation of a magnificent & brilliant painting of the <u>Madonna</u>, at the Roman Catholic Church of St Mary's, Hoboken; & the consecration of a Jewish Synagogue at the bldg No 78 Allen st, named Beth Hamedresch, or House of Learning, & was formerly a Methodist place of worhisp. 3-Among the 500 passengers for Calif in the mail steamer **Star of the West**, which sailed today for Aspinwall, were Hon John C McKibbin, Capt Cunningham, ordered to the command of the Navy Yard at Mare Island, Lt Nicholson, ordered to the command of the frig **Saranac**, Lts Thorburn & Brooks, & their assistants, ordered to the U S Coast Survey service in Calif, Rev Dr Scott & Rev Dr Peck.

The Newburyport Herald says that the old residents of Ward One were not a little surpised on Thus last by the advent in their midst of Mr Peter Fudge, after an absence of 46 years. It was supposed that he had long been an inhabitant of the spiritual spheres. In 1812 he sailed from there in a ship belonging to the late Moses Brown, since which time no tidings were had of him until his return. His wife was married twice after his departure, & some years since she died. –Boston Journal

The <u>Herndon House</u>, on the s w corner of F & 9th st, recently fitted up in the best style, is prepared to receive both permanent & transient guests. –P G Murray, proprietor

The brig **Leontine**, of Salem, Capt S Greenlaw, from Phil, with a cargo of coal, was run into & sunk on Fri night, when 10 miles from Highland Light, Capt Cod, by the U S store-ship **Release**, from Boston to Madeira. The captain & crew only had time to jump on board the **Release** before the brig went down, & they lost everything. She landed the crew of the brig at **Nauset Light**.

Died: on Jun 22, Frederick Livingston, aged 1 year & 22 days, only child of Wm T & Kate L Hines. His funeral will take place this evening at 6 o'clock, from the residence of his parents on 12th st, between Pa ave & H st.

Died: yesterday, Minnie, only daughter of Jas A & Mary A Magruder, of Gtwn, D C, in her 16th year. Her funeral will be from her parents' residence, 100 West st, today at 6 o'clock.

Died: on Jun 19, in Wash City, Robt J Roche, in his 40th year. He had been a patient sufferer for 2 years previous to his death from a pulmonary complaint. He was a good citizen, & twice elected to the ofc of City collector. We sympathize with his family in their deep affliction.

For sale: the beautiful homestead, the residence of the late Maj Howle, embracing the entire square bounded by C & D sts south, & by 14th & 15th sts, containing about 114,000 square feet of ground, improved by a large brick mansion, brick stable, carriage & smoke houses. This property is on the banks of the Potomac, & within 10 minutes' walk of Pa ave. Apply to H C Spalding, 338 north D st, Wash.

THU JUN 24, 1858
Two bldg lots on E st north, between 9th & 10th sts west, at public sale, on Jul 1, parts of lots 3 & 4 in square 377, fronting 24 feet each on north E st, between 9th & 10th sts, between the residences of Mrs Sargant & Mr Berry. Part of lot 4 is under a perpetual lease or ground rent, removable at the pleasure of the owner by paying about $450.
-Jas C McGuire, auct

Household & kitchen furniture at auction on Jun 28, at the residence of Dr Benj Rhett, on 11th st west, between E & F sts north. -Jas C McGuire, auct

Trustee's sale of improved property on the Island, on Jul 28, by deed of trust from D B Johnson, dated Oct 6, 1857, recorded in Liber J A S No 146, folios 283, of the land records for Wash Co, I shall sell lot 21 in square 267, with the improvements, consisting of a two story brick dwlg house. –F S Myers, trustee -Jas C McGuire, auct

Trustee's sale of all of lot 35 in square 100, with frame dwlg & steam mill, on 20th st, between L & M sts, by deed of trust from Nicholas Kuhland & wife, dated Apr 19, 1856, recorded in Liber J A S No 116, folio 17. Sale on Jul 27. –A Hyde, trustee
-A Green auct

N Y C, Jun 22, 1858. Violent storm in this city & Brooklyn. Mrs Duhaine, residing at Greenpoint, died this morning from fright. Mrs Bridget Farrell, residing on 5th ave, between Bergen & Wyckoff sts, was outside her door with an infant in her arms, when she was struck by lightning & killed. The infant was unhurt. Bernard Slane & Thos Gill were killed when the American Flint Glass Company was struck prostrating the bldg.

On Wed Wm H Spinney, of Eliot, N H, was accidentally shot by a young man, John R Hill. They were walking together, when Hill took out a pistol, intending to fire at some object. Just then Spinney passed in front of him & the ball struck him in the back of the head. He fell & never spoke or moved. The boys were each about 17 years of age.

On Friday John Lyons, residing in 494 Greenwich st, N Y, came home intoxicated & beat his wife. She lingered in great pain until Sat morning, when she died.

Mr J H Headley, a hitherto respectable citizen of Buffalo, has been convicted of passing counterfeit money. He once was a director of a bank.

Public sale of trust property. At the request of J H McCue, I, as his trustee, [for the benefit of John McCue,] will offer, on Aug 16, at public auction, on the premises, his residence near Staunton, considered to be one of the most desirable establishments in the Valley of Va: with 12 acres of land. –J D Imboden, trustee

Bricks. We are now manufacturing & have on hand a quantity of the best hand-made brick, which we offer at the lowest price. Our yard is near the Aqueduct, Va side. Apply to J Runey & Co or E Pickrell & Co, Gtwn.

The subscriber will sell at private sale that valuable property at Mass ave & 2nd st, being part of lot 30 in square 64, with a good 2 story frame house & back bldgs, school, carriage-houses & stable. –Wm Bayley

Orphans Court of Wash Co, D C. Letters testamentary on the personal estate of Philip Craver, late of Wash Co, deceased. –Fred'k Luff, exc

Valuable mineral & timber lands in Va for sale: the tract of land in Preston Co, Va, known as **Westphalia Tract**, comprising upwards of 5,000 acres of land, about 6 miles west of Oakland. This is the same property which, by decree of the Superior Court of Chancery, held at Clarksburg, Va, passed on Oct 21, 1824, was allotted to Chas F Mayer in partition of the lands mentioned in said decree, & was by the said Mayer assigned to Fred'k W Brune, jr, & others, trustees, by deed dated Jul 18, 1842, recorded among the land records of Preston Co, in book No 6, page 321. Apply to Geo Wm Brown, F W Brune, jr, 40 St Paul st. –Gibson & Co, aucts

Mrd: on Jun 22, at St Patrick's Church, by Rev Fr O'Toole, Dr H W Brent, of Md, to Miss Lavina, 2nd daughter of Jas Caden, of Wash City.

Mrd: on Jun 23, in Wash City, by Rev Mason Noble, at the 6th st Presbyterian Church, Mr J F McKim to Miss F M Ferree, all of Wash.

FRI JUN 25, 1858
Excellent household & kitchen furniture at auction on Jul 12, by deed of trust from Robt Cochran, jr, recorded in Liber J A S No 78, folios 347, dated Mar 15, 1854. Public auction at the residence of said Cochran, on B st south, between 13th & 13½ sts. –Andrew Wylie, trustee -A Green auct

News by the steamer **Persia** announces the death of Sir Philip Crampton, at his residence in Dublin, at the age of 86 years. He is succeeded in the Baronetcy by his eldest son, Sir John F Crampton, formerly British Minister at Wash, now stationed at St Petersburgh.

Died, on Jun 21, at the residence of his daughter, Mrs Benj F Thompson, in Hempstead, L I, Rev Zachriah Green, in his 99th year. First a soldier of his country in the hour of her peril, then, for more than 60 years a soldier of Christ. Honorably dismissed from the army because of wounds received at the battle of White Marsh, he entered Dartmough College, &, after finishing his studies, & was ordained a minister of the Presbyterian Church. He cherished the memory of his 2 great commanders, Washington & Greene.

Yesterday, about 11 o'clock A M, Mr Reeve Lewis, who, in company with Mr Entwisle, was shot by 2 ruffians on the Capitol Hill on Mar 27, died. Two persons, Barrett & Williams, are in jail for trial for the offence. Mr Lewis leaves a family of 7 children, most of whom are unable to support themselves. Their mother died about 6 months ago.
+
Died: yesterday, from the effects of a wound inflicted by the hand of a ruffian on the night of Mar 27, Reeve Lewis, aged 46 years. His funeral will be today at 4 o'clock, from his late residence, south B st, between N J ave & 1st st.

Sale of real estate. Wall & Barnard, aucts, sold yesterday, corner of 14th & G sts, in square 224, lot 1, to R Cruit, for $1.07 per foot; lot 2, to same for 98 cents; lot 3, to same, for 84 cents.

Died: yesterday, in Wash City, in the fullness of years, Mrs Eliz Lee, relict of Richd Bland Lee, one of the first Reps in Congress from the State of Va, & for many years an eminent politician of the Washington school. Mrs Lee was a native of Pa, where she was born on Feb 8, 1768, making her age at the time of her death nearly 91 years. Her funeral will take place today at 5 o'clock P M, from her late residence 468 6th st. [Aug 6th newspaper: Mrs Eliz Lee was the daughter of the late Stephen Collins, ont of the principal citizens & merchants of Phil during the Revolution. While at school an intimacy commenced between herself & Miss Dolly Payne, who afterwards became Mrs Todd; &, by a second marriage, the consort of the illustrious Jas Madison. This intimacy continued till the death of Mrs Madison. In Jun, 1794, Miss Collins was married by Bishop White to Richd Blanc Lee, a Rep from Va in the 1st Congress of the U S, Phil being then the seat of the Genr'l Gov't. Mrs Lee was also a friend of Mrs Hamilton, the relict of Alex'r Hamilton, whom she knew & loved. She enjoyed the friendship & society of Wm H Crawford, Chancellor DeSausseur, of S C; Senators Clay, Berrien, Webster, & other eminent men. Mrs Lee after her marriage removed with her husband to *Sully*, his estate in Va, & afterwards to Wash, D C, where Mr Lee died in 1827, & where his widow continued to reside during the residue of her life. In Nov, 1856, a severe fall disabled one of her limbs & ever after confined her to her chamber. She was a devoted Christian. She died on Jun 24, 1858, in her 91st year. Her faculties remained unclouded & active to the last. She lived, happy in her children & her friends. Her son, Judge Lee, was constantly with her. Mrs Lee left surviving her 2 sons & 2 daughters, viz: Maj Richd Bland Lee, U S Army; Judge Z Collins Lee, Md Judiciary; Mrs Ann Matilda Washington, relict of the late Dr Bailey Washington, surgeon in the U S Navy; & Mrs Cornelia McRae, wife of Dr McRae, of Va.]

Died: on Jun 24, of consumption, of a lingering illness, Thos W Osgodby, in his 34th year. His funeral is today at 8 o'clock, from his late residence, 441 K st, between 6th & 7th sts.

Died: yesterday, Robert Corrie, infant son of Wm C & Mary Lipscomb, of Wash City, aged 7 months. His funeral is this morning, at 9 o'clock from Mass ave, between 4th & 5th sts.

Died: on Jun 23, Louis Pinkney, only child of Sylvanus C & Eliza N Boynton, aged 15 months.

Died: on Jun 24, Caroline Haynes Grouard, youngest daughter of Ellen B & the late Geo M Grouard, in her 9th year. Her funeral will take place today at 4 o'clock, from her mother's residence on 6th st.

SAT JUN 26, 1858
Sale at auction, by decree of the Circuit Court of Wash Co, D C, made in the cause of John Hazle against Horatio R Maryman & others, [No 1,023, in equity,] public auction on Jul 24, of the following lots in Wash City: east half of lot 3 in square 728, fronting on East Capitol st, near 2nd st east. Lot 3 in square 730, fronting on Pa ave, south A st, & the public space. Lot 8 in square 758, on 2nd st east, midway between Md ave & north A st. Lots 1 thru 9 in square 867, fronting on north B & 6th sts east.
–Wm R Woodward, trustee -A Green auct

The trial of Gen Jas H Lane for the murder of Col Gaius Jenkins commenced in Lawrence, Kansas, on Jun 14, before the preliminary court of investigation, Mr Ladd, J P, presiding. Five lawyers are engaged on each side: Col Young, of Independence, Mo, Jas Christian, of Lawrence, Hugh & Thos Ewing, jr, of Leavenworth, & John Hutchinson, of Lawrence, for the defence; & for the prosecution, Messrs Coe, Collamer, Stafford, [prosecuting atty,] S N Wood, & ex-Sec Stanton. The medical testimony showed that Col Jenkins had died from wounds inflicted by the defendant, & that there were 98 shot wounds in the body, most of which were in the right side, the breast, & the abdomen. The trial was expected to last about a week.

Letter from a young lady residing in Lake City, on Lake Pepin, Minn, dated Jun 15. On Jun 5, two cousins, Rebecca & Julia, 2 Misses Stowell, from Mazeppa, cousin John, a young man named Crowin, & myself, took a sail over to Maidens' Rock. Soon after we left for home the wind began to blow & the boat capsized. Rebecca & Julia & the two Misses Stowell's were drowned. Mr Corwin did all he could to save them, but in vain.

On Sat last, Chas Ela, of Fryebrug, Me, age about 18 years, was killed when his pistol exploded. He walked or ran some 60 feet, when he fell dead.

Jacob G Ford, of Glenville, Schenectady Co, N Y, is the oldest lawyer living in the State of N Y, being now in his 98th year.

Baron de Watterstedt, the newly appointed Minister resident from Sweden & Norway, arrived at N Y in the steamer **Persia** on his way to Washington.

Died: on Jun 23, in Norfolk, John Jas Scipio Hassler, aged 59 years. Born in Switzerland, an assist in the U S Coast Survey, & son of the late F R Hassler, First Superintendent of the U S Coast Survey & Standarding of Weights & Measures.

N Y, Jun 24, 1858. Upon a suggestion that it would be well to invite the pall-bearers at Ex-Pres Monroe's funeral in 1831 to be present at the ceremonial on Jul 3, it is stated by the Commercial that not one of them is known to be alive. They were S L Southard, Col Richd Varick, John Watts, John Ferguson, David Brooks, John Trumbull, A Ogden, & Thos Morris. They are all though to be dead. [Jul 3rd newspaper: N Y, Jul 2. The remains of the late Pres Monroe were exhumed this morning, in the presence of the Va cmte, Mr Monroe, a nephew of the deceased, & others. The coffin was in an excellent state of preservation, & was then taken to the Church of the Ascension. The procession later passed down Broadway, to the City Hall, the 8th Regt of Nat'l Greys & a company of the 71st acting as an escort. The procession was a quarter of a mile long, & the sidewalks were densely crowded. Tomorrow the remains will be put on board for Richmond.]
[Jul 5th newspaper: The key to the vault has: James Monroe & Robert Tillotson, vault No 147, *N Y C Marble Cemetery*. A silver plate on the top of the coffin: James Monroe, of Virginia, died Jul 4th, 1831, aged 74. This plate was removed to the new one.]

Murder in Wash, D C, on Friday, near the Wash aqueduct at Powder-mill Branch. Mary Sheahy was murdered whilst she was sleeping, & the manner was cutting her throat with a knife. Wm Nugent, a large & very powerful man, has been arrested. He was jealous because she would not marry him. [Jun 28th newspaper: It seems that the murder was not committed in D C, but in Md. After careful survey, it came out that the District line passes directly through the house in which Mary Sheahy was butchered, & that the bed in which she & her little sister were lying at the time was by about 10 inches on the Md side of the line, & therefore in Montg Co. A Md coroner or magistrate is to be sent for to hold an inquest. The poor girl's remains were taken through the city on Sat afternoon on the way to burial.]

Montreal, Jun 25. Jean Baptiste Despriges & Ann Belisle were executed here today for the murder of Catherine Provost last winter. [Jun 30th newspaper: the execution took place on Jun 25, before a crowd of about 15,000, even though the thermomenter indicated 90 degrees in the shade. A Roman Catholic Bishop remained all night with Jean Bte Desforges & two Sisters of Charity with Widow Belisle. Rev Mr Villeneuve, spiritual adviser, asked Widow Belisle if she desired to see her children. She replied that she did not; adding that it would be very painful to her & to them. Mr Desforges & Widow Belise both admitted on the scaffold that they were guilty. Both prisoners kissed the crucifix. Desforges died instantly, but Widow Belisle, by some means the noose did not work correctly, & upwards of 7 minutes elapsed before she was pronounced dead. After the bodies had hung an hour they were cut down.]

Boston, Jun 25. Jas McGee was executed at the jail this morning for the murder of Deputy Warden Walker in the State prison some 18 months since.

Mrs P Hough, 452 Pa ave, between 3rd & $4\frac{1}{2}$ sts, has now vacant front & other rooms, with or without board.

The heirs of Chas McMicken, of Louisiana, have entered a suit in the U S Circuit Court for Ohio, to contest so much of the will of said McMicken as bequeathes $80,000 to the city of Cincinnati for the establishment of 2 colleges, on the ground that by the laws of Ohio the city has no power to accept such a devise, & that the terms of the bequest were otherwise repugnant to the laws of that State.

MON JUN 28, 1858
Letter addressed to Govn'r Wise by Mr Saml L Gouverneur, son-in-law of Mr Monroe: Petersville, Fred'k Co, Md, Jun 18, 1858. Reg: the removal of the remains of Jas Monroe, ex-Pres of the U S, from the public burying ground in N Y C to the cemetery at the city of Richmond. On Mar 4, 1825, he completed his 2nd Presidential term. As a private citizen he emerged from all his successive public trusts with poverty as the emblem of his purity & the badge of all his public honors. A loan from a near relative, reluctantly accepted, realized after his death, discharged the immediate demands in Washington, & bore him & his family to that residence in which he had fondly hoped to end his days. He struggled manfully with adversity for about 5 years. In the unexpected death of his devoted wife, in Sep, 1830, he realized the fact that his cup of earthly sorrows was full to the brim. His removal to N Y was the result of stern necessity, not of choice. At the solicitation of his family, in the residence of his youngest daughter, & in the society of his wife's relatives, herself a native of that city, he found all the beautiful sympathies which earth affords. On Jul 4, 1831, he ceased to live on earth. He was buried in a vault, originally purchased by his daughters, in a beautiful private cemetery surrounded by two sisters of his wife, one my own dear mother, with others, relatives of her family, that have slept around him. [James Monroe, of Va, Jul 4, 1831, aged 72 years.] Of the personal family associates of Mr Monroe, Mr Augustin Monroe, & Mr Jas Monroe, his nephews, & myself, his son-in-law, only survive. He left 4 grandchildren, of whom 3, the children of his younger daughter, are living. The youngest, Mr S L Gouverneur, jr, has, I learn from him, spoken for himself, & approves the removal; his eldest grandson, who bears his name, deeply afflicted by Providence, speaks through me. His only grand daughter will abide my action. Representing these interests, the memory of my late wife, sole executor of Mr Monroe, & possessed of his wishes in regard to the final disposition of his body, I trust I do not exceed the bounds of delicacy in addressing myself to you. We approve the removal. I will invite my son to accompany me at an early day to N Y. He will personally superintend the disinterment of the remains in the presence of all the members of the family who may be pleased to attend.
–Saml L Gouverneur.

Hon Wm R Harris, who was scalded by the explosion of the steamer Pennsylvania, died at Memphis on Sat. He was a judge of the Supreme Court of Tenn, & a brother of Gov Harris, of that State.

Boarding in the country: 8 miles from Wash & Alexandria, on the Leesburg turnpike. For further particulars address John Bartlett, Falls Church, Fairfax Co, Va.

The Cumberland [Md] Civilian says: Mr Geo Hinkle shot on Sat last, a few miles east of this city, a full grown porcupine. These animals are rarely to be met with in this region, & this fellow might indeed be termed a stranger.

Fatal affray at Centreville, King & Queen Co, Va, on Jun 17, between Mr Gogerty, a school teacher, & two Messrs Bristow, father & son. One of the elder Bristow's sons was a pupil of Gogerty, & being guilty of some misconduct, Gogerty flogged him. While the father held Gogerty in a clinched position, the young Bristow plunged a knife into the body of Mr Gogerty, killing him. The young assassin escaped.

The trial of Joshua H Arnold for the murder of his wife was held Jun 1, at the Jessamine circuit Court, at Nicholasville. A verdict of guilty was rendered, & the sentence of death pronounced against the prisoner that day. He is to be executed on Jun 24 of next month.
-Lexington [Ky] Observer

At a recent term of the Federal Court of the U S, Pontotoc, Miss, the father of Nancy Wilson, of Va, age about 16 years, obtained a judgment of $40,000 damages against Robt Wilson, of Miss, who was & is a married man, for decoying his daughter away from home. It is said that the dfndnt has transferred his property, so that nothing can be made out of him, although at the time he committed the deed he was a wealthy man.
-Memphis Bulletin

The trial of Geo W Harby for murder, in killing Chas H C Stone in Mar last, for the betrayal of his daughter, ended on Friday week in New Orleans, where the killing occurred. The result was a verdict of not guilty.

The death of Edw Moxon, the poets' publisher, is announced in the London papers. He was the friend of Chas Lamb, the elder d'Israeli, Saml Rogers, Barry Cornwall, Sheridan Knowles, Fanny Burney, Monchton Milnes, John Forster, & Tennyson. He was universally respected.

A <u>Fast Man</u>. Wm Simcock, of Wash Co, Pa, recently lost his wife in the morning, married his second wife before night, & followed the remains of his first wife, in company with the second, to the grave the day after.

Laws of the U S: 1-For erecting 30 additional <u>lamp posts</u> in Bridge & High sts, Gtwn: $810. 2-To John B Mutty, for compensation as acting secretary of the Territory of Nebraska during the vacancy created by the death of T B Cummings: $316.35.

Coroner's inquest was held yesterday on an elderly man, Thos Whelan, who, on Sat was arrested & committed to the workhouse for drunken & disorderly behavior; he died on Sat night. [An inquest on the body of a marine who had drowned on Sat; & an inquest was held on a little boy who drowned in the canal. No names on the latter.]

Died: on Jun 27, Townsend Washington, son of John S & Susan W Edwards, aged 1 year, 1 month & 7 days. His funeral will take place from the residence of his father, 442 F st, between 5th & 6th sts, this day at 5 o'clock P M.

A young man named Robinson, from Fred'k, Md, died on Sat last when he fell from the upper story of a new bldg under erection by Mr Jos Bryan, on N Y ave. He was at work on the cornice of the bldg, & was about to rig out some additional scaffolding to what had been left by the bricklayers, & supposing the latter to be safer than it was, prematurely entrusted his weight to it, when it fell outward into the street, carrying him with it upon a pile of bricks. He was taken to his boarding house, & died in about 2 hours.

Obit-died: on Jun 18, after a brief illness, *Mrs Mr P T Shepperd, consort of Hon A H Shepperd, at their residence near Salem, Forsyth Co, N C. The deceased was born in Gtwn, D C, & united in marriage with Mr Shepperd during his term of service as a member of Congress from this district. She was a kind mistress, an affectionate wife, & a devoted mother. The unexpected intelligence of the sudden death of her eldest & darling son, an officer in the U S Army, in the very flower of his youth, fell heavily upon her spirit. The pang of separation from the loved ones of earth would have been mitigated had it been vouchsafed to her to welcome back to his home her second son, a promising officer in the U S Navy, just landed in the country after a prolonged absence of several years. But an inscrutable providence had ordained otherwise, & with the other deeply afflicted members of the family & sympathizing friends around she gently passed away, in full communion with the Episcopal Church. Her mortal remains were laid to rest at sunset on Jun 19, in the new & beautiful woodland cemetery. –A Friend
*Copied as written.

Died: on Jun 22, in her 87th year, at Brunswick Place, Miss, the residence of her son, Alex M Gwin, Mrs Mary M Gwin, mother of Hon Wm M Gwin, of the U S Senate. She had been for more than 70 years a professing member of the Methodist Church, & her husband, Rev Dr Gwin, who died in 1841, was for more than 50 years a minister of that church, & its pioneer apostle in many of the Western & Southwestern States. He enjoyed the intimacy & confidence of Gen Jackson. The parents of the distinguished Senator from Calif were among the earliest emigrants from N C to Tenn.

Mrd: on Jun 2, by Rev Thos Hooper, Dr Thos H Kinney, of Staunton, to Miss Mary T, daughter of the late Wm T H Pollard, of Hanover Co, Va.

TUE JUN 29, 1858
Obit-died: yesterday, Judge Robt T Conrad, of Phil, at his residence on Sunday night. He was the first Mayor of Phil after the consolidation, & esteemed by all parties. He was only about 45 years of age.

Obit-died: yesterday, Hon Job R Tyson, after a brief illness. He was a member of Congress but a single term, yet his name was honorably connected with many measures of public interest. He was in his 55th year.

John Jackson, 87 years old, sought lodgings at a Cincinnati station house a few evenings since, having walked all the way from North Carolina, on his way to find a son at Indianapolis.

Montgomery Co. The Commonwealth of Pennsylvania to the Sheriff of Montg Co, greeting: We command you that you summon Rev Philip Slaughter & Ann Sophia his wife, late Anna Sophia Semmes, John M Forbes & Mary Eliz his wife, late Mary Eliz Semmes, Douglass Ramsey Semmes, Rev Wm M Nelson & Sarah W his wife, late Sarah W Semmes, & Thos Middleton Semmes, defendants, late of your county, so that they be & appear before our county court of common pleas to be holden at Norristown in & for said county of Montg, on Aug 16, 1858, to answer David Potts, jr, plnts, of a plea wherefore whereas the said plntf & the dfndnts together & undivided do hold the following described real estate: No 1: all that parcel of land in the borough of Pottstown, Montg Co, State of Pa, containing about 4 acres, more or less, being lot No 2 which was awarded to the heirs of John Potts, deceased, by the judgment of said court in a certain action of partition in the said court, wherein Thos Semmes & others are plntfs, & Jos Potts & others are dfndnts, of May, 1820, No 88, with the appurtenances. No 2: all that tract of land in Pottsgrove township, county & State aforesaid, bounded by the land now or late of Henry Smith; & near the land now or late of Jacob Malsberger, containing 23 acres & 17 perches, more or less. Together with the free right of passage forever reserved in common with the owner of lot 4, & the owners & occupants of lot 5. Witness the Hon Danl M Smyser, Pres of our said court at Norristown, May 29, 1858.
–F Sullivan, Prothonotary

Circuit Court of Wash Co, D C-in Equity. Jos Libbey vs Jas B Phillips, Jas Towles, Edw Owen, J M Carlisle, & Wm B Magruder. A special auditor will report the amounts due in the cause, & also state the trustee's account, on Jul 7 next, at City Hall. –Walter S Cox, special auditor

In Chancery. Virginia ss--Circuit Court of Rockingham Co, May Term, 1858. John C Beard, plntfs, vs David Beards' heirs, dfndnts. It is ordered that unless the dfndnts, Ann Bell & Mgt Kyle, or their decendants, if any they have, do appear here on the first day of the next term, & prove their right to share in the distribution of the estate of said David Beard, the court will, upon the presumption that the said Ann Bell & Mgt Kyle are dead, & died without leaving descendants, order & decree that their shares shall go to & be distributed among the other heirs of said David Beard. –A St C Sprinkel, clerk

On Sat Mr Cook, residing on 7th st, was the victim of sun-stroke & died on the same day.

Mrd: on Jun 24, in Wash City, by Rev Chas H Hall, at the Church of the Epiphany, Alex'r Henderson, U S N, to Kate, eldest daughter of L J Middleton.

Died: on Jun 27, Mr John McCauley, in his 53rd year. His funeral will be this afternoon at 4 o'clock, from his late residence on 4th st, between I & K sts.

Died: on Jun 5, at Malone, Franklin Co, N Y, after a protracted & painful illness of several years, Mrs Minerva Bradley, wife of Rev A C Treadway, & daughter of the late Judge Grant, of Oswego, N Y.

Died: on Jun 18, in Marilla, Erie Co, N Y, Mrs Mary Frances Kelsey, wife of Delose Kelsey, & daughter of J W & Mary Nye, of Wash, D C, in her 22nd year, leaving a husband & infant son to mourn their irreparable loss.

Died: on Jun 28, in Wash City, Julius E, infant son of J E & Kate Hilgard, aged 10 months. His funeral is this afternoon at 5 o'clock, from 361 F st, near 9th.

A telegraphic dispatch which announced the death of Maj Henry C Wayne, an esteemed officer of the army, reported as having died at Savannah on Sunday last, is a mistake. Maj Wayne is believed to be at Memphis, Tenn.

WED JUN 30, 1858
Army Court Martial: Gen Orders, No 6. War Dept, Adj Genrl's Ofc, Wash, Jun 24, 1858. The Court-Martial convened at San Antonio, Texas, Col Henry Wilson, 7th infty is president, & was tried Capt Seth M Barton, of the 1st regt of infty, on the following: Illegal conduct to the prejudice of good order & military discipline. Specification: The said Barton, at **Fort McKavett**, Texas, on Feb 24, 1857, being officer of the day in command of the police guard of said post, & adjutant of the 1st regt of U S infty, in command of the band of said regt, did then & there order & cause the sgt of said guard to tie up to a tree in front of the guard-house one Jos Heid, a citizen not subject to military authority, & did then & there order & cause certain soldiers of said band to flog said Heid on his bare back with wagon whips. Specification 2. The said Barton, at time & place aforesaid, having caused the flogging of said Heid, did then keep said Heid tied up to said tree for about 3 hours, more or less. Specification 3. The said Barton, at time & place aforesaid, did strike Private Louis Casten, of said regimental band, blows with a wagon whip to compel said Casten to flog said Heid. To which charges & specifications the accused pleaded as follows: No 1-guilty; No 2-guilty; No 3, not guilty, & not guilty to the charge. The Court find the accused: specification No 1-attaches no criminality thereto. Same for specification No 2. No 3-guilty & guilty of the charge. The court does sentence the said Capt Seth M Barton to be suspended from rank & command for 3 months, & to be confined to the limits of his post for the same period. War Dept, Jun 17, 1858. In this trial it was shown for the defence that the citizen who was flogged at the guard-house had entered the barracks, armed, & beat a soldier; that no civil tribunal to punish the offence was nearer than 170 miles. A Court-Martial has here adjudged that no wrong is done by an officer who causes his guard to flog a citizen-Therein the Court has manifested as little regard for the law as the officer on trial. The virtual acquittal on the 1st & 2nd specifications is disapproved. The finding on the 3rd specification & on the charge is confirmed. The sentence is confirmed, & ordered to be executed.
–John B Floyd, Sec of War.

Died: on Jun 28, in Wash City, after a short but painful illness, Mrs Julia A Goggin, in her 55th year. Her funeral will take place from her late residence, 481 10th st, this afternoon, at 5 o'clock.

Died: on Jun 27, at Edge Hill, Caroline Co, Va, in his 19th year, Jos Gales, son of Roger C Weightman, of Wash City.

Mrd: on Jun 24, at Harrisburg, Pa, by Rev Chas A Hay, at Zion's [Lutheran] Church, Peter A Keller, of Wash City, to Matilda R, eldest daughter of the late Henry Church, of Bridgeport, Pa.

Criminal Court-Wash-Tue. Two of the jurors, Thos H Miles & Geo H Johnson were unable to sit on account of ill health, & they were excused. John Scrivener & Jerome R Wroe were selected in their place. This is the trial of the Devlin brothers, charged with murder of Mr Thos B Berry. Witnesses: Dr A W Miller: knew the Devilin family since 1849; John S Devlin is of a rather excitable temperment & of weak intellect. Mr Saml E Smith was present at Berry's death, & was in the directory business with Mr Berry. Mr Thos A Scott lives on the opposite side of the avenue to Devlin; Mrs Devlin's shrieks were very loud. Geo W Conner & his brother were going to the navy yard, when they heard Mrs Devlin scream. Jas Conner, brother of the last witness, testified in similar manner. Mrs Catherine Shears was a servant in the Devlin family, & had lived there 14 months. She was upstairs at the time. [Jul 1st newspaper: The trial of Jas P & John S Devlin for murder contined yesterday: first witness was A E L Keese, who assisted Dr Miller in examing deceased's clothes. Found a weapon on him. Jos M Carrico testified: charged John Devlin with killing Tom Berry. Walter Benner testified: he had known Jas Devlin for 8 years-John not so long nor so well. Mrs Devlin, mother of the prisoners, was examined, & also Mrs Berry, the first wife of the deceased.] [Jul 2nd newspaper: Berry denied that he had another wife, but Mr Devlin had satisfactory proof that the charge was true; they were going to prosecute Berry for bigamy, but stopped the proceedings on his promise to leave the city. He went away, but soon came back. Mrs Mary Berry, first wife of Thos B Berry, being sworn, testified that she married the deceased, Thos B Berry, in Aug, 1851; lived at that time in Phil, & still resides there with her father; knew Mr Berry 4 months before her marriage with him. Berry spoke of his relatives in Wash, his step-father, Mr Ferguson, his mother & his sister. Jas Owner testified that he saw Berry on the day of his death. John Donoho testified that he is barkeeper at Hamlin's restaurant. Dr W G Phillips testified. Mr John Wallace testified. Mr Reilly, one of the guards at the jail, thinks John Devlin insane. Dr John Lynch had known the prisoner, John S Devlin, from a child. Wm H Langley lived near the Devlin's. Geo Shekells tended bar at different restaurants. Mr Patrick McKenna knew John Devlin & his father, the latter for 20 years. Mrs Fanny L Berry, [the second wife,] was married to the deceased in N Y C in 1852. When her father died, she was in N Y.] [Jul 3rd newspaper: Trial on Jul 2, 2004: Mr Rupp, Dr J W Stettinius, A E L Keese, & Mrs Fanny L Berry [the second wife,] testified.] [Jul 5th newspaper: on Jul 4th the jury returned a verdict of guilty of manslaughter against Jas P Devlin, & of not guilty in the case of John S Devlin-on the ground of insanity.]

Died: on Jun 23, in Winchester, Va, Miss Kate, 3rd daughter of Thos B Campbell.

Died: on Jun 27, in Wash City, Caroline Knowles, infant daughter of Hugh B & Eliza D Sweeny.

Rev Dr Jacob J Janeway died at his residence in New Brunswick, N J, on Sunday last, in his 84th year. For many years he was the pastor of the Second Presbyterian Church of Phil, & left that city to be installed as president of the Western Theological seminary at Alleghany, Pa, where he remained for some years. He was also president of the Board of Missions, trustee of the Princeton College, & prominent in numerous religious societies. He was a distinguished writer on theological subjects. –Phil American

THU JUL 1, 1858
Valuable business stand & dwlg in Gtwn at public auction, Jul 8, in front of the premises, High st, lately occupied by Mr Hamilton as a grocery store, improved with a commodious 3 story brick dwlg with ample back bldgs. –Barnard & Buckey, aucts, Gtwn

Ary Scheffer, the great painter of France, died at Paris about Jun 15. He was born in Holland in 1795; received his whole art education in France, receiving instruction from Guevin. He was a favorite of Louis Philippe when he was Duke of Orleans, & was instructor in art of his children, including the Princess Marie, who showed such talent as a sculptor.

Wash Corp-Jun 28, 1858: nominations by the Mayor:
Corp Atty: Jas M Carlisle
Messenger: Wm Q Locke
Tax Clerk: Wm J Donoho
Com'r of Health: Chas F Force, M D
Book-keeper: Edwin J Klopfer
Ward Physicians:
Philip C Davis, M D
J W H Lovejoy, M D
Geo M Dale, M D
J M Grymes, M D
J M Roberts, M D
J E Willett, M D
J M Toner, M D
Apothecaries to furnish medicines to the poor:
David G Ridgeley
Andrew W Hughes
Valentine Harbaugh
Jas N Callan
J B Gardiner
Jas O'Donnell
D B Clark
Intendant of the Asylum: John R Queen
Physician to the Asylum: W M Berry, M D
Com'rs of the Asylum: Geo W Emerson, Geo Mattingly, & Leonard Harbaugh
Com'r of the Eastern Section of the Canal, in place of John D Brandt, declined-Chas C Edelin.
Com'r of the Western Section of the Canal: Wm Wise
Sealer of Weights & Measures: Hiram Ritchie
Inspector of Fire Apparatus: John W Martin

Board of Health:
1st Ward: Dr P C Davis & J B H Smith
2nd Ward: Dr R K Stone & Jas I Dunawin
3rd Ward: Dr W G Palmer & Jos Bryan
4th Ward: Dr W P Johnston & Frs Mohun
5th Ward: Dr G McCoy & J P Ingle
6th Ward: Dr F S Walsh & John D Brandt
7th Ward: Dr J E Morgan & H A Clarke
Clerks of Markets: Centre Market, John Waters, Jos Lyons, assist; Eastern Market, Michl Conner; Western Market, Wm Walker; Northern Market, Geo D Spencer.
Com'rs of the Centre Market: Wm Orme Hudson Taylor, & Buckner Bayless.
Com'rs of the Western Market: Wm E Walker & Solomon Storer.
Com'rs of the Northern Market: Jas T Divine & Theodore Sheckels.
Com'rs of the Eastern Market: G W Johnson & Francis Jenkins.
Wood & Coal Measurers: Jos Z Williams, Saml C Mickum, Richd Wimsatt, John Cumberland, & Wm P Drury, vice Osgodby, deceased.
Measurers of Grain, Bran, etc: John Wilson & J Z Williams.
Jas Lawrenson, as trustee of the Public Schools for the second district, in place of Col W P Young, resigned. The Board proceeded to the consideration of the nominations submitted by the Mayor this day, & they were severally confirmed.

Martin Koszta, the Hungarian refugee, who was rescued from the Austrian authorities in 1858, by Cmder Ingraham, of the U S Navy, died recently in very indigent circumstances, on a sugar plantation near the city of Guatemala. -Panama Star, May 25.

A spiritual funeral was held at Lowell on Wed over the remains of J B Smith. Miss Emma Houston prayed & spoke in a trance, or the departed spoke through her. The wife & family of the deceased, instead of putting on black, dressed in white, with white shawls & bonnets trimmed with white.

The following are the officers who at present compose the Grand Council of the **Mount Vernon Ladies Association of the Union:**
Regent: Miss Ann Pamela Cunningham, S C
Vice Regents:
Mrs Anna Cora Ritchie, Richmond, Va
Mrs Alice H Dickinson, Wilmington, N C
Mrs Philoclea Edgeworth Eve, Augusta, Ga
Mrs Octavia Walton Le Vert, Mobile, Ala
Mrs Catharine A McWillie, Jackson, Miss
Mrs Margaretta S Muse, New Orleans, La
Mrs Mary Rutledge Fogg, Nashville, Tenn
Mrs Eliz M Walton, St Louis, Mo
Miss Mary Morris Hamilton, N Y C, N Y
Mrs Louisa Ingersoll Greenough, Boston, Mass
Mrs Susan L Pellet, Secretary, Richmond, Va
Geo W Riggs, Treasurer, Wash, D C.

Fatal duel at New Orleans on Jun 29 between Mr Hanlon, of the True Delta, & Mr Gibson, of the **Crescent**, in which the latter was killed.

Russel C Fowler, a printer by trade, a young man, died at Cincinnati on Sunday from taking an overdose of morphene. He arrived in Cincinnati from Mohoning Co, on his way to Indianapolis, last week, & complained of being unwell. It is supposed that he took so large a dose as to produce the fatal result.

Miles Greenwood, jr, accidentally shot himself at his father's residence near Cincinnati on Sat. He died in a few hours.

Mr Stofer, editor of the Lexington [Mo] Expositor, was shot dead last week, on board the steamer **A B Chambers**, on the Missouri river, by a professional gambler named Clark. Stofer had won money of Clark, & the latter shot him because he refused to play longer.

Local news- Wash. John H Goddard appointed Chief of Police, with Edw McHenry & Noble Thomas as lts.

Mrd: on Jun 30, at the Assembly's Church, by Rev Andrew G Carothers, Mr Robt Stewart Jordan to Miss Martha A Garrettson, daughter of N Garrettson, all of Wash City.

Mrd: on Jun 29, at the residence of Dr L D Gale, by Rev Dr Sunderland, Henry B Sheldon to Mary, daughter of the late Lewis Smith, all of Brooklyn, N Y.

Died: on Jun 30, Mrs Polly Wector, after a long illness. Her funeral will take place tomorrow evening at 6½ o'clock, from 254 F st.

Died: on Jun 30, Charles Edmund, youngest son of John E & Eliza T Norris, aged 5 months. His funeral is this morning at 10 o'clock at their residence on H st.

Crimes & casualties reported in the San Francisco Bulletin: Frank Quinn, shot at Princeton, near Mariposa, by Henry L Smith; Saml N Palmer, drowned in a mining tunnel at Junction Bluffs, Nevada Co; T S Wilson, Woolsey's Flat, Nevada, Co; L A Davis, El Dorada, Placer Co, & Ferdinand Maud, [a German,] Knights Ferry, each killed by caving in of banks while mining; Jas McPalmer, killed by falling from a cliff on Farallones Island; Lewis Lefeore, shot in self defence by deputy sheriff John L Smith, in Santa Barbara Co; Thos Buck, murdered by Thos Stewart at Douglass Flat, Calaveras Co; ___ Davis, who leaves a wife & family in the Atlantic States, died at Lawton's Mills, Siskeyou Co, from injuries received from a circular saw; Mr Mitchell, drowned at Placerville; Francis Fairchild, killed at Little Grass Valley, Nevada Co, by a bank of earth caving in; Wat Garten, shot dead at Minersville, Trinity Co, by John Morris; John Cowen, a thief, shot near Millerton; two Frenchmen, Messrs Baratier & Borel, & 2 hired men, massacred by Mexican banditti at a ranch in Tulare valley-one of the bandits was caught & hung; a negro hung by lynch law at Stockton, for having trespassed upon a white man.

Annual Commencement of Columbian College, D C, yesterday in the E st Baptist Church: oration by Mr Chas Wm Franzoni, of Wash, D C; oration by Mr Jos Darden Barnes, of Hertford Co, N C; oration by Mr Ashbel Floridus Steele, of Wash D C; discourse by Mr Henry Clay Upperman, of Wash, D C; sketch of America by Mr Isaac La Rue Johnson, of Columbia, N J; oration by Mr Edgar Williamson Tucker, of Morehouse parish, La; eulogy by Mr Thos Danl Jeffress, of Charlotte Co, Va. Address by Mr Thos Benton Shepherd, of Clarke Co, on the Dignity of Labor. The last address was by Mr Edwin John Cull, of Wash, D C, on the Philosophy of History. Degree of Bachelor of Philosophy was conferred on Chas Wm Franzoni, D C; Thos Fred'k Hampton, D C; Jas Landrum Holmes, Va; & Thos Danl Jeffress, Va. Degree of Bachelor of Arts conferred on Jos Darden Barnes, N C; Edwin John Cull, D C; Isaac La Rue Johnson, N J; Thos Benton Shepherd, Va; Ashbel Floridus Steele, D C; Edgar Williamson Tucker, La; & Henry Clay Upperman, D C. The degree of Master of Arts was conferred on Sydney H Owens, professor in Richmond College, Va; also on Wm J Martin, professor in the Univ of N C; also on Robt C Parkes, formerly of Columbian College, he now, by the same authority, conferred the degree of L L D on Hon Howell Cobb, & the degree of D D on Rev Geo W Samson. [Jul 3rd newspaper: The name of the 3rd gentleman who received the honorary A M on Wed is Robt C Fox, [instead of Parkes,] son-in-law of Hon A Kendall, & formerly an officer of the College.

FRI JUL 2, 1858
Hon Albert Hobart Nelson, late Chief Justice of Massachusetts, died on Sunday last, at the age of 46 years. On account of ill health he resigned his post in March last.

Rev Jabez Bunting, D D, the most eminent of he later Methodist divines of England, has just died. He was a native of Manchester, where he was educated by Dr Percival. He was called to the Ministry in 1799, & labored by the side of Dr Adam Clarke & Dr Coke.

Radford J Crockett was hung for murder at Atlanta, Ga, on Friday last, in the presence of 10,000 persons.

Mr Greer B Duncan died on Thu. Mr Duncan left here a short time ago, in a very feeble state of health, on a visit to Phil, & died, as stated above, on board the steamboat **Telegraph**, then lying at the Levee at Cincinnati. –New Orleans Picayune, 25th.

Lt Henry Brooks, the last surviving officer of the Kane Expedition, came to his death suddenly on Tue. While standing by the lyceum in the Brooklyn Navy Yard Mr Brooks was suddenly taken with a fit, & staggering fell backwards. His head struck the pavement with great force, so violent that the skull was fractured, indeed completely broken. He died a few moments afterwards. Mr Brooks was one of the most reliable & distinguished officer of the expeditions to the Arctic regions. At the time of his death he was acting boatswain in the navy yard, though his real position was that of lt. He wore medals from Queen Victoria, Pres Buchanan, & Lady Franklin. He has not been to sea since the Arctic voyage, because he lost part of both feet by the frost on that expedition. He was 45 years of age. N Y Express

Tragedy in Columbus Co, N C, on Jun 29. Joshua Rouse killed his father, his wife, & two of his small children, cutting off their heads with an axe. His eldest son ran over to the residence of Isaac H Powell & told him what had happened, who got W G Smith, & they went on towards Rouse's. When he saw Powell & Smith he dropped the axe. He is now in jail. He had been for some time in the Insane Asylum, but was taken out by his guardian some 3 or 4 weeks ago. –Wilmington [N C] Journal

Mrd: on Jun 30, at Alexandria, Va, by Rev Mr Dana, Dr S W Everett, of Quincy, Ill, to Mary, daughter of the late Dr S W Smith, of the former place.

Died: on Jun 30, in Gtwn, Mrs Eleanor Maria Forrest, relict of the late Geo P Forrest.

Died: yesterday, James N, youngest son of John W & Eliz R Nairn. His funeral will take place this evening at 5 o'clock, from the residence of the parents.

On Jun 28 Jos Ager, a hand on board the schnr **George Franklin**, Jabez Tyler, master, walked overboard when opposite Matthias Point, in the Potomac river, & was lost. The deceased was from Dorchester Co, & was unmarried.

SAT JUL 3, 1858
Household & kitchen furniture at auction on Jul 7, by order of the Orphans Court of Wash Co, D C, at the late residence of N A Randall, deceased, 426 north I st, corner of 10th st. -A Green auct

The contracts for supplying the Depts with stationery for the fiscal year ending Jun 30, 1859, have all been awarded to stationers of Wash City: State Dept: W F Bayly; Treas Dept: Franklin Philp; & Interior, War, & Navy Depts: Blanchard & Mohun

The President yesterday took up his residence at the Military Asylum for the summer. His official business will be transacted at the White House. Secretary Floyd moved out to the Asylum about a week since. -States

On Jun 14, the remains of Rev Elisha Mitchell, who lost his life on the Black Mountain about a year since, were removed from their resting place in the Presbyterian grave-yard in Asheville, N C, & on Tue conveyed to the highest peak on the mountain, which had been selected as their final resting place. The peak bears his name, & it the highest point of land in the U S east of the Rocky Mountains. A numerous calvacade of citizens accompanied the remains. A funeral oration was delivered by Rt Rev Bishop Otey, of Tenn. Hon David L Swain, Pres of the Univ, participated in the solemn ceremonies.

A daughter of John Camp, of Chambersburg, Pa, was killed by lightning on Sunday, while riding home from the meeting with the family. The others were severely stunned, but not injured.

Robt McMahon died suddenly at Ipswich on Jun 20th after eating a few raw clams. The bivalves are frequently poisonous in hot weather.

The Phil papers announce the death of Abraham Miller, a prominent citizen, who had for many years represented the city in the Legislature of Pa. He was 79 years of age.

Brazilian Legation, Wash, Jul 2, 1858. Messrs Jacob Humbird, *Bobert Harvey, & W Watts who engaged themselves, through their reps at Rio de Janeiro, in the construction of the second section of the D Pedro 2nd Railroad, are invited to appear in person as soon as possible at this Legation, for an object connected with their contract. By order of the Minister, A P Le Carvalho Borges, Sec of the Legation. [*Copied as written.]

Hon Richd Wayne, Mayor of Savannah, died at that city on Sunday last, after just a week's illness. He was a native of Savannah, & little over 54 years of age at the time of his death. He was educated at Union College, Schenectady, N Y, & graduated with the degree of M D, at the Medical College in Phil. He at one time held the appointment of Surgeon in the U S Army.

Mrd: on Jul 1, in Wash City, by Rev G W Samson, Mr Chas H Kane to Miss Ellen E Milburn, both of Fairfax Co, Va.

Mrd: on Jul 1, at the E st Baptist Church, Mr John Walling to Miss Mary E McGinnie, both of Wash.

Mrd: on Jul 1, by Rev Mr Holmead, Josiah Simpson to Miss Louisa Eliz Sage, all of Wash City.

Circuit Court for PG Co-in Equity, No 197. Thos O Thompson & Matilda his wife, vs Wm L Wall, Catharine M McKee, Martha J Townshend, Rebecca E Talbert, & Thos Talbert. The bill is to obtain a decree for the sale of the real estate being that which Theodore Wall, late of said county, died seized & possessed of. Theodore Wall was the father of said Matilda A, & died intestate some time in the year ___[blank,] leaving the said Matilda A, [who afterward in-married with said Thos O Thompson,] Wm L Wall, Catharine M McKee, Martha J Townshend, Rebecca E Talbert, [wife of Thos Talbert,] all of whom reside in PG Co; Saml T W H, & Danl R Wall, of Wash City, D C; Thos M Wall, & Adeline Barron, [wife of Saml B Barron,] of ___[blank,] in the State of Texas, his only heirs & legal reps, all of whom are of full age; & that the said Theodore Wall was seized & possessed at the time of his death in fee simple of certain real estate, lying & being near Brandywine, PG Co; that is to say, a tract or parcel of land adjoining Brandywine, & now in the possession of the said Catharine M McKee, supposed to contain 150 acres, name unknown; also, a piece or parcel, name unknown, containing about 40 acres; that the said real estate is incapable of division among the parties interested, & they have been entirely unable to agree among themselves to a sale & division thereof; & the said bill prays that a decree may pass for a sale of the said real estate, & a division of the property thereof, according to the respective interests of the parties interested, among the said parties. The absent dfndnts are to appear in this court, in person or by solicitor, on or before the first Monday of Nov next.
–Chs S Middleton, Clerk of the Cir Court of PG Co, Md.

Mrs Littles, tried in Rochester, N Y, for the murder of her husband, has been found guilty of manslaughter in the 2nd degree & sentenced to 7 years in the penitentiary.

Orphans Court of Wash Co, D C. Letters testamentary on the personal estate of Nicholas A Randall, late of Wash Co, deceased. –Eliz C Dorsey, excx

Died: on Jul 2, in Gtwn, D C, Augusta Ellen, in her 21st year, eldest daughter of Jacob & Ann Rebecca Ramsburg. Her funeral will be from Bridge st Church, Gtwn, today at 5½ o'clock P M.

Died: on Wed last, Ambrose, infant son of Michl R & Catharine Shyne.

Circuit Court for PG Co-in Equity, No 238. Arthur J West, Thos S West, Virginia O West, & John H Strider, adm of Eleanor West, against Wm D Bowie, Thos H Clagett, Biddell L West, Francis O M West, Helen M West, & Benj O West. The object of this suit is to procure a decree vacating & annulling certain deeds of trust of which the cmplnts' bill has the following description & particulars: on May 1, 1844, Arthur P West & Eleanor West, his wife, the father & mother of the three first-named cmplnts, who then resided in PG Co, by their deed of trust of that date, duly executed & acknowledged, to the consideration therein expressed, conveyed unto Wm D Bowie, of said county, & to Thos H Clagett, of Leesburg, Va, as trustees, a large & valuable real estate in PG Co, described in said deed, in trust for the sole & separate use of said Eleanor West & her heirs, free from the control of the said Arthur P West, & to be in no wise responsible for the debts he then owed or might thereafter contract, with power to the said Eleanor West, with the consent of the said trustees, to sell the whole or any part of the said real estate, & to execute the proper & necessary papers for the conveyance thereof, & the proceeds of sales to be invested for the purposes of said trust, or as the said Eleanor West should direct; & with the futher power to the said Eleanor West to dispose of said real estate or any part thereof, by last will & testament or other writing in the nature therof, executed in accordance to law, & in default of any such sale or disposition in trust after the death of the said Eleanor West for the use & benefit of her heirs. The bill further states that, on Jun 29, of the same year, the said Arthur P West, being then possessed of a large & valuable personal estate, did, by a deed of that date, for the consideration therein mentioned, convey the same unto the said Wm D Bowie & Thos H Clagett in trust to pay & satisfy all of the just debts of the said Arthur P West, & to indemnify & secure the said trustees for all loans & liabilities incurred for or on account of the said Arthur P West, & for all costs which had been or might be incurred by them in the execution of said trust, & the residue of said property & all moneys arising from the sale of any part thereof, after the payment of the just debts, liabilities, & expenses as aforesaid, to be held by them for the sole & separate use & benefit of the said Eleanor West, her executors, administrators, & assigns, free from the debts or liabilities of her said husband, which were then due or might thereafter be contracted, & free from his control, & subject to the same powers & provisions, by sale or last will & testament, as are before stated, as to the said real estate, copies of which said 2 deeds of trust are filed with said bill of cmplnt, as the said cmplnts exhibits, A & B, & prayed in said bill to be taken as parts thereof.

The bill further states that the said cmplnts are informed that the said trustees are now prepared to exhibit a full & final account of said trust estate, & to payover to the parties entitled to receive the same any balance of moneys in their hands from the sales of said property, & the residue of said property now in their hands, & are anxious to be discharged from said trust. The bill further states that said Eleanor West departed this life demetrine, in 1856, intestate, & without having disposed of any part of said trust estate, leaving the three first-named cmplnts in the bill, viz: Arthur John West, Thos S West, & Virginia O West, & Biddell L West, Francis O M West, & Benj O West her only children, [the latter of whom has since departed this life, leaving Helen West, his widow, & Helen M West & Benj O West, his only children,] & that letters of administration on the personal estate have been duly granted by the Orphans Court of Wash Co, D C, where the said Eleanor West resided at the time of her death, to John H Strider, who has duly qualified as such. The bill further states that a large portion of the aforesaid real estate has not been disposed of, & it will not be necessary to dispose of it for the purposes of said trust; that is to say, about 350 acres thereof known as *Pocosin*; & that the said real estate, in its present condition, is entirely unproductive & not capable of division among the parties entitled thereto, but it would be greatly to the interest & advantage of all of the said parties to have the same sold under the direction of this court. The bill prays that a decree may pass vacating & annulling said trust, & discharging said trustees therefrom, after they shall have exhibited in this court a full account of the sales of such portion of said trust estate as they may have sold, with the application of the moneys arising therefrom, & requiring the said trustees to hand over to the parties entitled thereto any balance of the money in their hands from the sale of said property, which my be unappropriated, with the residue of said trust estate now in their hands, & also for a decree for the sale of said real estate for division among the parties entitled to the same, & that all the parties interested may appear in this court & answer the premises & abide by such decree as may pass in the premises. Absent dfndnts are to appear at this court, in person or by solicitor, on or before said first Monday in Nov next.
-Chs S Middleton, Clerk of the Circuit Court for PG Co, Md.

I have this day, Jun 30, associated Dr B J Hellen with me in the Practice of Medicine & Surgery. Messages may be left either at my ofc, 397 C st, or at the ofc of Dr Hellen, Wash Infirmary. –Jno Fred'k May

MON JUL 5, 1858
The late Gen Chas Fenton Mercer-died after a very painful & protracted illness, at Howard, near Alexandria, Va, on May 4 last, in his 80th year. He was born in Fredericksburg, Va, Jun 16, 1778, very near *Marlborough*, the birthplace of his father, Jas Mercer, & for many years the residence of his grandfather, John Mercer, who emigrated when a young man from Ireland near the beginning of the last century. John Mercer was very successful as a lawyer, amassed a large fortune, published the first abridgment of the laws of Va, & died in 1769. James, the 3rd son, adopted the profession of his father, became Pres of the Genr'l Court of Va, & was translated thence to the Supreme Appellate Court, was a zealous Whig, & chosen by Conventions succeeding the extinction of the royal power in Va a member of the Cmte of Safely. He was elected a member of the Continental Congress, in which he served in 1779. He died while

attending upon his public duties as Judge of the Court of Appeals in 1798, leaving a large estate encumbered with heavy debts; all of which at a subsequent period were most honorably assumed by the subject of this notice, in the spirit of filial piety to the only parent he had known, his mother having died in his infancy; thus causing [to borrow his own words] to himself much suffering in after life. For 2 years after the decease of his father young Mercer found himself without means of completing his education; but in 1795 he entered the jr class in Princeton College, & in 1797, the first honors of his class were awarded to him by the unanimous vote of the Faculty & his class-mates, & at the commencement he delivered a Latin oration. In this class of 31 was Hon Richd Rush, Govn'r Troup, Govn'r Edwards, & Dr Beasly. On Jul 4, 1798, at age 20, while a student of law, when an invasion by the French was threatened, in a letter to Gen Washington, he tendered his services for the defence of the country; a little later a commission of 1st lt of cavalry, & soon after of captain, which, as all danger of war had ceased, he declined to accept, never intending to devote his life to the military profession. He was licensed to practice law in 1802; & in 1810 elected to the Gen Assembly of Va. Appointed during the session of the Gen Assembly a major general of the militia authorized by an act of Congress to be held in readiness for the public service, at his own request he was ordered to Norfolk, where he remained with a company of volunteers. He later resumed his seat in the Gen Assembly. His long Congressional career lasted 30 years. He was arrested by a dreadful & incurable malady, not immediately impairing sensibly his vigor of mind or body, & in the autumn of 1856 he returned from Europe & hastened to try the effect of the healing springs of his native State, deriving little or no benefit from them. He visited N Y & submitted to a surgical operation; followed by a 2nd surgery. A speedy death was inevitable.

Died: on Jun 16, near Marianna, Florida, Mr John G Roulhac, aged 61 years. He was a native of N C, a graduate of Chapel Hill, & a highly intelligent gentleman.

Died: on Jun 27, at Edge Hill School, Caroline Co, Va, of disease of the brain, Jo Gales Weightman, in his 19th year. He died far from his home; but kind friends stood by him in his last trying hour. –Caroline Co, Jul 1, 1858

In Mobile, on Jul 2, a fracas occurred between Mr H Warfield & Messrs John & David Reid, brothers, & of the firm of J Reid & Co. Both Reids were stabbed, John dangerously wounded. Warfield was arrested & committed to prison. The feud grew out of a feud 10 years' standing.

On Sunday, Alex McCoy, resident of Trimble Co, Ky, was shot dead by Savior Fry, of Saluda, Indiana, in a drunken frolic. Fry fled.

Orphans Court of Wash Co, D C. Letters testamentary on the personal estate of Robt J Roche, late of Wash Co, deceased. –Mary A Roche, Wm F Bayly, excs

WED JUL 7, 1858
Died: on Jul 5, of pneumonia, Jas Radcliffe Dunn, aged 33 years.

A row-boat, containing 2 sons & 2 daughters of Mr Wilson, of Poughkeepsie, N Y, & Mr Wilkins, a teacher in that city, was run down on Fri last by a river steamer & capsized. Mr Wilkins was drowned, but the others were saved, much bruised by contact with the wheel of the steamer.

Officers now in command at the Wash Navy Yard: Cmdor John Rudd, Capt Chas Turner, Lt Maury, Lt Patterson; Geo Wilmuth, boatswain; & Wm Hamilton, gunner. The copper rolling-mill is under the administration of Mr Wm Barbour.

Rudolf Cotton was killed by a stroke of lightning, on last Sat, at the house of widow McKay, in Indiana, opposite Carrollton, Ky. Two daughters of Mrs McKay were struck insensible by the shock, & the ear-rings of one of the ladies were melted from her ears. The girls are not expected to recover. –Louisville Courier, Tue

Trustee's sale of handsome property in Bladensburg at auction on Jul 28, by deed of trust from Jacob Brounstein & wife to the subscriber, dated Feb 24, 1857, one of the land records of PG Co, Md. Sale of one undivided moiety of a parcel of land, with bldg & improvements thereon, in the town of Bladensburg, which was heretofore conveyed to one Silbourn Mitchell by a certain Josiah Suit & his wife, by deed dated Feb 18, 1851, & duly recorded, & afterwards conveyed by said Silbourn Mitchell to Thos A Mitchell & Mary J Mitchell, now Mary J Brounstein. Also, one undivided moiety of each of those certain other parcels of land & improvements thereon in said town, known as lots 47 & 48, which was conveyed by the aforesaid Selbourn Mitchell to Thos a Mitchell & Mary J Mitchell, now Mar J Brounstein. –John Davidson, trustee -A Green auct
[2 spellings of Silbourn/Selbourn]

Mrd: on Jul 6, in Wash City, at the Nat'l Hotel, by Rev Dr Teasdale, Thos M Lomax to Miss Eliza Boteler, both of Fauquier Co, Va.

Died: on Jul 6, Mary, the beloved wife of Wm Wise, in her 50th year. Her funeral will be this afternoon at 4 o'clock, from her late residence, 83 4½ st.

Died: on Jul 5, Mary Martha, aged 23 months & 10 days, daughter of Eliza Frances & [tape covers the rest of the notice.]

Public attention called to the sale of 2 beautiful bldg lots, on 13th st, between K & L sts north, near the elegant residence of the late Major Lindsay. –John Marbury, trustee -Jas C McGuire, auct

Criminal Court-Wash-Tue. 1-Jas Cochran was found guilty of petty larceny, & sentenced to 6 months in the county jail. 2-Chas Carroll was found guilty of stealing a ham, & sentenced to 1 year in jail. 3-Robt Jones was convicted of stealing a Gtwn corporation bill & 2 gold quarter eagles, & sentenced to 1 year in the penitentiary. 4-Danl O'Connell was convicted of stealing one shirt & a josey of the goods & chattels of Bernard McGee: sentenced to 9 months in jail.

Orphans Court of Wash Co, D C. Letters testamentary on the personal estate of Henry Carl, late of Wash Co, deceased. –John Walter, exc

THU JUL 8, 1858
Beautiful farm, with the stock, crops, tools, & cattle, at auction, on Jul 15, on the premises, known as ***Springland***, late the property of W D Wallach, containing about 50 acres of land. The farm is about 6 miles from Alexandria & 4½ miles from the Washington market. The personal effects will be sold as well as the household & kitchen furniture. -Wasll & Barnard, aucts

Postmasters for N Y: appointments by the Pres:
Calvert Comstock, Albany
Geo M Chapman, Canandaigua
A S Johnson, Ithaca
Ashur Torrence, Lockport
Alfred B Getty, Oswego
Hiram A Bebe, Oweso
Nicholas E Paine, Rochester
Luker Dodge, Schenectady
Henry J Sedgwick, Syracuse
Jos M Lyon, Utica
Patrick Grattan, West Troy

Gen'l Land Ofc appointments:
Wm A Davidson, Register for New Mexico
Wm A Street, Receiver for New Mexico
Paschal Bequette, Receiver at San Francisco
Jas Guthrie, jr, Receiver at Oregon

On Fri J A Nettles was found dead in his room at the Girard House, Phil. It appears that he was about to pull the bell-rope, when he fell helpless. Papers in his pockets reveal he was from East Baton Rouge, La. The coroner's inquest rendered a verdict of apoplexy.

Supposed murder. On Monday, Coroner Sparklin was called to the boarding-house of Mr Stromberger, in Harrison st, to hold an inquest on the body of a man named John Eugard, who had died there suddenly. He was about 30 years of age. He thought he had been struck by a brick by some person in Franklin st. A bullet hole was found in the back of his head. His trunk revealed he had property in Calif & that he was from Texas.

Chas Williams, jr, a son of Chas Williams, paper-hanger, was drowned off Whitstone point, while returning in a schnr with a party of companions from an excursion down the river. He was between 14 & 15 years of age.

On Sunday the body of a man was found near Lansdale, Montg Co, Pa. His carpet-bag was lying near by, filled with good clothing, upon which was written Mark Boyd, Mauch Chunk, Pa, which is supposed to have been his name.

Jas Thompson, a youth, was executed at Columbus, Ga, on Friday last, for the murder of Mr J J Calhoun, about a year ago, in that city.

Orphans Court of Wash Co, D C. Letters testamentary on the personal estate of Geo S Neill, late of Wash Co, deceased. –Sarah A Neill, excx

Gtwn College annual commencement yesterday in the great hall in the College. Orations by Theodore J Dimitry; Henry W Clagett; Jos P Orme; Chas B Kenny; John F Marion; Jas F McLaughlin; Jas F Hoban. Prose pieces by Saml A Robinson; Caleb C Magruder; Edw Wootton; Francis X Ward; Cornelius J O'Flynn; Beverly C Kennedy, & Nichola S Hill. Degree of A M conferred on Fred'k L Smith, Pa; Geo Vadenhoff, Mass; Jas McShane, British America; Alex'r H Loughborough, D C; John S Rudd, Va; & Dominic Maguire, N C. Degree of A B conferred on Beverly C Kennedy, La; C John O'Flynn, Miss; Edw Wootton, Md; Chas B Kenny, Pa; Nicholas S Hill, Md; Jas A Wise, D C; Caleb C Magruder, Md; Saml A Robinson, D C; & Philip A Madan, Cuba. The degree of A B was also conferred the following students of the College of the Holy Cross, near Worcester, Mass: Wm J Denver, John Conlin, Jos Fallon, Geo Dillon, & Edw F Beahn, all of Mass. The Pres of the College, Rev Bernard A Maguire, said that the remarks he was making as president would probably be his last. He was anxious to be relieved of the often onerous care of so large a family, numbering nearly 400-& to return to private life.

On Wed, John Quenan, of Rondout, N J, was killed by the bursting of a cannon. He was about 30 years old, & leaves a wife & 2 children.

On Fri, Mr T G Clephane, a prominent citizen of Newport, Ky, was accidentally suffocated to death by the fumes of charcoal. His wife saw him fall into the cistern.

FRI JUL 9, 1858
Kansas Daily Ledger of Jul 2: Jas H Lane, tried before an Examining Court, for the murder of Gaines Jenkins, his neighbor, has been acquitted. Col Jenkins was the aggressor.

On Jun 5 the mortal remains of Jas Monroe were interred in **Hollywood Cemetery**, Richmond, Va. He was a country boy of Westmoreland, the county man of Washington. From the 18th to the 73rd year of his age he was almost incessantly in the public service. At 18 he left Wm & Mary College to enlist in the battle-fields of Independence. In the staff of Lord Stirling he was an aid-de-camp, & acquired the title of Colonel of a regt of Va, which was never raised. He was a Com'r of Va to the Southern camp; a legislator of Va; a member of the Continental Congress; twice Govn'r of Va; Minister to France, England, & to Spain, & again to England; twice elected Pres of the U S, & once almost unanimously.

Soldiers' of the war of 1812 recent celebration at Washington: Pres, Col Wm W Seaton; 117 names on the roll. 56 aged men walked at a slow pace to the Pres' House. Pres Buchanan, with Sec of State, Gen Cass, & Dr Blake, Comr of Public Bldgs, joined them. Col Seaton introduced the venerable John Sessford as the father of the city. He resided here before the Gov't; entered the ofc of the Nat'l Intelligencer in 1800. Saml B Beach read a patriotic ode, written by himself. Among the volunteer toasts were Col J S Williams; Gen St John B L Skinner & Maj Edw Simms.

A man named Sharp was killed on Jun 20th, on Pocahontas Co, Va, during an affray with another named Moore, who was arrested. Both parties are respectably connected.

A few weeks ago a constable Timmons was shot by a man, Kesler, in Gentry Co, Mo. He was arrested & put in the Albany jail. The prisoner was torn from the officers guarding him & borne off into the woods, allowed to say his prayers, & hung from a tree. The mob was composed of about 50 persons. –St Louis News

Bridget Callahen died in Newark on Sunday from the effects of an eye-wash, which she took inwardly instead of applying externally, as directed by the prescription.

Annual distribution of premiums at the Academy of the Visitation in Gtwn took place yesterday in the Odeon bldg, now much too small for the numbers. The distribution was by Rev Mr Maguire, Pres of Gtwn College. A gold medal was awarded to Miss A Frederick, of Augusta, Ga; 2nd honors to Misses A Ivey, Irene Godnow, J Potter, L De Launay, K Murphy, & Jane Turnbull; & queen of the jr circle was Miss M E Smith. Musical artists were Misses Mary Forsyth, Annie Weakley, Lecompte, Emily Bramhall, Dougherty, Bena Philips, & Kate Irving. Painting, drawing, embroidery, & needle-work by: Miss Libbie Pizzini; Miss A Frederick; Miss Bellenger; Miss Mabee; Miss Celeste Semmes-PG Co, Md; Miss Bramhall, of Rahway, N J; Miss Frederick; Miss Emily Long, of Garysburg, N C; Miss M Jones, of Ala; Miss L De Launay, of Ga; Miss C Semmes; Miss Lizzie Pizzini; Josephine Morse; Julia Potter, of Cincinnati; Miss Dillard; & Miss Dougherty. Handsome shirts were the handywork of Miss M Edelin, of Wash; & Miss Clements, of Chas Co, Md.

The new monument of Genr'l Brock, on Queenston Heights, C W, will be inaugurated on Oct 13 next, the anniversary of the battle of Queenston. The old monument was blown up by Letts, the pirate, during the Canadian rebellion, some 20 years ago.

Criminal Court-Wash-Wed. 1-Ferdinand Weisner was found guilty of assault & battery & sentenced to 2 weeks imprisonment in the county jail. 2-Jas P Devlin, convicted on Sunday last of the manslaughter of Thos B Berry, was sentenced to 4 years' imprisonment & hard labor in the penitentiary, to take effect from & after Jul 18 next.

For rent, the house, with the furniture, 261 G st, at present occupied by the Prussian Minister, Baron Gerolt. Apply on the premises or at 448 12th st. –Geo C Ames

Homes for Children. Wash Asylum, Jul 7, 1858. Several strong, hearty boys, from 11 to 15 years, will be bound to good masters upon application to the Com'rs of the Wash Asylum. Apply at the Asylum: Geo W Emerson, Geo Mattingly, Leonard Harbaugh.

Died: on Jun 26, at Goldsboro, N C, on his return from Mobile, John Hogan Douglass, in his 19th year. He was a son of the late Judge I R Douglass. A dutiful & loving son, an affectionate brother, a firm friend, have all been lost in him. –Charlestown [Va] Spirit

Died: on Jul 5, at his brother's residence, **Walnut Grove**, Alexandria Co, Va, Jas M Minor, of Wash Co, in his 46th year.

Died: on Jul 8, after a long & painful illness, Adeline E Davidson, in her 49th year, who leaves a husband & 8 children to mourn her loss. Her funeral is this afternoon at 4 o'clock, from her late residence of Pa ave, between 8th & 9th sts, Navy Yard.

Fruit of the Loom, bleached shirting cotton, represented as being the very best goods at 12½ cents per yard, for gentlemen's & boys shirts that are produced. –Perry & Bro, Central Stores, west bldg, opposite Centre Market.

SAT JUL 10, 1858
Beautiful farm, stock, tools, & crops, on Jul 22, at the residence known as *Springland*, owned by & at present the residence of E Yules, late the property of E D Wallach, containing about 50 acres. There is a comfortable dwlg & out bldgs. The farm is distant from Wash market 4½ miles by way of Gtwn. Personal effects will also be sold.
-Wall & Barnard, aucts

The Arkansas papers notice the death of Chas F Noland, a native of Va, but for more than 20 years a resident of Arkansas. He was well known throughout the State, having filled acceptably many places of trust & honor.

The Salem Register describes a magnificent elm in North Andover, on the Hubbard farm, which is supposed to be some 250 years old: 100 feet high & spreads over an area of about the same diameter.

Henry A Wise, jr, son of Govn'r Wise, [says the Va Herald,] was ordained a Minister at the Protestant Episcopal Theological Seminary, near Alexandria, on Jul 2.

Army Orders, Gen Orders No 8: War Dept, Adj Genrl's Ofc, Wash, Jul 8, 1878.
Promotions & appointments in the Army of the U S, made by the Pres, by & with the advice & consent of the Senate, since the publication of Genrl Orders, No 10, of Jul 7, 1857. Promotions: Corps of Engineers:
Brvt 2nd Lt John C Palfrey, to be 2nd Lt, Dec 31, 1857, the date of Capt Leadbetter's resignation.
Corps of Topographical Engineers.
Capt Campbell Graham, to be Major, Dec 9, 1857, vice Turnbull, deceased.
Brvt 2nd Lt J L Kirby Smith, to be 2nd Lt, Dec 9, 1857, the date of Capt Graham's promotion.
2nd Regt of Dragoons:
Lt Col Philip St George Cooke, to be Colonel, Jun 14, 1858, vice Harney, appointed Brig General.
Major Marshall S Howe, to be Lt Col, Jun 14 1858, vice Cooke, promoted.
Capt Lawrence P Graham, to be Major, Jun 14, 18558, vice Howe promoted.
1st Lt Wm D Smith, to be Capt, Jun 4, 1858, vice Calhoun, deceased. [Co F]
1st Lt Saml H Starr, to be Capt, Jun 14, 1858, vice Graham, promoted. [Co D]
2nd Lt Geo A Gordon, to be 1st Lt, Jun 4, 1858, vice Smith, promoted. [Co E]
2nd Lt John Mullins, to be 1st Lt, Jun 24, 1858, vice Starr, promoted. [Co D]
Brvt 2nd Lt Thos J Berry, to be 2nd Lt, Jun 4, 1858, vice Gordon, promoted. [Co A]

Brvt 2nd Lt Chas J Walker, to be 2nd Lt, Jun 14, 1858, vice Mullins, promoted. [Co I]
1st Regt of Cavalry:
1st Lt Edmund A Carr, to be Capt, Jun 11, 1858, vice Anderson, resigned. [Co I]
Brvt 2nd Lt Oliver H Fish, to be 2nd Lt, Jun 11, 1858, the date of 1st Lt Carr's promotion. [Co B]
2nd Regt of Cavalry:
Brvt 2nd Lt Fitzhugh Lee, to be 2nd Lt, Jan 1, 1858, vice Wood, resigned. [Co B]
Regt of Mounted Riflemen:
Brvt 2nd Lt Henry C McNeill, to be 2nd Lt, Oct 26, 1857, vice Wright, deceased. [Co C]
1st Regt of Artl:
Lt Col John Erving, of the 2nd Artl, to be Colonel, Oct 5, 1857, vice Crane, deceased.
Capt Robt Anderson, 3rd Artl, to be Major, Oct 5, 1857, vice Dimick, promoted to 2nd Artl.
2nd Regt of Artl:
Maj Justin Dimick, 1st Artl, to be Lt Col, Oct 5, 1857, vice Erving, promoted to 1st Artl
3rd Regt of Artl:
1st Lt Jas A Hardie, to be Capt, Oct 5, 1857, vice Anderson, promoted to 1st Artl. [Co G]
2nd Lt John Drysdale, to be 1st Lt, Oct 5, 1857, vice Hardie, promoted. [Co H]
Brvt 2nd Lt Abram C Wildrick, to be 2nd Lt, Oct 5, 1857, vice Drysdale, promoted. [Co C]
4th Regt of Artl:
1st Lt Gustavus A DeRussy, to be Capt, Aug 17, 1857, vice Grelaud, deceased. [Co K]
1st Lt John S Garland, to be Capt, Dec 29, 1857, vice Magilton, resigned. [Co I]
2nd Lt Edw F Bagley, to be 1st Lt, Aug 17, 1858, vice DeRussy, promoted. [Co F]
2nd Lt Fred'k M Follett, to be 1st Lt, Sep 10, 1857, vice Willcox, resigned. [Co C]
2nd Lt Geo S James, to be 1st Lt, Dec 29, 1857, vice Garland, promoted. [Co G]
Brvt 2nd Lt Geo A Kensel, to be 2nd Lt, Aug 17, 1857, vice Bagley, promoted. [Co L]
Brvt 2nd Lt Chas H Morgan, 3rd Artl, to be 2nd Lt, Sep 10, 1857, vice Follett, promoted. [Co A]
Brvt 2nd Lt Francis Beach, 2nd Artl, to be 2nd Lt, Dec 29, 1857, vice James, promoted. [Co E]
1st Regt of Infty:
1st Lt Seth M Barton, to be Capt, Oct 31, 1857, vice Miller, resigned. [Co F]
2nd Lt Walter Jones, to be 1st Lt, Oct 31, 1857, vice Barton, promoted. [Co H]
Brvt 2nd Lt Aurelius F Cone, 6th Infty, to be 2nd Lt, Jul 1, 1857, vice Ives, deceased. [Co G]
Brvt 2nd Lt Geo Ryan, 6th Infty, to be 2nd Lt, Oct 31, 1857, vice Jones, promoted. [Co B] [Since transferred to 7th Infty.]
2nd Regt of Infty:
2nd Lt John P Hawkins, to be 1st Lt, Oct 12, 1857, vice Wright, deceased. [Co D]
Brvt 2nd Lt Jos S Conrad, 4th Infty, to be 2nd Lt, Oct 12, 1857, vice Hawkins, promoted. . [Co E]
3rd Regt of Infty:
1st Lt Jas N Ward, to be Capt, Sep 28, 1857, vice Van Horne, deceased. [Co E]

2nd Lt Alex'r E Steen, to be 1st Lt, Sep 28, 1857, vice Ward, promoted. [Co A]
2nd Lt Matthew L Davis, jr, to be 1st Lt, Jan 14, 1858, vice Daniel, resigned. [Co A]
Brvt 2nd Lt Geo W Holt, 9th Infty, to be 2nd Lt, Sep 28, 1857, vice Steen, promoted. [Co F]
Brvt 2nd Lt Thos J Lee, 10th Infty, to be 2nd Lt, Jan 14, 1858, vice Davis, promoted. [Co I]

4th Regt of Infty:
Brvt 2nd Lt Edw J Conner, 5th Infty, to be 2nd Lt, Oct 22, 1857, vice Nugen, deceased. [Co A]

7th Regt of Infty:
2nd Lt Edmund C Jones, to be 1st Lt, Aug 1, 1857, vice Palfrey, resigned. [Co F]
2nd Lt Augustus H Plummer, to be 1st Lt, Jan 2, 1858, vice Van Bol_elen, who vacates his regimental commission. [Co K]
2nd Lt David P Hancock, to be 1st Lt, Apr 20, 1858, vice Pearce, resigned. [Co C]
Brvt 2nd Lt John S Marmaduke, 1st Infty, to be 2nd Lt, Aug 1, 1857, vice Jones, promoted. [Co B]
Brvt 2nd Lt Chas E Farrand, 2nd Infty, to be 2nd Lt, Jan 2, 1858, vice Plummer, promoted. [Co A] [Since transferred to 1st Infty.]
Brvt 2nd Lt Lafayette Peck, 8th Infty, to be 2nd Lt, Apr 20, 1858, vice Hancock, promoted. [Co H]

9th Regt of Infty:
1st Lt Thos C English, to be Capt, Dec 29, 1857, vice Guthrie, deceased. [Co H]
2nd Lt Philip A Owen, to be 1st Lt, Aug 1, 1857, vice Davis, resigned. [Co C]
2nd Lt Edwin J Harvie, to be 1st Lt, Dec 29, 1857, vice English, promoted. [Co H]
Brvt 2nd Lt Paul C Quattlebaum, 3rd Infty, to be 2nd Lt, Aug 1, 1857, vice Owen, promoted. [Co B]
Brvt 2nd Lt Robt H Anderson, 7th Infty, to be 2nd Lt, Dec 29, 1857, vice Harvie, promoted. [Co E]

Promotion of Brevet:
Co Albert S Johnston, 2nd Regt of Cavalry, to be Brig Gen by brevet, Nov 18, 1857, for meritorious conduct in the ability, zeal, energy, & prudence displayed by him in the command of the army in Utah.

II-Appointments:
Genr'l Officers:
Brvt Brig Gen Wm S Harney, Colonel of the 2nd Regt of Dragoons, to be Brig Gen, Jun 14, 1858, vice Smith, deceased.

Quartermaster's Dept:
1st Lt Wm L Cabell, 7th Infty, to be Assist Quartermaster, with the rank of Capt, Mar 8, 1858, vice Masten, resigned.
Wm H Gill, of Ohio, to be Military Storekeeper, Jun 12, 1858, vice McNutt, declined.
Jas C McCarthy, of Tenn, to be Military Storekeeper, Jun 14, 1858, vice White, deceased.

Medical Dept:
Jos C Baily, of Pa, to be Assist Surgeon, Oct 27, 1857, vice Byrne, resigned.

Pay Dept:
Capt Thos G Rhett, of the Regt of Mounted Riflemen, to be Paymaster, Jun 14, 1858, vice Walker, deceased.

Ordnance Dept:
Dennis Murphy, of Va, to be Paymaster & Military Storekeeper, Apr 7, 1858, vice Lucas, deceased.
Reappointments:
Alex'r W Reynolds, lately Assist Quartermaster in the U S Army, to be Assist Quartermaster, with the rank of Capt, to date from Aug 5, 1847, vice Brent, deceased, & to resume his former place on the Army Register, next below Capt Stewart Van Vliet.
7th Regt of Infty:
Matthew R Stevenson, lately 1st Lt in the 7th Infty, to be a Capt in the same regt, to date from Jan 2, 1858, vice Humber, deceased, & to resume his former place on the Army Register, next below Capt Jos H Potter.
III-Appointments made by the Pres since the adjournment of the Senate.
8th Regt of Infty.
Cadet Chas H Ingraham, to be 2nd Lt, Jul 1, 1858, vice Smith, resigned. [Co K]

The following-named Cadets, graduates of the Military Academy, are attached to the army with the Brevet of 2nd Lt, in conformity with the 4th section of the act approved Apr 29, 1812, to rank from Jul 1, 1858.
Corps of Engineers:
4. Cadet Wm C Paine.
Corps of Topographical Engineers:
2. Cadet Jos Dixon
4. Cadet Wm H Echols
Ordnance Dept:
2. Cadet Moses J White
Dragoon Arm:
10. Cadet Leroy Napier, jr: 1st Regt
11. Cadet Solomon Williams: 2nd Regt
12. Cadet Richd H Brewer: 1st Regt
Cavalry Arm:
15. Cadet Andrew Jackson, jr: 1st Regt
Regt of Mounted Riflemen:
18. Cadet Saml McKee
19. Cadet Edw P Cressy
Artl Arm:
5. Cadet John S Saunders: 2nd Regt
6. Cadet Jas H Hallonquist: 3rd Regt
7. Cadet Thos R Tannatt: 3rd Regt
8. Cadet Marcus P Miller: 4th Regt
Infty Arm:
14. Cadet Jas J Van Horne: 1st Regt
16. Cadet Chas G Harker: 2nd Regt
17. Cadet Sardine P Reed: 3rd Regt
18. Cadet Royal T Frank: 5th Regt
20. Cadet Asa B Carey: 6th Regt
21. Cadet Wm H Bell: 3rd Regt

22. Cadet Bryan M Thomas: 8th Regt
23. Cadet Wm J L Nicodemus: 5th Regt
24. Cadet Oliver P Gooding: 4th Regt
25. Cadet Wm G Robinson: 7th Regt
26. Cadet Geo N Bascom: 9th Regt
27. Cadet Chas E Jesup; 10th Regt

IV-Transferred:
Capt Horace Brooks, 2nd Artl, from Co A to Co H, Apr 8, 1858.
Capt W Austine, 3rd Artl, from Co K to Co B.
Capt Edw O C Ord, 3rd Artl, from Co B to Co K. No date.
Capt Wm F Barry, 2nd Artl, from Co H to Co A, Apr 8, 1858.
2nd Lt St Clair Dearing, 4th Infty, to 2nd Artl, Mar 17, 1858.
2nd Lt Thos E Turner, 2nd Artl, to the 4th Infty, Mar 17, 1858.
2nd Lt Alex'r B Montgomery, 3rd Artl, to the 4th Artl, Aug 27, 1858.
2nd Lt Lawrence Kip, 4th Artl to the 3rd Artl, Aug 27, 1857.
2nd Lt Geo Ryan, 1st Infty, to the 7th Infty, Jun 24, 1858.
Brvt 2nd Lt Thos J Berry, 1st Dragoons, to the 2nd Dragoons, Apr 13, 1858.
Brvt 2nd Lt Manning M Kimmell, 2nd Cavalry, to the 1st Cavalry, Apr 24, 1858.
Brvt 2nd Lt John T Magruder, 2nd Cavalry, to the 1st Cavalry, Apr 24, 1858.

V-Casualties.
Resigned, 13:
Capt Fred'k H Masten, Assist Quartermaster, Dec 31, 1857.
Capt Danville Leadbetter, Corps of Engineers, Dec 31, 1857.
Capt Geo T Anderson, 1st Cavalry, Jun 11, 1858.
Capt Andrew G Miller, 1st Infty, Oct 31, 1857.
Capt Albert L Magilton, 4th Artl, Dec 29, 1857.
1st Lt Orlando B Wilcox, 4th Artl, Sep 10, 1857.
1st Lt Nicholas B Pearce, 7th Infty, Apr 20, 1858.
1st Lt Robt H Davis, 9th Infty, Aug 1, 1857.
1st Lt Edw A Palfrey, 7th Infty, Aug 1, 1857.
1st Lt Junius Daniel, 3rd Infty, Jan 14, 1858.
2nd Lt Robt C Wood, jr, 2nd Cavalry, Jan 1, 1858.
2nd Lt Thos F Smith, 8th Infty, Apr 1, 1858.
Assist Surgeon John Byrne, Oct 11, 1857.
Commission vacated under the 7th section of the act of Jun 18, 1846.
By 1st Lt Wm K Van Bikelen, 7th Infty, Assist Quartermaster-his regimental commission, [only] Jan 2, 1858.
Commission vacated by new appointment:
By Brig Gen Wm S Harney, his commission as Colonel of the 2nd Regt of Dragoons, Jun 14, 1858.
Died:
Brvt Maj Gen Persifor F Smith, Brig Gen at **Fort Leavenworth**, K T, May 17, 1858.
Col Ichabod B Crane, 1st Artl, at Port Richmond, Staten Island, N Y, Oct 5, 1857.
Brvt Col Wm Turnbull, Major Corps of Topographical Engineers, at Wilmington, N C, Dec 9, 1857.

Brvt Maj Jefferson Van Horne, Capt 3rd Infty, at Albuquerque, New Mexico, Sep 28, 1857.
Capt Thos L Brent, Assist Quartermaster, at **Fort Leavenworth**, K T, Jan 13, 1858.
Capt Chas H Humber, 7th Infty, at **Fort Smith**, Arkansas, Jan 2, 1858.
Capt Patrick Calhoun, 2nd Dragoons, at Pendleton, S C, Jun 4, 1858.
Capt Presley N Guthrie, 9th Infty, at Newport, Ky, Dec 29, 1857.
1st Lt Thos Wright, 2nd Infty, at **Fort Randall**, N T, Oct 12, 1857.
2nd Lt John Nugen, 4th Infty, at **Fort Steilacoon**, W T, Oct 22, 1857.
2nd Lt Jas Wright, Regt of Mounted Riflemen, at Albuquerque, New Mexico, Oct 26, 1857.
2nd Lt Brayton C Ives, 1st Infty, at **Fort Clarke**, Texas, Jun 27, 1857.
Paymaster Benj Walker, at St Louis, Mo, May 28, 1858.
Military Storekeeper Edw Lucas, jr, Ordnance Dept, at Harper's Ferry, Va, Mar 5, 1858.
Military Storekeeper Chester B White, Quartermaster's Dept, at Benicia Barracks, Cal, Jan 12, 1858.
By order of the Sec of War, E D Townsend, Assist Adj Gen.

Mrd: on Jul 4, in Wash City, in St Mary's Church, by Rev Fr Alig, Mr Michl Esch to Miss Mgt Schaffeld.

Mrd: on Jul 8, by Rev Fr Alig, Mr Michl Huhn to Miss Mgt Jacob, both of Wash City.

Mrd: on Jul 6, at **Holland Point**, Calvert Co, Md, by Rev Mr Mitchell, Mr P A Bowen, of Gtwn, D C, to Rachel E, daughter of the late Wm Morton.

Died: on Jul 9, in Wash City, Mrs Tabitha Waters, in her 65th year. Her funeral will take place from the Church of the Ascension on Sunday at 3½ o'clock.

Grocery Store, Fixtures, Liquors, Household & kitchen furniture at auction on Jul 14, at the late residence of Mrs Lockrey, deceased, 5 East Capitol st, near 1st st. -A Green auct

Academy of the Visitation, B V M-Gtwn, D C. Annual distribution of premiums took place at this Institution on Jul 8. Premiums distributed by the Pres of the U S, assisted by B A Maguire, Pres of Gtwn College. Awarded premiums:

Kate Smith, Reading, Pa	Sybille Frederic, Augusta, Ga
Adelaide Frederic, Augusta, Ga	Louisa Walker, New Orleans, La
Jane Turnbull, Wash, D C	Victoria Pizzini, Richmond, Va
Susie Plowden, St Mary's Co, Md	Clara Gerald, N Y C
J Goodnow, Wash, D C	Emily Warren, Col Spring, N Y
Isabel Caulfield, Lexington Ky	Bettie Buckner, San Antonio, Texas
Kate Murphy, Florence, Ala	Eliza Sweeny, Wash, D C
Annie Horne, Milledgeville, Ga	Mary Soulard, St Louis, Mo
Alabama Robinson, Montg Ala	Blanche Soulard, St Louis, Mo
Amanda Ivy, Berwick City, La	Ida Ryon, Barnwell, S C
Hannah Maybee, Martinsville, Ind	Virginia Coolidge, Gtwn, D C
Barbara Sanders, Alexandria, Va	Harriet Butts, Montg, Texas

Josephine Murdle, Gtwn, D C
Annie Newall, Memphis, Tenn
Mary Forsythe, Wash, D C
Julia Potter, Cincinnati, Ohio
Emma Malbon, Gtwn, D C
Marietts Cullom, Carthage, Tenn
Jane Kelso, Kinderhock, Tenn
Eugenia Moore, Columbus, Geo
Mary Peters, Gtwn, D C
Maria Polk Walker, Memphis, Tenn
Maggie Owens, Phil, Pa
Mary Ann Kelly, Mountain Top, Va
Kate Irving, Wash, D C
Bessie Bellinger, Charleston, S C
Mary Callan, Gtwn, D C
Clementina Kirk, Sweet Springs, Va
Mary Van Riswick, Wash, D C
Mary Moxley, Gtwn, D C
Eliza Reeves, Richmond, Va
Sallie Major, Gtwn, D C
Alice Knight, Gtwn, D C
Lamar Horne, Milledgeville, Ga
Maria Offutt, Wash, D C
Mary Ivy, Berwick City, La
Emily Long, Garysburg, N C
Virginia Seymour, Gtwn, D C
Mary Waring, Montg Co, Md
Lucy Luckett, Canton, Miss
Sallie Weekley, Florence, Ala
Maggie Eddin, Wash, D C
Cecilia O'Donnoghue, Gtwn, D C
Clara Meem, Gtwn, D C
Mary Kennedy, Gtwn, D C
Clementina McWilliams, Chas Co, Md
Agatha O'Neale
Georgie Beebee, N Y C
Lucia Bellinger, Charleston, S C
Stella Clarke, St Mary's, Geo
Lizzie Woolard, Gtwn, D C
Isadora Hill, Gtwn, D C
Christina Leibrecht, New Orleans, La
Mary Ellen Smith, PG Co, Md
Augusta Goodwin, San Francisco, Cal
Mary Cleary, Wash, D C
Ellen Kelly, Mountain Top, Va
Lilly Risque, Gtwn, D C

Helen Clements, Gtwn, D C
Alice Seymour, Gtwn, D C
Fannie Petit, Gtwn, D C
Mary Jane Cannon, Wash, D C
Laura McPherson, Gtwn, D C
Lizzie Boucher, Gtwn, D C
Helen Brooks, Gtwn, D C
Emma Thocker, Gtwn, D C
Mary Liuber, Gtwn, D C
Agatha Roach, St Mary's Co, Md
Mary Rainy, Gtwn, D C
Jane Barbour, Gtwn, D C
Caddie Kirkwood, Wash, D C
Eliza Newman, Gtwn, D C
Maggie Chadwick, Newark, N J
Annie Davis, Richmond, Va
Mary Delaigle, Augusta, Geo
Virgina Lang, Gtwn, D C
Regina Sewall, Gtwn, D C
Elvira Offutt, Gtwn, D C
Teresa Keegan, New Orleans, La
Mary Pritchard, Gtwn, D C
Mary Keith, Boston, Mass
Amelia Ross, Gtwn, D C
Mary Waters, Gtwn, D C
Mattie Ould, Gtwn, D C
Katie Keegan, New Orleans, La
Josephine Morse, Natchitoches, La
Louisa Keegan, New Orleans, La
Celestia Semmes, PG Co, Md
Emma Keenan, Balt, Md
Ellen Walker, New Orleans, La
Pauline Seymour, Gtwn, D C
Sallie Davis, Wash, D C
Alice Waddell, Natchitoches, La
Maria Gormley, Gtwn, D C
Mary Semmes, Wash, D C
M Edelin, Wash, D C
L Lucket, Wash, D C
Mattie Jones, Enon, Ala
Octavia Prudhomme, Wash, D C
Helena Ward, Balt, Md
Bena Philips, Warrenton, Va
Mary Jane Robinson, Montg, Ala
Mary Maguire, St Louis, Mo
Anne Lecompte, Wash, D C

$150 reward for runaway Negro man John Henry, aged 42 years. He has a family living with Mr Wm C Clarke, Forest of PG, & a brother living with Mr Danl Clarke, near Upper Marlboro, Md. –A B Howard, living near Davidsonville, Md.

Richmond, Jul 9. The remains of the unfortunate Laurens Hamilton, of the 7th N Y Regt, were this afernoon placed in the Capitol, where they remained till 3 o'clock. They were then escorted by the Richmond regt to the steamer, & a guard of honor, composed of a member of each company, was detailed to accompany the body to N Y.

Norfolk, Jul 9. The capt & crew of the schnr **Francis French** are being tried in the Hustings Court at Smithfield for stealing slaves. Thompson, the steward, plead guilty, & has been sentenced to the penitentiary for 10 years.

Governess wanted to teach 5 children. One who can teach Music & French is required, & a Southern lady preferred. –Robt Beverley, Broad Run Station, Fauquier Co, Va.

MON JUL 12, 1858
Hon Jacob Thompson, Sec of the Interior, has gone to his home in Mississippi, & Mr Kelly, the chief clerk, has ben appointed acting Sec of the Interior during his absence.

Edw D Chamberlain, a freshman in Brown Univ, was drowned in Providence on Tue. He was 18 years old & the only son of his parents, who reside in Boston. He was being towed behind a boat by fellow-students, when the rope broke, & he sunk before they could reach him. He could not swim.

Mr Herman C Gilbert, the commercial editor of the Buffalo Commercial Advertiser, was suddenly killed in that city on Friday last. Some workmen were engaged in removing a platform in front of 14 Central wharf, when Mr Gilbert, happening to pass, seeing that they were short of help, undertook to assist them. The platform fell in a direction not expected, & a heavy timber struck him upon the head.

As the steamer **Ben Loder** was on a pleasure excursion on Geneva Lake, on the evening of the commencement exercises of the Hobart Free College of Geneva. While the party between four & five hundred gentlemen & ladies were in the midst of their hilarity, a young man, Jos A Clark, of Rochester, fell overboard & was drowned. He had been a member of Geneva College, & present at the commencement.

Fearful accident on Jul 4 at Michigan City, when a rocket just fired went into the crowd. Isaac Kennedy, age 13 years, had one cheek entirely carried away. The wife of Dr N G Sherman was struck in the side of the neck & the end stuck out some 6 or 8 inches. A physician was called & removed the rod. The wound is not as dangerous as feared. Dr Sherman is a wealthy & leading citizen of Michigan City, & is absent at Ogdensburg for his health. –Detroit Advertiser

Dr E W Fellows has just been convicted at Buffalo of robbing the mails in 1856. He had been out on bail ever since, & was confident of his acquittal. He is 47 years of age, & has a family. He did not deny his guilt. On hearing the verdict he became entirely prostrated.

On Wed Mr T Talbert was arrested in Nottingham district for an assault with intent to kill, & was taken before John A Goldsborough, magistrate, for examination. He was required to give bail. Talbert refused, & the Justice proceeded to write a commitment to jail. Talbert drew a revolver, &, placing it near Goldsborough's back, fired, causing death by hemorrhage in 5 minutes. Talbet was secured by constable Richardson, with the assistance of bystanders, & was taken to the Marlborough jail. –Star of Saturday

The commencement of the Oxford [Ohio] Female Institute-the first daughter of <u>Mount Holyoke Seminary</u>-occurred on Jun 18. <u>Eight</u> young ladies graduated. The second degree, Laureate of Literture, was conferred upon Miss Adaline Cary. –Springfield [Mass] Republican

U S Patent Ofc, Wash, Jul 9, 1858. Ptn of Fred'k E Sickles, of N Y, praying for the extension of a patent granted to him on Oct 19, 1844, for an improvement in opening & closing valves of steam engines, for 7 years from the expiration, which takes place on Oct 19, 1858. –Jos Holt, Com'r of Patents

Madame Jenny Lind Goldschmidt, with her husband & 2 children, [son & daughter,] arrived in London during the week ending Jun 19th, with the intention of residing in England for some time. The whole family, including domestics, have taken possession of a neat villa called **Rochampton Lodge**, situated on the south side of Barnes Common, & about a mile from Putney.

Explosion at the Manchester Print Works, in Smithfield, R I, on Thu. Killed were Patrick Clarke & David Stewart. Michl Kavanagh is badly injured.

Miss Harrover's School in Gtwn held its annual exhibition on Friday. Duet from Traviata, [instrumental] by Misses Kennon & Harrover; reading from the Gleaner, a school journal, by Misses Plater, Reeside, & Kennon; Life of a Bird, by Miss Annie Shirley; Conjugating Dutchman, by Miss Lizzie Brewer; American Flag by Miss Kate Boggs; Farewell, by Miss Susan Dougty. Miss Harrover's school is the successor of the long known & widely renowned establishment of Miss Lydia English, & since of Rev Mr Clark.

<u>Academy of the Visitation</u> in Wash: annual distribution of premiums took place on Jul 8. The premiums were distributed by Rev Dr Stonestreet, Pres of **Gonzaga College**, in Wash City. Honors were awarded to:

Senior circle:

Cecilia Hanna	Mary H Jones	Mary E Kearns
Emma Norris	Josephine Dyer	Louisa Keating
Kate McNeir	Emma Henning	Eulalia M Shyne

Catharine Gainor	Jane King	Anna Hanna
Rosolia Callan	Harriet Clarke	Mary M Melcher
Mary Kerr	Ellen Grouard	

Junior circle:
Williamanna Fitzpatrick	Catharine Dunnington	Alice Kerr
Virginia Laub	Rosetta Best	Laura Callan
Josephine Handy	Mary M Stuart	
Jane Lenthall	Eliza Stuart	

Honorably mentioned for their good deportment & general observance of the rules:
Rosa Fitzpatrick	Mary Joyce	Anna Handy
Juliana King	Mary V Bentley	Mary R Butt
Ann E Roach	Anna Bentley	Margaret Bentley
Eliz Beasley	Catharine Bates	

Mrd: on Jul 10, at St Matthew's Church, in Wash City, by Rev E Q L Waldron, Jas A Simpson, Artist, of Gtwn, D C, to Mrs Sarah Gibson, of Wash City.

Died: on Jun 28, in Gtwn, Eleanor, relict of the late Henry Paul, in her 76th year. She was a consistent member of the Episcopal Church.

Died: on Jul 1, Mrs Jane Lochrey, wife of Mr Hugh Lochrey, in her 38th year.

Italy: The Prince Royal of Sicily had been married to the Duchess Maria, of Bavaria.

Geneseo, N Y, Jul 9. This afternoon Isaac L Wood, convicted of the murder of his sister-in-law, was executed in the enclosure attached to the jail. He protested his innocence. He appeared to be in considerable agony.

Lexington, Ky, Jul 10. City Marshal Jos Beard was murdered by a man named Barker while endeavoring to arrest him. A crowd collected & hung the murderer, a few hours afterwards. [Jul 15 newspaper: Wm Barker, bully & thief, forced Mr John McChesney into a difficulty. Mr Beard interfered, & told Barker that he must go to the watch-house. Barker walked off some 20 paces with him, & then drawing a small bowie-knife stabbed him in the side, throwing him off the curb. He struck him again. Barker was conveyed to jail. The jailor, Mr Blincoe, was seized & the keys forced from him, & Barker was taken to the court-house. An effort was made by Mr Jas O Harrison, Judge Thomas, & Mr Roger Hanson to induce the mob to wait & let the prisoner be tried & hung by the action of the law, but their voices were drowned in shouts Hang him! Hang him! A beam was thrown out of the 2nd story window & a rope placed around their victim's neck. He was tossed out the window, falling some 6 feet. The rope breaking he fell to the pavement, fracturing his skull. He was again taken up on a ladder & thrown over. This time the rope held & he was left swinging for 2 hours. He was cut down & carried away. Mr Beard was the Democratic candidate for re-election. His leaves a wife & 5 children to mourn his loss, nearly or entirely destitute. Subscription papers are now in circulation, & a thousand dollars has already been raised.]

TUE JUL 13, 1858
Patents issued for the week ending Jul 6, 1858:
J B Benton & Co, of N Y: improvement in machines for raking & loading hay.
R M Berry, of N Y: for improvement in sewing machines.
G W Bishop, of N Y: for improvement in machines in gathering stones.
L R Blake, of Mass: for improvement in sewing machines.
E Brooks, of Pa: for improvement in breech-loading fire-arm.
Zenas Cobb, of Ill: for improvement in railroad car seats & berths.
M E Cronk, of N Y: for improvement in stoppers for bottles.
L A Dole, of Ohio: for improved boring machine.
Zina Doolittle, of Ga: for improved machine for upetting carriage axles.
W Drummond, of N J: for improvement in corn planters.
J Ericsson, of N Y: for improvement in steam engines.
G B Farnham, of Conn: for improvement in pumps.
J J Farrington, of N C: for improvement in mills for cutting, crushing, & expressing the juice from sugar-cane.
J Fleming, of Pa: for improved method of attaching lamps to lanterns.
S Fournier, of La: for improved registering attachment for clocks.
A A Genung, of Ohio: for improvement in pumps.
H Getty, of N Y: for improvement in faucets.
Ira Griggs, of N Y: for improved maching for turning the head & the nicking screws.
J P Harris, of Miss: for improvement in ploughs
R H Harrison, of Md: for improved washing machine.
S H Hartman, of Pa: for improvement in machines for testing the strength of springs.
Wm Hall, of Mass: for improvement in chairs for railways.
G Henderson, of Pa: for improved lathe for turning in metals.
J Hibbs, of Pa: for improvement in the running gear of wagons.
A P Holly, of N Y: for improved rotary pump.
L Holmes, of La: for improved method of constructing iron railings.
D C Hubbard, of Miss: for improvement in cultivators.
G Hubbard, of Mass: for improved measuring faucet.
S Ingersol, of Conn: for improvement in rotating shafts without using a crank.
A Kelly, of N Y: for improvement in skirt hoops.
A R Ketcham, of N Y: for improvement in steam boilers.
J Macnish, of Wis: for improvement in churns.
J P Manny, of Ill: for improvement in raking & binding attachments to harvesters. For improvement in harvesters. For improvement in track cleaners for harvesters. For improvement in harvester fingers. For improved mode of securing grain in bundles or sheaves.
J Mathewman, of Conn: for improved burglar's alarm clock.
T E McNeill, of Pa: for improved dust-pan.
M Maerk, of N Y: for improvement in hill-side ploughs.
J Mitchell, of N Y: for improvement in harvesters.
J J Parker, of Ohio: for improved maching for paring, slicing, & coring apples.
J G Perry, of R I: for improved sausage filler.
L Plonk, of N C: for improvement in machines for stuffing horse collars.

J H Quackenbush, of Mich: for improvement in railroad car couplings.
L Eacine, of Ill: for improvement in ventilating mill stones.
J Reed, of Mass: for maching for leathering tacks.
L O Rice, of Canada: for improvement in attaching carriage springs.
C L Russell, of Ct: for machine for leathering tacks.
E S Scripture, of Conn: for improved sash holder.
A Smith, of Ala: for improvement in cotton cultivators.
H B Smith, of Mass: for improved arrangement of devices for planing mouldings.
G H Soule, of N J: for improvement in breech-loading firearm.
W R Stace, of N Y: for tailor's measure.
W Staufen, of England: for improvement in treatment of fibre of Tampico hemp.
C A Stancliff, of Pa: for improvement in continuous chair-rails.
H W Taylor, of Pa: for improved nail machine.
J F Taylor, of S C: for improvement in rice hulling machines.
P P Taft, of Vt: for improvement in corn shellers.
R M Wade, of Va: for trunk protector.
R P Walker, of N Y: for improvement in machines for hulling rice.
W P Ware, of Ohio: for ear, cheek, & chin muff.
S W Warren, of N Y: for steam alarm & safety apparatus.
B H Washington, of Mo: for improvement in furnaces.
H E West, of Mass: for improvement in machines for pressing straw bonnets & other articles of varying thickness.
F Wolle, of Pa: for improvement in machines for making paper bags.
E S Wright, of N Y: for improved bedstead fastening.
H Yates, of Canada: for improvement in furnaces of steam boilers.
A Burnham, of Mass: for improvement in railway bridge signalizer.
W Darker, jr, of Pa: for improved water metre.
J Ewing, of N Y: for improved stopper for bottles.
J F Faust, of Ohio: for improvement in horse hay rakes.
W S Gale, of N Y: for improved valve regulator.
W J Granger, of Ill: for improved punch for perforating metal.
W C Grimes, of Pa: for improvement in water & steam indicators. For improved pressure gauge.
L A Grover, of Mass: for improvement in corn huskers.
J P Lipps, of N J: for improved lock.
J Lowe, of N Y: for improved magnetic steam-gauge.
G D Sargent, of Mass: for improved burglar's alarm clock.
N P Whittlesey, of Conn: for improved faucet.

Mrd: on Jul 7, at the Va Hot Springs, by Rev Dr Empie, of Richmond, Col Chas Hopkins to Miss Rose Baldwin, all of Bath Co, Va.

Orphans Court of Wash Co, D C. In the case of Francis S Walsh, exc of Venerando Palizzi, deceased, the executor & Court have appointed Aug 3 next, for the final settlement of the personal estate of said deceased, of the assets in hand.
-Ed N Roach, Reg/o wills

Information received of the sudden death of Lt Magruder of this city, while on his way to Great Salt with the Utah army. His death was caused by another man, a quarrel having arisen between them, which resulted in the shooting of Lt Magruder. His parents reside in this city. –States [Jul 14th newspaper: Headquarters 6th Column Utah Forces, Camp near the Blue, Jun 29, 1858. Brvt Lt John S Magruder, 1st cavalry, was killed in Marysville last night, in an unfortunate encounter with a citizen of Marysville named Poor. Lt Plummer, of the 7th infty, & Lt Wildrick, of the artl, both belonging to the 5th column, were present. Lt Berry, with 2 officers & 10 men, were immediately dispatched to bring in the body of Lt Magruder, & aid the civil authorites to bring the murderer to justice. -W H Emory, Maj 1st cavalry, commanding 6th column U F.]

New Orleans paper: A duel between 2 newspaper reporters in that city between Jos Hanlon, reporter for the True Delta, & Israel Gibbons, for the Crescent. The weapons were dueling pistols, distance 12 paces. Mr Gibbons received a ball that was not extremely dangerous. Mr Hanlon escaped uninjured, the ball cutting his coat.

Wash City police. The Board of Aldermen confirmed the Mayor's nomination of Noble J Thomas as a Lt of Police, & the following 40 additional policemen:

Danl Whalen	Thos J Edmonston	Alfred Henning
Robt H Harrison	Laurence Malone	John Barnes
John M Thornton	John G Stafford	Wm L Hatton
Jas Belt	Jas Scarff	Jos Luckett
John Kidwell	Thos Stone	John Joy
John W Coomes	Thos Sutton	Richd Evans
Thos J Kelly	Wm Owens Neale	John T Bradley
Jos S Norwood	Benj Kirtz	Peter Goodyear
Dennis Murphy	Wm Rabbit	Geo H Morgan
Fred'k Schafer	Philip Hutchinson	John Browers
Michl Fitzgerald	Jas R Gates	John J Lacy
Martin McNamara	Wm Johnson	Alex'r Humes
Thos Young	R H Digges	
John F Carter	Peter Kraft	

Died: on Jul 11, in Wash City, of pulmonary consumption, in his 21st year, Chas F M Grammer, a son of the late G C Grammer. His funeral will take place this afternoon at 6 o'clock, from his late residence, on 11th st, between G & H sts.

Died: at the residence of her grandfather, J F Caldwell, Fanny Wickliff, infant daughter of Col Lafayette & Francis C Caldwell, of West Baton Rouge, La. Her funeral is tomorrow at 10 o'clock, from 623 Md ave. [No death date given.]

Died: Joel D Fairbanks, aged 35 years. His funeral will take place from the Nat'l Hotel at 1 o'clock this day. [No death date given.]

Died: on Jul 12, of cholera infantum, little Harriet Penelope, infant daughter of Hom Wm F & Mary F E Pursell, aged 1 month & 22 days. Her funeral will take place this afternoon at 5 o'clock, at her father's residence, 316 Delaware ave, near the north gate of the Capitol.

WED JUL 14, 1858
N Y, Jul 12, 1858. 1-Vice-Pres Tompkins died on Jun 11, 1825, in his 51st year. His health had been failing for several years previous. 2-The body of Laurens Hamilton, a member of the 7th Regt, arrived with the Richmond escort, & arrangements for the funeral have been made. The relatives of the deceased requested that there be no military parade. It seems Mr Hamilton was sick when he went on board the boat at Richmond, & in the absence of his attendant, fainted & fell over the railing into the water.

Gen Ward B Burnett has accepted the Surveyor-Generalship of Kansas, & will shortly proceed to that Territory. –States

At the Patriotic Bank of Wash meeting of the stockholders on Jul 6, the following named gentlemen were elected Trustees for the ensuing year:

John Purdy	David Saunders	J F W Kenney
Wm Orme	C L Coltman	M G Emery
W J McDonald	John H Semmes	Edw Hall

The Irish papers announce the death of the Earl of Glengall on Jun 22, rather suddenly at Cowes, Isle of Wight. He was 64 years of age. In default of male issues the earldom becomes extinct. He was the author of the popular farce, The Irish Tutor, & other dramatic works.

Chicago, Jul 12. Mr Lincoln addressed a large concourse of people on Sat night, in reply to Senator Douglas' speech delivered the night before. There were an estimated 5,000 persons in attendance & considerable enthusiasm was manifested.

Trial on Monday of Barrett & Williams for the murder of Reeve Lewis. Jury formed, consisting mostly of talesmen from Gtwn: Alex M Smith, John F Campbell, Jas Murray, Wm Smith Hyde, Theodore Boucher, Geo Shoemaker, jr, W R Hurdle, Wm H Ernest, David W Oyster, Geo W Godey, Irwin S Barker, & Jas Fullalove. Witnesses: Jos M Carrico; Mr Isaac Entwisle; Mr Aug Klopfer; Ofcr Jos Williamson; Ofcr R H Degges; Capt Goddard; Mr Wm Mulloy; Wm Gibbs [residence on B st, Capitol Hill;] & Dr A W Miller-had known Henry Williams about 10 or 12 months. [Williams lived about a year in Washington, & had previously resided in Balt.] [Jul 15th newspaper: witnesses sworn: Wm H Thompson, a watchman at the Capitol; Wm A Mulloy, a watchman at the Capitol; & W W Bassett.] [Jul 16th newspaper: yesterday the jury returned with a verdict of guilty of murder in the case of Chas Barrett & manslaughter in that of Henry Williams. Barrett burst into tears. Williams appeared unaffected.] [Aug 7th newspaper: Barrett was sentenced to be hanged on Oct 22 next. Henry Williams was then sentenced to 8 years' hard labor & confinement in the penitentiary.]

Wedding Presents: M W Galt & Bro, Jewellers, 324 Penn av, Wash City. [Ad]

St John's College, Annapolis, Md, will resume on Oct 6, 1858. Rev C K Nelson, D D, Principal.

Leavenworth, Jun 8. Judge Cato has resigned his position as District Judge.

New Orleans, Jul 13. Gen Quitmen is lying seriously ill. Doubts are expressed of his recovery.

Com'r sale of valuable land in Alexandria Co, Va, by decree of the Circuit Court of Alexandria Co, rendered at its May term, 1858, in the case of Swann, etc, vs Dempsey & others: public auction on Aug 21 next, of a tract of land in said county, containing about 260 acres, being the property on which Dr R B Alexander resided, & of which he died seized. Also, a tract of land, adjoining, with the Factory Bldg & water power thereon. The property lies on the waters of Four Mile Run, about 3 miles from the city of Alexandria. –F L Smith, L B Taylor, I Louis Kinzer, Com'rs of Sale.

THU JUL 15, 1858
Household & kitchen furniture at auction on Jul 21, at the residence of C B Adams, on 10th st, between L & M sts. -Jas C McGuire, auct

Four brothers were accidentally drowned at Balt on Sunday last: John, Wm, Michl, & Thos Persley, respectively aged 26, 24, 22, & 19 years. They were all intoxicated & not in condition to navigate the boat they were in that capsized. –Exchange

The copartnership under the firm of Marsh & Voss is dissolved this day by mutual consent. O W Marsh will continue the Grocery business at the old stand, corner of 10th st & Pa ave. –O W Marsh, H H Voss

West Point Academy: members numbered according to the merit of their examination. The following order has been assigned to the five in each class who acquitted themselves best at the last examination:
First or Graduating Class: Wm C Paine, Mass; Moses J White, Miss; Jos Dixon, Tenn; Wm H Echols, Ala; John J Saunders, at large.
Second Class: Wm E Merrill, at large; Saml H Lockett, Ala; Chas R Collins, Penn; Orlando G Wagner, Penn; Chauncey B Reese, N Y.
Third Class: Walter McFarland, N Y; John A Tardy, jr, N Y; Horace Porter, Penn; Nicholas Bowen, N Y; Benj F Sloan, jr, S C.
Fourth Class: Henry A Dupont, at large; Henry W Kingsbury, N Y; Chas E Cross, Mass; Llewyllin G Hoxton, at large; Orville E Babcock, Vt.
Fifth Class: Arthur H Dutton, Conn; Francis U Farquhar, Penn; Patrick H O'Rooke, N Y; Chas C Parsons, Ohio; Richd M Hill, at large.

Mrd: on Jul 18, by Rev Dr Sunderland, Wm H Allen, son of Hon J W Allen, to Clara Augusta Gale, daughter of Dr L D Gale, all of Wash City.

Calif: the defeat of Col Steptoe is confirmed. His command fell into an ambuscade, & was attacked by a large number of Indians. He was formed to retreat with a loss of 7 killed & 15 wounded. The troops were not sufficiently supplied with ammunition. [Jul 16th newspaper: among the killed were 2 officers, Capt O H P Taylor & Lt Gaston. The officers of the command were Col Steptoe, Capts Winder & Taylor, Lts Wheeler, Fleming, Gaston, & Gregg. We were surrounded by six or eight hundred Indians. Sgt Ball, of Co H, is missing. Capt Taylor was shot through the neck, & Lt Gaston through the body. They both fell fighting gallantly. List of the killed or wounded: in Co C, 1st Dragoons, Brvt Capt O H Taylor, & private Alfred Barnes; in Co E, 1st Dragoons, private Chas H Hamish & Jas Crozet. Wounded: in Co C, 1st Dragoons, privates T C D May, Jas Lynch, Henry Montreville, & farrier E R Birch; in Co E, 1st Dragoons, 1st Sgt W C Williams; privates Jas Kelly, Wm D Misco_, Hariet Metchu, Jas Healy, Maurice Henly, Chas Hughes & John Mitchell; in Co E, 9th Infty, privates Ormond W Hammond, John Klay, & Gilbert Berger. Missing: in Co H, 1st Dragoons, 1st Sgt Edw Ball. Capt O H P Taylor was a graduate of West Point, of 1846, & brevet capt for gallant & meritorious conduct in conflicts in New Mexico. It is but a few weeks since he returned from the East with his wife & children, who are now widowed & orphaned. Lt Wm Gaston was a graduate of 1856, & an officer of great promise. We believe that Col Steptoe was decoyed into a position by the cunning treachery of Kamaikin & duplicity of friendly Indians, in whom the officers of the regular army place entirely too much confidence, where it was impossible to extricate himself.] [Jul 20th newspaper: Capt O H P Taylor was the youngest son of the late Capt Wm V Taylor, U S Navy, of this city, killed in the battle between Col Steptoe's command & a large body of Indians. His wife & little ones were with him at the time of the battle. –Newport [R I] Mercury]

Terrible affray in Lawrenceburg, Ky, in Anderson Co, on Fri last, two young men named Miller, from Wash Co, became excited with liquor, & on an attempt being made to quiet them, assaulted 4 men, there of whom were brothers by the name of Lurcy. Two of the Lurcys were killed, the 3rd mortally wounded, & the fourth man shot dead. The murderers have been arrested.

It will be rememberd by our readers that Mr Albert Sumner, of Newport, R I, his wife & child, some time since, were shipwrecked & all undoubtedly perished. By the presumptions of law, the wife & child died first, & the husband became entitled to the property. Mrs Sumner was a daughter of the late Walter Channing, of this city, & enjoyed the income of a large estate. Under these circumstances, more than $30,000 became legally vested in the late Mr Sumner, & through him came to his mother & sister & his 2 brothers, Chas Sumner, our Senator, & Geo Sumner. The estate was administered upon by Mr Geo Sumner, &, with the consent of all the heirs, the whole property which the deceased had derived from his wife has been surrendered to her relations. It gives us great pleasure to record an act so honorable to the parties, & prompted by so nice a sense of justice & equity. –Boston Granscript, Jul 10

FRI JUL 16, 1858
At Carmel, Maine, on Sat, the two only children of Lewis Robinson, aged 6 & 4 years, were drowned while bathing.

N Y, Jul 14. 1-Saml B Ruggles, a well known citizen of this city, has been appointed by Gov King as Canal Com'r to fill the vacancy occasioned by the death of Mr Whalton. 2-Fatal accident at 8 Gold st yesterday when a test by members of the Gas Co caused a cylinder to explode, killing J W Sharpe, breaking the right leg of Mortimer Lee, & wounding Thos Bent & Barney Elisler.

Artificial leather. Mr F C Jeune, of London, is the orginator of a process for producing an elastice material having the appearance of patent leather, but not liable like it to crack or peal on the surface.

A young man drowned. Douglas Harrington, age 22, residing with his father on 5th st, between G & H sts, was brought yesterday to Wash City, by his younger brother, Richmond Harrington, with whom he had gone to have a day's fishing on the Eastern Branch. It appears that Douglas undertook to swim across the river, where it is nearly a mile wide, & sank to rise no more. Douglas was a painter by trade.

Died: on Jul 14, in Wash City, Mrs Frances Jackson, wife of John Jackson, of Augusta, Ga. Her funeral will take place from the residence of her son-in-law, Lawson P Hoover, 160 G st, on Jul 16, at 4 o'clock.

Died: on Jul 4, at New Orleans, Mary Louisa, consort of Edw B Wheelock, & daughter of the late Capt Clack, U S Navy. Although young in years she was a bright example of the virtues which serve to adorn the female character. –R

Died: on Jun 19, in Calif, at Buena Ventura, the residence of Major Reading, Emily Montoya Briceland, wife of J N Briceland, of Shasta City, & daughter of the late S P Walker, of Wash City.

Health Report. Ofc of the Com'r of Health, Wash, Jul 15, 1858. Monthly report of deaths in Wash City for Jun, 1858: 137. –Chas F Force, Com'r of Health.

Dr T F Maury has removed his office to the s e corner of 4½ & C sts.

SAT JUL 17, 1858
Naval Court Martial recently in session in Wash City, for the trial of Cmder Boutwell, U S Navy, on certain charges & specifications, involving disobedience of orders while under Cmdor Mervine, in the Pacific squadron, which were brought against him by the Navy Dept. Cmder Boutwell was found guilty on all the charges & specifications, & sentenced to be dismissed from the service. Pres Buchanan has mitigated this punishment, by ordering in its stead, the suspension from the service of Cmder Boutwell for 5 years, on furlough pay. -Star

Stock & fixtures of a Family Grocery at auction, on Jul 19, at the store of Mr J McNew, 7th & K sts. [He is about to decline on account of ill health.] -Bontz & Coombs, aucts

Circuit Court of Wash Co, D C-in Chancery, No 1,397. Rebecca Williams vs Harriet Bodisco, Lloyd A Williams, Jas Beck, jr, et al. The object of the bill is to procure the appointment of a new trustee to carry into effect the trust & provisions of a certain deed of trust from Harriet Williams to Washington Beck, dated Jun 24, 1835,. The bill states that on Jun 24, 1835, Harriet Williams conveyed a certain tract of land in Gtwn, D C, with the bldgs & improvements thereon; upon certain trust fully set forth in said deed, & among others in trust upon the request in writing of said Rebecca, attested by 2 respectable witnesses, to sell & convey in fee said tract of land or any part or parts thereof. The bill of cmplnts further states that since the execution of said deed said Washington Beck has died intestate as to said property, leaving his brother, Jas Beck, his sole heir at law; that said Jas Beck has since died intestate as to the said real estate, leaving his only child & son, Jas Beck, jun, his heir at law. It appearing to the satisfaction of the Court that said Jas Beck, jr, son & heir at law of said Jas Beck, & Harriet Bodisco reside beyond the limits of the District of Columbia, & the absent dfndnts are to appear, by solicitor or in person, at the Clerk's ofc of said Court, on the first Monday of Dec next. -Jas Dunlop, Ch J -Jno A Smith, clerk

Army order: Maj Jeremiah Y Dashiell, pay dept, having failed to explain satisfactorily a deficiency in his accounts of public money, & having failed to obey repeated instructions from the Paymaster-Genr'l to pay over the balance acknowledged by him to be in his hands, the President directs that he be dismissed the service of the U S, in obedience to the act of Jan 31, 1823. Maj Dashiell accordingly ceases to be an officer of the army from this date-Jul 10, 1858. By order of the Sec of War. –E D Townsend, Assist Adj Genr'l

Louis Ran, of Cincinnati, a German, was caught by a hand on some machinery he was adjusting, & drawn through a narrow place & instantly crushed to death.

Rev R W Barnwell, of S C, has been elected Pres of Wm & Mary College, vice Mr Ewell, who resigned the position. Mr Taliaferro, of Gloucester, Va, has been elected professor of Latin & Latin Literature.

The bldg cmte of St Andrew's Free Church met on Friday at the ofc of Mr Chas Haskins, the architect, & awarded the contract for bldg this church to Mr Jos W Angus, of Wash City. The price is about $30,000. It is to be erected on the lot at the circle on 14th st, which was given to the church by Hon Caleb Cushing.

Criminal Court-Wash-Fri. 1-Michl Shea was put on trial for assault with intent to kill Jos Fletcher, on election day, by shooting at him with a pistol. The evidence was flimsy, & the jury acquitted the traverser. 2-John Falay, with 2 other aliases, & Andrew Kidwell were tried for arson & found guilty. The Court will grant a new trial because of the manner in which the premises were described in the indictment.

Mrd: on Jun 29, at **Monmouth**, near Natches, Miss, at the residence of the bride's father, by Rev J H Ingraham, Lt Wm S Lovell, U S Navy, to J Antonia, 2nd daughter of Gen John A Quitman.

Died: on Jul 15, at his residence, in Fairfax Co, Va, Rev Alonzo Hayes, formerly of N H, aged 48 years. His funeral is today at 1 o'clock P M.

Died: yesterday, Harriet Elizabeth, infant daughter of Henry C & Harriet Hepburn, aged nearly 12 months. Her funeral is this afternoon at 4 o'clock, from the residence of her grandfather, Mr Wm Cooper.

Died: on Jul 8, at Dalton, Ga, in his 33rd year, Lt John Dorsey Read, U S Navy, youngest son of the late Geo Read, of Newcastle, Delaware.

Died: on Jun 15, at *Longevity*, Chas Co, Md, Caroline E Pye, relict of the late John A Pye, in her 66th year. In her life she was a kind mother, an affectionate wife, & a sincere Christian.

Died: on Jul 10, at Salem, Fauquier Co, Va, Mr Thos Allen, in his 60th year, a highly respectable citizen, & esteemed by all who knew him.

Died: on Jul 14, at Cold Spring, Putnam Co, N Y, Fannie H M, daughter of Lt Col B L Beall, U S Army, aged 14 years & 5 months.

Died: on Tue, at his residence, near Marlboro, Md, Capt John Brookes, having nearly completed the 71st year of his age. In his earlier manhood he served his country, with fidelity & credit. He had been a most useful citizen. –Planter's Advocate

$300 reward for runaway servant man David Diggs, aged about 35 years, light copper color, last seen at Mr Queen's, on 7th st. –Josiah Harding, Cottage P O, Montg Co, Md

N Y, Jul 16. Disastrous railroad accident near Shin Hollow, 75 miles from N Y C, & 2 rear cars were thrown down an embankment 30 feet. Killed were: Mrs Adam Ray, Wm Childer- a boy; H Wood; a child of Mr Louis Lay, of New Orleans; & a child of Mr Brown, of Tioga Valley. Wounded: Mr Lay & wife, of New Orleans, slightly; Mr & Mrs Brown, of Tioga Valley, are badly hurt. [Jul 19th newspaper: the six persons killed outright are a son of Mr Brown, of Tiogo Co; the child of Mr R P Turner, of N Y; Mrs Ray, colored, of Binghampton; Mr G W Robertson, of N Y; Mr Harvey Wood, of Wellsburg, Tioga Co, Pa; & Mr Schultz, of Buffalo.]

MON JUL 19, 1858
We have received from the plantation of Mr Geo S Yerger, of Mississippi, a choice specimen of cotton yarn produced by the application of the famous invention of Mr Geo G Henry. We may confidently predict that, within a few years. Mr Henry's carding & spinning machinery will become an inseparable adjunct to the cotton gin.
-Richmond Enquirer

Luis G Osollo, cmder-in-chief of the Mexican army, died at San Luis Potosi on Jun 16, in his 30th year. He had been lingering for some time under an attack of fever.

The colossal Church of St Isaac, the largest in Europe, with the exception of St Peter's, in Rome, has just been finished & dedicated with great pomp & ceremony in St Petersburg. The church was commenced by Alexander I, in 1818. Under Emperor Nicholas great progress was made in the bldg, but he did not live to witness its completion. In the retinue of the Emperor, during the procession, was the aged but still robust & active architect of the edifice, Montferret, who has been presented with 40,000 rubles & an annual pension of 5,000 rubles, [to be continued to his wife in case she survives him,] & has been raised to the rank of an actual Councillor of State. There is no organ, as the Greek Church allows no instrumental music of any kind, & likewise interdicts female voices in the house of God. The bells too must only be sounded by striking, not ringing.

The fine steam-cutter **Harriet Lane** returned to Wash City Sat after a 5 day excursion upon the Potomac, James, York, & Chesapeake. The party on board: Miss Lane, Lady Ouseley & daughter, Miss Macalester, Mrs Clayton & daughter, Mrs Hughes, & the Misses Bright; Hon Howell Gobb, Sir Wm Gore Ouseley, Count Sartiges, Mr Aug Schell, Hon Elijah Ward, Hon J M Sandidge, Mr Macalester, Mr Henry, Mr Benj Ogle Tayloe, Mr Ro Magraw, Mr C H Scharff, Mr R W Hughes, & Master Wm Clayton.
-Union

Geo W Nesmith has prepared a very interesting memoir of Ebenezer Webster, the father of Danl Webster. It is published in the Concord [N H] Statesman. The office Ebenezer Webster last held at the time of his death in 1806, at age 67 years, was a judge of the court of Common Pleas which he held for 15 years. He served in the old French war, was a capt in the military during the Revolution, & a colonel in 1784. He was about 6 feet tall, of a massy frame, a voice of great compass, & eyes black & piercing.
-Boston Transcript

At N Y on Friday evening, 5 young women, named Azjaval Van Gilder, 14; Hannah H Bryan, 15; Ellen Smith, 15; Margaret Flynn, 16; & Louisa Ever, 19, all inmates of the House of Mercy under the care of Mrs Richmond, in 86th st, proceeded to the river for the purpose of bathing. They got beyond their depth, & being unable to swim, sank to the bottom. All were drowned. It is feared that the tide has carried the bodies further out into the river. -N Y Express

Criminal Court-Wash-Sat. 1-Jas P Alston, a young man, was tried for assault & battery with intent to kill John E Turner, also a young man, by stabbing him with a knife on Jun 11 last, in a quarrel. His mother & his brother were witnesses for the defence. A third brother was a witness for the prosecution. The jury found Alston guilty of assault & battery, but not of intent to kill. He was sentenced to 6 months' imprisonment in the county jail & a fine of $20. His widowed mother lies on a bed of sickness & in a great measure dependent on him. 2-Danl Moriarty, a man of remarkable size & strength, was charged with violently resisting ofcr Harrover in the execution of his duty on Jul 5, at a tavern, on Capitol Hill. The jury found him not guilty.

Died: on Jul 18, of diarrhoea, Eleanor Williams, youngest child of Mr & Mrs M H Miller, aged 4 months & 24 days. Her funeral is this evening at 6 o'clock, from the residence of the family, 512 M st.

Died: on Jul 8, at his residence, in Wmsburg, Lucian Minor, professor of law in the College of Wm & Mary. He will be mourned, not by his own immediate family alone, but by a large circle of attached friends.

Jas C McGuire has this day associated with him in the auction & commission business his son, F B McGuire, & Thos J Fisher, under the name of Jas C McGuire & Co.

New Orleans, Jul 17. Gen John A Quitman died this morning at his residence, near Natchez. [Jul 20th newspaper: Gen Quitman was about 60 years of age & a native of N Y; migrated at an early age to Mississippi, where he became a planter, & in political life one of the distinguished men of the State. In 1846-47 he volunteered for the Mexican war, & was appointed by Pres Polk a Major Genr'l.]

$100 reward for runaway negro boy John Campbell, aged about 17. –Hezekiah Brawner, Chas Co, Md.

Selling off all Fancy Dress silks, Berege & Lawn Robes, Swiss Muslins, Ginghams, & French Chintzes. -J W Colley, 523 7th st, 3 doors north of Penn ave.

Orphans Court of Wash Co, D C. Letters of administration on personal estate of John J S Hassler, late of Ripley, Jackson Co, Va, deceased. –Eliz S Hassler, Walter D Davidge, adms

TUE JUL 20, 1858
Cleveland Herald. Tribute to public virtue. Judge McLean is one of the most eminent of the Justices of the U S Supreme Court on the bench of the Circuit Court, now in session in Hoffman's block. He is now about 73 years of age, born in Morris Co, N J, in 1785; admitted to the bar in 1807; in 1812 became a candidate for Congress & was elected; & in 1814 re-elected to Congress. Pres Monroe appointed him a Com'r of the Genr'l Land Ofc in 1822 & Postmaster Genr'l in 1823. In 1829 he was appointed by Pres Jackson a Justice of the U S Supreme Cout, & entered upon his duties at the Jan term of 1830, & he has been in service over 28 years.

Trustee's sale by deed of trust from Henry Carl & wife, recorded in Liber J A S No 151, one of the land records for Wash Co, D C: auction on Aug 23, the following real estate in Wash City: lot 26 in square 499, fronting on 4½ st 47 feet, with a two story brick house. –Chas Walter, trustee -A Green auct

Chancery sale of valuable property on D st, next to the Nat'l Intelligencer Ofc: by decree of the Circuit Court of Wash Co, D C, passed in the cause of Shuster & Clagett vs I F Mudd et al, No 1,301, on Mar 12, 1858: public auction on Aug 12, part of lot 3 in square 431, with the bldg thereon. –Wm R Woodward, trustee -A Green auct

Ambrose S Skeeles, formerly of Lockport, N Y, murdered his wife by cutting her throat, at Cedar Rapids, Iowa, on Jul 1st, & then committed suicide by the same operation. They had been married some 15 years, & on the 3rd year of their marriage they separated. Mrs Skeeles lately took measures to procure a divorce. Mrs Skeeles' maiden name was Bulah C Vinton.

Last week in Marshall Co, Ky, a tree on the farm of Mr Thos Reed was struck by lightning. Two sons of Mr Reed were instantly killed, & two others were severely injured, one of whom is not expected to recover. Two horses were killed by the stroke.

I will sell at private sale the Farm upon which I now reside, called **Montazile**, on Hanson's Branch, PG Co, Md, 6 miles from Wash, containing 150 acres. The dwlg is a large & handsome frame bldg; & two barns capable of curing 25,000 weight of tobacco. Address, Wash, D C, J H Bowling.

Valuable real estate for sale: by decree of the Circuit Court of Montg Co, Md, in Equity. Private sale of the real estate of Thos Hunter, late of said county, deceased, called **Windsor**, containing 500 acres of land, more or less, with a commodious dwlg, & all the necessary out-bldgs for a farm. This farm is on the west side of the road leading from Wash to Fredericktown, 1½ miles from Rockville. Apply to the undersigned, near Rockville, Montg Co, Md. S G K Hunter, trustee

Mrd: on Jul 15, by Rev Mr Morsell, John H Sothoron to Virginia D, daughter of the late Notely L Adams, of Wash City.

Died: on Jul 1, at **Fort Moultrie**, near Charleston, S C, *Abert Byrne, aged 13 months & 1 day, the youngest son of Louisa A & Surgeon B M Byrne, U S Army.
[*Abert as written.]

WED JUL 21, 1858
N Y C, Jul 19. The death of Alderman Wm Murray is the second of the Board which has occurred since Jan 1st.

Wm T Porter, well known for his long connexion with the "Spirit of the Times," died at N Y on Monday last.

Geo E Dunham, a junior of **Yale College**, drowned in the Conn river on Sat, while practicing for the regatta of Jul 23, when a collision occurred with another boat.

On Fri Dr O D Wilcox committed suicide at Elmira, N Y. He had amputated a leg for a man, Mr Hammond, in Chemung, who soon afterwards died. Dr Wilcox was charged with mal-practice, & criminal proceedings were instituted against him. He took some deadly poison & died in half an hour.

Criminal Court-Wash-Tue. Trial of Augustus Heisler & Geo Johnson for the murder of Marcellus Stoops, on Apr 3 last. Jury: Adam Gaddis, Jas F Scott, Terence Drury, Henry C Purdy, John G Dorry, Esau Pickrell, Benj Darby, A W Delzell, John Cruikshank, Wm Dowling, Benj H Sothoron, & Geo W Bohrer. The prisoners were remanded to jail.

Yesterday a young man, Tobias Rawlings, at work in the Gov't marble-cutting yard near the jail, dropped suddenly down, & in a few minutes expired. Cause supposed to be disease of the heart. He was about 24 years of age, & leaves a wife & 2 children.

Orphans Court of Wash Co, D C. In the case of the heirs of Wm Ferguson, deceased, the trustee reported he sold part of lot 8 in square 51, for $347, & the purchaser was Michl Donohoe, who paid one-half of the said sum in cash, & gave his note for the balance, payable at 6 months from this date, with interest until paid. –Wm F Purcell

Equity, No 1,075. John F Sharretts, exc of Saml Brereton, against Wm H Brereton, Saml Brereton, John Hoover, & Eliza Ann Brereton. I am directed to state the account of the late Saml Brereton, & to distribute the assets among his reps: at my ofc in the City Hall, Wash, on Aug 12 next. –W Redin, auditor

Mrd: on Jul 6, at the residence of Mrs Sterling Clairborne, Nelson Co, Va, by Rev Mr Martin, Robt Taylor Berry to Miss Mattie J, daughter of Jos K Irving.

Mrd: on Jul 20, at Charlestown, Jefferson Co, Va, by Rev C E Ambler, Thos K Wallace, of Wash City, to Helen V, daughter of Saml Stone.

Died: on Jul 20, in Wash City, Joanna Auchmuty, infant daughter of Major & Mrs E D Townsend. Her funeral will take place from her father's residence, 339 21st st, this afternoon at 5½ o'clock.

Died: on Jul 17, in Wash City, in Christian triumph, Rosina E Vermillion, formerly of Chas Co, Md, wife of Clinton Vermillion, in her 23rd year.

Died: on Jul 19, at Richmond, Va, in his 33rd year, Mr Robt J Wiglesworth, printer, foreman of the "South" newspaper, & formerly a mail agent.

Died: on Jul 19, at Hampstead, Stafford Co, Va, Samuel J, infant son of John & Louisa E Potts, of Wash City. His funeral is this morning at 10 o'clock, from the residence of his father, 497 17th st.

Died: on her way, with an aged mother, to visit a sister in Ky, near or at Portsmouth, Ohio, Miss Abilgail Gillett, daughter of the late Rev Eliphalett Gillett, D D, of Hallowell, Maine. She left this city in feeble health on Wed last. Her last hour came, & her widowed parent, alone among strangers, stands a mourner by her grave. To that mother one only of eleven children survives. This beloved daughter had been a companion, solace, support, & joy. [No death date given.]

THU JUL 22, 1858
The Mobile Register announces the death, on Jul 13, at Macon, Miss, of J H Dunn, lately appointed Consul at Havana.

Govn'r Ujhazy, the Hungarian patriot & exile, has been in N Y a few days, & left Sat to return to his home in Texas. He was on his way from Europe, whither he has been to visit the members of his family. As the Austrian Gov't would not allow him to enter Hungary, his relatives were obliged to meet him in Belgium. The interview took place in Ghent. His daughter, Madame Madrasz, accompanied him back to America.

Criminal Court-Wash-Wed. 1-The case of the U S against Augustus Heissler & Geo Johnson, charged with the murder of Marcellus Stoops on Apr 3 last. Thos Brown & Edw Meads are included in the indictment. Mr W B B Cross, one of the prosecuting attys; & Mr Norris, for the defence. Witnesses examined: Wm Johnson; Fred'k Manayette; Mrs Martha Hensley was standing at the corner of 9th & N Y ave; Nicholas Drummond was an officer at the time; John Houck saw Wm Johnson; Justice T C Donn called by defence; & Mr F Augustus Klopfer testified. [Jul 23rd newspaper: witnesses of Tue: Patrick Gormley; Ofcr Suit; Van Loman Johnson, brother of Geo Johnson, one of the dfndnts; Mr Ratcliffe; Dr Butt; Ofcr Birkhead; Washington Dougherty; & Mr Ould.] [Aug 7th newspaper: Heissler & Geo Johnson were sentenced to 8 years each in the penitentiary on the verdict for manslaughter, & an additional 7 years each, to take effect after the expiration of the term of the former sentence, on their conviction of the robbery of John C Cornell.]

U S Patent Ofc, Wash, Jul 20, 1858. Ptn of Philos B Tyler, of Springfield, Mass, praying for the extension of a patent granted to him on Jan 16, 1845, for an improvement in steam cotton presses, for 7 years from the expiration of said patent, which takes place on Jan 16, 1859. –Jos Holt, Com'r of Patents

Mrd: on Jul 20, at Phil, by Rev Thos J Shepperd, Jacob Gideon, of Wash City, to Miss Julia Hewitt, of Phil, eldest daughter of the late John Hewitt, formerly of Wash.

Died: on Jul 16, in Wash City, in his 45th year, John H Somervell, formerly of Anne Arundel Co, Md.

Died: on Jul 21, Robert, 2nd son of A H & Emma Derrick, in his 11th year. His funeral is this afternoon at 4 o'clock, from the residence of his parents, 82 Pa ave.

Died: on Jul 20, in Gtwn, in his 69th year, Richd Jeffries, of Richmond, formerly Clerk of the U S Court for the Eastern District of Va.

Died: on Jul 20, suddenly, Alex'r Rollings, in his 26th year. His funeral is this afternoon at 4 o'clock, from his late residence, on F st, between 1st & 2nd sts. The Journey-men Stonecutters' Association is respectfully invited to attend.

Phil, Jul 21. An accident occurred today on the Lehigh Valley railroad, which has been greatly exaggerated. The bridge broke down & Joel Fields & Wm Landis were killed.

D J Bishop & Co have purchased all Mr S Decamp's interest in the Book & Stationery business, 438 Pa ave, & will continue to do business at the old stand.

Armand Jardine against Henry Naylor, Jas C McGuire, Thos Berry, W S Cox, Wm Emmert, Honorine Jardine, Albertine, Louisa, Miriam, Agricola, Malvina, & Theresa Favier. The parties above named & the creditors of the late A Favier are notified that on Jul 30, at my ofc, in the City Hall, Wash, I shall state the trustee's account of further assets received & distribute the same among the creditors & parties. –W Redin, auditor

FRI JUL 23, 1858
Executor's sale of horse, carryall, cart, harness, & furniture, at the residence of the late Henry Carl, 4½ & K sts, [Island,] by order of the Orphans Court of Wash Co, D C.
-Jno Walters, exc -Jas C McGuire, auct

Trustee's sale of very superior 3 story & basement brick house & lot on north M, next to 10th st, at auction: on Aug 16 next, by deed of trust from Jos B Tate, dated Apr 28, 1857, recorded in Liber J A S No 133, folios No 144 thru 147, of the land records for Wash Co, D C: sale of all of lot 6 in Davidson's subdivision of square 368, with improvements.
-John M Jameson, trustee -A Green auct

Jas Milligan, who was accessory with Kesler, who was hung a short time since by a mob in Gentry Co, Miss, for killing constable Timmons, was likewise taken out of jail on Jul 5 & hung until dead.

Col Alex'r Wilson, of Phil, has been appointed U S district atty for Utah.

Mr Henry Fitz, of N Y, a most accomplished optical instrument maker, has prepared a special telescope to be used by Lt Gilliss in observations of the Sept eclipse of the sun, & offers it freely to the Smithsonian Institution.

The monument erected by Napoleon III over the remains of Queen Hortense, in the Church of Ruell, was consecrated on Jun 27. The same church contains the mausoleum of the Empress Josephine.

Criminal Court-Wash-Thu. 1-John Mardis was charged with resisting an officer, & was fined by the Court $8 & costs.

A party, consisting of Gabriel Labonty, Geo Robbins, Bernard Flanigan, & Benj Ralston, encamped on a maroon, on Tybee Island for some days. A scuffle occurred in camp over a gun, which went off, killing Ralston instantly. The party returned with the dead body of their companion to the city. –Savannah Republican, 20th

Sad calamity at a Methodist Church picnic at N Y on Wed, resulting in the death by drowning of Mrs Isabella Ferguson, 115 Lewis st; Mrs Emma Demilt, 113 Lewis st; & Mrs Ann Eliz Jacobs, 57 Gouverneur st. Miss Magnum, of 258 Delancey st, was rescued alive & taken to her residence, but her recovery is deemed highly improbable.

Chas Letcher, the printer of the free-love paper at Berlin Heights, Ohio, has committed suicide. His mother, an excellent woman, living in Iowa, did all she could to win her son from the seductive influence of a sensual fanaticism, but in vain.

Greenbrier White Sulphur Springs, Va, will receive visiters till Sep 1 next.
–G W C Whiting, Pres of the Company

Mrd: on Jul 20, by Rev Wm L Dalby, Wm Burke, of Madison, Wisc, to Sallie C, daughter of Wm D Drish, of Leesburg, Va.

Died: on Jul 20, Mary L Dean, wife of Felix Dean, in her 27th year.

SAT JUL 24, 1858
Hon Wm F Gordon, formerly for several years a prominent & much respected member of Congress from the Albemarle district of Va, died at his residence in that county on Jul 21. He was standing conversing with his son, when, feeling faint, he requested to lay down, which was done, & he immediately expired. He served only one term in Congress, but that sufficed to give him an historic name, for he proposed the Subtreasury system.

Jas Nolan was hung at New Orleans on Jul 16 for the murder of John Renon, whom he assassinated at a coffee house in Aug last. He made every effort to escape the penalty due to his crime. Before the execution he was visited by Fr Dufau, of the Jesuit College, in prayer. With him were Tripp, Lindsay, & Haas, likewise under sentence for murder, engaged in pleas for forgiveness at the Court of Heaven.

The youngest son of Rev B Frost, lately pastor of the Unitarian Church in Concord, Mass, have been living for several months with Mr F's family at Fayal, & about Jun 1 became one of a pary to visit the Peak of Pico, a mountain upon the island. Miss Fuller was one of the party. On their return he was heard to scream that he was falling. The company rushed to his aid, but too late. He had fallen from a precipice 70 feet high. His back was broken, & he received other injuries from which he died 3 days afterwards.

On Sat Albert Eldridge, of Toledo, a promisig young man, formerly of Cleveland, Ohio, fell from the steamer Northern Light into Saginaw Bay, & was drowned. Ladies on the main deck begged him to retire from standing upon the narrow ledge on the outside of the steamer, but he disregarded the warning. He was one of an excursion party.

Mount De Sales Academy of Visitation for Young Ladies, near Catonsville, 5 miles west of Balt, Md: founded in 1852. It sets on 76 acres of ground & affords ample space for exercise. The course of instruction comprises numerous subjects.
–A Friend of Education

Boarding & Day School for Young Ladies, Alexandria, Va, Miss E Tebbs, Principal. The Session will begin on Sep 15, & close the last of June. The Principal is a graduate of the Virginia Female Institute, & has had considerable experience in teaching. [Recommended by Richd H Phillips, Principal of the Va Female Institute.]

Valuable farm of 1,233 acres on York River, called *Capahosie*, offered for sale. The dwlg & out-houses are in tolerably good order. –Goddin & Apperson, Richmond, Va

Died: on Jul 23, of disease of the lungs, in his 17th year, Claudius A Wells, youngest son of Thos C Wells, of Wash City. His funeral will take place from his father's house, 3rd & East Capitol st, this afternoon at 4½ o'clock.

MON JUL 26, 1858
Marine Telegraph-Capt Hudson's report: U S steam frig **Niagara**, Queenstown, Ireland, Jul 8, 1858. I am mortified & disappointed to report the arrival of the **Niagara** at this port on Jul 5, after 3 unsuccessful attempts at laying down the telegraphic cable.
-Wm L Hudson, Captain, to Hon I Toucey, Sec of the Navy, Washington

Orphans Court of Wash Co, D C. In the case of Titus Bastinelli, adm of Fred'k Casali, deceased, the administrator & Court have appointed Aug 17 next, for the final settlement of the personal estate of said deceased, of the assets in hand. -Ed N Roach, Reg/o wills

Orphans Court of Wash Co, D C. In the case of Simeon Garratt, adm of Charlotte Garratt, deceased, the administrator & Court have appointed Aug 17 next, for the final settlement of the personal estate of said deceased, of the assets in hand.
-Ed N Roach, Reg/o wills

Died: on Jul 25, after an illness of one week, of an affection of the brain, Witte Landy, aged 7 months & 22 days, son of J J & M G Mulloy. His funeral will be this afternoon at 2 o'clock, from the residence of his parents, 507 north C st, Capitol Hill.

Died: on Jul 25, Frank Breckenridge, infant son of E N & M E Leonard, aged about 5 weeks. His funeral will be from the residence of his parents, 6 Missouri ave, at 4 P M.

Obit-died: on Jul 8, at Dalton, Ga, en route from Arkansas to Orange Court-house, Va, Lt J Dorsey Read, U S Navy, aged 33 years. May our widowed friend, his wife, ever find true & sympathizing friends in this her sore affliction. -A

TUE JUL 27, 1858
Rugby Academy, 14th st, opposite Franklin Square, will be resumed on Sep 1 under the charge of the undersigned. –Rev Jas A Harrold, Wash

The ninth session of the Southern Female Institute, Richmond, Va, will commence on the first Monday in Oct next. –D Lee Powell, Principal

Wanted, a situation as a Teacher or Tutor to a private family by a gentleman, a Presbyterian, who has had considerable experience in teaching. Address J H Williamson, Romney, Hampshire Co, Va.

The trustees of Transylvania Univ, being about to establish a High School in Lexington, Ky, wish to engage the services of a Principal Teacher: salary will be $1,500 per annum, with the use of a residence on the College grounds, with a percentage on the tuition fees. Address W A Dudley, Sec of Transylvania Univ.

Sad Accident. Saml Sylvester, druggist, H & 6th sts, met with an accident on Friday from which it is feared he will lose his sight. He was endeavoring to uncork a bottle of ammonia, during which the neck of the bottle broke, & a portion of its contents flew in his face. He has not been able to open his eyes since then. –States

Died: yesterday, Cornelia, daughter of Wm B & Eliz Dennison, aged 8 years & 10 months. Her funeral will be from the residence of her parents, 333 5th st, between G & H, today at 4 o'clock.

Died: on Jul 17, at the Bay of St Louis, where he had gone for the benefit of his health, Wm Locke Chew, aged 80 years, 3 months & 6 days, a native of Calvert Co, Md, & emigrated to the State of Mississippi in 1806; since then he has resided in that State, enjoying the domestice happiness of a married life, & rearing a large & estimable family, many of whom were present at the close of his earthly pilgrimage. He left 4 sons, 1 daughter, & several grandchildren. –G [This remarkable gentleman was a constant & regularly paying subscriber to the Nat'l Intelligencer for 52 years to the day of his death.]

Subscriber has for sale 84 acres of land in the District divided into 5 lots of from 10 to 20 acres, all within 3 miles of Wash City & one from Rock Creek Church, in a good & rapidly increasing neighborhood. He also has 150 acres with a small house on it that joins the farms of Messrs Dundas, Tucker, Bates, & Wiltberger. Apply to E J Middleton, City Hall, or the subscriber. –Henry Queen, near Wash

Trustee's sale of valuable farm in Greenbrier Co, near the White Sulphur Springs, called **Jericho**, containing 900 acres. By deed of trust executed by Saml D Leake & wife, dated Nov, 1857, duly recorded in Greenbrier Co Court: public auction on Aug 24, on the premises. There is a large brick dwlg, just completed, & out-bldgs. Mr Vance, the manager, will show the place. –N B Keane, Trustee -Goddin & Apperson, aucts

For sale: a rare chance for a highly improved country seat, the subscriber, about to remove out of the District of Columbia. It is called **Prospect Hill**, 1 mile west of Gtwn, upon the Little Falls' new road. The dwlg is built of brick, large & conveniently arranged; out-houses are a servant's house & cottage for gardener; large stable, corn-house, ice-house, meat-house, poultry house, & springhouse. I will also sell a small farm about 2½ miles from Gtwn. Apply to B T Hodges, living at the place, or Wm R Riley, Wash City. –B T Hodges

Obit-died: on Jul 3, after a long & painful illness, Mrs Susan R Page, relict of the late Dr R P Page, of *The Briars*, Clarke Co, Va. She was a devoted mother, fondly attached sister, & a consistent Christian, for many years a communicant in the Episcopal Church. To her orphan girls & only boy is left the memory of her virtues. –A Friend

WED JUL 28, 1858
Cincinnati Gaz of Jul 26. The old mansion of the late Pres Harrison at North Bend was destroyed by fire on Jul 25. It was occupied by Col Wm H H Taylor, [who married a daughter of Gen Harrison] & family, & they barely escaped in their night clothes. Historical papers, & portraits of Mrs Harrison, painted by Beard, taken at different periods of his life, are probably destroyed. Mrs Harrison, the widow of Pres Harrison, was not in the dwlg. She at present is at the residence of her son, Hon J Scott Harrison, a few miles from the homestead. [North Bend was the first landing place of John Cleves Symmes, the original patentee of all the land between the two Miamis & was at one time regarded as the rival of Cincinnati or *Fort Washington*.]

Two sons of Mr John Nout, of Orange Co, N J, were drowned in the Mongany river on Sat. Their father, being unable to swim, was unable to rescue them.

Charleston South Carolinian of Jul 10. Robt Wilson was killed by his stepson, John O Darby, on Jul 9. Wilson was essaying to handcuff his wife, Darby's mother, & take her upstairs to cowhide her, when Darby [age 19] interfered. Liquor had a large share in this deplorable business. Darby came to town last night & surrendered himself.

In Maine village, in this county, about 16 miles from Binghampton, on Jul 16, Oliver Howard, about age 30 years, murdered two of his children, boys, by cutting their throats with a razor. –Binghampton Rep

Last week Jacob Barks drank a quart of whiskey & died in the course of half an hour, at Mercerville, Va, on the Chesapeake & Ohio Canal.

Appointment of Postmasters by the Pres:
Jacob Isaacs, Columbus, Miss, re-appointed.
Freeman Brady, sen, Wash, Pa, vice Aiken, removed.
John C Riley, Quincy, Ill, vice Brooks, removed.
E B Collings, Wilksbarre, Pa, vice Sorber, resigned.
Jas G Dickie, Buffalo, N Y, re-appointed.
Jas R Fonda, Troy, N Y, vice Whitman.

Orphans Court of Wash Co, D C. Letters of administration on the personal estate of John H Somervell, late of Wash Co, deceased. –Sarah J Somervell, admx

Orphans Court of Wash Co, D C. Letters of administration on the personal estate of Isaac Stoddard, late of Wash Co, deceased. –Eliz Stoddard, admx

THU JUL 29, 1858
An old pioneer gone. On Jul 16 the venerable Josiah Hedges, of Tiffin, Ohio, died, at the advanced age of 80 years & 3 months. He was born in Berkeley Co, Va, on Apr 9, 1778. He left home at an early age to carve out his own fortune. In 1801 he settled in Belmont Co, Ohio; was the first sheriff of Belmont; & Clerk of the Court. He then entered into the mercantile business at St Clairsville. In 1820, at the land sales at Delaware, Ohio, he bought the land which was an unbroken forest, a vast solitude, a tangled wild woods; where now the spires of elegant churches & fine bldgs rear their heads. Mr Hedges in his younger days was a stout, athletic, vigorous man, & retained his manly sense in his old days, up to his last & fatal attack. As a husband he was kind, & as a father, generous & indulgent. –Ohio paper [At the time of his death this venerable citizen had been a constant subscriber for the Nat'l Intelligencer for upwards of 40 years.]

Pullen, who was sentenced last year to the penitentiary for 8 years for robbing the Richmond custom-house of $25,000, died of consumption, last Friday in prison.

Notice of co-partnership. I have this day associated with me in the Wall Paper & Upholstery business Mr L J Rothrock. It will hereafter be conducted under the firm of Franklin & Rothrock, corner of 9th & D sts. –S P Franklin -Jul 29, 1858

Farm on the Orange & Alexandria Railroad at auction: on Aug 28, I will sell at auction my **Walnut Branch Farm**, containing 295 acres of land, with good bldgs.
–R B Williamson, Warrenton, Va

Died: on Jul 27, at his residence in Chas Co, Md, Chas F Dement, in his 61st year.

$100 reward for runaway negro man Geo Lee, about 23 or 24 years of age.
–J A Osbourn, Upper Marlboro, PG Co, Md.

The Boston Journal records the death on Sunday last of a little girl, daughter of Wm G Lewis, from hydrophobia. She had been bitten by a mad dog 4 weeks ago & the symptoms appeared on Thu last, when she complained of a sore throat. Convulsions became very frequent & she suffered intense agony.

Orphans Court of Wash Co, D C. Letters of administration on the personal estate of Lemuel A Rollings, late of Wash Co, deceased. –Emily E Rollings, admx

FRI JUL 30, 1858
A boy, 10 years old, Geo Prickner, the son of a German widow, residing in Brooklyn, disappeared on Friday last, & was missing until Monday, when his dead body was found in a large trunk or chest in the house of his mother. He evidently got into the trunk to conceal himself, when a self-adjusting lock closed the lid upon him & he was smothered.

Mrd: on Jun 15, at Oakland, Calif, Maj Saml Woods, U S Army, to Jennie G Kirkham.

Mrd: on Jun 17, in San Francisco, Mr Jerdon Bowers to Miss Delilah Lancaster-the former of Ky, the latter of Wash, D C.

Died: on Jul 29, in Wash City, Mrs Catherine Lyons, wife of Chas Lyons. Her funeral will be this afternoon at 4 o'clock, from her late residence on 10th st, south of the ave.

SAT JUL 31, 1858
A letter from Montevideo of May 29 brings intelligence of the death of a remarkable Frenchman, M Aime Bonpland, the naturalist, who died a few days ago previously at San Borja, at age 85; born at Rochelle in 1773. –London paper

Maj John Sanders, of the U S Engineers, died at **Fort Delaware** on Jul 29, after a short illness. He was a native of Ky, son of Lewis Sanders, the distinguished agriculturist of that State, & brother of Geo N Sanders, Navy Agent of this city. He graduated second in his class at West Point, & was the chief engineer under Gen Worth in the brilliant attack upon the Bishop's Palace, & also at Vera Cruz. He was, at the time of his death, superintending the constuction of **Fort Delaware**, the principal defence of Phil.
-N Y Commercial

A son of Hon C J Faulkner, aged about 10 years, accidentallyshot himself with a pistol on Monday last. The ball took effect in the leg. At latest accounts it had not been extracted.
-Va Free Press

Three young men drowned at Chicago, while on a pleasure excursion, by the upsetting of their boat. They were G Wentworth Scott, formerly of Montreal; Haviland Peck, of Toronto, & ___ Palmer, of N Y.

Miss Margaret Allen, residing in Mechlinburg Co, N C, was instantly killed by lightning on Jul 20. She was standing in the door of her father's dwlg, & was much injured by splinters from the door posts. The balance of the family in the house experienced a severe shock.

The barque **Sebois** arrived at Boston quarantine on Tue from Cienfuegos with yellow fever on board. Capt McNeil, Henry Mason, the 2nd mate, Jos Wood, a passenger, & 2 seamen, all died on the passage. The barque **Iola**, St Mary's, & brig **Spitfire** are also at quarantine with the fever on board.

London correspondent of the North American says, on Jul 9, a telegram was received with an account of the suicide committed by Rev Dr Sadlier, one of the Senior Fellows of Trinity College, & the Senior dean of the year. He hung himself on a tree, while on a visit to his brother at Castle Kevick, the other side of Phoenix Park. He was the eldest son of the late Provost Sadlier. He was 50 years of age. No cause assigned for the act.

Sanford Van Hensler, of Montg Co, N Y, recently raced with another man, but fell, blood gushing from his mouth & nostrils from a burst blood vessel. He died soon afterwards.

Falling of a railroad bridge on Sat last over the bridge over Todd's Fork, on the Cincinnati, Wilmington, & Zanesville railroad. The fireman, Mr John Bangham, of Wmsport, was killed; Saml Slack, a brakeman, was so injured that he soon died.

Calvert College, near New Windsor, Carroll Co, Md, will commence on Aug 20 & end on the last Tue of June. –A H Baker, A M, Principal

Teacher wanted to take charge of a small school in his own family. –Richd H Carter, Post Ofc, Salem, Fauquier Co, Va.

Died: on Jul 29, in Wash City, after a short but painful illness, Mary Adeline, daughter of John Fred'k & Mary O'Bryon, aged 20 months & 14 days. Her funeral is on Sunday next at 4 o'clock, from their residence, 484 10th st, south side of Pa ave.

Died: on Jul 29, in Wash City, Seth Jewett Barton, aged 15 years, son of S W & Lucy A Barton.

Died: on Jul 18, in Shepherdstown, Va, Mrs Eliz B Towner, in her 59th year, relict of the last Benj T Towner-a lady of estimable qualities, & a long & patient sufferer from disease.

MON AUG 2, 1858
Jas Kelly, aged 44, was executed at Brooklyn on Friday last for the murder of his wife.

Spots on the Sun. The British Astronomical Society, have presented their medal to M Heinrich Schwabe, of Deneau, who is stated to have made daily observations of the phenomenon for a period of 30 years.

Political Items: Wm E Niblack has been nominated for re-election to Congress by the Democrats of the first district of Indiana. Wm H English has been nominated for re-election in the second district. Martin Gray has been nominated by a Democratic Convention in the sixth district. In the ninth district, John C Walker, editor of the Laporte Times, has been nominated to oppose Mr Colfax. Hon John Sherman has been unanimously re-nominated to Congress by the Republicans of the thirteenth district of Ohio.

Naval: The brig **Dolphin**, Lt John N Maffit commanding, was to sail from Key West on the 26th for a cruise on the north side of Cuba. The sloop **St Mary's**, Cmder Davis, which has been lying at Mare Island, Calif, for some months past, was expected to sail for Panama about Aug 1. Many of her men deserted. She will probably return home in Jan next.

John G White, postmaster at Colfax, Ia, was shot by Saml Duke, & died in a few hours. Duke kept a groggery & the people were abating the nuisance, when Duke fired into the crowd, wounding White, who was only a spectator. Duke is held for trial.

To Hall Neilson, Pres of the Great Falls Manufacturing Co & all others whom this notice of condemnation may concern: you are notified that Geo R Braddock, Justice of the Peace in & for Montg Co, Md, has this day, on my application as the authorized agent of the U S, issued his warrant, directed to the Sheriff of said county, commanding him to summon a jury of 18 good & lawful men to meet on your land at or near the Great Falls of the river Potomac, lying in said county, on Aug 9, 1959, for the purpose of valuing & condemning a portion of said land as of an absolute estate in perpetuity in the said U S, & assessing all damages which the owner or owners thereof have sustained, & do & shall sustain by reason of the erection & construction of a dam upon & through said land, for the use of the Washington Aqueduct, when & where you will please attend, if to you it shall seem meet. –M C Meigs, Capt of Engineers, Chief Engineer Washington Aqueduct.

A murderous affray occurred at Poestenkill, 8 miles from Troy, N Y, on Wed, between two brothers, Wm Diamond & Henry Diamond, both aged men, one 74 & the other 60. They engaged in a dispute, when Henry stabbed Wm in the neck. He died in about 4 hours. They drank a good deal of whiskey during the evening. Henry is in jail.

Mrd: on Jul 31, by Rev Geo W Samson, D D, Jason R Hopkins, of Bangor, Maine, to Miss Phebe Bishop, of Wash City.

Died: on Jul 31, in Gtwn, Amanda, wife of Dennis O'Neill, in her 49th year. Her funeral is on Tue at 9 o'clock, from the residence of her husband, 1st & Fred'k sts.

Mrs Helen Key Blunt, of this city, will give readings from British & American poets at the Smithsonian Institution on Wed evening next.

TUE AUG 3, 1858
Appropriations made during the First Session of the 35th Congress:
1-For compensation of the Pres of the U S: $25,000.
2-For compensation for the Vice Pres of the U S: $8,000.
3-For compensation to the secretary to sign patents for lands: $1,500.
4-For compensation to the private secretary, steward, & messenger of the Pres of the U S: $4.600.
5-For contingent expenses of the Executive ofc, including stationery therefore: $350.
6-For compensation of the Sec of State & Assist Sec of State, clerks messenger, & laborers in his ofc: $57,800
7-For the relief of Gardner & Vincent, & others. To audit & settle the several accounts of Gardner & Vincent, A S Gardner, A F Holmes, G B Murphy, C C Carlton, N E Crittenden, O A Brooks, & Co, & W Bingham & Co, for good furnished the U S marine hospital at Cleveland, Ohio, during the superintendency of John Coon: indefinite.
8-To pay Jennett H McCall, only child of Capt Jas McCall, of Gen Pickens' brig, in the S C regt during the war of the Revolution, the 7 years' half pay of a captain: $2,100.
9-To pay the widow of Cmder Wm Lewis Herndon a sum equal to 3 years' full sea-service pay of a cmder in the navy: indefinite.
10- Relief of John Hamilton: for his time & services during his imprisonment with the Indians in the war of 1812 with Great Britain: indefinite.

11-Relief of Dr Chas D Maxwell, a surgeon in the U S Army, the difference of pay between that of passed assist surgeon & a surgeon, from Dec 22, 1845, to Jul 7, 1848, being the period during which he performed said duties on board the U S ship **Cyane**: indefinite.

12- Relief of the owners of the barque **Attica**, of Portland, Maine: the amount imposed on said vessel as tonnage duty by the collector of N Y, in 1855: $174.62.

13-To pay the heirs of Alex'r Stevenson the amount due to said Stevenson from the time of his enlistment, Jan 1, 1776, until the time of his discharge, 1783: $654.

14-Relief of Duncan Robertson: for moneys paid by him to the navy yard at Gosport, for repairs of the Norwegian barque **Ellen**, for damages encountered in aiding & rescuing the passengers of the steamer **Central America**: $749.

15-Relief of Capt Jas Mac McIntosh, U S Navy: to pay him the difference between the sum paid to him at the Treasury as cmder on other duty & that which was due to him as such officer attached to a vessel for sea service, & being in full for his services as an ofcr of the West India squadron from Aug 14, 1837, to Sep 3, 1838: $204.95.

16-To refund to Elijah F Smith, Gilman H Perkins, & Chas F Smith, or survivors of them, composing the firm of Smith, Perkins & Co, of Rochester, N Y, the amount paid by them to the U S on one debenture bond, executed by John B Glover & Co, dated Apr 2, 1857, as penalty over & above the regular duties on the merchandise therein mentioned: $837.

17-Relief of Geo A O'Brien: to pay him for his services as clerk in the ofc of the 2nd Auditor from Jul 5, 1845, to Mar 3, 1846: $549.83.

18-To the heirs of John B Hand: $1,340.

19-Relief of Rufus Dwinel: for interest at the rate of 6% annum, on $13,037.72, from Mar 4, 1837, when the latter sum was due from the U S to said Dwinel's assignor, to Mar 11, 1852, when an appropriation was made for its payment: $11,748.03.

20-Relief of Jonas P Keller: for his services as a watchman or overseer of the Executive bldg at F & 17th sts from Apr 1, 1849 to Sep 30, 1850: $750.

21-Relief of Susanna T Lea, widow & admx of Jas Maglenen, late of the city of Balt, deceased: for the value of a horse & equipment belonging to said Jas Maglenen impressed in Sep, 1814, for the purpose of sending an express to North Point, & all was lost in said service: $130.

22-Relief of J Wilcox Jenkins: for the difference between the pay of capt's clerk & a purser of a 1st class sloop-of-war from Jan 1, to Apr 30, 1856, during which time he was the acting purser of the sloop-of-war **Germantown**: indefinite.

23-Relief of Wm B Trotter: for all demands of Trotter growing out of the emigration & subsistence of Choctaw Indians in Mississippi, in 1831, under a contract with the U S: $1,680.

24-Relief of the heirs or legal reps of Richd D Rowland, deceased, [of Alabama,] & others: to the them $3,200; & to the heirs, excs, adms, or legal reps of whomsoever possesses whatever title the U S gave to Cureton, Smith, & Heifner to the s e quarter of secion 2, township 14, range 8 east, of the lands selected in Ala, & sold under treaty of Mar 24, 1832, with the Creek Indians, for the benefit of the orphans of the tribe, $2,260, with interest at the rate of 5½%, upon both aforesaid sums, from Nov 1, 1836: indefinite.

25-Relief of Saml W Turner & Alvin A Turner: for their services in transporting the U S mail on their steamers from Cleveland, Ohio, & Detroit, Mich, to Mackinaw, Saut Ste

Marie, Marquette, Copper Harbor, Eagle Harbor, Eagle River, & Ontonagon, Mich, & La Pointe, Bayfield, & Superior City, in the State of Wisconsin; $23,825.

26-Relief of D O Dickinson: for services rendered in connexion with keeping a light in Waukegan harbor, Ill: $108.75.

27-Relief of Thos Phenix, jr: for acting as paymaster's clerk in the employment of D Randall, deputy paymaster general, the sum of $3 a day; but from this compensation is to be deducted the salary of $500 per annum, already received by him: indefinite.

28-Relief of Lewis W Broadwell, for transporting the U S mails, from Sep 4, 1854 to Apr 17, 1857, at the rate of $5,000 per annum: $12,938.

29-Relief of Benj L McAtee & Isaac N Eastham, of Louisville, Ky: for transporting extra mail matter between Jul 1, 1846, & Jun 30, 1850: $6,000.

30-Relief of Benj Wakefield: difference of pay between master's mate & boatswain, from Jan 1, 1848, to Jan 19, 1850: indefinite.

31-Relief of Susannah Redman, widow of Lloyd Redman: amount adjudged as due for 3 horses lost by him while in the service of the U S during the Mexican war: $170.

32-Relief of Simeon Stedman: who served in Capt Chritopher Ripley's company of the 37th infty during the war with Great Britain in 1812, such sum or sums as may have accrued to him from the time of his last receiving payment for services till the end of the war: indefinite.

33-Relief of Oliver P Hovey: for printing the Kearny Code of laws for New Mexico in 1846: $1,555.

34-Relief of Geo W Biscoe: for indemnification for the loss of the schnr **Speedwell**, captured in the Patuxent river by the British naval forces on Aug 22, 1814, & which was in the waters & within the territorial jurisdiction of the U S on Feb 17, 1815, the day of the exchange of the ratifications of the treaty of Ghent, & was carried away out of the said waters & territorial jurisdiction of the U S, in violation of the 1st article of the said treaty: $2,000.

35-Relief of Richd B Alexander: for the value of one horse & one mule lost by him during the Mexican war: $250.

36-Relief of Wm Heine, Artist in the Japan Expedition under Cmdor Perry, compensation at the rate of $1,800 per annum during the time he was actually employed in such service: indefnite.

37-Relief of Alonzo & Eldridge G Colby: for the balance due them on their contract with the U S, dated Jul 24, 1855, for constructing a breakwater at Owl's Head harbor, Penobscot river, Maine: $2,502.11.

38-Relief of David McClure, adm of Jos McClure, deceased: for the amount of interest collected from said Jos McClure, in his lifetime, on a judgment in favor of the U S Gov't, which it was afterwards ascertained the said McClure did not properly owe, & the amount of which judgment has been previously refunded to him by Congress: $107.64.

39-Relief of Jas Rumph: in full compensation for medical aid rendered to soldiers in the service of the U S in 1837: $760.

40-Relief of John Dearmit: to pay him, in addition to the amount already paid by the Gov't under his contract for carrying the mail, from Jun 2, 1844, for 4 years: $295.

41-Relief of Stuckey & Rogers, mail contractors, at the rate of $333 per annum for transportation of the mails, deducting therefrom whatever payment may have been made, at the rate of $138 per annum, by the Post Ofc Dept: indefinite.

42-Relief of Peter Parker: for his services as charge d'affaires ad interim at Canton, China, at various periods between May 26, 1852, & May 4, 1855: $2,603.19.
43-Relief of the legal reps of Danl Hay, deceased: to pay them a sum equal to 2% on all moneys disbursed by him as agent for paying pensions, from & after Apr 20, 1836, with interest on the same, from Apr 30, 1856: indefinite.
44-Relief of Dr Thos Antisell: from services rendered a acting assist surgeon to the command [co G, 3rd artl,] escorting Lt Parke's party of survey, from Calif to New Mexico, in 1855: $274.65.
45-Relief of the heirs of Richd Tarvin: for losses sustained by Richd Farren, or Richd Tarvin, during the war of 1813-1814: $600.
46-Relief of Mrs Harriet O Reid, excx of the late Brvt Col A C W Fanning, of the U S army: to pay her the amount claimed to be due the estate of said Col Fanning, as commissions of 2½% upon the sum of $50,000 disbursed by him in 1827 & 1828, at the U S arsenal, in Augusta, Ga: $1,250.

N Y: Mrs John Ryan & a little child were burned from the explosion of a camphene lamp. Both died in consequence.

Died: on Jul 30, of typhoid fever, Maria Meehan, wife of Robt H Broom, & daughter of John S Meehan, Librarian of Congress.

Died: on Aug 1, in Gtwn, Mrs Mary E Offutt, daughter of the late John I Adams, aged 18 years. Her funeral will take place from the residence of her mother, corner of 2nd & High sts, this afternoon at 4 o'clock.

Died: on Fri, in Cecil Co, Md, whither she had gone for her health, Mrs Isabella West, widow of the late Capt Job West, of Balt, & eldest sister of Rev John C Smith, of Wash City. "With Christ."

WED AUG 4, 1858
The English papers note the decease of two well-known female writers, Mrs Marcet, age 90 years, & Mrs Loudon. Mrs Loudon enjoyed a pension of L100 per annum from the civil list.

The Signers of the Declaration of Independence: out of the whole of 56, 4 lived beyond the age of 90, Chas Carroll of Carrollton reached the advanced age of 95 years, 1 month & 24 days. Ten exceeded the aged of 80; ten lived beyong 70 years; 15 exceeded the age of 60; ten passed their 50th year; 6 died past 40; & one is supposed to have perished at sea, aged 30. Franklin was born in 1706 & died in 1790. Carroll was born in 1737 & died in 1832. –Phil Press

Criminal Court-Wash-Tue. 1-Wm Quigley was put on trial for assault & battery, but in consequence of an error in the name of the principal witness, as reported by the Grand Jury, a nolle prosequi was entered. 2-Geo Barker, colored, tried for assault & battery, was acquitted.

Young Ladies' Institute, Wilmington, Del: opens the first Monday in Sept. Address Rev Thos M Cann, A M, Principal & Proprietor.

Mrd: on Aug 3, at *Giesborough*, during the celebration of Mass, by Very Rev N D Young, O P, Mr Hugh B Ewing, son of Hon Thos Ewing, of Ohio, to Miss Henrietta E Young, daughter of Mr Geo W Young, of the District of Columbia.

Mrd: on Aug 3, in Wash City, by Rev Dr F Swentzel, Amos Lovejoy, of Balt, to Kate V, daughter of the late Capt Jas Moncrieff, of N Y C.

Mrd: on Aug 3, at the residence of the bride's father, near Bladensburg, PG Co, Md, by Rev Wm Pinkney, D D, Saml T Williams, of Balt, to Miss Carrie, daughter of John C Rives.

Died: on Aug 3, at *Oakwood*, near Alexandria, Va, after a painful & lingering illness, Wm Henry Grammer, son of the late G C Grammer, of Wash City, in his 19th year. His funeral is this afternoon at 5 o'clock, from 446 11th st, above G.

Miss Brooke's English & French Boarding & Day School, Seven Bldgs, 138 Penn ave, Wash, D C. The duties of this establishment will be resumed on Sep 13, 1858.

Private tuition & board in the country, at the north. Rev & Mrs H L Myrick, of Brooklyn, Conn, receive into their family several children to instruct according to the wishes of parents, giving to each particular attention & affectionate care. Terms: $300 per annum, payable semi-annually in advance.

THU AUG 5, 1858
Household & kitchen furniture at auction on Aug 7, by order of the Orphans Court of Wash Co, D C: the personal effects of Jas Handly, deceased, at my auction store, 526 7th st, corner of D st. –Jos Hodgson, W Flaherty, adms -A Green auct

A telegraphic dispatch from Detroit says that Senator Chandler, of Mich, was seriously, though it is believed not dangerously, injured on Mon by the explosion of gas at his residence in that city.

The illness of Chief Justice Duer, of the Superior Court of N Y, who has been confined to his house for some time with a broken leg, has taken a very serious turn. On Sunday last he was smitten with a severe stroke of apoplexy, which left him speechless, & there is now little hope of his recovery.

Orphans Court of Wash Co, D C. In the case of Wm T Duvall, surviving adm, with the will annexed, of John Smith, deceased, the administrator & Court have appointed Aug 26 next, for the final settlement of the personal estate of said deceased, of the assets in hand. -Ed N Roach, Reg/o wills

Orphans Court of Wash Co, D C. Letters of administration on the personal estate of Thos Hurst, late of Wash Co, deceased. —Thos Hutchinson, adm

Wash Corp-Aug 2: 1-Ptn of W W Corcoran, asking to be reimbursed the expense of guttering on 3 fronts of square 186: referred to the Cmte on Improvements. 2-Ptn of Jacob Fleishell & others, asking that the curbstone may be set & the footway paved on 4th st east, between East Capitol st & A st north: referred to the Cmte on Improvements. 3-Ptn of Peter Shepard; & ptn of Isaac Mister: praying the remission of fine: referred to the Cmte of Claims. 4-Ptn from F Dainese, asking to be relieved from a certain assessment: referred to the Cmte of Claims. 5-Cmte of Claims: bill for the relief of Frances Jane Jones & Jas F Divine: affirmative.

Early yesterday Henry Folkz, a German, aged 66 years, was found dead [accidentally hung] in the ice-house of his son-in-law, west of Hyde Park. During the night he had evidently fallen down a hatchway, & at a distance of 10 feet brought up against some iron hooks used for lowering & raising meat. One hook had caught his clothes at the back of the neck. The strong collar band of his shirt was thus drawn so tightly against his front neck as to cause his death. —St Louis Democrat

Died: on Aug 4, in Wash City, Mrs Clarissa Hall, relict of the late Dr Fred'k Hall, of Wash City, in her 73rd year. Her funeral will be this afternoon at 6 o'clock, from the residence of her son-in-law, Mr H B Sweeny. Her remains will be transferred to Balt tomorrow for interment.

Trustee's sale of valuable property: by decree passed on Nov 6, 1857, by the Circuit Court of PG Co, Md, sitting as a Court of Equity, in a cause wherein Mgt S A Cumming, next friend to Edmund B Cumming & others, is cmplnt, & Edmund B Cumming & others are dfndnts: public sale on Aug 26, all the residue of the real estate, in said county, conveyed to Hon Thos W Cumming, deceased & intestate, by one Martin Buell & Lucy Ann, his wife, in fee simple, containing 162 acres, more or less. This estate is within 2 miles of the Soldier's Home. The dwlg & out-houses are large & in excellent order. -Danl C Digges, trustee

FRI AUG 6, 1858
On the first Sabbath in Jul, at the communion of the Congregational Church in Woodstock, John McClellan, was admitted to the church on profession of his faith. He is 93 years old, the oldest living graduate of **Yale College**, of the class of 1785.

The late Amos Lawrence gave away for charitable purposes, during the last 24 years of his life, from the close of 1828 to the close of 1852, $639,000. –Boston Courier

Seven slaves, who escaped from Dorchester Co, Md, on Sat night week, were on Sat arrested in Caroline Co, together with a white man, Hugh Hazelett, [a resident of Dorchester Co for 2 or 3 years,] who was found in their company. They were all taken to Cambridge on Mon last in the steamer **Kent**, under the charge of the sheriff & deputy of Caroline Co. Hazelett was committed to jail.

On Sunday, at Gloucester, N J, a lad, Jas McKeon, was instantly killed & another one, Hermann Aurenfricht was so seriously injured that it will be impossible for him to recover. They were enjoying themselves on a swing when the weights of the swing fell, hurling the boys 50 feet to the ground. McKeon died instantly.

A picnic party from Wash City were returning from an excursion to the Great Falls on the packet **Flying Cloud**, on Tue last, the steersman, a young man, Geo Ludick, fell overboard & was drowned. The body was recovered.

Mrd: on Jul 14, by Rev Wm S White, D D, Prof Jas J White, of Wash College, to Miss Mary Louisa, daughter of Col S McD Reid, of Lexington, Va.

Mrd: on Jul 13, at Alexandria, Va, by Rev Elias Harrison, Geo T Baldwin to Maggie J, youngest daughter of W H McKnight, all of Alexandria.

Mrd: on Aug 4, at the Methodist Episcopal Church South, Wash City, by Rev Mr Granbery, Mr Jas Southgate, jr, to Miss Delia Haywood Winne, both of Norfolk, Va.

Criminal Court-Wash-Thu: Auguste Heisler & Geo Johnson found guilty of the robbery on the highway of Mr John C Connell, on Apr 3 last. Two others, Thos Brown & Edw Meads have also been indicted for the same offence, but have not yet been apprehended.

Phil, Aug 5. Trinity Bay, Aug 5. To the Pres of the U S: Dear Sir: The Atlantic Telegraph cable on board the U S frig **Niagara** & her Britannic Majesty's steamship **Agamemnon** was joined in mid-ocean on Jul 29 & has been successfully laid; & as soon as the two ends are connected with the land line Queen Victoria will send a message to you. The cable will then be kept free until after your reply has been transmitted. With great respect, I remain your obedient servant, Cyrus W Field. [Aug 7th newspaper: Cyrus W Field, Trinity Bay: My Dear Sir: I congratulate you with all my heart on the success of the great enterprise with which your name is honorably connected. Under the blessing of Divine Providence I trust it may prove instrumental in promoting perpetual peace & friendship between the kindred nations. I have not yet received the Queen's dispatch. Yours, very respectfully, James Buchanan]

By writ of fi fa, issued by Jas Cissell, one of the Justices of the Peace, Wash Co, at the suit of Wm Johnson, against the goods & chattels of Francis A Kirby, I have seized one threshing machine, the property of said Kirby: public sale of same, on Aug 7, on the corner of Md ave & 4½ st. –J H Wise, Constable

SAT AUG 7, 1858
The Telegraph is still down between Port Hood & Capre Breton. There is the least doubt, however, of the absolute correctness of Mr Field's report of yesterday. The weather is west & disagreeable.

The citizens of Craytonville, Anderson district, the birth place of Hon Jas L Orr, Speaker of the House of Reps, have tendered him a public dinner to take place on Aug 12.

St John's College, Annapolis: commencement on Wed last. The following are the graduates: John W Dorsey, of Howard Co, Md; Chas A Johnson, of Mississippi; Jas H Wilson, St Mary's Co, Md; Seaton Munroe, Wash, D C; Jonathan Maiben, Alabama; Wm O Eversfield, PG Co, Md; Andrew G Chapman, Chas Co, Md.

Tragedy at Deer Creek, Calif, on Jul 2. Dr McMurtha & his brother owned a quartz vein there, which was jumped by 12 men. Dr McMurtha was shot dead. His brother killed 4 & wounded 7. He gave himself up to the officers of the law, & after examination he was held to have acted justifiably & was discharged.

Jos Wright, alias Tripp, was hung at New Orleans on Fri last. He was an old offender, being upwards of 50 years of age. He murdered, some time ago, Henry Keene.

Criminal Court-Wash-Fri: 1-John Roach, 15, & Thos Hanahan, 16, found guilty of assault & battery with attempt to kill Mr Thos C Magruder on Jun 12 last, whilst engaged in robbing his cherry orchard, armed with pistols, revolvers, & a gun, & were shown to have been very violent. They shot at Mr Magruder lodging a buckshot in his hand. Sentenced to 3 years each in the penitentiary. 2-Geo Jones, tried for a 2nd time for resisting Ofcr Frere on election day, was found guilty & sentenced to 2 months in jail & $10 fine.

A coroner's inquest held yesterday at the site of the old Nat'l Theatre on the body of Thos Fahey, a laborer engaged in pulling down the dismantled walls of the theatre. The wall toppled over before he could extricate himself from danger. He leaves a wife & several children.

I offer my farm for sale, near Warrenton, containing 250 acres; dwlg house & out-bldgs are in good repair. Apply to my atty, Rice W Payne, Warrenton, Va. –Mgt A Combs

Five men went from Pawtucket to Central Falls, R I, on Sunday, got intoxicated, got into a quarrel, & Wm McKanna, fell to the ground & was taken up lifeless. No injury found.

Miss Harriet Lane, of Ellenville, Ulster Co, N Y, went into the mountains on Thu last to gather whortleberries & became lost. She was found 3 days later, more dead than alive.

Died: on Aug 6, Mrs Sophia Jones, aged 21 years, daughter of John & Sophia Wahl, after a short but painful illness. Her funeral will take place on Sunday at 4 o'clock, from her residence on F st, between 2nd & 3rd sts.

The subscriber, having had 2 years' experience in teaching, desires a situation as a Tutor in a private family or as Principal of an academy. –T H Lee, Montg, Orange Co, N Y.

MON AUG 9, 1858
Brookeville Academy, Montg Co, Md, will commence on Sep 6. –E B Prettyman, A M, Principal. –A Bowie Davis, Pres Board of Trustees

Stephen H Branch has been convicted before the Recorder's Court at N Y of a gross libel on Mayor Tiemann, Peter Cooper, & Simeon Draper. He was sentenced to be imprisoned in the penitentiary at Blackwell's Island for 1 year & be fined $250, & stand committed till the fine be paid.

Affray last night in the neighborhood of Carpenter's & Virgin Alleys. It appears that Mr Robt McCurdy, an old & well known citizen of Carpenter's Alley, was married yesterday to a young lady some 23 or 24 years of age. A group of boys started pelting the residence of Mr McCurdy with brickbats & stones. Mr McCurdy seized a pistol & fired upon the crowd, wounding 8 of the boys. He was arrested & held to bail. He has been a resident of this city nearly 40 years. –Pittsburg Journal of Friday.

Shooting affrays in Ky: 1-On Tue, Mike Hermann, became involved in a difficulty at the coffee-house & was shot 3 times. He died this morning. Jas White surrendered himself & is now in custody. 2-On Tue John Gatton was killed & John Alligator was wounded at the Six-Mile House, on Bardstown road, by a man named Owen, the bar-keeper. Verdict: Owen shot in self defence. –Louisville Journal

At the commencement of Bowdoin College, Maine, on Aug 4, the honorary degree of Dr of Laws [LL D] was conferred upon Hon Jefferson Davis, of Miss, & Hon Wm Pitt Fessenden, of Maine. At the 54th commencement of the Univ of Vt, on Aug 4, the degree of LL D was conferred upon Jas Melville Gillis, of Wash, D C.

J L Page, formerly of Salem, Mass, resident among us for 20 years, now in his 80th year, & with his wife enjoying the sea breezes of old Salem, writes thus to his son, Prof Page, of his mother's sisters: "The eight sisters are all here together, & their average age is 71 & a fraction, making an aggregate of 568 years; & they talk over their young days & old days with such volubility that I cannot undertake to call them to order."

Mr Eliphalet Greeley, Ex-Mayor of Portland, Me, died in that city on Wed night. He held various offices of trust; was mayor from 1840 to 1848, & Pres of the Casco Bank for 30 years, until his death.

Sale at auction by decrees of the Circuit Court of Wash Co, D C, passed in the cause of John Hazel vs Horatio R Maryman et al, No 1,023 in equity: public auction on Aug 31 of the east half of lot 3 in square 728, on East Capitol st, between 1st & 2nd sts east; lot 3 in square 730, on Pa ave & south A st; lot 3 in square 758, on 2nd st, between Md ave & north A st; lots 1 thru 9, in square 814, on north B & 4th st east; & lots 14, 15, 17, & 18 in square 867, on north B & 6th sts east. –Wm R Woodward, trustee -A Green auct

Criminal Court-Wash-Sat. 1-Danl Stewart guilty of an assault & battery with a stick on a Pole named Anthony Gymnaski, in Apr last. Stewart was put under arrest. 2-Edw Quinlan, age 14 years, one of the parties who assaulted Mr Thos C Magruder, was charged with assault & battery with intent to kill by throwing stones at & striking Mr Magruder severely on the head. Verdict: not guilty.

Mrd: on Aug 4, at West Point, N Y, at the Church of the Holy Innocents, by Rev John W French, Chaplain & Professor of Ethics U S Military Academy, Lt John T Greble, 2nd U S Artl, to Sarah Bradley, daughter of the officiating clergyman. [See Aug 11th newspaper notice.]

For sale, a Classical School on C st, between 4½ & 6th sts. The Principal wishing to retire from teaching. Inquire of A F Kimmel, or of the Principal, Geo W Dorrance, A M.

Yesterday Mr Bernard Brien, an old & well known citizen of Wash, dropped down whilst attending divine service in St Matthew's [Catholic] Church, & almost immediately died. The cause assigned was an attack of apoplexy.
+
Died: on Aug 8, of apoplexy, Mr Bernard Brien, an old citizen of the District. His funeral will take place from his late residence [Miss Ann Briscoe's] on Pa ave, between 17th & 18th sts, this afternoon at 4 o'clock.

Died: on Aug 7, Chas Bell, in his 85th year. His funeral will take place from his late residence this afternoon at 3 o'clock.

Died: on Aug 3, at the residence of Wm H Cassaday, Loudoun Co, Va, of pulmonary disease, Miss Sarah Edmonia Denham, in her 30th year. –B

Trinity Bay, [N F] Aug 7. Since our arrival here on the morning of the 5th I have been constantly receiving telegraphic messages asking for full particulars in regard to the laying of the Atlantic cable, to which it is impossible for me to reply, as every moment of my time will be fully occupied while I remain here; & I have handed to Mr McKay, the superintendent of the N Y, Newfoundland, & London telegraph Company's lines my daily journal, & given him full permission to send from the same any extracts that he might think of interest to the public, expecially those portions which will reply to the communications that I have received. –Cyrus W Field
+
Trinity Bay, Aug 7. The Atlantic Telegraph cable was successfully landed here yesterday morning, & is in perfect order. The steamship **Agamemnon** has landed her end of the cable, & we are now receiving signals from the telegraph house at Valencia. The U S steamer **Niagara** & her Majesty's steamer **Gorgon** & steamer **Porcupine** leave for St John's tomorrow. Due notice will be given when the Atlantic telegraph line will be open for public business. –Cyrus W Field

TUE AUG 10, 1858
Mrs Jas Price published a romance in the Ohio Farmer, a year ago, in which the real & unenviable characters were very plainly intended for Jas Gay & wife. A difficulty occurred between Mr Gay & Jas Price & son, in which the son was killed & the father wounded. Gay has just been tried in Clark [Ky] Circuit Court for murder & acquitted.

The Valley Female Institute, Winchester, Va: 5th annual session will commence on Sep 1st. –S P York, A M -G La Monte, A B, Principals

A son & daughter of Mr W Sabin, of this city, went to Onondaga Creek on Monday, where the boy ventured upon a log & fell into the water. His little sister ran home to inform her father. He got hold of the boy's leg & pulled him out. He was laid out as dead, but an hour later he was observed to breathe. Every effort was made by his parents for his recovery, & at 12 o'clock the lad was conversing with them. He is doing well. This is the most singular case of resuscitation after drowning that we can recollect hearing of. –Syracuse Courier

The dwlg house of Mrs Jones, widow of the late Evan Jones, about 1 mile from Rockville, Md, was entirely destroyed by fire on Aug 1, with nearly all its contents, & no insurance. The fire originated by a servant carelessly igniting a match in an upper room, when the whole box took fire, & she threw them on the floor. The bldg was soon ablaze.

On Monday week, at a barbecue in Madison Co, Ky, near Rockcastle, Mr Moore, constable, summoned Messrs Roberts, Mullin, Jones, & brother to help him arrest 2 Haileys; the Haileys resisted; killed the constable & the brothers Jones, & wounded Mullin, who is not expected to live, & Roberts slightly in the hand. One of the Jones', after he had been cut across the stomach, told them he could not live, but one of them held him by the head while the other cut his head nearly off with bowie knives. The murderers escaped, but one of them has since been arrested.

Metropolitan Collegiate Institute, a Boarding & Day School for Young Ladies, 464 E st, between 6th & 7th sts, will be resumed the first Monday of Sep next. The Fletcher property on E st, [formerly occupied by Messrs Fleischman & Noble, for several years past by the Misses Rooker as a young ladies boarding school,] has been secured for the future sessions of the institute. –Mrs & Mrs T H Havenner, Principals

Gtwn Classical & Mathematical Academy will be resumed on Sep 6.
–P A Bowen, Principal

Mrd: on Aug 8, by Rev Andrew G Carothers, Mr L Stewart to Miss Eliz E Lewis, both of Wash City.

Died: on Aug 8, at the Navy Yard, Wash City, Thos Wainwright, 2nd son of Lt T H & Maria M Patterson, aged 4 years & 1 month. His funeral will take place from the Navy Yard at 5 o'clock this afternoon.

Died: on Aug 7, near Wash City, at the cottage, the residence of his aunt, Geo R Carroll, in his 46th year.

Trustee's sale of a piece of land & house in the country, near Wash City, under a deed of trust, dated May 31, 1858, recorded in Liber J A S No 157, folio 25, of the land records for Wash Co, D C: public auction on Aug 21, all of lot 2 in Geo Taylor's subdivision of a part of the orginal tract of land called **Pleasant Plains**, containing 5 1/16th acres of land, more or less, with a frame house & out bldgs. –W H Ward, trustee -Jas C McGuire, auct

Orphans Court of Wash Co, D C. In the case of Francis R Triay, exc of Raphael R Triay, deceased, the executor & Court have appointed Aug 31 for the final settlement of the personal estate of the deceased, of the assets in hand. -Ed N Roach, Reg/o wills

WED AUG 11, 1858
On Thu Mr Hugh David, on the banks of the Delaware, near Tacony, was cleaning his revolver, when he was called out of the room. On his return he found his step-daughter Helen B Souberbielle, aged 18 years, lying dead on the floor. It was an accidental death.

On Thu in Cincinnati, Ohio, a lad named Hatmaker was killed when a loaded pistol he was examining exploded. He died almost instantly.

Two sons of Chauncy Donaldson, 16 & 20 years were hunting ducks in the marsh in West Swanton, Vt. The elder fired as the younger brother was raising his head, & some of the shot passed through his neck killing him. The afflicted father was almost paralyzed with grief.

Trustee's sale: by deed of trust from Messes Asbury F Fawsett & Geo E Deneal, dated Aug 2, 1856, recorded in Liber J A S No 120, folio 37, & by the direction of the Messrs Pickrell, the assignees & holders of the note at 2 years secured thereby, I shall expose at auction, on Sep 15, the property: part of *White Haven*, in D C, between Gtwn & the Little Falls, being No 2 of the division between the heirs of the late Abnor Cloud, containing 36 acres & 2 roods of land, more or less, as now occupied by said Fawsett & Deneal, beginning on the upper line of the canal road, marked B No 2, running the courses & distances described in a deed from Hellen M & Jas Carberry to Geo Meem, dated Nov 2, 1849, Liber J A S No 9, folio 501. –Richd Pettit, trustee
-Edw S Wright, auct

Mortality at sea. The Boston ship **Sparkling Wave**, Capt Thos Saunders, arrived at N Y quarantine on Sat after a melancholy voyage. She left N Y in Dec last for ports in Cuba to load for England. While at Havana, the 2nd mate, Thos Patterson, stewardess, Ann Hunter, & a seaman, John McCanna, died of yellow fever; & while at Matanzas, Duncan Tolman & Jas Myers & 2 other seamen died. Capt Saunders, first ofcr Danl Moore, & 2nd ofcr John Penny died of the same disorder. The ship sailed in June last for Falmouth, England; put into Savannah, but before arriving there Mr Jordan, the new chief ofcr, the 2nd ofcr, & one seaman died. On Aug 5 Geo F Carpenter, the 3rd captain, died after 3 days' sickness; but before expiring gave orders to shape the ships course for N Y, where she arrived in charge of Capt Isaac Beebe & a disabled crew. Six of the crew of 14 are down with the fever.

On Sat, at Hastings, 20 miles from N Y, Mrs Dean, Mrs Lyle, & Miss Lyle, were riding in a one-horse wagon when the girth-band broke, frightening the horse, who ran at full speed down the hill into a tree. Mrs Dean & Miss Lyle were instantly killed. Mrs Lyle's injuries, it is hoped, will not prove fatal.

Col Henry King, a native of N C, who fought as a private at New Orleans, & was on the electoral ticket of Alabama in Gen Jackson's first Presidential campaign, died on Jul 13, in Marengo Co, Ala. He was for many years a member of the Alabama Legislature.

Lafayette Institute, Pa ave, above 7th st. The undersigned, late Pres of Wilmington Female College, Delaware, assisted by Miss Maria D Halsted, late Preceptress of the same institution, & Miss Mary Williams, late acting Preceptress of the Genesee Seminary, N Y, will open a school for Young Ladies at 159 & 161 Pa ave, on Sep 6. –L C Loomis, A M

Upperville Academy will commence its 7th annual session on Sep 6. –J Welby Armstrong, Principal, Upperville P O, Fauquier Co, Va.

Mrs Bell's English & French Seminary for Young Ladies, corner of L & 10th sts, Wash, will commence on the first Monday in Sep, 1858.

Alexandria High School [Va] will commence on Sep 20. –Caleb S Hallowell

Orphans Court of Wash Co, D C. Letters of administration on the personal estate of Eleanor M Forrest, late of Wash Co, deceased. –Ed Chapman, adm

Mrd: on Aug 4, at West Point, by Rev J W French, Chaplain & Professor of Ethics at the Military Academy at that place, John T Greble, 2nd U S Artl, to Miss Sarah Bradley, daughter of the officiating clergyman.

Mrd: on Aug 4, in Bristol, R I, Edw Winslow Lincoln, of Worcester, Mass, to Kate Von Weber, daughter of Maj Ward Marston, of the U S Marine Corps. [See Aug 9th newspaper notice.]

Died: on Jul 21, at Coos, Coos Co, N H, C B Adams, of Wash City.

Died: on Aug 10, after a short illness, Boyle Ramsay, youngest son of Andrew H & Eliz S Smith, in his 6th year. His funeral will be this afternoon at 4 o'clock, from the residence of his parents, 436 N st, corner of 13th.

Died: on Aug 3, near Petersburg, in her 24th year, Mrs Mary G Judkins, wife of Rev Wm E Judkins, of the Va Conference, & eldest daughter of Wm Waring Ball, of Fairfax Co, Va. She was a loving daughter, devoted wife, & fond mother.

Died: on May 25, in Phil, Mrs Esther White Harris, wife of Dr Thos Harris, U S Navy. Mrs Harris was the grand-daughter of Bishop White, whose home was one of the loveliest on earth, & she was its crowning ornament. Of commanding beauty & impressive dignity, she did honors of the most hospitable house to universal admiration. Her married life, in Wash, & then Phil, was distinguished for its genuine charity. Mrs Harris died after a painful & lingering illness; she would cheer & console her invalid husband.

THU AUG 12, 1858
Members of Congress elect from Missouri:
St Louis district: J Richd Barret
Boone district: Thos L Anderson
Lewis district: John B Clark
Platte district: Jas Craig
Lafayette district: Saml H Woodson
Greene district: John S Phelps
Wash district: John W Noell

Hon Isaac Toucey, Sec of the Navy, has left Wash City with his family to sojourn a short time at his home in Connecticut. His official duties, during his absence, devolve on Chas W Welsh, the Chief Clerk of the Dept.

On Aug 13th, at 355 Pa ave, known as Werner's Restaurant, we shall offer for sale all his stock of fine liquors, to make room for improvements. –C R L Crown & Co, aucts 357 Pa ave

Edgehill School, Princeton, N J. –Rev Jas I Helm, or Rev Jas P Hughes, Principals.

Obit-died: on Jul 31, at the residence of his father, Rev Jos T Moore, in Gtwn, John S Moore, in his 31st year, after a distressing illness of several weeks. He was the eldest child of his parents, & was born & educated in this District. For many years he was a faithful & efficient officer in one of the bureaus of the War Dept. May he rest in peace!

Died: on Aug 11, Mary Fitman, aged 9 months & 11 days, daughter of John & Margaret Fitman. Her funeral is this morning at 10 o'clock, from L & 1st st north.

Died: on Aug 11, Sarah Louisa, infant daughter of Benj & Mary Reiss. Her funeral is this evening at 4 o'clock from her fathers' residence on G between 14th & 15th sts.

The funeral of Mrs Mary Wiseman will take place this evening at 6 o'clock, from Christ Church, near the Navy Yard. [No death date given.]

FRI AUG 13, 1858
The celebrated racing stallion "Ambassador" was killed by lightning on Thu last, on the plantation of Mr Chas N Merriwether, about 10 miles from Clarksville, Tenn.

Hon John McLellan, of Woodstock, Conn, died at his residence on Sunday, in his 93rd year. He was the oldest living graduate of **Yale College**. Among his surviving children is the wife of Prof Benj Silliman, sr.

Mrs Mary Massey, the oldest white inhabitant of King Geo Co, Va, aged 92 years, died on Tuesday last.

Boarding & Day School for Young Ladies-French & English: 309 F st, Wash, D C. The next academic term will begin on the 2nd Monday of Sep, & end on Jun 30th following. -Principal, Donald Macleod, A M, Univ of Glasgow

Select Classical School, on C st, between 6th & 4½ sts, formerly under the management of Mr G W Dorrance, will hereafter be conducted by J S Stowes. Long experience in teaching. School will be resumed on the first Mon in Sep, 1858. References: J Green, M D, Wash; Geo W Dorrance, A M; S G Dodge.

Cincinnati Gaz: terrible accident Tue, near College Hill. Mr Squire J John, of the furniture warerooms on 4th st, passed from his sleeping room to the rear part of his dwlg, & on opening the kitchen door discovered a large hawk flying about his barn. He called to the girl at work in the room to bring his gun, as it was handed to him he inquired if it was loaded. The girl replied that she thought it was not, & turned to procure some percussion caps, as directed. Mr John raised the hammer of the gun, & placed the butt upon the floor, to blow into the barrel, when a favorite house-dog came bounding through the open door, & springing to his master, he exploded the gun, the contents entering the face of Mr John, killed him instantly. He was an enterprising & industrious mechanic & by his own energy built an extensive business. He was about 40 years of age. Mr John left a wife & 8 daughters, the youngest an infant.

Hon Theodore S Fay, U S Minister to Switzerland, was married to Anna Lentwein, at Berne, on Jun 15. At the same time & place Dr Francis P Abbott, of Berlin, Prussia, [formerly of the State of Maine,] was married to Miss Caroline L, only daughter of Hon T S Fay.

Wm Rawle, an old & esteemed member of the Phil bar, died there on Aug 10.

Died: on Aug 12, Charles Michel James Enthoffer, aged 19 months, son of Jos & Eliz Ann Enthoffer. His funeral is this afternoon at 4½ o'clock, from the residence of the parents, 447 D st.

SAT AUG 14, 1858
The death of Most Rev Wm Walsh, Roman Catholic Archbishop of Halifax, N S, is announced as having occurred at his residence there on Tue. He was in his 54th year.

The wife of Geo Snow, of Arkansas, gave birth to 3 children Jul 26.

Fair Hill Boarding School for Girls, Sandy Spring, Montg Co, Md, will commence the 11th term on Sep 13th, & continue 42 weeks. –Richd S Kirk, Wm Henry Farquhar, Olney P O, Montg Co, Md. References: Benj Hallowell, Robt H Miller, W B Richards, Alexandria; Thos Scrivener, & Jos Libby, Gtwn.

Female Academy, I st, between 18th & 19th sts, will commence its 4th annual session on the first Monday in Sept. –E E Janney, Principal

Emerson Institute, H st, between 12th & 13th sts, select classical & mathematical school for boys, will resume on Sep 1. Number of students limited. –Chas B Young, Principal

I offer for sale my Farm, about 5 miles from Warrenton, containing 512 acres; with a frame dwlg & the usual outbldgs. Mr Courtnay, residing on the place, will show it, or Mr Geo B Williamson, near Warrenton. For price & terms, I refer to my atty, Rice W Payne, at Warrenton, Va. –Sarah Williamson

My farm for sale near Warrenton, Va, containing 540 acres; the dwlg house & out-bldgs are new. Refer to my atty, Rice W Payne, at Warrenton, Va. –Geo E Williamson, near Warrenton, Va.

Wm F Clary, Justice of the Peace & Genr'l Agent, Ofc 381 F st, between 8th & 9th sts, opposite the Patent Ofc. [Ad]

Late Mexican papers announce the death, on Jul 2, of ex-Pres Don Valentine Gomez Farias, at age 77 years. He had been feeble for a long time & inactive in politics.

Mrd: on Aug 12, at the residence of Govn'r Floyd, by Rev Dr Hall, Chas Ripley to Margaret Breckenridge Drake, both of Louisville, Ky.

Died: on Aug 12, Charles, infant son of Charles & Esther Ann Stott, aged 25 days.

Gtwn friends & citizens of Wash: Mrs Harriet Key Blunt is to give a course of her fine Readings from eminent authors at Forrest Hall, this evening. She is the daughter of the gifted author of the Star Spangled Banner. At the Hall of the Union Hotel, Gtwn, at 8 o'clock: tickets 50 cents, to be had at the door.

Rev J H Allen, formerly of Wash, having established himself in the delightful village of Jamaica Plain, Mass, will receive a limited number of pupils into his family.

MON AUG 16, 1858
Household & kitchen furniture at auction on Aug 31, by deed of trust from Wm H Faulkner to the subscriber, dated Aug 6, 1857, recorded in Liber J A S No 139, folios 263 thru 265, of the land records for Wash Co, D C. –M Thompson, trustee -A Green auct

Army orders, Headquarters of the Army, West Point, N Y, Aug 10, 1858, have just been promulgated by Gen Scott. The march, in the depths of winter, of Lt Col [now Col] P St Geo Cooke, commanding the 2nd Dragoons, from *Fort Laramie*, through the South Pass, to Green River; & that of Capt R B Marcy, of the 5th Infty, from Camp Scott over the mountains, to New Mexico, deserve, as they have already received, special commendation. Brvt Brig Gen Johnston has had the honor to be supported by officers of great intelligence, zeal, & experience. Yet it is not to be doubted that to his own high soldierly qualities, untiring exertions, tact, & sound judgment the credit for the condition & high tone of his army is pre-eminently due. By command of Brvt Lt Gen Scott. Irvin McDowell, Assist Adj Gen

John A Jones, formerly a member of the Md Legislature from St Mary's Co, died on Jul 12 in Texas, whither he emigrated in 1819.

Eleven **Sisters of Mercy**, from the house of the Order in Kinsale, Ireland, & destined for Cincinnati, arrived in N Y in the ship **Arago**. The Superior of the house in Kinsale is the lady who conducted the Sisters of Mercy to Crimea. The Sisters now arrived propose opening in Cincinnati a house similar in its objects to the Convent of Mercy in N Y. A company of Sisters of the Poor of St Francis, from their mother house at Aiz-la-Chapelle, are expected in a few weeks, also on their way to Cincinnati. They devote themselves in many ways to the poor & forlorn, & in Prussia have the care of the inmates in many of the public prisons.

The death of Rev E Smalley, of Troy, is a painful affair. He was the pastor of Union Church, in Worcester. He took a relaxation from the Church in Troy & went to Europe. He was sick all the voyage out, & on the return from Europe his sea-sickness came on again, & from it he never recovered.

Peter Williams, under sentence of death at Auburn, Maine, with a colored man, Abraham Cox, for the murder at sea of the captain, 2 mates & 1 man of the brig **Albion Cooper**, of Portland, has made a confession, admitting that himself & Cox committed the murders they were charged with. The motive appears to have been ill-treatment on the part of the mate. The weapon used in dispatching their victims was a hatchet.

Jas Farrell, of Andover, stopped at the Exchange Hotel in Providence on Fri, climbed out of the window in his room on the 3rd floor & dropped to the ground. He fractured his hip, jaw, & wrist. An empty liquor bottle in his pocket was probably the original cause.

Mr Logan met with a terrible death at Carpentersville, Ia, a few days ago. While erecting a lightning rod to the Presbyterian Church he was precipitated 100 feet by the breaking of one of his ladders, fracturing his skull in the most horrible manner.

On Sat week Augustus & Saml Gilchrist, & a Scotchman, McVicker, of Thomaston, & Miss Mary Flinton, of George's Island, Me, were upset in a boat by a sudden squall, & sunk with all on board. Miss Flinton's father witnessed the accident from the shore.

On Thu last week Dr John Malehorn, residing near Westminster, Md, had one of his legs & foot terribly mashed by falling between the seat & main beam of the horse-power of a threshing machine, which he was attending. No bones were broken, however.

Last week a little son of Judge Donaldson, in Montezuma, Indiana, was bitten on the arm by a spider while sleeping in a cradle. Inflamation spread to other parts of the body, & the 2nd day after the injury the child died.

Admx's sale in Phil: the estate of Gen Persifor F Smith, deceased: furniture, rifles, guns, pistols, swords, & uniform clothing: on Aug 23: including an antique Military Chair, made of wood, from the fortifications of the Castle of San Juan d'Uiloa.
–M Thomas & Sons, aucts, 139 & 141 south 4th st, Phil.

Groceries, Wines, & Liquors: 393 Pa ave. –Henry C Purdy, successor to Thompson & Hamilton.

Orphans Court of Wash Co, D C. In the case of Eliza T Berry, excx of Washington Berry, deceased, the executrix & the Orphans Court of Wash Co, D C, appointed Sep 7 next, for the final settlement of the personal estate of said deceased, with the assets in hand. -Ed N Roach, Reg/o wills

Mrd: on Aug 4, at Lecompton, Kansas, by Rev C M Callaway, Maj T W Sherman, of the U S Artl, to Miss Mary H, daughter of Hon Wilson Shannon, ex-Govn'r of Kansas, formerly of Ohio.

Died: on Aug 15, near Wash, David Miller, infant son of G Alfred & Sallie M Hall, aged 10 months & 26 days. His funeral will take place from the residence of Mr J A Bartruff, *Prospect Hill*, at 4 o'clock this evening.

Died: on Aug 11, at the residence of his grand-father, Rev Geo L Machenhimer, Calvert Co, Md, Arthur, eldest son of John W & Nannie C Baden, aged 20 months & 19 days.

Died: on Aug 15, in Wash City, Eugene, infant son of Fannie R & Dr Cornelius Boyle

Died: on Aug 13, Mr Andrew Mille, aged 54, a native of Marseilles, France, but for 25 years a resident of Wash City.

Goshen, Orange Co, N Y, Aug 14. Last night at the house of Chas Reeves, in Hamptonburg, Mr Reeves & his family were absent from home, leaving their house in the charge of 3 servants, Wm Saunders, Peter Shorech, & Mgt Shealy. Peter & Mgt were to be married next week. Wm Saunders, without a word, shot & killed Peter. He then shot Mgt who is still alive, but cannot survive but a few hours longer. Saunders has not yet been arrested.

TUE AUG 17, 1858
The Govn'r of Ky offers a reward of $600 for the arrest of Wm Healey, Archibald Healey, Jas Healey, & Noah Wiggins, or $150 each of the men, for their delivery to the jailer in Rockcastle Co. They are charged with killing Wm S Moore, Wm A Jones, & Jas H Jones.

N Y C, Aug 15. The ceremony of laying the corner-stone of the new St Patrick's Cathedral, by Bishop Hughes, has brought to mind the fact that the first church erected by the Catholics was the old St Peter's in Barclay st, 75 years ago. There are now 28 Catholic Churches in the city, 76 in the diocese, & in the arch-diocese 636 churches, & a Catholic population of 875,000. The ceremony was performed on Assumption Day, Aug 15, before an immense concourse of people.

The triumph complete! The Queen's message to the Pres of the U S & the Pres' reply. Greeting between the English & American Directors.
Trinity Bay, Aug 10.
To the Directors of the Atlantic Telegraph Co:
Europe and America are now united by Telegraph. Glory to God in the highest; on earth peace & good will towards men!
Directors of the Atlantic Co of Great Britain.
Trinity Bay, Aug 16-P M.
To the Associated Press:
The Cable is now finished & the communication perfected. You may look out for the Queen's Message this evening or tomorrow morning.
The Queen to the President.
Trinity Bay, Aug 16.
Honorable the Pres of the U S:
Her Majesty desires to congratulate the Pres upon the successful completion of this great international work, in which the Queen has taken the deepest interest. [No Signature.]
N Y, Aug 16.
We have a positive assurance from Mr McKay, the superintendent of the Newfoundland Telegraph line, that the message sent to the Pres actually came over the Atlantic Cable this afternoon, & that the cable is now in good order to transmit any reply the Pres may wish to send.
D H Craig, Agent Associated Press
+
The Pres of the U S received the first intimation of the working of the cable at the Soldiers' Home through the Associated Press by the hands of Govn'r Bigler. He immediately came to the city, found here the Queen's message. The following is his reply:
Pres' Message to the Queen.
Wash, Aug 16, 1858. The Pres cordially reciprocates the congratulations of her Majesty the Queen on the success of the great international enterprise accomplished by the science, skill, & indomitable energy of the two countries. It is a triumph more glorious, because far more useful to mankind, than was ever won by conqueror on the field of battle. May the Atlantic Telegraph, under the blessing of Heaven, prove to be a bond of perpetual peace & friendship between the kindred nations, & an instrument destined by Divine Providence to diffuse religion, civilization, liberty, & law throughout the world! In this view, will not all the nations of Christendom spontaneously unite in the declaration that it shall be forever neutral, & that its communications shall be held sacred in passing to the places of their destination, even in the midst of hostilities?

Danl O'Connell, a lad, fell from the roof of the Trimountain House, Boston, on Thu, while flying his kite, fell 5 stories to the sidewalk, & died the next day.

Day School for Young Ladies, 435 D st, between 2nd & 3rd sts, will commence on the first Monday in Sept next. –Misses Koones

Trust sale of valuable mill property: by deed of trust executed by Wm H Harrison & wife, for benefit of Meixsel & Grafton, of Balt City, dated Sep 22, 1857, recorded in the clerk's ofc of Warren Co, Va, the undersigned will offer at public auction, in front of the Front Royal Hotel, Warren Co, Va, the large brick Merchant Mill called Warren Mills & other bldgs, on the Shenandoah river, in said county. –Giles Cook, trustee, Warren Co, Va.

The subscriber offers for sale a number of bldg lots in & near Staunton, Va. Staunton is a thriving village; the society is polished & refined; the morning papers from Richmond, Balt, & Wash are received at Staunton by 2 o'clock every day, & the telegraphic wires afford means of instant communication with the cities of the East & South. The prices of lots will vary from one to four hundred dollars per acre. –Alex H H Stuart

Orphans Court of Wash Co, D C. Letters of administration on the personal estate of Bernard Brien, late of Wash Co, deceased. –Seraphim Masi, adm

Died: on Aug 16, George Knott, in his 55th year. His funeral will be at 1 o'clock from his late residence on the corner of Green & Dunbarton sts, Gtwn.

WED AUG 18, 1858
Trinity Bay, Aug 17, 1858. The Queen's message was completed this morning. It was commenced yesterday, & during its reception the telegraphers at Valentia desisted from sending it in order to make some slight repairs to the cable. Through a mistake, the part received was sent South as if it constituted the whole message. The following is the message entire: Valentia, [via Trinity Bay,] Aug 16, 1858. To the Pres of the U S: The Queen desires to congratulate the Pres upon the successful completion of the great international work in which the Queen has taken the deepest interest. The Queen is convinced that the Pres will join with her in fervently hoping that the electric cable which now connects Great Britain with the U S will prove an additional link between the nations whose friendship is founded upon their common interest & reciprocal esteem. The Queen has much pleasure in thus communication with the Pres, & renewing to him her wishes for the prosperity of the U S.
+
N Y, Aug 17, 1858. To the honorable Pres of the U S: I beg leave to transmit a message, this moment received from Trinity Bay, explaining the cause which prevented the whole of the Queen's message from being telegraphed from Valentia, together with the complete message itself. Shall we consider your message to her Majesty a full reply, & date it this day accordingly? The operators at Trinity Bay await our answer. –P Cooper
+
The Pres, upon receipt of the above, immediately authorized his dispatch of Monday night to be transmitted without change.

The Norfolk Herald newspaper celebrated its 64th anniversary on Fri last. The "Stars & Stripes" were raised to the flag-staff of the establishment.

Fire yesterday entirely destroyed the carpenter's shop on Wash st, between G & H sts, the property of Mr Thos W Birch.

Died: Aug 9, at Vicksburg, Miss, suddenly, Lt A A Holcomb, U S Navy, aged 46 years.

Local: the application of Mrs Sarah E Hess for a teacher-ship was referred to the Cmte on Examinations. Also, applications from Miss Lyida M Potts & Mrs O'Brien. Miss Amanda Baird was elected sub-assist teacher to the Female Dept of the 3rd district. In the same district the former teachers were re-elected except Misses Mirick, Moss, Sanderson, & Mesdames Clark & Freeman, who are suspended until the next meeting on account of having failed to furnish the tabular statements of their schools.

THU AUG 19, 1858
Wm Saunders, who murdered his fellow-servant, Peter Shorock, & attempted to kill Margaret Shealy, in Orange Co, N Y, has been arrested near Chester. It is said to be untrue that he committed the deed through jealousy. It is thought that Margaret will recover.

Remaining stock of grocers & fixtures at auction on Aug 25, at the store of T N Adams, 544 north M st, between 8th & 9th sts. -A Green auct

Wash Corp, Aug 16, 1858. 1-Cmte of Claims: bills for the relief of Jas T Ferry; of Albert Hart; & of Wm Forsyth, passed. Same cmte: asked to be discharged from the consideration of the ptns of of Edw P Walsh & Ellen Fitzgerald.

Valuable property for sale: the beautiful property of the late Edw Fitzgerald, corner of I & 18th sts, consisting of 5 lots & a 2 story brick bldg in square 106. Also lot 2 in square 685. –Thos Carbery, exc

Locust Grove Academy, 5 miles from Mechum's River Depot, Albemarle Co, Va. Instructors: Edw B Smith, A M, Principal; Summerfield Smith, A M. This School is preparatory to the Univ of Va, or to any college. Next session begins on Sep 6. Address at Yancey's Mills Post Ofc, Albemarle, Va.

Trustee's sale. The subscriber, as surviving executor & trustee of the will of David Peter, deceased, will sell at auction, on Sep 8, at the Circle in Wash City, lot 17 & 18 in square No 1; lot 1 in square 13; lots 16, 19, & 21 in square 24, & part of lot No 1 in square 2. -Geo Peter

Died: on Aug 18, Charles M, son of Thos & Phebe Sanderson, in his 27th year, leaving a wife & one child to mourn their irreparable loss. His funeral to tomorrow at 4 o'clock, from the residence of his father, corner of 10th & N sts, Navy Yard.

Died: on Aug 16, near Warrenton, Va, Mary Rosetta, only daughter of Henry B & Rosetta Otterback, aged 18 months. Her funeral is this afternoon at 4 o'clock, from the residence of her parents, at the Navy Yard.

New Orleans, Aug 17. The number of deaths reported from <u>yellow fever</u> for the week is 285. The number of deaths yesterday was 58.

FRI AUG 20, 1858
There is now a prospect that Col Fremont will be left in the undisturbed possession of his splendid domain in Calif. His lands, amounting to 45,000 acres, & containing inexhaustible mines of auriferous quartz, are situated in Mariposa Co, & he has already established a mill, which is producing gold to the amount of $2,600 per week. The lands of Col Fremont were held by him under a patent from the U S, but this did not deter trespassers from attempts to take possession of such choice portions as they thought likely to prove productive. More than a year ago an association, the Merced Mining Co, seized upon a part of the *Pine Tree Vein*, a rich gold mine in *Bear Valley*, where Col Fremont & his family are at present residing. An action was commenced, & Fremont recovered judgment in the justice's court, where the case was decided in his favor.

Wm S Pilcher, Mayor of the city of Louisville, Ky, died on Aug 14, after several months' illness. He was a native of Va, & a resident for several years of Shepherstown, in Jefferson Co. He had long been a leading politician in Ky, first as a Democrat & last as an American.

Mr Doolittle, of Chicago, who hired 2 men to whip the schoolmaster, Keith, because the latter had sent the boy home to wash his face, has been fined $500 & sent to the city prison for 6 months. Doolittle is a man of property.

On Monday night a large steam factory in Attleborough, Mass, owned by V H Capron, took fire in the boiler room & was entirely destroyed. The factory was occupied by Everett, Dean & Co, jewellers, Hayward & Briggs, jewellers, & Godfrey Wheelock, manufacturer of spool sewing cotton. The whole amount of property destroyed was about $30,000. Nearly 150 workmen have been thrown out of employment.

A new infty company has just been organized in Gtwn under the command of Capt J H McHenry Hollinsworth, who saw actual service in the war with Mexico, & had their first out-door parade on Monday. The company at present numbers between 40 & 50. Other ofcrs are: 1st Lt J S McKenny; 2nd do, E Cummins; 3rd do, Jno Cruikshank; 1st Sgt, Wm Cruikshank; 2nd do, J R Offley; 3rd do, S Robinson; 4th do, J Waters. The uniform will consist of dark blue, with blue facings, the same as the Infty of the U S Army. Arm-rifle musket.

Yesterday the ceremony for the laying of the corner-stone of a new hall for the use of the Potomac [Masonic] Lodge No 5 of Gtwn, took place on High, near Bridge st. The stone was laid by Grand Master Geo C Whiting.

Eugene Carusi, Atty at Law, ofc 483 6th st, one door south of Louisiana ave. [Ad]

Chauncey Warriner, Watchmaker & Jeweller, 34 4½ st, 3 doors north of Pa ave. [Ad]

Died: Aug 18, suddenly, at his residence, in PG Co, Md, Jas R Brent, aged about 56 years. His remains will be removed to St Peter's Church, in Wash City, where the funeral services will take place at 9 o'clock A M this day.

Died: Aug 19, in her 6th year, Julia Blatchford, daughter of Wm & Julia Linton. Her funeral will be on Aug 20 at 11 o'clock from the residence of her father, on 6th st, between D & E.

Chicago. Messrs Boggs & Smith were engaged in erecting brick stores on State st, above Van Buren st, next door to a frame bldg, 292, owned by John B Busch, & occupied by Jacob Rohm as a lager-beer saloon below & a residence above. Mr Boggs was some 3 inches over their line & he did not comply when asked to clear the line. Mr Busch's son, Frank Busch, pointed a loaded pistol through an open widow of the saloon & frightened the workers away. He was arrested & to stand trial, his father going his security in the sum of $500. He returned to the spot, & after consulting with his mother, Rohm, & others, the latter gave him a pistol, where he walked to where his victim was with other workmen, busy erecting a scaffold, & without speaking, shot him dead in his tracks. He was at once seized & disarmed & taken to the armory & locked up. His father & Rohm were also arrested as accessory before the fact. –Chicago Tribune.

SAT AUG 21, 1858

Detective officer Edw G Carlin, within an hour of the robbery of the U S Mint, at Phil, on Wed, arrested Chas Mervine & Chas Morris, & by positive evidence succeeded in fixing the crime upon them. The prisoners are both young men of refined address. It is thought that the names given are assumed ones. They were committed in default of $2,500 each.

A cow, belonging to Mr Follen, near **Spring Vale**, Fairfax Co, Va, lately brought forth, at one birth, four well formed vigorous calves, which are all doing well.

The Columbian College, Wash, D C, will commence on Sep 29. –J G Binney, President

Warwick School for Boys, 5 miles from Wash, & 3 from Alexandria. Rev E B Lippitt, Rector. Mr C E Wiedmayer, Associate Principal & Instructor in Modern Language.

The Misses' Hawleys' English & French Boarding & Day School, 167 Pa ave, between 17th & 18th sts, will be re-opened on Sep 13 & close Jul 1.

Gunpowder accidents. 1-Shocking accident at Buffalo, N Y, on Tue, during the celebration of the Atlantic cable. A wrought-iron mortar belonging to Mr Palmer, the pyrotechnist, & used by him in the display of fireworks, exploded. Joshua Dusenbury had his thigh crushed & later died. John Lancanshire was injured & suffered some hours from concussion of the brain. Geo Prime, about 16, was struck in the back of the neck, the missile buried itself about 2 inches deep. E Buckley, about 12, received a severe wound. Mr Mauer received a foot wound. 2-At Phil, an artl company fired a salute of 100 guns, & Geo Lowber & Thos Snyder were seriously injured. They both have families. 3-At Portland, Me, on Thu, in honor of a visit from a military corps of Montreal, Canada, Lt Proctor, of the Boston Fusiliers received a blank cartridge in his arm; Chas Sutherland, member of the Highlanders, was shot in the thigh; & Cpl Lautler, of the Montreal Rifles, narrowly escaped death, a charge passing through his chapeau.

The Female English & French Collegiate Institute has a through & practical knowledge of the French language are not equaled or surpassed by any other institution in Wash City. Institute: 182 I st, Gadsby's Row. –Hiram Corson, Principal. -M'me Caroline Rollin Corson, Vice principal.

Mrd: on Aug 19, in Wash City, by Rev Wm Edwards, Mr Jos S Graves to Miss E J Glover, both of Gtwn.

Died: on Aug 18, at Rippon, Jefferson Co, Va, Mrs Sidney Turner, the estimable wife of Wm F Turner, of said county, & daughter of Edw Patterson, of Balt.

MON AUG 23, 1858

Celebration at Louisville, Ky, on the news of the Atlantic telegraph were accompanied by some painful accidents. A watchman, Geo Coulter, in interfering with some boys who had a bonfire in the street, was shot by Wm *Gilman & died in half an hour. *Gilmore was also shot in the breast, & it is doubtful that he will recover. *Copied as written. The wife of Mr Nick Deamer, while standing with a child in her arms, at 3rd & Main sts, was struck in the face by a rocket. Both eyes were burnt & she may loose one & perhaps both eyes. Mr Murdoch, of the firm of Bell & Murdoch, was seriously burnt.

On Fri the body of John W Young, a butcher in the Alexandria market, was found dead in Hooff's run, at the upper end of King st. He left town in his cart to go to his home, near the cemetery, on Thu night, & it is supposed he drove off the unprotected platform called a bridge, & hence the accident. The cart was lying on him, & the horse still attached to it.

Paul Juneau, son of Solomon Juneau, the first white man that settled in Milwaukee, was accidentally shot & killed at Horicon, Wisc, on Fri, by a boy with whom he had been shooting at a mark. He was a member of the Legislature, & leaves a wife & children.

Died: on Aug 15, at the residence of his father, Wm H Hebb, in St Mary's Co, Md, Dr Thos Wm Hebb, aged 26 years & 4 months.

Died: on Jul 20, at his residence, **Piney Branch**, Fairfax Co, Va, after a protracted & severe illness, Chas Stewart, in his 77th year.

Desirable residence on H st at private sale: the dwlg, adjoining the residence of Col Emory, & nearly opposite that of Hon Mr Faulkner. Apply to Geo Gordon, 1st house north of the Pension Ofc, or to Maj Thomas, of the War Dept.

TUE AUG 24, 1858

Col Ed Yarboro, son of the proprietor of Yarboro's Hotel, in Raleigh, N C, committed suicide in that city on Tue night.

Household & kitchen furniture at auction on Sep 1, at the residence of Rev G D Cummins, 21 Indiana ave. -Jas C McGuire, auct

A bloody tragedy at St Mary's, Mo, on Aug 10. An old man, John Shaaf, killed his own son, Henry Shaaf, by shooting him with a gun loaded with 16 buckshot & a slug. He shot him it appears without provocation. The old man was arrested & taken to St Genevieve, where he was committed to jail. The son leaves a wife & a family of children.

Mrd: on Aug 17, in Wash City, at Trinity Church, by Rev H J Kershaw, Mr E G W Hall, of Upper Marlboro, Md, to Isabel, youngest daughter of Horatio C Scott.

Mrd: on Aug 23, in Wash City, by Rev J N Coombs, Capt J D Cornwall, of N Y, to Miss Mary E Ulmer, of Rockville, Md.

Died: on Aug 23, Mary Jane, only daughter of Wm & Matilda Rutherford, aged 17 months & 3 days. Her funeral will take place this afternoon at 4 o'clock, from the residence of her parents, 410 13th st, between G & H sts.

English & Classical Academy for Young Gentlemen, Principal, J H A Bridge, M D. The Academy was opened in Apr, 1858 & will begin the 2nd scholastic year on the first Monday of Sep, 1858. Location: 9th & H sts until the new Academy is completed.

Subscriber wishing to retire from farming, offers at private sale the farm on which she now resides, on the river road, from Gtwn, D C, to Seneca Mills, Montg Co, Md: contains 225½ acres; comfortable dwlg house & kitchen, & necessary out-bldgs. –Amy C Fisher

Orphans Court of Wash Co, D C. Letters of administration on the personal estate of Thos Reade, late of Wash Co, deceased. –Robt Clarke, adm

Miss O'Driscoll's French & English Boarding School, 1626 Summer st, near Logan square, Phil, is now ready for the reception of pupils. Apply at the academy.

WED AUG 25, 1858
The U S sloop-of-war **St Louis** was launched on Sat at the Brooklyn Navy Yard. She is to carry 18 guns.

Administrator's sale of household & kitchen furniture at auction on Sep 1, at the late residence of John H Somervell, deceased, 518 north H st, between 6th & 7th sts.
-Sarah J Somervell, admx -A Green auct

M Alexis Soyer, one of the most energetic, intelligent, & remarkable enthusiasts in the culinary science, has died at Paris of renal apoplexy.

The death of Lt Holcombe, U S Navy, by apoplexy, at the Prentiss House in Vicksburg, is announced. Lt Holcombe married a daughter of the late Geo Watterston, of Wash City. Lt Holbombe's wife & several children survive him.

Chas Radiminski, 1st Lt of 2nd Cavalry, died at Memphis on Aug 18. He had many friends in Wash City, & was warmly esteemed. The War Dept has received information of the death of Maj St Clair Denny, paymaster in the army. He died at Pittsburg.

Williams & Cox, the murderers of the ofcrs & one of the crew of the brig **Albion Cooper**, are to be executed at Lewistown Falls, Me, on Fri next. This will be the first execution in Maine for near a quarter of a century.

Orphans Court of Wash Co, D C. In the matter of the ptn of the children & heirs at law of Wm W Whitmore, deceased. Richd H Laskey, trustee, reported the sale of the real estate of Wm W Whitmore, deceased, [other than the sale made to Frances Guest, which is hereby absolutely rejected,] be ratified. The report states the amount of sales, including the sales to said Guest, to be $1,426.74, & excluding said sale to be $1,041.74. –Wm F Purcell. -Ed N Roach, Reg/o wills

Obit-died: Geo P Blevins died a few days since near Selma, Ala, from injuries received by being thrown from a buggy. He is said to have been one of the finest classic scholars in the South. At Princeton College, he & Chas G Leland & other talented young writers, edited the College Magazine. In after years he was a favorite contributor to the Knickerbocker.

Died: on Jul 31, at **Woodland**, his residence in Loudoun Co, Va, Mr Landon Carter, in his 85th year. About 15 years ago he united himself with the Protestant Episcopal Church, of which he died a member. His last illness was tedious & painful, & continued a little over 3 weeks. Precious in the sight of the Lord is the death of his Saints. –J L

Died: on Aug 22, Ann McKay, wife of Geo McKay. She was a native of Perthshire, Scotland, & lived for many years in Montreal, Canada, where she raised her family of children, but for the past 3½ years she has been a resident of Wash. She was a faithful wife & mother, & lived & died in peace with God & an example to all who knew her.

Alexandria, Aug 24. Jas Green killed Carver, at Mobile, at Warrenton Springs, Va, last night, with a bowie knife in a rencontre. They had made arrangements to fight a duel, but were arrested in Wash. Both were young men. Green has been arrested.

THU AUG 26, 1858
Wash Corp-Mon. 1-Ptn of Peter Emrich for the remission of a fine: of Chas B Queen; & Saml Walcup, for the same: all referred to the Cmte of Claims. 2-Benj Hodges, resident student at the Wash Asylum, asking indemnity for losses sustained by the fire on Mar 2, 1857: referred to the Cmte on the Asylum.

Valentia, Aug 25. I send my warmest congratulations on the success of the Atlantic Telegraph, & God be praised. –Saml Gurney, Chairman of Atlantic Telegraph Co.

Died: on Aug 15, at New Orleans, of yellow fever, Henry E Senstack, aged 33 years. The deceased was a native of Wash, D C.

Arrival of the U S steamer **San Jacinto**, Cmder H H Bell, arrived at N Y on Tue from Hong Kong May 14, Batavia May 24, Simon Bay [Cape Good Hope] Jun 29, St Helena Jul 22. All well. The **San Jacinto** has been absent from the U S 2 years & 11 months. List of her ofcrs: Cmder, H H Bell; Lts, H H Lewis, J C Williamson, John Rutledge, Jas M Duncan, Walter W Queen, R T Bowen; Purser, J O Bradford; Capt of Marines, John D Simms; Chief Enginer, B F Isherwood; Chaplain, R Govin; Assist Surgeons, R P Daniel & J E Semple; 1st Assist Engineers, Andrew Lawton & E S De Luce; 2nd do, Henry W Spooner & Wm B Brooke; 3rd do, Ten Eyck Biles, Henry C Victor, & Chas H Baker; Capt's clerk, Ernest Clifford; Purser's clerk, D A Edwards; Boatswain, Chas Johnston; Gunner, John C Ritter; Carpenter, Asa Poinsett; Sailmaker, Stephen Seaman; Acting Masters Mates, Chas H Berret & Virginius L Bracey.

Western Academy, corner of 17th & I sts, Wash. A select school for boys will commence Sep 6, & close Nov 15. Dept of Math: Silas L Loomis, A M. Dept of Languages: A Geo Wilkinson, A B.

A rencontre took place on Monday, at Warrenton Springs, between Mr Jas Green, son of Jones Green, deceased, & Mr Quentin Carver, of Mobile, which resulted in the instant death of Mr Carver. Mr Green is under arrest. –Alexandria Sentinel [Oct 4th newspaper: Carver is about 30; Green about 25. Examination in the County Court, Warrenton, Va, Sep 30, 1858. Sworn in & testified: Walter H Ratcliffe; Mr Douglas Tyler; Mr Wm H Dulaney; Mr W Green; Mr John Linton-of Wash City; Mr Yeatman, a police ofcr from Wash; Robt H Hutton; John Green; Geo Tyler; C W Ashton; Moses M Green, manager of the Springs; Capt Green; Littleton Tyler; John S Fant; John M Fant; justice of the peace; Richie Green; Geo H Shumate; Jas R Shirley; Dr S C Smoot-of Wash; Thos Skinner, barkeeper at the Springs; Jos M Kennedy; & David Waddell. The magistrates decided to send the prisoner for trial before the next Criminal Court, to be holden in April next. -Reporter]

Died: on Aug 25, after a severe illness, Wm E Crossfield, in his 48th year, a native of Wash City. His funeral will take place this afternoon at 4 o'clock, from his late residence, 344 9th st, above N Y ave.

The subscriber offers at private sale the property known as the **Bakery**, on the south side of the canal, near the Alexandria aqueduct, together with the wharf, which is about 210 feet deep from canal to river-the tow-path being included in this property. The **Bakery** has a front of 64 feet on the canal. Also, a Wood & Coal Yard, now in the occupancy of Kurtz & Orme & Mr Barron. This property has a front of 120 feet on the canal & 102½ feet on the west side of Green st. –Thos Brown, or S T Brown, Wash, or to Barnard & Buckey, Gtwn.

Desirable Farm for sale: I offer my farm, **North Bend**, in Amherst Co, on Buffalo river, containing 400 acres; with a new 2 story brick house. All the bldgs are new. I can sell the above Tract of Land on very favorable terms. –Wm T Barret, New Glasgow, Amherst Co, Va

FRI AUG 27, 1858
Trustee's sale of 2 valuable lots on Pa ave, between 19th & 20th sts west: on Sep 14, on the premises, by deed of trust, dated Aug 22, 1857, recorded in Liber J A S No 141, folios 334: part of lot 5 in square 118, fronting 15 feet on Pa ave, s w of the lot conveyed by Saml Harkness to J S Higdan & J R Rhodes; running to lot 6, with the same to the n w corner of said J S Higdan & J S Rhodes' lot. Also, part of lot 5 in the same square, bounded by a lot conveyed by Uriah Forrest to Benj Coombes. –Thos J Fisher, trustee -Jas C McGuire, auct

In Gtwn, Ky, a few days since, a little son of Hon Alvin Duvall met his death when the father & mother were away from home. A little negro girl got a vial of hartshorn & was playfully holding it to the noses of the children. It accidentally spilled into the mouth & nose of the little boy. He died in 30 hours after suffering intense pain.

Central Academy, E & 10th sts, L Merchant, A M, Principal: will resume on Sep 1.

Ordered by the Orphans' Court of PG Co, Md, upon the suggestion of W Parker Griffen & Susannah P Bryan, two of the sureties upon the bond of said E Pliny Bryan, as adm of the late Wm Bryan of Richd, that they are in danger of suffering from said securityship; that the said E Pliny Bryan indemnify & counter secure the said securities, as required by the act of assembly in such case made & provided, on or before Oct 4 next, the counter security to be approved by this court. –Wm A Jarboe, Reg o/wills

Mrd: on Aug 23, at Stonington, Conn, in Calvary Church, by Rev Mr Weston, his Excellency Theodore Marinas Roest Van Limburg, Minister Resident of his Majesty the King of the Netherlands to the U S, to Isabella, daughter of Hon Lewis Cass, U S Sec of the State.

Mrd: on Aug 26, by Rev Mr O'Toole, of St Patrick's Church, Richd B Darnall, of Anne Arundel Co, to Fanny Maria, relict of the late Dr O'Leary, daughter & grand-daughter of the late John & Wm Walshe, Atty at Law, Dublin, Ireland.

Mrd: on Aug 25, in Wash City, by Rev Mr Granbury, Mr Columbus Beach to Miss Caroline V Starr.

Died: on Aug 16, at the residence of his daughter, Mrs Amelia Sanders, at Sarcoxie, Jasper Co, Missouri, Maj Thos Moseley, jr, [father of Wm S Moseley, of the Genr'l Land Ofc,] in his 67th year of his age. Maj Moseley was born in Woodford Co, Ky, on Jul 12, 1792; emigrated to the Territory of Missouri in 1819; upon the organization of the State gov't was appointed Clerk of the Circuit Court of Madison Co, which office he held 14 years. He removed to New Madrid Co, elected to the Genr'l Assembly of the State & served as a Rep during the sessions of 1834 & 1835. In 1848 he was appointed by Pres Taylor Indian Agent for the Wyandottes, Shawnees, & the Delawares. He was an honored member of the Masonic Fraternity, & received the rites of Masonic burial. His disease was consumption, from which he suffered many years. He left behind him a wife & 4 children, besides grand children & a large circle of friends.

Depredators arrested yesterday on the farm of Dr Henry Haw, charged with robbery of corn, potatoes, & turkeys: Wm Dowling, 20; Wm Moore, 30; & Edw Humphrey, 20. Dowling & Moore were committed to jail, Humphrey is out on security. They live on plunder by day, like gypsies, & use the grave-yards for sleeping in at night.

Died: on Aug 24, in Hamilton Village, West Phil, Maria L Horner, wife of John W Horner, & daughter of the late Wm M Lansdale, of Md.

Yazoo plantation & 100 negroes for sale: about 65 miles above Yazoo city: containing 4,640 acres of land; with a new gin-house, overseer's house, comfortable quarters for 100 negroes, & other out-bldgs. Mr Jos B Willis, now on the place, will show the property. Apply to A Burwell, E B Willis, C A Manlove, Vicksburg, Miss, or Messrs Martin, Cobb & Co, New Orleans.

SAT AUG 28, 1858
Improved property on the Island at auction, on Sep 1, part of lot No 5, in square 585, with a frame house & a small back bldg. The property belongs to J G Nichols, Mary Nichols, wife of said J G Nichols, will not agree to join with her husband in the execution of a deed to the purchaser, wishing to reserve her right to dower. -A Green auct

Gonzaga College: the course of studies is substantially the form of teaching [*Ratio studiorum*] followed for more than 300 years in the Jesuit Colleges in Europe, & since 1790 in our own country. No one is admitted even to the preparatory who cannot read & write. No attendance at our religious exercises is exacted or expected of non-Catholic students. The examinations are in Feb & Jun. The Scholastic Exercise of this Institution, favorably known heretofore as the Washington Seminary, will be resumed on Sep 6. –Chas H Stonestreet, Pres

Circuit Court of Wash Co, D C: Wm G Pearson vs Augustus Jay. About 1834 Jos Pearson died seized & intestate of certain real estate in Wash, viz: lots 1, 2, 12 thru 18 in square 772; lots 1, 2, 13 thru 20 in square 773; all of square 775 except a lot 144 feet 2 inches at the n w corner thereof; lots 2 thru 6 in square 804; lots 2 thru 9 in square 805; lots 2 thru 5 in square 806; lots 2 thru 5 in square 807; all of square 710; lot 1 thru 33 in square 672; lots 1 thru 25 in square 711; lot 1 in square 712; lots 5 thru 23 in square 855; lots 1, 3 thru 7, 10 thru 12, & 17 thru 19, & half of 8 in square 266; & all of square 931; that said Jos Pearson left surviving him a widow & 9 children; that one of his said children, Josephine Pearson, intermarried with P Augustus Jay, & they have both since died, leaving one child, Augustus Jay, who is a minor & resides out of D C; that, by the deaths of several of said children & conveyances from others & from said widow, which are particularly set forth in the bill, all of said property has become vested in the cmplnt & said infant, Augustus Jay, viz-7 undivided tenths in cmplnt & 3 undivided tenths in said Augustus Jay. The object & prayer of the bill is to have a partition made of said real estate between the cmplnt & said minor; or, if a partition cannot be made, to have the property sold & the proceeds divided. Absent dfndnt to appear in this Court, in person or by solicitor, on or before the 2nd Monday of Jan next. –Jas S Morsell, Assist Judge Circuit Court D of C -Jno A Smith, clerk

Gtwn Female Seminary-Boarding & Day School, will resume on Sep 15 next.
-M J Harrover, Principal

Died: on Aug 20, of consumption, at Strattsville, Clarion Co, Pa, Richd Dillon, [printer,] of Wash, in his 21st year of his age.

Mrd: on Aug 26, at the residence of the bride's mother, by Rev Mr Finckel, Hermann H Voss to Miss Lucy, 2nd daughter of the late Julius Peters.

MON AUG 30, 1858
The sloop-of-war **St Louis** "launched" at N Y a few days ago, is 30 years old, having been built at the Wash navy yard in 1828. She is a 2nd class sloop, carries 20 guns, has been on the stocks repairing for some time, & goes into the dry-dock to be coppered.

Thu at Phil: 1-Jas Freas, a young man, was murdered in West Phil by a dissolute fellow, Chas Stiles. 2-Louis Orr, a lad, was crushed to death at Broad & Girard ave by the falling of a marble slab. 3-A son of Saml Smith, 4 years old, was scalded to death by falling into the gutter in Cherry st, which receives the waste hot water from Wells & Webster's steam saw mill in Sterling alley. 4-Augustus Schnackenberger died in convulsions in Parrish st. 5-A daughter of Mrs Buckingham, age 10 years, was burnt to death by the explosion of a camphene lamp, at her residence near 3rd & Poplar.

Capt Jos Dowd, of Madison, [a promising young shipmaster,] was trolling for blue-fish near the Race-in company with Capt Post, of Essex-he was knocked overboard by the boom of the sail boat, or pulled into the water by a large fish, & instantly disappeared. Capt Post spent several hours looking for him, without effect. Capt Dowd was in command of a Liverpool packet, was 26 years old, & had been married 3 weeks.
–New Haven Register

New Female Academy is about to be opened by Miss Violetta Jones & her accomplished associates, offering the best guarantees for superior personal training & literary instruction. –Local Item

Obit-died: on Aug 23, at Stafford, Conn, Hon Calbin Willey, formerly U S Senator from Conn. He would have been 82 years of age if he had lived till Sep 15 next; was born at East Haddam, Conn, Sep 15, 1776; commenced the study of law at Hebron in Jun, 1795, with John Thompson Peters, late a Judge of the Supreme Court; in 1798 was admitted to the bar in Tolland Co, & practiced law that year. Represented Stafford in the Gen Assembly of his State twice; in 1806 was appointed the first postmaster at Stafford Springs, until he removed to Tolland in 1808. While in Tolland he was 8 years postmaster & 7 years Judge of Probate for Stafford district; was an Elector of Pres & Vice Pres of the U S in 1824, 7 times represented the town in the Gen Assembly, was 2 years a member of the State Senate, & 6 years a member of the U S Senate, which time expired Mar, 1836. Since then he held no public office, save that of justice of peace, but pursued with assiduity his profession.

Notice of copartnership: Nat'l Lime Kilns, formerly E S Smoot's: corner of N Y ave & 20th st. Orders to be left at P W Dorsey's, 7th & I sts; F Wheatley's, 37 Water st; Dorsey & Earnest, High st, Gtwn; or at the Kilns, will receive prompt attention.
–Wheatley & Dorsey

Obit-died: Hon Wm Graham, at his residence, a few miles from Valorica, Ind, in his 77th year. He was born upon the frontier, where schools were almost unknown, & where the labor of the pioneer was divided between subduing the forest & defending his hearth-stone from the fury of the savages. He obtained the elements of a common-school education. He was a member of the first Constitutional Convention of Indiana, & served for many years in both branches of the Legislature. In 1820 he was elected presiding ofcr of the House of Reps. In 1837 he was elected a member of Congress, & at the close of that Congress he retired to private life. [No death date given-appears current.]

Died: on Thu, ex-Govn'r Ralph Metcalf, in Claremont, N H, of erysipelas, aged about 65 years. He was a man of considerable education & ability, & leaves a handsome fortune the result of frugal habits & careful management. He was president of a bank at Newport, N H, & had recently built one of the finest houses in Claremont, his native town.

Died: on Aug 20, Mr Edw Philbrick, who was the oldest citizen but one of Concord, N H, 89 years of age. For 23 years he was one of the door-keepers to the N H Legislature, & for many years was a messenger in the Merrimac Co Courts.

TUE AUG 31, 1858
Aaron J Patterson, landsman, born at Wash, aged 19 years, who had just entered the naval service, fell overboard from the U S ship **Pennsylvania**, at Norfolk, on Sat, & was instantly killed, his head coming in contact with the chains & gangway in his descent.

Richmond Enquirer-Gloucester Co, Aug 19, 1858. Whale fishing in the Chesapeake. On Aug 4 a Whale was spotted at the mouth of North & Ware rivers, on Mobjack bay. On the Monday following an extraordinary noise on the North river, near the residence of Warner T Taliaferro, attracted that attention of the family. On Aug 11th the whale was off the residence of Dr P A Taliaferro, & that gentleman, with his brother Edwin Taliaferro, accompanied by Mrs ___, took off after the whale. Pulling the boat within a few feet of his body, far enough off to escape a blow from his tail, Dr Taliaferro leaped overboard into 5 feet water, & boldly attacked him with an impromptu lance, made of an old Toledo blade that had done service in several wars. Though mortally wounded, the whale would not yet yield; exhausted & unable to escape, the boat, pulling fearlessly upon him, headed him within a few hundred yards of shore, where cables & ropes with fastened to his tail & he was dragged to the shore by a force of over 150 negroes, who had assembled to witness the sport.

Mrd: on Aug 24, by Rev G W Samson, Mr French Graham to Miss Amanda Courtney, both of Wash.

Died: on Aug 30, in Wash City, Anna Jane Hawke, in her 18th year, after an illness of 5 days. Her funeral is on Sep 1 at 3 o'clock, from the residence of her aunt, Mrs C Evans, on E st, between 6th & 7th sts, Navy Yard. The funeral service will take place at St Patrick's Church.

WED SEP 1, 1858
The chair of Greek in the Lynchburg College has been filed by the appointment of Patrick Henry Cabell, a graduate of Emory & Henry College, Va. The chair of Mental & Moral Science will be filled by Rev W W Walker.

The Lexington [Miss] Advertiser announces the death, in Holmes Co, of Rev Mr Cooper, the original dreamer of Cooper's Well, an eccentric, but eloquent & good man. The celebrated waters, Cooper's Wells, were his discovery & once his property.

The Corp of Gtwn on Monday ratified the condemnation of the property occupying the site of the newly projected Aqueduct st, between Pa ave, near 26th & Green sts, Gtwn, which was valued by a jury a few days since at $6,615. It is thought that about $4,000 more of adjacent property will be taken in, so as to render the improvement of the place as complete & handsome as possible.

Yesterday an alarm was raised by a domestic in the house of Mr Arthur Scott, on Capitol Hill, that a burglar was on the premises. A watchman, Alfred Henning, in the neighborhood, gave chase, but the burglar made for the woods & escaped.

Died: on Aug 31, in Wash City, at the residence of her daughter, Mrs Mary Ann Jones, in her 83rd year, after a long & painful illness, Mrs Anne Page, relict of the late Wm Byrd Page, of Clarke Co, Va. Her funeral is tomorrow at 12 o'clock M, from Christ's Church, Alexandria, Va.

THU SEP 2, 1858
A Telegraphic despatch announces the death at Baton Rouge, La, on Sunday last, of Dr Harney, of the U S Army, & a brother of Gen Harney. [Sep 8th newspaper: Dr B F Harney died on Aug 29, at his residence at Baton Rouge, La: he was born in the State of Delaware, removed to Mississipi, & soon after completed his medical educaton; received into the U S military service as surgeon & shared in the hardships & glories of the campaign of 1815. His age is about 80 years, the oldest surgeon in the U S army, & was, by seniority, entitled to the rank of Surgeon Gen, which we understand he twice declined accepting.]

A son of Mr Ephraim Clement, of Wheelock, aged about 15, was accidentally shot on Wed last, in St Johnsbury, Vt, by carelessly handling a pistol. A fatal result is anticipated.

Steam engine, lathes, tools & iron at auction: on Sep 8, at the Machine Shop of Mr C Buckingham, on C st, between 10th & 11th sts, his entire stock. –Wall & Barnard, aucts

Extensive sale of superior household & kitchen furniture at auction on Sep 6, at the residence of Mrs Col Broom 373 3rd st, between D & E sts. –A Green auct

Petersburg Express. Fatal encounter in Dinwiddie Co, on Thu, between 2 highly esteemed citizens: Mr Morgan Burns, of Dinwiddie, & Mr W W Battle, of Sussex. Mr Burns had unsettled accounts standing against Mr Battle. A heated quarrel ended over the matter, when Battle shot Burns, who fell dead upon the spot.

John Nehastic, a Bohemian, but one month in this country, has been arrested in Chicago for killing his daughter Marie, 5 years old, to save her from starvation, a fate which had overtaken a younger child a day or two before.

Marcellus Roe, one of the most esteemed & successful farmers in Cecil Co, Md, died on Aug 22, as it is supposed, from drinking water conveyed through leaden pipes. He had suffered for a year or two past from this cause, & had been warned by his physician against the use of the water, but he continued to use it. –Elkton Democrat

Geo Combe, the great champion of philosophical phrenology, & author of the Constitution of Man, died at the hydropathic institution at Moor-Park, Surry, on Aug 14. He was born in Edinburgh in 1788, where he has always resided. In 1833 he married Miss Cecilia Siddons, & with her, in 1838, went to the U S, where he remained until 1840. The latter period of his life was one of very infirm health.

Orphans Court of Wash Co, D C. Letters of administration on the personal estate of John A F Todstchinder, late of Wash Co, deceased. –Williminer Todstchinder, admx

Mrd: on Aug 31, in Wash City, by Rev Mr Swentzell, Mr Wm A Caldwell to Miss Margaret A Duvall, all of Wash City.

Mrd: on Aug 31, by Rev B J Bittinger, Mr Alex'r Garden to Miss Ann Andrews.

$4 reward for strayed or stolen Red Buffalo Cow, giving milk. –Timothy O'Brien, in the alley between 2nd & 3rd st & F & G sts.

U S Patent Ofc, Wash, Aug 31, 1858. Ptn of Henry Stanley, of Albany, N Y, praying for the extension of a patent granted to him on Jan 4, 1845, for an improvement in coal stoves, for 7 years from the expiration of said patent, which takes place on Jan 4, 1859. –Jos Holt, Com'r of Patents

FRI SEP 3, 1858
Miss Mary Myers, aged 16 years, an accomplished girl, was burnt at Chicago on Tue last, & died in 6 hours, by the explosion of a lamp filled with camphene.

St John's Academy will be open for the reception of Boys & Young Gentlemen on Monday, at 405 15th st, between H & I sts. –L J Draper, M D, President

The Duke of Mecklenburg-Strelitz has placed a laurel crown of gold on the tomb of Mme Sontag, who lies buried by her sister Nina's side in the chapel of the convent at Mariental, a village near Dresden. Inscription: "To the best of wives and of mothers, the most faithful of friends, the most beautiful and amiable of women, the greatest of songstresses, this crown is dedicated by George, Grand Duke of Mechlenburg-Strelitz."

The corner-stone of the Md Agricultural College was laid on Aug 24 by Chas B Calvert, on the site selected for the purpose, n w of Bladensburg village, on the property known as **Rossburg**, purchased by the Association from Mr Calvert. Trustees of the institution present: Col J A Sothoron, St Mary's Co; Col Chas Carroll, Howard Co; John Merryman, Balt Co, [the Pres of the State Agricultural Society;] W W Corcoran, Wash City; Jas T Earl, Queen Anne' Co, [late Pres of the State Agricultural Society;] Hon J Dixon Roman, of Wash Co; & W T Mitchell, of Chas Co.

Yesterday Mr Fuller Darnell, for the past 4 years in the employ of Messrs Barnes & Mitchell as book-keeper, left their store to go to his boarding-house. He had complained a little during the day, & went home to use some remedy. He died a few minutes after he arrived there, lying on his bed. The cause assigned by his medical attendant is disease of the heart. Mr Darnell was verging on 60 years of age, & was much respected.

Mrd: on Aug 25, in Warrenton, N C, at the residence of the bride's father, Miss Catharine V Williams, daughter of John T Williams, to Dr J Chambliss, of Mississippi.

Died: on Aug 30, at **Welbourn Hall**, Loudoun Co, Va, in her 30th year, Mrs Rebecca Ann Dulany, the wife of Richd Henry Dulany. Mrs Dulany was a consistent member of the Methodist Episcopal Church from the time she was 15 years old till she died.

Died: on Sep 2, Wm B Worthington, in his 29th year. His funeral will take place from his father's residence, on L, between 8th & 9th sts, today at 3½ P M.

Died: on Aug 7, suddenly, at the U S Hotel, Long Branch, N J, Mr Jas Bingham, aged 34, late of Boston.

Pittsburg, Sep 2. Accident last night on the Allegheny Valley Railroad near Hutton's Station, when the last car, containing a large party returning from a camp-meeting, was thrown from the track. Miss Mary Kincaide was killed. 20 others were injured. [Sep 4th newspaper: Mrs Mary Anne, daughter of J T Kincaid, of this city, was instantly killed. John Rockley had his skull fractured & J M McCleneary had his arms broken.]

SAT SEP 4, 1858
Hon F K Zollicoffer, member of Congress from the Nashville district, Tenn, has been appointed Pres of the Nashville & Chatanooga Railroad.

Superior Cabinet Furniture: Edwin Green, at his Metropolitan Cabinet Ware rooms, 178 & 180 Pa ave, between 17th & 18th sts. [Ad]

Rev Eleazer Williams, more generally known, perhaps, as claiming to be the Dauphin of France, died at Hogansburgh, N Y, on Aug 28. For some time back we announced his indisposition. [Sep 8th newspaper: Rev Eleazer Williams was for many years a missionary of the Episcopal Church among the St Regis Indians. He was between 70 & 80 years old when he died, & in the war of 1812, was a bold & skillful leader of the St Regis Rangers, under Gen Dearborn. Mr Williams' father, Thos Williams, was, if I mistake not, of a Massachusetts family, &, though a white man, became the principal chief of the St Regis Indians, then inhabitants of Canada. –J F P]

Prof John Wilson, of South Wood School, Talladega, Ala, died on Aug 22, from taking a dose of morphine instead of quinine. The druggist had sent the wrong drug.

Distribution of premiums at St Mary's Female Institute, near Bryantown, Chas Co, Md: on Aug 29, by Rev R J O'Toole, of St Patrick's, Wash; awarded to:

Jane McGarr, Wash, D C
Lizzie McGarr, Wash, D C
Alice Berry, PG Co, Md
M Louisa McLean, Wash
Mgt Bagnem, Wash, D C
Anna Surratt, PG Co
Martha Sasscer, PG Co
Mary M Dyer, Wash, D C
Mgt McGarr, Wash, D C
Regina Gardiner, Chas Co
Mary Dobbyn, Wash, D C
Isabella Bowling, Chas Co
Mary L Wilson, PG Co
Nellie B Digges, Chas Co
Hannah Sasscer, PG Co
Jane Ratcliff, Chas Co
Mary J Campbell, Chas Co
Maggie Bowling, Chas Co
Nannie Jenkins, Chas Co
Nannie Jameson, Chas Co
Zorah Mattingly, Chas Co
Mary Holmes, Chas Co
Louisa Burroughs, Chas Co
Estelle Gardiner, Chas Co
Mittie Carrico, Chas Co
Sallie Keleher, Wash, D C
Ellen Keleher, Wash, D C
Mary E Spalding, St Mary's Co
Symphronia Bryan, PG Co,
Kate Montgomery, Chas Co
Mary A Langley, Chas Co
C Warren, Chas Co

Tornado in Ulster Co last week. At Dewittville the two dwlg houses of Mr J Smith & Mr Hoyt were blown down. Mrs Hoyt & her 3 children were on a visit to the house of Mr Smith at the time. Mrs Hoyt was instantly killed, & Mrs Smith lived but a few hours. Another lady, named Hunbeck, was injured to such an extent that her life is despaired of. The 3 children of Mrs Hoyt were badly hurt.

At Fincastle, Botetourt Co, Va, on Aug 26, Jas McDowell, Pres of the Farmers' Bank of that place was shot in the office by Henry W Bowzer, a wealthy farmer of the county. The assailant gave himself up to the officers of justice. The cause was a domestic difficulty between their families.

Died: on Sep 3, in Wash City, Emma Rebecca, daughter of G A & Harriet Sage, in her 17th year. Her funeral will take place from her father's residence, 527 Md ave, near 6th st, this afternoon at 4 o'clock.

Hollidaysburg, Sep 2. Miss Matilda Caldwell, daughter of Judge Caldwell, met with a shocking death last night. She was returning from a wedding at the house of Rev Lloyd Knight, in a vehicle driven by a young man named Wertz. The horse took fright & ran off. Miss Caldwell leaped out & fell with violence upon her head. She was carried home & expired this morning.

Mrd: on Sep 4, in the 7th st Presbyterian Church, by Rev B F Bittinger, Quincy L Page to Mary E, eldest daughter of Danl E Davidson, all of Wash City.

Died: on Sep 2, in Wash City, suddenly, Mr Fielder Darnal, in his 61st year, formerly of Montg Co, Md, but for the last 5 or 6 years a resident of Wash. His funeral is this afternoon at 3 o'clock, from Mrs Beck's corner of Pa ave & 11th st.

Died: on Aug 24, Maria Lansdale, wife of John W *Horton, of Phil, & daughter of the late Wm M Lansdale, of Harford Co, Md. [*Possibly Horton/Hor___.]

Died: on Aug 26, in Brunswick Co, Va, Hugh L Percivall, jr, in his 14th year. The victim of an unfortunate accident-the discharge of a gun in the hands of a companion. He lingered 17 days. He spoke words of comfort to his distressed parents; & to the unhappy author of the misfortune. –J R J

$10 reward for the return or information that will lead to the discovery, of certain papers concerning the services of Col Jas Innes in the Revolutionary war, which papers were at one time in the possession of Gen Wm Lambert, ex-Mayor of Richmond, Va, & by him delivered to some person to the undersigned unknown. –Jas J Randolph

MON SEP 6, 1858
John G Barr, of Alabama, lately appointed U S Consul at Melbourne, died on his way to his station, on May 18 last, from sun stroke.

Chas Meyer was arrested at Milwaukee on Aug 28, charged with embezzlement of $20,000 from Simon Levy. The account of Levy is that when in business in London in 1850 he sent Meyer to Paris as his agent to purchase goods, & Meyer absconded with the money, & he had neither seen nor heard of him till he met him in a barber's shop at Milwaukee.

Saml Hoffman, aged 22 to 24 years of age, a bricklayer by trade, drowned yesterday whilst bathing, he sunk to rise no more. He had been in a pleasure party of some 18 men who left Wash City early in a sloop to spend the day at the White House, down the river.

Four men drowned in Milwaukee due to a heavy storm on Aug 27, rendering the lake very rough. Robt P Jennings, a merchant, & John H Sullivan, a young lawyer, were in a small sailboat. The boat was found but not the men. Their bodies were found on Sat. A fishing vessel owned by Henry Buchraid, & manned by himself & 2 others, was capsized & 2 of the men drowned. Names not given.

Farm of 220 acres for sale, with good bldg improvements, near the Gtwn & Rockville turnpike, near Wash. Also a farm of 130 acres 5 miles from Gtwn. Apply to W S Holliday, No 2 Todd's Bldg.

Orphans Court of Wash Co, D C. Letters testamentary on the personal estate of Jas M Minor, late of Wash Co, deceased. –John R Minor, exc

Obit-died: on Aug 26, at her residence, near Mobile, Ala, Mrs Martha Toulmin, widow of the late Hon harry Toulmin, a Judge of the U S Court, aged 87 years. She came to the U S from England, her native place, in the latter part of the last century. After a few years' residence in Ky she was married to Judge Toulmin. This was a second marriage for the sons & daughters of another; but this much may be said, those step-children never knew the want of a mother; they blessed the hour to her latest day that gave them a mother such as their second mother proved. Mrs Toulmin lived & died a Unitarian, the faith of her fathers, the faith of her husband. -P

Boston, Sep 4. During a severe thunder squall this afternoon, a sailboat from Quincy, containing Geo F Spear, his wife & niece, capsized. Mrs Spear was saved, the other 2 were drowned. The bodies were recovered. A boat from Hingham, containing 2 sons of Maj Joshua Hersey was also capsized off Crown Point. One was drowned & the other swam ashore.

TUE SEP 7, 1858
Personal effects of Gebhardt Bergmann, deceased, [formerly of Wash st] consisting of household & kitchen furniture, wearing apparel, cabinet-maker's tools, & lathes, at auction, on Sep 9, by order of the Orphans Court of Wash Co, D C. –J T Downs, auct

Miss Henrietta Chapin, daughter of Bennet Chapin, of Chicopee st, was injured lately by being thrown out of the rail-car that goes up the summit of Mount Holyoke. She remained at the Mountain House 8 days after the accident, but it was believed she would be able to be removed home in the course of the week. Her spine & head are most seriously affected. Miss Augusta F Kneeland, of West Springfield, struck the ground on the outside of the railing, & escaped injury. Near the summit the gentlemen on the rear of the car commenced shaking & jostling the car for the purpose of frightening the ladies, when the front portion of it rose about 18 inches & swung to the south, striking against & breaking the railing. The two ladies became greatly alarmed & jumped out or were pitched out. -Springfield Republican

On Aug 27, at Key West, 2 boys bathing near the bath-house belonging to Senator Mallory, discovered a body floating on the inside. On examination it proved to be that of Mr Sales, the Spanish Consul. He entered the bath-house about 12 M, & was discovered drowned near 2 hours later.

I offer for sale my place near the first toll-gate on 7th st plank road, 1 mile from Wash, containing 13 acres of land, with a substantial dwlg, with 8 rooms & out bldgs.
–J P Dickinson

Orphans Court of Wash Co, D C. Letters of administration on the personal estate of Thos J Massie, late of Wash Co, deceased. –Sarah A Massie, admx

Oysters, oysters. Fresh oysters received this day, fine, fat, & luscious. Served up in every style at Lloyd's Nat'l Restaurat, s e corner of 7th & E sts.

The wife of Mr Geo Stoddard of Brookline, Mass, having a violent headache, took a dose of morphine in the hope of obtaining relief. She soon became aware that she had taken an overdose, but she feared no serious ill effects. She died in the evening.

On Fri last John Burns was executed at Wheeling for the murder of Mary Ann Montony on May 14 last. He was hung upon the spot where the foul deed was perpetrated.

On Thus last a fire at Easton, Md, originating in a stable belonging to A B Pritchett, spread to the stabling of the Union Hotel, & also the residence of Dr Saml Harper, all of which was destroyed.

A little child of Mr Babock, of Mercer Co, Pa, died on Tue from drinking a decoction of fly-powder, which its mother had prepared & left in a saucer for killing flies.

Mrd: on Sep 2, by Rev W H Chapman, Mr Leoanrd Wesley Harvey to Miss Charity Ann Jones.

Died: on Sep 6, in Wash City, of typhus fever, Sarah Jane, wife of Joshua Banks, in her 46th year. Her funeral will take place from the residence of her husband, corner of 5th & H sts, on Wed morning, at 10 o'clock.

Died: on Sep 5, suddenly, Saml R Hoffman, in his 22nd year. His funeral is this morning at 10 o'clock, from his mother's residence, H st, near 12th st.

WED SEP 8, 1858
Trustee's sale of improved property on north N, between 14th & 15th sts, by deed of trust from Wm H Smallwood & wife, dated Dec 18, 1856, of the land records of Wash Co, D C: lot 4 in square 211, with a good dwlg house, it being the same parcel or property conveyed to the said Wm H Smallwood by Edw Knight & others by deed dated May 29, 1854, & duly recorded. –Edw C Carrington, trustee -A Green auct

Stock of retail grocery at public sale on Sep 10, at the store of Jeremiah McKnew, corner of 7th & K sts, by virtue of a distrain for house rent due & in arrears.
–A E L Keese, bailiff -Jas C McGuire, auct

Household & kitchen furniture at auction on Sep 17, by deed of trust from Danl E Groux, dated Oct 1, 18_7, recorded in Liber J A S No 143, from folios 413 to 422 of the land records of Wash Co, D C, & also a deed recorded in Liber J A S No 149. All the furniture in the house at 225 Pa ave. –R P Jackson, trustee -Jas C McGuire, auct

The 3 year old daughter of Mr Henry Baker, of Harwich, Mass, died on Thu last from the effects of eating the ends of 3 dozen friction matches.

On Sunday, during divine service in St John's Church, at Richmond, Va, Mr Solyman, the organist, fell down insensible, & almost instantly expired. He had been ill of asthma.

The 3 Washburnes [brothers] again in the field. Israel Washburne, jr, has been renominated for Congress in the 5th district of Maine; Elihu B Washburne is up again in the 1st district of Ill; & C C Washburne is in nomination for another term in the 2nd district of Wisc. They are all Republicans.

A poor man named Thos Nichols, a hod carrier, yesterday fell from the scaffolding of the new Church of the Ascension on H, near 9th st, the scaffolding itself having given way under him. The contents of the hod fell upon the poor man's skull & so injured it that he died in a few moments after having been taken to the infirmary.

Sixty Scotch girls have just been imported directly from Scotland to work in the factories at Holyoke, Mass.

Six Cents Reward for runway, John Jas McGuire, an indentured apprentice to the coach painting business. All persons are cautioned against harboring or employing said apprentice at the peril of law. –M McDermott, 455 Pa ave

Mrd: on Aug 31, in Wash City, at St Peter's Church, by Rev Mr Knight, David Potts, of Va, to Mrs Ann E Addison, 2nd daughter of the late Notely L Adams, of Wash City.

Mrd: on Sep 7, at St Patrick's Church, by Rev Mr Boyle, B J Neale, of Wash City, to Miss Mary H, daughter of the late Edw J Hamilton, of Chas Co, Md.

Died: on Sep 7, in Wash City, Mrs Louisa Worthington, wife of L W Worthington, in her 48th year. Her funeral is this afternoon at 4 o'clock, from her late residence on L, between 8th & 9th sts.

Child lost, supposed to have been carried off. Jas H O'Leary, a white boy, 5 years old, has been missed from his home, on C st, between 3rd & 4½ sts, since about 10 o'clock yesterday [Tue] morning. He is well grown & smart for his age, & has brown hair & blue eyes. Any information concerning him will be thankfully received.

THU SEP 9, 1858
The chess contest between Paul Morphy & Herr Lewenthal, now in progress in London, is exciting considerable interest on both sides of the Atlantic. The last accounts the score stook Morphy-7; Lewenthal-2; draw-1. The purse is for $1,000.

Wash Corp: Sep 6. 1-Cmte of Claims: bills for the relief: of Saml Statcup; of Peter Emerich; & of Foster Henshaw: all passed.

Mr Kellum Myers, aged 28 years, accidentally killed himself on Monday last near Burlington, N J, while in a boat gunning. The trigger caught in something & discharged the contents into his right side.

Sale privately of valuable city property in Petersburg. The undersigned, intending, at the end of the current year, to remove permanently to another part of the State, desires, in the interval, to sell out to one or more persons, the whole of his real estate in Petersburg, Va. The limits of an advertisement forbid a detailed description of an estate so large, varied, & valuable. The city lots offered all lie within the city; the dwlgs are of brick & wood, some very valuable; & there is a family residence of brick, with all the modern improvements, on a large lot. Petersburg has a population of 18,000. Apply in person or letter to my agent, Mr Hugh Nelson, or to subscriber. –Robt B Bolling, Petersburg, Va

The West-Chester Academy, at West-Chester, Pa, will commence on Nov 1 next. For catalogues address Wm F Wyers, A M, Principal, at West-Chester, Pa.

Wanted a situation as teacher in a private family, or as assist in some academy, by a graduate of one of the first institutions in Va, who has had 3 years' experience in teaching Latin, French, English, & Mathematics. Satisfactory testimonials as to character & qualifications in possession. Address Jas Finlay, Shepherdstown, Va.

Mrd: on Sep 2, at St John's Church, Maury Co, Tenn, by Rev Jas Hildebrand, Henry C Yeatman, of Nashville, to Mary Brown, daughter of Gen Lucius J Polk.

Mrd: on Sep 1, at Portland, Maine, Chas H Boyd, U S Coast Survey, to Miss Annette M, daughter of the late Col G Dearborn, U S Army.

Died: on Sep 7, in Gtwn, Mrs Angeletta Lowndes, wife of Francis Lownds. Her funeral is this afternoon at 4 o'clock, from St John's Church, Gtwn.

Orphans Court of Wash Co, D C. In the case of John Marbury, adm of Otho M Linthicum, deceased, the administrator & Court have appointed Sep 28, for the final settlement of the personal estate of said deceased, of the assets in hand.
-Ed N Roach, Reg/o wills

Chambersburg, Pa, Sep 6. An affray last evening near Waynesboro, in this county, I which a man named Osborn was shot dead by two brothers, Danl & David Funk. The dispute arose from Osborn carrying water from Funk's well. Both brothers are in prison.

Cincinnati, Sep 7. A train on the Hamilton & Dayton Railroad ran into a carriage containing D P Fessenden, his wife, & 2 nieces today. Mrs Fessenden was killed & the others were severely injured.

Dayton, Sep 7. Two young men, sons of Dr Ritley, whilest attempting to cross the track of the Dayton & Western Railroad, were run into by a passing train. The younger brother was instantly killed; the other escaped slightly injured.

FRI SEP 10, 1858
On Tue last -Jas C McGuire & Co sold all of square 326, fronting Md ave, between 11th & 12th sts west, at prices ranging from 16 to 31 cents per foot, to G W Riggs & Co.

Washington Theatre: Proprietor, W D Stuart
Sole Lessees & mgrs, Geo Kunkel, John T Ford, T L Moxley-Kunkel & Co.
Acting Manager, Mr C W Tayleure
Stage Manager, Mr Jos W Dawson
Assist Treasurer, Mr J S Sessford
Fifth Night & Benefit of Edwin Booth. Friday, Sep 10, 1858,
Shakspeare's sublime tragedy of Hamlet.
Hamlet-Edwin Booth
Ghost-H F Daley
Gravedigger, W M Fiske
Ophelia, Miss Parker

Mrd: in Wash City, on Sep 8, by Rev John Ross, Mr Wm G Pugh, formerly of Balt, to Miss Julia E Morrow, of Wash City.

Mrd: on Sep 9, in Wash City, by Rev G W Samson, Mr Wm P Greenlow, of King Geo Co, Va, to Miss S V B Perkins, of Stafford Co, Va.

Died: on Sep 8, in Wash City, Jennie, only daughter of J W & Mary Jane Colley, aged 5 years & 6 months. Her funeral will take place this morning, at 10 o'clock, from her grandmother's residence, Mrs Jane Taylor's, 411 3rd st.

SAT SEP 11, 1858
Henry Addison, Claim Agent & Broker, opposite the Treasury Dept, Wash City. [Ad]

Young Ladies Institute, a Boarding & Day School, English & French, 40 E st, Wash, D C, will commence on the 2nd Mon in Sep. -Chas H Norton, A M, Principal

On Sat the house of Richd Lombard, on Brown Brook Island, off Wellfleet, Mass, was struck & almost completely wrecked by lightning. His family was not injured. During the same shower the house of Christopher Champlain, on Block Island, & thoroughly torn to pieces by the lightning. The inmates were only stunned.

Dr Jas Sinclair, an eminent physician, died of yellow fever in New Orleans on Wed of last week. He was attending the sick & fell victim in the discharge of his duty. Dr V Deschamps, one of the physicians employed by the Howard Association, died of the fever on the same day.

Explosion on Wed as the steamboat **Aurora** was on her regular trip from Keyport, N J, to N Y. John Merenus, one of the firemen, died instantly; another fireman died in the afternoon.

The death of Geo Newbold, Pres of the Bank of America, in N Y, is announced.
[No date given-current item.]

Died: yesterday, in Wash City, Franklin Pierce, aged 1 year, son of Southey S & Isabella Parker. His funeral is today, at the residence of his parents, at half past 3 o'clock.

Died: on Sep 10, Caroline Louisa, infant daughter of Elias & Mary E Travers, aged 13 months & 2 weeks.

To Physicians. I desire to sell or lease, with the good will, my dwlg & position in practice, a situation unsurpassed in advantages. A desire to change business for agricultural pursuits only determines the offer. Inquire at the Loan & Property Commission Agency of P M Pyfer, 428 E st, Wash City.

Superior Musical Instruction. Prof De Coeniel will open his new Musical Repository in a few days on the corner of 11th & Pa ave.

MON SEP 13, 1858
Dr Abiel A Cooley, the inventor of friction matches, died at Hartford, Conn, on Aug 18, aged 76 years. His genius has probably conduced as much to the convenience of his fellow-men as that of any other inventor.

Edw Tucker, the engineer of the New Haven railroad train which ran off the drawbridge at Norwalk 5 years ago, & resulted so disastrously in the destruction of human life, committed suicide in N Y C on Thu, by severing with a razor the main arteries of his left arm. He has not run any engines since the Norwalk disaster. He was 40 years of age, & has left a wife & 2 children residing in the vicinity of Troy.

Several months since the remains of a human being were discovered in the woods 15 miles from Detroit. A valise & letters were found & showed the body to be that of John Hickey, a railroad freight conductor. He had befriended a poor man, John Kennedy, & Kennedy is suspected of being the murderer of Hickey. He has not yet been found.

A young lady, 18 or 19 years of age, daughter of Mr Haywood, gardener of John Jacob Astor, jr, at Esopus, near Rondout, N Y, died on Tue from the effects of fright. She was riding in a wagon when the horse took fright & ran with great speed for about a mile, when it was stopped. The young woman was taken from the wagon in a dying condition, & lived but a few minutes.

Henry M Howard, for many years naval officer of the port of Charleston, died on Thu last. His age was about 40 years.

Jacob Clute, aged 65, died on Fri, at his residence in N Y, from injuries received the evening previous while in an altercation with his son David, aged 23. The father was intoxicated & got into a quarrel with his son, who, in return for a blow, struck the old man & knocked him down. In the fall Mr Clute struck the back part of his head violently.

Mary Ann Pecard, 10 years of age, living in the family of John Bartlett, at Albany, accidentally shot herself on Sunday. She died in less than an hour.

Died: on Sep 11, in N Y, at the City Hospital, Danl Cronin, in his 27th year. His funeral will take place from the residence of his mother, 388 D st, between N J ave & South Capitol st, this afternoon at 2 o'clock.

Died: on Sep 11, at Mount Pleasant, Fauquier Co, Va, Eddie, infant son of John R & Ellen G Ashby, of Wash City.

Circuit Court of Wash Co, D C–in Equity. Alex'r Close, Adolphus Schneiwind, Wm F Heins, Robt McEldowney, Jno McEldowney, Francis Dundelet, Mathew T Gosnell, et al, creditors of Baruch Hall, vs Baruch Hall, Richd Wallach, the trustees of the Bank of Washington, Matthew W Galt & Wm Galt, Jos Gales & Wm W Seaton, D R Wall, ___ Maxwell, Jas Sears, & Jos Colley, Thos B Gray, Saml B Anderson, adm of Chas Wallace, Wash City Savings Bank, & Wm B Bowie. The parties interested are to appear before me at the Auditor's room, City Hall, on Sep 22, at the City Hall.
–Walter S Cox, Special Auditor

Obit-died: Aug 31, at the residence of her daughter, Mrs Roger Jones, of Wash City, Mrs Ann Page. Mrs Page was the youngest child of the late Henry Lee, of Va, & sister to the Ofcr of that name of Revolutionary memory, & of Chas Lee, Atty Gen under Washington. In early life she was united in marriage to Richd Byrd Page, of Va, who she long survived, reaching the advanced age of 84 years. Her funeral rites were performed in Christ Church, Alexandria, within whose venerable wall she had for many years been a constant worshipper.

Cincinnati, Sep 11. Railroad accident on Sep 10 occurred to the Steubenville & Cincinnati express train, going west on the Steubenville & Indiana road. The rear engine jumped off the track, knocking out timbers of the bridge. The bridge broke & the baggage & front passenger cars fell some 10 or 12 feet. Jos Fleming, of Zanesville, was fatally injured; Mr Roach, of Louisville, had both legs broken; some 20 or 30 persons were bruised more or less severely.

$200 reward for runaway negro men, Henson, about 40, & Gusta, about 21 or 22.
-Levi Pumphrey, Livery Stable, Wash.

TUE SEP 14, 1858
From Calif. 1-Mr Thos Doyle is the only passenger known to have been lost by the recent disaster to the steamship **Oregon**, which ran ashore on Point Reyes. 2-On Aug 5, the Anti-Lecompton Convention at Sacramento nominated for Supreme Judge, John Currey, of Solano Co; for Comptroller, L N Dawley, of Nevada; for Supreme Court Clerk, H U Jennings, of Batte Co. Hon Jos C McKibbin was renominated for Congress, & Wm L Dudley, of Calaveras, was nominated for Congress. The Republican State Convention endorsed the nomination of Currey for Judge, but nominated F P Tracey, vice Dudley. They also nominated Dr S C Gunn, of Tuolumne, as Comptroller.

Yellow fever: deaths in New Orleans during 24 hours to noon Sep 10th: 85. Deaths last week in Charleston: 103.

Mr Morphy, the American chess player, played 8 games blindfolded, at one time, at the Birmingham Chess Congress, recently, winning all but one against Mr J Kipping, jr, of Manchester..

The copartnership existing under the name of Clagett, Newton, & May & Co, is this day dissolved by mutual consent. Jos J May will settle up the business. John B Clagett intends to continue the Dry Goods business, Pa ave & 9th st, having bought out the stock of the late firm. -John B Clagett, A L Newton, Jos J May, Darius Clagett [Sep 14, 2004]

Mrd: on Aug 25, at Shortwood Chapel, Somerset, by Very Rev Canon McDonnell, Edwin De Leon, U S Agent & Consul-Genr'l for Egypt & Dependencies, to Ellen Mary Nowlan, youngest daughter of the late Jas Nowlan, of Rathgar, near Dublin.

Died: on Sep 13, in Charlottesville, Va, Emma Frances, aged 2 years & 3 months, youngest daughter of Henry Polkinhorn, of Wash City. Her funeral will take place from her father's residence, 147 B st, Island, this morning at 11 o'clock.

Died: on Sep 13, Rosina, aged 2 years & 9 days, only child of Geo & Mary E McClelland. Her funeral will take place today, at 3½ o'clock, from the residence of Mr A R Allen, Mass ave, between 4th & 5th sts.

Board & comfortable rooms may be obtained at Miss Morley's, 276 Pa ave, near the Kirkwood House. The parlors occupied by Hon Mr Dimmick last session; also, the rooms occupied by Dr Loomis, as a dental ofc, are for rent, with or without board.

$150 reward for runaway negro man who calls himself Nace Shaw, aged 45 years. He has a mother living in Wash City, at 212 south B st, Island. -Sarah Ann Talburtt

Valuable West River farm for sale: by decree of the Circuit Court of Anne Arundel Co, in a cause in which Lucy Mitchell & others are cmplnts & Henry J Thompson & others dfndnts: public auction, on Oct 1, of the real estate, being the dwlg & plantation of the late Jas Mitchell, on which his widow resides, lying near the South River Church, adjoining the lands of Frank H Stockett, Mrs Susan Boyle, Benj O'Hara, Jacob W Bird, & Thos Holliday, consisting of parts of the tracts of land called or known by as **Taylor's Choice**, **Larkin's Hill**, **Taylor's Triangle**, **Right Angle Triangle**, & **Mary's Mount**. This farm is about 10 miles from Annapolis & 5 miles from Galesville steamboat landing, & contains about 190 acres of land, more or less. The improvements consist of a modern 2 story brick dwlg, with slate roof & back bldg, kitchen, & other necessary bldgs. The healthfulness is undoubted, as can be ascertained by reference to the family physician, Dr Murray. -Randall & Hagner, trustees

WED SEP 15, 1858
Naval Intelligence. Capt Rich, of the marines, has been detached from the steamer **Niagara**, that the charge of violating the N Y quarantine laws, in connexion with Ray Thompsons, may be investigated by a court of inquiry. Lt Heywood takes Capt Rich's place on board of that vessel.

The U S brig **Dolphin** took to Boston Capt Saml Townsend, cmder of the American brig **Echo**, captured off Cuba with 318 slaves on board. On Sat he was taken before the U S Com'r Loring, & was committed for examination on Sep 21. [Sep 16th newspaper: the crew of the steamer **Echo**, alias Gen Putnam, having been brought up on habeas corpus before Judge Magrath, of the U S District Court at Charleston, S C, their discharge from custody was moved on the grounds-1-That the proceedings of the Com'r were irregular & insufficient to justify a commitment. 2-That the commitment is in itself improper & illegal. Judge Magrath denied the motion.]

Hon Jas Mullett, one of the Justices of the Supreme Court for the 8th Judicial District of N Y, died at Fredonia, Chatauque Co, on Sep 10. He was respected by his professional brethren for his acquirements & esteemed for his genial disposition.

Mr Robt Morris, the colored lawyer of this city, recently bargained for a residence in Caryville, Chelsea, for $5,000, but the inhabitants of the locality sent the owner of the estate a remonstrance against Mr Morris settling there. The owner of the house felt the force of the remonstrance, & Mr Morris cannot have the estate. –Boston Courier

Mrd: on Sep 14, at the Church of the Epiphany, by Rev Chas Hall, F F Myer to Mary V, eldest daughter of J D Orr, all of Wash City.

Mrd: on Sep 2, at St John's Church, Ashwood, by Rev Mr Hildebrand, Henry C Yeatman to Mary Brown Polk, daughter of Gen Lucius J Polk, of Maury Co, Tenn.

Mrd: on Sep 13, in Wash City, by Rev Raymond Young, Col Wm Henry Daingerfield, of Wood-Cot, PG Co, Md, to Mary, daughter of the late Maj P G Howle, of the Marine Corps.

Mrd: on Sep 14, at Wesley Chapel, by Rev L F Morgan, Robt Cohen, jr, to Miss Mary Eliz Stallings, of Wash City.

Died: on Sep 10, Willie B, aged 6 years, 9 months & 19 days, youngest son of Mrs Julia E Sanford, widow of the late Chas H Sanford, of Westmoreland Co, Va.

Supreme Court of the U S, No 146, Dec Term, 1857. In error to the Circuit Court of the U S for the district of Indiana. Enoch McCarty, plntf in error, vs Guernsey Y Roots et al. Mr Gillet, of counsel for the dfndnts in error, having suggested the death of Enoch McCarty, the plntf in error, now here moved the Court of an order of publication to make the proper reps parties, on consideration whereof it is now here ordered by this Court that unless proper reps of the said Enoch McCarty, deceased shall voluntarily become parties within the first 10 days of the ensuing term, the dfndnts in error shall be entitled to open the record & have the judgment affirmed, if it be not erroneous.

THU SEP 16, 1858
Three prisoners escaped from the Columbia Co, Wisc jail, a few days ago, & John Murray, under confinement for murder, who escaped, returned to jail after a few hours.

Wallawalla Aug 6: contemplated military movements against the Indians in Oregon. Ofcrs: Staff: 1st Lt P A Owen, Acting Assist Adj Gen; Capt T W Kirkham, Assist Quartermaster; Assist Surgeon J F Hammond & 1st Lt J Mullen, Assist Topograpical Engineers. First Dragoons: Brvt Maj Wm N Grier; Lts Wm D Pender, H B Davidson, & D McM Gregg. Third Artl: Capts E D Keyes, Edw O C Ord, Jas A Hardie, & F O Wyse; Lts H G Gibson, Geo F B Dandy, G H Hill, M R Morgan, Jas L White, Lawrence Kip, D B Ransom, Robt O Tyler, H B Lyon, Geo P Ihrie, & Jas Howard. Ninth Infty: Capts Fred'k T Dent & Chas S Winder; Lt H B Fleming.

A Telegraph announces the sudden death on Sep 10, of Rev A W Black, D C, of Pittsburg, an eminent divine of the Reformed Presbyterian Churc. For over 30 years he exercised the ministry in Western Penn, in the same neighborhood where his father, Rev Dr John Black, labored for half a century.

M Poitevin, the intrepid aeronaut, whose excursions on horseback caused so much excitement in London, has met the fate of his predecessors. He fell into the sea near Malaga, when descending with his balloon, & was drowned.

Four men killed at the new glaze mill of the Hazardville powder works at Endfield, Ct, that exploded on Monday. Killed: John A Garesche, superintendent, & 3 others, not named.

Richd B Washington, intending to remove from Jefferson Co, has authorized me to sell his valuable landed estate in said county: 3 tracts: **Blakeley**, containing about 340 acres, with a fine brick dwlg & out bldgs; The **Grubb Farm**, containing about 250 acres of fine limestone land, with a comfortable frame dwlg, & convenient out-houses; adjoining **Blakeley**. A tract of timber land, containing about 130 acres, a part of the **Richwood Tract**. Apply at Charlestown, Jefferson Co, Va. –S Howell Brown, Real Estate Agent

Died: on Sep 14, Jas O'R, aged 3 years & 1 month, son of John & Agnes McDermott. His funeral is this morning at 10 o'clock, from the residence of his parents, 67 Missouri ave.

Died: on Sep 14, Josephine Ruth, infant daughter of Geo S & Clotilda J Gillcrist, aged 1 year & 3 months.

Died: on Wed, Mrs Christiana Handley, relict of the late Jas Handley, in her 52nd year. Her funeral will be on Fri at 2 o'clock, from the house of her son-in-law, Jos F Hodgson, 405 7th st.

Died: on Sep 9, at her brother's, near Augusta, Ill, Mrs Mary Slade Tufts, in her 38th year, daughter of J E & N O Weems, late of Wash, D C.

The second lecture in the course before the Catholic Beneficial Total Abstinence Association of D C, will be delivered by the First Vice Pres, H C McLaughlin, at Temperance Hall, E st, on Sep 19, at 8 o'clock. Admittance free.
–J J Kane, Jos Walsh, M D, Cmte on Lectures

FRI SEP 17, 1858
Excellent household & kitchen furniture at auction on Sep 28 & 30, at the residence of Miss Janney, corner of 8th & Pa ave. -Jas C McGuire, auct

Handsome household & kitchen furniture at auction on Sep 23, at the residence of Dr Binney, Pres of Columbia College, on College Hill. -Jas C McGuire, auct

On Sep 10th, near Harrison & Jefferson sts, Mrs Smith, wife of Geo W Smith, & her sister, Mis Catharine McCreesh, & a 9 year old boy, were enveloped in flames when the can of fluid for a lamp exploded. Mrs Smith was horribly burnt, but still alive yesterday, & cannot possibly recover. Miss McCreesh, age 18 years, will die. The boy, it is thought, will survive. -Chicago Times, 12th

Died: on Sep 15, Mrs Mary Eliot, relict of the late Saml Eliot, in her 74th year. Her funeral will take place at the residence of her son-in-law, Lemuel J Middleton, 12th & F st, this evening at 4 o'clock.

Died: on Sep 12, in Charlestown, Jefferson Co, Va, James Brown, in his 85th year.

Horticultural exhibition awards persent on Wed: fruits: John N Trook, Mr Raub. Foreign grapes: Thos Blagden; John B Turton & J K Vernon. Native grapes, C G Page. Freestone peaches: Wm Cammack; eating pears, John N Trook; & Clement Hessler & C G Page. Apples, Thos Brown, & J C Clark. Canteloupes, Geo Talbert; & John Perins. Cabbage, Frank Boyle; lettuce, Clement Hessler; carrots, Alfred Ray; corn, Wm Little; celery, Clement Hessler; & Wm Little; turnips, C G Page; cucumbers, Alfred Ray; onions from sets, Clement Hessler. In plants & flowers the awards went to: for petunias, C G Page; phloxes, John Saul; cut roses, Jerome Degges; & C G Page; best centerpiece, Clement Hessler; dahlias, Prof Page. Handsomest centerpiece: Mr John Watt, in charge of the Pres' conservatory & garden. The gardens of Mr Corcoran are under the able care of Mr Spence. Mr Wm Cammack & Wm Wm Hughes also exhibited interesting plants.

SAT SEP 18, 1858
The anniversary of the primitive Methodist Chapel, Walsall, was held recently, on the Sabbath. Mrs Colley, of Madely, occupied in the pulpit in the morning, Rev Thos Parr preached in the afternoon; & in the evening the sermon was delivered by Theophilis Parr, age 10 years. –London Patriot

Notice to Trespassers. All persons are forewarned from trespassing, in any manner, with or without dog or gun, upon my farm, near Good Hope, as the law will be most certainly & rigidly enforced against all who disregard this notice. –Lucy B Walker

Obit-died: on Sep 3, at his residence in Winchester, Ky, Hon Chilton Allen, of Ky, at age 73 years. Mr Allen was born in Albemarle Co, Va, on Apr 6, 1786, & moved to Ky, then the far West, to try his fortune among the noble pioneers, when he was quite a boy. He first settled in Bath Co, following his humble trade of wheelright, & studied at night to get his education. In Oct, 1807, he moved to Winchester, where he has resided every since, teaching school, then entered upon the practice of law. He served in both branches of the Legislature for several years. During 1837 && 1838 he filled the arduous ofc of Pres of the Board of Internal Improvement.

On Sat in Pittsburgh, Pa, Thos Smithson, 19, a painter, had been desirous for some time of paying his addresses to Eleanor Henry, aged 17, daughter of a respectable widow woman, Mrs Harriet Henry, residing on Second st. Miss Henry was a young lady of excellent reputation, & a member of the Liberty St Methodist Church, & had been away for some time to avoid the dfndnt, & had just arrived home when Smithson called on her. Mrs Henry was doing domestic work when she head the report of a gun. Her daughter was shot in her back, the ball passing through the lung. Smithson was seen running from the house & was caught by a crowd who pursued him. –Pittsburg Gaz

Orphans Court of Wash Co, D C. Letters of administration on the personal estate of John S Moore, late of Wash Co, D C. –J B Moore, adm

Ira Young, professor of mathematics, natural philosophy, & astronomy, in Dartmouth College, N H, died at his residence, on Sep 14, after an operation for a disease which had baffled the skill of the most eminent physicians.

Mrd: on Sep 14, at Grace Church, by Rev Alfred Holmead, J E F Holmead to Hannah, eldest daughter of Jos N Gordon.

Died: on Sep 16, in Wash City, Mrs Fanny Munroe, relict of the late Thos Munroe, in her 85th year. Her funeral will be from the residence of her son-in-law, H K Randall, F & 18th sts, on Sat at 4:30 P M.

Richmond, Sep 17. Duel this morning between Mr O Jennings Wise, of the Enquirer, & Hon Sherrard Clemens, of Wheeling. Mr Clemens fell, but the wound is not considered a dangerous one. [Sep 20th newspaper: The duel was over certain strictures in the Enquirer on Mr Clemens' course in connexion with the claims of Mr Letcher & Judge Brockenbrough to the Governorship. –Richmond Whig]

Augusta, Sep 17. Serious disaster yesterday on the Augusta & Savannah railroad: Luther Northey, the engineer, a native of N H, & 2 firemen were killed.

N Y, Sep 17. Wm H Monoghan, of Charleston, S C, fell from a window of the N Y Hotel last night & was killed.

For sale: 5 bldg lots on 14th st west, in square north of the residence of Chas Hill. -John F Ennis, atty, 22 Louisiana ave.

MON SEP 20, 1858
Several years ago Jas Young, a wealthy citizen of Milford township, Butler Co, Pa, deceased, left property valued at $105,000 to be equally divided between his 5 children. The homestead was sold to a Mr Williamson, who has resided upon it since the sale. A few days ago Mrs Williamson was sweeping near the chimney & found an old Spanish half dollar; as she swept she found more coins. She called to her husband, & in searching the chimney, found a deposite of $1,700 in old Spanish silver coins of all denominations, each piece of which was dated as far back as 1828. The heirs of the deceased were sent for, & the coins surrendered to them. The heirs insisted paying Mr Williamson & his lady $50 each, making a reward of $250 each. –Phil Press

Geo H Lamb, who drowned his wife in the Mississippi river, at St Louis, & alleged that she died a natural death in Memphis, has been convicted at St Louis of murder in the first degree, but an appeal will be taken to the Missouri Supreme Court. The murder was detected by the father of the victim.

Railroad accident on the Balt & Ohio railroad on Thu, by which the fireman, Wm Dodson, was instantly killed, & the engineer, Wm Mobley, was injured, but not seriously. -Martinsburg Republican

Mr Wm Manegault, a planter, from Charleston, S C, was killed on Thu by a fall from a window of the N Y Hotel, N Y C. He was a native of the U S, aged about 78 years.

Mrd: on Sep 18, by Rev B A Maguire, D D, Pres of Gtwn College, assisted by Rev F E Boyle, Dr B J Hellen to Virginia E, daughter of Col W F Phillips, of Wash.

Died: on Sep 18, in Wash City, after a long affliction, Mrs Dorothy H Knott, aged 70 years. Her funeral will be from her late residence, 450 F st, this morning at 10 o'clock.

Died: yesterday, in Wash City, George W, in his 18th year, son of John W & Rebecca W Smith. His funeral is this evening at 4 o'clock, at 227 Pa ave, between 14th & 15th sts.

Health report: Ofc of the Com'r of Health, Wash, Sep 17, 1858. Deaths in Wash City for Aug, 1858: 72. -Chas F Force, Com'r of Health

Edw Dolan, Merchant Tailor, sign of the Golden Fleece, 14th st & Pa ave. [Ad]

TUE SEP 21, 1858
New Orleans, Sep 20. The deaths by yellow fever on Saturday were 74. The total number during the week was 460.

The subscriber, rendered by age incapable of attending to business, has determined to make public sale of his Farm, crop, & all his lands in Lafayette & Cass Counties, Mo; with 25 servants, cattle, farming utensils; brick dwlg; small tracts of land: sale in Lafayette Co on Oct 18. The lands in Cass Co will be sold on Oct 26. Address subscriber at Tabo Post Ofc, Lafayette Co, Mo. –M W Flournoy

Executor's sale of a valuable farm: execs of the last will & testament of the late Wm Easby, will sell at public auction, on Mar 17 next, at the auction rooms of J C McGuire: ***Chillon Castle Manor***, containing in all 62 acres of land, more or less: with a small frame dwlg house & a large well built & nearly new barn; about 3 miles from the center Market. –Agnes M Easby, Horatio N Easby, John W Easby, excs -J C McGuire, auct [The above auction was also advertised in the Feb 23, 1857 newspaper.]

Valuable improved & other real estate for sale in Gtwn, D C, by assignment made to us by F & A H Dodge, we offer the following: warehouse & wharf, Water & High sts, presently occupied by Mr Stribling. Warehouse, opposite the above, under rent to Mr W R Edes. Storehouse on Water st; warehouse on High st; storehouse & dwlg on High st; 2 tenements on High st; wharf lot on Water st, now occupied by Myers & Son; frame house on Jefferson st; cottage & garden on Wash & Stoddert sts; frame house on Stoddert st & lot; vacant lot on Wash st, adjoining the house of Mr McDaniel, on the north side. -H C Matthews, Ed Chapman, trustees

Four young Spaniards, from the Island of Cuba, Vicenti Ramalie, Jean Granier, Louis Fernandez, & Emanuel Ramalie, were arrested on Mon last at Mobile on information sent by telegraph from New Orleans, where they are charged with stealing 600 ounces of Spanish gold, & also with the murder of a young Cuban named Francisco Biancho.

Ordered by the Orphan's Court of PG Co, upon the suggestion of Walter P Griffin & Susan P Bryan, 2 sureties upon the bond of E Pliny Bryan, as adm of the late Wm Bryan, [of Richard] that they are in danger of suffering from said suretyship, that the said E Pliny Bryan indemnify & counter-secure the said securities, as required by the act of Assembly in such case made & provided, on or before the third Tue in Oct next, the said counter-security to be approved by this court; warning the said E Pliny Bryan of this order. State of Md, PG Co: I hereby certify that the aforegoing court order is truly taken & copied from the court proceedings of the Orphans' Court of said County. Sep 14, 1858. –Wm A Jarboe, Register

Mrd: on Sep 14, at Jefferson City, Missouri, by Rev Mr Lefturich, Robt J Lackey, of Wash City, to Mrs Eliz Moore, daughter of ex-Govn'r King, of Missouri.

Phil, Sep 1, 2004. Whereas Letters of Administration upon the estate of Rebecca Karrick, deceased, late of Wash City, have been granted to the undersigned, all persons indebted to said estate will please make payment, & those having claims will present the same to J S McMullin, adm, 1231 Spruce st, Phil.

Desirable residence for sale. The undersigned, having purchased a farm to which he designs removing, offers for sale his beautiful residence in Charlestown, Jefferson Co, Va: situated on the main st of the outskirts of the town; a beautiful brick dwlg containing 10 rooms, & all necessary out-bldgs. I will sell this beautiful property for the low sum of $3,500, provided I can find a purchaser between this & Jan 1st next. This is far less than the cost of the bldgs. For further information address Dr R S Blackburn, Charlestown, Jefferson Co, Va.

WED SEP 22, 1858
Mobile, Sep 21. Arthur P Bagby, Ex-Govn'r of this State & formerly U S Senator, died here of yellow fever. [No death date given-current news item.]

For several weeks the most painful anxiety has prevailed respecting the fate of the Australian passenger ship **Ultonia**, Capt Wm S Baker, which left the Thames for Melbourne with 180 souls on board in the early part of last Nov. There is too much reason to fear that the ship will never again be heard of, & the scenes daily witnessed at Lloyd's by the frequent visits & anxious inquiries of the relatives & friends of those on board are most distressing. –Liverpool paper

Orphans Court of Wash Co, D C, Sep 21. In the case of Wm G Palmer & Wm Towers, adms of John T Towers, deceased, the administrators & Court have appointed Oct 12 next, for the settlement of the personal estate of said deceased, with the assets in hand. -Ed N Roach, Reg/o wills

Dr Lane, a candidate for the Legislature from Polk Co, in the recent Arkansas election, was arrested while canvassing his district by an officer from N C, on a charge of having committed a murder in that State many years since, from which time until recently his whereabouts had been unknown. Lane is said to be a man of learning & talents.

Mrd: on Tue, by Rev John C Smith, Oliver B Denham to Miss Eliz J Bartlett, all of Wash City.

Died: on Sep 15, at Springfield Parsonage, Carroll Co, Md, Henry, youngest child of Rev T W & Mary C Simpson, aged 13 months & 29 days.

Died: on Sep 17, Richard Findly, infant son of Chas H & Susan E Lane, aged 2 months.

I wish to employ a Lady as Governess who is capable of teaching all the usual English branches. Address Aquila Turner, Bryantown, Chas Co, Md.

THU SEP 23, 1858
The Richmond papers announce the death of Thos R Joynes, of Accomac Co, a prominent member of the State Convention of Va in 1829, & an eminent lawyer. [Sep 24th newspaper: Thos R Joynes, senior, died on Sep 12, in his 69th year. An able lawyer, who rose to success & fortune by his own exertions.]

The U S steam frig **Niagara** sailed for Liberia on Monday. List of her ofcrs: Cmder-John S Chauncey. Lts-J R Mullany, Edw A Barnett, A J Drake, Wm Nelson, Wm Mitchell, [Acting Master] Surgeons-Edw Hudson, M P Christian. Purser-Chas C Upham. Engineers-John Faron, [Chief[Wm S Stamm, Edw D Robie, Geo R Johnson, Mortimer Kellogg, J H Bailey, W G Bachler, F Cronin, G W Rogers. Lt of Marines-Chas Heywood. Acting Boatswain-John K Bartless.

On Sep 16 at Adrian, a man, Mr Ira Thurston, one of the aeronauts, seated on the valve of a balloon was carried into the clouds. He was using his weight to hold the balloon down, while the car was detached. This proved a calamity. He was in a perfectly helpless situation and the fatal ascension took place in Blissfield, Lenawee Co, & it was seen going up & on. The exact fate baffles conjecture. He was an experienced balloonist, formerly a resident near Lima & Rochester, in Western N Y, but latterly resided in Adrian. He was a widower, having lost his wife last winter. He leaves an interesting daughter, about 17 years of age. [Sep 27th newspaper: Mr Bannister, the associate of Mr Thurston, the lost aeronaut, has seen the balloon which descended near Baptiste Creek, but not his friend. This recalls a similar one which occurred in 1855, when Timothy Winchester made an ascent from Norfolk, Ohio, in Aug, starting in good spirits & amid the cheers of a large concourse of people, since which time he has not been heard from. When last seen he was near & going in the direction of Lake Erie. No tidings have ever been received of him or his balloon. This balloon, too, belonged to Mr Bannister.]

Thos Swann has been nominated for re-election as Mayor of the city of Balt, Md.

Ex-Govn'r Geo T Wood died at his residence on Trinity river, Texas, on Sep 5. He was colonel of a regt of Texas volunteers at the storming of Monterey, & distinguished himself by the coolness & courage of his bearing. He had been a Rep in Congress of Texas, & in 1847 elected Govn'r of the state. Since then he has been in private life, residing at his plantation.

Wash Corp-Sep 20: 1-Bills taken up & referred to the Cmte of Claims: for the relief-of Chas R Queen; of C W Boteler; of Saml Statcup; of Peter Emrick; of Dr Johnston Eliot; of Foster Henshaw; of Richd H Gault; of Robt Payne; of John T Killmon; & of Margaret Edwards.

Mrd: on Sep 20, in Wash City, by Rev B F Bittinger, Mr Wm Pearsons to Miss Nancy Rezin.

Died: on Sep 12, at his residence, in Accomac Co, Va, Thos R Joynes, sr, in his 69th year.

From Europe. Halifax, Sep 22. The American ship **J J Hawthorne** & the barque **Margaret** came in collision in the mouth of the Mersey, & the latter sunk. All perished except the captain & pilot.

Edgeworth for sale: the residence of the late Gen Wm F Gordon, of Albemarle Co: contains about 1,300 acres, with a comfortable dwlg & other out-houses. If not sold previously it will be offered at public auction this fall, when I expect, as the administrator of Gen Gordon, to sell some 70 or 80 valuable slaves, together with the other personal estate usually found on a large farm. Inquire to me at Charlottesville, & Mr Geo L Gordon, who is now residing on the land, will show the same. –Wm J Robertson

Circuit Court of Wash Co, D C-in Chancery. John Simon vs Jos Davis, Geo W Garrett, & Banner Graves. The cmplnt, about Mar 16, 1852, sold to the dfndnts, Davis & Garrett, a part of lot of ground numbered 41, in reservation 10, in Wash City, for $709, & took the 4 promissory notes of said Davis & Garrett for the purchase money, all of said notes dated Mar 16, 1852, each for the sum of $177.25, & payable respectively in 1, 2, 3, & 4 years after date, with interest; that the cmplnt, on Mar 16, executed & delivered to the dfndnts, Garrett & Davis, a bond of conveyance for & also gave them actual possession of said piece or parcel of ground; that but 2 of said notes have been paid in full, although all of them have long since been due; that on or about Oct 13, 1856, the said Davis & Garrett made an assignment in writing, whereby they assigned & transferred the said bond, & all their right, title, & interest to the same to the dfndnt Graves; that the cmplnt bound himself by said bond to make or cause to be made, upon the payment of said notes & interest, a good & sufficient deed of conveyance, conveying unto said Davis & Garrett, their heirs & assigns, a good, sure, & absolute estate in fee simple, clear of all incumbrances of, in, & to said piece or parcel of ground. That neither of the dfndnts have paid either of the 2 notes, which were drawn payable in 3 & 4 years after day; but the said dfndnt Graves, who resides out of D C, paid at sundry times on account of the first of said 2 notes, the sum of $120, & that the residue of said note, together with the whole of the other notes, is still due & unpaid. The object of the bill is to obtain a decree against the dfndnts, requiring them to pay the balance of the purchase money & interest due to the cmplnt by some short day; & in default of payment, then, that the said piece of parcel of ground & premises be sold, & the said balance paid out of the proceeds of such sale. Absent dfndnts are to appear in this Court, in person or by solicitor, on or before the first Monday in Feb next. –Jas S Morsell, Associate Judge -Jno A Smith, clerk

FRI SEP 24, 1858
On Sat week at Nashville, Tenn, a young lady, the daughter of Rev Dr Summers, editor of the Southern Methodist Book Concern, met with a sudden death. Dr Summers with his family spent the day with the family of Col M G L Claiborne, in the Nashville, near the water works. After dinner Dr Summers left for his office. The ladies proposed to walk to the reservoir, a short distance from the dwlg of Col Claiborne. The reservoir fire bells sounded an alarm for fire, when Clara, the daughter of Dr Summers ascended the wall that she might have a view of the burning bldg, but lost her balance & fell into 8 to 10 feet of water, & was drowned. She was 13 years of age, the eldest living child of her bereaved parents, a lovely girl, full of life.

The Boston papers announced the death of the richest man in New England, Ebenezer Francis, who died at his residence in Pemberton square, on Sep 21. He was born at Beverly, Mass, Oct 15, 1775, & at his death was nearly 83 years of age. He was the only son of Col Ebenezer Francis, who was killed in the battle of Hubbardtown, near Ticonderoga, Jul, 1777. He came to Boston in Jan, 1787, a poor boy, & obtained a situation in the counting room of the late Jonathan Harris, with whom he was subsequently several years connected in business. His estate is estimated at nearly four millions of dollars.

Piano forte, household & kitchen furniture, at auction on Sep 30, at the residence of Rev Dr Teasdale, 429 13th st, next to G st. –A Green auct

The telegraph announced the death of Hon Arthur P Bagby, of Alabama. He died on Sep 21, at Mobile, of yellow fever.

A child of Mr Vaule, living at the Navy Yard, was yesterday scalded to death by oversetting on itself a vessel of boiling water.

Mrd: on Sep 5, at St Stephen's Church, Phil, by Rev Dr Ducachet, Jos J May, of Wash, D C, to Miss Anne Heath Henderson, of St Louis, Missouri.

Orphans Court of Wash Co, D C. Letters testamentary on the personal estate of John McCauley, late of Wash Co, deceased. –Eliz McCauley, admx

SAT SEP 25, 1858
Naval: 1-Lt Wm M Murdaugh, Flag-Lt of the Paraguay squadron, left Norfolk yesterday to join Cmdor Shubrick. 2-The sloop-of-war **Water-witch**, on of the Paraguay fleet, Lt R B Pegram commanding, arrived at Nofolk yesterday. She will speedily be followed by the steamer **Fulton**. 3-Cmder Alex'r M Pennock has received orders to take command of the steamer **Southern Star**, now fitting out with all dispatch at the Gosport navy yard for the Paraguay expedition. 4-The sloop-of-war **Cyane**, Capt Lockwood, sailed on Sep 21 for the Pacific, all her officers having reported.

Vessels of the Brazil squadron & Paraguay expedition: W B Shubrick, Flag-Ofcr; frig **Sabine**, Capt J B Hull; sloop **Falmouth**, Cmder Farrand; brig **Perry**, Lt R L Tilghman; brig **Bainbridge**, Lt F B Renshaw; brig **Dolphin**, Cmder Chas Steedman; steamer **Fulton**, Lt J J Almy; steamer **Water-witch**, Lt R B Pegram; storeship **Supply**, Lt F Stanly; steamer **Memphis**, [chartered,] Cmder J B Marchand; steamer **Atalanta**, [chartered,] Cmder D B Ridgely; steamer **Caledonia**, [chartered,] Cmder A L Case; steamer **Southern Star**, [chartered,] Cmder A M Pennock; steamer **Western Port**, [chartered,] Cmder T T Hunter; revenue steamer **Harriet Lane**, Capt J Faunce. -States

Trustee's sale of improved property on the Island: on Oct 26, on the premises, by deed of trust from D B Johnson, dated Oct 6, 1857, & recorded in Liber J A S No 146, folios 283, of the land records for Wash Co. I shall sell lot 21 in square 267, with a 2 story brick dwlg house. –F S Myer, trustee -Jas C McGuire, auct

The case of Geo H Hickman, indicted for altering a land warrant issued by the U S Gov't came up on Sep 23, in the U S District Court, Balt, on a motion to quash the indictment. The grounds upon which that was asked were that the court had no jurisdiction, no offence having been commiteed against the U S; &, that there was no law of Congress making such alleged alteration a criminal offence. Judge Giles will render his decision on the motion in the morning.

Rosewood Chickering Piano Fortes, & household & kitchen furniture at auction on Oct 1, at the residence of John W Allen, 14th st, between F & G sts. –Jas C McGuire, auct

Augustus P Shutt has received an independent nomination for the ofc of Mayor of Balt, & has accepted the honor.

Gen Scott had a very severe fall on the stairs at Cozzens' Hotel, West Point, last week, when about to attend a dinner party given to him at Col Delafield's. Having had a bullet through one shoulder, & a sword thrust through the other arm during his campaigns, he was unable to break the fall & his back was severely injured. He cannot move without great pain. He has been cupped & leeched. At his age, with so ponderous a frame, it is a serious affair. –N Y Express

Col Bee's btln of volunteers reached **Fort Leavenworth** on Sep 13, & were paid off on Sep 15. Col Cook, Capt Gove, Capt Donevent, & Lts Buford, Pegram, Hill, & Merrill, had also arrived at the fort.

A woman named Shelling, at Groveport, Ohio, committed murder on Sep 22, by throwing into a well 35 feet deep, her 4 children, one a boy, the others 3 girls, the oldest 12 years, & the youngest 2 years. She afterwards jumped in herself. All were taken out dead. The woman is supposed to have been insane.

Workmen yesterday began removing the brick wall at the Christ Church burying ground at 5th & Arch sts. It was removed to allow the grave of Franklin to be seen from the street. –Phil Inquirer, Sep 21

Died: on Sep 14, in Hunter's Bottom, Ky, at the residence of her son, Wm White, Margaret Hoyt, aged 91 years. She was a native of N Y, & landed in Maysville, Ky, 70 years ago. She was the first white woman in Cincinnati.

St Mary's Female Seminary will re-open on Oct 18. The institution is beautifully situated on the St Mary's river, the site of the old city of St Mary's. Mad. Despommier & Miss Blades transferred from Balt to St Mary's. –C Billingsley, President

MON SEP 27, 1858
N Y papers state that the description given of a vessel burnt, on Sep 13th, midway between Halifax & Ireland, was either the steamship **Austria** or the steamship **Alps**, while the figure-head would seem to show that the former is the ill-fated steamer. The **Austria** had on board about 250 persons, including Germans resident in America, who had been spending the summer in the old country. List of her cabin passengers, amongst whom are T Eisfeld, the well known musician & conductor of the Philharmonic concerts in N Y; Theodore Glanbenskee, Prof of German in the Free Academy, Md; & Hermann Thorbecke, a well-known German of Phil. Herm Sondheim, wife, & 5 children, N Y; S Kititaff, Minden; Miss Bridget Loughlin, Carl Nettman, N Y; J Bogel & wife, New Orleans; Mrs Emilie Vezin & 3 children, Phil; Miss Therese Von Mengershausen, Arnsberg; T Eisfeld, Mrs Julie Ebbinghaus & daughter, A Weissenborn, N Y; Mrs Anna

Paypers & 3 children, Miss Maria Herkin, St Louis; Gustav Kohn, Konigsberg; A E Wiedmann, N Y; Jacob Frindly & wife, Wittelsdorf; E Weisker, N Y; Wilh Stachel, Cincinnati; Miss Hedwig, Dormitzer, Hamburg; Mrs Sophie Jagel & child; A M Starmunt, N Y; Miss Caroline Howitz, Copenhagen; F Gorrissen & wife, Hamburg; Miss Helene Wulf, Copenhagen; W Rosenthal, wife, & 5 children; Miss Lena Myer, Miss Minna Smith, Th Glaubenkslee, N Y; Fr Bartels, San Francisco; C D Trott, J B Massury, Zanzibar; Hermann Thorbecke, Phil; Jos Hope, Ed Adelsdorfer, Ed Bogel, N Y; R V Durfeddt, Dresden; Ad Hermann, wife, & 7 children, Igelo; Julius Busch, N Y. Besides these, the **Austria** had a large number of steerage passengers. Her freight is very valuable, consisting in great part of velvet & silk winter dry goods. [Sep 28th newspaper: the barque **Lotus** arrived at Halifax on Sep 26, with 12 of the 67 passengers saved from the steamer **Austria**, which was burnt at sea on Sep 13. List of the saved: L Kuhn, 1st ofcr; B Hertman, 2nd do; S Bernett, 3rd do; C Meihaelis, boatswain's mate; C Plate, quartermaster; N Surgerizen, sailor; H Richter, boy; S Freibold, fireman; Edw Avindolph, steward; C Poll, engineer's assist. Passengers-females: Maria Friedrich, from Tray; Rosalie St Zig, Lobsenz; Bettery Ergen, Lemburg; Catherine Tinokel, N Y; B Rovendamon, Scharbeck; Trina Hoschel, Bremen. Males: Forde Stauz, Mesmer; Chas Tras, Nicaragua; Theodore Isfeld, N Y; ___ Durfield, Dresden; D Cohn; F Reinlanmer, Koln; Jacob Rill, Baierk; Frauz Fitz, Maine; Emil Tasz, Engar; Dr Sheck, Koln; Wm Becker, N Y; T Wepfer, N Y; Ellen Velle, N Y; C Lonic, Chicago; Leopold Thillier, Pochlowitz; G Luklemann, Cincinnati; T Hohental, Rubons Wildniss; F P Retke, Lenzeu; G Vollerson, Cappelen; Fred'k Stabner, Ferdinand Stabner, Zarinkon; H Osbar, Bremerbeck; C Becker, Blomberg; A Lars, Cappelen; N Sicks; H Wendell; C Buchalt; F Rendsburg; S Hess, Holzzen; W Haso, Berlen; Peter Ivagnar, Worms; Wilif Minsicu, Worns; Levy Bock, Tudorf; S Pollack, Rutzden; Philip Muller, Kran; Ernst Witte, Weden; A Bionsteil, Manheinn; E Wunnschmann, Ligen; Lyon Wolfk, N Y; Freidhel Vagner, Cassel; Jas Smith; ___ Murray, Alexandria, Va. The following were transferred to the ship **Lotus**: Chas Brew, England; Jean Polikeruski, N Y; Phillip Berry, Hackensack, N Y; H Arandus & C Hogguist, Sweden; C V T Rosin, Richmond, Va; Henry Augustus Smith, Chelsea; J F Cox, Boston; Alfred Verin, Phil; Theodore G Glaubenskier, N Y; Thompson, Calif. Capt Waters, of the ship **Prince Albert** tendered to those at Halifax a free passage to N Y, & 10 accepted. The **Prince Albert** sailed thence on Sunday.]

The Boston papers mention the sudden disappearance of Mr John Etheredge, formerly chief clerk in the Navy Dept. He left his home on Sep 13th & has not since been heard from. His friends are apprehensive that he has committed suicide. His watch & other valuables were left in his room. Any information concerning him should be addressed to M A Etheredge, 254 Tremont st, Boston. -Union

Wm C Clark was executed at Danville, Pa, on Friday last for the murder of his wife by poison.

Jas Adger, an eminent merchant of Charleston, S C, died in N Y on Fri last after a brief illness of pneumonia. He was about 83 years of age, & had been for 65 years a resident of Charleston, whither he emigrated from Ireland.

Rochester Union of Thu. An old man, Saml C Albro, who resided at Whitestown, Oneida Co, for many years, & at the time of the last war was attached to a company from that place, has been largely engaged in making bogus land warrants. Some 5 years since he resided here, through A G Mudge he obtained a pension & a land warrant, to both of which he was entitled. He moved to Jerusalem, Yates Co, & to other counties, making warrants for dead soldiers, names on the muster-rolls, & even living soldiers; from 75 to 100 warrants. On Tue Deputy Marshal Dryer went to Jerusalem & arrested Albro, together with a justice of the peace, Chas H Vail, & 3 young men named Tomer, Spencer, & Casey. Deputy Marshal Omstead went to Whitestown, Oneida Co, & arrested Morris Wilcox, a justice of the peace residing there, & some others, we believe H H Bostwick, a well-known lawyer of Auburn, & escorted them to this city. Judge Barriger, of Tioga, & Mr Hudson, of Schuyler Co, had their names each forged to a land warrant. [Sep 29th newspaper: Albro was held & fully committed to answer charges that will consign him to prison for life. Wilcox & Vail were held to answer at the next U S Court in the sum of $2,000 each, which bail they promptly entered & went their way. The subscribing witnesses were held in the sum of $500 each to answer, & all recognized to appear. –Rochester Union]

A procession of German citizens, preceded by a band of music, marched through & from Wash City to dedicate the new **Prospect Hill Cemetery**, on the northern edge of the city, close to the **Glenwood Cemetery**. It is the property of the German Evangelical Church.

Died: on Sep 25, after a short illness, Mr Levi Pumphrey, aged 68 years. He resided in Wash City about 40 years, & was appreciated by his fellow citizens for his unbending integrity in all the vicissitudes through which he passed. His funeral is this afternoon at 3½ o'clock, from his late residence on C st, between 4½ & 6th sts.

New Haven, Sep 24. Geo Mercer, an Englishman, & a cutler by trade, was killed in an amateur prize-fight in this city last night by Wm Houston, another Englishman. There was but one witness present. They fought 5 rounds. On the last 3 Mercer fell, & did not rise from the last; his brain was congested. Houston is committed for examination today.

Orphans Court of Wash Co, D C. Letters of administration on the personal estate of Jas R Dunn, late of Wash Co, deceased. –Richd H Laskey, adm

TUE SEP 28, 1858
Excellent household & kitchen furniture at auction on Oct 4, at the residence of Mrs Eliza Lake, on Pa ave, between 2nd & 3rd sts. -Jas C McGuire, auct

Charleston "Times" of Sat announces the death of Rev Reuben Post, who died of the prevailing fever yesterday. He had nearly reached his 67th year. He was the pastor of the Circular Church for 21 years, beloved by his congregation. Dr Post was a native of Vt, in which State he graduated in 1814, subsequently proceeded to a theological course at Princeton, N C. He was ordained in Jul, 1819, & was pastor of the First Presbyterian Church in this city until Feb, 1836, when he accepted a call to Charleston.

Household & kitchen furniture at auction on Sep 28, at the residence of Rev J B Eckard, 346 N Y ave, between 9th & 10th sts. –C W Boteler, auct

Eleventh St Cabinet Establishment, Wm McL Cripps, near Pa ave. [Ad]

Naval: The sloop of war **Cyane** went to sea from Norfolk Fri last. She is bound for the Pacific. List of her ofcrs: Capt-Saml Lockwood Lambert; Lts-J H Spotts, T S Phelps, Geo N Morris, J Stillwell, A G McCartney, [Acting Master.] 2nd Lt of Marines-A N Baker. Surgeon-L J Williams. Assist Surgeon-Chas E Living. Purser-J D Murray. Capt's Clerk-T W Upshur. Purser's Clerk-Chas F Float.

List of ofcrs attached to the steamer **Fulton**, of the Paraquay expedition: Lt Commanding-J J Almy. Lts-M R Warrington, Robt B Stewart, Robt Seldon, Marshall C Campbell. Purser-Rob H Clark. Surgeon-Mayo. Chief Engineer-Newell. Assistants-John A Grier, W P Burrow, J B Houston, & DeCraft. Purser's Clerk-John Powers. The marines are in charge of Sgt Thos Bowe.

On Sep 18, as Archbishop Blane, of Louisiana, was getting on board the steamer at Donaldsonville, for New Orleans, he got his foot accidentally in a hole in the deck of one of the boats, & fell in such a manner as to break both bones of his left leg.

Died: on Sep 26, in Wash City, Miss Mary G Handy, in her 76th year. Her funeral is this afternoon at 3 o'clock, from the Rev Dr Smith's Church, [4th Presbyterian,] on 9th st.

Died: on Sep 23, at Ashland, Hanover Co, Va, Mrs Frances B Robinson, wife of Edwin Robinson, of Richmond.

Died: on Sep 26, Laura Cornelia, infant daughter of Thos H & Marion E Maddox.

WED SEP 29, 1858
The sculptor Hart has finished his model of the statue of Henry Clay, ordered by the Clay Monumental Association of New Orleans. The likness is said to be perfect. The model goes from Florence to Munich, where it will be cast in bronze, & the inauguration will probably take place in New Orleans on the anniversary of Mr Clay's birthday in 1860.

The Abbeville [S C] Banner records the decease of Wm Lowndes, youngest son of the late John C Calhoun, who died on Sep 19, on his plantation, in Abbeville District. Since the death of Mr Calhoun 3 sons & a daughter, we believe, have followed him to the tomb. -Charleston Courier

$100 reward for strayed or stolen, from the commons near F st, a bay Horse. The reward will be paid to any person delivering said horse to J B Greenwell, 167 South F st, Island.

On Wed last, in Concord, Mass, the wife & son of Mr Edw Barrett, were shockingly burnt by the explosion of a fluid lamp.

The number of the passengers who embarked from Hamburg on the ill-fated steamer **Austria** amounted to 420, viz: 49 men & women & 19 children in the first cabin; 103 men & women & 8 children in the second cabin; & 211 men & women & children as steerage passengers. In addition it is supposed that a number of passengers were taken on board at Southampton, & the ofcrs & crew numbered about 100 persons. It appears that only 67 of the more than 500 souls, have been saved. The flames pressed closely to the passengers & many jumped into the sea. Two sisters jumped overboard together; a missionary & wife leaped into the sea together; the stewardess & assist steward followed; one Hungarian gentleman, with 7 fine children, 4 of them girls, made his wife jump in, then blessed his 6 eldest children, made them jump in one after the other, & followed them with the infant in his own arms. The French barque **Maurice**, Capt Ernest Renaud, of Nantes, rescued 40 persons of the burning steamer, & acted with the utmost kindness. He gave clothes as far as he could furnish to the suffering passengers, & acted as nurse, doctor, & surgeon to the burnt people, delicately & with tenderness. The fire is known to have arisen from very culpable negligence of some of the crew. The captain & surgeon considered it expedient to fumigate the steerage with burning tar. The operation was to be performed by the boatswain, under the superintendence of the 4th officer. The boatswain heated the end of a chain to dip in tar to produce smoke; the end became too hot to hold, & he let it drop upon the deck, to which it set fire; the tar upset, & immediately all was in flames. A feeble attempt was made to extinguish it, but without effect.

+

It appears but too certain that Mrs Willian, wife of Mr Willian, proprietor of the millinery, & lace store on Pa ave, near 8th st, together with her 2 children, were of the number of the victims on board the steamer **Austria**.

+

N Y, Sep 28. The two young ladies Keittner, passengers of the steamer **Austria**, are not among the saved.

The announcement of the death of Hon L J Sigur, at Pass Christian, on Sep 18, took his acquaintances & friends by surprise. He was a member of one of the oldest & most respected families in the State. –New Orleans Picayune

P S Turley, formerly a clergyman, was executed on Friday week in Kanawha Co, Va, for the murder of his wife. On the gallows he made a speech, attributing the commission of the crime to intemperance.

Orphans Court of Wash Co, D C. Letters of administration on the personal estate of Jacob Towne, late of Worcester Co, Mass. –Foster Henshaw, adm

Mr John T Ford, manager of Holliday Street Theatre, Balt, is now in Washington for the purpose of erecting a new theatre.

Mrd: on Sep 21, by Rev T W Greer, Mr West Scott to Miss Margaret Purceel, all of Wash City.

THU SEP 30, 1858
Wash Corp-Wed: 1-Ptn from Thos Irwin; from Michl Mooney; & from John Straining: each for the remission of a fine: referred to the Cmte of Claims. 2-Ptn of Saml Norment & others for a foot-bridge across the Tiber at 3rd st: referred to the Cmte on Canals. 3-Cmte of Claims: bills for the relief-of Peter Emrick; of Dr Johnson Eliot; of Richd H Gault; of Chas R Queen; & of Saml Statcup: passed.

Jas J Hatch, one of the Editors of the Charleston Courier, died on Sep 25, after 5 days' illness with the yellow fever. He was a native of Maine, & was only about 25 years of age. He was first connected with the Charleston Standard, & in the early part of 1857 entered the editorial service of the Courier, & acquitted himself with credit.

Ordnance Sgt Thos Wilson died at **Fort McHenry** on Tuesday. He was 40 years old, & the last 20 years of his life have been spent in the army. He was with the American army under Gen Z Taylor in Mexico, & fought in the battles of Monterey, Vera Cruz, Cerro Gordo, & the bloody engagements in the valley of Mexico. He was remarked for his bravery, & the late Gen F Persifor Smith mentioned him by name in his general dispatches to the Gov't at Washington, & at the conclusion of the war he was presented with a certificate of merit. The deceased leaves a family. -Sun

Rugby Institute, a Select Boarding School for boys & young gentlemen, at Mount Washington, 6 miles from Balt, will commence on the first Monday in Nov. For circulars address E Arnold, LL D, Mount Washington, Balt Co, Md.

For rent, the house of Mr Ellet, 288 H st, between 17th & 18th sts. Apply to the owner, on the Heights of Gtwn, or by letter through the City Post Ofc.

Died: on Sep 29, in Wash City, after a protracted illness, Geo Thomas, in his 67th year, a citizen of Wash for upwards of 40 years, part of which time he was Cashier of the Bank of the Metropolis. His funeral will take place tomorrow at 3½ o'clock, from his late residence on E st, between 9th & 10th sts.]

Died: on Sep 29, Mary F, wife of Michl Green, & daughter of Owen Leddy, aged 34 years. Her funeral will be on Oct 1, at 8:30 A M, from her husband's residence, 13th L sts.

N Y, Sep 29. The ship **Prince Albert**, from Halifax, with several of the rescued passengers of the steamer **Austria**, arrived here this forenoon. The names below of the survivors is correct, but the names of S Peterson & F Thompson were omitted. Mr Rosen, of Richmond, & Mr Berry, of Hackensack, N J, give statements of the **Austria**'s disaster. Mr Peterson, a Swede, says the captain was the first to jump overboard, & no ofcr or engineer was to be found; all discipline was at an end. Mr Rosen says his father was in the boat when it was cut from the davits & fell out, but afterwards supported himself with an oar. When the boat righted his father caught hold of the stern, but being exhausted fell over & was drowned. He wished to jump over & save his father, but was prevented by those in the boat.

FRI OCT 1, 1858
The German newspapers of N Y contrast the condition of the steamer **Austria** with that of the several American steamers lost at sea. When the ship **Artic** & the steamship **Central America** went down there were instances of self-command & of heroic courage. No ordering & leading hand, such as distinguished the never to be forgotten Capt Herndon, executed with unflinching courage & calmness; all was wilde & mad, crowding hither & thither, loss of self possession & despair. Capt Heydtman is dead; well for him that he is so. For-this is the most painful part of the catastrophe, the disaster was incurred by the most criminal negligence. The list of persons saved which has been furnished to the N Y papers by the passengers brought thither by the steamer **Albert** differs materially in the spelling of names from the list published as telegraphed from Halifax: Passengers: Chas Brew, of England; Jean Polekrusen, N Y; Phillip Berry, Hackensack; H Render, S Peterson, C Hogginst, Sweden; C V T Rosin, of Richmond, Va; Henry Aug Smith, Chelsea, Mass; John I Cox, of Boston; Alfred Vezin, Phil; T G Glanbenskier, of N Y; F Thompson, of Calif; S Wepper, Ellenville, N Y; C Lomke, Chicago; G Sichlman, Cincinnati; Jas Smith Murray, Alexandria, Va; Franz Medade, N Y; Theodore Eisfield, N Y; Lyon Woff, N Y; Maria Frederich, of Prague; Rosalia Stizig, of Lotzenz; Betty Ergen, of Lemberg; B Rosendamm, of Schaunbech; Trina Hoschlet, of Bremerford; Chas Tras, of Nicaragua; ___ Durofeld, of Dresden; B Solin, of Breslau; Wm Folker, of Luchen; T Remlander, of Koln; Jacob Rill, of Barern; Franz Zitz, Maine; Ernest Tasse, Fulgar; Dr Scheck, Koln; Wm Beeker, Solingen; Leopold Thiller, Rockowitz; T Honenloe, Rubows Wildness; F Pletke, Leuzen; G Nottersen, Cappelin; Friederich Stabner, Tarnckew; Ferdinand Stabner, Tarnckew; H Osbar, Bremerbech; C Becker, Blomberg; A Lars, Cappelin; A Sichs, of H Wendel, Rendsberg; C Buchhole, Rendsberg; S Hess, Holgeson; H Haase, Berlin; Peter Wagner, Worms; Wulf Milslow, Worms; Levy Boch, Indorf; S Tollock, Rutseden; Phillip Mullen, of Aarow; Ernest Witte, Weden; A Biernstell, Manuheim; E Wunschmann, Liggeh; Freidhef Watner, Cassel. Crew: L Hahn, 1st ofcr; B Hertmann, 2nd do; J Bernett, 3rd do; C Necharles, Boatswain's mate; C Plate, quartermaster; N Surgenson, sailor; ___ Richter, boy; ___ Friebold, steward; ___ Pole, engineer's assistant.

Wharves & warehouses for rent, from Jan 1 next, with the adjoining lots & warehouses, on the Eastern Branch. The undersigned may be seen almost every day at the Franklin Ins ofc, in the Patriotic Bank bldg, 7th st. –Thos Blagden

Extensive sale of horses, cattle, carriages, wagons, corn, hay, oats, & straw, blacksmith's shop, & tools, on Oct 7, at the **Highlands**, for many years the residence of the late Robt Y Brent, 9 miles from Wash, between the Gtwn & Rockville & the Wash & Brookeville Turnpike. –Theodore Mosher

Orphans Court of Wash Co, D C. In the case of Saml A Peugh, adm of Eliz Slater, deceased, the administrator & Court have appointed Oct 19th next, for the final distribution of the personal estate of said deceased, of the assets in hand.
-Ed N Roach, Reg/o wills

Butcher's stand for sale at Centre Market on Sat next, to the highest bidder for cash, fronting on 7th st. By order of the Mayor. –John M Waters, M M

Yesterday Mr F J Hieburger was shot by Winant Streng, a German, from Calif, on D st. Streng was seen pacing up & down the street talking incoherently about the Masonic order. He pulled out a five barreled revolver & discharged it in the direction of the door of the Masonic Hall, one of the shots hitting Mr Hieburger in the foot. Streng was arrested by ofcr King & committed to jail for examination. [Oct 2nd newspaper: Mr Streng on being examined said that he had no defence; none that would help him. He is about 40 years of age, by birth a Prussian. He was remanded to jail for trial at the Criminal Court. Dr Holston stated that Mr Hieburger has suffered intensely, & has been compelled to submit to the amputation of the great toe of the left foot, & that the season is such as to make lockjaw not unlikely.]

Mrd: on Sep 29, in St Luke's Church, Bladensburg, Md, by Rev Dr Pinckney, Rev Wm Christian, of Wash, D C, to Eliz Marshall Marbury, of PG Co, Md.

Mrd: on Wed, by Rev John C Smith, Mr Thos F Cissell to Miss Jane V D McFarlin, all of Wash City.

Died: on Wed, in Wash City, after a long & painful illness, Teresa, wife of Dennis O'Donnoghue, in her 28th year. Her funeral is this afternoon from the residence of her husband, 437 G st. [The time was not given.]

SAT OCT 2, 1858
Hon Henry Bedinger, late Minister to Denmark, has arrived at his home in Jefferson Co, Va, & has been cordially greeted by his numerous friends of all parties.

Died: on Oct 1, in Wash City, after a brief illness, Henry Meredith, aged 2 months & 11 days, 2nd son of Lt N H & Jane Henry Meredith Van Zandt. His funeral will take place at 2 o'clock on Sunday next, from the residence of its grandparents, 404 H st, between 12th & 13th sts.

Departure of missionaries for China. The ordination of Rev S L Baldwin, missionary for China, will take place on Fri in the Clinton st M E Church. Mr Baldwin & wife, with Miss Beulah & Sarah Wolsten, of Trenton, & Miss Porter, of N Y, who go out as teachers, are expected to embark on Oct 4, in the clipper ship **Empress**. Three missionaries from the Dutch Reformed Board, Rev Alvan Ostrom & wife, [formerly Miss Webster, of this city,] & Rev Mr Rappaljee, for Amoy; & Rev AL B Peet & wife, of The American Board, for Fuh Chau, will also sail in the **Empress**. The present force of the Methodist mission in Fuh Chau consists of Rev H S Maclay, of the East Balt Conference, Mrs Maclay, [formerly a teacher in the Newark Wesleyan Institute,] Rev Dr Wentworth, of the N J Conference, Rev Otis, of the Genesee Conference, & Mrs Gibson.
-Newark Advertiser of Sep 29.

On Thu, Lt Hagner, at the U S Arsenal, Bridesburg, was testing a mortar with one ounce of powder, to ascertain how far it would throw a 24 pound ball. The mortar was stationed on Frankford creek, & discharged in the direction of the river road. Mrs Pickett, wife of the Superintendent, left her house, about 100 yards from the mortar station, & the sgt called to warn her to take care as the mortar has just fired. She began to run, but towards the ball, & was struck, breaking one of her arms & mangling her body so badly that she died in about an hour. The deceased was about 20 years of age, & had been married about 2 years. –Phil Ledger

Died: on Thu last, in Gtwn, D C, Miss Mary Heugh, in her 91st year. Her funeral will be this afternoon at half-past 4 o'clock, from her late residence, 70 Congress st.

Died: on Sep 10th last, in Montgomery, Ala, John B Morton, formerly of Chester Co, Pa.

MON OCT 4, 1858
Trustee's sale, by deed of trust from Jas Crutchett, dated Oct 14, 1857. Auction on Oct 14, on the premises, lots M & N, in the Balt & Ohio Railroad Co's subdivision of lot 4 in square 574, fronting on Indiana ave. –Walter S Cox, trustee -Jas C McGuire, auct

The agent of the Nashville Bible Society, Mr R M Hawkins, has recently been distributing Bibles in Macon Co, Tenn, & met with the old family Bible that found a place in Gen Washington's chamber. The gentleman who has the Bible told me that at the General's death his niece fell heir to the Bible. Previous to leaving Va her son died & he waited on him until death. The old lady told him that she was getting old, & that she had nothing to give him for waiting on her son save the old family Bible. He gladly received it & brought it to Tenn with him on horseback. He said he would not take $3,000 for it. The gentleman lives in the town of Lafayette, Macon Co, & his name is Col Claiborne.

Aaron Ogden Dayton, the 4th Auditor of the Treasury Dept, died very suddenly in Phil on Friday. His health for a long time has been delicate. He was a native of N J, & appointed to ofc from N Y. He held the postion of Auditor of Naval Accounts since 1838-20 years- having received his appointment from Mr Van Buren. -Union

Excellent household & kitchen furniture at auction on Oct 8, at the residence of Richd E Simms, 668 H st, between 4th & 5th sts. -A Green auct

A dispatch dated at Staunton, Va, on Fri says: R W Bushnell, late of Wash City, while laboring under temporary derangement, caused by ill health, shot himself this morning at the American Hotel. He still lingers this evening & is perfectly conscious. He states the act was committed while under mental aberation.

Mrd: on Oct 1, in Wash City, by Rev G W Samson, Mr Robt Yancy to Miss Mary E Threalkil, both of Culpeper Co, Va.

Died: on Sep 29, George Thomas, of Wash, aged 67 years. He was one of our oldest & worthiest of our citizens, who rose to success & fortune by his own exertions, & was an able cashier in the Bank of the Metropolis for many years. He was born in St Mary's Co, Md, & came to Wash at an early period of his life, where he resided for the last 40 years. He leaves a brother & sister to enjoy the fruits of his labors from a well spent life.

Orphans Court of Wash Co, D C. Letters of administration de bonis non on the personal estate of Geo Phillips, late of Wash Co, deceased. –Jas Lynch, adm D B N

Orphans Court of Wash Co, D C. Letters testamentary on the personal estate of Fanny Munroe, late of Wash Co, deceased. –Cols Munroe, exc

Orphans Court of Wash Co, D C. Letters of administration on the personal estate of Levi Pumphrey, late of Wash Co, deceased. –Wm H Thomas, Jos Bensley, adms

Orphans Court of Wash Co, D C. Letters testamentary on the personal estate of Lucinda Simms, late of Wash Co, deceased. –Thos Nicholls, exc

TUE OCT 5, 1858
On Sep 25, Jas Malony, a deck hand on the propeller **Globe**, which runs between Buffalo & Cleveland, lay down & went to sleep upon a sofa which was loosely laid among some other freight near the engine hatch. Suddenly awakening, he upset the sofa, & was precipitated through the hatch, some 12 feet, & fell upon the engine while in full motion. He was instantly crushed to death.

Capt Townsend, of the slaver **Echo**, has been fully committed for piracy. His trial will take place on Oct 15, at the Circuit Court. A new complaint has been entered against him for misdemeanor, which subjects him to a fine of from $1,000 to $5,000, & imprisonment for from 3 to 7 years.

Household & kitchen furniture at auction on Oct 7, at the residence of the late Mrs Goggin, on 10th, between D & E sts. -Jas C McGuire, auct

Levi Long, Postmaster at Pleasant Union, Pa, was arrested on Monday last on a charge of purloining money letters from the mails. He was committed to jail.

The following have been admitted [upon examination] as Acting Midshipmen at the Naval Academy at Annapolis:

Jas A Merriwether, Ga	Mortimer M Benton, Ky
Chas L Huntingdon, Ill	Wm W Read, Va
Henry Jones Blake, Mass	Smith W Nichols, Mass
Silas W Terry, Ky	Ivey Foreman, N C
Francis M Roby, Mo	David D Wemple, Wis
Wm Henry Harrison, Ga	Fred'k R Smith, Me
Edwin Tracy Brower, Pa	Robt P Huntington, Ind
Elliott C V Blake, Ohio	Edw N Kellogg, Ill

Fred'k H Crandall, Ill
Jas Williams Ahl, Penn
Wm Hy Winslow, Maine
David Alex Telfair, N C
Wm E Pinckney, La
Mortimer G McWilliams, Ala
Edw J McDermote, Tedas
H Beverly Littlepage, Va
Henry T Grafton, Ark
Chas H Daniels, N Y
Chas S Cotton Wis
John K Carrothers, Ill
Wm O'Hara Robinson, Pa
David Moody, Ohio
Chas St C Huston, N Y
Chas H Humphrey, N Y
Moreau Forrest, Md
Algernon S Worth, N Y
Chas F Shoemaker, New Mexico
Edw S Ruggles, Utah

John Jos Read, N J
Wm S Moon, Ohio
Henry Clay Holt, Tenn
John Bradley, N Y
Chas Wm Zimmerman, Md
Geo W Sumner, Ky
Eug B Sturgeon, Penn
Archibald N Milchett, Ill
Henry H Mannaduke, Mo
Roswell H Lamson, Oregon
Geo Aug Howard, Tenn
Wm H Hivling, Ohio
Robt Chester Foute, Tenn
Berga F Day, Ohio
David Barnum, Minn
Geo A Crall, Ohio
Giles Frank Appleton, N H
Harvey H Dougherty, Ky
Kobert Payne, Mo

I will offer at public sale, on the premises, on Nov 1, part of **Wollaston's Manor**, containing about 200 acres of land, on the Potomac river, at the mouth of Cackhold's creek, in Chas Co, Md; with good bldgs. Address J C C Hamilton, Atty at Law, Wash City, D C, or Dr F M Lancaster, Tompkinsville, P O, Chas Co, Md.

Obit-died: on Sep 28, of yellow fever, Rev Henry Mandeville Denison, Rector of St Peter's Church, in Charleston, S C, after a brief illness. He was a native of Wyoming Valley, Pa, & was theologically educated at the Protestant Episcopal Seminary in Fairfax Co, Va. He married a daughter of Hon John Tyler, of Va, who died several years since. He leaves a surviving daughter, at present residing in Brooklyn.

Rev Chas Wellbeloved died at York, England, in his 90th year & in his 67th in his ministry to the Presbyterian Church of that city.

Orphans Court of Wash Co, D C. Letters of administration on the personal estate of Martin Foley, late of Wash Co, deceased. –Jas O'Brien, adm

Mrd: on Oct 2, by Rev Mr Swenzel, Philip Boteler, of Wash City, to Mrs Isabella Taylor, of Gtwn, D C.

Balt, Oct 4. The railroad train from Phil was detained when the mail car struck a horse & was thrown down the embankment. Mr Reuben Jamar, one of the oldest conductors on the road, but not in charge of the train at the time, was severely but not dangerously injured; Mr McDuffie, baggage master, was cut on the head & arm; Mr Peter McGirk, baggage agent, was instantly killed. It is thought that he jumped from the platform.

WED OCT 6, 1858
Adm's sale of land warrant on Oct 7, in front of our store, Revolutionary Land Warrant No 2,499, for 200 acres, issued to Jacob Town. Terms cash, in gold. –Foster Henshaw, adm -Wall & Barnard, aucts

Jacob Dammert, age about 15 years, & late an employe in the post ofc at San Antonio, was arrested at Indianola on Sep 13, with fifty or sixty thousand dollars in drafts, bank stock, lottery tickets, which he had abstracted from letters passing through that office. He is a German, whose parents live in San Antonio. His intention was to go back to his uncle in Germany, & not use the drafts in this country, believing they would be converted into money there without any sort of difficulty.

On Thu Miss Anna Bell, age 18 years, of West Troy, N Y, was instantly killed by the falling of a piece of coping from the bldg occupied by Mr Robbins. She was standing on the sidewalk, & the falling stone struck her head, penetrating the skull 2 inches.

Mrd: on Oct 5, in Wash City, at Waugh Chapel, by Rev T M Carson, Mr John Patch to Miss Margaret Little, all of Wash City.

Mrd: on Aug 19, in the Second Presbyterian Church, Strabane, Ireland, by Rev W A Russell, brother to the bride, Andrew Dunn Hemphill, of Wash City, U S, to Eliz, daughter of Mr Alex'r Russell, Burnside, Raphoe.

Died: on Oct 5, Ann Elizabeth, wife of Geo T Raub. Her funeral will take place from her husband's residence, C & 15th st, at 3 o'clock, this afternoon.

Died: on Oct 5, in Wash City, Miss Adelaide V C Bradford, in her 20th year. Her funeral will take place from her mother's residence, 368 8th st, between K & L sts, this afternoon at 3 o'clock.

Died: on Oct 5, in Wash City, of remittent fever, in her 7th year, Mary Malvina, only daughter of Ann Rosina & John H Trenholm. Her funeral will take place at St Patrick's Church, on Oct 7, at 9 o'clock.

Quebec, Oct 4. The Norwegian ship **Catarina**, Capt Funnemark, for Fowey, 43 days out, arrived yesterday. On Sep 14 she fell in with the steamship **Austria**, & took from the wreck 22 persons in all, 16 passengers & 6 of the crew. Passengers: G Stepel, Andrew Lindensheim, Conrad Eiffert, Jorgen Fitchen, Wilhem Brannsdorff, Heinrich Fourier, Irachim Pless, Edw Ahlers, Jos Swertzeck, Christopher Barcker, Sven Neilson, Peter Svensen, ___ Widsentz, Johannes Danmuller, Christopher Danike. Crew: Martin Folige, Jos Karze, Fred'k Thefeldt, Heur Rieper, Johan Rohmondt, Johan Heinrich, & __ Jake.

N Y, Sep 5. Edmund Burns & Patrick Tracey, two of the Irishmen who were wounded in the affray with the Italians at the Cosmopolitan Garden here on Sunday night, are dead.

Orphans Court of Wash Co, D C. Letters testamentary on the personal estate of Geo Thomas, late of Wash Co, deceased. –Jas Dunlop, exc

U S Patent Ofc, Wash, Oct 4, 1858. Ptn of J B Thaxter, adm of John Hatch, deceased, of Hingham, Mass, praying for the extension of a patent granted to said John Hatch, on Feb 20, 1845, for an improvement in "buttons" for 7 years from the expiration of said patent, which takes place on Feb 20, 1859. –Jos Holt, Com'r of Patents

THU OCT 7, 1858
The contract of Mr Lawrence Myers, of Phil, for cast-iron pipes for the Wash aqueduct, was yesterday forfeited, because he has not complied with its provisions by delivering the 30 inch pipe within the time specified, Oct 1. –Union, Oct 4 [Oct 8th newspaper: in 1853, at Paris, the Minister of Agriculture & Commerce issued a letter to the Prefects forbidding in breweries & liquor stores the use of lead, copper, or zinc pipes, & cites the numerous cases of poisoning arising from the employment of such pipes.]

Chancery sale, by decree of the Circuit Court of Wash Co, D C, passed in a cause wherein B W Kennon is cmplnt & Martha C Kennon & others are dfndnts: auction on Nov 10 next, on the premises, of a parcel of land, namely, parts of lots 2 & 3 of the original subdivision of **Mount Pleasant** between the Peter family, on the main county road leading from 20th st, in Wash City, by Vevan's, Little's, & Estlin's; binding also upon Rock Creek & **Jackson Hill**, Walbridge's, Holt's, & Estlin's. It contains about 40 acres. Inquire of the subscriber, or of Lewis Carbery, County Surveyor.
–W Redin, trustee -A Green auct

In the Court of Quarter Sessions of Phil, on Monday, Wm Nixon was pronounced guilty of manslaughter for having left his horse & cart standing unattended in a public street, by which negligence a child was killed.

Horses, oats, negroes, & household & kitchen furniture at auction on Oct 14, at the residence & stables of Levi Pumphrey, deceased, on C st, between 4½ & 6th sts, by order of the Orphans Court of Wash Co, D C. . –W H Thomas, Jos Beasley, adms
-A Green auct

Alex'r Buchanan died in Smyth Co, Va, at the advanced age of 98 years. He had voted for every Pres of the Republic since its foundation. Capt Brown, of Russell, the adjoining county, is 101 years old, & still in health.

Governess wanted, a young lady to teach 2 or 3 small children. –Jos R Roberts, living near Bladensburg, PG Co, Md.

The murderer of Mr Grant, of Texas, late of Orange Co, N C, & son-in-law of the late Prof Mitchell, has been detected, proving to be Washington Garner, the son of a wealthy but very much dreaded neighbor of Mr Grant's. Washington was jailed, but about 200 enraged citizens assembled, broke open the jail, took him our, & shot him to atoms.

On Thu last Mr Richd W Bushnell, of Wash, arrived at this place & took lodgings at the American Hotel. He had an interview with Dr Stribling, the Superintendent of the Western Lunatic Asylum, stating he wanted to place himself under the Dr's care. On Friday a boarder heard the report of a pistol from Mr Bushnell's room. He had shot himself behind the right ear. He is still alive, & says he feels pretty well except for a headache. Mr Bushnell is a native of Rockingham Co, unmarried, & about 40 years of age. He graduated at the Univ of Va some 18 or 20 years ago with great distinction. He taught school in Richmond, & removed from there to Wash City. He is a member of the Episcopal Church. –Staunton [Va] Spectator, Oct 5

Rev Bernard Maguire, Pres of Gtwn College, has retired, having served one term longer than is usual with the heads of that excellent institution. Fr John Early comes here from Balt to fill the vacated chair. -States

The Richmond Dispatch the statement that Rev Moses D Hoge, of that city, has accepted the pastorate of the Second Presbyterian Church in Wash City.

Orphans Court of Wash Co, D C. In the case of Helen M West, admx, with the will annexed, of Benj O West, deceased, the administratrix & Court have appointed Oct 26th next, for the final settlement of the personal estate of said deceased, of the assets in hand. -Ed N Roach, Reg/o wills

U S Patent Ofc, Wash, Oct 5, 1858. Ptn of Eleazer Carver, of Bridgewater, Mass, praying for the extension of a patent granted to him on Jan 4, 1845, for an improvement in saw cotton gins, for 7 years from the expiration of said patent, which takes place on Jan 4, 1859. –Jos Holt, Com'r of Patents

Mrd: on Oct 5, by Rev Andrew G Carothers, Mr John T Miller, of Wash City, to Miss Catherine R Sheid, of Loudoun Co, Va.

Mrd: on Oct 5, in Wash City, by Rev G W Samson, Mr Nelson C Driver to Miss Margaret A Beall, both of Wash City.

Mrd: in Wash City, at St Patrick's Church, by Rev Fr Boyle, Mr Philip Hill to Miss Anna V Crauford, both of PG Co, Md. [No marriage date given-appears to be a current item.]

FRI OCT 8, 1858
A lad, Edw Mulligan, whose parents reside in Ritchie Co, at Petroleum, on the Northwestern Va road, came to his death last week from the bite of a rattlesnake. It was found in the bed of his father & mother, & he was lying on the floor nearby, when the snake struck him. He lived 24 hours after being bitten.

Farm & farm stock at auction on Oct 20; the farm of F Vincenti, on the Wash & Balt Turnpike, 3 miles from Beltsville. Also, the crops. There is a small dwlg with requisite out-bldgs. –Wall & Barnard, aucts

The explosion on the steamship **Hammonia** occurred at sea, a few hours after leaving the Elbe for N Y. The ship was turned round to retrace her steps to the Elbe. Dr Neander, one of the cabin passengers & the surgeon of the **Hammonia**, assisted the injured. Madame Andre, from Offenbach, residing at Phil, had a slight contusion of the right hip; Herr Barth, from Costa Rica, dislocation of the left knee cap; Miss Fanny Biermann, from Furth, slight wound on the left cheek; Herr Friedrich Muller, from Oldenburg, lower part of left thigh bone broken & fracture of right leg below the knee, rendering the amputation of both legs necessary.

Mrs R G Etchison has received her entire Stock of Fall Goods: No 12 Penn ave, Wash. [Ad]

The subscriber offers for sale 77½ acres of land on the east side of the **Piney Branch** or 14th st road, nearly opposite to the old Bodisco place, now owned by Mr Blagden. This farm has also a front on the Wash & Rockville Turnpike, directly opposite the highly improved residence of Mr Mosher. Apply to me through the Wash post ofc, or to Mr Walter S Cox, 40 Louisiana ave. –Wm Gaston Pearson

Orphans Court of Wash Co, D C. Letters of administration on the personal estate of Henry F English, late of Wash Co, deceased. –Eliz V English, admx [Mr David English is authorized to pay out & receipt for all moneys due to or from the above estate. E V E]

Mrd: on Oct 6, in Wash City, by Rev Wm F Clark, S J, Pres of Loyola College, Balt, Richd H Clark to Ada, daughter of the late Raphael Semmes, of Gtwn.

Meeting of Junior Class of Columbia College, D C, Oct 6, 1858, on the death of esteemed classmate, Alfred McDaniel, of Missouri. –J C L Hatcher, Pres -D A Chambers, sec

N Y, Oct 7. The barque **Thales**, of New Orleans, arrived here with Wm Briggs & 4 seamen who were picked up in a boat belonging to the wrecked ship **Pelican State**.

SAT OCT 9, 1858

Excellent household & kitchen furniture at auction on Oct 11, at the residence of W W Breckenbaugh, on Pa ave, opposite the Nat'l Hotel. -Jas C McGuire, auct

On Wed at the house of Mr Oliver, about 4 miles from Balt, Mr Wm Hebdin & friends, gathered after returning from a gunning excursion. They decided to shoot chickens, & were followed by a son & daughter of Mr Oliver. Mr Hebdin had his gun, which was half-cocked, when the gun exploded, the greater portion of its contents passing into the breast of the boy, killing him instantly. Another portion of the charge passed into the little girl, injuring her severely. John Clough, a young man, received about 130 shot in various portions of his body. Mr Hebdin remained at the bedside of the wounded administering to their wants until a late hour in the night, & has taken upon himself the duty of liquidating all the expenses. -Clipper

The Sec of the Navy received intelligence of the death of Surgeon B Ticknor, at Ann Arbor, Mich, in his 71st year. His total service amounted to 35 years, of which 15 were spent at sea & 20 in various naval hospitals. He returned from his last voyage in 1848.

M Crepin, at Lyons, France, who was furnished with 2 meals a day by an old widow for 35 centimes, left his fortune, three million francs, to this guardian angel over his misery.

Suitable reward will be paid for the recovery of a coal black pointer Dog, which strayed or was stolen from 424 E st. He wears a steel collar with my name engraved upon it, & answers to the name Milo. –John A Linton

Yesterday, Mr Felix Richard, a native of France, & for about 3 years in the employ of Mr C Gautier, as clerk in his restaurant, was taken suddenly ill whilst attending to his duties. He was removed to another room, & in a short time died. Death was caused by disease of the heart. He was between 50 & 60 years of age, esteemed by all who knew him.

Mrd: on Oct 5, in Wash City, by Rev Mr Morsell, Thos Benton Rector, of Fauquier Co, Va, to Miss Mary L Weber, of Wash City.

Mrd: on Oct 7, at the Church of the Ephiphany, by Rev Wentworth L Childs, Albert Melbourne Pett, of Beloit, Wisc, to Miss Margaret Fountain, of Wash.

Died: on Oct 1, at New Orleans, of yellow fever, Mr John F McCarthy, a native of Wash City. He graduated at Gtwn College & afterwards at the Law School of Harvard Univ. He was professor of mathematics & ancient languages in the Wash Seminary, & a practioner of law in Wash City & the city of St Louis.

MON OCT 11, 1858
New Orleans Bulletin: The great criminal offender Paulin C Lebleu, the cold blooded murderer of Ewing & Parsons, the cold-hearted wife seducer & kidnapper, the lawless desperado of the parish of Caleasieu, has at last met that fate he so richly deserved. On Sep 13 the District Court commenced its regular session at Lake Charles, the seat of justice of the parish of Calcasieu. On Wed Lebleu rode up to the rack of the hotel, descended from his mule, & started towards the house with a pair of dragoon pistols, a repeater, & a bowie knife in his belt. He almost reached the steps when he was shot from the front of the very same steps, 4 different times, by a man named Eugene Foux & others, who had all been victims of the depravities of Lebleu. He expired almost instantly. The men who shot him were set at liberty the next day.

Mr Dermott Dempsey, supposed to be the wealthiest man in Macon, Ga, died on Sep 20, leaving an estate of $500,000. He was a member of the Roman Catholic Church. He leaves a will, which divides $5,000 between his 2 children, & gives the remainder, $495,000 to the Catholic Church. [Oct 14th newspaper: Mr Dempsey's estate is valued at somewhere about $250,000, & all goes to his children, not a cent to the Catholic Church.]

Advertisement in the St Louis Republican: engaged-Miss Anna Gould to John Candal, City Marshal, both of Leavenworth, K T. From this time henceforth & forever-until Miss Anna Gould becomes a widower-all young gentlemen are requested to withdraw their particular attention.

Mr Judson Warner, residing on Bridge st, Gtwn, was sitting reading a newspaper to his wife when all at once he stopped, coughed, threw up blood from his chest, & in a few minutes was a corpse. His health has been infirm for some time. Aged about 40 years, he leaves a wife & 7 children.

On Sat night, a seaman, Wm H Lisby, from Balt, one of the crew of the barkantine **Ephraim Williams**, Cornwall master, lying at the west Wash wharves, fell from her bow, & it is feared he was drowned. His body has not yet been found. [Oct 12th newspaper: The body of Lisby was recovered on Sunday. It appears from the darkened appearance of one side of the face & head that he struck on the anchor in falling from the vessel's bow, & being stunned was unable to save himself.]

I have this day associated with me in the Dry Goods business Jos J May. The business will be conducted in the name of Clagett & May. –John B Clagett

Orphans Court of Wash Co, D C. Letters of administration on the personal estate of John T S McConchie, late of Wash Co, deceased. –Thos P Morgan, adm

Died: on Oct 8, Mrs Magdalena P Kinchy, in her 52nd year, a native of Switzerland, but for the last 25 years a resident of Wash City.

Died: on Oct 4, at St Louis, Mo, Philip Mauro, for some years past a resident of that place, but formerly & for many years a much esteemed resident of Wash City.

Died: on Sat, at the residence of her parents, in Brooklyn, N Y, Florence, daughter of Mr & Mrs D H Craig. Nineteen months ago she came, with her mother, as far south as Richmond for the benefit of her declining health. She peacefully passed from earth.

Obit-died: Edw H Pendleton. As a husband he was most devoted, as a son & brother affectionate & kind; his memory will be cherished by a wide circle of relatives & friends. [No other information.]

St Louis, Oct 10. On Aug 25 a fight occurred between a small detachment of troops under Maj McLean & the Indians at Bear Springs, in which Maj McLean was severely wounded & 6 or 8 Indians killed. Col Loring's command was expected at **Fort Union** in a few days. Gen Garland, Maj Nichols, & Capt Easton had left for the States.

TUE OCT 12, 1858
Household & kitchen furniture at auction on Oct 15, at **Rock Spring Farm**, formerly the residence of Mr Dashiel, on High st, about 1 mile from Gtwn. -Jas C McGuire, auct

Rev E C McGuire, D D, was struck down with paralysis yesterday morning. Last Sunday was the 45th anniversary of his ministerial labors. –Fredericksburg Herald

A Pennsylvania paper announced that death has at last divided the oldest pair in the U S. Mrs Ludwick Snyder died a few days since in Burnside Township, Clearfield Co, Penn, at age 108. Her husband, who is 112 years old, survives her.

The subscriber has 84 acres of land in the District, divided into 5 lots, for sale. He also has 150 acres, with a small house on it. It joins the farms of Messrs Dundas, Tucker, Bates, & Wiltberger. Apply to E J Middleton, City Hall, or the subcriber, Henry Queen, near Wash, D C, who will show the property.

An ancient Church. The "First Church in Hartford," Conn, has been in existence 225 years, & has never dismissed a pastor. It has had 10 in all, 9 of whom have lived & died among their people; & the 10th, Dr Hawes, has now been in charge for 40 years.

Mrd: on Oct 9, in Wash City, in the Fourth Presbyterian Church, by Rev John C Smith, Mr Jacob Grimly to Miss Mary Jane Wilson, all of Wash City.

Mrd: on Oct 5, by Rev D Ball, Benj Burns to Mary A Basset, all of Wash City.

Mrd: on Oct 7, by Rev S Rodgers, Mr Geo White to Miss Marion A Harris, all of Wash City.

Mrd: on Oct 6, at Brooklyn, N Y, by Rev Mr Howland, at the residence of the bride's father, Alfonso A De La Figaniere, 4th son of his Excellency the Minister Plenipotentiary of Portugal to the U S, to Eliz H, eldest daughter of Wm Pitt Palmer.

Died: on Oct 4, in N Y C, Fannie K, wife of Lt N Michler, of the Topographical Corps of Engineers of the U S Army, & daughter of the late Judge Kirtland, of that city.

Died: on Sat last, at Balt, in his 77th year, Col Nicholas Burke, who commanded a company in the war of 1812. He was highly respected by all who knew him.

Died: on Oct 11, in Wash City, Mary Josephine, infant daughter of Paulus & Parthene Thyson.

Orphans Court of Wash Co, D C. Letters of administration, with the will annexed, on the personal estate of Jas F Morton, late of Wash Co, deceased. –Ellen Morton, admx w a

WED OCT 13, 1858
Mrd: on Oct 5, at the residence of Dr J F Faunt LeRoy, of Clarke Co, Va, by Rev Jos Jones, Geo Davidson, of the U S Coast Survey, San Francisco, Calif, to Ellinor, daughter of the late Robt Henry Faunt LeRoy, of the U S Coast Survey, & grand-daughter of Robt Owen, of New Lanark, Scotland.

Mount Vernon Ladies Association of the Union: officers now appointed:
Regent, Miss Ann Pamela Cunningham, S C
Vice Regents:
Mrs Anna Cora Ritchie, Richmond, Va
Mrs Alice H Dickinson, Wilmington, N C
Mrs Philoclea Edgeworth Eve, Augusta, Ga
Mrs Octavia Walton Le Vert, Mobile, Ala
Mrs Catharine A McWillie, Jackson, Miss
Mrs Margaretta S Morse, New Orleans, La
Mrs Mary Rutledge Fogg, Nashville, Tenn
Mrs Mary Boott Goodrich, Southbury, Conn
Mrs Eliz M Walton, St Louis, Mo
Miss Mary Morris Hamilton, N Y
Miss Phebe Anne Ogden, Eliz, N J
Mrs Louisa Ingersoll Greenough, Boston, Mass
Mrs Abba Isabella Little, Portland, Maine
Mrs Catherine Willi_ Murat, Tallaassee, Fla
Mrs Alice Key Pendleton, Cincinnati, Ohio
Mrs Abby Wheaton Chace, Providence, R I
Sec-Mrs Susan L Pellet, Richmond, Va
Treas-Geo W Riggs, Wash, D C
The contract with Mr Washington for the sale of the property to the Association was signed on Apr 6, 1858. The sum to be paid was $200,000. $18,000 was paid at the signing of the contract. The first instalment of $57,000, due Jan 1, 1859, is now ready to be paid, & it is hoped to raise the entire purchase sum during the present year, in order to take possession on the coming Feb 22. By the terms of the charter & contract the remains of Washington are never to be removed from their present resting place, which is on the spot chosen by himself. –Susan L Pellet, Sec -Richmond, Va, Sep 21, 1858

Information wanted of Mary Ryan, residing in Wash, D C, by her sister, Johanna Ryan, from Dublin, Ireland. Address her, care of Hugh Ford, 409 Penn st, Phil.

THU OCT 14, 1858
Trustee's sale: by deed in trust to the late John W Maury, dated Jul 25, 1842, recorded in Liber W B No 96, at folios 273, of the land records of Wash Co, D C, & by decree of the Circuit Court of D C appointing the subscriber trustee to execute the trusts in the said deed contained, in the stead of said John W Maury, deceased, the subscriber will, on Oct 25, sell at public auction, lot 2 in square 267. –W A Maury, trustee -A Green auct

A new military post, named **Fort Quitman**, in honor of the late Gen Quitman, has been located on the San Deigo mail route, 60 miles beyond **Fort Davis**, & at the point where the road first touches the Rio Grande.

The Providence Journal announces the death in that city on Sunday of Stephen Harris, age 72 years, one of the most eminent manufacturers in Rhode Island. He was one of the founders of the Rhode Island Medical Society.

The late Ebenezer Francis, of Boston, says the Boston Gaz, has left nearly five millions of dollars. He wills to each of his daughters, Mrs Mason & Mrs Bowditch, $200,000 outright; $100,000 he gives in legacies to various persons. The balance he places in trust for the benefit of his 9 grandchildren, the interest, however, to go to his daughters during their lives. This interest amounts to about $234,000 per annum, or $117,000 each.

At Naugatuck, N Y, Aug 29, Edwin L Hopkins, son of Truman & Julia Hopkins, aged 22; Sept 7th, Harriet A, wife of Merit Wooding, & daughter of Truman & Julia Hopkins, aged 32; Sep 9th, Truman Hopkins, aged 54; Oct 2nd, Julia, wife of Truman Hopkins, aged 53; & in Prospect, Oct 4, Clarissa, wife of Albert Young, aged 33 years, daughter of Truman & Julia Hopkins. All members of the same family. [No other information. Appears to be a notice of recent deaths in the same family.]

On Sat an accident occurred on the Ohio & Miss railroad, about 150 miles from Cincinnati. A freight train from the East & another from the West came into collision. The conductor, J W Brown; the engineer, J Redman; a brakesman, Mr Dryon, & a fireman, [unable to learn his name,] were all killed. –Cin Gaz

Died: on Oct 13, Miss Melinda Barker, of Westmoreland Co, Va. Her funeral will take place from the house of Jos F Hodgson, 405 7th st, this day at 3 o'clock.

Died: on Sep 13, India May, infant daughter of Louisa P & John B Ward. Her funeral is this afternoon at 4 o'clock, from their residence, 443 C st.

FRI OCT 15, 1858
Valuable farm near Wash City at auction on Nov 1: the beautiful farm of Mr Jos Gingle, containin 49½ acres, located about 7 miles from Wash, on the 7th st road leading to Colesville, & adjoining the farms of Messrs Thos Wilson, Geo W Riggs, & Dr Condict, being the first farm after passing over the Sligo branch. -A Green auct

Chancery sale of very valuable 4 story brick house, by a decree passed May 17, 1858, by the Circuit Court of Wash Co, D C, in a cause, No 1312, pending in said court between F H Newman et al cmplnts, & Edw W Newman et al, dfndnt: public auction on Nov 8, of the north half of lot 26 in square 254, on 13th st west, near Pa ave, with a 4 story brick dwlg house on the same. –J B H Smith, trustee -A Green auct

Duel fought near Memphis, Tenn, recently, between Mr Waters, of Va, & Dr J E Nagle, formerly of Lancaster, Pa. Mr Waters died the same night, & Dr Nagle will probably die from his wounds.

The steamer **Empire State** came in collision with the sloop **Exchange**, of Dartmouth, cutting her in two, on Tue. The person supposed to be lost is John H Ford, a trader of Bristol, R I.

The Detroit Tribune notices the death of Mr Hiram Becker, of St Paul, Minn, who was found dead in his bed. He was the U S Marshal for Michigan under Pres Fillmore, & was elected to Congress from Minnesota, but through some irregularity did not get his seat.

Capt Isaac Bowen, U S Army, attached to the Commissary Detp, died at Pass Christian, La, on Oct 4.

The sudden death of the beloved & gifted wife of Hon John Hickman, on Oct 12, has created a profound sensation at West Center, Pa. She was attacked with hemorrhage of the lungs. –Phil Press

Saul's Nursery: the stock of autumn trade is very extensive; every article guaranted as to accuracy. –John Saul, 896 7th st, corner of H st, Wash City, D C.

Mr Wm Bayley, one of our best & most useful citizens, a slater by profession, was engaged to roof the house of Francis T King, on Liberty road, & whilst upon a scaffolding this morning with his son Geo & a tinner named Hetzell, the scaffoding gave away, precipitating all upon it to the ground, & Mr Bayley, falling upon his head was instantly killed. His son, Mr Geo Bayley, aged 20 years, received a compound fracture of the right leg, & Mr Hetzell was only slightly injured. The deceased was one of the oldest members of the Order of the Odd Fellow. –Balt Patriot of last evening.

Mrd: on Oct 12, in Wash City, at the F st Presbyterian Church, by Rev P D Gurley, D D, Mr John B Bloss, of Detroit, Mich, to Miss Sarah R, daughter of John M Gilbert, of Wash City.

Mrd: on Oct 12, in Leesburg, by Rev O S Kinsolving, Alex'r H Rogers to Julia, only daughter of Dr Thos H Clagett, all of Loudoun Co, Va.

Nashville, Oct 13-fight on the fair grounds today, originating in a family feud. Sandy Owen was killed, & his brother was dangerously wounded. Gen J A Battle & Saml Cowan were mortally & several others severely wounded.

SAT OCT 16, 1858
Andrew Kessecker, the compositor who set the first type in what is now the State of Iowa, is worth $50,000. He located at an early day in Dubuque, stuck to his business, & now reaps the reward. He still acts as compositor in the Times' ofc.
–Indianapolis Citizen

Rev S N Evans, pastor of the Presbyterian Church at Lane, De Kalb Co, Ill, was instantly killed by lightning, a few yards from his own door, on Sep 30.

Jas R Bellville, a clerk in the Chicago post ofc, was arrested at Chicago a few days ago upon the charge of stealing from the mail. He was employed in the ofc about 3 months & registered letters were found upon his person. He offered no defence, & was committed to await trial in default of $2,000 bail.

Powell's Hotel for rent or lease; now occupied by T W Epes, situated in the city of Petersburg, Va, for rent or lease from Jan 10, 1859. –Chas Corling, Pres of Powell's Hotel Co.

Mrd: on Oct 12, by Rev Wm H Chapman, Mr Thos Hickey to Mrs Emily Gill, all of Wash City.

Mrd: on Oct 13, by Rev Wm H Chapman, Mr Albert B Lacey, of Wash City, to Miss Angeline Holly, of Chas Co, Md.

Mrd: on Oct 14, by Rev Wm H Chapman, Mr John Thos Gorsuch to Sarah Rebecca Griffin, all of Wash City.

Mrd: on Oct 14, by Rev Wm H Chapman, Mr Philip A Cawood to Miss Sarah E Green, all of Wash City.

Mrd: on Oct 14, in Wilmington, Del, by Rev Wm Aikman, Mr Thos B Thruston, of Greenville, S C, to Miss Annie Bush, daughter of Geo Bush, of Wilmington, Del.

Mrd: on Oct 12, at St James' Church, Richmond, Va, by Rev Dr Woodbridge, Virginius Dabney, of Miss, to Maria, daughter of Jas E Heath, of Richmond, formerly Auditor of the State, & more recently Com'r of Pensions at Wash.

St Louis, Oct 16. A battle took place between a detachment of the 2nd cavalry & a band of Camanche Indians, near Witchita village, on Oct 1, in which Lt Van Camp & 4 men were killed & Maj Van Dorn & 10 men wounded. The Camanches had 40 killed.

MON OCT 18, 1858
Parker Cleveland, Professor of Chemistry & Mineralogy in Bowdoin College, Maine, died on Friday, aged 79 years.

Nashville Union of Oct 14. Affray at the Fair Grounds. It appears that a bitter feud has for some time existed between John, Jas, & Sandy Owen, sons of Everett Owen, of Williamson Co, & Sam & Geo W Cowan, sons of Mr Owen's wife by a former husband. Sam Cowan met Jas Owen, who had his wife leaning upon his arm, at the fair Oct 13, & spat in his face. Owen commenced an attack & Cowan drew a pistol & shot Owen through the heart, killing him instantly. A melee ensued & Jas Owen was shot, his wounds thought to be mortal. Sam Cowan was mortally wounded. Gen Joel A Battle was horribly mangled about the head from blows inflicted with a heavy stick; his wounds may prove fatal. Mr Thos Battle & Mr W A Davis were slightly wounded.

Mr E M Ryland, one of the oldest & most eminent merchants of St Louis, died in that city on Oct 13. At the time of his death he was Pres of the Chamber of Commerce.

Orphans Court of Wash Co, D C. Letters of administration on the personal estate of Aaron O Dayton, late of Wash Co, deceased. –Mary B Dayton, admx

New Dry Goods Store: A L Newton, late of the frim of Clagett, Newton, & May & Co: located on 7th st.

Cheap & Elegant Furniture. Saml Kirby, manufacturer of superior & fashionable furniture, announces that his warehouse is well stocked: located on 8th st near Pa ave.

Valuable & well stocked farm at private sale, owned & occupied by Geo C Siebel, within 2 miles of Beltsville, Md, containing about 180 acres of land, with new dwlg house, barn, stable, corn-house, & other out-bldgs, together with crops, stock of farming implements, which are of the most superior character. Inquire of -J C McGuire, auct

Articles taken on Friday last by the police from the house of Mrs Dobbins, mother of Dolly Dobbins, have been identified by different persons in Wash & Gtwn. Mr Geo Waters, of Gtwn, identified his wheat sacks; Mr Vanderwerken indentified his property. Dobbins stands fully committed for trial at the Criminal Court.

Mrd: on Oct 12, at Winchester, Va, by Rev Jas R Graham, Geo M Gordon, of Wash, to Miss Virginia, daughter of Col John P Riely, of the former place.

Died: on Oct 17, after a lingering illness, Thos B Goddard, formerly of St Mary's Co, Md, but for many years a resident of Wash City. His funeral will be from the residence of his mother, Steamboat Wharf, Island, on Mon at 3½ o'clock.

TUE OCT 19, 1858

Hon Wm Jay, of Bedford, Westchester Co, N Y, died on Sep 14, in his 70th year. He was son of the celebrated John Jay, one of the fathers of the Republic, & was himself a man of distinction. The greater part of his life has been spent at the family country-seat, near Bedford, which he inherited on the death of his father in 1829. He was appointed the first Judge of Westchester Co by Govn'r Tompkins, & his reappointmen to that ofc was successively made by Govn'rs Clinton, Marcy, & Van Buren.

Dissolution of partnership by mutual consent, under the firm of Murray & Randolph. Stanislaus Murray is authorized to settle the business. –Stans Murray, Wm M Randolph, Wash, Oct 19, 1858.

For sale, the beautiful country residence called **Mount Pleasant**, which is in PG Co, Md, about 4½ miles n e of Wash; with a new modern built house, & all necessary out-bldgs. A bargain may be had if early applied for. –R Brice Hall, 373 7th st

A beautiful new hearse arrived on Sat last to the establishment of Mr Fred'k Lakemeyer, proprietor of the livery stable on G st, near 17th. It surpasses every thing we have hitherto had in Wash. It was built for Mr Lakemeyer in Phil, by Messrs Beckhaus, Allgaier & Petry, it being understood that Mr Allgaier is its designer & the principal mechanic. The panels on the sides, front & back are inserted with plates of glass, painted in appropriate tints well executed representations of the Saviour of the World & figures emblematic of the hopes & glories of the life to come. These are by Mr P Kraus, of Balt.

Mrd: on Oct 12, in Phil, by Rev Dr Townsend, Allison Nailor, jr, of Wash City, to Maggie L DeHaven, youngest daughter of J DeHaven, of Phil.

In the decease of Mrs Jas Maher, for many years the worthy & industrious conductress of the Union Hotel on Pa ave & 13½ sts the community has lost a useful member of society, & a large & dependent family an affectionate & excellent wife & mother. At her house the numerous delegations of Indians who have for long years past gathered here to transact business with the Executive Gov't have always met with the treatment of a hospitable home, & it is no matter of doubt that amongst the members of almost every one of the numerous tribes on our frontier the most sincere mourners of Mr Maher will be found.
+

Died: on Oct 17, in Wash City, Mrs Bridget Maher, wife of Jas Maher, Public Gardner, in her 56th year. Her funeral will be this afternoon from the Union Hotel, at 2½ o'clock.

Died: on Oct 17, in Wash City, Mary, infant daughter of the late Edw Quinn, aged 14 months & 9 days.

Died: on Oct 18, in Gtwn, Margaret, daughter of the late John Laird. Her funeral will take place on Oct 20, from her late residence on Gay st, Gtwn, at 10 o'clock.

For sale, the estate on which I reside, being nearly half of the tracts given by Col Ed Carter, of **Blenheim**, to his sons John, Champ, & Hill Carter, containing 1,670 acres, about one-fifth bottomland. To a cash purchaser, who would take the slaves, [100] stock, & crop, much less than the value would be accepted. –Danl Warwick, Amherst

Trustee's sale of the valuable real estate of the late J P C Porter. By decree from the Circuit Court for Montg Co, as Court of Equity, in the case of Sarah E Peter & others vs J P C Peter, the subscribers, as trustees, will offer at public sale, at the farm houses of the late John P C Peter, on the road leading from Seneca Mills to Edwards' Ferry, on Nov 1, the following real estate, containing 1,215¾ acres, divided into 5 lots. Lot 2-1st & 2nd part-contains 364 acres of land with a log dwlg-house & barn. Lot 4 contains 316¼ acres. Lot 5 contains 391 acres, & is known as **Oakland Farm**, with a frame dwlg & out-houses. Lot 6 contains 144½ acres. The property will be shown by Mr Thos Peter. –John Brewer, Geo Peter, trustees [*Porter as copied.]

WED OCT 20, 1858
Judge Wm Lowe, Judge of the Orphans' Court for Fred'k Co, Md, died on Oct 8. He was striken down with paralysis on Oct 7. He had been Judge for upwards of 6 years, & a resident of this city twenty odd years. –Fred'k [Md] Herald

Mr Eastgate, of Ellenville, Ulster Co, N Y, was accidentally shot on Friday, & died shortly after. Mr Eastgate & Mr Shultz were returing home in a one-horse wagon, when the horse became unmanageable, & Mr Eastgate either fell or was thrown from the wagon. The double-barrelled gun in the wagon, struck the ground & discharged its contents into the side of Mr Eastgate.

Wm Sander, convicted at Newburgh, N Y, of the murder of Peter Shork, was on Friday sentenced to death by hanging on Dec 3 next, at the county jail at Gohsen, N Y.

A letter from Judge R W Sherrard, of Marysville, Calif, to his father, Jos H Sherrard, at Winchester, Va, communicates the intelligence that Jas Krebs, formerly a citizen of Winchester, was drowned in Fraser river, at the new gold discoveries, a short time since.

A man named Kersey committed a wholesale human slaughter at a horse race in Texas, a short time since, with a bowie-knife. Some difficulty occurred & he killed Rev Mr Shaw, Mat Shaw, & T Hughes, & wounded two others. He escaped but not before he was shot & wounded.

Stock of superior groceries at public sale on Oct 25, at the family grocery store of O W Marsh, Pa ave & 10th st. –Jas C McGuire, auct

Sale by order of the Orphans Court of Wash Co, D C. Auction of the household & kitchen furniture on Oct 25, the personal effects of Mary A Perkins, at the late residence of Mr Henry Perkins, **Blue Plains**, known as the ***Head of Frazier***. –A Green auct

Orphans Court of Wash Co, D C. Letters of administration on the personal estate of Mary A Perkins, late of Wash Co, deceased. –John Costigan, adm

Orphans Court of Wash Co, D C. In the case of Alice Fox, admx of Jos Fox, the administratrix & Court have appointed Nov 9 next, for the final settlement of the personal estate of said deceased, of the assets in hand. -Ed N Roach, Reg/o wills

Died: on Oct 19, in Wash City, after a short illness, Capt Lafayette Boyer Wood, of the Eighth Regt of Infty. His brother officers & friends are invited to attend his funeral this day at 12 M. from his late residence, 289 G st, between 13th & 14th sts.

Died: on Tue last, in Wash City, Franklin Webster, aged 4 years & 6 months, son of Mary E & Geo A Baker.

Boots, Shoes, & Gaiters: E Edmonston, 491 7th st, between D & E sts. [Ad]

THU OCT 21, 1858
Vessels which are destined for Paraguay; the largest fleet that has been dispatched from our shores since the sailing of Cmdor Perry for Japan.
The frig **Sabine**, [flag-ship:] Flag Ofcr Wm B Shubrick, cmder-in-chief; Cmder Thos J Page, fleet capt; Cmder P Drayton, aid to flag ofcr; Lt Wm H Murdaugh, flag Lt; Thos J Page, jr, sec to flag ofcr; Capt, H A Adams; Lts, Mr Woodhull, Chas S McDonough, G P Welsh, W Gibson, R F R Lewis, L H Newman, & W P McCann; fleet surgeon, Jas M Green; passed assist surgeon, J F Harrison; assist surgeon, J C Bertolette; purser, J F Steele; chaplain, J Blake; brevet capt of marines, Robt Tansill; 1st Lt of marines, C A Henderson; 2nd Lt of marines, T S Wilson; boatswain, P Atkinson; gunner, Jas M Cooper; carpenter, W D Jenkins; sailmaker, John Joines. Armament, 50 guns.

The sloop **Preble**: Cmder, Thorton A Jenkins; Lts, A Bryan, Robt D Miner, K Randolph Breese; passed assist surgeon, JY Taylor; purser Wm W J Kelley; 2nd Lt of marines, H L Ingraham; acting boatswain, H P Grace; acting gunner, Jos Swift; carpenter, J G Myers; sailmaker, D C Brayton. Armament, ten 32 pounders & 1 nine inch gun.
The steamer **Memphis**: Cmder, John B Marchand; Lts, Chas W Hays, J B Smith, A Pendergrast, & O F Stanton; purser, C C Jackson; assist surgeon, E R Denby; 2nd assist engineer, Wm Roberts; 3rd assist engineers, J McElmell, Thos Cronin, & Geo H Riley. Armament, two 19 inch guns.
The steamer **Atlanta**: Cmder, Danl B Ridgley; Lts, John Downes, Geo H Bien, J R Eggleston, & H M Garland; passed assist surgeon, J M Browne; 2nd assist engineer, Thos J Jones; 3rd assist engineer, W S Thompson, E B Latch, & W H Glading. Armament, two 9 inch guns.
The steamer **Caledonia**: Cmder, Augustus L Case; Lts, Wm A Webb, N H Vanzandt, Henry Wilson, & Edw P McCrea; passed assist surgeon, Washington Sherman; 2nd assist engineer, J S Albert; 3rd assist engineer, G F Kutz, Z K Rind, & F J Lovering. Armament, two 9 inch guns.
The brig **Dolphin**: Cmder, Chas Steadman; Lts, L Paulding, John V McCullom, Chas W Flusser, & E P Williams; assist surgeon, A L Gibson. Armament, one 9 inch gun & two 32 pounders.
The steamer **Southern Star**: Cmder, A M Pennock; Lts, J Wilkinson, J H Rochelle, B E Hand, & Jas A Greer; assist surgeon, John Vansant; 1st assist engineer, A Henderson; 3rd assist engineer, L Campbell, O H Lackey, & R A Copeland. Armament, two 9 inch guns.
The steamer **Westernport**: Cmder, Thos T Hunter; Lts, T S Phelps, J Young, A E K Benham, & Chas H Cushman; purser, Jas K Harwood; 2nd assist engineer, M P Jordan; 3rd assist engineer, Geo J Barry, M H Plunkett, & Wilson K Purse. Armament, two 9 inch guns.
The steamer **Fulton**: Cmder, John J Almy; Lts, Miles K Warrington, J B Stewart, Robt Selden, & M C Campbell; purser, R H Clark; passed assist surgeon, H O Mayo; 1st assist engineer, Harman Newell; 2nd engineer, J A Grier; 3rd engineer, W P Burrow, J P Houston, & J DeKraft. Armament, four 9 inch guns.
The steamer **Water-Witch**: Lt commanding, Robt B Pegram; Lts, A Barbot, D A Forrest, E T Spedden, & F H Baker; passed assist surgeon, Chas F Fahs; 1st assist engineer, W C Wheeler; 2nd assist engineer, R W McCleery; 3rd assist engineer, R B H Wharton, B E Chassain, & C A Chipley. Armament, one 9 inch gun.
The storeship **Supply**: Lt commanding, Fabius Stanly; Lts, A Reed, Jno Kell, J D Blake, & J H Gillis; purser, Geo W Clarke; passed assist surgeon, P J Horwitz. Armament, 4 guns.
The storeship **Release**: Lt commanding, Wm A Parker; Lts, T S Fillebrown & J G Maxwell; midshipman, G S Perkins. Armament, 1 gun.
The steamer **M W Chapin**: Lt commanding, Wm Ronckendorff; Lts, Jas E Jouett, John Walters, & J W Dunnington; acting master, A F Crossman; 2nd assist engineer, Ten Eyck Biles; 3rd assists engineer, Geo D Lining & K L Dick. Armament, one 9 inch gun.
The Brazil Squadron;
The frig **St Laurence**: Flag ofcr, French Forrest; capt, J B Hull; Lts, P C Murphy, J H Parker, H C Blake, W P Buckner, J G Walker, W H Dana, & E C Potter; fleet surgeon,

S Barrington; passed assist surgeon, Geo Peck; assist surgeon, F L Galt; purser, C W Abbott, chaplain, M R Talbot; major of marines, J G Reynolds; 2nd Lt, A W Stark; midshipmen, R L Phythian; R R Wallace, W E Evans, W S Shryock; boatswain, Wm Smith; gunner, Asa Curtis; carpenter, W F Laighton; sailmaker, Geo Thomas. Armament, 50 guns.

The sloop **Falmouth**: Cmder, E Farrand; Lts, Ed W Rogers, W W Pollock, S R Franklin, Geo Brown, & W A Kirkland; surgeon, J J Aberenthy; assist surgeon, W M Page; 2nd Lt of marines, C A Hebb; boatswain, E B Bell; gunner, F A Cunningham; carpenter, John Stimpson; sailmaker, John Wadsworth. Armament, 20 guns.

The brig **Perry**: Lt commanding, R L Tilghman; Lts, W T Truxton, J J Cornwell, E C Grafton; passed assist surgeon, J W B Greenhow; midshipmen, T K Porter & W N Allen. Armament, 6 guns & one 9 inch.

The brig **Bainbridge**: [ordered from Africa to Brazil.] Lt commanding, Francis B Renshaw; Lts, Geo A Stevens & S E Bassett; acting master, A Hopkins; passed assist surgeon, E Wysham. Armament, 6 guns, one 9 inch.

Accounts from Greece announce the death of Prince Alex' Mavrocordato, a patriot Greek, who has been prominent in the affairs of his country for many years. He was born in 1787, at Constantinople; descended from an ancient Fanariot faily.

A man named Rooney was convicted at Albany, N Y, a few days ago, of arson, & sentenced to be hung on Dec 3. In the dead of night he deliberately fired the dwlg house of 2 widowed females, in which, at the time, were locked in sleep, no less than ten human beings. You could have had no malicious feelings to indulge against these widows & these helpless children. They had never injured you.

Prince Chika, of Moldavia, was thrown from his carriage in Paris a week or two ago & killed.

The funeral of Miss Laird, sister-in-law of his honor Judge Dunlop, which took place yesterday from her late residence on Gay st, Gtwn, was attended by a numerous retinue of friends of the family. Her remains were deposited in the family burial ground near Bladensburg.

Mrd: on Oct 19, at the Assembly's Church, by Rev Andrew G Carothers, Mr Thos Thompson to Miss Josephine C Davis, daughter of Saml Davis, both of Wash City.

Mrd: on Oct 19, in Bridge st church, Gtwn, by Rev J H Bocock, D D, Chas G Talcott, of Wash City, to Theodosia Lawrence, daughter of the late Robt Barnard, of Normanston, D C.

Died: yesterday, suddenly, Scott, son of Robt & Mary S Widdicombe. His funeral will take place this morning at half past 1 o'clock.

Excellent household & kitchen furniture at auction on Oct 28 & 29, the effects of J H Knott, on north G st, near 15th st west, including a superior Rosewood 7 octave Wm Knabe & Co piano forte, but little used. -Jas C McGuire, auct

Executor's sale of desirable house & lot on 11th st, Island, on Oct 27, being part of square 353, with a substantial brick dwlg. –Henry Lyles, Gilbert Simpson, execs -C W Boteler, auct

Six months ago a statement went the rounds of the press that 4 graduates of Dartmouth College, all of them clergymen, still survived. Hardly has this fact become known then death commenced its work. Rev Mr Parsons, of N J, died at age 99; Rev Labin Ainsworth, for three-quarters of a century minister of Jeffrey, N H, died about the same time, having more than completed his century; Rev Zacahriah Greene, of Hempstead, L I, followed in his 99th year, & now we chronicle the death of Rev John Sawyer, of Bangor, Me, who died on Oct 14, aged 103 years & 5 days. In early life he served in the Revolutionary army, & was wounded in one of the battles in which he took part. Rev Danl Waldo, recently Chaplain of the Nat'l House of Reps, is, if we mistake not, the oldest clergyman in the country engaged in the active duties of his profession. His age is about 94 years.

Orphans Court of Wash Co, D C. Letters of administration on the personal estate of Alfred Pennington, late of Wash Co, deceased. –Eliz M Pennington, admx

FRI OCT 22, 1858
On Tue Austin Dalrymple attempted to get upon the car next to the last on the railroad train, at Newton Corner, upon the Boston & Worcester Railroad. He fell & rolled beneath the cars, the wheels passed over his body, killing him almost instantly.

Disaster to the fishing fleet. The Bath[Me] Tribune of Monday reports the loss on North Cape, Prince Edward's Island, during the week before last, of over 30 sail of fishing vessels belonging all along the coast of this State & Mass. The only definite relate to the new mackeral schnr **E Atwood**, Stinson Jewett, master, of Westport, which was lost with every soul on board. The crew consisted of 10 persons, including the officers.

A cannon prematurely discharged on Tue during the military display at Natick, terribly lacerated Geo W Sanborn & Levi Elkins, who were in the act of ramming down the charge, also badly wounding Jos Blake, who was in the range of the wadding. Sanborn & Elkins lose each an arm, but it is thought that all may survive.

In the Orphan's Court of Lancaster Co, Pa, estate of Mary Lorentz, late of Lancaster city, State & county, aforesaid, deceased, the undersigned auditor, to audit & make distribution of the balance in the hands of Peter L Grosh, adm, de bonis non, C T A, to & among the heirs & those legally entitled, on Dec 14, 1858, at the court-house in Lancaster city. -David W Patterson, auditor

A printer by the name of Ohr was fatally injured last week at Pekin, Ill, by the premature discharge of a cannon he was loading.

Messrs Jas C McGuire & Co sold yesterday 5 bldgs lots, on E st, between 2nd & 3rd sts, for 55½ & 60 cents per square foot, purchased by Messrs Geo W Cochran & Chas E Walker. Also, 2 small frame houses on 11th st west, between I & K sts, to P M Dubant for $795 & $905.

Orphans Court of Wash Co, D C. Letters of administration de bonis non on the personal estate of Martin Foley, late of Wash Co, deceased. –Mgt Foley, admx d b n

Orphans Court of Wash Co, D C. Letters testamentary on the personal estate of Clarissa Hall, late of Wash Co, deceased. –H B Sweeny, exc

Meeting of the Gtwn College Cadets to pay tribute to the late Nicholas C Parsons, a worthy & esteemed member. Copy of resolutions to be sent to the family of the deceased.
-Jos P Orme, Alphonse Rost, Henry Cruzat, cmte [Oct 25th newspaper: Tribute of respect to the late Mr Nicholas C Parsons, by the Philonomosian Society of Gtwn College.
–T A Lambert, J K Taylor, J B Laloire, cmte, Gtwn College, Oct 24, 1858]

Mrd: on Sep 14, in Oakland, Calif, at the residence of J Ross Browne, by Rev Mr Aeklee, Gustavus Mix to Miss Kate Browne.

Mrd: on Oct 20, by Rev Andrew G Carothers, Mr Wm Furmage to Miss Mary Aiken, both of Wash City.

Mrd: on Oct 21, at the MeKendree Parsonage, by Rev D Ball, Mrs Jas M Devan to Miss Mary A Mangum, both of PG Co, Md.

SAT OCT 23, 1858
Entire furniture of a large boarding-house at auction on Nov 4, of Mrs Searles' boarding-house, 383 Pa ave, south side. –Wall & Barnard, aucts

The Union announces that Hon J Glancy Jones, of Pa, has accepted the appointment of Minister to Austria.

The Pension Ofc has received information of the conviction at Albany of Andrew Baird & Geo Hamilton, before the U S District Court, of frauds committed upon the Gov't in connexion with the business of that office.

The execution of Chas H Barrett was postponed by the Pres for 2 weeks, to afford the Executive time to fully examine all the facts of the case.

First Ward Livery Stable on G st, between 17th & 18th sts, Fr Lakemeyer, agent [Ad]

Md State Agricultural Society: meeting on Thu at Balt, John Merryman, of Balt, unanimously re-elected its Pres; & the following gentlemen for other offices, viz:
Vice Presidents:
John H Sothoron, St Mary's Co
John S Sellman, Anne Arundel Co
Chas Ridgely, Hampton, Balt Co
Robt Dick, Montg Co
Richd Cooke Tilghman, Queen Anne's Co
Teagle Townsend, Worcester Co
Odin Bowie, PG Co
J M Jacobs, Harford Co
John C Brune, Balt City
Chas Carroll, Howard Co
Edw Lloyd, jr, Talbot Co
L T Brien, Wash Co
Dr S P Smith, Alleghany Co
Jas Tilghman, Somerset Co

Geo R Dennis, Fred'k Co
G M Eldridge, Cecil Co
S T C Brown, Carroll Co
John W Jenkins, Chas Co
R T Goldsborough, Dorchester Co
Edw Wilkins, Kent Co
W Hardcastle, Caroline Co
J H Gary, Calvert Co
Allen Dodge, Dist of Col
J W Ware, Western Va
Thos R Joynes, Eastern Va
Gen Cadwallader, Pa
Bryan Jackson, Del

Curators:
Wm Crichton, Balt City
Frank Cooke, Balt City
Jas H Goldsborough, Talbot Co

J Mulliken, PG Co
N B Worthington, Anne Arundel Co
Corr Sec: J Howard McHenry, Balt Co

A section of coping fell from a new bldg on Franklin st, Boston, on Tue, & striking Saml Colton, foreman of the carpenters, killed him instantly.

Bernard McIntire, age 8 years, was killed at the depot in Manchester, N H, on Monday. His head was entirely severed from his body by the wheels of the car.

Mrd: on Oct 20, at the M E Church South, by Rev Mr Granbery, Mr John Richard Sothoron to Miss Roberta Skidmore, both of Wash City.

Died: on Oct 15, in New Orleans, of yellow fever, John A Werckmuller, a native of Norfolk, Va, & for many years a clerk in a mercantile house in that city. When the yellow fever broke out, in 1855, he came, with his mother & sisters, to this city, where he was employed in the Gen Land Ofc; afterwards went to New Orleans & was book-keeper in the Picayune ofc. –D L D

Died: Oct 16, in Staunton, Va, in her 8th year, Harriet Irwin, daughter of Saml Forrest, U S Navy.

Died: on Oct 22, in Wash City, of congestive fever, Mary Alice Pettit, aged 6 years, 8 months & 18 days, daughter of Chas W & Gertrude Pettit. Her funeral will be Sunday afternoon at 3 o'clock, from the residence of her parents, 398 Mass ave, between 9th & 10th sts.

Died: on Oct 22, Willie Boteler, infant son of Wm H & Mary A Falconer, aged 11 months. His funeral will be this afternoon at 3 o'clock, from his father's residence, 506 I st, between 9th & 10th sts.

Heirs Wanted. State of N C, Orange Co: Court of Equity, Sep Term, 1858. Nelson B Hall, adm of Danl Trurentine, deceased, vs Danl Trurentine, et al. Bill of interpleader. In obedience to a decree of the Court of Equity for the county & State aforesaid, advertisement for all persons claiming to be next of kin of Danl Trurentine, deceased, late of Orange Co, N C, to appear at the next term of this court, to be held at Hillsboro, on the 2nd Mon of Mar, 1859, & show their relationship & identity. Witness: Thos Webb, clerk & master in equity. –Thos Webb, C & M E

MON OCT 25, 1858
Rosewood piano forte, household & kitchen furniture at auction on Nov 1, at the late residence of Gov Bigler, 12th & H sts. -J C McGuire, auct

Chancery sale of valuable real estate known as the <u>National Theatre</u>, by decree of the Circuit Court of Wash Co, D C, between Jas A Lenman & John T Lenman as cmplnts & Wm H Winder & others as dfndnts: public sale on Nov 16, of the whole of lot 4 & all that part of lot 3 in square 254, not heretofore conveyed to Allison Nailor, the whole property fronting 88 feet 10½ inches on E st, between 13th & 14th sts. –Chas S Wallach, Walter D Davidge, trustees -Jas C McGuire, auct

Constans F Daniels, late editor of the New London Chronicle, died on Wed, aged 69 years. He was educated for the legal profession, which he pursued only for several years. He was attacked with severe illness about a year ago which compelled him to retire.

On Wed last 3 little children of Mr Sullivan, a boy & 2 girls, at Springfield, Walworth Co, Wis, were left alone in the house. By some means the bed took fire & the children were burnt so severely that they died. The eldest was 5 & the youngest a helpless babe.

Warning about playing with fire-arms. Rockford [Ill] Democrat. On Oct 17, Frank, the 11 year old son of Jas L Loop, a member of the bar in that city, was accidentally shot & killed by his brother, Matt, while playing soldier.

Mrs Mary Twiggs was hung at Danville, Pa, on Fri last, as a punishment for having poisoned with arsenic Mrs Catherine Clark, whose husband was convicted of the same charge & hung on Sep 20. The black cap was drawn over her face, the fatal spring was touched, & her spirit passed away.

Ira Stout was executed on Friday last, at Rochester, N Y, for the murder of Mr Little, his brother-in-law. His death was painful to witness. His neck was probably not dislocated, & he died by a slow process of strangulation. His afflicted mother was hopeful to the last that the Govn'r of the State would grant the commutation of the punishment; there being no doubt of his guilt, the Govn'r declined to interpose.

An arrest was made on Sat last by Ofcr Daw of Terence Carrigan, for some time employed as a watchman at the new Gashouse on G st, near the river. He was charged with stealing iron, the property of the Gas Co, his employers. He had offered the iron for sale.

The subscriber offers for sale a Farm of 260 acres, lying on both sides of the Railroad from Wash City to Balt, 1 mile from the depot at Beltsville. Also, a farm of 270 acres, with all necessary bldgs, 1½ miles from the depot at Beltsville. –Wm S Holliday, Broker, No 2 Todd's Marble Bldg, Wash.

Died: on Oct 23, in Wash City, Mrs Abigal Sullivan, aged 74 years. Her funeral will take place from the residence of her brother-in-law, John G Law, this day at 3 o'clock, on G, between 4½ & 6th sts, Island.

Died: yesterday, Alexander John, infant son of A L & Mary Newton, aged 23 days. His funeral is this afternoon at 3 o'clock, from the residence of his parents, 512 G st.

Orphans Court of Wash Co, D C. Letters of administration on the personal estate of Felix Richard, late of Wash Co, deceased. –C Gautier, adm

TUE OCT 26, 1858
Household & kitchen furniture, & effects, at auction on Oct 29, at the residence of M Willian, 6th & E sts. –Wall & Barnard, aucts

The War Dept received information of the death of Brvt Col Francis Taylor, major of the 1st artl, of yellow fever, at Brownsville, Texas, on Oct 11. He served with distinction in the Mexican war, & was honorably mentioned in the despatches of Gen P F Smith, after the battle of Churubusco.

The numerous friends of Mr Nicholas Cleary, formerly of Wash, but now of Calif, will be gratified at learning of his recent election as Judge of the 13th judicial district of that State, which is one of the mountain districts, including the town of Mariposa. He has been a resident in Calif for 3 years.

The clergy of New Orleans who have fallen at their posts since the appearance of the yellow fever this year-bulletin of Oct 18. Rev Gaylord D Moore, of the Third Presbyterian Church, has been attacked, but is rapidly convalescing; Rev Dr Palmer, of the First Presbyterian Church, & Rev Dr Walker, the presiding elder, [of the Methodist Episcopal Church] of this district, are both down with the fever.

Yellow fever at Brownsville: mortality among the sick is heavy. The Americans named in a list published are, Jas Kennedy, Marianne Reed, Mr Reed, John Alsback, Mr Johnson, J L Knott, David Arroyo, Miss Bloom, Robt Doyle, Edw McKane, Mr Parker, Phoebe Mears, Robt Leoder, Geo Dye, jr, & E L Barre. –New Orleans Picayune

Letter dated Brownsville, Oct 6. The disease is very fatal in the garrison: Col K L Harralson, collector of customs, died yesterday; also, a young man by the name of Davis, one of the employees in the custom-house. Among those dead are Leroy Basse & Felter Johnson. Mrs Scarborough is at the point of death. Our physician in this is Dr Watson, who is nearly broken down.

Judge O'Neal, in the Yorkville Enquirer, tells the following of Judge Wm Smith, of S C. He had the rare blessing to win the love of one of the purest of women. He married Margaret Duff, who spent the nights doing the work of the Judge while he was on a spree, carousing. He found her asleep at his desk one night & promised her never to drink another drop while he lived, & he faithfully kept this promise. From that day every thing which he touched turned to gold. No better eulogy could be pronounced on Mrs Smith than has been given in the words of her distinguished husband.

Circuit Court of D C–in Chancery, 1,152. Sewell & others, creditors of John Brereton, against Eliza Ann Brereton & John Hoover, adms of said John Brereton, & Mary, Eliz, Ellen, Anne, John, & Flora Brereton, heirs-at-law of said John Brereton. Wm Redin, trustee, reported the sale to Prestley F Dorsey, of 107 acres 3 roods & 13 perches, part of the tract of land called **Granby**, decreed to be sold, at the price of $5,935.05, the agreed purchase money; & that the trustee convey the same to the said purchaser, taking from him a deed of trust on the land, in the usual form, to secure payment of the deferred instalments of the purchase money. –Jno A Smith, clerk

I would rent to a good tenant, for 4 to 6 months, or a year, my property in Gtwn, consisting of square 12 in the plot of the town, on which is a roomy & convenient dwlg, ready furnished with the best furniture, together with stables & other out-bldgs. The terms are $125 a month, or $1,200 a year. Apply on the premises, Louis Mackall.

On Friday last Mr Meyenberg, of Alexandria, returned to that city from Europe, whence he came in the ship **Saxonia**. He reports having seen his sister [Mrs Willian] & her two children embark on the steamship **Austria** at Hamburg; also Mr Jacob Brodbeck, late of Alexandria, formerly of Wash. He himself was strongly urged by them to go in the same ill-fated vessel, but declined & took passage in the **Saxonia**.

Died: on Oct 17, Martha Virginia, wife of W A Taylor, of Cumberland, Md, & eldest daughter of F Wheatley, of Gtwn.

Louisville, Ky, Oct 25. Horace Bell, who released his father & brother from the Brandenburg, Ky, jail last July, [to which they were committed on the charge of running off negroes,] was taken last Sat from the fair grounds at New Albany, Indiana, without a warrant, & brought into Ky by Louisville police officers. Upwards of a 100 persons have chartered a ferry-boat & intend leaving for Brandenburg today to rescue Bell. Govn'r Willard, of Indiana, has promised a requisition on the Govn'r of Ky for the men who captured Bell. A public meeting has been called here to denounce the proceedings of the officers.

N Y, Oct 25. Prof Doremus has submitted an analysis of the body of Sophia Stephens, who was supposed to have been murdered by her husband a year ago. The result proves that an abundance of arsenic was found in her body. The husband, Stephens, has been fully committed for trial.

WED OCT 27, 1858
Dept of State, Wash, Oct 18, 1858. Information has been received from B Squire Cotrell, U S Commercial Agent at San Juan del Norte, of the death at Bluefields, on Sep 18, of Benj Mooney, a citizen of the U S.

Oscar Myers, charged with Burns [who was recently executed for the crime] with the murder of Mary Ann Montony, at Wheeling, Va, was tried on Oct 18 & convicted of murder in the 2nd degree. He was sentenced to the penitentiary for 15 years.

The first celebration of the settlement of Cuyahoga Co, Ohio, was held on Wed, under the auspices of the Cuyahoga Historical Society. Of the pioneers present was Mr Culver, the sole survivor of the surveying party & of those who put up the first cabin where Cleveland now stands. Mrs Govn'r Wood presided at a flax wheel which was presented to her in 1820. –Cleveland Herald

Executrix's sale of household & kitchen furniture at auction on Nov 2, at the late residence of Geo H Dunlop, deceased, at 305 Md ave, between 6th & 7th sts, by order of the Orphans Court of Wash Co, D C. –Harriet Dunlop, excx -A Green auct

Orphans Court of Wash Co, D C, Oct 19, 1858. In the case of Basil Brooks, exc of Stepney Forrest, deceased, the executor & Court have appointed Nov 13 next, for the final settlement of the personal estate of said deceased, of the assets in hand. -Ed N Roach, Reg/o wills

Died: on Oct 25, in Wash City, after a lingering illness, Jas Seneca Pettit, aged 26 years, 5 months & 23 days, son of the late Chas Pettit. His funeral is this afternoon at 3 o'clock, from the residence of his mother, 484 E st, between 5th & 6th sts.

Died: at the residence of Mr Henry Stark, near Beltsville, Md, Richd Randolph, of Va, in his 76th year. [No death date given-appears to be a current item.]

THU OCT 28, 1858
The venerable Robt Fulton, recently arrested on the charge of stealing money letters deposited in his office, has been honorably discharged from custody, the U S Grand Jury having failed to find any evidence to warrant his detention. This matter now wears the aspect of a villainous conspiracy, designed to destroy the character of an old & worthy citizen, & we trust that it will be sifted to the bottom. A man who has arrived at the age of 73 years with an unblemished character should not be thus maligned with impunity. -Rochester Union of Oct 23.

Dr Fred'k Dorsey, sr, died at his residence in Hagerstown, Md, on Oct 24, in his 83rd year. He was the oldest practicing physician in the State, if not in the whole country. His career as a physician extended over half a century, & in Western Md, where he was more intimately known, he was regarded with the highest esteem. -Sun

Orphans Court of Wash Co, D C. Letters testamentary on the personal estate of Edw H Pendleton, late of Wash Co, deceased. –Philip P Pendleton, H B Tyler, excs

Died: yesterday, in Wash City, Mrs Edw Simms, the devoted wife of one of our most estimable citizens, a pious Christian & a kind mother. Her funeral will take place tomorrow at 10 o'clock, from the residence of the family, on C st, near 4½ st. High mass will be offered in St Patrick's Church.

N Y, Oct 27. Horrible butchery was perpetrated last night on West 30th st. The victims are the family of Francis Gouldy, lumber merchant, consisting of himself, wife, 2 sons, a daughter, & 2 servant girls. None of them are yet dead. The would be murderer, is the oldest son of Mr Gouldy, Francis A Gouldy-19 years of age, who returned home to his father's house in a state of delirium & attacked his father first, beating in his skull so that he cannot live. The mother came to the rescue of the father & was badly wounded. The two young brothers, 9 & 13, were next attacked, & the eldest cannot live. A married sister of the murderer, with a babe in her arms, was attacked, but escaped without serious injury. Two servant girls were horribly butchered & neither can recover. The assassin then locked himself in his own chamber & blew out his brains with a pistol. The family is highly respectable, & the father is an officer in the 30th st Methodist Church. [Oct 29th newspaper: the son, Francis A Gouldy, had long been a subject of grief & annoyance to his parents. He told a friend that he had a dispute with his father about money. He was sober when he left the saloon that night, where he ate oysters, but did not drink intoxicating liquor. On arriving home the door was opened by his father, & he was charged with abstracting a Savings' Bank book from his private desk & procuring money thereon. The young man replied that it was in his name, & he had a right to take the book. Soon after young Gouldy retired. He changed his clothes & then taking a hatchet in his hand descended the stairs in his stockings, entered the room where his father has just tunred off the gas, & dealt him a blow on the head. Mrs Gouldy, who had just gone to bed, heard the heavy fall of her husband. The son went to her room, seized her hand & exclaimed, "Mother, oh, Mother!" & dealt her a severe blow upon the head with the hatchet. He struck his two younger brothers as they slept, one mortally. The two servant girls, who had heard the noise, with attacked in the hall. One was mortally wounded. Mary, the eldest sister of the murderer, did not recognize her brother who was covered with blood, & thought he was a burglar. She retreated into her room & locked the door, opened the window & shouted for the police. The police arrived to a scene of horror. Jane Gouldy, duly sworn, deposes & says that the deceased was her stepson, & since July last he was unemployed; he was at tea, in his usual good health & spirits at 6 o'clock. My son Nathl, 14 years of age, was kneeling by his father & kissing him; he was also wounded in the head. I hoisted the window & cried for help. Joanna Murphy & Eliz Carr are the names of the servants.]

Mrd: on Oct 27, in Wash City, at the Sixth Presbyterian Church, by Rev Mason Noble, Mr Albert B Norton to Miss Mary Jane Ellis, daughter of Jonas B Ellis, all of Wash.

FRI OCT 29, 1858
At a recent session of the U S Circuit Court, in Vt, Judge Smalley presiding, the grand jury found 4 bills: one against W Swett, of Thetford, bound over in the sum of $3,000; one against Rev Isaiah Huntley, of Essex, bound over in the sum of $1,500; & two against Dr Asa George, of Calais, bound over in the sum of $2,500, all for procuring land warrants fraudulently.

John Cobb, jr, has been convicted at Atlanta, Ga, of the murder of a man named Landrum. Landrum was an old & inoffensive man, that he wantonly attacked & murdered.

Ordination of a Colored Bishop. The last Gen Conference of the Methodist Episcopal Church, held at Indianapolis, Indiana, authorized the election & ordination of a Bishop for the Republic of Liberia, if the Annual Conference of that expanding African State should so determine. Rev Francis Burns has been elected. He was ordained on Oct 14 at Perry, N Y. He is, we believe, a native of Newburg, N Y, but has resided in Liberia since 1831. He married & has raised a family there, a son being now in his 3rd collegiate year at Wesleyan Univ, Conn. He returns in the packet ship **Mary Caroline Stevens**, on Nov 1 next, from Balt. -Ledger

Mrs R G Etchison is now selling off her entire stock of goods at cost for cash, to close up business, she being unable to continue on account of her health. Her stock consist of French embroideries, ribands, laces, & trimmings. No 12 Market-space, Pa ave, between 8th & 9th sts, Wash.

The famous seventeen-hoop skirts, in white & gray, made of the best watch-spring steel. They are much lighter, more flexible, & produce less inequality in the set of the dress than any other skirt now in use. –Perry & Brother, Central Stores, west bldg, opposite Centre Market.

Died: on Oct 27, at her residence, in Alexandria Co, Va, in her 35th year, Mrs Martha A Gibson, the wife of Joshua Gibson, of Wash City. Her funeral will take place this morning at 10 o'clock, from her late residence in Alexandria Co.

Died: on Oct 26, in Wash City, Stephen H Mullowny, son of John F & Amanda L Mullowny, aged 2 years, 10 months & 16 days.

Advices from Japan. It is stated that an important treaty had been concluded by Townsend Harris, the American Consul at Jeddo, & that a son of Capt Tatnall, of the Navy, had been dispatched to Wash, via China, with the treaty. It is rumored that the Japanese will open a new port in the Bay of Jeddo for the use of American commerce, & that a Japanese Prince was to start immediately for Wash.

SAT OCT 30, 1858

Last heard of the Gouldy family was that the father is in a comatose condition; Nathl's injuries are severe; his brother Charles is more hurt & can hardly recover; Mrs Gouldy will do well if inflammation can be prevented; Joanna Murphy, one of the servant girls, is pronounced beyond hope; & Eliz Carr, the other girl, is getting better. [Nov 1st newspaper: Francis A Gouldy, would have been 19 years of age next Apr 19. He had been in a boarding school, to sea, clerk in a hardware store-lost that position, addicted to late hours & immoral practices, morose & revengeful at times, & had an uncontrollable temper. His father finally decided to embark him once more in his former business as a partner. He withdrew $10 from his father's account. The slightest opposition would thrown him into excitement. –N Y paper]

Battle of the Four Lakes: the U S troops, under Col Wright, against a large party of hostile Indians on Sep 1st. The enemy numbered from 300 to 500 warriors.
Field & Staff: Col G Wright, 9th Infty; Lt P A Owen, 9th Infty, Act Asst Adj Gen; Capt R W Kirkham, Quartermaster & Commissary; Assist Surgeon J F Hammond & Assist Surgeon Randolph, Medical Dept; Lt J Mullan, 2nd Artl, Topographical Engineer.
Dragoon: 1st Regt, 4 companies: Maj Wm Grier, commanding; Lt H B Davidson, commanding company; Lt W D Pendler, do; Lt D McM Gregg, do.
Artl: 3rd Regt 4 companies: Capt E D Keyes, commanding btln; Capt E O C Ord, commanding company; Lt R O Ryler, commanding howitzer detachment; Lt D R Ransom, commanding company; Lt G P Ihrie, do; Lt M R Morgan; Lt J Howard; Lt L Kip, adj of btln.
Infty: 9th Regt, 2 companies: Capt F T Dent, commanding btln; Capt C S Winder, commanding company; Lt H B Fleming.
Capt J A Hardie, being the field ofcr of the day, was charged with the care & defence of the camp & train. Co M, 3rd Artl, Lt H B Gibson commanding, & Lt G F B Dandy, a grand guard under Lt H B Lyon, & detachment of the dragoons, artl, & infty companies constitute the force for the protection of the camp & train.
It is said that Col Wright had captured two noted hostile chiefs, & had them promptly shot. There was no sign of the war coming to a speedy close. The wife of Maj Garnett died at **Fort Simcoe**, Wash Territory, on Sep 17.

Circuit Court of Wash Co, D C-in Chancery, No 1,267. Selden, Withers & Co, against Augustus A Nicholson's widow, heirs, & administrators. W Redin reported he has sold to Henry M Morfit lot 1 in square 573, for $4,113.46; J T Mitchell lot 1 in square 844, for $338.05; W R Woodward lots 2 & 3 in square 844, & lot 19 in square 795, for $248.28; John P Murphey lot 23 in square 296, for $542.48; Wm B Todd lots 5, 6, & 7 in square 719, for $1,022.24; & that all the said purchasers have complied with the terms of sale. -Jno A Smith, clerk

Hartford, Oct 29. A letter has been received from Lt Tyler, of the army, to his father here, dated Sep 15, stating that the Spokan & Peluse Indians had been defeated after 2 days' fighting. Col Steptoe's pistol was found on the body of a dead Indian. The letter was expressed to **Fort Taylor** by Indian runners.

Mrd: on Oct 29, in Wash City, by Rev Dr Nadal, Mr Bishop Cooper, of Balt, to Miss Sarah Ellen Babb, of Bangor, Maine.

Mrd: on Oct 28, by Rev Mr Morsell, E Irenee De Pont, of Delaware, to Charlotte Shepard, youngest daughter of Gen Henderson.

Died: on Oct 29, in Wash City, Charles Henry, infant son of Albert M & Julia Noyes. His funeral will take place from the residence of his parents, 437 8th st, between G & H sts, on Sunday afternoon, at 2 o'clock.

MON NOV 1, 1858
San Antonio [Texas] papers publish accounts of the Military Court of Inquiry, instituted at the request of Capt W R Bradfute, 2nd cavalry, to investigate the shooting of private Murry, Co K, 2nd cavalry, by Capt Bradfute, which assembled on the Clear Fork of Brasos, on Sep 26. Liquor had been sold at the house near the camp of companies G & K, 2nd cavalry, within the extended limits of the Indian reservation. Capt Bradfute visited this place to get this whiskey seller removed; on arriving at the grocery, he found several soldiers there, among them private Murry, Co K, 2nd cavalry, under the influence of liquor; he ordered them to their camps; the order was not obeyed at once by private Murry; that Murry exhibited indications of resistance to the captain's authority; that it became necessary to employ force, he, the said Bradfute, being in the execution of his office at the time; that he struck Murry, & again repeated the order, Murry resisted the captain by striking him, staggering him back several steps, at the same time advancing with determination of following up the first blow, whereupon Capt Bradfute drew his pistol & fired, killing the said Murry. The Court is of the opinion that Bradfute was justified for his own safety, to take the measures that he did; the opinion is that no other proceedings are necessary in this case.

Executor's sale of superior furniture, gilt frame mirrors, carpets & curtains, furniture & china, etc, on Nov 11, at the establishment of the late E H Pendleton, on Pa ave, adjoining the U S Hotel. –H B Tyler, Philip P Pendleton, excs -Jas C McGuire & Co, aucts

Superior cabinet furniture, elegant brocatelle curtains, French plate mirrors, chandeliers, French clocks & vases, rich table furniture, excellent piano forte, etc, at public auction, on Nov 15, at the residence of his Excellency Cavalcanti de Albuquerque, Brazilian Minister, I & 17th sts, the entire effects of this elegant establishment.
-Jas C McGuire & Co, aucts

Accidental shooting of a pistol gallery keeper named Taylor, in the hands of John Travers, a hackman, is given in the San Francisco Bulletin of Sep 25. Travers was looking at some Derringer pistols to purchase one, & carelessly picked up a Colt's revolver, not noticing it was loaded, & snapped it in the direction of Taylor. Taylor died from the fatal shot in a minute or two, without uttering a word. He was unmarried, age about 46 years, & a native of Mississippi. Travers delivered himself up to the Sheriff, & was put in prison until the circumstances of the death should be made to appear to the satisfaction of all.

Buffalo Advertiser of Thu. Railroad accident, about a mile east of Conesus, when the night train from N Y, coming west, was found to have the passenger & baggage cars off track. Accident followed killing instantly, O Hurd, a drover from N Y; S M Reed, Greene, Chenango Co; a women & an infant, who are unknown.

Centre-Market: On Mar 2, 1799, Pres Washington addressed a cummunication to Thos Beall, of Gtwn, & John M Grant, trustee, requesting them to convey to the Com'rs, appointed under the act of Congress for establishing the permanent seat of government of the U S, the streets, the several squares, parcels, & lots of ground appropriated to the use of the U S, in which he particularly described by numbers & lines the public appropriations or reservations. No 7 is the reservation now occupied by the Centre-market, extending from 7th to 9th st. The purposes for which the reservations were specially intended are not mentioned in the communication to which reference has been made. The plan of the city, published in Phil in 1792, known as Ellicott's map, has a diagram upon reservation No 7, indicating that it was intended to be occupied by some public bldg; but the nature of it is not printed in letters, as is the case with the Pres' square & Capitol grounds; nor is there any printed designation of the object for which the reservation was intended either on Major L'Enfant's plan or on the original plan approved by Pres Washington. In the minutes of the Commissioners on Jul 31, 1801, there is: "The Board agree to pay $500 towards making a good market south of square 408, near the canal, & to furnish such freestone as may be wanted for the base & cornices of the piers; provided this stone will not answer for any of the outside work or hearths of the Capitol:" & on Feb 13, 1802, it appears by the journal that the balance of this subscription was paid. The first act to incorporate the city of Washington was approved by Pres Jefferson on May 3, 1802; & on Oct 6th following the Corporation passed an act entitled "An act to establish & regulate markets," the first section of which is in the following words: "Be it enacted by the First & Second chambers of the City Council of Washington, that, after the first day of Nov next, there shall be established & held in the said city a market on or near the south side of Pa ave, between 7th & 9th sts west; & the market there erected & holden shall be called the Centre-market. [From the foregoing facts the following deductions result: 1-The ground on which the Centre Markethouse stands is a public reservation, & the title is in the Gov't, inasmuch as Congress has never passed any act authorizing it to be alienated. 2-That no inference can be fairly drawn from the diagram of a bldg on Ellicott's map that reservation No 7 was originally designed for a market place. 3-The market-house was erected before the city had been chartered, & that soon after the Corporation was created a general law was enacted establishing & regulating markets, which embraced the Centre-market & gave to it the name it now bears. In the early history of the city it used to be called the <u>Marsh-market</u>, which is no doubt the name it bore before the present name was given to it by law.] Our city authorities had better go to work & erect a new bldg upon the site occupied by the present market. –Civis

On Fri Edw L Houghton, Cashier of the Litchfield Bank, Conn, was arrested in N Y, charged with the embezzlement of $10,000, by means of false entries. He had decamped to that city, & a requisition had been obtained from Gov King for his arrest.

Mrd: on Oct 27, at the residence of Henry Harding, Rockville, Md, by Rev Mr Dougherty, Wm Kilgour, of Cumberland, Md, to Miss Ellen Rose, daughter of the late Chas I Queen.

Mrd: on Oct 28, in Trinity Church, New Haven, Conn, by Rev Prof Harwood, Lt H K Stevens, U S Navy, to Grace, daughter of Gen Jos G Totten, Chief Engineer U S Army.

Circuit Court of Wash Co, D C, in Chancery, Oct Term, 1858. Edw M Linthicum, cmplnts, vs John C McChesney & others, dfndnts. Chas A Buckey, trustee, sold the southern half-part of lot 190, in Beall's addition to Gtwn, to the Gtwn Gas Co, for $790; same to be ratified. –John A Smith

Orphans Court of Wash Co, D C. In the case of Margaret Eaton, admx, with the will annexed, of John H Eaton, deceased, the Court & administratrix have appointed Nov 16th next, for the final settlement of the personal estate of the deceased, of the assets in hand. -Ed N Roach, Reg/o wills

Died: on Oct 31, in Wash City, Robert Greenhow Moore, aged 14 months & 3 days, son of Florence G & S T Moore, U S Army. His funeral will take place this afternoon at 3 o'clock, from the residence of Mrs Greenhow, 398 16th st.

Died: on Sat, in Wash City, Mr Jos R Willett, formerly of Pa, but for the last 20 years a resident of Wash City, aged 80 years. His funeral is on Nov 1, at 11 o'clock, from the residence of his son, on Indiana ave, between 1st & 2nd sts.

Circuit Court of Wash Co, D C-Oct Term, 1858, in Chancery. Geo W Beall & others, cmplnts, vs Rachel Beall, Ninian Remuck, & others, dfndnts. Geo W Beall, trustee, reported to the court that he has sold the farm being part of a tract called ***Friendship***, situated partly in Wash Co, D C, & partly in Montg Co, Md, containing 53½ acres, 2 houses & lots in Gtwn, in said District, on the south side of Bridge st, the estate of Ninian Beall, deceased; that the said farm was sold to Philip J Buckey for $5,142; one of the said houses & lots to Dorcas Robey for $800; & the other said house & lot to Jas Mannague for $800; that the purchasers have complied with the terms of sale. -John A Smith, clerk

TUE NOV 2, 1858
Gen Paez arrived in Wash City on Thu last, accompanied by Messrs Pedro J Rojas, Manuel Paez, N Mujica, & N Mujica, jr. On Fri they were presented to the President, & through him they bade adieu to the U S, Gen Paez expressing for himself his gratitude for the hospitality & proofs of sympathy extended to him in this country, which he called his second home. They left for Phil & will depart in one of our war vessels for Venezuela.

Rev Francis B Jamison is announced by the Catholic Mirror as having died recently at St Vincent's College, Cape Girardeau, Mo, in his 58th year. He was a descendant of the early Catholic settlers of Md, & was born near Fred'k city. In his early youth he entered Mount St Mary's College, Emmettsburg, where he distinguished himself by his talents & the facility with which he advanced in the paths of literature & science.

One Hundred Years. One hundred years ago there was not a single white man in Ohio, Ky, Indiana, & Illinois Territory. It is now a flourishing part of America. It was not until 1769 that the "Hunter of Ky," the gallant & adventurous Boone, left his home in N C to beome the first settler of Ky. The first pioneers of Ohio did not settle until 20 years later. A hundred years ago Canada belonged to France; there were but 4 newspapers in the U S; & the great Frederick of Prussia was performing those great exploits which have made him immortal in military annals, & with his little monarchy was sustaining a single-handed contest with Russia, Austria, & France, the 3 great powers of Europe combines.

Aaron Nigers, a teamster residing in Watertown, died from hydrophobia at the Mass Genr'l Hospital Thu. He was bitten 6 months since by a dog supposed to be mad. His wife & friends said he showed no anxiety, but he said he suffered intense mental agony all this time. He died when in an unconscious state. –Boston Trav'r of Fri

On Oct 29 the roof of a three story house, owned by R M Bryan, in course of erection by the Sextons, on Wash ave, gave way & fell, & David Messer, a carpenter, received a severe wound. Four slaters were on the roof: Thos Hayden & Peter Riley were injured; Thos Gagan had one of his feet almost severed by falling on the sharp point of slate. He was also otherwise injured & died in the City Hospital soon after he arrived there. Michl Dermady had his chin mashed, both jaw bones broken, & bruised. He was conveyed to the Sisters' Hospital almost speechless. –St Louis Republican, 30th

Four inmates of the Rockville [Montg Co, Md] jail broke loose on Sat last & escaped. One of the four is Wm Nugent, who stands charged with the bloody & unprovoked murder of Mary Sheahy, near the reservoir of the Wash aqueduct. $100 for his arrest.

Mrd: on Oct 28, by Rev C C Mador, John C, eldest son of the late Benj F Chew, of Augusta, Ga, to Miss Hannah, eldest daughter of Andrew Van Bussum, of Wash.

Died: on Nov 1, in Wash City, B Schad, a native of Germany, but for the last 25 years a resident of Wash City, in his 47th year. His funeral will take place from his late residence, on Pa ave & 3rd st, on Nov 3, at 3 o'clock.

WED NOV 3, 1858
The Indian war in New Mexico: officers & troops under Col Miles, about 335 men, left **Fort Defiance**, New Mexcio, on Sep 9, in pursuit of hostile Indians, & returned on the 14th bringing with them 5,000 head of fine large sheep & 6 prisoners. Six Indians were killed during the scout, also 2 soldiers, Fisher, the bugler of Co I, mounted rifles, & Sweeny, of Capt Elliott's company. Several others were slightly wounded. Col Miles issued orders for 2 columns to be ready to march on Sep 19. Maj Brooks & Lt Averelle & Capt Lucero go to Colitas. Capt Elliot accompanies Lt Willard to meet Capt Lindsay; Lts Hildt & Whipple to remain at **Fort Defiance**, & also Capt McLane's company mounted rifles. Capt McLane is recovering from his wounds.

Fire on Monday in a row of 2 story houses on F st, near 22nd, belonging to Mrs Mary Bevan, under the name of Lewis' row. It is pretty certain that they were set on fire.

Emigrants for Liberia. The Liberian packet ship **Mary Caroline Stevens**, under the command of Capt John B Heaps, sailed from Balt yesterday for Liberia, carrying out between 70 & 80 passengers, & miscellaneous cargo. Among the cabin passengers are the following missionaries: Rev Mr Stone & wife, recently of Alabama, but formerly of Va, who proceed out under the auspices of the Southern Baptist Missionary Board; Rev Mr Rambo & wife, Rev Mr Messenger & wife, & Rev Mr Hubbard & wife, all of the Protestant Episcopal Board of Missions. These are designed for the Carvalha field of labor. Rev Messrs White & Elliott, of the Mendi Mission; they are sent out by the American Missionary Board, an independent organization of N Y. Also, Rev Bishop F Burns, [colored,] of the Methodist Episcopal Church, who, having been ordained to the bishopric by the Methodist Bishops of this country, will officiate as Bishop of the Republic of Liberia. Rev John Seys, of the Methodist Episcopal Church, proceeds with the party as the U S agent for the return of the Africans recently captured & returned to Africa.

Richmond Enquirer of Monday: death of John M Patton. His loss is a public one & will be long felt by the community in which the latter years of his life have been spent. [No other information-current item.] [Dec 6th newspaper: John Mercer Patton was not educated in the first place for the profession of the law, but that of medicine. He passed through his academic & collegiate course at Princeton, & graduated in the Medical College of Phil. He then commenced the study of the law, & came to the Bar. A few days ago a tribute to Hon John M Patton was held by the Members of the Bar of the Circuit Court for Culpeper Co, on motion of John S Pendleton, Hon Richd H Field, Judge of this Judicial Circuit & of the Special Court of Appeals of Va, was called to the chair, & Henry Shackelford appointed Sec.]

On Monday Mr Danl Walsh, living at the Navy Yard, was quite seriously injured when the mail wagon, laden with mail matter, containing 4 men, rushing down 3rd st towards Pa ave at a rapid pace, overtook 2 ladies, & Mr Welsh, who were passing. The ladies escaped being struck, but Mr Walsh was not so fortunate. He suffered simple fractures of his thigh & ankle. He is said now to be doing pretty well. [Nov 4th newspaper: Mr Danl Walsh was yesterday under the influence of delirium, & his left ankle was much more serious than at first supposed.]

Mrd: on Oct 13, in Milton, Pa, by Rev Wm Simonton, of Wmsport, Hon Alex'r Jordan, of Sunbury, Judge of the 8th judicial district, to Miss Hannah H Rittenhouse, of Phil.

Mrd: on Tue, in the Fourth Presbyterian Church, by Rev John C Smith, Philip W Killinger, of Lebanaon, Pa, to Miss Mary Eliz, daughter of Nicholas Halter, of Wash City.

Mrd: on Nov 2, at the second Presbyterian Church, by Rev Mr Krebs, Mr John D McKenney to Miss Anna Croggon, both of Wash City.

Died: on Nov 1, suddenly, Mr Jacob Hall, in his 50th year. His funeral will be at the residence of his brother, 424 F st, between 6th & 7th sts, this morning, at 10 o'clock.

Died: on Monday last, in his 63rd year, in Wash City, Isaac Holland, formerly the efficient & gentlemanly clerk of Messrs Blair & Rives, when they published the Daily Globe, & for many years past the Doorkeeper of the U S Senate. He was a native of Md, & came to this city some 25 years ago. He was much esteemed by all who knew him.

Orphans Court of Wash Co, D C. Letters of administration on the personal estate of Capt Lafayette B Wood, late of the U S Army, deceased. –Margaret A Wood, admx

Orphans Court of Wash Co, D C. In the case of Jane Campbell, excx of Danl Campbell, deceased: the executrix & Court have appointed Nov 23 next, for the final settlement of the personal estate of the deceased, of the assets in hand. -Ed N Roach, Reg/o wills

THU NOV 4, 1858
Mr Hiram Robinson, his wife, & 2 children, were consumed in a house fire in the vicinity of Grand Rapids, Mich, on Oct 19. They were found near where the door had been, indicating that the unfortunate inmates were awakened, but suffocated before reaching it.

On Oct 22, John Dowling Terrett, son of Col Wm H Terrett, formerly of this city, aged about 9 years, while gunning with Mr Jas Lloyd, in the neighborhood of Jackson, Miss, was accidentally shot by the latter, whose gun went off while climbing a fence, lodging in the head & breast of the youth, producing almost instant death.

Stock & fixtures of Cigar Store at auction on Mar 6, at the Cigar Store of August Kropp, on 11th st, near Pa ave. -Jas C McGuire, auct

It is announced that Lord Bury, son-in-law of Sir Allan McNab, of Dundrun, in Upper Canada, just arrived from England, will shortly visit Washington in connexion with the affairs of the Galway line of steamers, of which he is one of the directors.

The Florence correspondent of the Newark Advertiser writes: The second bronze cast of Powers' Webster is just finished. If possible it is more perfect than the one lost at sea. It should be exhibited at Washington before being placed on its pedestal in Boston. Mr & Mrs Franklin Pierce are expected here within a few days from Switzerland, en route for Rome, whither his friend & biographer, Mr Hawthorne has preceded him. Mr Hawthorne passed the summer in a pleasant villa in this vicinity with his family. The reading public will not be disappointed in its expectation of another book from his pen.

A humane friend calls attention to the deplorable cicurmstances of a poor women named Shananhan, living on H st, near the iron bridge over the Tiber. She has 6 little children, is sick & destitute, & her husband is an inmate of the Lunatic Asylum. Who could have a harder fate?

Boarding: Mrs M Patrick, late of Balt, has taken the house on 8th st, long & favorable kept by Miss Janney. [Ad]

Mrs Jourdan has been convicted at Rome, N Y, of poisoning her husband in Ava, in Aug, 1857. The jury recommended that the sentence be imprisonment for life.

N Y, Nov 3. The British barque **Claude**, from Quebec, for Sunderland, was wrecked in a gale last month. The Capt's wife & 7 of the crew perished. The remainder arrived here. [No names given.]

FRI NOV 5, 1858
N Y, Nov 3, 1858. 1-Something out of the common run in the way of panoramic exhibitions is promised before long from the skillful pencil of Mr John Bandar. 2-In Fulton, on Tue, arrived Mr Jerome Napoleon Bonapart, grand nephew of the Emperor Napoleon the First. It is understood he is on a visit to his father & friends in Balt. Mr Bonaparte holds a commission in the French army, & served in the Crimean war. 3-A day or two since the captain & part of the crew of the British barque **Claude**, waterlogged at sea on Oct 29, were brought into this port by Capt Johnston, of the American ship **Isaac Bell**. The name of the captain of the British vessel is Chessell, &, in a letter to the Courier & Enquirer, he describes in warm terms the humane & gallant conduct of Capt Johnston in saving him & 5 others from impending death. On the **Isaac Bell** was Capt Johnston, & chief ofcr, Mr Oldaker, & the 2nd ofcr, Mr Pidgeon; also, Mr Lickens & Mr Thos Fudge, passengers. Capt Chessell had the misfortune to lose his wife, who, when his vessel first filled with water, had gone into the rigging for safety, but, the vessel falling on her beam-ends, the poor woman was drowned in her place of retreat; after which the vessel righted. When the **Claude** was finally abandoned, the dead body of the captain's wife remained aloft, visible to the eyes of all, but beyond their power to reach it.

Circuit Court for PG Co, in Equity. Sewall & others vs Brereton's heirs. Ordered that the sale by W Redin, trustee in said cause, as made to Prestly F Dorsey of 107 acres 3 roods & 13 perches, part of the land called **Granby**, decreed to be sold for $5,935.05, be ratified. –Chas S Middleton, clerk

Negro contest for social equality. A suit was brought in Michigan by Day, a negro, against Owen, the owner of a steamboat, for refusing to carry him as a cabin passenger on his boat from Detroit to Toledo The dfndnt said that by the regulation of said boat colored persons were not received as cabin passengers, & were not allowed to use the cabin as such passengers. The plntf demurred, holding that such a regulation could be no defence. The circuit court over-ruled the demurrer, & a writ of error took the case to the supreme court, & the supreme court unanimously sustained the decision of the circuit court overruling the demurrer. Both courts said the facts stated in the notice were a good & sufficient defence to the plntf's action. The judgment below [which was against Day's right to be carried in the cabin] must be affirmed with costs. This decision as to the social status of the free negro in the free States is made by a Republican court. -Union

The steam-frig **Roanoke** arrived at Aspinwall on Oct 18 from San Juan del Norte, whence she sailed on the previous day. All were well except Lt Lanier & Assist Engineer Greer, who, being unwell, are to return to the U S in the sloop-of-war **St Louis**.

The journals of Nantes publish a report, sent by Capt Renaud, of the ship **Maurice**, to the owners, Messrs E le Boterf & Chas Gresle, of Nantes, with details respecting the steamer **Austria**, afire on Sep 13, & the individuals saved. He transcribed the report to his two officers, Messrs Nivert, 2nd mate of the **Maurice**, & Berraud, 1st mate, who had charge of the boats, & whose conduct is beyond all praise. The **Austria** was on fire from stem to stern; we saw from 250 to 300 perish. At least 150 to 200 were hanging overboard by means of ropes tied to the ship's rails. They were here & there from 20 to 30 holding on by the same rope. It would catch fire from the heat within, & the whole of the poor wretches disappear without the possibility of helping them. Two of my officers' conduct was beyong all praise. I have to say the same of my whole crew, & especially name Hamon, Gendron, & Mauvilain, who all rivaled each other in their zealous efforts to save more victims from the sea. And now, this day, Sep 14, 1858, I have 67 shipwrecked passengers on board, several of whom are seriously ill. I am making for the Azores, either Flores or Fayal. God grant me a safe passage & complete the deliverance I have begun.

Dr Lincoln has removed to 510 12th st: ofc hours from 9 till 10 A M, & from 4 to 5 P M.

Mrd: on Oct 27, at the Plains, by Rev Jas W Hoskins, Barnes Compton, of Chas Co, to Miss Margaret Holliday Sothoron, daughter of Col John H Sothoron, of St Mary's Co, Md.

Mrd: on Oct 23, in Phil, by Rev E D Newberry, Edw Shoemaker, of Wash City, to Frances, daughter of the late Benj L Walton, of Frankford, Pa.

Died: on Nov 4, in Wash City, Mrs Ann Dunawin, in her 68th year, relict of the late Wm Dunawin, a native of Fred'k City, Md, but a resident of Wash City for the last 30 years. Her funeral will take place from her late reidence, 15th & Mass ave, today at 3 o'clock.

New Orleans, Nov 4. R H Chilton, cotton broken, committed suicide this morning.

Notice. Application made to the proper authority for the renewal of a certificate of stock of the Corp of Wash for $402.41, issued on Aug 2, 1832, in the name of Mary Jamesson, the original certificate has been lost or mislaid.

SAT NOV 6, 1858
The Pres has commuted the sentence of death against Chas Barret for the murder of Reeve Lewis into imprisonment for life in the penitentiary of Washington. The jury which convicted Barret have earnestly besought me to commute his punishment to the term of life in prison; the crime was not committed with premediation or deliberate design; but under the effects of intoxicating liquor. -Union

Law Office: H Loughborough & A H Loughborough practice in the D C Courts, & give particular attention to claims against the Gov't. Ofc: 30 La ave, between 6th & 4½ sts

Prolific. Born at South Windsor, [Wapping,] Conn, Oct 22, 1857, two daughters & a son, & Oct 18, 1858, two sons, to J F Strong, making 3 sons & 2 daughters born within a year.

For rent: the dwlg house of Mr John H Gordon as a boarding house, situated on Pa ave & 7th st, over the Hardware Store of Messrs Harvey & Adams. Apply to Campbell & Coyle, or Fitzhugh Coyle, or Chas Bradley..

I will sell or exchange for improved Wash City property 83½ acres of land about 1 mile beyond Rock Creek Church & 4½ miles from Wash. Inquire of John F Coyle, or W W Cox, 6th Auditor's Ofc, Post Ofc Dept.

Mrd: on Nov 2, in Phil, by Rev W R Dewitt, D C, Hon John W Geary, Ex-Govn'r of Kansas, to Mrs Henderson, of Cumberland, Pa.

Balt, Nov 6. Henry Gambrill, one of a notorious gang of rowdies who infest the southern part of the city, & who murdered Policeman Benj Benton about a month ago, was this afternoon convicted of murder in the first degree. This evening Policeman Geo W Rigdon, who was the principal witness in the trial of Gambrill, was shot dead about an hour ago in the western part of the city by one of the same gang. The murder was committed in the officer's house in the presence of his wife & children. Rigdon was an active & faithful officer. The murderer's name is Corre. Threats are made of lynching him. [Nov 8th newspaper: Rigdon was shot as he was standing leaning on the mantel-piece, with his back to the window, in his sitting room, talking to his wife. Also in the room was a little lost child, which he had picked up in the street. The assassin was Peter Corre, a butcher, an associate of Gambrill. Rigdon had been on the force 2 years, was a stout athletic man, & leaves a wife & no children to mourn his loss. He was 35 years of age, & today would have been the 7th anniversary of his marriage.] [Nov 25th newspaper: Henry Gambrill was on Wed sentenced to expiate his offence upon the scaffold. He is scarcely 21 years of age.]

Died: on Oct 3, at Pass Christian, Miss, of yellow fever, Capt Isaac Bowen, Commissary U S Army. At the same place, Oct 5, of yellow fever, Catharine Cary Bowen, his wife; at the same place, Oct 15, of cholera infanutm, Robt, their infant son, aged about 8 months.

MON NOV 8, 1858
N Y, Oct 6, 1858. Mr Everett will lecture on Nov 12th, at Niblo's, in behalf of the **Mount Vernon Association**. Miss Agnes Robertson has promised one of her charming representations for the benefit of the Association. Miss Juliana May, the distinguished singer, [who is the grand-daughter of Richd Henry Lee,] has offered her voice & talent to the cause.

Orphans Court of Wash Co, D C. Letters of administration on the personal estate of Asa Curtis, late of the U S Navy, deceased. –Ann Curtis, admx

Redemption of Va stock at 5 & 6%: holders of said certificates are required on Feb 10, 1859, to surrender the stock at the ofc of the 2nd Auditor; whether surrendered or not the interest will cease on that day. Under an act to provide for the construction of a Turnpike road from Winchester to some point on the Ohio river, passed Mar 19, 1831, 5%.
1832: Jas Govan, Edw Govan, & Archibald Govan, excs of Jas Govan, deceased: $2,000
1832: Wm Williams, of Waling st, London: $15,000
1833: do: $15,000
1834: The Most Noble Geo Granville, Duke of Sutherland: $5,000.
1836: N M Rothschild & Sons, of London: $60,000.
1840: Norman Stewart, of Richmond, Va: $5,000.
1854: Benj Moses, of London: $5,000.
1856, Mar: Garret F Watson: $1,000.
1856: Abraham D Pollock: $2,000.
Under an act directing an examination of the Winchester & Parkersburg Road, with a view to widen & partially McAdamize the same, passed Mar 29, 1837.
1854: Wm J Albert, trustee for the children of Chas Fischer, deceased: $10,000.
Under an act further to provide for the construction of the Northwestern Turnpike Road, passed Mar 30, 1857, 6%.
1837: John V Willcox, of Petersburg, Va: $15,000.
1837: Dr Austin Brockenbrough, of Tappahannock: $40,000.
1837: Jno Coles, of Albemarle, Va: $2,500.
1837: Mary Johnson, wife of John Johnson, Annapolis: $10,000.
1837: Pres & Professors of the College of Wm & Mary in Va: $400.
1839: Jas Cornick, of Norfolk: $1,000.
1841: Mrs Mary W Cabell, wife of Jos C Cabell: $500.
1842: John V Willcox, of Petersburg, Va: $2,000.
1843: Hill Carter, trustee, under will of Beverly Randolph, for the benefit of Nancy Kennon & others: $1,500.
1844: Thos R Nalle, U S N: $300.
1844: Miss Eliza Coles: $100.
1848: Mrs Frances Todd Barbour, Orange Co: $100.
1848: Albert G Wortham, of Richmond: $500.
1848: Winfield Cosby, Louisa: $500.
1849: Edmund H Flournoy: $1,000.
1852: Wood Bouldin & A A Morson, Com'rs etc, in the case of Waller vs Gilliam: $2,000.
1853: Nicholas Mills, Com'r in the suit of Mills vs Robinson & others, etc: $2,000.
Do: John G Pollock, of Stafford: $200.
1854: Jas H Paxton, exc of A T Barclay: $600.
1856: R W Flournoy, com'r, Fleming's exc, vs Perkins' exec, etc: $200.
1857: Martha L Nelson, guardian of W H Nelson: $200.
1857: John S D Cullen, trustee for Marg't Otelia Cullen, under the will of John Cullen, deceased, etc: $1,000.
1858: W G Cazenove, trustee of Mary E Cazenove: $2,000.

Under an act further to provide for the construction of the Northwestern Road, passed Feb 6, 1834.
1839: Thos Cadett, of Riegate, Surry, England: $4,000.
1841: Dr Saml Webb: $1,150.
1841: Peacock, Handley, & Co, of Sleaford, Lincolnshire, England, Bankers: $3,000.
1841: Jas Haskins, cmte of John Haskins, sen, etc: $700.
1843: John V Willcox, of Petersburg: $1,000.
1844: Jas Haskins, cmte of John Haskins, sen, etc: $500.
1846: Olivia Johnston, of Richmond: $500.
1846: Mo Hon Richd Seymour Conway, Marquis of Hertford, Great Britian: $5,000.
1847: Emily T Morris: $800.
1847: Lucilla Wallace, of Fredericksburg: $100.
1847: Thos Stevenson, of Richmond: $100.
1848: Hiram Sims, of Standardsville: $200.
1848: Timothy Taylor, of Loudoun Co: $1,200.
1848: Wms Carter, guardian of Georgiana Wickham: $700.
1848: Peter H Anderson, of Chesterfield: $3,900.
1849: John Rutherford, trustee for Margaret Blair & Maria Blair, children of T R Blair: $800.
1850: Wm H Hubbard: $700.
1850: Mrs Pamela Hobson, of Richmond: $400.
1854: Mrs Juliet Drew: $400.
1854: Jas M Swann, of Powhatan: $400.
1854: John Lester, of Richmond: $400.
1855: Henry Cox, ex, & com'r: $1,000.
1855: Wm Frayser, surviving exec of J a Frayser, in trust for Miss A Sanderson: $50.
1855: Thos Page, of Cumberland, trustee for Edw C Fisher & Lavinia A, his wife & their children: $300.
1855: Mary & Eliz D Vass: $118.
1855: Poval Turner, cmte Randolph Turner: $200.
1855: H L Brooke, adm de bonis non, with the will annexed of Judith Randolph, deceased: $266.
1855: Wm D Sims: $181.
1856: Thos Pratt, of Spotsylvania: $1,500.
1856: Hugh W Sheffey, trustee of Peter Sheets: $860.
1856: Margaret C Hanson: $170.
1856: Miss M G Chevallie: $100.
1856: Jas H Behan: $8,000.
1856: John D G Browne, adm of G N Clough, deceased: $60.
1857: L Masters, Com'r Amelia Co, Ct Court in the case of J N Vaughn's adms vs Hunt & wife, etc: $100.
1857: Mrs A M Holladay: $400.
1857: John A Gordon, guardian of Fanny F Gordon: $300.
1857: Miss Eliza S Atkinson: $250.
1857: Martha L Nelson, guardian of W H Nelson: $200.
1858: Edw C Bishop: $100.

1858: Kent, Payne & Co: $100.
1858: Saml S Wegler: $500.
Under an act to provide for the construction of a turnpike road from Staunton to Parkersburg, passed Mar 16, 1838.
1839: Mary B Latane, of Essex Co, Va: $1,300.
1839: Thos Stevenson, Richmond: $1,000.
1853: Francis L Smith, com'r in suit Hepburn vs Hepburn & others: $300.
1853: Sally N Berkeley, of Essex Co: $600.
1854: C J Beirne: $400.
1854: Jonathan T Cowherd, com'r under decree Louisa circuit court, Apr 24, 1854, etc: $400.
1854: Jonathan T Cowherd, of Louisa: $150.
1858: Rosalie P Aylett: $500.
1858: B H Harrison: $500.
1858: Emma Marx, of Richmond, Va: $500.
-J M Bennett, Auditor of Public Accounts. S H Parker, Register. Geo W Munford, Sec of the Commonwealth. Com'rs of the Sinking Fund. Richmond, Va, Nov, 1858.

Orphans Court of Wash Co, D C, Nov 6, 1858. In the case of Benj L Jackson, adm of Geo W Bowie, deceased, the administrator & Court appointed Nov 30, for final settlement of the personal estate of the deceased, of the assets in hand.
-Ed N Roach, Reg/o wills

Died: on Nov 6, Eliza, daughter of A E L & Catharine Keese, aged 7 years & 5 months. Her funeral is today at 3 o'clock, from her parents residence, 628 N st, between 4th & 5th.

Died: on Nov 7, in Wash City, John C Smith Parker, youngest daughter of Thos & Caroline Parker. His funeral will be on Tue at 11 o'clock, from the residence of his father, on 6th st.

I shall publish the Daily Globe & the Congressional Globe & Appendix during the next session of Congress. Copy of the Daily Globe for 4 months: $3. –John C Rives, Wash.

TUE NOV 9, 1858
On Sat in the N Y harbor the propeller **Petrel**, built for a pleasure yacht, but lately employed as a tug on the North river, suddenly burst her boiler. On board at the time was Henry Brink, engineer; Edw Downey, fireman; & a pilot & deck hand, whose names could not be ascertained. Downey had a severe wound in the head, but the others were killed instantly.

A few days since Mr Jas Wright, of Sandusky, Ohio, while gunning for wild ducks, near the head of Sanduskey Bay, was drowned by the upsetting of his skiff, which was occasioned by the firing of a large swivel fowling piece.

Thos Walls, charged with killing Harrison King, at Oldtown, Allegheny Co, Md, last May, was convicted last Tue of murder in the 2nd degree & sentenced to 8 years & 6 months in the penitentiary.

Excellent household & kitchen furniture at auction on Nov 17, at the residence of Wm H Upperman, on Pa av, between 3rd & 4½ sts. -Jas C McGuire & Co, aucts

On Oct 30 Mr Ransom Gaston was thrown from a lumber wagon at Oberlin, Ohio, & was run over, & so injured, that he died the next day. His son was also thrown from the wagon, & had one arm broken, & was otherwise badly injured.

Peter Brown & a friend were riding in a wagon in Breck's Lane, Christiana Hundred, Del, were thrown from the vehicle by the running away of the horse. Mr Brown was instantly killed & his companion was severely injured. [No date given-current item.]

Burlington College commenced on Nov 1. During the vacancy of the Rectorship, occasioned by the resignation of Rev Mr Chetwood, it will be carried on under the personal supervision of the undersigned. Burlington College is a Christian household. -G W Doane, Pres

Occoquan Mills for sale: located in Prince Wm Co, Va. We will sell with the mills, or separately, a frame dwlg, used as the miller's house, & a large stone Mansion, with all the necessary out-bldgs. Possession given on Jul 1, 1859. –Jos Janney & Co, Occoquan Post Ofc, Prince Wm Co, Va.

Wash, Nov 8, 1858. A few days since I saw a statement in the local Star newspaper relative to the new banking institution recently established in Wash City, of which Chas E Russ, late of N Y, is Pres. The Star warns its readers against taking the notes of this bank-"The Bank of the District of Columbia" & calls it a bogus concern. In this a great injustice is done. If the editor of the Star had taken the trouble to make himself acquainted with the affairs of this institution, he would have found that the gentlemen connected with it are responsible men, & fully able to redeem their notes.
-A Citizen of Wash

Desirable residence for lease or rent on F st north, available on Nov 15. Apply to Mrs Wm Speiden, on the premises.

Died: on Nov 8, in Wash City, David V Kurtz, in his 39th year, 2nd son of David & Eliz Kurtz. His funeral will be this afternoon at half past 3 o'clock, from the residence of his father, 349 F st, between 9th & 10th sts.

Boston, Nov 8. Capt Dobson, late master of the brig **Isle de Cuba**, which recently arrived here in charge of the mate, was arrested in New Bedford yesterday & brought to this city for examination on the charge of being engaged in the slave trade.

WED NOV 10, 1858

N Y, Oct 8, 1858. The venerable Josiah Quincy was on Monday struck to the ground by a vehicle & run over as he was walking in Tremont st, Boston. So severe are his injuries that his life is in imminent danger. His injuries are on the back of his head. Both his legs were also run over by the vehicle which came in collision with him. [Nov 12th newspaper: Josiah Quincy, sen, is now 86 years of age, in full vigor of his intellect, as will be shown in his soon to be published biography of John Quincy Adams. The telegraphic report of his accident was exaggerated. He will be about the streets as usual in a few days. –N Y Post]

The following Passed Midshipmen have been promoted to Masters [in the line of promotion,] from Nov 4, 1858: Philip Porcher, Alfred Hopkins, Montgomery Sicard, Edmund O Matthews, T McKean Buchanan, Geo E Law, Edw P Lull, Edw Lea, Alex F Crossman, Chas S Norton, & Hamilton H Dalton.

Trustee's sale of part of lots 20 & 21 in Cabot's subdivision of square 677: by deed of trust from Michl Macnaman to the subscriber, dated Aug 2, 1855, recorded in Liber J A S, No 165, folios 230 thru 233, of the land records for Wash Co, D C, having a front of 14 feet on G st, between North Capitol & 1st st, with improvements. –Geo S Donn, trustee -A Green auct

Mrd: on Nov 9, at **Zoar**, Montg Co, Md, by Rev Danl Motzer, Geo A Munro to Lizzie Hall, only daughter of Jos Thompson, of the former place.

Mrd: on Nov 2, by Rev Septimus Tustin, D D, of Wash City, John S Maxwell to Miss Sallie M, daughter of Robt T Magaw, both of Harford Co, Md.

Died: on Nov 8, in Wash City, after a protracted illness, Mrs Mary S, consort of Geo H Fulmer, in her 60th year. Her funeral will take place today at 2 o'clock, from the residence of the family, 461 I st, between 4th & 5th sts.

Died: on Nov 9, Justin, infant son of Justin H & Emma Sergeant Howard.

Orphans Court of Wash Co, D C. Letters of administration, de bonis non, with the will annexed, on the personal estate of Jos H O'Brien, late of Wash Co, deceased. –Sarah J O'Brien, admx de bonis non, with the will annexed.

THU NOV 11, 1858

Extensive sale of new & superior cabinet furniture, lace curtains, & gilt cornices, on Nov 25, at the House Furnishing establishment of G T Smallwood, 508 7th st. -Jas C McGuire & Co, aucts

Wm Fell Giles, jr, appointed by the Pres to the consulship of the U S at Geneva, Switzerland. Mr Giles is a son of Hon Wm F Giles, Judge of the District Court of Md.

Jacob Wells, aged 13, while on a visit to a relative in Lenhartville, Berks Co, Pa, was playing in a barn last Fri, with a chain across a beam, & by some means became suspended, & was quite dead when found. It is not thought that the act was intentional.

Wm Cameron, who resides near Oquaka, Ill, purchased a shot gun that had a load in it, & a few days thereafter shot if off, when it kicked with such force as to rupture his abdomen & cause his death in a few hours.

Cmdor Sinclair, of the U S ship **Vandalia**, while searching for 3 men belonging to the ship **Wild Wave**, which had been wrecked on the Island of Oene, & who afterwards reached Tahiti in a boat of their own construction, visited the little Island of Rooahoogah, where he found 6 white men, 3 Americans & 3 Englishmen, who have lived there 14 years, & had so completely identified themselves with the natives as not to desire to leave.

The death of Lord Chas Wellesley has directed attention to the danger of the Dukedom of Wellington becoming extinct; for it now depends upon the lives of the 2 sons of Lord Charles, after the present Duke of course. It is suggested that the title should be enlarged & made heritable by the collateral branches of the house of Wellesley.

Boarding: Mrs Turpin, 485 12th st, near F, has several vacant rooms suitable for families & single gentlemen. Table boarders can also be accommodated.

I offer for sale the place on which I live, in PG Co, Md, 8 miles from Wash: contains 700 acres of land, divided into 6 fields. The bldgs consist of a small but comfortable dwlg house, overseer's house, several tenant houses, & other out-bldgs. –Henry B Bird, Piscataway Post Ofc, PG Co, Md.

On Sep 20 Eldred Ward met W W Smith on the street in Shreveport, La, in broad daylight, & deliberately discharged both barrels of a shot-gun into his body, causing instant death. He mounted his horse & fled. Rewards of three or four thousand dollars were offered for his arrest. Ward made it to Texas; changed his course, & Mr Oglesby, of New Orleans, passed him near Woodville, & rode on, stopped at Mr Battle's, & informed him that Ward was coming. A posse collected by Mr Redwine went to Tatum's Hotel, where they expected him to stop. Mr Tatum before their arrival had stopped Ward from leaving his room by presenting a double barreled shot-gun at his breast. When the party with Redwine, [10 men,] arrived Ward was summoned to surrender. He replied that he was innocent & unarmed, & they approached him without suspicion. He instantly drew a pistol in each hand & shot John F Barnes through the heart & dangerously wounded John F Walker. He then rushed the door, but was shot down by Mr Tatum. Ward was finally induced to throw aside his pistols & surrender & taken to Shreveport, & lodged in jail. –New Orleans Courier

Orphans Court of Wash Co, D C. Letters of administration on the personal estate of Jacob Hall, late of Wash Co, deceased. –Absalom A Hall, adm

Orphans Court of Wash Co, D C. Letters testamentary on the personal estate of Ann Simms, late of Wash Co, deceased. –Jane E Gray, excx

Mrd: on Nov 9, at *Pine Grove*, near Wash, by Rev John Lanahan, Alex'r Elliott, jr, of Mount Vernon, Ohio, to Mary Lavinia, daughter of Selby Scaggs, of the former place.

Died: yesterday, in Wash City, Mrs Susan B Ringgold, relict of the late Lt Thos Lee Ringgold, U S Army, & daughter of the late Hon A P Upshur. Her funeral will take place at the Church of the Epiphany, G st, today, at 3 o'clock.

Died: on Nov 6, at the residence of her father, D Rokohl, in St Louis, Mo, Mary Juliet Kibbey, wife of Wm R Kibbey, aged 20 years.

Died: on Nov 9, Charles Williams, [colored,] aged 85 years. His connexion with the auction business for the last 25 years has made old Uncle Charles well & favorably known to the public. His funeral will take place today at 2:30 o'clock, from his late residence, 366 15th st, between L & M sts.

Worcester, Mass, Nov 10. The city marshal, Fred'k Warren, was today accidentally shot in the chest by a pistol, & it is feared cannot live.

Obit-died: on Monday last, Geo W Strong, at his residence in this village, of consumption. He was in times past extensively connected with the railroad enterprises of Vt, & was one of the Presidential Electors for this State in 1856. He was a son of the late Hon Moses Strong, & died at the early age of about 40 years. –Rutland Herald

Lost, a young Pointer Dog, having a steel collar marked with the name of M N Falls. Reward of $5 will be given for his delivery at this office.

FRI NOV 12, 1858
Army Gen Orders, No 21, Headquarters of the Army, N Y, Nov 6, 1858. Assistant Chas H Page, now at *Fort Leavenworth*, will accompany the companies of the 1st Cavalry to *Fort Smith* & *Fort Washita*, taking post at the latter named station. Sgt Stewart & Cpl Underhill were tried & convicted by Garrison Court-martial on a charge of disobedience of orders; that execution of the sentence, confirmed by the garrison cmder, was suspended by special order of the cmder of the department, in pursuance of a general order from the Headquarters of the Army, May 8, 1852, denying the jurisdiction of a garrison court of such charge. The question is not clear upon the authority of the text writers. I incline to the opinion of the Gen-in-Chief. Disobedience of a lawful command of a superior officer in the execution of his office, is a capital case, & not triable by a garrison court, &, however that may be, the order of the Gen-in-Chief is mandatory to garrison cmders, & does, in effect, forbid any such cmder to send any such case to a garrison court, or to execute their sentence in such case. These proceedings, in violation of his order, are null & void. -War Dept, Nov 1, 1858 -J B Floyd

Mrd: on Nov 10, in Wash City, at the 7th st Presbyterian Church, by Rev Mr Bittenger, Mr S W K Handy to Miss Annie E Vernon, all of Wash City.

Died: on Nov 10, in Wash City, Jerome Beron, aged 62 years. His funeral will be from the residence of his son, on Ga ave, near 11th st, this afternoon at 2 o'clock.

On Wed at N Y officer Robt Cainnes arrested a man who had threatened to kill the captain of a vessel, & was proceeding with him for the Tombs, when the man dealt the officer a severe blow on the left cheek & fled. The officer recovered & shot 3 times at him, the last took effect in his right side. He was taken to the City Hospital & died there. [No name given for the man who was arrested & died.]

A new constituent of the atmosphere, which within a few years been discovered, will become as familiar to the rising generation as oxygen, hydrogen, & nitrogen are to the present. The name applied to this newly discovered substance is <u>ozone</u>. It is oxygen electrified, & was discovered by Prof Schoenbien, the discoverer of gun-cotton, about 19 years ago. Van Marum, near the end of the 18th century, noticed its existence, but the matter had been forgotten.

N Y, Nov 11. Henry Reed, a night clerk in the post ofc, was arrested today in the act of purloining letters. He confessed to the robbery 3 weeks ago of a package containing over 100 letters, directed to Brooklyn.

Proclamation-State of Md. Information received that Wm Nugent, [an Irishman,] committed for the murder of Mary Sheahy, & Andrew Martin, [colored,] charged likewise with murder, did break out of & escape from the jail of Montg Co on Oct 30, 1858, & are still at large. I, Thos Holliday Hicks, Govn'r of Md, offer a reward of $150 in each case for the apprehension & delivery to the Sheriff of Montg Co of said Nugent & Martin. Nugent is about 30, 6 feet high, & stout built, with a large scar from a blow on his forehead. Martin is about 45, 5 feet 10 inches high, little darker than copper color. -Thos H Hicks, Nov 10, 1858. –Jas R Partridge, Sec of State

Whereas Bounty Land Warrant No 39,957, for 40 acres, issued to Margaret Sutton, widow of Thos Sutton, deceased, dated Feb 7, 1852, has been stolen, lost, or otherwise destroyed, this is to give notice that a caveat has been filed to prevent said warrant from being patented, & application will be made to the Pension ofc for a duplicate thereof, by John Johnson, Atty.

Savannah, Nov 11. The ship **Fanny Fosdick** was burnt here last night.

SAT NOV 13, 1858
The Circuit Court of PG Co, [Md] was adjourned on Sat last by Judge Crain, as a mark of respect to the memory of Jno Contee Mullikin, a member of the PG Bar &Auditor of the Court. Resolutions were formed expressing sympathy to his relatives, & a sense of the loss of the officer sustained by the Court, & of a friend & professional brother by the members of the Bar. [No other information-current item.]

There being a lack of engineers in the service, the Sec of the Navy has appointed the following acting engineers to sail in the steamer **Arctic** & the steamer **Metacomet**, viz: for the **Arctic**, Mr Wm S Montgomery, with the pay of a 2nd assist engineer, & Mr Jas Shaughnessy, with the pay of 3rd assist engineer. For the **Metacomet**, Mr Saml Montgomery, with the pay of 2nd assist, & Messrs Wm Selden & Geo Farren, with the pay of 3rd assists. Jas Wallace, of Phil, appointed a 3rd assist engineer in the navy, vice Z K Rind, resigned.

N Trautwein & A Leit, 2 youths indicted at St Louis for the murder of H Downey, were on Monday found guilty of murder in the 1st degree. He was murdered for his money.

$20 reward. A small Parian Marble Figure, representing a Female kneeling, was stolen from the **Oak Hill Cemetery** on Nov 10. One of the arms of the figure was broken. A reward of $20 will be paid by the Cemetery Co for the detection of the thief & recovery of the figure. –Henry King, Treasurer

A suit which had been in progress for some time at Columbus, Ia, in which Wm Mewherter, an old & well known citizen of the county, was dfndnt, terminated by the jury rendering a verdict that the dfndnt, who had been an agent for Shrewsbury & Price, millers, has in hand unaccounted for over $10,000. At the time of the announcement of the verdict, Mewherter stood to the right of the Judge's desk, drew a pistol & shot himself in the head.

Trustee's sale, by decree of the Circuit Court for Fred'k Co, Md, as a Court of Equity, the undersigned, trustees, will offer at public sale, at the Catoctin Iron Works, on Dec 15, 1858, all that valuable real estate, to wit: The ***Catoctin Iron Works***, & lands belonging, containing 7,000 acres, situated in said county; with a commodious dwlg house; grist mill; saw mill; village of about 60 houses for workmen; & other out bldgs.
–John B Kinkel, Wm J Ross, trustees -W B Tabler, auct

Artesian well now in course of sinking on the property of Amos Kendall, at **Kendall Green**; so far as known, this is the first attempt in this city at such an enterprise. The engineer is Mr J H Stearns, & the depth already attained is 50 feet.

The first number of a daily new paper to be printed & published in Gtwn has just appeared, under the title of the Gtwn Ledger, by Messrs H A Keefer & Co.

St Louis, Nov 12. Col Miles had another encounter with the Navajos, 10 of whom were killed. Kit Carson, with a band of Utahs, passed through Santa Fe on his way to fight the Navajos. The Mohave Indians attacked an emigrant train while crossing the Colorado, killing 3 men, 2 women, & 4 children.

N Y, Nov 12. The ship **John Elliott Thayer**, of Boston, was burnt in the Gulf of Calif. The crew was saved.

MON NOV 15, 1858
Combats with hostile Indians. 1-May 24, 1857-Gila expedition: commanded by Col W W Loring, Mounted Riflement: killed: the notorious Mogollon chief Cuchillo Negro. 2-Nov 8, 1857: 2nd Lt J B Witherell, 2nd cavalry: in pursuit of a party of Camanche Indians. Lt Witherell was slightly, & privates Gehrung, of Co C, & Chas Morris & Patrick Connell, of Co K, were severely wounded. 3-Nov 28, 1857: Capt Parkhill, with 1st Lt & Adj W S Harris, 1st Lts DaCosta & John Canova, & 75 men of Col S St Geo Rogers' regt of Fla mounted volunteers, landed from Chokolisco Key, Fla, in search of hostile Seminoles. He was attacked by a party of Indians, who fled after the first fire. Capt Parkhill was killed, & privates M M Mason, John A Stevens, & Thos Posey, of his company, privates A McAlphin & O'Neill, of Capt Hardee's company, severely though not dangerously wounded. 4-Jan 28, 1858: 1st Sgt W McDonald, of Co D, 2nd Cavalry, with 14 men sent out from Camp Verde, Texas, surprised a party of Indians: killed 2. Privates Stroacher & Hughes severely, & Private Tenny slightly wounded. The sgt speaks in commendation of hospital steward, Arnold Stubb. Praise to the guide, Polycarpio Rodrigue, for his untiring exertions & sagacity in the pursuit. 5-May 16, 1858: at To-hots-nim-me, Wash Territory, companies C, E, & H, 1st Dragoons, & E, 9th Infty, aggregate 159 men, were attacked & overpowered by some 1,200 of the Spokan, Pelouzue, Coeur d'Alone, Yakima, & other Indian tribes. Brvt Capt O H P Taylor, & 2nd Lt W Gaston, both of the 1st Dragoons, were killed. Co C, 1st Dragoons: 1st Sgt J A Hall, Bugler R A Magan, Farrier E R Birch, Privates R S Montague, Alfred Barnes, killed; Victor C DeMay mortally wounded, since dead. Co E, 1st Dragoons: 1st Sgt Wm C Williams, mortally wounded, since dead; Private R P Kerse, who gallantly defended the body of Brvt Capt Taylor [lying mortally wounded,] when the Indians made a desperate charge to get possession of it. [Doesn't say so, but it appears that Kerse was also wounded.] Co H, 1st Dragoons: 1st Sgt Edw Ball, with a few men, repulsed the attempt of a large number of Indians; Privates Francis Poisell, who assisted in rescuing & bearing off Capt Taylor under a heavy fire from the enemy; C H Harnish & Jas Crozet, Co H, 1st Dragoons, both killed. Co C, 1st Dragoons: wounded: Privates Jas Lynch & Henry Montrevill. Co E, 1st Dragoons: wounded, Jas Kelly, severely; Wm D Micon, Hariet Sneckster, severely; Jas Healy, Maurice Henley, Chas Hughes, & John Mitchell. Co E, 9th Infty: wounded, Privates Ormond W Hammond, severely; John Klay & Gotlieb Berger, slightly. 6-Aug 15, 1858: a party of 15 mounted men, commanded by 2nd Lt Jesse K Allen, 9th Infty, surprised hostile Indians on the Upper Yakima river, Wash Territory: the gallant young leader lost his life. 7-Aug 29, 1858: Capt McLane, Mounted Riflemen, commanding 12 men of his regt & a company of 52 New Mexican guides & spies, was attacked by a party of 300 Navajo Indians near Bear Spring, New Mexico: Capt McLane was severely though not dangerously wounded. 8-Sep 9 to 15th, 1857: Lt Col Miles, 3rd Infty, in pursuit of hostile Mavajoes, had several skirmishes: Bugler Ezekiel Fisher, was killed. Wounded: Co A, Mounted Riflemen: Sgt Jas Watson, slightly, & Private Manus Sweeney, mortally, since dead. Co I, Mounted Riflement: Private G Dunn, wounded. Co C, 3rd Infty: Private Wm Mauk, slightly wounded. 9-Oct 1, 1858: Bvt Maj Van Dorn, Capt 2nd Cavalry, commanding, came upon a camp of hostile Camanches, between four & five hundred: painful to record the death of 2nd Lt Cornelius Van Camp, 2nd Cavalry, a promising young officer, who was shot through the heart with an arrow while charging the enemy. Sgt J E Garrison, of Co F; Privates Peter

Magar & Jacob Echard, of Co H, were killed. Private Henry Howard, of Co H, missing, supposed to have been killed. Wounded: Co A: Bvt Maj Van Dorn, severely, 4 wounds Cpl Jos P Taylor, dangerously. Co H: Private C C Alexander, severely; Sgt C B McClellan, Cpl Bishop Gordon, & Bugler M Aborgast, slightly. Co F: Privates C C Emery & A J McNamara, severely, & W Frank, slightly. Co K: Private Smith Hinckley, slightly. The sutler, Mr J F Ward, was slightly wounded, & the special agent in charge of the friendly Indians, Mr S Ross, was severely wounded. During the combat Capt N G Evans, 2nd Lts Harrison & Phifer, each killed two, & Lt Major killed 3 Indians in hand to hand encounters. –L Thomas, Assist Adj Gen

N Y: upon a tombstone in the church yard of the Reformed Dutch Church in Sleepy Hollow, near Tarrytown, can be found an inscription: "in memory of Capt John Burkout, who parted this life, Apr 10, 1785, aged 103 years, & behind him when he died 240 children & great-grandchildren. Also Mary, the wife of John Burkout, who died Aug, 1755, aged 73 years. The church itself was erected in 1609, & is one of the oldest churches in the country.

Adms sale of stock, horses, corn, farming utensils, farming implements, & household & kitchen furniture at public auction on Dec 1, on the farm belonging to the estate of L B Hardin, deceased, in Alexandria Co, near Bailey's Cross-roads.
–Geo D Fowle, Wm P Johnston, adms -Saml J McCormick, auct, Alexandria, Va
+
Adms sale of likely negroes, on Nov 22, at the tavern of Saml Catts, belonging to the estate of the late L B Hardin. –Geo D Fowle, Wm P Johnston, adms
-Saml J McCormick, auct, Alexandria, Va

Mr John Craver & his son, of Fred'k City, Md, were bringing a load of straw in a one-horse wagon from the country on Wed, both being on top of the load, the son driving, when coming down the hill in the west end of Partick st, some of the gearing broke & the horse commenced kicking. The father tried to grasp the lines, but missed them & pitched off on his head, & the wagon passed over him, causing his death the following day.

Wm Porter, age 18 years, committed suicide by taking strychnine, at Jackson, Tenn, a few days ago. He had recently married a young lady, & being under age & dissipated, according to his own account, his parents or guardian refused to put him in possession of property coming to him. –Columbus [Geo] Enquirer

Public sale of his farm, *Fruitland*, 2½ miles s w of Beltsville, containing 100 acres; with a frame tenement, cottage, & out-bldgs. –John T C Clark -J C McGuire & Co, aucts

Accident at New Orleans on Sat, when 2 painters, Jas Naylor & Dick Reed, were painting the cornice of the upper windows of Old Fellows' Hall. The platform they were on that was suspended by ropes in some way, one side precipitated downwards. Naylor was dashed to death, a distance of some 70 or 80 feet. He was but 21 years of age, & born in Limerick, Ireland. Reed managed to hold on til rescued.

Jas Rodgers, who deliberately murdered Mr Swanston, by stabbing him, while the latter was quietly walking through 9th ave with his wife, was hanged in the city prison at N Y on Fri last. His age was 20 years.

Orphans Court of Wash Co, D C. Letters testamentary on the personal estate of Bonaventura Schad, late of Wash Co, deceased. –Chas Mades, exc

Dept of State, Wash, Nov 11, 1858. 1-Information received from R B Campbell, the U S Consul at London, of the death, on board the American ship **Nathan Hanan**, of Kingston, on the passage from New Orleans, Ebenezer Pierce, master, of Edmund Gruth, F S Norton, & L E Abraham, all of yellow fever. 2-Information has been received from B Squire Cotrell, the U S Commercial Agent at San Juan del Norte, of the death of Henry S Kelly, at the Machuca Rapids, on the San Juan river, on Sep 23 last. The deceased is represented to have been a naturalized citizen of the U S, & to have spent several years in the States of Ohio & Calif.

N Y papers: Prof Isaac B Woodbury, a prominent N Y music teacher died at Columbus, S C, on Oct 26, aged only 39 years. He was formerly a teacher in the public schools of Boston, whence he removed to N Y some 8 or 10 years ago. He had been in ill health for the past few years.

Died: on Nov 13, in Wash City, Mr John H Trenholm, son of Sir John Trenholm, a captain in the British Royal Navy. The deceased was born at Sobreves, Normandy, France, in 1811, & was in his 47th year. He was well & favorably known in this city, & was foreman in the offices of the Globe, Union, & States, in the latter of which he was employed at the time of his death. He had been a resident of Wash City for more than 20 years, & leaves a wife & 2 children to lament his death.

Died: lately, at Phil, whither he had gone to prosecute his medical studies, Mr Robt Hooe, son of Towson Hooe, of Fauquier Co, Va, in his 24th year. He died of typhoid fever.

TUE NOV 16, 1858
Mr Jas B Anderson, printer, met his death at New Orleans on Nov 7, by being accidentally run over by a horse car. He has been employed for 20 years on the Picayune, whose editors pay a handsome tribute to his memory.

Mrd: on Nov 19, by Rev W Howe, Mr Wm E Chandler, of Wash, D C, to Miss Mattie A, youngest daughter of John Finley, of Castle Fin, Pa.

Mrd: on Nov 9, in Gtwn, D C, by Rev Mr Tillinghast, of St John's Episcopal Church, Benj Prescott, of the Parish of St Landry, La, to Miss Kate E Taylor, of the former place.

Died: on Nov 15, Mr Saml L Brown, late of Howard Co, Md, in his 27th year. His funeral will be from the residence of Mr Jos Harbaugh, on 7th st, this afternoon at 3:30.

Died: on Nov 15, at his sister's, Mrs Caroline E Sanders, near Wash, Thos Snowden, aged 56 years. He will be buried on Wed at 10 o'clock, at *Oakland Place*, Md, [*Contee's station*,] in the family burial ground.

WED NOV 17, 1858
The steamer **Fulton**, bound from Pittsburgh to St Louis, struck a stump at Buffington Island on Tue & sunk in 16 feet of water. 12 deck passengers were drowned. The boat, which was valued at $18,000, is a total loss. The passengers lost all their baggage.

The case of the State vs Andrew Thompson, indicted for the murder of Henry Fletcher, on trial in Harford Co Court at Bel Air, Md, the jury on Sat brought in a verdict of murder in the 2nd degree. Judge Price sentenced him to 21 years in the penitentiary.

David S Evans, tried at Pittsburgh for the murder of his wife, was on Sat found guilty of murder in the first degree.

Official, Dept of State, Wash, Nov 15, 1858. Information received from Wm Miles, the U S Consul at Callao, Peru, of the death of the following American seamen, viz: Date/native or resident of/vessel/where deceased.
1858:
Apr 3, Danl Hussey, Mass, vessel **Casual** at Callao
Apr 10: Jos Johnson, N Y, vessel **Casual** at Callao
Apr 11: Robt Wilson, Boston, vessel **Rapid** at Bella Vista
Apr 20: Robt White, N Y, vessel **Casual** at Callao.
Apr 21: Thos King, U S, vessel **Susan Fitzgerald** at sea.
Apr 28, Thos Atkinson, N Y, vessel **Casual** at Guadaloupe Hospital.
Apr 30: Jos Richards, U S, vessel **Shakspeare**, Callao.
May 1: Geo Wilson, U S, vessel **Lawrence Brown** at Bella Vista.
May 13: Robt Smith, unknown, vessel **Casual** at Callao.
May 17: Thos Hoskins, N Y, vessel **Casual** at Guadaloupe Hospital.
Mary 24: Richd Williams, U S, vessel **John Bryant** at sea, Oct 22, 1857.
May 24: Francis Revir, U S, vessel **John Bryant** at sea, Oct 27, 1857.
May 24: Jno Boyd, U S, vessel **John Bryant** at sea, Dec 15, 1857.
May 24: Stephen Nash, U S, vessel **John Bryant** at sea Jan 29, 1858.
Jun 3: Henry Hibbert, unknown, vessel **Casual** at Bella Vista Hospital.
Jun 5: Wm Jackson, unknown, vessel **Casual** at Bella Vista Hospital.
Jun 8: Theodore West, U S, vessel **Callao** at Callao.
Jun 14: Geo H Davis, U S, vessel **Casual** at Bella Vista Hospital.
Jun 14: Jno Awson, U S, vessel **Harraseeket**, at sea Jun 18, 1858.
Jun 21: Alex Nickerson, unknown, vessel **Casual** at Guadaloupe Hospital.
Jun 24: Jas Wiland, U S, vessel **Casual** at Lima.

Circuit Court of Wash Co, D C-the case of Wilson vs Lieberman, has occupied the Court for a week, & brought to a close yesterday. Prior to 1807 Clotworthy Stephenson was the owner of lots 16 & 17 in square 254; in 1807 he built a house, 3 stories high, on lot 17, with a gable end towards lot 16, having stacks of chimneys & fireplaces protruding towards lot 16, for the convenience of building against it. In the same year he conveyed to Mrs Wheaton, under whom the plntf claims, "one divided & ascertained moiety of lot 17 in square 254," & on the back of the deed was endorsed a memorandum [as appears by the record, for the original deed was not produced] of the same date with the deed, signed by the grantor & by Jos Wheaton, the husband of the now grantee, & who, as there was evidence tending to show, bought the property for her, & caused it to be settled upon her, by which memorandum the terms upon which the grantor should have the use of the wall in bldg on the adjoining lot were stated. Stephenson, the grantor, after the Wheatons went into possession, continued to reside on the residue of his property there, having it enclosed, & part of the enclosure being the wall in question. In 1821 the dfndnt's house was built, having this for one of its walls. In 1853 the plntf purchased the Wheaton title, & took a deed conveying by metes & bounds the half of lot 17 adjoining lot 16. The dfndnt's deed, & the deeds of those under whom he claimed, described his property, by metes & bounds, as part of lot 16, with the appurtenances. After the plntf's purchase, in 1853, an accurate survey of the square showed that the division wall stood wholly 9 inches or more within lot 17. The plntf claimed the land according to survey. For the purpose of bldg on it he caused the old house to be torn down, intending to build, & to make the wall next to the dfndnt 14 inches thick, instead of 9, as it had been before; & to place the center of the new wall, with the increased thickness, precisely on the line ascertained by the survey, which would bring it some distance inside of all the dfndnt's fireplaces. On the other hand, the additional width to the plntf's lot would add greatly to its value. It seems not unreasonable, therefore, that a narrow strip of land, in itself of small value, should have given rise to so much litigation. In 1853 Lieberman procured an injunction against Wilson to prevent the taking down of the old wall, unless it should be found unsound, & to prevent his bldg a new wall otherwise than on the site of the old one if it should be taken down. The old wall was unsound, & was taken down, & rough boards nailed up in its place; & so the premises [vacated by Lieberman] continued for about a year, when Lieberman rebuilt the wall &, as was stated by his counsel, rebuilt it 14 inches thick, instead of 9 inches, as the other walls of his house are, in order to be sure that it should be strong enough to support Wilson's projected house. But when the new wall was about 10 feet above the pavement Lieberman was stopped by an injunction at the suit of Wilson, preventing him from rebuilding any other than a 9 inch wall. He dropped off to a 9 inch wall. Wilson then brought this suit for a trespass; & Lieberman brought his suit to recover damages for cutting away the site of the house, & leaving it for a year without rebuilding it. It has resulted, as to the law, in the Court's having restricted the plntf, Wilson, to damages for the alleged trespass in occupying, for several days before the bringing of the suit, so much of the ground as was not covered by the old 9 inch wall. The points of law interesting to the public in Wash City are: first, that a man may enjoy the comforts of his own hearth, when he had done so for more than 20 years, without fear of an action for damages founded upon an accurate survey, made by his neighbors; &, secondly, that when a 9 inch party wall is torn down it cannot be rebuilt a 14 inch wall, whatever the bldg regulations may be supposed to say to the contrary; the first builder being the person who exercise the power under these regulations. Verdict for the plntf, one cent damages.

Died: on Nov 16, in Wash City, in her 61st year, Mrs Susan Benson, consort of Wm B Benson, of Wash City. The deceased was an exemplary & pious Christian. Her funeral will take place on Oct 18 at 2 o'clock, from her late residence, 8th, near L st.

Circuit Court of Wash Co, D C-Chancery, No 1,302. John Van Riswick vs Michl Muntz & others. Chas S Wallach, trustee, reported that on Jul 9, 1858, he with Jas C McGuire, auct, employed by him for that purpose, sold lots 21 & 22 in square 625, to Jas Fowler, trustee, for $763.33; part of lot 7 in said square, with improvements, to John Van Riswick, for $615; lot 6 in said square to John Van Riswick, for $663.81; & part of lot 7 & the whole of lot 8 in said square & improvements, to Martin McNamara, for $660, & the several purchasers have complied with the terms of the sale. –Jno A Smith, clerk

Chestnut Hill School, for Young Gentlemen, 3 miles north of Balt, Md, has been in full operatio since Nov, 1848. **Chestnut Hill** is a country seat of 100 acres, unsurpassed in natural beauty & healthfulness. For circulars address the Rector, Rev Fred'k Gibson, M A, Balt, Md. References: Hon Jas B Clay, Ky; & Dr Wm P Johnston, Wash, D C.

Private Select Dancing Academy, at Temperance Hall, E st, between 9th & 10th sts, Profs Antonio & Marini. [Ad]

THU NOV 18, 1858
The chartered steamer **Westernport** sails on Sat, with Gen Paez on board, for Venezuela. Her officers are: Cmder, Thos T Hunter; Lts, T S Phelps, J Young, A E Benham, & Chas E Cushman; Purser, Jas R Harwood; 2nd Assist Engineer, M P Jordan; 3rd Assist Engineers, Geo J Barry, M H Plunkett, & Wilson K Purse. Her crew consists of about 60 sailors & 12 marines. She carries two large nine-inch guns.

Judge Eckler, of Utah, has arrived at St Louis, having in his charge Henrietta Polidore, a young girl, who was four years ago abducted from Gloucester, England, & who has lately been rescued from the Mormons by a writ of habeas corpus, at the request of the British Government.

Wash Corp-Mon: 1-Ptn from Gilbert Vanderwerken, & from Danl Collins, each for the remission of a fine: referred to the Cmte of Claims. 2-Ptn from E Loeffler, asking payment for painting & hanging street signs: referred to the Cmte of Claims. 3- Cmte on Improvements: bill to authorize E G Queen to re-occupy a certain recorded alley in square 425: determined in the negative.

John H Turton returns his sincere thanks to the Fireman of Wash & his also his neighbors for their prompt assistance in saving his property from destruction on H st, on Sat last.

Miss Euphrasia Beverly, being on a visit to Richmond, was on Monday standing before the parlor fire of her friend, Miss Duval, when the draft of the flue wafted her skirts against the blazing coals. In an instant she was enveloped in flames. She was badly burnt & after a night's suffering she breathed her last.

Died: on Oct 28, at Medford, Mass, Susan L Mann, in her 24th year. When the U S steam-frig **Minnesota** was launched from the navy yard in Wash City, Miss Mann performed the ceremony of christening that vessel. She was distinguished by unusual personal beauty, & a rare degree of intellectual superiority.

FRI NOV 19, 1858
Jos Balestier, who a few months ago took up his residence in York, died in that place on Sat last after a brief illness. He was about 70 years of age. He has been for a number of years U S Consul at Singapore.

Govn'r of Md appointed Benj P Smith, Com'r of Deeds for the State of Md in D C.

The ship **Eastern City**, 1,368 tons, bound from Liverpool to Melbourne, left the ship **Mersey** on Jul 10th last, having on board 180 passengers, 47 men, officers & crew, & more than 1,600 tons of general cargo. On Aug 23, after passing the equator, fire was discovered in the fore-hold. Capt Johnstone's conduct throughout the transaction appears to be above all praise. All passengers & crew were ordered on deck. Peter McLean did not obey, & was found suffocated in his berth. Within a half an hour from the time a ship was sighted in the afternoon, the ship **Merchantman** passed under the stern of the burning ship. In a brief space the boats were got out from either ship, & first the women & children were transported on board the troopship, then the rest. 227 persons were thus rescued.

N Y, Nov 17. 1-Mr Robt Strong, late cashier of the City Bank of N Y, died on Monday, a bank officer for more than 40 years. 2-A verdict of $4,250 has been obtained against the Eighth Ave Railroad Co, in consequence of the death of Gilbert Sandford, caused by his forcible ejection from the cars because he refused to pay his fare. 3-Policeman Cairnes, who shot Hollis, a prisoner, has been admitted to bail by Judge Russell, on the ground that there was not that premeditation before the shooting which is necessary to constitute the crime of murder. The bail was fixed at $10,000. 4-Henry Reed, one of the night clerks in the post ofc in N Y C, had been arrested for embezzlement of letters, & committed for trial. [Nov 22nd newspaper: The grand jury ignored the bill against Cairnes for manslaughter on the ground that the homicide was justifiable.]

The trial of Rev Danl Downey, a Catholic priest, on a charge of the murder of a man named Kelley, by shooting him with a pistol at Staunton, Va, resulted on Monday last in the jury finding him guilty of murder in the 2nd degree. The term of imprisonment in the penitentiary was fixed at 8 years.

In pursuance of a resolution of the Board of Chosen Freeholders of Monmouth Co, N J, the clerk published a statement of the expenses incurred in the trial & execution of Jas P Donnelly: it foots up to $3,759.49.

Nathl Sunderland, convicted of the murder of Patrick Colbert, who made his escape from the Richmond, Va, jail on Sunday, has been recaptured & lodged in prison again.

Eliz Carr, one of the domestics wounded in the Gouldy tragedy, is dead. Mr Gouldy still remains in a precarious condition. He is at times quite rational, & often inquires after his son Frank, whom he supposes to be alive & in prison. Nathl is rapidly recovering, as is also his mother; but it is feared Charles, the youngest boy, will never recover from the effects of his injuries. He appears to be the only member of the family that is in any immediate danger.

Wash Ordnance: Wm S Morris & Co, granted permission to erect telegraph posts in Wash City. Morris & his associates, forming a Magnetic Telegraph Co for connecting Washington with the Southwest, to erect posts & suspend wires from some convenient point on Pa ave, running to B st north, thence along B st to 14th st west, thence along 14th st to its junction with the Potomac Bridge. Approved, Nov 12, 1858.

Wash Ordnance: Act for the relief of John M Roberts, M D, Thos Miller, M D, & Wm D Butt, M D: Roberts to be paid $32; Miller $15; & Butt $12, for professional services rendered police officer Thos H Robinson. –Approved, Nov 12, 1858.

Kimmel House has just been completed, & will be open on Nov 23 for the reception of guests. Situated on C st, between 4½ & 6th sts. –A F Kimmel, Proprietor
–E V Campbell, Superintendent

In Equity, No 1,302. Michl Muntz, John C Brent, Mary H Elliott, admx of Wm P Elliott, Silas Hill, J B H Smith, Geo M Davis, David Myerle, & Jos S Cabott. I am directed to state the account of Chas S Wallach, the trustee, & the claims of the several parties above named, & of any creditors of said Michl Muntz, on Dec 11 next, at 10 o'clock.
–W Redin, auditor

Mrd: Nov 18, in Wash City, by Rev P D Gurley, Chas Demond, of Boston, Mass, atty-at-law, to Miss Ada B Campbell, eldest daughter of Mason Campbell, of the Treasury Dept, Wash.

Died: on Nov 18, in Wash City, Mr Danl Walsh, [recently injured by the mail stage on Pa ave.] His funeral will take place from the residence of Mr J W Robertson, on Pa ave, between 9th & 10th sts, tomorrow at 2 o'clock.

Com'rs & adms sale of valuable real & personal estate, in Albemarle Co, Va; Circuit Court of Albemarle, in the case of Robertson, guardian, etc, vs Gordon, etc, & as administrator of Gen Wm F Gordon, deceased, will offer for sale, on Dec 15, the real & personal estate in said county, of which the said Wm F Gordon died seized & possessed. The said land is *Edgeworth*, being the residence of the late Gen Gordon: contains 1,300 acres, with a comfortable brick dwlg, & out bldgs, cabins sufficient for the accommodation of a large number of negroes. I will also sell 71 very valuable slaves, together with the stock of horses, mules, cattles, farming implements & crop. Mr Geo L Gordon, now residing on the premises, will show the land. –Wm J Robertson, Com'r & adm of W F Gordon, deceased. –H Benson & Co, aucts

Detroit, Nov 18. The captain of a schnr shot his stevedore, Danl Flynn, in an altercation, & John Miller shot his brother-in-law, Peter Shaner, killing him instantly. Both the murderers have been arrested. [No other information.]

SAT NOV 20, 1858
Hugh Hazlitt, a white man, charged with enticing & persuading slaves to run away from Dorchester Co, Md, was tried this week at Cambridge, & found guilty on 7 indictments. He was sentenced by the Court, on the first indictment, to the penitentiary till May, 1867, & on each of the others for 6 years, making a total of 45 years.

Letters have been missing from the mails the past few months on the route between Washington, the county seat of Fayette Co, & Columbus, Ohio. Wm S V Prentiss, special mail agent, investigated the matter; dispatched a decoy package containing about $45 & then followed its route. After it passed the post ofc at Duff's Forks, Fayette Co, it became missing. Mr Prentiss immediately called upon the postmaster, W A Phelps, demanded the package. Phelps denied all knowledge of it. His daughter, aged 15, acknowledged that the package had been taken by her & her sister Sarah. The parties were all arrested & held for examination. Mr Phelps, the father, is nearly 60 years of age, owns a farm of 140 acres, where he resides, & has always stood well in the community. [Nov 23rd newspaper: There was no evidence to implicate Mr Phelps or Jennie. Sarah was required to give bail in $500 to answer the charge at the Dec term of the U S Court, & bail was promptly given by her friends.]

A little boy, 7 or 8 years old, understood to be the son of Mr W W Tyler, was yesterday run over by a wood cart on H st, near 9th, & killed. The horse had run away, & was passing up the street furiously, when he came in contact with the child, one of the wheels passed over the child's head, crushing it in a shocking manner. [Nov 22nd newspaper: The little child reported to have been killed was not a son of Mr Tyler's, but of Dr Brooke Jones, of the City Post Ofc. He was not killed, but is living, with considerable hope of recovering. More distressing is that Mrs Jones is on a bed of sickness & in no condition to suffer the painful excitement caused by so severe an injury to her son.]

Dept of State, Wash, Nov 17, 1858. Information received from Gideon Nye, the U S Vice Consul at Macao, of the death of Mr Saml Burge Rawle, the Consul of the U S at that port, in his 71st year.

Mrd: on Nov 9, by Rev Theodore M Carson, Mr Wm H Nally to Miss Jane M Wagoner, both of Wash City.

Mrd: on Nov 9, by Rev Wm H Chapman, Richd Smith to Miss Rebecca Ann King, both of PG Co, Md.

Mrd: on Nov 17, at the Ebenezer Methodist Episcopal Church, on Fourth st east, by Rev Wm H Chapman, Mr John T Cook, formerly of Wash City, to Miss Anne R, daughter of the late Robt Hunter, of Alexandria, Va.

Mrd: on Nov 18, by Rev Wm H Chapman, Mr Chas T Berkley to Miss Emma Meachan, all of Wash City.

Mrd: on Nov 15, in Cincinnati, by Rev Dr C M Butler, Wm E Hood to Mary W, only daughter of Benj Homans, formerly of Wash.

Died: on Nov 18, Rebecca, widow of the late John McLeod, in her 80th year. She was the revered member of a devoted family, ever the companion of her grandchildren; a fond & devoted mother, self sacrificing to a fault. Her funeral will be on Sat at 2 o'clock, from the residence of her son-in-law, Junius J Boyle, corner of 21st & H sts.

MON NOV 22, 1858

Gen Robt Hanna, of Indiana, an old citizen & the last surviving member of the Indiana Consttitutional Convention of 1816, was killed on Thu last while walking on the track of the Peru & Indianapolis railroad.

Orphans Court of Wash Co, D C. Letters testamentary on the personal estate of Jos Balestier, late of Wash Co, deceased. –J N Balestier, exc

$15 reward for stolen bay Mare. –Sarah Ann Talburtt, living near Upper Marlboro, Md.

Died: on Nov 20, after 2 days of severe suffering from the effects of a burn, Louisa Edwards, youngest daughter of Christina C & Wm Ballantyne, aged 9 months & 9 days.

Died: on Nov 21, in Wash City, Carrie Lawrence, infant daughter of Jacob C & Mary A Gibson. She will be buried at 2 o'clock today, at 371 6th st, near H st.

Circuit Court-Wash. Wm Campbell's heirs were plntfs & Wm H Gunnell dfndnt. It involves the proprietorship of a large square of land on the Island, or the 7th Ward of Wash, now nearly all studded over with dwlgs. The plntfs made out their title by showing that on Oct 18, 1794, a large amount of property, including square 465, in which lie the lots in dispute, was conveyed by the U S Com'rs to Jas Greenleaf; that Jas Greenleaf, by deed dated May 10, 1796, reciting that this property was in fact owned by him jointly with Robt Morris & John Nicholson-each one-third, conveyed all his interest in all property in Wash, with that purchased from the Gov't & that purchased from individuals, to said Morris & Nicholson, as tenants in common; that Wm Campbell, as a creditor of Morris & Nicholson, caused writs of foreign attachment, issued from the Genr'l Court of Md, to be levied, on Apr 22, 1797, on all the property of Morris & Nicholson, including this square & many others, which resulted finally in a judgment of condemnation on Jun 10, 1800, in the Court of Appeals of Md, of all the interest of Morris & Nicholson in the property, & a sale of that interest under execution, at which sale Wm Campbell, the plntf in the suite, was a purchaser; &, finally, that the plntfs in this suit were the heirs at law of Wm Campbell. This was the whole title of the plntfs. But for a better understanding of the case, & to remove an erroneous impression as to the extent of Campbell's title acquired as above, it will be necessary to allude to certain other suits of older origin. The interest of Morris & Nicholson bought by Campbell proved not to be as extensive as might have been supposed from the quantity of the property. More than a year before the attachment Greenleaf, Morris & Nicholson had mortgaged all this property to John Law, to secure certain contracts with him. In 1800 commenced certain suits by Pratt, Francis, & others, the assignees of Morris & Nicholson, against Law & Campbell, claiming to redeem the property from the mortgage, & by law against the others, claiming the forclosure of the mortage. In these suits the validity of Campbell's title was contested. They were finally decided in the Supreme Court in 1815. That Court held Campbell's title good to whatever interest Morris & Nicholson had, subject to the incumbrances on the property created before Campbell's purchase. They directed a sale of the property to satisfy the mortgage unless the debt to Law should be paid, & accordingly the whole of the property mortgaged to law, except 6 squares, was sold to pay the debt to Law, & was insufficient to pay it. Northing was left to Campbell except what he could realize out of these 6 squares, which were Nos 465, 468, 469, 470, 495, & 498, the situation of which will now be explained. About 1796 an agreement was made between the U S Com'rs, Morris & Nicholson, & Thos Law, that the com'rs would make a good title to Law in certain property which Morris & Nicholson had bought from the Gov't & sold to Law, [but which they had not paid the Gov't for,] in exchange for which Thos Law was to release certain of the property mortgaged to him to Morris & Nicholson, & they were to convey it to the Gov't, to stand in the place of that which the com'rs would convey as aforesaid to Thos Law. The com'rs did convey certain squares to Law, & in exchange Law released the 6 squares aforesaid to Robt Morris, & Robt Morris conveyed these by atty to the com'rs. This conveyance was considered to be defective, & Wm Campbell claimed that the title remained in Morris & Nicholson, & was covered by attachment. The U S filed a bill in chancery in 1813 against Campbell, Morris & Nicholson's assignees & others, claiming to have these squares conveyed to them by a good deed. This suit was finally settled last year, when the Circuit Court decreed that the U S were entitled to a lien upon a certain number of square feet in these squares for the balance of Morris & Nicholson's indebtedness to them, that the ground should be selected by Morris' heirs, or, they failing to do so, by the U S. The U S made their selection, taking 5 of the squares & 3 lots in the 6th one, which was square 465, & the property so selected was sold under the decree of W S Cox, as trustee. The result was that out of the whole of the property bought by Campbell, nothing was left to him, because of the mortgage & liens prior to his attachment, but part of square 465. The satisfacton of the lien of the U S left this free of incumbrances, & in Jan, 1858, his heirs brought ejectment suits against the parties in possession. This was the case under trial from Tue to Thur last. The main defence was adverse possession. It was claimed that Mr Greenleaf had had this property enclosed, claiming it as his own, from a period anterior to 1818, to the time of his death in 1843, & the dfndnts claimed under a deed from his heirs. It was shown that Wm Campbell, who resided in Md, was in the District in 1817 & about 1819, & it was contended that the adverse possession commenced against him at that time. Evidence was offered on these points, but the Court held that no adverse possession could commece pending the suit of the U S against Campbell & others aforesaid, especially as Greenleaf seemed to be substantially a party to the suit. Under instructions from the Court, the Jury rendered a verdict for the plntfs. Counsel for the plntfs was Walter S Cox, assisted by Hon Henry Winter Davis, & the counsel for the dfdnts Jos H Bradley.

Calif Intelligence: 1-Col Wright had returned to Walla-Walla. 2-Ebenezer Thayer, of Boston, committed suicide on Oct 24.

Benj Gwinn, a Philadelphian, was arrested on Sat for robbing a valuable overcoat, the property of Mr Joshua B Moore, druggist, & other property. He came here as an iron worker on the roof of the new gas-house.

Augusta, Nov 20. Hon Wm Schley died here this afternoon, aged 72. He was a native of Md, & formerly the Govn'r of this State, as well as a member of Congress. [Nov 24th newspaper: Mr Schley was born in the city of Fred'k, Md, on Dec 10, 1786; was educated in the academies at Louisville & Augusta, & admitted to practice law in this city in 1812. He was a devoted husband & parent; thoroughly a Georgian.
–Augusta Constitutionalist, Nov 21.]

TUE NOV 23, 1858
At the age of 61, Ida Pfeiffer, the well-known traveler, departed on that journey from whence none returns in this world. In middle life, on the death of her husband & the settlement of her children, she commenced her series of tours. Madame Pfeiffer was more than 40 years old before she took up her pilgrims' staff. During the following 21 years she was the incarnation of feminine restlessness. -Phil Press

Death from Freight. The wife of Thos Roper was frightened to death last night by the fire which was near her dwlg. She was age 38 years. –Hartford Times

On Nov 13, on Tallahatchee river, Mr David Carnes went out in a skiff with 2 ladies, Mrs Welch & Miss Henrietta Jenkins, on a fishing excursion. In the middle of the river the skiff upset, & Mr Carnes was able to right the boat & rescue Mrs Welch. He approached Miss Jenkins who clasped him so tightly that he could swim no longer, & they both sunk to rise no more. Mr Carnes was 21 years of age, & leaves behind him a family.

Administrator's sale of household & kitchen furniture at auction on Nov 26, at the residence of the late Boneventura Schad, 3rd & Pa ave. –Chas Medes, exc
-Jas C McGuire & Co, aucts

Clifton, England: recently Miss Mary Richmond, 18, understood to be a grand-daughter of Rev Leigh Richmond, was on a visit to a connexion of her family, residing near Richmond Park, Clifton. On Friday she accidentally wandered off the cliff, called the Lion's-head Cliff, to her death some 300 feet to the road below.

Persons known to have drowned on the steamer **Fulton City**, when she sunk at Buffington, Ohio, on Nov 12, were Jos Johnston, wife & child, deck passengers bound for Leavenworth city; Tim Donahue, deck passenger, bound for Canton, Tenn; Milton Thompson, deckhand, resided at Gtwn. Mr Johnston was a resident of Pittsburgh.

A man named Flynn was convicted of murder at Lockport last spring, but resorted to the insane dodge & was sent to the Utica Asylum. He has been returned as of sound mind, & on Sat was sentenced to be hung on Jan 7.

WED NOV 24, 1858
Pierre Descombe, a Frenchman, died at St Roch, Canada, on Nov 15, at age 112 years. He retained full possession of all his faculties, down to the hour of his death.

Col Saml B Sibley, long connected with the press of Ga & Fla, died at Savannah Nov 18. John B Trinchard, commercial editor of the Moblie Register, died suddenly Nov 16.

Chancery sale of very valuable improved property near the Post Ofc Dept: by decree of the Circuit Court of Wash Co, D C, passed in a cause wherein John F Boone, jr, is cmplnt, & Wm C Boone & others dfndnts, dated Nov 13, 1858: public auction on Dec 17, of the south half of lot 12 in square 406 in Was City, improved by a commodious 3 story dwlg house with the modern conveniences, on 8th st, near F. –A Austin Smith, trustee -J C McGuire & Co, aucts

Having permanently left Wash City, I have closed my Wood & Coal Yard. Mr Saml H Young, Wood & Coal dealer on 9th st, is authorized to receipt for me & sell the stand & stock. –H B Riehle, N Y ave, between 13th & 14th sts.

Orphans Court of Wash Co, D C, Nov 23, 1858. In the case of Wm Redin, Walter S Cox, & Wm P Maulsby, adms of Stephen Cassin, deceased, the Court & administrators have appointed Dec 14 next, for the final settlement of the personal estate of said deceased, of the assets in hand. -Ed N Roach, Reg/o wills

Thanksgiving Day. In obedience to the request of the municipal authorities, & with a full conviction that all should render thanks to the Great Almighty of Heaven, who made all & governeth all, & wishing to atone for errors of the past, & asking mercy for the future, I issue this my card, informing all, of every name or denomination, rich or poor, high or low, that my Restaurant will be closed as to all spirituous or vinous liquors on that day; & I hope no one professing to be my friend will aske me to violate this determination. -W Rupp, 484 Penn ave

Mrd: on Nov 18, at the residence of Dr S J Cooke, PG Co, by Rev E A Knight, Francis N Brent, of Wash City, to Miss I A, daughter of the late Jas Magill, of Md.

Mrd: on Nov 17, at St Paul's Church, by Rev Joshua Peterkin, Wm F Owens, of Balt, to Nannie J, daughter of T Tinsley Johnson, of Richmond, Va.

Mrd: on Nov 21, at Havre-de-Grace, Md, by Rev Septimus Tustin, D D, of Wash City, G Taylor Lyon to Miss Maria L Pennington.

Mrd: on Nov 17, in Wash City, by Rev C W Hall, Thos C Donn to Miss Mary A Webb.

Died: on Nov 23, after a lingering illness, John T Cole, a native of Loudoun Co, Va, but for the last 15 years a resident of Wash City. His funeral will take place from his late residence, on I st, between 4th & 5th sts, this afternoon at 3½ o'clock.

Died: on Nov 22, Mrs Eliza Ann, wife of Mr John T Clements, of Wash City, after a protracted illness, in her 53rd year. Her funeral will take place on Thu afternoon, at 2½ o'clock, from the Second Presbyterian Church.

Died: on Nov 23, Robert S, only son of Robert L & P A Teel, aged 3 years, 5 months & 17 days. His funeral is this day at 3½ o'clock, from the residence of his parents, on C st, between 4½ & 6th st. Friends of the family & of Hinton & Teel are invited to attend.

St Louis, Nov 22. From Oregon & the Gold Region. 1-David Harris, of Balt, was burnt to death at San Francisco on Oct 22. 2-The remains of Capt Taylor & Lt Gaston have been buried at Walla-Walla. 3-Michel, nephew of Kamiakin, the leading murderer of the Indian Agent, Bolow, 3 years since, had been captured by Major Garrett & confined at Yakima. 4-An Indian chief was killed while attempting to escape from Col Wright's command.

For rent: residence of the late Maj Howle, on 14th st west, contains 12 rooms, attached stable, carriage-house & smoke house. Apply to P C Howle, Patent Ofc, or on premise.

THU NOV 25, 1858
Jas Fulton, of Tenn, has been appointed a Purser in the Navy, vice J B Danforth, jr, resigned.

Columbus Post Ofc: John Miller has been appointed postmaster at Columbus, Ohio, vice Saml Medary, appointed Govn'r of Kansas. –States

Lamentable occurrence in Greenfield, Saratoga Co, N Y, in the family of Albert Close. He accidentally shot his 12 year old daughter, when he was shooting at squirrels. She died the next day. The squirrels were destroying his harvested corn. [No date given- current item.]

Wash Corp-Mon. 1-Ptn from John Connelly, praying to be allowed an additional sum for burying Hillery Lemons, a pauper, who died May 5, 1858, of smallpox: referred to the Cmte of Claims. 2-Cmte of Claims: asked to be discharged from the consideration of the ptn of O C Humphreys & Geo Jueneman, & of Danl Collins, for the remission of fines: cmte was discharged accordingly.

From Los Angeles we hear of a stampede among the <u>camels</u> lately introduced by Gov't into that region, by way of Texas, in use by Lt Beale. During a snow storm on Oct 2, which at the Tejon was very violent, the U S camels at the rancho of S A Bishop, strayed away. Mr Griffith Williams, who went in search of them, returned to San Bernardina on Nov 17 with 9 of them, which he overtook on the desert. Some 6 are missing.

Continuation sale of superior household & kitchen furniture at auction on Dec 1, at the establishment of Geo T Smallwood, 508 7th st. We shall close out the residue of stock. –Jas C McGuire & Co, aucts

The 6th Infty arrived at Carson Valley, & will reach Placerville Thu next. Ofcrs of the 6th: Col Geo Andrews; Brvt Lt Col W Hoffman; Dr J J Milhan, assist surgeon; Lt J L Corley, adj; Lt C G Sawtelle, quartermaster; Capt W S Ketchum; Capt C S Lovell; Brvt Maj E Johnson; Capt R W Foote; Capt F Hendrickson; Capt R B Garnett; Cast F F Flint; Brvt Maj L A Armstead; Lt E J Marshall; Lt J A Smith. There are also about 300 recruits in charge of Lt Bootes, who are now probably about the Sink of the Humboldt, & may be expected in this place in about ten days.

Orphans Court of Wash Co, D C. Letters of administration on the personal estate of Isaac Holland, late of Wash Co, deceased. –Geo F Barrett, adm

Frank Hill, a clerk in the Little Rock, Ark, post ofc, has been sentenced to hard labor in the State penitentiary for 6 years for robbing the mails.

M W Galt & Bro have removed to their new store, 354 Penn ave, between 6th & 7th sts.

Mrd: on Nov 23, in Emmanuel Church, Balt, by Rev H V D Johns, D D, Arthur Lee Rogers, of Leesburg, Va, to Charlotte, daughter of the late Gen Geo Rust, of Loudoun Co, Va.

Mrd: at Oaken Brown, Va, Wm Lawson Waring to Miss Rosalie V Tayloe, daughter of the late Chas Tayloe. [No date given. Under Marriage column.]

Chicago, Nov 24. Hon Thos L Harris, Rep in Congress of the 6th district of Ill, died of consumption this morning. [Nov 27th newspaper: Col Harris was born in Norwich, Conn, Oct 29, 1816; graduated at Trinity College, Hartford, in 1841; studied law in Conn with Govn'r Isaac Toucey, & was admitted to the bar in Va in 1842; commenced his practice in Menard Co, Ill; in 1846 he raised & commanded a company, & joined the 4th regt of Ill volunteers to serve in the war with Mexico.]

From New Mexico: Lt Averill was wounded by a ball passing through his tent while encamped between **Fort Defiance** & Albuquerque, but the wound was not dangerous.

SAT NOV 27, 1858
N Y: Govn'r King has commuted the sentence of death passed upon Dennis Tanner, of Columbia Co, to imprisonment for life. Tanner cut his wife's throat with a butcher knife & then kicked her down stairs. In regard to the too frequent exercise of Executive clemency, in this instance there would seem to be some excuse, Tanner being nearly 80 years of age.

N Y: The death of Hon B F Butler has been noticed in the several courts of the city.

Wash City Ordinance: Act for the relief of Wm Linkins & B F Moxley, assignees of Alfred Collins: to pay each $75, as assignees of Alfred Collins, to whom the sum was due for constructing a sewer under the footway in front of lots 7 & 8 in square 117. –L Tree, Pres of the Board of Common Council pro tem. –Wm T Dove, Pres of the Board of Aldermen. Approved, Nov 26, 1858. –Jas G Berret, Mayor

Cmdor Chas Stewart has applied to be relieved from command of the Phil Navy Yard, preparatory to resigning his commission in the U S Navy. The Cmdor has been led to this course by the action of the "Board of Fifteen." This Board placed him upon the retired list, an act which roused the indignation of the entire country. Cmdor Stewart has been over 60 years in the cause of his country. –Phil Argus

Mrs L L Sigourney furnished 50 poor familes with turkeys or fowls, & best quality pumpkin pies, for a Thanksgiving dinner.

On Nov 22, on the Central Ohio railroad, Mr Alfred H Davis, U S mail agent from Balt to Cincinnati, was killed. Mr Davis started from the first baggage car to reach an adjoining apartment of another car by walking along an 8 inch wide platform, when a stick projecting out caught his clothes & caused him to fall under the wheels of the cars. He was about 30 years of age. A water-boy on the train saw the accident as it happened.

Mrs Rachel Hunt & Mrs Rachel Ayres, one aged 104 years & the other 101 years, died in Harford Co, Md, last week. Both died the same day.

Mrd: Nov 24, in Wash City, by Rev G M Samson, Mr Jos W Franklin to Miss Mary A Cranston, both of Wash.

Mrd: Nov 25, at the residence of the bride's father, by Rev Septimus Tustin, D D, John D W Moore, of Montg Co, Md, to Miss Sarah B, daughter of Chas L Coltman, of Wash City.

Died: on Nov 26, in Wash City, suddenly, Mrs Mary S Edwards, consort of Alpheus L Edwards, of the First Comptroller's ofc, formerly of Chattanooga, Tenn. She was a consistent member of the Methodist Episcopal Church South, & died as she lived, a consistent Christian. Her funeral will take place from her husband's residence, 22, corner of 8th & K sts, on Oct 28, at 2 o'clock.

Died: on Nov 25, suddenly, in Balt, Mrs Isabella Foushee Ward, wife of Wm J Ward, of that city, & daughter of Thos Green, of Wash.

In Equity, No 1,268. Robt A Cassin vs Stephen J Cassin & others, heirs at law of Cmdor Stephen Cassin, deceased. By order of the Circuit Court of Wash Co, D C, I am to inquire whether the real property left by Cmdor Cassin is susceptible of partition among his heirs; & if not, whether it will be to the benefit of his minor heirs that it be sold. Examination on Dec 8 next, at the Auditor's room. –Wm R Woodward, special auditor

Died: on Nov 23, of pneumonia, Robert S Teel, aged 3 years & 5 months, only son of Robert L Teel, merchant tailor, of Wash City. The mortal remains of this beautiful child were on Tue, taken to Richmond, Va, & there committed to the silent tomb.

Comrs' sale of valuable land in Alexandria Co, Va, on Dec 28, about 247 acres, being the property on which Dr R B Alexander resided, & of which he died seized. Also a tract adjoining with the Factory Bldg & Water power thereon; contains about 2½ acres. This property lies on the waters of Four Mile Run. –F L Smith, L B Taylor, I Louis Kinzer, Comrs of sale.

MON NOV 29, 1858

The executors of the will of Hon John M Niles, of Hartford, Conn, [Messrs Gideon Welles & Calvin Day,] have paid over to the city treasurer the sum of $20,000, devised by Mr Niles as a fund the interest of which is to be annually expended in assisting heads of families, especially poor widows, in the payment of rents & the purchase of fuel.

The telegraph brings us intelligence of the sudden death of Hon Henry Bedinger, on Nov 26, at his residence adjoining Shepherdstown, Va. He had but lately returned to his home, after an absence of 5 years as Minister to the Court of Denmark during which service he had been successful in bringing about a treaty for the abolition of the Danish Sound Dues, so long a subject of complaint & vexation. His sickness was pneumonia, with which he was attacked on Nov 23.

Hon Jonathan Knight, but lately a Rep in Congress from Wash Co district in Pa, died on Nov 22. He was in his 70th year.

Mr Thos Baltzell, jr, son of the esteemed Chief Justice of Fla, who resided at the navy yard at Pensacola, where he held the important post of assit civil engineer, was returning to his home on board the steamer **Calhoun**, together with his wife, from Tallahassee, where he had been on a visit to his father's family. The steamer stopped at Apalachicola Bay on Oct 30th, & lay at the West Pass anchorage waiting for the mails. A little girl, a daughter of Mrs Hazard, one of the deck passengers, fell from her chair on the hurricane deck & rolled overboard, & the gallant Baltzell jumped overboard to save the child, & was drowned himself in his noble effort. The child was saved by the mate of the steamer. His body was recovered after being in the water 1½ hours. He was about 24 years of age. -Apalachicola advertiser

Edwin J Dickens committed suicide at the American Hotel, in Jersey City, on Tue night. He arrived in this country about 6 weeks ago, & expressed a wish to find employment in a newspaper ofc. He represented himself as a distant relative of Chas Dickens. He registered his name as Henry Anson, England. Mr Archibald, the British Consul, ordered that the body be interred at his expense in the *N Y Bay Cemetery*. Letters in his trunk were from London & other parts of England. He appeared to be without money. In his pocket was found a bottle of the solution of cyanide of potassium.

On Monday a heavy iron truss roof, in course of erection over the rolling mill of Messrs Brown Brothers at Waterbury, Conn, fell instantly killing Mr Thos J Paine.

State Dept, Wash, Nov 24, 1858. Information received from Oliver H Perry, the U S Consul at Canton, of the death of Jas Upton, a native of Great Britain, but a citizen of the U S, on Jun 15 last, having been killed in an encounter with the Chinese in the passage from Canton to Whampoa.

Mrd: on Oct 12, in Thomasville, Ga, Aeneas Armstrong, U S Navy, to Miss Henrietta E Vickers, only daughter of the late Jas M Vickers, of Thos Co.

Died: on Nov 28, in Wash City, Wm Burdine, in his 78th year. He has been employed in the navy yard for the last 55 years. His funeral will take place tomorrow at 2 o'clock, from the residence of his son, near the Navy Yard Bridge.

Died: on Nov 27, John J, son of Sophia & John Vierbuchen, aged 1 year & 4 months. His funeral will be this afternoon at 2 o'clock, from the residence of his father, 345 First st east.

$5 reward will be paid for the recovery of a small dark red cow, strayed from the premises of the subscriber about a week ago. –J R McGregor, E, between 2nd & 3rd sts.

Family Grocery Store, Penn ave, s e corner of 10th. –Hermann H Voss [The accounts of the late firm of Marsh & Voss are left with Mr H H Voss for collection. –O W Marsh]

Orphans Court of Wash Co, D C. Letters of administration, with the will annexed, on the personal estate of Peter Schio, late of Wash Co, deceased. –Josephine Schio, admx, w a

Orphans Court of Wash Co, D C. Letters of administration on the personal estate of Saml L Brown, late of Wash Co, deceased. –Ellen A Brown, admx

TUE NOV 30, 1858
The entire stock of jewelry, watches, plated ware, & showcases, at auction, on Dec 2, of Mr John Robinson, at the store at 349 Pa ave. N B: I intend to keep exclusively a Clock Store. –John Robinson, 349 Pa ave. –Wall & Barnard, aucts

Trustee's sale, on Dec 10, of property on the Island, by deed of trust from P A B Meister, dated Aug 4, 1855, recorded in Liber J A S No 102, folios 195, in the Land Records of Wash Co, D C: sale of lot 8 in square 535, situated on the east side of 4½ st, between south C & D sts. -Bernard Hooe, trustee -Jas C McGuire & Co, aucts

The London Watchman announced the death of Rev John Hickling, the oldest Methodist preacher in the world, & the last survivor of the Helpers of John Wesley. He died on Nov 9, in the 71st year of his ministry, & would have been 93 years old had he lived 3 weeks longer.

Thos L Higdon, late a draughtsmen in the navy yard at Portsmouth, Va, committed suicide on Friday, by blowing out his brains with a musket. He was a native of Wash, D C, but had been formerly all his life a resident of Portsmouth, having been for several years employed in the ofc of Naval Constructor Hartt, at the yard. He was an excellent workman; 28 years of age, & unmarried.

Thos O Larkin, one of the oldest of the pioneer citizens of Calif, a man of great wealth, died on Oct 27, after a brief illness, at his house in San Francisco, in his 57th year. He emigrated to Calif in 1832, & was appointed U S Consul, to reside in Monterey, in 1844. He was married in 1833, & his children are the first of American parentage, paternal & maternal, born in Calif. –Calif paper

Orphans Court of Wash Co, D C. Letters of administration on the personal estate of E D Leazer, late of Wash Co, deceased. –Nathan S Lincoln, adm

Mrd: on Nov 25, at the residence of Mr Luther R Smoot, by Rev Dr Norwood, of Gtwn, Mr J Courthope Lawton, of Powhatan Co, Va, to Miss Nellie A Laub, of Wash City.

Mrd: on Nov 10, at **Rose Hill**, Wash Co, Md, by Rev Dr Creigh, Alonzo Berry, of PG Co, Md, to Virginia, daughter of Otho Williams, of the former place.

Mrd: on Nov 24, by Rev J W Diller, rector of St Luke's Church, Brooklyn, N Y, at Red Bank, N J, Dr J W H Lovejoy, of Wash, D C, to Maria L, youngest daughter of Wm A Greene, of the first named place.

Died: on Nov 28, suddenly, Capt Benj E Brooke, U S Marine Corps. His funeral will take place from the residence of his brother-in-law, Mr Wm S Darrell, 498 I st, on Dec 1 at 11 o'clock.

Died: on Nov 26, at Florence Height, N J, Maria C, wife of Jos West, of Phil.

Died: on Nov 27, Jessie T, infant daughter of Thos R & Mary C Suter, aged 6 months.

Three days from Europe. Robt Owen, late Minister to Naples, is dead. [Dec 1st newspaper: In announcing the decease in England of the venerable philanthropist, Robt Owen, who had reached the aged of 88 years, the telegrapher added that he was ex-Minister to Naples. It was his son, Robt Dale Owen, who was the minister.]

Sale of **Dawson Farm**, in Albemarle Co, Va, by act of the Gen Assembly of Va, passed Mar 15, 1858, giving authority to the Rector & Visiters of the Univ of Va to sell the lands devised to the Univ by the late Martin Dawson, & by direction of the Board of Visiters, I shall offer at public auction, before the court-house door in Charlottesvile, on Feb 7, the tract of land lying on the main road from Charlottesville to Scottsville, containing by survey 538½ acres. –Robt B Prentis, Proctor Univ of Va

Straudsburg, Pa, Nov 29. The locomotive on the Delaware & Lackawana road exploded today & Thos Lonergan, the fireman was killed, & Edw Hawley fatally injured.

WED DEC 1, 1858
On Sat Jas Cowles, an old, wealthy, & respected citizen of Farmington, killed himself by cutting his throat. He was about 55 years of age. –New Haven Journal

The steamship **Indian Empire**, of the Galway & N Y line, which left N Y on the 23rd & Halifax on the 29th of last month, for Galway, had not been heard from up to the time the ship **Europa** sailed from Liverpool, on the 20th inst, when she was 21 days out from Halifax. Names of her cabin passengers are: Rev Mr Hennessy, Timothy Harrison & wife, E J Rooney, W S Keebill, Richd Wallace & wife, Hugh McDowell, Jane Kennedy, Patrick Dalton, E Reyloff, P Reardon, F McGovern, Michl Clifford, David Hennessy. Passengers in the forward cabin: H A Manley, Wm M Creeney, Mgt Zaliousky, Mary J Evans, Anne Hughes, Mary Muncy, John Delany, Catharine Canon, Jeremiah Hactnell, wife, & 2 children; Edw Cauwee, Edw Peter Carroll, Jane Bradley, Timothy Kelly, Thos Tiemann & wife, Anne McGiven, Mary Jane McGiven, Geo Greenfield & wife, Jas Connor, Robt Reed, Denis Hannigan, Wm Kennedy, John Jennings, Jas Kelly, Geo Eades, Michl McHansen, Jas Dinman, Jas Walsh, Jos Bingham, Mary May, John Grogham, John McGiven, Michl McLaughlin, Patrick McHealy, Michl Warde, Hugh Knox, Robt Scullen, Mary Ann Murphy, Mary Ann Lynch, Jas Auell, Mary Auell, May Auell, Eliz Auell, Jas Auell, Mgt Foley, Robt Clarke, Honora Clarke, Thos Collins, Eugene Daly, Thos Healey, John Kiemann, Eliz Kiemann, Ellen Kiemann, Wm Kiemann, Mary Jane Kiemann, Tobias Boyce, Michl Doherty. Her officers: Capt Courtenay; Mr Berry, 1st ofcr; Mr Hastings, 2nd ofcr; Mr Coslett, 3rd ofcr; Mr Read, 4th ofcr; Mr Gallimore, 5th ofcr; Dr Partington, surgeon; Mr Hewston, purser; Mr Wagstaff, purser; & Mr Ashley, engineer. The names of the men comprising the crew of the vessel are not given. The total number of souls on board when the vessel left N Y was 177.

Col Steptoe, Maj Garnett, & Lts H H Walker, Jesup, Ihrie, Gregg, Peader, & J Mullin, of the U S Army, arrived at N Y in the ship **Illinois** from Calif.

Adm's sale of household & kitchen furniture at auction on Dec 3, at the late residence of Isaac Holland, deceased, 515 17th st west, by order of the Orphans Court of Wash Co, D C. -G F Barrett, adm -Wall & Barnard, aucts

Mr Gouldy, the father of the family who were victims to the ferocity of the son, is likely ro recover from his dangerous wounds. He has been informed of the suicide of his son. The other members of the family are doing well.

Lt F Allen, U S Navy, has tendered his resignation, to take effect from Dec 1st, for the purpose of accepting a position offered to him by the U S Mail Steamship Co, running between N Y & New Orleans.

Mrd: on Nov 24, in N Y, by Rev T H Taylor, Vicompte Jules Treidhard, First Sec of the French Legation at Wash, to Sarah Austin, daughter of Philip V Hoffman, of N Y C.

Died: on Nov 30, Capt John W Dellaway, in his 70th year. He was born in the State of Rhode Island, but for the last 40 years has been a resident of the District of Columbia. His funeral will take place this morning at 10 o'clock, from his late residence, 310 19th st.

Died: on Nov 30, in Wash City, Jas Bayard Clarke, late clerk in the Bank of the Metropolis, in his 43rd year. His funeral will take place at the E st Baptist Church on this day, Dec 1, at 2 o'clock.

Died: yesterday, in Wash City, Elisha M, son of Hon Elisha Whittlesey, in his 37th year. According to his request, his remains will be conveyed to Canfield, Ohio, the place of his birth, for interment. The procession that may attend it to the railroad depot will move from his late residence, 454 D st west, at 4 o'clock this afternoon.

Died: on Nov 30, Alexander Forrest, youngest son of Robt M & Catharine C Combs, aged 8 years, 3 months & 7 days. His funeral will be this afternoon, at 4 o'clock, from the residence of his parents, 611 8th st east.

Circuit Court of Wash Co, D C-in Chancery, No 1,301. W M Shuster et al vs Ignatius F Mudd et al. Wm R Woodward, trustee, reported that he sold part of lot 3 in square 431, in Wash City, on Aug 12 last, to Robt S Wharton, for $2,850, & hath complied with the terms of the sale. –Jno A Smith, clerk

THU DEC 2, 1858
Trustee's sale of machinery & fixtures of the Island Brewery, Dec 9, at the Brewery, on Maine ave, between 4½ & 6th sts. –Thos J Fisher, trustee -Jas C McGuire & Co, aucts

Adms sale of the personal effects of the late Felix Richards, at the auction rooms, on Dec 4, consisting of guns, clothing, tools, watches & chains, & trunks, etc. –C Gautier, adm -Jas C McGuire & Co, aucts

The survivors of the Kane expedition are rapidly thinning, & it is our duty today to chronicle the demise of another, Mr Francis C Walton, who was one of the bravest men under Dr Kane's command. He was about 55 years old when he died. His last months on earth were passed in the midst of destitution. –Phil Press

Two murderers, Jas McCormick & Thos Mulroe, who were sentenced to be hung at Haverstraw, N Y, on Dec 16, for murder, & who escaped from the Rockland Co jail 2 weeks ago, have been recaptured near Newcastle, Westchester Co, & taken back to the Rockland jail. The sentence of the law will be executed on the above day, in the yard of the court-house, at Haverstraw, in Rockland Co.

Mrs Mary Adams, Pa ave, opposite Brown's Hotel, has several unoccupied rooms, & can accommodate families & single gentlemen with board.

Died: on Sep 17, at **Fort Simcoe**, Wash Territory, Marianna Eaton, in her 27th year, wife of Maj Robt S Garnett, U S Army, & daughter of Geo S Nelson, of N Y C. Also, at the same place, on Oct 23, Arthur Nelson, her infant son, aged 7 months & 5 days.

Died: on Oct 6, in New Orleans, La, in her 58th year, Mrs Sarah Devaughn, for many years a resident of Wash.

FRI DEC 3, 1858
Circuit Court of Wash Co, D C-in Equity. Margaret Chandler, Danl T Chandler, Mary Chandler, & Joshua Humphreys & Margaret Ann his wife, against Wm Chandler, Walter Hay, Benj E Gantt, Walter C, Mary S W, Ann H, Edw C, Lucy, Richd, Catharine T, & Jane C Gantt, Margaret R Chandler & Mary J, & Wm L Chandler, & [blank] Browne & [blank] Taylor, & Mary his wife. The late Walter S Chandler died seized of divers real estate in this District, which was divided among his heirs at law, & upon such division, lots 18 thru 24, & another lot north of the above, all in Gtwn, D C, at the n w intersection of West & Congress sts, with the dwlg-house thereon, were assigned to said Margaret Chandler, his widow, for her dower in his estates; that the said house stands on said lots 18 & 19, & that the residue of said lots, except a portion of the lot on Congress st, are not necessary to said house; that they are unimproved, produce no income to the said widow, but, on the contrary, are an annual charge & expense to her in the taxes, & it would be advantageous to sell the same, & distribute the proceeds among said widow & heirs according to their rights. The bill further states that the dfndnts above named do not reside in this District, but in different & distant States; & the object of said bill is to have the unimproved lots 20 thru 24, & so much of the other lot on Congress st, which it is not necessary to attach to the said lots, & also lots 18 & 19, to increase the depth of the whole to 125 feet, sold, & the proceeds arising from such sale distributed among said cmplnts & dfndnts, under the direction of the Court, according to their rights, leaving the said house & lots 18 & 19 & part of the ground north thereof still to be enjoyed by said Margaret Chandler for her dower right. Absent dfndnts are to appear in this Court on the first Monday of May next to answer said bill. –Jno A Smith, clerk

Shocking murder at Boston on Tue: Johanna Crowley was killed at her residence by her husband, John Crowley, a laborer, in a fit of intoxication. Their 2 children witnessed the deed. Cowley made his escape. The deceased is represented as having been a quiet & industrious woman.

At Balt on Wed, in the public house of Mr Lawson P Keach, on Gay st, known as the Green House, two brothers, John & Thos Connery, had come to town in search of a missing animal belonging to their father. They failed to find it, & drank too many strong drinks & became intoxicated. John tried to get Thos to leave, when Thos immediately drew a pistol & shot his brother dead upon the spot, the ball entering near the left eye. The deceased was a single man, age about 26 years. Thos escaped. –Balt Patriot

Equity, No 1,301. Shuster & Clagett against Ignatius F Mudd & wife, Wm Dennesson & wife, & Messrs Smith, Hill, & Davis, reps of the Wash Bldg Association. The parties above named, the trustee, & creditors of Agnes Hammel, are notified that on Dec 24, at City Hall, Wash, I shall state the trustee's account, & the distribution of the fund. -W Redin, auditor

Calif: Edw H Sergent & Thos Brooks were playing cards at Shaw's Flat, Oct 23, when a quarrel ensued, during which Brooks seized a piece of stove-wood & struck Sergent over the head, fracturing his skull, the effects of which he died the next morning.

Equity, No 1,251. Hanson Gassaway's heirs against David Ott's heirs. I am directed by an order of the Circuit Court of Wash Co, D C, to state first the trustee's account with the trust fund; second, the amount due the dfndnts; third, the surplus in the trustee's hands; & to report whether the debt of the U S against said Ott's estate has been fully paid. All parties interested are to attend at the Auditor's room, in City Hall, Wash City, on Dec 13, 1858. —Wm R Woodward, special auditor

SAT DEC 4, 1858
The dwlg-house of Mr Richd O Mullikin, about 3 miles from Upper Marlborough, PG Co, Md, was entirely consumed by fire on Friday last. The loss is heavy, there being but partial insurance, about $1,800.

On Wed Thos Marsh, a gas inspector in the employ of the Manhattan Gaslight Co, came before Justice Quackenbush & made affidavit that he suspected P Muller, doing business at 426 Hudson st, was fraudulently using the company's gas. Upon inspection a lead pipe which supplied gas, as suspected, was attached to the company's service pipe, distributing pipes fixed in the house. The connecting pipe was detached & taken into court, as was also Muller; the latter committed for examination. –N Y Express

Detroit Free Press of Nov 30. Henry Jones, an American Lake captain, of the brig **Concord**, was shot in the head with a revolver on Nov 29, on board his vessel, lying near Port Sarnia, Canada, by Wm H Tyler, U S Deputy Marshal, of this city. Capt Jones also belonged to Detroit, having a residence about 9 miles out on the Grand River road, where his wife & one child are living at present. The ofcr was attempting to broad the brig to serve a writ of attachment on her, which was resisted, by the captain & crew. The writ grew out of the suit of the owner of the propeller **General Taylor**, from a collision between those 2 boats near Whitefish Point, Lake Superior. When Tyler boarded the brig he was met by Jones, who had an axe raised, as if to strike him. The crew was armed with handspikes & clubs. Jones died about an hour after he was shot.

For rent or lease, a small farm of about 20 acres on the Chesapeake & Ohio Canal, 2 miles above Gtwn. Inquire of Mr Andrew McLaughlin, Barnum's Hotel, or Mr Fred'k Wehr, 53 Fountain st, Fell's Point, Balt. Apply to the subscriber, 45 1st st, Gtwn. -H L Steuart

Chancery, No 1,227. John R Woods, cmplnt, against Jos S Clark, Edwin C Morgan, adm, & Anna Josephine Briscoe, Richd C Briscoe, Walter C Briscoe, Maria Jane Briscoe, & Theodore H Briscoe, heirs of Richd G Briscoe; Jos H Bradley, Wm B Kibbey, John A Linton, Augustus E Perry, Richd H Clarke, Aloysius N Clements; the Trustees of the Bank of Metropolis, Wash; Chas Stott, Moses Kelley, Thos Purcell, Geo Parker, Thos Parker, Benj L Jackson, Wm B Jackson, Thos T Barnes, John R Mitchell; Selden, Withers & Co, Isaac Clarke; Trustees of the Bank of Wash, David M Mahon, Jos L Peabody, Ann M Smith, Mary McDaniel, Devere O'Brien, Geo W Graffin, Geo P Frick, Robt Close, Francis Dandelet, Jas Sangster & Co, Isaac Pollard, Pitman & Baldwin, Jos & W C Simms & Co, & Jos S Clarke, guardian ad litem of Maria Jane & Walter C Briscoe, dfndnts. By order of the Circuit Court of D C, I am directed to state the amount due to the cmplnt on his judgment against the late Richd G Briscoe, & an account of all other judgments & debts of all his other creditors, & of Briscoe & Clarke; & to take an account of the personal estate of said Richd G Briscoe, & also the real estate, & the value thereof, held by him & by said Jos S Clarke, & the liens & encumbrances charged thereon, & now due & unpaid; & to report if it be necessary to resort to said real estate, & what part thereof is liable for the debts of said cmplnt & of said creditors. The investigation will be commenced on Dec 28, in my ofc, in the City Hall, Wash.
–W Redin, auditor

Died: on Nov 3, William Buchanan Burch, youngest son of Thos W & Martha Burch, aged 2 years & 3 months. His funeral is this afternoon at 3 o'clock, from the residence of his parents, 368 5th st.

Died: in Orange Co, Va, in his 39th year, Marcus Bull, a kind father, devoted husband, & a faithuful friend. Through a protracted illness he was patient & uncomplaining.
–W [No death date given-appears to be a current item.]

Died: on Nov 13, in Handsboro, Miss, Saml J Fowler, in his 48th year, a native of Wash City, but for the last 18 or 20 years a resident of Mississippi.

Circuit Court of Wash Co, D C, in Chancery. Newman et al vs Newman et al. The trustee sold lot 8 in square 288 to J M Graham for $945; part of lot 5 in square 243 to Jas Carroll for $600, being the part of said lots belonging to the estate of the late Eliz W Newman; & on Nov 8, 1858, he also sold the north half of lot 26, in square 254, & improvements, to Dr Chas H Lieberman, for $8,324, & that the purchasers complied with the terms of sale. –Jno A Smith, clerk

Brookhill School, 6 miles north of Charlottesville, Va, begins Sep 1st. Chas Minor, M D, A M, U Va. Assistants: Rhodes Massie & Wm R Abbott.

MON DEC 6, 1858
Mrd: on Nov 30, at St George's Church, N Y, by Rev Stephen H Tyng, D D, Henry Everdell to Mary H, daughter of Thos Ewbank, of that city.

Died: on Dec 5, in Wash City, Charlotte Bleecker, relict of the late Vinal Luce, in her 70th year. Her funeral will be from the residence of her son, Lt S B Luce, U S N, 394 20th st, on Dec 7 at 2 o'clock.

Died: on Dec 4, in Wash City, after an illness of 24 hours, of scarlet fever, Fannie Stillwagon, aged 3 years, 9 months & 4 days, youngest daughter of J J & M G Mulloy. Her funeral will be this afternoon at 3½ o'clock, from the residence of her parents, 507 north C st.

Died: on Nov 26, Mrs Susan Armstrong, wife of John B Sherrard, & daughter of David Gibson, aged 30 years. Long forewarned of her approaching end, they marked with painful solicitude the steady progress of her insidious disease as it gradually undermined her constitution, enfeebled her strength, & caused her beauty to consume away like a moth. Months ago, convinced that her recovery was hopeless, by a deliberate act, she gave up her children, four in number, the eldest 10, the youngest 2 years of age, into the hands of her covenant God, claiming on their behalf the fulfillment of his promise, I will be a God to thee & to thy seed after thee; & thenceforward endeavored to divest her mind of all anxious care respecting them. After one of her severest paroxysms, her children assembled at her bedside & each received a Bible from her trembling hand.

Equity, No 1,116. Thos R Bird, against Jas C McGuire, adm, & Rebecca E Brown, widow, & Jos Brown, heirs of John D Brown & of Alice Brown. Trustee's account to be stated & the funds in hand distributed among the creditors of John D Brown, deceased, on Dec 27, City Hall, Wash. -W Redin, auditor

Orphans Court of Wash Co, D C. Letters of administration on the personal estate of Wm Roberts, late of Wash Co, deceased. –E Owen, adm

TUE DEC 7, 1858
Mrd: on Oct 8, 1858, at Astoria, Oregon Territory, by Rev Dr McCarty, Chaplain U S A, Lt Geo H Mendell, U S A, to Miss Ellen, daughter of Gen John Adair, of Astoria.

Mrd: on Nov 29, at the residence of the bride's father, near Columbus, Tenn, by Rev Dr Pise, Jos Branch to Miss Mary Jones, daughter of Dr J W Polk.

Died: on Nov 24, in All Saints Parish, S C, Charles Calvert Stuart Post, aged 15 months & 15 days, son of Dr Wm M & Mary L Post. Suffer little children to come unto me, & forbid them not, for of such is the kingdom of Heaven.

Criminal Court-Wash, Mon. Grand Jury sworn:

Geo W Riggs, foreman	Buckner Bayliss	Enos Ray
Judson Mitchell	Wm J Stone, sr	Joshua Pearce
Jas Towles	Geo A Bohrer	Chas R Belt
Wm Orme	Benj F Middleton	John Purdy
Gregory Ennis	Jas C McGuire	Jos N Fearson
Geo Chipman	Wm F Bayly	Ham Loughborough

Chas L Coltman
Dr Chas Nichols
Petit Jury:
Notley Moreland
Wm Cleary
Edw H Edelin
Wm Flenner
Wm B Evans
John R Murray
Thos Young
John F Bridgett
Vincent Masi
David A Gardiner

Geo S Gideon
Dr Thos Miller

Thos B Entwisle
Francis Mattingly
John F B Pursell
Wm Egan
John B Ward
Robt K Nevitt
John B Turton
John Van Reswick
John S Magee
John T Clements

Geo Mattingly
Wm B Todd

Peter Berry
Jas Rhoades
John H Trunnell
Geo B Smith
John R McGregor
Wm Sanderson
Leonidas Bowen
Jas Murray
Robt H Watkins
Jas S Barnard

The Fisher Girl, the beautiful marble statue by Mr Barbee, a native citizen, has been brought from Richmond some days ago, is still at the Capitol, & will be found in the artist's studio, & can be seen seen & admired.

WED DEC 8, 1858
Senate: 1-The Vice Pres laid before the Senate a report from the Chief Clerk of the Court of Claims, transmitting the opinions of that court adverse to the claims of Thos C Nye, of Mary E D Blaney, admx of Geo Blaney, of Alex'r M Cumming, of S Bowman & Geo Brinker, surviving exec of Isaac Bowman, & of the State of Alabama against the U S, under the act of her admission into the Union; also opinions in favor of the claims of Thos Allen, of John Peebles, of Nancy M Johnson, admx of Walter R Johnson, & of Emilie G Jones, excx of Thos P Jones, deceased; which were severally ordered to lie on the table for the present. 2-Mr Cameron gave notice of his intention to introduce a bill granting a pension to the widow of Gen Persifer F Smith. 3-Mr Seward gave notice of his intention to introduce a bill granting a pension to Mrs Myra Clarke Gaines.

House of Reps: 1-Ptn of Thos Price for bounty land. 2-Ptn of Orrin Abbott for pension. 3-Bill for the relief of Wm Lyon late pension agent of Knoxville, Tenn.

Tally-ho Razors: shaving cream, brushes, Razor Strops, & perfumery & toilette articles, just received & for sale. –E K Lundy, 390 Pa ave, Nat'l Hotel Bldg.

J M Ainsa, who was attached to Crabbe's party of invaders of the Mexican province of Sonora, & nearly all of whom were massacred at the mission of Santa Inez, has been released by the gov't of Sonora, & returned to San Francisco.

Rt Rev Henry U Onderdonk died at his residence in Phil on Monday last. He was a native of N Y; at one period the rector of St Ann's Church, Brooklyn; in 1827 chosen Assist Bishop of Pa; succeeded Bishop White as head of the diocese, after the decease of Bishop White; & in 1845 Bishop Onderdonk resigned his office & was succeeded by Bishop Potter. –Phil American

Judge Hart, city solicitor of Cincinnati, was run over on Wed by a railroad train at Loveland, Ohio, & died the next day. He attempted to jump on the train while in motion.

A St Petersburgh journal, by one of the late arrivals, announces that the tenor Malmanoff, while on the stage, murdered prima donna Averonich. No details are given.

Among the visitors now in Wash City is Hon Volney E Howard, formerly a member of Congress from Texas, & now a citizen of Calif.

Information wanted of Mr Eugene Secretan, a native of Switzerland, about 40 years of age, near 5 feet 7 inches in height, slender built, fair complexion, speaking English quite imperfectly, & a gentleman in his bearing & address. He left St Louis, Mo, for Paducah, Ky, en route for Knoxville, Tenn, on Oct 17, 1857, on board the steamboat **Daniel Boone**. He is known to have reached Paducah, but further nothing is known of him, nor whether he be living or dead. A reward of $100 will be given for authentic information of him, if alive, or of his death, if not, to Rev Frederic Esperandien, Knoxville, Tenn, or Hon Horace Maynard, Wash.

On Wed, at the village of Salem, Wash Co, N Y, Martin Wallace was executed for the murder of Barney McEntee. The parties were friends, & Wallace committed murder for money.

Mrd: on Tue, by Rev John C Smith, Mr Chas H Morgan to Miss Georgiana Shackelford, both of Fairfax Co, Va.

Died: on Dec 2, at Chapel Hill, N C, Sue, wife of Prof Wm J Martin, & youngest daughter of the late Wm McCoy, of the Univ of Va.

Died: last evening, after a brief & painful illness of scarlet fever, little Ridie, daughter of Edmond & Eugenia Brooke, aged 6 years & 1 month. Her funeral will take place from the residence of her grandmother, Mrs Maria A Queen, 289 7th st, between L & M sts, on Thu at 10 o'clock.

Died: on Dec 6, at Alexandria, Thos C Atkinson, a native of Balt, but for the last 9 years a resident of Alexandria. He was the chief engineer of the Orange & Alexandria railroad from the commencement of the work; & was eminent in his profession, & generally beloved & esteemed by all who knew him.

THU DEC 9, 1858
Hon Fred'k Nash, Chief Justice of the Supreme Court of N C, died at his residence in Hillsborough on Dec 4. He had but just overcome a recent attack of sickness, & was in fine health; had just returned from a visit to his native town, Newbern, where he was a member of the Synod of the Presbyterian Church, which recently met in that place. He was born in Newbern in 1781.

Excellent household & kitchen furniture at auction on Dec 15, at the residence of Baron Gerol_, Prussian Minister, on G st, between 14th & 15th sts. -Jas C McGuire & Co, aucts

Rev John T Roddan, pastor of the Catholic Church in Purchase st, Boston, died there on Friday. He was a graduate of the College of Propaganda at Rome, & was a man of ability. He was a native of Boston, & lacked just one month of being 40 years of age. -Boston Post

Mrs Mary Beall, wife of the late David Beall, who assisted in cutting the logs for the first house ever built in Cumberland, Md, died there a few days ago, aged 90 years. Her husband, to whom she was married 70 years ago, died a couple of years since.

On Sat near Portland, the 5 year old daughter of Mr Nathan W Smith was so dreadfully burnt, that she died in a few hours. She had been fastened in a room with her younger brother while her mother was temporarily absent, & it appears that in attempting to light a lamp her clothes caught fire, as did also the clothes of the little boy. A man heard the screams & broke the window to get to the little girl. She was enveloped in flames & died that evening. The little boy was only slightly burnt.

Wm Schwitzer, alias Sanders, was hung on Friday at Goshen, N Y, for the murder of a German man-servant employed in the family of Mr Chas Reeves, & the attempted murder of a German woman in the same family. He was tried on Oct 14 at Newburgh, when the woman testified against him & he was sentenced to death.

Mrd: on Dec 7, in Wash City, by Rev Dr Smith Pyne, Mr Sydney A Legare, of S C, to Miss Emily S Green, daughter of Thos Green, & grand-daughter of the late Thos Ritchie.

Mrd: on Dec 7, in Wash City, at St Matthew's Church, by Rev Mr Boyle, Alphonso T T Donn to Miss Charlotte Rainey, all of Wash City.

Died: on Dec 8, in Wash City, Mrs Eliza J Wheat, wife of J H Wheat, in her 48th year. Her funeral will take place from St Paul's Lutheran Church, H & 11th sts, Fri, 3 o'clock.

Died: on Tue, after an illness of 48 hours, Chas Capner Coltman, in his 23rd year. His funeral will take place this afternoon at 2 o'clock, from the residence of his father, Chas L Coltman, & will proceed to the 2nd Presbyterian Church on H st, between 13th & 14th.

Died: on Dec 6, John Burr, in his 73rd year, many years a resident of Wash City.

Died: on Dec 6, in Wash City, after a few hours' illness, of croup, Americus M C Zappone, eldest son of Margaret Ann & Americus Zappone, in his 4½ year.

A bill has passed the House of Reps of Georgia, by a vote of 56 to 52, prohibiting the <u>intermarriage of first cousins</u>, under a severe penalty, & cutting off the inheritance of issue.

Died: on Dec 5, at Warren Green Hotel, in Warrenton, Va, from an injury sustained by a fall on the previous day, Dr Jas D Hitt, in his 58th year. Dr Hitt was a native of the Edgefield district, S C. After graduating in his profession in early life he settled near Rectortown, Fauquier Co, Va, where he married & spent several years; removed to Georgia until the death of his wife, when he returned to the place of his early adoption. A short time after which that awful scourge, the yellow fever, visiting Norfolk, leaving its inhabitants almost at the mercy of the humane from a distance, Dr Hitt fearlessly left his home & devoted his time & talents to the relief of that striken population. He has left many friends in this community to sympathize with his 2 children, the only survivors of his name, who, away in the sunny clime of the South, will hear the tidings of their said bereavement, -J H R

A fire occurred on the farm of Mr Wm D Prather, about 4 miles from Annapolis, Md, on Wed last, & destroyed a new barn, wheat, corn, & farming utensils. Loss about $1,500.

Mrs Johanna Klingeman, in a suit against the N Y & N H Railroad Co, for damages for the loss of her husband, caused by carelessness of their employees, got a verdict in the Supreme Court, Westchester Co, at White Plains, before Judge Ingraham, on Nov 22, for the sum of $5,000.

Wash Corp-Mon: 1-Ptn from Mary Childs, asking to be remunerated for certain services rendered by her: referred to the Cmte on the Asylum. 2-Ptn from Robt W Middleton for the remission of a fine imposed on his son, Henry Middleton, a minor, for carrying dangerous weapons: referred to the Cmte of Claims. 3-Ptn of Jos Gerhardt; of M Pinkin; & of Wm Boyd, each for the remission of a fine: referred to the Cmte of Claims. 4-Bill for the relief of Agnes Reagan: passed.

Orphans Court of Wash Co, D C. In the case of Jno H G McCutchen, adm of Thos Hawkins, deceased, the Court & administrator appointed Jan 4 next, for the final settlement of the personal estate of said deceased, of the assets in hand.
-Ed N Roach, Reg/o wills

Criminal Court-Wash-Wed. 1-Thos Gorman convicted of larceny of a silver fruit basket from John H Wheeler. 2-Albert Parris found not guilty for assault & battery with intent to kill Jas O'Day on Jul 5 last. 3-Alex'r H Loughborough was today admitted to practice at the bar of this court. [Dec 10th newspaper: Thos Gorman was sentenced to 2½ years in the penitentiary.]

Circuit Court of D C-in Equity. Augusta McBlair, by John H McBlair, her next friend, & Julia Ten Eyck, by John C Ten Eyck, her next friend, plntfs, versus John G McBlair, Virginia G McBlair, John H McBlair, jr, Julia T McBlair, Chas R McBlair, Andrew J McBlair, Augusta Ten Eyck, Julia Ten Eyck, Jane Ten Eyck, Mary Ten Eyck, John C Ten Eyck, & Wm Gadsby, Ann Sophia Newton, Margaret S Chapman, & Alexander McIntire, dfndnts. This suit is to obtain a decree for the sale of certain real estate in Wash City, D C, of which the late John Gadsby died seized & possessed. John Gadsby devised the same by his will & testament to his trustees, to wit: His wife, Provey Gadsby,

& his friends, Jas Eakin & Alex'r McInitre, the survivor & survivors of them, & to the heirs of said survivor, to be held by them as by the said will was declared; that is to say, that they should permit his wife, Provey Gadsy, for & during her natural life, to occupy & possess all that real estate in the Corp of Wash, in square 167, with all bldgs thereon, & to take the profits & issues, without interference of any person & without impeachment of waste, & at her death then that the said excs, trustee, & their survivors should hold the same & every part thereof for the benefit of his two daughters, Augusta McBlair & Julia Gadsby, [now Julia Ten Eyck,] in equal moieties; for life, respectively, with remainders over, &, in the event of either dying without issue living at her death, with cross remainders over to the issue of said daughters, respectively, living at the time of their death, respectively, or to the survivor for life & to the issue of said survivor living at the time of her death, if one should died leaving no living issue & the other surviving her, & that in the event that both said daughters should die leaving no issue of either living at the time of the death of either, the said estate, as the plaintiffs are advised & charge, would revert to the right heirs of said John Gadsby. That the said Provey Gadsby & Jas Eakin are dead; that said Augusta McBlair hath issue, to wit, 6 children; that said Julia Ten Eyck hath issue, to wit, 5 children; that said John Gadsby left as his right heirs, besides his said daughters, Augusta & Julia, his children, Wm Gadsby, Ann Sophia Newton, & Margaret S Chapman; that of the real estate in said square 167 a large portion, [about 50,000 or 60,000 square feet] are vacant & unimproved, which, together with that part that is improved & built upon, embracing the whole property left by testator in said square, the plaintiffs desire to be sold by a decree of the Court, under & by virtue of an act of Congress entitled "An act to authorize the Circuit Court of D C to decree the sale of real estate in certain cases," approved Aug 18, 1856, [2 vol Statues at Large, page 118;] that the said property is unproductive as to a part of it, being vacant & unimproved, &, as to that improved & built on, is less beneficial in its present condition to the life tenants than it would be if the same were sold & the proceeds invested in more profitable securities, & that the sale of the same would not impair or injure the rights of any other persons; that, in order to effect these objects, the bill prays that the trustees may be appointed to make sale of said property, under the decree of the Court, on such terms & with such notice as to time & place of sale as the Court in its wisdom may appoint, & that the said Court will invest the said proceeds for the interests of the parties as it may think best. Dfndnts John H McBlair, jr, & Augusta, Julia, Jane, May, & John C Ten Eyck, children of John C Ten Eyck, are non residents of D C; said absent dfndnts are to appear in this Court on the First Mon in May next & answer said bill. –Jno A Smith, clk -Chilton & Magruder, solicitors

FRI DEC 10, 1858
Senate: 1-Memorial of Chas Abert, atty-at-law, asking to be allowed the balance of his fees for professional services in connexion with the Wash Aqueduct, rejected by Capt Meigs on the settlement of his account. 2-Two memorials from Capt D G Farragut, of the U S Navy-one asking to be allowed the amount of compensation estimated by the Navy Dept for the commandant of the Calif navy yard, during the time he was in command; the other, to be allowed an amount paid by him to two master's mates enlisted by him under authority of the Navy Dept & rejected on the settlement of his accounts.

Mr Foster Hale, the inventor of raised letters for the use of the blind, fell down dead on a pavement in Selma, Ala, on Nov 26. [No other information.]

On Friday last Mr McElroy, of Salisbury Mills, Orange Co, was killed on the Erie railroad by jumping from a freight train on the Newburg Branch Road. He jumped off just as the train was passing his house, & lost his life.

Died: on Dec 8, in Wash City, Mary Ann Wall, aged 63 years, a member of the religious Society of Friends, & mother of Wm Wall, of the firm of Wall, Stephens & Co, & of Capt Nicholas Wall, of St Louis, Missouri. The deceased has been a resident of Wash City for many years, & one of its oldest teachers. Her funeral will take place on Sat at 2 o'clock, from 542 H st, near 6th.

SAT DEC 11, 1858
Chas Tallian, Henry G Daun, & Chas Memott have been arrested in Europe as a part of the gang concerned in the forgery of the bills of the Nat'l Bank of Austria.'

Wm R Harris, a resident of Albany, but stopping with his brother in Troy, N Y, died very suddenly on Sat from drinking valerian. Coroner's verdict: Wm R Harris came to his death from gangrenous inflammation of the stomach, produced by intemperate habits. He was 31 years of age, & leaves a wife & 2 children. –Troy Whig, Dec 6

Capt T J Brittain, of the Ordnance Dept, has resigned. His resignation has been accepted by the Pres, to take effect on Dec 20 next.

Miss Abbie Summers, of Livingston Co, N Y, who had been connected with the Female College at Oberlin, Ohio, was most shockingly burnt on Friday. While putting fluid in her lamp, the fluid caught fire & she was instantly enveloped in flames.

Members of the Ladies' Union Benevolent Society to relieve the Poor of Wash:
Managers:

Mrs E B Mills	Rev Mrs J B Harold
Rev Mrs Wm McLain	Mrs T F Harkness
Mrs M A Cox	Rev Mr Mason Noble
Mrs De Noble Young	Mrs De Selding
Mrs P D Gurley	Mrs Wm H Winter
Mrs Enoch Tucker	Mrs S W Houston
Mrs Columbus Munroe	Mrs J C G Kennedy
Miss Mary Scott	Mrs Bolivar Knox
Mrs Stephen P Hill	Mrs G W Samson
Miss Kitty Smith	Mrs Capt Woodhull
Mrs Capt Talcott	Mrs T U Walter
Mrs Wm Bell	*Mrs Brown
Mrs Danl Ratcliffe	

[Dec 29th newspaper: this list is repeated in the Dec 29 newspaper, except the name of Mrs Brown is replaced by that of Mrs Brawner.]

Sister Mary Eleanor, of St Francis Xavier, died on Dec 4, at the Carmelite Convent in Balt. She was of one of the old Md families. Her sister, Mrs Ann Mattingly, is known by many, as is her brother, Thos Carbery, Pres of the Bank of the Metropolis, Wash. At the time of her death, Sister Eleanora was in her 86th year, & the 47th of her conventual life. A requiem mass was offered for the repose of her soul on Monday last; & her burial, with the usual religious rites, took place on the same day. –Catholic Mirror

Senate: 1-Ptn of Carl Beoher, of N Y, praying for an increase of pension: laid on the table. 2-Ptn of E B Boutwell, a cmder in the navy, praying compensation for certain extra services while in command of the U S steamer **Colonel Harney** & the U S ship **John Adams**: ordered to lie on the table until the cmtes shall have been appointed.

We have before us an extra of the Mount Vernon Record, published in Phil, which announces the payment on Dec 2, through Geo W Riggs, of Wash City, Treasurer of the *Mount Vernon Ladies' Association*, the sum of $57,000 with interest, to John A Washington, that sum constituting the first bond due him by the association. The eloquent appeal of the Regent of the Association, [Miss Cunningham,] is now before the public. Clubs of 10, 20, or more persons can remit to the Regent; Mrs Susan L Pellet, Corr Sec, Richmond, Va; or Vice Regents representing the *Mount Vernon* interest in other States.

Died: on Dec 9, in Wash City, Mrs Mary A Lee, in her 40th year, relict of the late Hon E Smith Lee, of Detroit, Mich. Her funeral is at 3 o'clock on Sunday, from the Church of the Epiphany, on G st, between 13th & 14th sts.

Died: in Wash City, Jane Appleton Means Pierce Perry, aged 2 years & 3 months, infant child of Chas M & Susan E Perry. Her funeral will take place on Sunday at 2 o'clock, from 533 M st. [No death date given.]

Salem, Mass, Dec 9. The boiler in the tannery of Mr J B Lord, of Salem, exploded today killing Mr Henry Miller, engineer of the concern. The bldg was demolished.

MON DEC 13, 1858
Splendid parlor suites, mattresseses, household furniture, & window shades at public auction on Dec 10th, at the establishnent of Geo T Smallwood, 508 7th st.
-Jas C McGuire & Co, aucts

Judge John McLean, of Wash Co, N Y, died a few days ago. He was an intimate personal & political friend of Silas Wright & ex-Sec Marcy, & filled many offices of distinction, conferred upon him while they occupied the Gubernatorial chair of N Y.

The Michigan papers announce the conviction & sentence of Fuller & Walker for the murder of Mr Holden, at Ann Harbor. This man's life was insured for $29,000, the payment of which was resisted by the companies on the ground that the deceased had committed suicide. Such resistance was made that Mrs Holden compromised the case of $20,000, & so lost $9,000.

Dissolution of the partnership between the subscribers, under the title of Harvey & Adams, by mutual consent, on Nov 1. The books of H & A may be found at the store of F L Harvey & Co, at the old stand, 325 Pa ave. F L Harvey will continue the Hardware business. -F L Harvey, Geo R Adams, Thos J Adams

Orphans Court of Wash Co, D C. Letters testamentary on the personal estate of Thos H Benton, late of Wash Co, deceased. –M Blair, exc

At St Louis, on Dec 8, a respectable German, Henry Linhoff, killed Dr Edw Van Der Roecke, who had been some 2 years in this country, & for 7 or 8 months acquainted with Mary Ann Costanz, to whom he was married one month ago. She was a widow; her maiden name was Mary Ann Linhoff, & Henry Linhoff is her brother. Before marrying her Van Der Roecke practiced in the country in this region, but on his marriage received from her money, with which he furnished an office in good style. On the 3rd day after the wedding he began to abuse his wife by scurrilous reproaches. He appeared to have only wished her money & was going to abandon her. She checked into his past & found letters written to him from Wurtemburg, Germany, showing he had forsaken a wife who was still living in that city. Her brother, Henry Linhoff, reproached the Doctor for deceiving his sister, when the Doctor replied that he also had found himself deceived in her. At this remark Linhoff drew his revolver & shot the Doctor through the heart, & then surrendered himself into custody.

Died: on Dec 6, at the Eutaw House, Balt, John Elgar, inventor & mechanician, aged 75 years. He was truly a friend, a man of childlike simplicity & modesty. –G W

Died: on Dec 11, in Wash City, John Florentius Cox, aged 76 years. His funeral is on Tue at 2 o'clock, from 466 13th st, near Pa ave.

TUE DEC 14, 1858
Stribling Springs School, Augusta Co, Va, is preparatory to Univ of Va: session begins the last Monday in Sep & ends the first Fri in June each year. Apply to the Principal or Proprietor: J Hotchkiss, Principal; C Kinney, Proprietor; P H Woodward, Hotel-keeper. References: Rev B M Smith, D D, U T Seminary, Va; T C Walker, Wash, D C; A A Chapman, Wash, D C; Rev U H Ruffner, Harrisonburg, Va; N C Kinney, Staunton, Va.

Criminal Court-Wash-Mon: 1-John McConn found not guilty for stealing a watch, because the act was committed within limits of the State of Va; he was held for a requisition from the Govn'r of Va. 2-John G Nichols not guilty in beating his wife. 3-Arthur Thynne, a marine, acquitted of stealing gold coins. 4-Convicted of a rout at the Park: Geo Beall, in consideration of having been 5 months in jail already, to a fine of $1; Burnett West to a fine of $15, & prayed in commitment until paid; sentence of John Hammond is suspended in consequence of his illness at this time.

House of Reps: 1-Memorial of Gregory Patti, praying that a pension may be granted him: referred.

Senate: 1-Ptn from Oscar J E Stuart, setting forth that his slave was the inventor of a useful agricultural machine, for which the Com'r of Patents refused a patent, on the ground that a machine invented by a slave, though it be new & useful, could not be in the present state of the law patented; & asking that the patent laws may be so amended that a patent may issue to the master: referred. 2-Ptn from Jonas P Levy, asking immediate attention of Congress to his claim against Mexico: referred. 3-Ptn from Ellinor Gardiner, asking compensation for property destroyed during the war with Great Britain: referred. 4-Ptn from Wm E Haskill, asking to be allowed the commutation pay due his ancestor: referred. 5-Ptn from Jas E Holmes, asking an extension of his patent for an improvement in the construction of chairs for invalids: referred. 6-Ptn from the heirs of John Waire, a soldier of the Revolution, praying to be allowed a pension: referred. 7-Ptn from Mary Featherston, widow of a boatswain in the navy, asking to be allowed a half-pay pension: referred. 8-Ptn from Benj Chadbron, asking to be allowed the difference between the amount of pension he received & the amount he should have received for a total disability: referred. 9-Bill for the relief of Henry G Carter, adm of Curtis Gull, deceased. 10-Bill for the relief of Wm Wallace, of Ill: referred to the Cmte on Pensions. 11-Bill for the relief of Lewis Cass Forsyth: referred to the Cmte on Military Affairs. 12-Bill for the relief of Francis Dainese: referred to the Cmte on Foreign Relations. 13-Bill for the relief of Jane Perry: referred to the Cmte on Pensions.

Mrd: on Monday, by Rev John C Smith, Mr Jas W Deale to Miss Barbara Ann Brumback, both of Va.

Mrd: on Dec 9, in Columbus, Ohio, Mr Bertram Woodward, formerly of Wash City, to Miss Harriet Overmeyer, of Columbus.

Died: on Dec 13, of scarlet fever, William, son of William H & Eliz Dennesson, aged 4 years & 10 months. His funeral is this afternoon at 3 o'clock, from the residence of his parents, 383 5th st, between G & H sts.

Died: on Dec 13, after a painful illness of a few months, Emma, wife of Dr W Brooke Jones. Her funeral is Dec 15 at 3 o'clock, from the residence of her husband, 9th & G sts.

St Louis, Dec 13. Hon Saml Medary has arrived in this city, on his way to Kansas, to enter upon his duties as Govn'r of that Territory.

WED DEC 15, 1858
Gen G J Pillow, of Tenn, is in Wash City, a guest at the residence of his brother-in-law, Hon A V Brown, Postmaster General.

Lt J M Gilliss, U S Navy, whom the Smithson Institution some time since dispatched on an astronomical expedition to South America, has returned home.

Hon Thos Ruffin, of Alamance Co, has been chosen to fill the vacancy on the bench of the supreme court of N C, occasioned by the death of Chief Justice Nash.

Capt Jas N Ward, 3rd regt of U S infty, died at St Anthony, Minn, on Dec 6. He was a native of Georgia, & was a gallant & worthy officer. His disease was consumption.

Senate: 1-Ptn from Jos Stockbridge, a chaplain in the U S Navy, complaining of certain persecutions to which he had been subjected in consequence of refusing to use the Episcopal liturgy, in the performance of public worship on board the U S frig **Savannah**, under the command of Saml Mercer, & bearing the broad pennant of Cmdor W D Salter, in the Rio de la Plata: referred to the Cmte on Military Affairs. 2-Ptn from Haym M Salomon, asking to be reimbursed certain moneys advanced by his father to Jas Wilson, Jas Madison, Arthur Lee, Jno T Mercer, Theo Bland, jr, Jos Jones, Edmund Randolph, & others, with a note from Mr Reed, Pres of the Continental Congress, to Haym Salomon: referred. 3-Ptn from J Hosford Smith, that he is engaged in the establishment of a line of screw steamers on a coasting route from the port of N Y, & desires to be allowed to purchase them in England or Scotland [where he can avail himself of their experience in the construction of iron vessels] free of duty: referred.

House of Reps: 1-Memorial of Archibald Mereman, a soldier of the war of 1812, asking Congress to grant him a pension: referred. 2-Memorial of Capt Jonas P Levy, asking Congress to empower the Pres to take such steps as may be necessary to obtain from the Gov't of Mexico indemnity for seizure of the Pedrigal Mines, in Tasco; also for indemnity for false imprisonment & illegal duties exacted: referred.

Daring robbery on Monday night upon the jeweller's & silversmith's store of Mr N Jensen, 9th & D sts, one door south of Mr Geo S Gideon's printing ofc. No clue to the perpetrators has yet been found.

Died: on Dec 14, Arthur, son of Jas & Eliz Bowen, aged 2 years & 9 months. His funeral is tomorrow at 10 o'clock, from the residence of his father, 606 Md ave, south.

Died: on Dec 7, at her residence in Keokuk, Iowa, Mrs Anne Clark Belknap, widow of the late Brvt Brig Gen Belknap, U S Army, in her 58th year.

Died: on Nov 20, in the city of Lexington, Missouri, in her 51st year, Mrs Sarah Ann Middleton, wife of Mr Jas H Middleton. She was a native of Wash City, of which Mr Mr was also formerly a resident. She was an exemplary Christian.

Died: on Dec 5, in St Louis, Missouri, at an advanced age, Mrs Jane Patterson, relict of the late Dr Thos Patterson, & for many years a resident of Montg Co, Md.

THU DEC 16, 1858
Trustee's sale by decree of the Circuit Court of D C, on Jan 6, 1859, of a spacious frame house & the land attached, being the late residence of Thos Perkins, deceased, adjoining Good Hope, on the Marlboro road, about 1 mile from the Anacostia or Navy Yard bridge: contains 15 acres of ground. –John Costigan, trustee -A Green auct

Household & kitchen furniture at auction on Dec 20, at the residence of Gov Walker, who is about leaving Wash, corner of I & 20th sts. –C W Boteler, auct

By virtue of the Orphans Court of Wash Co, D C, the undersigned will sell at public sale on Dec 21, for cash, at Huseville, Chas Co, Md, 40 likely negroes.
–Violet A Williams, admx of Wm H Williams.

New Orleans, Dec 13, 1858. Lt Geo F White, who was carried off on board the schnr **Susan** from Mobile, arrived here this day, by the barque **Oregon**, from Barbadoes, having been put on board that vessel on Thu last, 2 days out from Mobile Point. He reports that, on finding the schnr under way, he ordered the captain to come to anchor; which order was refused, & the vessel proceeded to sea. She was commanded by Capt Maury, & had on board Frank Anderson, Col Bruneau, Col McDonald, Maj Elli, Col Rudler, Capt West, & other officers, & about 250 men, armed with revolvers, side-arms, & rifles. They declared that they were going to Greytown, in Nicaragua. Lt White will be dispatched to Mobile tomorrow, & will probably be called thence to Wash to report to the Gov't in person.

Lord Napier's successor, Hon Richd Brickerton Pemell Lyons, has been resident Minister at Florence since June last. He is the eldest son of Adm Lord Lyons, & has been regularly trained in the diplomatic service, having entered it in 1839, being then 22, as attaché at Athens, where his father, then Capt Sir Edmund Lyons, represented the British Crown. He was long resident in Greece, a short time at Dresden; & for several years lately at Florence, whence he was sent to Naples in Mar, 1856. –Albion

Col John Lind Smith, Maj of Engineers, U S Army, died in N Y on Dec 13. He served with distinction in the Mexican war under Lt Gen Scott, & received the brevets of colonel & lt-colonel for his services. He was a native of Charleston, S C.

Saml Barnes, for many years the able editor & conductor of the newspaper at Fred'k, Md, died at his residence in Balt Co yesterday at the advanced age of 72 years. He has filled many positions of honor & trust in his native State & city, & always with marked credit & ability.

F W Lincoln, jr, was re-elected Mayor of Boston on Monday by over 2,000 plurality. He was the Citizen's candidate, Moses Kimball, Republican, has 4,372 votes, & Julius A Palmer, Temperance, 1,130 votes.

Court of Claims, Dec 15, 1858. The case of Wm H Wigg vs the U S, was interrupted by Hon Judge Gilchrist being called home by the sickness & death of his mother.

Rev John Larkin, one of the ministers of the Roman Catholic Church at St Francis Xavier, in N Y, died very suddenly on Sat.

Senate: 1-Ptn from Pierre Ogilvie Beebee, asking the aid of Congress in publishing a book on American law: referred. 2-Ptn from Jas Roye, of Ark, styling himself freeman & real estate holder in Marion Co, urging the influence of the Senate against the admission of Kansas as a slave State, because there is no clause in the Declaration of Independence, Articles of Confederation, or in the Constitution of the U S warranting the slavery of human beings: referred. 3-Ptn of Mrs H B Macomb widow of Gen Alex'r Macomb, for a pension: referred. 4-Ptn of Fred'k Griffing, praying payment of an amount claimed to be due to him for land purchased by the Sec of the Navy for the navy yard at Brooklyn: referred. 5-Ptn from Ann Scott, widow of Wm B Scott, deceased, praying that authority be given the accounting officers of the Treasury to allow her a commission upon the disbursements of her said husband as pension agent: referred.

In the U S District Court at Portland on Friday John A Miller was sentenced to 10 years hard labor, in the State prison for mail robbery. Chas Foster, his accomplice, received a 3 years' sentence.

Adm Lord Lyons, who was the Cmder-in-Chief of the British Navy in the Black Sea, died on Nov 23, at the age of 68. He entered the navy at age 11 years. One of his sons was killed before Sebastopol. He was one of the most respected advisers in the great war council of Paris, & has been created a Baron for his achievements in the Crimea.

Mrd: on Dec 8, in Christ Church, Nashville, by Rev Leonidas Smith, Prof John Kimberley, of the Univ of N C, to Miss Bettie Meredith, daughter of Hon Thos Maney, of Nashville.

Died: on Dec 15, in Wash City, at the residence of her father, Sarah Anna Maria Wheaton, wife of Lt Frank Wheaton, 1st Cavalry, & daughter of Col Cooper, Adj Gen of the Army. Her funeral is on Dec 17 at 12 M.

Died: on Dec 13, in Wash City, after a few days' illness, Mrs Eliza T Hickey, wife of the late Davl G Hickey, in her 60th year.

Died: on Dec 15, in Wash City, Josephine Borrows, infant daughter of the late Jos B & Mary A S Tate, aged 6 months & 9 days. Her funeral is this afternoon at 3 o'clock, from the residence of her grandfather, Mr Jno Mills, 406 D st.

Orphans Court of Wash Co, D C. Letters testamentary on the personal estate of John Hopkins, late of Wash Co, deceased. –G W Hopkins, J S Hopkins, excs

FRI DEC 17, 1858
Died: on Dec 15, Clara Virginia, infant daughter of John & Sarah E O'Donnel, aged 2 years & 6 months. Her funeral will be from the residence of her parents, 644 7th st. [Funeral: No date or time given.]

Senate: 1-Ptn from Vincent Kokowski, an old soldier of the Military Asylum in D C, asking to be allowed a pension, to enable him to live with his family: referred. 2-Ptn from John A Ragan, proposing a plan to prevent the overflow of the Mississippi & its tributaries, & asking a grant of land to enable him to effect that object: referred. 3-Ptn from Lewis Purdy & others, officers & soldiers in the Black Hawk war, asking such amendment of the county land laws as will include those who served in said war less than 14 days: referred. 4-Ptn from L W Bogg, asking an appropriation to be made that he may be paid his salary as alcalde & judge under the military gov't of Calif: referred. 5-Cmte on Foreign Relations: joint resolution authorized Townsend Harris & H C J Hensken, to accept certain presents from the Majesty the Queen of Great Britain & Ireland, reported it back without amendment & recommended its passage. 6-Cmte on Military Affairs: adverse reports on the memorials of Jos Verbiski, of Augustus Moor, & of Wm Merrihew: ordered to be printed. 7-Bill for the relief of O H Berryman & others: indefinitely postponed. 8-Act to authorize the Sec of the Treasury to issue a register or enrollment to the vessel **James McIndoe**, now owned by Thos Coatsworth, Jas G Coatsworth, & Wm Coatswoarth, of Buffalo, N Y: indefinitely postponed. 9-Bill for the relief of Eliz E V Field; of Jane Perry; & of Jeremiah Wright: each indefinitely postponed.

Diplomatic appointments: confirmed on Wed last by the Senate:
Wm Preston, of Ky, Minister Plenipotentiary to Spain.
John E Ward, of Georgia, Minister Plenipotentiary to China.
J Glancy Jones, of Pa, Minister Resident to Austria.
[Dec 18th newspaper: The title of Hon J Glancy Jones should have been Envoy Extraordinary & Minister Plenipotentiary to America.]

Obit-died: on Aug 18, at the Gayoso House, Memphis, of consumption, Lt Chas Radziminski, U S Army. He came to the U S a mere lad, yet in his native country, Poland, he had attained a cadetship in a military school, were was laid the basis of an excellent eduction. After a short residence in a Northern city, he proceeded with letters to Richmond, Va & was employed as a civil engineer; went to Va a youth & a stranger; attained a perfect knowledge of the English language; & removed to Wash City. The Mexican war commenced & he obtained an appointment to the 3rd dragoons. When 4 new regts were added to the army in 1855, he was induced to ask for appointment, which was conferred on him in the 2nd cavalry. The seeds of disease developed. He met his fate in Memphis. He was the accomplished gentleman & model soldier. –S

Criminal Court-Wash-Thu. 1-Thos Hughes convicted of stealing a ham from Mr C F E Richardson. 2-Wm Hooper, alias Jones, was convicted of stealing a horse, valued at $100, the property of Jas B Greenwell, & recommended by the Jury to the mercy of the Court. Court adjourned.

50 or 100 acres of land for sale, east of Wash. For information inquire of Col Naylor, at the City Hall, or Alex McCormick, at the Patent Ofc. –S B Scaggs

SAT DEC 18, 1858
Superior household & kitchen furniture at auction on Dec 23, at the residence of Sir Wm Gore Ouseley, all his furniture. –C W Boteler, auct

Criminal Court-Wash-Fri. 1-Timothy O'Driscoll was acquitted on a charge of assault. 2-John Faley & Andrew Kidwell, tried a 3rd time for arson, in an unoccupied house, were acquitted. 3-Thos T Malein, colored, was tried for larceny of property to the value in all of several hundred dollars from Adams' Express Ofc.

Health Report: Ofc of the Com'r of Health, Wash, Dec 16, 1858. Deaths in Wash City for Nov, 1858, from all causes: 74. –Chas F Force, Com'r of Health

MON DEC 20, 1858
Superior household & kitchen furniture at auction on Dec 23, at the residence of Mrs Bird, corner of Md ave & 11th st, all the furniture & effects. -J C McGuire & Co, aucts

Gen Wm O Butler, of Ky, declines the Democratic nomination for Govn'r of that State.

Ex-Govn'r Slade is lying dangerously ill at his house in Vermont.

On the death of Lt Strain his scientific instruments, his journals, & personal effects were taken to N Y, where they were placed among unclaimed goods, & after the usual interval were advertised for sale. The Navy Dept is not aware that Lt Strain left any connexions. By order of the Collector the effects of Lt Strain have been withdrawn from public sale, in the hope that some one may appear authorized to take them in charge. –Cin Adv

House of Reps: 1-Ptn of Thos M Hope, praying a settlement of his account upon the principles of equity & justice: referred. 2-Memorial of Hester Sergeant Barton, widow of Wm P C Barton, M D, deceased, late a surgeon in the U S Navy, praying Congress to pass a law granting her a pension: referred. 3-Memorial from Mrs Abigail Paxon, widow of Geo Paxon, Florida War, for a pension during widowhood: referred.

Criminal Court-Wash-Sat: 1-John Carberry, a hackman, was tried for stealing a shawl from Mr Arth, whom he had carried in his hack, was acquitted. 2-Moses Mozine, charged with John Carberry as above, was found guilty of larceny. 3-Anthony or Arthur Duckett was found guilty of stealing some screw stocks & dies the property of John Duvall. 4-Thos McGuire, charged with assault, submitted his case, & was fined $5 & costs. The Court adjourned.

U S Patent Ofc, Wash, Dec 16, 1858. Ptn of John Fowler, of N Y, praying for the extension of a patent granted to him as assignee of Henry Jones, of Bristol, England, on May 14, 1845, for an improvement in the preparation of flour for bread making, for 7 years from the expiration of said patent, which takes place on Mar 13, 1859. -Jos Holt, Com'r of Patents

U S Patent Ofc, Wash, Dec 16, 1858. Ptn of Edw Maynard, of Wash, D C, praying for the extension of a patent granted to him Mar 22, 1845, for an improvement in percussion primers, for 7 years from the expiration of said patent, which takes place on Mar 22, 1859. —Jos Holt, Com'r of Patents

TUE DEC 21, 1858
Hon Timothy Pillsbury died at his residence, near Danville, Texas, on Nov 23, in his 69th year. He was long a resident of Brazoria Co, & occupied a leading place in the Congress of the Republic of Texas. He also represented the Western district of Texas for 4 years in the U S Congress.

Senate: 1-Ptn from Lt T Harmon Patterson, asking to be allowed the pay given to certain other officers under the acts of Mar 3, 1853: referred. 2-Ptn from Sheldon McKnight, asking additional compensation for carrying the mails on the Cleveland, Detroit, & Lake Superior routes: referred. 3-Ptn from Margaret N Halsey, former widow of Capt Cushing, of Ohio, asking to be allowed a pension: referred. 4-Ptn from the widow of Peter L Morris, for a pension. 5-Ptn from Richd Roman, commissary of subsistence during the war with Mexico, asking to be credited with an amount disallowed in the settlement of his accounts: referred. 6-Ptn from Richd Cheney, asking payment for a paving the street in front of the custom-house in San Francisco: referred. 7-Ptn from Thos Coward, asking a pension for services on board a privateer during the last war with Great Britian: referred. 8-Ptn from the administrator of Geo Fisher, asking an amendment of the joint resolution of last session devolving upon the Sec of War the execution of the act of Dec 22, 1854: referred. 9-Ptn from Sarah Hatton, asking to be allowed a pension on account of the services of *Thornas Baker in the navy of the Revolution: referred. [Thornas copied as written.] 10-Ptn from A Payne, asking the passage of a law repealing the condition of settlement & cultivation imposed upon purchasers of lands graduated at 12½ cents per acre: referred. 11-Ptn from Jacob Whitman, a soldier of the war of 1812, for a pension: referred.

The trial of Allibone & Newhall at Phil, on a charge of conspiracy against the Bank of Pa, terminated on Sat last in a verdict of not guilty.

On Tue last the dwlg of Robt Dutton, in Davenport, was destroyed by fire. Mr Dutton was at his store, & Mrs Dutton went out to get some milk & locked the door, leaving her 3 children inside. Two were lost in the fire, & one was very much burnt. The children were aged 1, 5, & 7 years; & before night the rescued infant also died. —Chicago Times

Criminal Court-Wash-Mon: 1-Benj Gwin found guilty of stealing overcoats belonging to Mr J B Moore, druggist, & Mr James, his assistant. Sentenced to 2 years in the penitentiary on each conviction. 2-Laura Herbert, colored, convicted of stealing a sack of flour: sentenced to 6 months' imprisonment. 3-Wm Patterson, guilty on 2 charges of larceny: sentenced to 2 years in the penitentiary for the former, & 3 months in jail for the latter. 4-Timothy Smith submitted his case for assault, & was fined $5. He had been 5 weeks in jail. The Court adjourned.

The subscriber offers his farm in PG Co, Md, for sale: 2 miles from Bladensburg depot: contains 100 acres; improvements in good repair. Also, adjoining the same, 100 to 240 acres will be sold if desired. Refer to D C Digges, atty at law, Upper Marlborough, or to the undersigned, who will show the premises. –Chas Digges, near Bladensburg

Died: on Dec 20, in Wash City, Mr Ferdinand Grenup, aged 74 years, father of the late Benj C Grenup. His funeral will take place from the Columbia Engine-house on Dec 11 at 3 o'clock.

Died: on Dec 19, in Gtwn, D C, at the residence of her father, Jos N Fearson, Mary Elizabeth, the only child of her parents, & the dearly beloved wife of Fred'k W Jones. Also, on Dec 18, Fred'k Fearson Jones, the infant son of Mary Eliz & Fred'k W Jones. The friends & relatives are requested to attend the funeral at 17 Congress st, Gtwn, on Tue at half past 2 o'clock P M.

Died: on Dec 3, at Warrenton, Va, Mrs H E Bacon, wife of Rev J S Bacon, late Pres of the Columbia College of Wash City. Mrs Bacon was a lady of varied accomplishments. After a protracted illness she sank in death, calm & resigned, in hope of a blessed resurrection.

Died: on Dec 18, at Guilford, Conn, in her 81st year, Mrs Anna Lay, widow of the late Richd Lay, a native of Conn, & for many years a resident of Gtwn, D C.

Halifax, Dec 20. The steamship **Ariel**, from Southampton on Dec 1, arrived here today short of coal, & in charge of the 1st ofcr. On Dec 8, during a heavy gale, a sea struck the ship, killing Capt Ludlow & severely injuring the 2nd ofcr & 2 seamen. The **Ariel** proceeds to N Y tomorrow afternoon.

WED DEC 22, 1858
Senate: 1-Ptn from Jeremiah Thornton, asking to be allowed an invalid pension for a wound received in the last war with Great Britain. Mr Foot remarked he was personally acquainted with the Mr Thornton, & having investigated the case, found it to be meritorious one: referred. 2-Ptn from Theodore Lewis, military store-keeper at the Wash arsenal, praying compensation for performing the duties of assist commissary of subsistence: referred. 3-Ptn from Geo C Johnson, asking the passage of a law to test the validity of a *Mexigan grant by the district court of the U S for the northern district of Calif: referred. 4-Ptn from Gilbert Vanderwerken, asking that the bill passed by the House of Reps in relation to a railroad along Pa ave, in Wash City, may become a law: referred. 5-Cmte on the Library, to which was referred the bill to authorize the Pres to make advances to Hiram Powers, reported it back with a recommendation that it pass. 6-Cmte on Pensions: bill for the relief of Wm Wallace, of Ill, with an amendment. Same cmte: adverse report on the ptn of Wm Welch, a soldier in the last war with Great Britain 7-On the motion of Mr Shields, the Senate proceeded to the consideration of the bill for the relief of Thos Laurent, surviving partner of the firm of Benj & Thos Laurent.
[*Mexigan as written]

Robt M Riddle, for many years the able & popular editor of the Pittsburgh Commercial Journal, died on last Sat after an illness which has afflicted him for at least 7 or 8 years. He was a son of the late Judge Riddle, at one time a politician of note in Western Pa, & a brother of Jas Riddle, of Phil. He was also brother-in-law of Judge Shaler, of Pittsburgh. Mr Riddle was a native of Pittsburgh & spent the best years of his life in advocacy of its interests. He was in his 47th year. –Phil Bulletin

Army Intelligence: War Dept, Adj Gen's Ofc, Wash, Dec 10, 1858. Promotions & appointments in the Army of the U S made by the Pres since the publication of Gen Orders No 8, of Jul 3, 1858: Promotions:
Medical Dept: Assist Surgeon Jas Simmons to be surgeon, vice Harney, deceased; to date from Aug 29, 1856, & to take place on the Army Register next below Surgeon David C DeLeon.
Corps of Engineers: Brvt 2nd Lt Richd K Meade, jr, to be 2nd lt, Jul 29, 1858, the date of Capt Sanders' death.
1st Regt of Dragoons: 2nd Lt Wm D Pender, to be 1st lt, May 17, 1858, vice Taylor, killed in action. Co C
Brvt 2nd Lt Saml W Ferguson, of the 2nd dragoons, to be 2nd lt, vice Pender promoted; to date from Jun 14, 1858. Co I
Brvt 2nd Lt Marcus A Reno to be 2nd lt, vice Gaston, killed in action; to date from Jun 14, 1858. Co E
2nd Regt of Cavalry: 2nd Lt John B Hood to be 1st lt, Aug 18, 1858, vice Radziminski, deceased. Co K
Brvt 2nd Lt Manning M Kimmel, of the 1st cavalry, to be 2nd lt, Oct 1, 1858, vice Van Camp, killed in action. Co D
Regt of Mounted Riflemen: 1st Lt Robt M Morris to be capt, Jun 14, 1858, vice Rhett, appointed paymaster. Co G
2nd Lt Jos G Tilford to be 1st lt, Jun 14, 1858, vice Morris, promoted. Co E
Brvt 2nd Lt Ira W Claffin to be 2nd lt, Jun 14, 1858, vice Tilford, promoted. Co H
3rd Regt of Artl: 2nd Lt Lyman M Kellogg to be 1st lt, Jul 31, 1858, vice Mowry, resigned. Co A.
Brvt 2nd Lt Wm Sinclair, of the 2nd artl, to be 2nd lt, Jul 31, 1858, vice Kellogg, promoted. Co K
8th Regt of Infty: 1st Lt Lafayette B Wood, to be capt, Jul 19, 1858, vice Longstreet, appointed paymaster, deceased. Co I
2nd Lt Thos M Jones, to be 1st lt, Jul 19, 1858, vice Wood, promoted. Co A
Brvt 2nd Lt Jas J Van Horn, of the 1st infty, to be 2nd lt, Jul 19, 1858, vice Jones, promoted. Co G
9th Regt of Infty: Brvt 2nd Lt Chas G Harker, of the 2nd infty, to be 2nd lt, Aug 15, 1858, vice Allen, died of wounds received in action. Co C
10th Regt of Infty: 1st Lt Cuvier Grover to be capt, Sep 17, 1858, vice Pitcher, deceased. Co F
2nd Lt Jas Deshler to be 1st lt, Sep 17, 1858, vice Grover, promoted. Co H
Brvt 2nd Lt Sardine P Reed, of the 3rd infty, to be 2nd lt, Sep 17, 1858, vice Deshler, promoted. Co E

Appointments:
Subsistence Dept: 1st Lt Wm W Burns, of the 5th infty, to be commissary of subsistence, with rank of capt, Nov 3, 1858, vice Bowen, deceased.
Medical Dept: J Cooper McKee, of Pa, to be assist surgeon, Oct 2, 1858, vice Simons, promoted.
Pay Dept: Brvt Maj Jas Longstreet, capt in the 8th regt of infty, to be paymaster, Jul 19, 1858, vice Dashiell, dismissed.
Danl McClue, of Indiana, to be paymaster, Oct 28, 1858, vice Denny, deceased.
Ordnance Dept: Richd Fatherly, of Arkansas, to be military storekeeper, Aug 9, 1858, vice Andrews, deceased.
Transferred:
Brvt 2nd Lt John S Saunders, 2nd artl, to the Ordnance Dept, Sep 1, 1858.
2nd Lt Lafayette Peck, 7th infty, to the 8th infty, Nov 30, 1858.
2nd Lt Chas H Ingraham, 8th infty, to the 7th infty, Nov 30, 1858.
Casualties:
Resigned, [2]: 1st Lt Sylvester Mowry, 3rd artl, Jul 31, 1858.
2nd Lt Edgar O'Connor, 7th infty, Oct 22, 1858.
Commissions vacated by new appointments:
By Paymaster Jas Longstreet, his commission as capt in the 8th infty, Jul 19, 1858.
By Paymaster Thos G Rhett, his commission as capt in the regt of mounted riflemen, Jun 14, 1858.
Died:
Brvt Lt Col Francis Taylor, major 1st artl, at *Fort Frown*, Texas, Oct 12, 1858. [*Frown as written.]
Brvt Maj John Sanders, capt corps of engineers, at **Fort Delaware**, Del, Jul 20, 1858.
Capt Isaac Bowen, commissary of subsistence, at Pass Christian, Miss, Oct 3, 1858.
Capt Mathew S Pitcher, 10th infty, at N Y, N Y, Sep 17, 1858.
Brvt Capt Oliver H P Taylor, 1st Lt 1st dragoons, killed in action, on Colville Trail, Wash Territory, 85 miles north of Snake river, May 17, 1858.
1st Lt Chas Radziminski, 2nd cavalry, at Memphis, Tenn, Aug, 1855. [No day given.]
2nd Lt Newton F Alexander, Corps of engineers, at Biloxi, Miss, Oct 10, 1858.
2nd Lt Cornelius Van Camp, 2nd cavalry, killed in action, near the Wichita Village, Texas, Oct 1, 1858.
2nd Lt Jesse K Allen, 9th infty, of wounds received in action on the Upper Yakama river, Wash Territory, Aug 15, 1858.
2nd Lt Wm F Gaston, 1st dragoons, killed in action on Colville Trail, Wash Territory, 85 miles north of Snake river, May 17, 1858.
Brvt 2nd Lt John T Magruder, 1st cavalry, at Marysville, Nebraska Territory, Jun 28, 1858.
Surgeon Benj F Harney, medical dept, at Baton Rouge, La, Aug 29, 1858.
Paymaster St Clair Denny, at Pittsburg, Pa, Aug 18, 1858.
Military Storekeeper Wm R Andrews, Ordnance Dept, at Little Rock Arsenal, Ark, Aug 2, 1858.
Dismissed: Paymaster Jeremiah Y Deshiell, Jul 10, 1858. –S Cooper, Adj Gen

Rev Mr Schenck does not accept the call of the Trinity Church, Wash. He will continue his labor, as he has already for some years done, in our midst. –Chicago Times

In the case of Cartzany vs Shaw, which is a breach of promise case, the plaintiff obtained an order yesterday from Hon Judge Heber for leave to amend her petition by increasing her damages from $20,000 to $100,000. A large number of witnesses, between 40 & 50, have been summonded on both sides. –St Louis Republican, Dec 15

At Rappahannock Co, Va, a day or two since, a little son of Mr John T Corder, near Flint Hill, left the house with a negro to drive some cows to a point not far distant. In a few minutes the negro returned & stated that the little fellow, who was about 9 years old, had tied himself to a cow's tail, & had been badly hurt. The father found the little boy tied to the tail of a cow by a rope around the waist. He was dead, having been dragged some distance, & his body shockingly mutilated.

Criminal Court-Wash-Tue: 1-Winnett Strong, the man who created a disturbance in Sep last in front of the Masonic Hall on 9th st, was tried for assault & battery with intent to kill & found not guilty. Strong was found to be out of his mind at the time the act was committed.

Nearly 300 persons were assembled in the Union Hall, at Warren, Mass, last Wed, to give a donation party to Rev D Sherman, pastor of the Methodist society that worships in that bldg, when half the floor gave way, precipitating at least 100 persons into the store below. Mrs Calvin Cutter had her ankle broken & was scalded by the upsetting of a boiler of water nearby, while in the act of making tea & coffee for the guests. Her recovery is a matter of much doubt. Mrs Weaver, morther-in-law of L J Knowles, complained of pain, & died at 2 o'clock that night. She was 62 years of age.
–Springfield Republican

THU DEC 23, 1858
Senate: 1-Memorial from Andrew Stoddard, cmder in the U S navy, relative to his pay: referred. 2-Ptn from Simpson P Moss, asking to be allowed the benefit of the act of Jul 21, 1852, fixing definitely the compensation of the collector at Astoria in the settlement of his accounts as collector of the district of Puget's Sound: referred. 3-Ptn from Jas Varney, a soldier in the war of 1812, asking to be allowed a pension on account of a disability contracted in the service: referred. 4-Ptn from A M Tabb, clerk of the navy yard at Gosport, Va, praying that the pay of clerks of navy yards may be increased: referred. 5-Ptn from Gillum Baley & Wm R Baley, praying indemnity for losses by the Mohawk Indians: referred. 6-Ptn from G R Barry, a purser in the navy, praying compensation for services as judge advocate: referred. 7-Cmte on Military Affairs: adverse reports on the bill for the relief of Lewis Cass Forsyth, & on the memorial of Dr Israel Moses for an improved ambulance for the transportation of the sick & wounded: ordered to be printed. 8-Cmte on Naval Affairs: joint resolution authorizing Wm L Hudson & J R Sands to accept certain testimonials awarded to them by the Gov't of Great Britain. [A snuff-box & medal to be presented to them as a memorial of their services in laying the Atlantic cable.] 9-Cmte on Patents & the Patent Ofc: bill for the relief of Jas E Holmes. [Patent for an improvement in chairs for invalids.]

The Theatre was well attended last evening to witness the interesting play of Ingomar, in which Mrs Julia Dean Hayne took the part of Parthenia. The piece was handsomely gotten up, & formed a pleasing spectacle.

W J Herring ranks with Landseer & Rosa Bonhjeur as a painter of animals. One of his latest & greatest works, the Village Blacksmith, is now on free exhibition at Messrs Taylor & Maury's bookstore in Wash City.

Criminal Court-Wash-Wed: 1-Terrence Carrigan was convicted of grand larceny. 2-Lewis Frank found guilty of stealing money & clothing, constituting grand larceny, & sentenced to 2½ years in the penitentiary. 3-John D Baptiste was convicted of stealing clothing at a ball on the Island, & sententnced to 2½ years in the penitentiary. 4-John Dandridge, colored, was convicted on 2 charges of grand larceny at the same time as Baptiste's crime, & sentenced to 1 year & 3 months on each conviction, being 2½ years in all. The Court adjourned.

Died: on Dec 21, Mrs Mary Ann Scrivener, in her 82nd year. Her funeral is this morning at 10 o'clock, from the residence of her son-in-law, Grafton Powell, 516 14th st.

Died: on Dec 5, at his seat in Franklin Co, N C, John D Hawkins, only surviving child of the late Col Philemon Hawkins, of Warren Co, N C. The deceased was born on Apr 15, 1781, received a liberal education at the Univ of the State, & was admitted to the bar. He was the father of a large family; his house was the abode of hospitality, ever open.

Died: on Dec 20, of scarlet fever, Cornelia, daughter of Hon Thos G & Anna C Clemson, of PG Co, Md.

Died: on Nov 8, at Winchester, Va, after a protracted illness, Thos B Campbell, in his 63rd year. He was respected among the active business men of Winchester; he served 21 years as Treasurer of the Lutheran Church there. After an appropriate funeral discourse by Rev W Baum, pastor of the Lutheran Church, his remains were interred on Sabbath in the Cemetery in Winchester. His bereaved family & friends mourn his loss.
+
Died: on Nov 29, of typhoid pneumonia, at the residence of his brother, Chas W Campbell, near St Josephs, Missouri, John Theodore Campbell, in his 21st year. He was the youngest daughter of the late Thos B Campbell. In later years, while yet a youth, he left the paternal roof to seek a home in the far distant West, where he early manifested great promise. The wounds so recently inflicted upon this deeply bereaved family are again re-opened & bade to bleed afresh; & thus, within a very brief period indeed, has this one happy family been called to mourn the loss of a kind & affectionate father, 2 lovely sisters, & now an affectionate son & brother. Be ye also ready. –W

FRI DEC 24, 1858
Mrd: on Dec 22, by Rev Mr Swentzel, Mr Geo W Taylor, of Wash City, to Miss Louisa Ellen Stone, of Gtwn, D C.

Nominations Confirmed. The following is a list of the retired Naval Ofcrs nominated & confirmed by the Senate on Wed.
Capts: Thos Paine, Wm Inman, & Wm Ramsey to the active list; F P Voorhees to the leave list.
Cmders: Wm M Armstrong, A K Long, T D Shaw, F Johnson, to the active list; L W Lecompte to the leave pay list.
Lts to Cmders: W D Porter, G G Williamson, John C Carter, S B Bissell, J J Glasson, A H Kilty, W Chandler, R W Meade, A Gibson.
Lts: Henry C Flagg, J J B Walback, J A Doyle, M C Marin, R B Reill, M C Perry, Henry Rolando, F A Parker, W B Fitzgerald, A C Rhind, R B McArann, A T Byrens, J P Hall, to the active list; Jas M Watson, S Chase Barney, J F Abbott, J Brownell, G W Harrison, to the leave pay list.

House of Reps: 1-Bill for the relief of Maria Sevart & Eliz Sevart, heirs of Harlan Sevart: referred. 2-Bill to grant bounty land to the companies of Capts Britton & Davis, of the war of 1812: referred. 3-Joint resolution of thanks to Capt Saml C Reid for having formed & designed the present flag of the U S. 4-Bill for the relief of Mrs Ferguson Smith.

Senate: 1-Memorial from Geo Washington Greene, grandson of Gen Nathl Greene, who has been engaged for more than 10 years in collecting & arranging the documents of his grandfather-during the period of the Revolution, & asks Congress to give its aid to the publication of the same. He points out also to the resolution of Congress of Aug 8, 1786, directing a monument to be erected to the memory of Nathl Greene at the seat of the Federal Gov't, yet that monument was never erected, & not a stone remains to show where the ashes of the hero of the South mingled with the soil of the country which he saved: referred. 2-Memorial from Gen Leslie Combs, asking that the money appropriated by Congress for the satisfaction of the Texas bonds, now remaining in the Treasury, may be distributed pro rata, & also asking the payment of Texas bonds formerly held by him which have been lost: referred. 3-Ptn from Hester Stoll, widow of an old soldier, asking a pension. Mr Shields stated that the petitioner was the widow of an old soldier who served 26 years, & had, previous to his death as well as since, served as hospital matron in the Florida war, & afterwards in that of Mexico; that he knew personally that her services were of the most invaluable kind to the sick & wounded officers in the city of Mexico; that she was now old & destitute, & involked a favorable consideration of her case at the hands of the Cmte on Pensions: referred. 4-Ptn from Wm H Crabbe, clerk in the navy yard at Phil, asking an increase of salary: referred. 5-Ptn from the administrator of John Ferguson, asking to be paid his portion of the proceeds of certain work which has been paid into the Treasury: referred. 6-Bill for the relief of Jane Turnbull, which gives her a pension of $50 a month. The motion being agreed to, Mr Crittenden spoke in glowing terms of the services of Capt Turnbull, & said that his death was occasioned by disease contracted in the service of his country during the Mexican war. Mr Clay moved to amend the bill by reducing the pension to $30 per month, which was agreed to. Mr Houston said he would vote with pleasure for the amount granted in this bill, or even a larger amount. The question being taken, the bill was passed by 26 yeas, & 18 nays.

Thos Henderson & Albert Cummings, two young men of excellent character, were suffocated to death a few days since at West Flamboro, Canada West, by placing burning coals in their sleeping room.

R W Woolley, of Ky, was confirmed as Sec of the Legation to Spain. Lt Col R E DeRussy, corps of engineers, has been assigned the command of the corps, & to the charge of the Engineer bureau of the War Dept.

List of patents issued last week:
W Ager, Pa, improvement in cleaning rice.
H L Arnold, Wis, improvement in car seats & couches.
J Badger, Ill, improvement in seeding machines.
T D Bailey, Mass, improvement in pegging jacks.
J A Barrington, Ohio, improvement in harvesters.
R W Belson, Pa, improvement in stoves.
C A Bremner, N Y, improvement in compostion for roofing.
J Broughton, N Y, improved cut-off gear for steam engines.
C Bullock, N Y, improvement in harvesters.
M M Camp, Conn, improved propeller for life-boats.
E G Chormann, Pa, improved ellipsograph.
E Claude, N Y, improvement in breech-loading revolving fire-arms.
H T Clawson, N C, improved pepper cruet.
H T Clay, Me, improvement in shingles.
P H Cotton, Ala, improvement in preserve cans.
J Cumberland, Ala, improvement in buckles.
F Daunoy, La, improvement in bagasse furnaces.
R DeCharms, Pa, improved carpet fasteners.
A Douglas, N Y, improved slide & fastening for skirt hoops.
J Fairclough, Ky, improvement in balancing mill stones.
S P Francisco, Pa, improvement in hydrants.
S Friend, N Y, for extension finger-rings.
P C Fritz, N Y, improvement in machines for separating garlic from grain.
E M Fuller, N Y, improvement in horse-power for driving reciprocating saws.
P W Gates, Ill, improvement in cut-off gear for steam engines.
H Glynn, Md, improvement in medicated fabrics.
E K Godfrey, N Y, improvement in paper files.
P B Green, Ill, improvement in seats & sleeping couches for railroad cars.
T F Hall, Ohio, improvement in hanging window sash.
J C Hall, Miss, improved manufacture of portable fans.
H Havell, N J, improvement in the manufacture of scissors.
O Hussey, Md, improved method of gathering grain upon & discharging it from the platform of harvesters.
E A Jeffery, N Y, improvement in hoop lock.
T Lewis, Mass, improvement in bottle-stoppers.
T S Lewis, Me, improved folding bench.
J C McGrew, Ohio, improvement in machinges for elevating hay.

J Montgomery, N Y, improved buoyant propeller.
A W Morse, N Y, improvement in seeding machines.
J Peckham, Conn, improvement in draughting shirts.
A Plinta, N Y, improvement in railroad rails.
D D Porter, U S Navy, improvement in quoins for gun-carriages.
J Redhead, Miss, improved self-adjustable leveling instruments.
G F Rice, Mass, improved maching for boring wood.
H C Sergeant, Ohio, improved governor for steam engines.
R Shaler, Conn, improved brush.
E Skelly, La, improvement in boiler furnaces.
O B Smith, N Y, improvement in harness buckles.
I Speight, Miss, improvement in hominy mills.
J Stevens, N Y, improvement in buckles for skirt hoops.
A F Tarr, Mass, for improved mitre box.
E Thoms, Va, improvement in corn press.
W Tucker, Mass, improved dynamometer.
R Vincent, Ill, improvement in ploughs.
W W Wade, Mass, for labels for trees, etc.
A Walker, N H, improvement in apparatus for purifying gas.
D Wells, Mass, improvement in stoves.
E Wells, Pa, improvement in manufacture of glass furnaces & pots.
N S White, Vt, improved method of attaching cutting lips to auger shanks.
J A Woodward, Iowa, improvement in smut machines.
G S Ayling, Mass, improved instrument for measuring altitudes, etc.
S Baldwin, N J, improvement in watch faces.
W Hathaway, Mass, improved clothes frame.
R Heneage, N Y, improvement in hemp brakes.
R K Huntoon, N H, improved maching for turning tapering twists on wood.
C Marzonie, N Y, improvement in the manufacture of paper, pulp from wood.
M Robins Ohio, improvement in faucets.
J L Roe, N Y, improved ice pick.]
Reissue: C H McCormick, Ill, improvement in reaping machines; reissued May 24, 1853; reissued Dec 21, 1858.

We understand that Hon Jas A Pearce, U S Senator, & Hon Jas L Orr, Speaker of the House of Reps, have been solicited, & accepted, the invitation of the Burns' Club, in Wash City, to preside at the centennial celebration of the birthday of Robt Burns on Jan 25 next. We believe that Mr Pearce is a lineal descendant of the house of Ramsay, represented by Lords Dalhousie & Panmure, 2 eminent British statesmen. Mr Orr is Scotch & Irish descent, & full appreciated the poetical genius of Scotland's great bard. Sir Archibald Alison, the historian of Europe, is to preside at a similar celebration in Glasgow, & Lord Macaulay, the historian of England, will preside in London. The versatile Lord Brougham does honor to Scotia's peasant bard, & will preside at the Edinburgh festival. Cols Wm & Jas Burns, sons of the poet, are to be present at the Dumfries celebration. Burns' genius belongs not alone to Scotchmen, but to humanity.

Mrd: on Dec 23, at Trinity Church, by Rev Mr Wentworth L Childs, Dr Jas M Grymes to Mary E Peyton, eldest daughter of Jas M Torbert.

Mrd: on Dec 21, in Wash City, by Rev G W Samson, Mr Alfred L Bullock to Miss Eliz E Kyle, both of Va.

Died: on Dec 23, in Wash City, of scarlet fever, Henry, son of Wm H & Eliz Dennesson, aged 2 years & 5 months. His funeral will take place from the residence of his parents, 383 5th st, between G & H, this afternoon at 3 o'clock.

Died: on Dec 23, in Gtwn, D C, Mrs Frances E Smith, wife of Jeremiah J M Smith, in her 39th year. Her funeral is this afternoon at 2½ o'clock, from the residence of Saml Fearson, corner of Congress & Water sts, Gtwn.

Died: on Dec 23, in Wash City, Mrs E J Dove. Her funeral is this afternoon at 2½ o'clock, from her late residence, 187 F st, between 17th & 18th sts.

Criminal Court-Wash-Thu: 1-Jno D Baptiste was sentenced to 1 year & 3 months in the penitentiary for theft. 2-John Runnels convicted of larceny, sentenced to 6 months in jail. 3-Robt Ardry, convicted of larceny in the same case as Runnels, sentenced similary. 4-Saml Barnes, convicted of the assault & battery without intent to kill, sentenced to one year in jail. 5-Robt La Bille submitted his case for an assault & battery on officer Wise, & was sentenced to 3 months' imprisonment.

SAT DEC 25, 1858
Hon Chas B Phelps, of Woodbury, died suddenly at Roxbury, on Tue. He was there with other members of a cmte appointed to erect a monument to the memory of Col Seth Warner, the compatriot of Ethan Allen at Ticonderoga & Crown Point. –New Haven Jrnl

Restoration in the Naval Service: correct list from an official source, of the naval nominations recently acted upon by the Senate, together with the position in the service which has been assigned to each ofcr.
Captains transferred:
Philip F Voorhees, on furlough pay, to leave pay; Thos Paine, on furlough pay, to the active list, to take rank next after Capt Thos Crabbe; Wm Ramsay, dropped, to the active list, to take rank next after Capt French Forrest; Wm Inman, on leave pay, to the active list, to take rank next after Capt Josiah Tattnall.
Cmders promoted or transferred:
Saml W Lecompte, on furlough pay, to leave pay; Wm M Armstrong, on leave pay, to be a capt, on active list, to take rank next after Capt J R Jarvis; Andrew K Long, on furlough pay, to be a capt, on the active list, to take rank next after Capt Henry Eagle; Zach F Johnston, dropped, to be a capt, on the active list, to take rank next after Capt Geo S Blake; T Darrah Shaw, on leave pay, to active list, to take rank next after Cmder W C Whittle.

Lts promoted or transferred:
Wm D Porter, on furlough pay, to leave pay, to be a cmder on the active list, to take rank next after Cmder H K Thatcher; G G Williamson, on furlough pay, to be a cmder, on the active list, to take rank next after Cmder F Chatard; J C Carter, on furlough pay, to be a cmder, on the active list, to take rank after Cmder G A Prentiss; S B Bissell, on leave pay, to be a cmder, on the active list, to take rank next after Cmder J P Gillis; J J Glasson, on leave pay, to be a cmder, on the active list, to take rank next after Cmder S Swartwout. A H Kilty, on furlough pay, to be a cmder, on the active list, to take rank next after Cmder C S Boggs; Wm Chandler, on leave pay, to be a cmder on the active list, to take rank next after Cmder A H Kilty; Richd W Meade, on furlough pay, to be a cmder, on the active list, to take rank next after Cmder J R Tucker; Alex'r Gibson, on furlough pay, to be a cmder, on the active list, to take rank next after Cmder E M Yard; Henry C Flagg, on furlough pay, to leave pay. J B Walbach, dropped, to be a lt on the active list, to take rank next after Lt W H Ball; Thos Brownell, on furlough pay, to leave pay; Jas A Doyle, on furlough pay, to the active list, to take rank next after Lt J R M Mullany; M C Marin, on leave pay, to the active list, to take rank next after Lt Jas A Doyle; S Chase Barney, dropped, to be a lt on the reserved list, on leave pay, to take rank next after Lt M B Woolsey. R B Riell, on furlough pay, to active list, to take rank next after Lt T B Huger; M C Perry, on furlough pay, to active list, to take rank next after Lt R B Riell; Henry Rolando, on furlough pay, to active list, to take rank next after Lt Danl Ammen; F A Parker, on furlough pay, to active list, to take rank next after Lt J M Wainwright; J F Abbott, on furlough pay, to leave pay; W B Fitzgerald, on furlough pay, to active list, to take rank next after Lt C M Fauntleroy. A C Rhind, dropped, to be a lt on the active list, to take rank next after Lt A Read; R M McArann, on furlough pay, to active list, to take rank next after Lt W Nelson; Jas M Watson, H N Harrison, & Chas Hunter, on furlough pay, to leave pay.

Passed Midshipmen promoted:
J P Hall, dropped, to be a lt on the active list, to take rank next after Lt J W Bennett; A T Byrens, dropped, to be a lt on the active list, to take rank next after Lt W K Mayo; Wm R Mercer, dropped, to be a lt on the active list, to take rank next after Lt E E Stow. This list is the only correct one which has been published. -States

Circuit Court of Wash Co, D C-in Equity. Sewell & others, creditors of John Brereton, vs Eliz Brereton & John Hoover, adms of said Jno Brereton, & Mary, Eliz, Ann, John, & Flora Brereton, his heirs at law. The above named are to appear before me on Jan 18 next, City Hall, & the creditors of said Jno Brereton to file their claims with me on or before the said date. —Walter S Cox, special auditor

Recently in Dane Co, Ill, a German, Melchion Stoppel, who had been proved guilty of deliberate murder, was convicted of manslaughter. Judge Dixon said-in my opinion, if any man was ever guilty of willful, premeditated murder, it was you, in taking the life of John Ritmeir. You stabbed him with a butcher knife after informing him that "he must die." The highest punishment prescribed by law is 4 years in the penitentiary. The sentence in your case is that you be confined in the State prison at hard labor for 4 years from this day at noon, & that you be solitarily imprisoned for the first 10 days of each & every month of the said term.

At *Edge Hill*, the property of Hon J W Crisfield, near Centreville, Queen Anne's Co, Md, was destroyed by fire on Sunday last. The fire originated accidentally. Half the loss of about $2,000, is secured by the Mutual Fire Ins Co, of Cecil Co.

Circuit Court of Wash Co, D C-in Equity. Richd W Bryan & Sarah Ann his wife, Ruel K Compton & Rachel J his wife, Geo W Tubman & Laura his wife, Chas H Lane & Susan his wife, & Mary E Briscoe, cmplnts, vs Jane H Dement, widow & admx of Richd Dement, John P Dement, Wm B Dement, & Thos Dement, dfndnts. Richd Dement, late of Wash City, deceased, was at the time of his death seized in fee of lots in said city numbers 20 & 21, in reservation number 11, which he held under 2 deeds from the Mayor of Wash, D C, dated Apr 6, 1847; that said lots are improved, having on them 2 good 3 story brick houses of an equal value; that said Richd Dement died intestate, leaving a widow, the above name Jane H Dement, & 8 children, namely, the above named Sarah Ann Bryan, Rachel J Compton, Laura Tubman, Susan Lane, Mary E Briscoe, John P Dement, Wm B Dement, & Thos Dement, his only heirs at law; that said property cannot be divided among the said heirs at law without loss & injury to them; that it is subject to the dower right of said widow, & also to the payment of the debts of said Richd, whose personal estate proved to be insufficient to pay the claims of his creditors. The bill states that it would be for the advantage of all persons interested therein that the said described real estate should be sold free of the dower-right of the said widow, & suggests that with her consent the same should be so sold, & that the Court allow her an equitable equivalent therefore out of the proceeds of the sale thereof. The object of the bill of cmplnt is to obtain a decree of the said Court for the sale of the said real estate, & the application of the proceeds of sale, first, to satisfy the said widow for her dower in said premises; secondly, to pay the balances due the several creditors of the said Richd Dement; &, thirdly, to distribute the residue of such proceeds of sale among the heirs-at-law of said Richd according to their several just claims & rights. It appears that John P Dement & Wm B Dement, do not reside in D C, & are in fact out of the reach of the process of this Court. The absent dfndnts are to appear in this court on the first Monday in May next, & answer said bill. –Jas S Morsell, Assist Judge Circuit Court D C. –Jno A Smith, clerk

Boston, Dec 24. The ship **Margaret Tyson**, from N Y, bound to San Francisco, [date & position unknown,] & the entire crew, with one exception, are supposed to have been lost. One man was picked up on the ships house, who reported that he had been floating on it for 17 days.

TUE DEC 28, 1858
Capt Saml C Reid, the hero of the battle of Fayal, in the gallant fight which he made in command of the private armed brig **General Armstrong**, in 1814, has been noticed for having made & designed the present flag of the U S. The design was adopted in cmte, & the bill passed Congress on Apr 4, 1818. The new flag, as designed by Capt Reid, was made at his house, in N Y, by his wife & a number of young ladies, & first hoisted over the hall of the House of Reps on Apr 13, 1818.

Christmas day was delightful, clear, bright, & just cool enough to invite a pleasurable degree of exercise. The Churches thew open their doors & were well attended.

Col J A Tucker, Democratic nominee for judgeship of the southwestern circuit, & also Senator to the late Legislature of Georgia, from Stewart, committed suicide at Dawson, Ga, last week by taking morphine. He was a man of fine genius, strong mental powers, & possessed of qualities of heart that attached to him most warmly a host of friends.

Jacob Shuster alias Tom Hand, who has spent some 30 years of his life in prison, was again convicted in Phil on Fri last charged with forging a bank note plate of the Bank of Delaware Co, Pa, & a $10 note on the same institution. The three daughters of the dfndnt watched the progress of the trial. He was stamped as a felon, yet to his daughters he was pure & spotless

Mrd: on Dec 24, by Rev A G Carothers, Mr Edw Moulden, of Montg Co, Md, to Miss Sarah Jane Howell, of Wash City.

Mrd: on Nov 16, by Rev A G Carothers, Mr Chas W Spencer to Miss Lizzie S Miles, both of Wash City.

Mrd: on Nov 23, at Fairview, Montg Co, Md, the residence of the bride's father, by Rev E A Colburn, Mr Alpheus Middleton, of Wash, to Miss F Eugenia, youngest daughter of Dr Washington Duvall.

Died: on Dec 25, J H T Werner, in his 55th year.

Died: on Dec 26, in Gtwn, Elizabeth Summerville, in her 6th year, youngest daughter of John & Juliet Marbury.

Information received in this city of the death at New Orleans on Dec 23, of ex-Chief Justice Geo Eustis, of La. He was a native of Mass, & a graduate of Harvard College. He reached New Orleans about 1822. He has left a widow & several children, one of whom, Hon Geo Eustis, jr, has, during the last & present Congress, been the Rep from the 1st Congressional district of Louisiana.

John A Miller, convicted at Portland, Me, of robbing the mail, has been sentenced to the State prison for 10 years. Chas Foster, convicted of cutting open a mail bag, was sentenced to 3 years.

Trustee's sale: the undersigned, as trustee of Francis Thomas will sell at public auction, at the City Hotel, in Fredericktown, on Jan 17, 1859, that valuable farm called **Montevue**, on Fred'k & Harper's Ferry Ridge road, adjoining the village of Petersville, in Catoctin Valley, the residence of ex-Gov Francis Thomas, containing 307½ acres of land; with a commodious brick house & numerous out-bldgs. For further information call on the subscriber residing in Fred'k city, Md. –Geo Smith, trustee

Boston, Dec 27. Capt Townsend, of the slaver **Echo**, in charge of 2 U S Deputy Marshals, left here today for Key West, to be tried for piracy.

St Louis, Dec 27. The Jeffersonville City Examiner learns from a reliable source that **Fort Scott** in Kansas, on Dec 15, was attacked by Montgomery at the head of 200 men, the town taken, & 5 or 6 persons killed. The object of the attack was to release one of Montgomery's men confined there on a charge of murder. A band of thieves & assassins from Kansas entered Vernon Co, Missouri, killed David Cruse & stole a lot of cattle & horses. About the same time 2 parties, under Brown & Montgomery, entered Missouri on the Little Osage river, stole a negro woman & took Wm Larne prisoner, but released him the next day. An express had been sent to the Govn'r of Missouri for assistance to protect life & property.

Miss Margaret Dyer, Dress-maker, has removed to the Wheeler & Wilson Sewing Machine Agency, 354 Pa ave, over Messrs Galts' new Jewelry Store, & invites the ladies to call & leave their orders.

WED DEC 29, 1858

Excellent household & kitchen furniture at auction on Dec 30, at the residence of W W Jacobs, 525 I st, between 6th & 7th sts. —Bontz & Coombs, aucts

Gen Jas Gadsden died at Charleston, S C, on Sunday last, aged about 60 years. He was appointed Minister to Mexico in 1853, & in the following year negotiated with that country the treaty which bears his name. Since his retirement he has taken no active part in national affairs.

Superior Court at Cincinnati: Rev Geo W Quinby against Fred'k Eckstein, jr, the plntf claiming damages to the amount of $10,000, alleging that, by the negligence of the dfndnt, or his agent, belladona was put up in a prescription instead of dandelion, by which the health of the plntf was materially injured & his life put in jeopardy. The jury returned a verdict for the plntf for $2,500.

Within the past 3 weeks 5 deaths have occurred in the family of Hamilton Easter, at his country residence upon the Liberty road. Within that period have died his mother-in-law, father-in-law, wife, his wife's aunt, & his son, Hamilton Scott Easter, aged 23 years, & a partner in business, who deceased yesterday morning. Last winter Jos Easter, an interesting son, died in the flush of youth after a few days' illness. Last evening we learned that Mr Easter himself had been stricken down with disease. —Balt Sun

It is stated that Washington Irving has made a donation of $500 to the ladies' fund for the purchase of **Mount Vernon**.

St Paul's Pioneer of Dec 5, reports the sudden death of John H Brownson, atty of that city, & son of Dr Orestes A Brownson, whose remains were found under the rear window of his office, from which he had leaped or fallen in the course of the night.

Handsome Dinner & Evening Dresses: W M Shuster & Co, 38, opposite Centre Market, between 7th & 8th sts, Wash. [Ad]

THU DEC 30, 1858
Appointments by the Pres, by & with the advice & consent of the Senate:
Registers of Land Ofcs:
Leland Wright, at Booneville, Mo.
Saml M Hankins, at Grenada, Miss.
Jas G G Garrett, at Wash, Miss.
Edmund P Hart, at Visalia, Calif.
Wm A Davidson, at Santa Fe, New Mexico.
Berryman Jennings, at Oregon City, Oregon.
Wm B Rankin, at Olympia, Territory of Washington.
Receivers of Public Moneys:
Sidney M Forbert, at Demopolis, Ala.
Robt D Haden, at Columbus, Miss.
T Rush Spencer, at Superior, Wisc.
Christopher Graham, at Henderson, Minn.
Paschal Bequette, at San Francisco, Calif.
Jos Hopkins, at Marysville, Calif.
Wm A Street, at Santa Fe, New Mexico.
A Lawrence Lovejoy, at Oregon City, Oregon
Surveyor Gen: Ward B Burnett, for Kansas & Nebraska.

Col Abraham Van Buren, of Columbia, S C, recently sold to Col Elisha Worthington, of Chicot Co, Ark, his whole plantation of slaves, numbering 210, for $147,000, or an average of $700 each. Col Van Buren is a son of ex-Pres Van Buren, & married the daughter of Col Singleton, of S C. Mrs Van Buren is the sister of the late Mrs Govn'r McDuffie. -Journal of Commerce

Circuit Court of Wash Co, D C-in Equity. Pairo & Nourse, vs Chas H Van Patton, R T Chew, Ann G Wight, Geo W Phillips, Isaac D Tol, & John E Kendall. Statement of trustee's account on Jan 10, at the Auditor's room, City Hall, Wash.
–Walter S Cox, Spec Auditor

Last Thu a circular saw flew out of its bearings while running in a shingle mill & struck John Wretholm, a Swede, on his side, cutting him diagonally in two.

Mrd: on Dec 27, at Sunnyside, Dedham, Mass, by Rev J Chaplin, D D, J E Gowland, of England, to Miss Kate S, only daughter of Hon Wm S Damrell.

From Calif: N Y, Dec 29. 1-Joel McDonald, an ex-policeman, & John Leary were killed by some thieves whom they were attempting to arrest at Columbia. One of the murderers was captured & hung. 2-Benj F Moulton, a well known expressman, was killed at San Francisco by Jos W Brewer.

Died: yesterday, suddenly, at the Nat'l Hotel, in Wash City, of congestion of the brain, Mr Chas F Aikin, formerly of Mass.

FRI DEC 31, 1858
Naval Intelligence: The ship **Roanoke** was at Aspinwall on Dec 20. Thos Arkwright, fireman, died on Nov 23, & Jas Donnavan died on Dec 16. 2-The ship **Savannah** was at San Juan Del Norte on Dec 4. On that day Jas Fitzgerald, seaman, died.

Supreme Court of the U S: Dec 30, 1858: Nicholas St John Green, of Mass, was admitted an atty & counselor of this Court.

The most appropriate things for Holyday Presents: Claggett & May, Pa ave & 9th st. [Ad]

Obit-died: on Dec 23, in N Y, Sister William Anna Hickey, formerly a resident of Wash City. She had for many years past devoted her life to religion as a **Sister of Charity**, & was a useful member of an important institution in the State of N Y, whose members have devoted themselves to works of charity & mercy. Requiescat in pace!
+
Died-on Dec 23, after an illness of 8 months, Sister Williamanna, **Sister of Charity**, & member of the Society of Mount St Vincent, N Y, in the fullness of years spent in the perfect discharge of every duty imposed by her beloved vocation. Twenty-eight years ago she left Wash City for the purposes which have resulted in her full accomplishment of all the aims & ends of a devoted & pious Christian.

Mrd: on Dec 28, in Gtwn, D C, by Rev Dr Norwood, Wm D Cassin, of Chicago, Ill, to Mary Amelia, eldest daughter of Dr Grafton Tyler.

Died: on Dec 30, in Wash City, after a long & painful illness, which he bore with Christian patience & resignation, John Geo Eichhorn, in his 73rd year, a native of Baden, Germany, but for the last 27 years a citizen of this country. He leaves a wife & 3 children to mourn his loss. His funeral will take place on Jan 1 at 10 o'clock, from his late residence, on Third, between F & G sts.

Died: on Dec 29, Catharine E, wife of the late Wm A Williams, of Wash City. Her funeral will take place this Friday, Dec 31, from her late residence, 379 Pa ave.

Orphans Court of Wash Co, D C, Dec 28, 1858. In the case of Augustus E L Keene, adm of Chas Schussler, deceased, the administrator aforesaid has, with the approbation of the Court, appointed Jan 21 next, for the final settlement & distribution of the personal estate of said deceased, with the assets in hand. -Ed N Roach, Reg/o wills

A

Abbey, 215
Abbot, 34
Abbott, 62, 329, 395, 447, 449, 469, 473
Abel, 2
Aberenthy, 395
Abert, 63, 239, 304, 453
Aborgast, 425
Aborn, 20
Abraham, 426
Abrahams, 19, 44
Academy of the Visitation, 291
Acosta, 87
Acton Hall, 150
Acton Place, 149
Adair, 240, 448
Adams, 9, 22, 31, 63, 66, 122, 128, 144, 229, 233, 242, 243, 250, 297, 304, 318, 327, 335, 353, 393, 414, 419, 444, 456, 462
Adamson, 154, 231
Addison, 25, 41, 63, 64, 205, 215, 353, 355
Adelsdorfer, 370
Adger, 370
Aeklee, 397
Ager, 63, 64, 274, 470
Agricultural College, 348
Ahlers, 380
Aiken, 311, 397
Aikin, 478
Aikman, 390
Ainsa, 204, 449
Ainsworth, 396
Albaugh, 60
Albert, 218, 394, 415
Albro, 371
Alcock, 46, 203, 204
Aldrick, 38
Aldridge, 6
Alexander, 3, 11, 76, 89, 94, 95, 122, 137, 149, 164, 178, 191, 203, 204, 213, 214, 225, 226, 235, 238, 246, 250, 256, 297, 317, 425, 440, 466

Alexander I, 302
Alig, 288
Alison, 471
Allard, 196
Allcock, 237
Allen, 34, 38, 43, 63, 76, 127, 132, 136, 152, 155, 164, 166, 168, 191, 213, 223, 231, 233, 237, 238, 240, 242, 243, 247, 297, 301, 313, 330, 358, 362, 369, 395, 424, 443, 449, 465, 466, 472
Allgaier, 391
Alliance, 119
Allibone, 27, 463
Alligator, 323
Allsop, 100
Allston, 212
Almy, 368, 372, 394
Alsback, 400
Alston, 302
Altemus, 146, 158, 202
Alvarez, 22
Alvord, 25, 36, 76, 163
Alworth, 143
Ambler, 225, 305
Ambush, 46, 162
Ames, 282
Ammen, 473
Analostan Island, 1
Anderson, 3, 32, 33, 38, 53, 63, 150, 162, 183, 193, 240, 247, 284, 285, 287, 328, 357, 416, 426, 459
Andover, 150
Andre, 383
Andrew, 63
Andrews, 63, 174, 178, 182, 189, 227, 347, 438, 466
Andrus, 33
Angel, 22
Angus, 210, 300
Ansart, 137
Ansel, 27
Anson, 440
Anthon, 207
Anthony, 82

Antisell, 130, 136, 223, 228, 230, 235, 318
Antonio, 201, 429
Apperson, 130, 309, 310
Appleby, 10, 11, 63, 210
Appleton, 22, 152, 183, 207, 379, 455
Appointments by the Pres, 13, 18, 20, 22, 53, 151, 191, 214, 237, 240, 245, 252, 254, 477
Appollo Hall, 131
Araktsheef, 207
Arandus, 370
Arbogost, 105
Archer, 54, 237, 242
Archibald, 440
Arctic voyage, 273
Ardgowan, 217
Ardry, 472
Areadia, 203
Arfwedson, 203, 204
Argout, 47
Arguello, 205
Arista, 207
Arkwright, 478
Arlshton, 135
Armitage, 63
Armstead, 438
Armstrong, 63, 93, 95, 105, 130, 197, 199, 327, 441, 448, 469, 472
Arnold, 63, 105, 115, 122, 189, 252, 265, 374, 470
Arnot, 48
Arnu, 34
Arny's Confectionary, 40
Arredondo, 50
Arroyo, 400
Arth, 462
Arvine, 63
Asbury, 163
Aschwanden, 1
Asel, 27
Ashburton, 207, 216
Ashby, 357
Ashcraft, 227
Ashford, 63
Ashley, 36, 203, 443

Ashmore, 240
Ashton, 116, 341
Astor, 356
Atchison, 48, 207, 232
Atkins, 241
Atkinson, 40, 63, 151, 189, 393, 416, 427, 450
Atlantic cable, 324, 467
Atlantic Telegraph, 321, 333, 340
AtLee, 189
Atocha, 4
Atz, 98
Auchmuty, 305
Audubon, 207
Auell, 443
Augus, 231
Auld, 205
Aulick, 251
Aurenfricht, 321
Austin, 13, 14, 26, 63, 77
Austine, 287
Averelle, 409
Averill, 438
Averonich, 450
Avery, 37
Avezzana, 207
Avindolph, 370
Awson, 427
Ayer, 4
Aylett, 188, 417
Ayliff, 76
Ayling, 471
Ayott, 55
Ayres, 208, 439
Ayton, 63

B

Babb, 406
Babbit, 130
Babbitt, 17, 24, 223, 247
Babcock, 297
Babock, 352
Babson, 13
Baby, 65
Bache, 191, 194
Bachler, 365

Bachman, 207
Bacon, 91, 136, 149, 207, 231, 235, 243, 256, 464
Baden, 65, 175, 332
Badgeley, 105
Badger, 207, 470
Baehr, 257
Baeschlin, 64
Bagby, 365, 368
Bagget, 64
Baggett, 231
Bagley, 284
Bagnem, 349
Bagwell, 102
Bailey, 2, 64, 175, 207, 231, 365, 470
Baily, 249, 285
Bainbridge, 26, 27, 147, 203, 204, 207
Baird, 44, 105, 189, 335, 397
Baker, 15, 31, 83, 90, 167, 169, 175, 240, 241, 248, 314, 341, 353, 365, 372, 393, 394
Bakery, 341
Baldwin, 30, 34, 49, 101, 183, 203, 214, 220, 294, 321, 376, 447, 471
Bale, 64
Balestier, 160, 430, 433
Balestieri, 201
Baley, 467
Ball, 2, 53, 62, 64, 65, 92, 105, 138, 156, 229, 231, 232, 298, 327, 386, 397, 424, 473
Ballantyne, 146, 433
Ballard, 102, 230
Ballinger, 64
Ballot, 188
Balmain, 64
Baltzell, 440
Bancroft, 34, 152, 207, 218
Bandar, 412
Bandico, 169
Bandoouin, 44
Bangham, 314
Bangor City Greys, 99
Bangs, 207
Bankhead, 132
Banks, 11, 26, 101, 106, 207, 237, 352

Bannister, 366
Baptiste, 468, 472
Baratier, 272
Baratte, 101
Barbaria, 119
Barbee, 449
Barber, 198, 237
Barbot, 394
Barbour, 207, 279, 289, 415
Barcker, 380
Barclay, 87, 415
Bard, 188, 210, 215, 236, 247
barge **G W P Custis**, 226
Barger, 209
barkantine **Ephraim Williams**, 385
Barker, 14, 64, 85, 101, 119, 124, 167, 183, 207, 209, 232, 241, 292, 296, 318, 388
Barks, 311
Barlow, 34, 234
Barmeister, 18
Barnard, 11, 36, 51, 84, 99, 114, 122, 130, 207, 210, 223, 247, 261, 395, 449
Barnes, 2, 20, 34, 35, 52, 115, 273, 295, 298, 348, 420, 424, 447, 459, 472
Barnett, 365
Barney, 30, 118, 469, 473
Barnum, 379
Barnwell, 288, 300
barque **Attica**, 37, 84, 157, 247, 316
barque **Claude**, 412
barque **Ellen**, 111, 316
barque **Iola**, 313
barque **Lotus**, 370
barque **Margaret**, 366
barque **Maurice**, 373
barque **Oregon**, 459
barque **Sebois**, 313
barque **Thales**, 383
Barr, 230, 232, 350
Barraga, 188
Barre, 400
Barret, 20, 328, 341, 413
Barrett, 64, 65, 261, 296, 372, 397, 438, 443
Barriger, 371

Barringer, 207
Barrington, 395, 470
Barron, 5, 6, 122, 162, 174, 275, 341
Barry, 52, 64, 90, 105, 181, 182, 209, 232, 242, 287, 394, 429, 467
Bartels, 370
Barth, 383
Bartholomew, 224
Bartless, 365
Bartlett, 94, 104, 144, 188, 228, 265, 356, 365
Bartly, 90
Bartoll, 240
Barton, 268, 284, 314, 462
Bascom, 196, 287
Basham, 97
Basse, 401
Basset, 386
Bassett, 55, 135, 162, 296, 395
Bastinelli, 309
Batchelor, 122, 189
Bateman, 62, 64
Bates, 49, 65, 207, 252, 292, 310, 386
Batson, 10
Battle, 106, 347, 389, 390, 420
Baudoin, 224
Baudowin, 228
Baughman, 102
Baum, 62, 468
Bautschen, 248
Bawden, 99, 115
Baxter, 7, 135
Bayard, 164, 205, 223, 224, 238, 444
Bayless, 271
Bayley, 260, 389
Bayley's Purchase, 114
Bayleys, 52
Baylis, 258
Bayliss, 64, 107, 242, 258, 448
Baylor, 63, 133, 246
Bayly, 256, 274, 278, 448
Bayly's X Roads, 89
Bayne, 67, 86, 115
Beach, 64, 65, 233, 281, 284, 342
Beach Hill, 175
Beahn, 281

Beale, 90, 92, 135, 164, 207, 209, 242, 437
Beall, 6, 64, 90, 107, 149, 226, 246, 256, 301, 382, 407, 408, 451, 456
Bean, 164, 223, 227, 232, 235, 247
Bean, Benj, 64
Beane, 105
Bear, 104
Bear Valley, 336
Beard, 16, 233, 267, 292, 311
Beaseley, 64
Beasley, 292, 381
Beasly, 278
Beatley, 46
Beatrice Cenci, 123
Beatty, 17, 24, 56, 105, 253
Beauchamp, 150
Bebb, 58
Bebe, 280
Beck, 39, 46, 180, 300, 350
Becker, 370, 375, 389
Becket, 65
Beckhaus, 391
Bedinger, 376, 440
Bee, 369
Beebe, 103, 126, 326
Beebee, 289, 460
Beeker, 375
Beelen, 19, 26
Beers, 84, 136, 232
Behan, 416
Beirne, 417
Beitinger, 210
Belafield, 204
Belden, 80, 191
Belisle, 263
Belknap, 135, 458
Bell, 29, 46, 55, 64, 88, 140, 144, 161, 198, 237, 244, 267, 286, 324, 327, 338, 341, 380, 395, 401, 454
Bellefonte Cemetery, 162
Bellenger, 282
Bellerjean, 76
Bellinger, 289
Bellville, 389
Belmont, 96

Belson, 470
Belt, 11, 12, 13, 141, 172, 231, 295, 448
Bemiss, 189
Benedict, 3
Benham, 214, 394, 429
Benjamin, 3, 155
Benner, 269
Benneson, 252
Bennet, 252
Bennett, 26, 27, 36, 51, 64, 130, 135, 199, 245, 417, 473
Bennett, Alex'r, 64
Benning, 114
Bensley, 378
Benson, 37, 107, 429, 431
Bent, 162, 299
Bentley, 292
Benton, 17, 24, 48, 65, 136, 151, 152, 153, 156, 162, 171, 223, 293, 378, 384, 414, 456
Beoher, 455
Bequette, 280, 477
Beresford, 168
Berger, 298, 424
Bergman, 49, 254
Bergmann, 351
Berkeley, 417
Berkley, 433
Bernard, 91, 155
Bernett, 370, 375
Beron, 422
Berraud, 413
Berrell, 241
Berret, 16, 341, 439
Berrett, 35, 237
Berrien, 64, 156, 261
Berry, 13, 24, 31, 34, 65, 98, 104, 143, 175, 178, 256, 259, 269, 270, 282, 283, 287, 293, 295, 305, 307, 332, 349, 370, 374, 375, 442, 443, 449
Berryman, 41, 89, 159, 461
Bertolette, 393
Besancon, 148
Best, 292
Bestor, 228, 232
Beth Hamedresch, 258

Bettman, 197, 208
Betts, 103
Betzar, 117
Beurre, 34
Bevan, 410
Beverley, 290
Beverly, 429
Beyner, 16
Biancho, 364
Bias, 64
Bibb, 23
Bickford, 193
Bicksler, 65
Biddle, 104
Bien, 394
Biermann, 383
Biernstell, 375
Bigelow, 203, 204, 221
Biggs, 192, 230
Bigler, 22, 333, 399
Bigley, 65, 162
Biglow, 64
Biles, 341, 394
Billings, 254
Billingsley, 76, 369
Bingey, 65
Bingham, 44, 315, 348, 443
Binney, 91, 337, 361
Bionsteil, 370
Birce, 131
Birch, 2, 64, 114, 118, 136, 145, 158, 227, 230, 298, 334, 424
Bird, 53, 64, 65, 249, 358, 420, 448, 462
Birdette, 130
Birge, 157
Birkhead, 306
Birth, 65
Biscoe, 26, 160, 225, 235, 246, 250, 317
Bishop, 42, 97, 215, 220, 221, 293, 307, 315, 416, 437
Bissell, 30, 469, 473
Bittenger, 422
Bittinger, 146, 205, 347, 350, 366
Black, 6, 48, 63, 106, 156, 248, 360
Blackburn, 34, 142, 364
Blackiston, 34

Blacksnake, 235
Blackwell, 251
Blades, 369
Blagden, 65, 361, 375, 383
Blagrove, 228
Blair, 34, 153, 411, 416, 456
Blake, 105, 169, 177, 191, 241, 281, 293, 378, 393, 394, 396, 472
Blakeley, 360
Blakey, 214
Blakistone's Pavilion, 257
Blanchard, 11, 45, 122, 274
Bland, 458
Blandin, 168
Blane, 372
Blaney, 449
Blatchford, 337
Blattenberger, 94
Blauvert, 43
Bleecker, 448
Blenheim, 392
Blevins, 340
Blewitt, 196
Blincoe, 292
Bliss, 91, 245
Blocker, 104, 230
Blocking, 168
Blodgett, 199
Blood, 34, 215, 240
Bloodworth, 87
Bloom, 400
Bloss, 389
Blount, 122
Blow, 237
Blue Plains, 393
Bluford, 225
Blunt, 315, 330
Boarman, 42, 64
boat **Friend**, 242
Boch, 375
Bock, 370
Bocock, 190, 395
Bodfish, 13
Bodisco, 300, 383
Body, 163, 223, 225, 235, 247
Boen, 65

Bogan, 95
Bogel, 369, 370
Bogg, 461
Boggs, 154, 291, 337, 473
Bohrer, 30, 84, 189, 239, 305, 448
Boileau, 153
Boiles, 122
Bolin, 131
Bolles, 168, 201
Bolling, 354
Bolow, 437
Bolton, 189
Bomford, 64, 103
Bonapart, 412
Bond, 45, 64, 97, 134, 166, 251
Bone, 60
Bonham, 156
Bonhjeur, 468
Bonner, 164
Bonpland, 313
Bontz, 299, 476
Bonzinska, 164
Booker, 174
Boon, 171
Boone, 64, 65, 409, 436
Boose, 229
Bootes, 438
Booth, 201, 355
Boott, 387
Bootz, 168
Borden, 20
Borel, 272
Borgershausen, 64
Borges, 275
Borreman, 64
Borrows, 136, 145, 158, 239, 460
Borry, 160
Bortolette, 201
Boss, 38, 64, 88
Bosse, 65
Bossier, 81
Boston, 46, 191
Bostwick, 371
Boswell, 220
Boteler, 27, 97, 119, 141, 195, 209, 253, 279, 366, 372, 379, 396, 399, 459, 462

Boucher, 289, 296
Boudinot, 30
Bouldin, 415
Boultbee, 163, 223, 228
Boutwell, 299, 455
Bowden, 213
Bowditch, 388
Bowdoin College, 323
Bowds, 105
Bowe, 372
Bowen, 11, 57, 64, 66, 79, 102, 119, 232, 240, 288, 297, 325, 341, 389, 414, 449, 458, 466
Bowers, 30, 154, 313
Bowie, 84, 139, 276, 357, 398, 417
Bowlegs, 31
Bowlen, 166
Bowles, 120, 248
Bowling, 64, 221, 224, 304, 349
Bowman, 11, 45, 64, 163, 165, 449
Bowne, 215
Bowzer, 349
Boyce, 443
Boyd, 55, 78, 110, 138, 202, 280, 354, 427, 452
Boyden, 191
Boyer, 160, 177
Boyle, 52, 64, 224, 229, 232, 332, 353, 358, 361, 363, 382, 433, 451
Boyne, 46
Boynton, 262
Boytington, 135
Bracey, 341
Braddock, 315
Braden, 241
Bradford, 20, 213, 241, 247, 341, 380
Bradfute, 406
Bradley, 49, 61, 64, 65, 77, 91, 103, 126, 136, 142, 158, 167, 206, 231, 232, 233, 256, 268, 295, 324, 327, 379, 414, 434, 443, 447
Bradly, 143
Brady, 64, 65, 132, 134, 249, 311
Brake, 33
Bramhall, 282
Branch, 323, 448

Branda, 87
Brandt, 146, 158, 270, 271
Branham, 254
Brannsdorff, 380
Bransford, 153
Branson, 169
Brant, 9
Brashears, 217
Brawley, 12, 240, 252
Brawner, 303, 454
Brayton, 176, 197, 206, 394
Brazie, 193
Brazleton, 236
Breast, 159, 213
Breathett, 81
Breckenbaugh, 383
Breckenridge, 65, 309, 330
Breckinridge, 64
Breese, 18, 394
Breevort, 162
Breggeman, 11
Breisach, 119
Bremner, 470
Brenan, 131, 169
Brengle, 120, 136
Brenner, 219
Brent, 21, 64, 130, 188, 260, 286, 288, 336, 375, 431, 436
Brenten, 140
Brereton, 64, 158, 202, 233, 251, 305, 401, 412, 473
Brest, 103, 144, 159
Brevoort, 48
Brew, 370, 375
Brewer, 123, 169, 286, 291, 392, 477
Brewster, 223, 230, 235, 247
Briars, 311
Briceland, 299
Bridge, 339
Bridgett, 64, 230, 449
Bridgwood, 181
Briel, 242
Brien, 157, 324, 334, 398
Brier, 163
brig **Adams**, 48
brig **Albion Cooper**, 331, 340

brig **Bainbridge**, 368, 395
brig **Caledonia**, 95, 113, 156
brig **Chippewa**, 95
brig **Concord**, 446
brig **Dolphin**, 213, 314, 359, 368, 394
brig **Echo**, 359
brig **General Armstrong**, 224, 474
brig **Isle de Cuba**, 418
brig **Leontine**, 258
brig **Perry**, 368, 395
brig **Prometheus**, 88
brig **R W Packer**, 10
brig **Spitfire**, 313
Briggs, 34, 336, 383
Bright, 64, 202, 233, 302
Brink, 417
Brinker, 22, 449
Brintnall, 199
Brisco, 220
Briscoe, 14, 64, 65, 66, 244, 324, 447, 474
Bristol, 248
Bristow, 265
Brittain, 454
Brittingham, 102
Britton, 469
Broadwell, 223, 228, 235, 247, 317
Brobst, 174
Brock, 146, 282
Brockenbrough, 196, 362, 415
Brodbeck, 401
Brodhead, 10, 90, 232
Bromberg, 210, 213
Bromley, 240, 255
Bron, 214
Bronaugh, 64, 65
Bronson, 17
Brooke, 18, 24, 34, 94, 104, 105, 319, 341, 416, 442, 450
Brookes, 235, 301
Brooks, 48, 64, 96, 98, 104, 130, 146, 158, 162, 190, 223, 227, 258, 263, 273, 287, 289, 293, 311, 315, 402, 409, 446
Broom, 318, 347
Broombee, 134

Brou, 183
Brouchard, 196
Brougham, 471
Broughton, 197, 470
Brounstein, 279
Brousard, 174, 183
Broussard, 3, 27, 169, 214, 246
Brouwer, 79
Brower, 63, 378
Browers, 232, 295
Brown, 8, 11, 13, 19, 27, 34, 35, 41, 43, 64, 65, 77, 82, 93, 97, 102, 104, 105, 109, 111, 112, 113, 114, 117, 142, 144, 147, 149, 151, 155, 172, 175, 176, 181, 183, 201, 212, 213, 218, 230, 231, 232, 239, 240, 258, 260, 301, 306, 321, 341, 354, 359, 360, 361, 381, 388, 395, 398, 418, 426, 441, 448, 454, 457, 476
Browne, 38, 87, 121, 126, 176, 186, 394, 397, 416, 445
Brownell, 30, 469, 473
Browning, 93, 100, 136, 202
Brownlee, 99
Brownson, 476
Brubacker, 87
Bruce, 30, 33, 46, 120, 153, 217, 224, 230, 235, 246
Bruckner, 144, 220
Bruff, 69
Brumback, 457
Brune, 260, 398
Bruneau, 459
Bruns, 256
Brush, 64
Bruzy, 52
Bryan, 64, 138, 178, 266, 271, 302, 342, 349, 364, 394, 409, 474
Bryant, 64, 102, 136, 162
Buchalt, 370
Buchanan, 18, 48, 188, 214, 273, 281, 299, 321, 381, 419, 447
Buchhole, 375
Buchley, 64
Buchly, 84, 239
Buchraid, 350

Buck, 272
Buckalew, 250
Buckey, 341, 408
Buckfield, 138
Buckhanan, 39
Buckhart, 252
Buckingham, 110, 186, 344, 346
Buckles, 55
Buckley, 169, 201, 337
Buckner, 30, 252, 288, 394
Budlong, 78
Buel, 106
Buell, 11, 110, 320
Buford, 179, 369
Bulgar, 152
Bulkley, 182
Bull, 64, 104, 204, 447
Bullock, 23, 164, 223, 470, 472
Bulow, 44
Bunnell, 26, 27, 203, 204
Bunting, 105, 273
Burch, 32, 37, 68, 146, 230, 231, 233, 447
Burche, 64
Burdett, 65
Burdine, 195, 232, 441
Burgess, 28, 49, 124
Burgey, 152
Burgin, 92
Burgwyn, 187
Burhman, 105
Burk, 3
Burke, 160, 168, 201, 308, 386
Burkhead, 231
Burkout, 425
Burley, 65
Burlingham, 194
Burnett, 56, 154, 192, 201, 296, 477
Burney, 231, 265
Burnham, 26, 27, 101, 224, 294
Burns, 62, 64, 155, 160, 229, 231, 237, 248, 347, 352, 380, 386, 402, 404, 410, 466, 471
Burnside, 57
Burr, 10, 93, 451
Burroughs, 122, 199, 349

Burrow, 372, 394
Burrows, 132
Burrus, 14
Burt, 93, 141
Burton, 247
Burwell, 98, 186, 343
Bury, 64, 230, 411
Busch, 337, 370
Busey, 104, 136
Bush, 65, 390
Bush Hill, 141
Bushnell, 377, 382
Buswell, 193
Butcher, 64
Butler, 4, 26, 27, 43, 55, 64, 104, 111, 131, 144, 162, 169, 251, 433, 438, 462
Butt, 62, 90, 292, 306, 431
Butterfield, 225, 237
Butterworth, 113, 140
Butts, 288
Buttt, 154
Byington, 64, 67, 242
Byles, 5
Byng, 61, 193
Byrd, 110, 199, 346, 357
Byrens, 469, 473
Byrne, 23, 64, 98, 169, 213, 231, 285, 287, 304
Byrnes, 114

C

Cabell, 285, 346, 415
Cabot, 66, 109
Cabott, 431
Caden, 260
Cadett, 416
Cadwallader, 167, 398
Cainnes, 422
Cairnes, 430
Caldwell, 116, 200, 201, 225, 230, 295, 347, 350
Calef, 122
Calhoun, 22, 29, 47, 156, 162, 280, 283, 288, 372
Callaghan, 142
Callahan, 42, 46, 65, 127, 143, 232

Callahen, 282
Callan, 65, 66, 90, 98, 231, 270, 289, 292
Callaway, 332
Calvert, 27, 40, 48, 61, 348
Calvert College, 314
camels, 92, 437
Cameron, 34, 52, 55, 161, 233, 420, 449
Cammack, 107, 137, 233, 256, 361
Camp, 44, 274, 470
Camp Scott, 178
Campbell, 47, 49, 65, 66, 79, 94, 127, 138, 139, 189, 236, 237, 270, 296, 303, 349, 372, 394, 411, 414, 426, 431, 433, 468
Cancemi, 3
Candal, 385
Candler, 166
Canfield, 11, 55, 214, 215, 247
Cann, 319
Cannady, 122
Cannon, 65, 133, 204, 217, 289
Canoll, 61
Canon, 155, 443
Canova, 424
Cantwell, 76
Capahosie, 309
Capers, 196
Capron, 45, 336
Caradine, 106
Carberry, 326, 462
Carbery, 66, 90, 114, 185, 245, 335, 381, 455
Carden, 252
Carey, 286
Caris, 24
Carl, 280, 303, 307
Carlin, 233, 337
Carlisle, 66, 267, 270
Carlton, 315
Carman, 140
Carmelite Convent, 455
Carmichael, 173
Carnes, 435
Carney, 243

Carothers, 4, 144, 190, 272, 325, 382, 395, 397, 475
Carpenter, 46, 138, 203, 204, 213, 233, 246, 326
Carr, 10, 28, 154, 164, 169, 201, 284, 403, 405, 431
Carrell, 188
Carrico, 65, 119, 126, 143, 269, 296, 349
Carrigan, 400, 468
Carriger, 34
Carrington, 154, 352
Carrol, 145
Carroll, 65, 81, 108, 158, 178, 225, 230, 279, 318, 325, 348, 398, 443, 447
Carrollton Manor, 202
Carrothers, 379
Carson, 55, 105, 144, 225, 380, 423, 432
Carter, 8, 13, 23, 30, 36, 61, 62, 76, 135, 154, 155, 167, 194, 208, 211, 215, 231, 249, 251, 295, 314, 340, 392, 415, 416, 457, 469, 473
Cartzany, 467
Carusi, 21, 41, 222, 336
Caruthers, 151
Carver, 62, 164, 223, 227, 340, 341, 382
Cary, 20, 291
Casali, 309
Case, 185, 368, 394
Casey, 13, 103, 371
Caskey, 216
Caskie, 153
Caslo, 155, 211
Cass, 250, 255, 281, 342
Cassaday, 324
Cassady, 199
Cassell, 146, 158
Cassey, 168
Cassiday, 65, 104
Cassidy, 157
Cassilis, 92
Cassin, 28, 58, 66, 436, 439, 478
Casteel, 65
Castell, 232
Casten, 268
Castillo, 59
Castine, 167

Castle, 76
Castleman, 239
Casto, 60
Catholic Church, 87
Catholic Churches, 332
Catlett, 244
Catlin, 110
Cato, 47, 186, 297
Catoctin Iron Works, 423
Caton, 11, 19, 66, 231
Catonsville, 308
Catts, 425
Caulfield, 188, 210, 215, 236, 288
Causee, 32
Cauth, 164
Cauwee, 443
Cavenaugh, 4, 65
Cavendish, 57
Cawood, 390
Caxxillo, 24, 215
Cazeau, 203, 204, 221
Cazenove, 175, 415
Cecil, 199
Cenci, 123
Chace, 80, 171, 387
Chadbron, 457
Chadwick, 289
Chaffee, 8, 95, 122, 236
Chafin, 136
Chamberlain, 55, 290
Chambers, 65
Chambliss, 348
Champe, 8, 38, 151
Champion, 105, 202, 232
Champlain, 355
Chandler, 17, 30, 45, 66, 175, 250, 319, 426, 445, 469, 473
Channing, 298
Chapin, 17, 116, 163, 231, 351
Chaplin, 477
Chapman, 21, 34, 40, 65, 85, 105, 122, 131, 164, 177, 195, 208, 220, 221, 222, 280, 322, 327, 352, 364, 390, 432, 433, 452, 456
Chappel, 210
Chappell, 234

Charles, 11
Charpenning, 207
Chase, 26, 37, 157, 164, 223, 235, 247
Chassain, 394
Chassaing, 220
Chatard, 5, 473
Chatelier, 161
Chaudonet, 160
Chauncey, 29, 365
Chauvenet, 191
Cheatham, 142
Chedell, 11
Cheever, 82
Cheney, 463
Cheshire, 65
Chessell, 412
Chester, 42, 65
Chestnut Hill, 429
Chetwood, 418
Chevallie, 416
Chevis, 3, 183
Chew, 104, 310, 409, 477
Chika, 395
Childer, 301
Childs, 65, 110, 384, 452, 472
Chillon Castle Manor, 364
Chillon Castle Manor Farm, 116
Chilton, 66, 83, 413, 453
Chipley, 394
Chipman, 448
Chippewa Chief, 38
Chisholm, 33, 50, 65, 232
Chism, 230
Chittenden, 66
Chittum, 105
Chomel, 177
Chormann, 470
Chorpenning, 113, 183, 210
Choteau, 65
Chowpening, 94
Christian, 201, 262, 365, 376
Christmas day, 475
Chubb, 65
Church, 65, 269
Church of St Isaac, 302
Churchill, 52, 97, 123, 204, 235, 246

Cissel, 56
Cissell, 70, 321, 376
Clack, 299
Claffin, 465
Clagett, 73, 75, 276, 281, 303, 358, 385, 389, 391, 446
Claggett, 478
Claiborne, 367, 377
Clairborne, 305
Clampitt, 66, 136, 230
Clanton, 106, 127
Clapdore, 65
Clapp, 43, 94
Clark, 39, 46, 65, 66, 93, 104, 124, 145, 158, 207, 213, 231, 233, 235, 242, 244, 245, 270, 272, 290, 291, 328, 335, 361, 370, 372, 383, 394, 399, 425, 447, 458
Clarke, 11, 14, 20, 28, 35, 39, 62, 65, 66, 98, 99, 106, 114, 115, 142, 146, 158, 162, 194, 197, 199, 205, 214, 237, 257, 271, 273, 289, 290, 291, 292, 339, 394, 443, 444, 447
Clary, 330
Claude, 470
Clawson, 470
Claxton, 11, 56, 96, 242
Clay, 152, 160, 253, 372, 429, 469, 470
Clayton, 94, 122, 144, 182, 302
Clear, 147
Cleary, 289, 400, 449
Clemens, 179, 362
Clement, 168, 252, 346
Clements, 21, 65, 77, 179, 230, 282, 289, 437, 447, 449
Clemm, 104
Clemson, 468
Clephane, 27, 281
Clermont, 50
Cleveland, 89, 390
Clifford, 18, 253, 341, 443
Clingman, 192
Clinton, 8, 163, 166, 191, 234, 240, 391
Clitherall, 151
Cloakey, 65, 66
Clopper, 136

Close, 164, 223, 235, 247, 357, 437, 447
Cloud, 326
Clough, 383, 416
Cloutier, 97
Clover Dale, 92
Clowes, 9
Cloze, 227
Cluskey, 65
Clute, 356
Clymer, 137
Coale, 93
Coates, 36, 183, 241
Coatsworth, 89, 461
Cobb, 273, 293, 343, 404
Cochran, 11, 65, 66, 128, 133, 260, 279, 397
Cocke, 153
Cocking, 66
Codrington, 65
Coe, 105, 121, 262
Coffee, 34
Coger, 87
Coghlin, 102
Cogswell, 11
Cohen, 62, 124, 167, 359
Cohn, 370
Coke, 66, 273
Cokendorfer, 66
Colbert, 430
Colbly, 157
Colburn, 475
Colby, 223, 228, 235, 247, 317
Colclazer, 65
Colcock, 101
Coldes, 255
Cole, 65, 76, 437
Coleman, 66, 136
Coles, 415
Colfax, 314
Colgrere, 8
Colgrove, 19, 23
Collamer, 191, 262
Collar, 65
Collet, 110
Colley, 121, 177, 228, 230, 303, 355, 357, 361

Collier, 198, 213, 228
Collings, 311
Collingsworth, 66
Collingwood, 110
Collins, 65, 66, 104, 105, 168, 170, 217, 261, 297, 429, 437, 439, 443
Collison, 76
Colloway, 116
Collum, 14
Colored Bishop, 404
Colt, 9, 168, 220, 406
Coltman, 230, 256, 296, 439, 449, 451
Colton, 398
Columbian College, 194, 204, 337
Combe, 347
Combs, 47, 322, 444, 469
Compare, 94
Compton, 65, 413, 474
Comstock, 20, 143, 151, 280
Condict, 388
Condit, 215
Cone, 284
Coney, 210
Congressional Cemetery, 133, 248
Congressional Globe, 417
Conington, 65
Conlan, 92
Conlin, 281
Connell, 138, 149, 241, 321, 424
Connelly, 66, 437
Conner, 96, 146, 158, 269, 271, 285
Connery, 445
Connolly, 65, 66, 94, 96
Connor, 65, 181, 232, 443
Conover, 248
Conrad, 18, 266, 284
Conservatory, 6
Considine, 65
Contee's station, 427
Converse, 82, 168
Conway, 22, 27, 160, 169, 174, 192, 196, 214, 246, 416
Conzaga, 26
Cook, 24, 34, 55, 65, 66, 103, 176, 201, 232, 267, 334, 369, 432
Cooke, 91, 178, 199, 283, 330, 398, 436

Cookman, 222
Cooley, 356
Coolidge, 288
coolies, 42
Coombe, 65
Coombes, 65, 342
Coombs, 62, 65, 105, 230, 232, 299, 339, 476
Coomes, 168, 295
Coon, 315
Coonrod, 122
Cooper, 16, 28, 90, 134, 154, 199, 200, 233, 301, 323, 334, 346, 393, 406, 460, 466
Cope, 65
Copeland, 132, 157, 394
Corbin, 162, 181
Corcoran, 66, 71, 113, 248, 320, 348, 361
Corder, 467
Cordier, 83
Corey, 113
Corley, 146, 438
Corling, 390
Cornelius, 105
Cornell, 306
corner-stone, 336
Cornick, 415
Cornwall, 265, 339, 385
Cornwell, 175, 395
Corp of Gtwn, 346
Corre, 414
Corrie, 262
Corse, 65
Corson, 338
corvette **Concord**, 95
Corwin, 58, 262
Cosby, 415
Coskery, 181
Coslett, 443
Costa, 53
Costanz, 456
Costigan, 65, 140, 393, 458
Costtin, 66
Cotrell, 402, 426
Cotton, 279, 379, 470

Coudon, 59
Coulter, 338
Coumbe, 66
Count Fersien, 253
Countess of Effingham, 254
Coursey, 232
Courtenay, 443
Courtnay, 330
Courtney, 175, 232, 345
Cousins, 88
Cowan, 162, 389, 390
Coward, 463
Cowen, 272
Cowherd, 417
Cowles, 443
Cowperthwait, 139
Cox, 53, 55, 57, 62, 66, 76, 122, 125, 152, 189, 231, 251, 267, 307, 331, 340, 357, 370, 375, 377, 383, 414, 416, 434, 436, 454, 456, 473, 477
Coxe, 129, 176, 228, 236, 238
Coyle, 35, 38, 90, 98, 108, 145, 414
Cozzens, 203, 204, 369
Crabb, 204
Crabbe, 33, 37, 60, 449, 469, 472
Craig, 65, 94, 97, 99, 123, 230, 328, 333, 385
Crain, 422
Crall, 379
Cram, 200
Cramer, 28
Crampton, 46, 164, 260
Cranch, 31, 66
Crandall, 379
Crandell, 62, 65, 90
Crane, 78, 122, 284, 287
Cranston, 439
Crauford, 382
Craven, 18, 215, 249
Craver, 260, 425
Crawford, 90, 148, 185, 261
Creager, 195
Creaser, 231
Creeney, 443
Creigh, 442
Crepin, 384

Crescent, 272
Cressy, 286
Cribbet, 40
Crichton, 398
Crinian, 44
Cripps, 23, 39, 372
Crisfield, 474
Crispin, 171
Crittenden, 97, 123, 191, 315, 469
Crocker, 99
Crockett, 128, 273
Croggan, 66
Croggon, 410
Crogham, 248
Croghan, 60
Crompston, 208
Crompton, 215
Cromwell, 106
Cronan, 137
Cronin, 106, 232, 357, 365, 394
Cronk, 293
Crook, 156
Cropley, 11
Crosby, 46, 219, 235
Crosman, 199
Cross, 35, 65, 66, 88, 89, 208, 297, 306
Crossfield, 341
Crossman, 18, 168, 394, 419
Crosson, 56
Croswell, 114
Crouch, 112, 255
Crow, 91
Crowin, 262
Crowley, 445
Crown, 65, 165, 328
Crozet, 298, 424
Cruickshank, 214
Cruikshank, 99, 156, 305, 336
Cruit, 66, 261
Cruse, 476
Crutcher, 81
Crutchett, 65, 233, 256, 377
Cruzat, 397
Culbertson, 22
Culican, 242
Cull, 273

Cullen, 162, 415
Cullom, 289
Culpepper, 124
Culver, 82, 231, 402
Culverwell, 12
Cumberland, 233, 271, 470
Cumming, 4, 28, 106, 133, 320, 449
Cummings, 105, 265, 470
Cummins, 82, 117, 181, 235, 237, 336, 338
Cunlberg, 8
Cunningham, 11, 13, 29, 58, 78, 97, 101, 104, 184, 196, 202, 253, 258, 271, 387, 395, 455
Cupples, 87
Cureton, 164, 316
Curran, 202, 232
Currey, 357
Currier, 254
Curry, 65, 121, 241
Curtin, 8
Curtis, 2, 18, 65, 66, 102, 222, 395, 414
Cushing, 182, 300, 463
Cushley, 65
Cushman, 130, 165, 201, 223, 225, 235, 246, 249, 394, 429
Custis, 184
Cutter, 467
Cutting, 187
Cutts, 33
Cuyahoga Historical Society, 402
Cyrus, 214

D

D'Ivernois, 143
d'Orleans, 234
Dabney, 390
DaCosta, 424
Dade, 21, 199
Daggett, 14
Dahlgren, 169, 218
Daily, 168
Daily Globe, 417
Dainese, 320, 457
Daingerfield, 359
Dalby, 308

Dale, 270
Daley, 67, 355
Dalhousie, 471
Dally, 104, 105
Dalrymple, 396
Dalton, 67, 419, 443
Daly, 66, 443
Daman, 94
Damburghy, 119
Dameron, 191
Dammert, 380
Damrell, 477
Damron, 254
Dana, 274, 394
Dandelet, 447
Dandridge, 91, 468
Dandy, 360, 405
Dane, 187
Daney, 53
Danforth, 437
Daniel, 147, 153, 166, 186, 285, 287, 341
Daniels, 150, 379, 399
Danike, 380
Danmuller, 380
Dannoy, 50
Darby, 305, 311
Darden, 231, 273
Dardenne, 108
Dare, 34, 48
Darker, 294
Darly, 28
Darnal, 350
Darnall, 342
Darnell, 348
Darnes, 256
Darrell, 442
Dart, 44, 66, 91, 127, 159, 213
Dashiel, 51, 163, 385
Dashiell, 94, 104, 115, 132, 203, 247, 300, 466
Datcher, 212
Daun, 454
Daunoy, 470
Davenport, 223, 227, 235, 247
David, 66, 326

Davidge, 66, 67, 107, 197, 223, 228, 303, 399
Davidson, 22, 66, 67, 107, 112, 143, 231, 279, 280, 283, 350, 360, 386, 405, 477
Davies, 12, 175
Davis, 11, 30, 41, 42, 43, 56, 66, 67, 72, 78, 93, 102, 105, 111, 135, 137, 142, 143, 145, 158, 188, 201, 202, 203, 204, 211, 225, 230, 231, 232, 256, 270, 271, 272, 285, 287, 289, 314, 322, 323, 324, 367, 390, 395, 401, 427, 431, 434, 439, 446, 469
Davison, 104
Daw, 400
Dawes, 152
Dawley, 102, 357
Dawson, 36, 355, 442
Dawson Farm, 442
Day, 33, 83, 379, 412, 440
Dayton, 66, 193, 377, 390
de Albuquerque, 406
de Arguello, 205
De Armas, 89
de Bodisco, 177
de Bonne, 155
De Bow, 50, 80
De Coeniel, 356
de Gammond, 61
De Groot, 220
De Haven, 211
De La Figaniere, 386
De Lannby, 223
De Lanney, 247
De Lannoy, 99, 130
De Launay, 282
De Leon, 358
De Luce, 341
De Mercy, 161
De Pont, 406
de Repentigny, 155
De Ronceray, 56
De Selding, 454
de Visser, 203
De Visser, 38
de Watterstedt, 263

dead, 168
Deakins, 175
Deale, 105, 457
Deamer, 338
Deamit, 163
Dean, 172, 233, 308, 326, 336
Deans, 194
Dearborn, 69, 349, 354
Dearing, 122, 176, 287
Dearmit, 223, 227, 247, 317
Deavenport, 164
Debbes, 214
Decamp, 307
Decatur, 55, 88, 226
DeCharms, 470
Declaration of Independence, 318
DeCraft, 372
Deeth, 87
Degges, 67, 296, 361
DeHaven, 392
Deigenhart, 13, 24
DeKraft, 394
Delafield, 369
Delaigle, 289
Delane, 252
Delaney, 18
Delany, 443
Delcross, 248
DeLeon, 465
Delhi, 148
Dell, 101
Dellaway, 444
Delphy, 39, 56, 226
Delzell, 305
Deman, 94
DeMay, 424
Dement, 67, 312, 474
Demers, 160
Demilt, 308
Demond, 431
Dempsey, 76, 183, 238, 297, 384
Denaise, 94
Denby, 102, 394
Deneal, 326
Dener, 55
Denham, 67, 231, 324, 365

Denison, 379
Denman, 103, 144
Dennesson, 446, 457, 472
Dennet, 221
Dennett, 91
Dennis, 237, 398
Dennison, 49, 62, 133, 155, 196, 310
Denniston, 138
Denny, 48, 54, 77, 122, 340, 466
Densley, 66
Dent, 20, 66, 94, 360, 405
Denver, 48, 248, 281
Dermady, 409
Dernelle, 121
Derrick, 108, 170, 194, 306
Derringer, 406
DeRussy, 284, 470
Deschamps, 355
Descombe, 436
Desforges, 263
Deshiell, 466
Deshler, 465
Desmond, 20
Despommier, 369
Despratt, 35
Despriges, 263
Determan, 229
Detwiler, 12
Devan, 397
Devaughan, 138
DeVaughan, 107
Devaughn, 11, 49, 445
Develin, 134
Deveraux, 139
Devereux, 52
Devers, 67
Devidine, 246
Devidrein, 227
Devidrine, 130, 223, 235
Devin, 145
Devine, 91, 170, 219
Devlin, 143, 269, 282
Dewees, 67
Dewey, 101
Dewitt, 414
Diamond, 67, 315

Dice, 104
Dick, 25, 76, 130, 199, 223, 247, 394, 398
Dickens, 66, 440
Dickerson, 71, 196
Dickie, 311
Dickinson, 107, 129, 164, 223, 246, 271, 317, 351, 387
Dickman, 188
Dickson, 66, 97, 103, 105, 187, 188
Diefendorf, 47
Digges, 51, 106, 136, 295, 320, 349, 464
Diggins, 175
Diggs, 106, 132, 301
Digney, 66
Dillard, 130, 282
Diller, 442
Dillon, 164, 281, 344
Dimick, 97, 284
Dimitry, 281
Dimmick, 103, 358
Dimond, 20
Dink, 53, 77
Dinman, 443
Dinney, 122
Diomatari, 53
Disharoon, 188, 210, 219
Disher, 67
Distorges, 171
Ditmas, 55
Divine, 27, 158, 271, 320
Divorce in England, 79
Dix, 126
Dixon, 36, 54, 74, 126, 183, 286, 297, 348, 473
Doane, 78, 85, 418
Dobbin, 3
Dobbins, 391
Dobbyn, 349
Dobson, 66, 418
Dodd, 104, 163
Dodge, 40, 47, 93, 122, 194, 232, 240, 254, 280, 329, 364, 398
Dodson, 66, 363
Doherty, 443
Dohnar, 8

Dolan, 141, 363
Dole, 168, 293
Doll, 67
Dolliver, 240
Dolman, 146
Donaghue, 66, 72
Donahue, 435
Donaldson, 33, 60, 66, 132, 163, 223, 230, 242, 246, 247, 326, 331
Donelan, 66, 67
Donevent, 369
Doniphan, 249
Donn, 31, 67, 81, 231, 237, 306, 419, 436, 451
Donnavan, 478
Donnell, 142, 257, 270
Donnelly, 4, 9, 21, 102, 430
Donnoghue, 67
Donoho, 11, 67, 90, 108, 230, 255, 269, 270
Donohoe, 305
Donohoo, 123
Donovan, 67
Doolittle, 17, 293, 336
Doone, 115
Doran, 199
Doremus, 402
Dorn, 34, 390
Dorrance, 324, 329
Dorris, 248
Dorry, 305
Dorsay, 54
Dorsett, 11, 49, 136
Dorsey, 3, 54, 63, 140, 145, 201, 240, 257, 276, 301, 322, 345, 401, 403, 412
Doty, 163, 223
Dougherty, 66, 100, 149, 232, 282, 306, 379, 408
Douglas, 44, 52, 66, 134, 166, 296, 470
Douglass, 198, 230, 282
Dougty, 291
Dove, 29, 35, 66, 67, 80, 155, 190, 232, 239, 439, 472
Dow, 55
Dowd, 26, 89, 344

Dowling, 11, 108, 127, 234, 305, 343, 411
Downer, 18, 231
Downes, 394
Downey, 417, 423, 430
Downing, 67, 137, 203
Downs, 116, 213, 351
Doyle, 67, 231, 357, 400, 469, 473
Draine, 108
Drake, 109, 122, 130, 365
Draper, 164, 213, 223, 225, 323, 347
Drayton, 393
Drew, 213, 247, 416
Drish, 308
Driver, 382
Droman, 13
Drout, 103, 205
Drueken, 67
Drummond, 34, 293, 306
Drury, 28, 66, 127, 185, 231, 256, 271, 305
Dryer, 371
Dryon, 388
Drysdale, 284
Duane, 137, 178
Dubant, 397
Dubois, 137
Dubose, 166
Ducachet, 368
Duchess Maria, 292
Duchess of Orleans, 229, 234, 241
Duckett, 72, 462
Dudley, 93, 188, 233, 310, 357
Duer, 15, 228, 319
Dufau, 308
Duff, 401
Duffy, 146, 158, 231
Dufief, 66
Duhaine, 259
Duke, 314
Duke of Mecklenburg, 348
Duke of Orleans, 270
Dulaney, 341
Dulany, 348
Duley, 67
Dulin, 66

Dumbar, 43
Dunawin, 271, 413
Dunbar, 66, 172
Duncan, 51, 111, 161, 223, 273, 341
Duncanson, 136, 161, 227
Dundas, 310, 386
Dundelet, 357
Dunham, 304
Dunlop, 153, 300, 381, 395, 402
Dunn, 214, 278, 306, 371, 424
Dunnington, 11, 239, 292, 394
Dupont, 297
Durand, 160
Durfeddt, 370
Durfee, 161
Durfield, 370
Durham, 14, 217
Durkee, 94
Durofeld, 375
Durr, 67
Duryee, 253
Dusenbery, 111
Dusenbury, 236, 337
Dutton, 4, 297, 463
Duvail, 66
Duval, 196, 429
Duvall, 40, 43, 85, 130, 214, 319, 342, 347, 462, 475
Dwight, 107, 201
Dwinel, 100, 223, 224, 247, 316
Dwinell, 188
Dye, 400
Dyer, 31, 66, 67, 144, 230, 231, 291, 349, 476
Dyson, 238

E

Eacine, 294
Eades, 443
Eagle, 472
Eakin, 105, 453
Eakle, 67
Earl, 230, 348
Earl of Glengall, 296
Early, 382
Earn, 230
Earnest, 345
Easby, 67, 114, 115, 116, 136, 142, 158, 364
East, 111
Easter, 476
Eastgate, 392
Eastham, 52, 203, 204, 225, 235, 317
Eastman, 23, 199
Easton, 385
Eaton, 67, 81, 92, 94, 177, 408, 445
Ebbinghaus, 369
Ebbittt House, 119
Eccleston, 165
Echard, 425
Echols, 286, 297
Eckard, 372
Eckler, 429
Eckloff, 67
Eckstein, 476
Eddin, 289
Eddy, 42, 102, 168
Edelin, 67, 149, 216, 270, 282, 289, 449
Edes, 10, 29, 185, 364
Edge Hill, 474
Edgerton, 2
Edgeworth, 366, 387, 431
Edmonds, 241
Edmondston, 111
Edmonson, 90, 231
Edmonston, 11, 137, 230, 239, 295, 393
Edwards, 58, 67, 78, 84, 87, 99, 105, 106, 137, 139, 149, 189, 211, 223, 225, 230, 266, 278, 338, 341, 366, 392, 433, 439
Effinger, 104
Egan, 122, 449
Eggleston, 105, 143, 164, 174, 394
Eichhorn, 478
Eiffert, 380
Eisenbise, 60
Eisfeld, 369
Eisfield, 375
Ela, 262
Elam, 23
Elder, 34
Eldredge, 10

Eldridge, 59, 308, 398
Elgar, 456
Eliot, 167, 210, 361, 366, 374
Elisler, 299
Eliza Frances, 279
Elkins, 48, 396
Ellet, 176, 374
Elli, 459
Ellicott, 407
Ellicott's Mills, 127
Elliot, 67
Elliott, 34, 47, 68, 176, 241, 409, 410, 421, 431
Ellis, 62, 67, 153, 179, 404
Ellman, 146
Elvans, 67
Elwyn, 191
Ely, 142
Emans, 193
Emerich, 353
Emerick, 67
Emerson, 18, 270, 282
Emery, 296, 425
Emmerson, 230
Emmert, 98, 307
Emory, 196, 295, 338
Emperor Nicholas, 302
Emperor of Austria, 211
Empie, 294
Empress Josephine, 307
Empress Regent, 86
Empy, 172
Emrich, 340
Emrick, 366, 374
Endlich, 20
Engle, 105
English, 7, 11, 67, 143, 162, 231, 239, 285, 291, 314, 383
Ennis, 76, 98, 108, 145, 158, 231, 362, 448
Enthoffer, 329
Entwisle, 133, 143, 230, 232, 261, 296, 449
Epes, 390
Eppes, 226
Ergen, 370, 375

Erickson, 36
Ericsson, 203, 293
Ernest, 296
Erving, 284
Esch, 288
Esperandien, 450
Espey, 67
Essex, 21, 161, 167, 172, 210
Estep, 53
Estlin, 381
Etchison, 105, 383, 404
Etheredge, 370
Etheridge, 55
Etting, 177
Eugard, 280
Eustis, 475
Evans, 67, 80, 115, 117, 131, 151, 191, 212, 233, 295, 346, 389, 395, 425, 427, 443, 449
Eve, 189, 271, 387
Ever, 302
Everdell, 447
Everett, 82, 134, 274, 336, 414
Eversfield, 322
Ewans, 105
Ewbank, 447
Ewe, 255
Ewell, 300
Ewing, 10, 67, 122, 149, 262, 294, 319, 384
Eyre, 12

F

Fabens, 245
Fagot, 102
Faherty, 68
Fahey, 68, 322
Fahs, 394
Fair, 250
Fair Hill Boarding School, 329
Fair View, 139
Fairbanks, 9, 229, 295
Fairchild, 272
Fairchilds, 129
Fairclough, 470
Fairfax, 97, 98

Falay, 300
Falconer, 399
Fales, 67
Faley, 462
Fallon, 281
Falls, 421
Fanning, 135, 159, 163, 236, 247, 318
Fant, 341
Farias, 330
Faries, 148
Farley, 122
Farmer, 77
Farnham, 293
Farnsworth, 52
Faron, 365
Farquhar, 68, 297, 329
Farragut, 30, 453
Farran, 252
Farrand, 285, 368, 395
Farrar, 67
Farrell, 67, 79, 81, 195, 259, 331
Farren, 318, 423
Farrington, 293
Farrow, 135
Fassett, 51
Fast Man, 265
Fatherly, 466
Fatio, 67
Faulkenberger, 68
Faulkner, 68, 118, 186, 313, 330, 338
Faunce, 368
Fauntleroy, 123, 473
Faust, 294
Favier, 67, 176, 240, 307
Faw, 67
Fawsett, 326
Fay, 20, 329
Fearson, 230, 256, 448, 464, 472
Featherston, 457
Fellins, 82
Fellows, 62, 164, 223, 227, 235, 247, 291
Felt, 55
Fendall, 231
Fenne, 67
Fenton, 21, 186

Fenwick, 149, 229
Ferguson, 1, 27, 53, 105, 168, 228, 231, 232, 263, 269, 305, 308, 465, 469
Fernandez, 364
Ferrar, 109, 110
Ferree, 260
Ferris, 67
Ferry, 335
Fessenden, 191, 213, 215, 323, 354
Feuchtwanger, 44
Fewill, 201
Field, 26, 27, 85, 203, 204, 213, 226, 321, 324, 410, 461
Fields, 67, 307
Fife, 10, 55
Fifield, 58
Figh, 217, 238
Fillebrown, 394
Fillmore, 57, 80, 86, 389
Fills, 35
Finch, 67, 150
Finckel, 344
Findlay, 47, 48, 147
Findly, 365
Fines, 167
Finkman, 231
Finks, 210
Finlay, 354
Finley, 102, 127, 426
Finotti, 175
First Church in Hartford, 386
First Colony, 109
first cousins, 100
first house, 451
first of American parentage, 442
first white woman, 369
Fischer, 68, 229, 415
Fish, 284
Fisher, 4, 20, 34, 35, 48, 67, 78, 127, 150, 206, 230, 239, 303, 339, 342, 409, 416, 424, 444, 449, 463
Fisk, 67
Fiske, 355
Fitch, 235, 240
Fitchen, 380
Fitman, 107, 328

Fitz, 242, 307, 370
Fitzgerald, 67, 99, 129, 155, 197, 245, 295, 335, 469, 473, 478
Fitzhugh, 173, 284, 414
Fitzpatrick, 35, 98, 191, 204, 213, 228, 232, 292
flag of the U S, 474
Flagg, 23, 133, 469, 473
Flaherty, 172, 206, 231, 319
Flanigan, 307
Flanner, 102
Flannery, 68
Flansburg, 219
Fleet, 67
Fleischman, 325
Fleishell, 232, 320
Fleming, 18, 153, 196, 197, 213, 222, 223, 225, 235, 247, 293, 298, 357, 360, 405, 415
Flemming, 80, 225
Flenner, 449
Fletcher, 34, 49, 145, 158, 162, 230, 231, 254, 300, 325, 427
Fleury, 196, 215
Flinn, 125, 133, 173
Flint, 67, 438
Flint's Hotel, 118
Flinton, 331
Float, 372
Flood, 46, 213, 233
Floor, 12, 159
Floridus, 273
Flournoy, 363, 415
Floyd, 84, 120, 152, 198, 200, 268, 274, 330, 421
Flussar, 249
Flusser, 394
Flye, 237
Flynn, 160, 201, 302, 432, 436
Fogg, 271, 387
Foley, 379, 397, 443
Folige, 380
Folk, 238
Folker, 375
Folkz, 320
Follansbee, 67

Follen, 337
Foller, 67
Follett, 284
Fonda, 311
Fontaine, 181, 199
Fooks, 164
Foot, 6, 200, 464
Foote, 80, 86, 251, 438
Foran, 98
Forbert, 477
Forbes, 102, 182, 267
Force, 11, 49, 68, 164, 270, 299, 363, 462
Ford, 67, 68, 139, 146, 157, 262, 355, 373, 387, 388
Fore, 223, 227
Foreman, 378
Forest Hill, 257
Forester, 207
Forests, 214
Forrest, 48, 67, 68, 106, 141, 232, 274, 327, 342, 379, 394, 398, 402, 444, 472
Forster, 57, 265
Forsyth, 24, 108, 211, 214, 238, 282, 335, 457, 467
Forsythe, 289
Fort, 68
Fort Bridger, 255
Fort Brown, 103
Fort Clarke, 288
Fort Crawford Reservation, 198
Fort Davis, 387
Fort Defiance, 409, 438
Fort Delaware, 313, 466
Fort Des Moines, 99
Fort Dodge, 250
Fort Drane, 103
Fort Frown, 466
Fort Gaines, 142
Fort Gilleland, 23
Fort Laramie, 15, 330
Fort Leavenworth, 23, 39, 109, 116, 120, 239, 287, 288, 369, 421
Fort McHenry, 374
Fort McKavett, 268
Fort Moultrie, 304

Fort Quitman, 387
Fort Randall, 288
Fort Riley, 99
Fort Scott, 476
Fort Simcoe, 405, 445
Fort Smith, 288, 421
Fort Smith Times, 194
Fort Steilacoon, 288
Fort Taylor, 405
Fort Union, 385
Fort Washington, 311
Fort Washita, 421
Fort Wayne, 190
Fort Wm Henry Hotel, 225
Forward, 163
Foster, 34, 42, 68, 99, 189, 460, 475
Fougeray, 160
Foulkes, 67
Fountain, 384
Fourier, 380
Fournier, 293
Foute, 379
Foux, 384
Fowke, 67
Fowle, 164, 230, 425
Fowler, 2, 37, 67, 164, 227, 247, 272, 429, 447, 462
Fox, 20, 59, 67, 93, 190, 273, 393
Foy, 42, 43, 67, 172
Frahluk, 175
Frampton, 105
Francis, 94, 216, 367, 388, 434
Francisco, 180, 194, 470
Franck, 185
Frank, 67, 87, 230, 286, 425, 468
Frankinberger, 34
Franklin, 11, 90, 273, 312, 318, 369, 395, 439
Franzoni, 11, 273
Fraser, 67, 68
Frasier, 23, 68, 91
Frayser, 416
Freas, 344
Frederic, 288
Frederich, 375
Frederick, 282

Frednock, 27
Freeburger, 232
Freeland, 48
Freeman, 67, 185, 194, 204, 335
Freibold, 370
Freitas, 169
Fremont, 48, 153, 155, 336
French, 10, 67, 125, 167, 202, 232, 256, 324, 327
Frere, 231, 322
Frick, 447
Friebold, 375
Friedrich, 370
Friend, 73, 132, 470
Friendship, 408
frig **Colorado**, 199
frig **Congress**, 18, 147
frig **Constellation**, 88
frig **Guerriere**, 147
frig **Java**, 147
frig **Macedonian**, 88, 176
frig **Merrimack**, 245
frig **Minnesota**, 430
frig **Niagara**, 1, 309, 321, 365
frig **President**, 95
frig **Roanoke**, 413
frig **Sabine**, 368, 393
frig **Saranac**, 258
frig **Savannah**, 458
frig **St Laurence**, 394
frig **St Lawrence**, 94
frig **Susquehanna**, 160, 165, 168, 176, 201
frig **United States**, 95
frig **Wabash**, 162, 176
frigs Niagara, Wabash, & Minnesota, 177
Frikard, 197
Frindly, 370
Frink, 188
Frisby, 197
Fritz, 470
Frizel, 164
Frizzle, 141
Frost, 89, 177, 199, 213, 308
Fruit of the Loom, 283

Fruitland, 425
Fry, 30, 67, 252, 278
Frye, 67
Fudge, 258, 412
Fugate, 130, 223, 224, 227, 235, 247
Fugitt, 67, 68, 232, 249
Fugleman, 184
Fullalove, 296
Fuller, 42, 130, 210, 308, 455, 470
Fulmer, 148, 419
Fulton, 248, 402, 437
Funk, 354
Funnemark, 380
Furmage, 397

G

Gaddis, 136, 305
Gadsby, 54, 68, 112, 338, 452
Gadsden, 476
Gaeble, 257
Gagan, 409
Gagliardi, 108
Gagnon, 44, 203, 204, 210, 246
Gaines, 10, 45, 211, 213, 245, 449
Gainness, 164
Gainor, 292
Gale, 34, 225, 272, 294, 297
Galena, 168, 201
Gales, 11, 269, 278, 357
Gallagher, 25, 68
Gallant, 68, 145, 158
Galligan, 90
Gallighan, 68
Galligher, 39
Gallimore, 443
Galloway, 106, 129, 191
Galt, 193, 202, 231, 232, 237, 239, 297, 357, 395, 438
Galtier, 55
Galts, 476
Gamble, 226
Gambrill, 414
Gammon, 164, 215, 223, 227
Gansevort, 29
Gantt, 445
Garber, 150

Garden, 347
Gardener, 123
Gardiner, 20, 129, 140, 144, 270, 349, 449, 457
Gardner, 68, 106, 199, 223, 230, 235, 247, 315
Garesche, 360
Garland, 68, 284, 385, 394
Garner, 40, 42, 68, 231, 381
Garnett, 55, 199, 405, 438, 443, 445
Garratt, 309
Garret, 147
Garrett, 47, 48, 67, 68, 147, 179, 367, 437, 477
Garrettson, 272
Garrison, 424
Garten, 272
Garvin, 162, 168
Gary, 398
Gassaway, 5, 6, 446
Gaston, 68, 298, 418, 424, 437, 465, 466
Gates, 42, 77, 213, 232, 295, 470
Gatton, 323
Gaul, 42
Gault, 366, 374
Gautier, 384, 400, 444
Gaver, 105, 128
Gawler, 136, 230
Gay, 55, 324
Gay Mont, 155
Gaylord, 34
Gazeli, 103
Geary, 6, 78, 85, 87, 221, 233, 414
Gebhardt, 164
Geddes, 68, 256
Gedney, 58
Gehrung, 424
Genand, 61
Gendron, 413
Genealogies, 45
Generous, 248
Gentin, 81
Gentry, 131
Genung, 293
George, 148, 404
Gerald, 288

Gerard, 177
Gerhardt, 452
German, 232
Gerol_, 451
Gerolt, 282
Gerson, 246
Getty, 205, 280, 293
Geyger, 160
Gibbon, 171, 191
Gibbons, 104, 295
Gibbs, 50, 201, 296
Gibson, 48, 68, 105, 153, 167, 182, 240, 251, 260, 272, 292, 360, 376, 393, 394, 404, 405, 429, 433, 448, 469, 473
Gidding, 231
Gideon, 11, 49, 66, 306, 449, 458
Giesborough, 319
Gift, 254
Giggy, 38
Gila, 424
Gilbert, 2, 104, 109, 166, 290, 389
Gilchrist, 180, 191, 199, 254, 331, 459
Giles, 148, 368, 419
Gill, 68, 90, 233, 258, 259, 285, 390
Gillcrist, 360
Gillet, 359
Gillett, 305
Gilliam, 415
Gillis, 30, 68, 323, 394, 473
Gilliss, 307, 457
Gills, 166
Gilly, 122
Gilman, 39, 42, 57, 90, 92, 144, 256, 338
Gilmore, 338
Gilpatrick, 34
Gilpin, 140
Gindart, 217
Gindrat, 238
Gingle, 388
Girard, 91, 280
Givens, 23
Givizandi, 168
Gladding, 20
Glading, 394
Gladmon, 68
Glanbenskee, 369

Glanbenskier, 375
Glanding, 37, 173, 213
Glanz, 20
Glass, 94
Glassell, 123, 135
Glasson, 30, 469, 473
Glaubenkslee, 370
Glaubenskier, 370
Gleason, 248
Glen, 188
Glen Ross, 32
Glenn, 87
Glenroy, 11
Glen-Welby, 251
Glenwood Cemetery, 371
Glick, 147
Glover, 68, 87, 116, 129, 316, 338
Glynn, 29, 470
Gobb, 302
Gobright, 231
Goddard, 21, 34, 44, 68, 88, 98, 149, 203, 204, 210, 231, 272, 296, 391
Goddin, 309, 310
Godey, 179, 296
Godfrey, 191, 470
Godnow, 282
Godon, 29
Godwin, 175
Goff, 108, 223
Gogerty, 265
Goggin, 269, 378
Goheen, 104
Golden, 115
Goldsborough, 68, 291, 398
Goldschmidt, 291
Goldsmith, 33, 36
Gondomar, 109
Gonter, 68
Gonzaga, 26
Gonzaga College, 41, 177, 192, 247, 291, 343
Gonzago, 26
Gonzales, 169, 201
Gooch, 26
Good, 108
Goodell, 188

Goodin, 28, 87
Gooding, 287
Goodman, 202
Goodnow, 288
Goodrich, 26, 27, 224, 387
Goodsel, 215
Goodwin, 163, 241, 289
Goodyear, 230, 295
Gordon, 19, 26, 68, 76, 83, 115, 132, 136, 283, 308, 338, 362, 366, 391, 414, 416, 425, 431
Gorgan, 189
Gorham, 183
Gorman, 180, 221, 235, 452
Gormley, 154, 289, 306
Gorrissen, 370
Gorsuch, 390
Gosnell, 102, 357
Gough, 111
Gould, 10, 59, 385
Gouldy, 403, 405, 431, 443
Gouley, 227
Gouverneur, 255, 264
Govan, 415
Gove, 369
Govin, 341
Gowland, 477
Grace, 249, 394
Grady, 35, 154, 231
Graffin, 447
Grafton, 30, 189, 334, 379, 395
Graham, 30, 34, 68, 105, 122, 232, 233, 283, 345, 391, 447, 477
Grammer, 68, 127, 295, 319
Gramp, 169
Grampp, 183
Granbery, 321, 398
Granbury, 27, 46, 79, 342
Granby, 251, 401, 412
Grandin, 104
Grandy, 124
Granger, 14, 242, 294
Granier, 364
Grant, 45, 94, 189, 268, 381, 407
Granville, 415
Grassland, 132

Gratiot, 168, 220
Grattan, 153, 280
Graves, 68, 97, 215, 338, 367
Gray, 27, 68, 156, 184, 188, 232, 241, 314, 357, 421
Grayson, 204, 214, 246
Grebble, 145, 158
Greble, 324, 327
Greeley, 323
Greely, 48
Green, 4, 37, 41, 55, 59, 68, 104, 136, 173, 256, 261, 329, 340, 341, 348, 374, 390, 393, 439, 451, 470, 478
Greene, 102, 261, 396, 442, 469
Greenfield, 443
Greenfield Mills, 202
Greenhow, 395, 408
Greenlaw, 258
Greenleaf, 68, 74, 433, 434
Greenlow, 355
Greenough, 387
Greenwell, 175, 372, 461
Greenwood, 94, 272
Greer, 199, 373, 394, 413
Gregg, 68, 78, 298, 360, 405, 443
Gregory, 11, 195, 205
Greig, 162
Grelaud, 284
Grenacker, 68
Grenan, 68
Grenup, 464
Gresle, 413
Gretter, 153
Grier, 165, 201, 360, 372, 394, 405
Griffen, 342
Griffin, 8, 38, 40, 55, 68, 128, 138, 139, 194, 364, 390
Griffing, 460
Griffith, 65, 105, 164, 175, 223, 232, 235, 247
Griggs, 293
Grignon, 103, 159
Grimes, 45, 175, 294
Grimly, 386
Grimsley, 34
Grindall, 68

Grinter, 47, 48, 147
Grisby, 34
Griswold, 83, 104, 175
Gritzner, 25, 213
Groenveldt, 68
Groff, 68
Grogham, 443
Groman, 176
Grosh, 396
Gross, 88, 233
Grosvenor, 217
Grosvenor Square, 149
Grosvernor, 39
Grouard, 262, 292
Groux, 352
Grover, 19, 294, 465
Grubb, 55, 108, 219
Grubb Farm, 360
Grund, 232
Gruth, 426
Grymes, 270, 472
Gtwn Ledger, 423
Guess, 233
Guest, 104, 251, 340
Guevin, 270
Guillary, 130
Guinon, 214
Gull, 457
Gunn, 357
Gunnell, 36, 68, 69, 141, 152, 159, 433
Gunton, 68, 229, 248
Guppey, 137
Gurley, 230, 389, 431, 454
Gurney, 340
Gussell, 140
Gustis, 13
Guthrie, 280, 285, 288
Guyot, 191
Gwathmey, 153
Gwin, 204, 266, 463
Gwinn, 68, 435
Gwynn, 39
Gymnaski, 323

H

Haas, 308
Haase, 375
Habicht, 213
Habiteht, 169
Hachtel, 117
Hackney, 230
Hactnell, 443
Haddock Hills, 158
Haddock's Hill Farm, 158
Haden, 477
Hadley, 240
Hagner, 83, 144, 241, 358, 377
Hahn, 375
Haileys, 325
Hain, 199
Haislip, 69
Haldeman, 240
Hale, 48, 55, 91, 230, 454
Hales, 91
Haley, 36
Haliday, 35, 134, 180
Hall, 2, 11, 15, 20, 24, 35, 44, 68, 76,
  129, 152, 153, 168, 183, 188, 199,
  210, 220, 224, 237, 255, 267, 293,
  296, 320, 330, 332, 339, 357, 359,
  391, 397, 399, 411, 419, 420, 424,
  436, 469, 470, 473
Hallett, 47
Halliday, 11
Hallonquist, 286
Hallowell, 214, 327, 329
Halsay, 33
Halsey, 130, 140, 463
Halsted, 327
Halter, 410
Hamacher, 11
Hamburg Lime-kilns, 116
Hamer, 196
Hamill, 86
Hamilton, 6, 34, 38, 52, 57, 68, 69, 95,
  98, 99, 100, 104, 111, 115, 122, 126,
  131, 154, 157, 164, 169, 223, 227,
  240, 246, 247, 250, 257, 261, 270,
  271, 279, 290, 296, 315, 332, 353,
  379, 387, 397
Hamish, 298
Hamlin, 127, 139, 269

Hammel, 446
Hammond, 26, 54, 101, 118, 155, 220, 298, 304, 360, 405, 424, 456
Hamon, 413
Hampton, 58, 273
Hamtramck, 173, 190
Hanahan, 322
Hancock, 101, 231, 285
Hand, 19, 59, 163, 192, 193, 223, 236, 247, 316, 394, 475
Handley, 117, 146, 172, 360, 416
Handly, 206, 319
Handy, 29, 81, 136, 231, 292, 372, 422
Hanen, 14
Hank, 104, 105
Hankins, 477
Hanlon, 272, 295
Hanmer, 150
Hanna, 104, 291, 292, 433
Hannay, 69
Hannigan, 443
Hannum, 142
Hansell, 8, 59
Hanson, 238, 292, 416
Haraday, 206
Harbaugh, 232, 233, 270, 282, 426
Harby, 265
Hardcastle, 398
Hardee, 424
Harden, 164
Hardenbrook, 15
Hardesty, 163, 219, 245
Hardie, 284, 360, 405
Hardin, 128, 131, 425
Harding, 301, 408
Hardon, 232
Hardy, 9, 69, 113, 129, 155, 211, 221, 229
Hare, 216
Hargraves, 238
Hark, 205
Harker, 286, 465
Harkness, 68, 69, 342, 454
Harman, 69, 131
Harmar, 190

Harney, 23, 109, 120, 123, 209, 283, 285, 287, 346, 465, 466
Harnish, 424
Harold, 170, 454
Harper, 22, 49, 104, 352
Harralson, 401
Harrell, 30, 173
Harrington, 148, 177, 299
Harris, 11, 94, 95, 113, 131, 135, 140, 154, 163, 213, 224, 233, 236, 242, 248, 264, 293, 327, 367, 386, 387, 404, 424, 437, 438, 454, 461
Harrison, 21, 69, 80, 130, 134, 160, 179, 194, 205, 220, 230, 233, 250, 252, 253, 292, 293, 295, 311, 321, 334, 378, 393, 417, 425, 443, 469, 473
Harrold, 199, 309
Harrover, 161, 232, 291, 302, 344
Harry, 194
Hart, 42, 170, 237, 240, 335, 372, 450, 477
Hartman, 293
Hartnett, 28
Hartstene, 218
Hartt, 442
Harvey, 68, 98, 159, 166, 230, 275, 352, 414, 456
Harvie, 285
Harwood, 121, 249, 394, 408, 429
Hasam, 223, 235, 247
Haskell, 7, 9, 27, 78
Haskill, 457
Haskins, 5, 89, 209, 226, 300, 416
Haslup, 27
Haso, 370
Hassam, 230
Hassened, 149
Hassler, 66, 194, 263, 303
Hastings, 97, 116, 119, 443
Hatch, 374, 381
Hatcher, 383
Hatfield, 214
Hathaway, 47, 471
Hatmaker, 326
Hatton, 295, 463
Havell, 470

Havelock, 32, 86, 146
Haven, 83
Havener, 68
Havenner, 7, 69, 325
Havens, 151
Haviland, 187
Haw, 68, 185, 256, 343
Hawes, 386
Hawke, 346
Hawkins, 15, 69, 76, 109, 151, 284, 377, 452, 468
Hawks, 54, 98
Hawley, 69, 106, 246, 443
Hawleys, 337
Hawthorne, 411
Haxall, 153
Hay, 137, 211, 214, 247, 269, 318, 445
Hayden, 55, 102, 409
Hayes, 44, 51, 78, 85, 155, 191, 301
Hayfields, 243
Hayne, 78, 118, 156, 189, 212, 245, 468
Haynes, 19, 196, 262
Hays, 34, 41, 103, 151, 165, 183, 254, 394
Hayward, 59, 336
Haywood, 321, 356
Hazard, 440
Hazel, 323
Hazelett, 320
Hazle, 230, 262
Hazlitt, 432
Hazzard, 27
Head of Frazier, 393
Headley, 260
Headly, 86
Heald, 55
Healey, 332, 443
Health report, 363
Health Report, 299, 462
Healy, 298, 424
Heap, 8
Heaps, 410
Heard, 130
Heart, 239
Heath, 69, 368, 390
Heaton, 126, 144, 219

Hebb, 338, 395
Hebdin, 383
Heber, 467
Hectig, 161
Hedding, 196
Hedge, 15
Hedges, 312
Hedrick, 232
Hedwig, 370
Hefferman, 11
Heid, 268
Heifner, 316
Heights of Gtwn, D C, 194
Heine, 27, 224, 227, 235, 246, 317
Heinrich, 380
Heins, 357
Heise, 69
Heiskel, 136
Heiskell, 34, 121
Heiskill, 5
Heisler, 305, 321
Heiss, 11
Heissler, 306
Heitmiller, 68
Hellen, 43, 277, 363
Helm, 11, 122, 328
Hemphill, 380
Hendebert, 51
Hendee, 110
Henderbert, 176
Henderson, 15, 47, 53, 89, 91, 135, 147, 165, 201, 233, 267, 293, 368, 393, 394, 406, 414, 470
Hendley, 205
Hendricks, 104, 218
Hendrickson, 438
Heneage, 471
Henke, 69
Henley, 424
Henly, 298
Hennessy, 69, 443
Henning, 166, 241, 291, 295, 346
Hennon, 9
Henry, 17, 41, 69, 111, 134, 162, 168, 185, 191, 201, 230, 290, 301, 302, 362
Henshaw, 353, 366, 373, 380

Hensken, 461
Hensley, 227, 306
Henson, 357
Hepburn, 69, 90, 146, 158, 177, 195, 233, 301, 417
Herbert, 18, 69, 78, 109, 120, 207, 228, 230, 463
Herd, 69
Hereford, 34
Herkin, 370
Hermann, 323, 370
Herndon, 102, 132, 174, 186, 229, 241, 246, 315, 375
Herndon House, 258
Herold, 68, 76
Herrick, 68, 210
Herring, 250, 468
Herrity, 69
Hersey, 351
Hertman, 370
Hertmann, 375
Herty, 69
Hess, 232, 335, 370, 375
Hesse, 168
Hessler, 361
Heth, 23
Hetrick, 105
Hetzel, 68, 69
Hetzell, 389
Heugh, 377
Hewitt, 306
Hewston, 443
Heydtman, 375
Heywood, 189, 358, 365
Hibbard, 165, 218, 238
Hibbert, 427
Hibbs, 293
Hickey, 69, 211, 356, 390, 460, 478
Hickling, 135, 441
Hickman, 368, 389
Hickory Hill, 226
Hicks, 69, 76, 165, 173, 422
Hieburger, 376
Higbee, 12, 98
Higdan, 342
Higdon, 442

Higgason, 122
Higgins, 14, 69, 148
Highlands, 375
Hilbus, 170
Hildebrand, 105, 354, 359
Hildebrandt, 166
Hildeburn, 139
Hildreth, 15, 194
Hildt, 409
Hilgard, 21, 91, 268
Hill, 42, 48, 68, 69, 157, 158, 159, 209, 237, 259, 281, 289, 297, 360, 362, 369, 382, 431, 438, 446, 454
Hillary, 140
Hillborn, 44
Hilliary, 10
Hills, 99, 237
Hilton, 90, 154, 163
Hinckley, 425
Hinds, 94
Hines, 40, 68, 229, 258
Hinkle, 265
Hinton, 140, 437
Hirst, 104
Hitchcock, 53, 164, 191, 223
Hitt, 452
Hitz, 63
Hivling, 379
Hoban, 68, 281
Hobson, 416
Hock, 86
Hodge, 201
Hodges, 310, 340
Hodgson, 172, 206, 231, 243, 257, 319, 360, 388
Hodnott, 160
Hoemiller, 113
Hoff, 29
Hoffman, 69, 105, 141, 185, 210, 350, 352, 438, 444
Hofnagle, 232
Hoge, 382
Hogginst, 375
Hogguist, 370
Hohental, 370
Hohl, 59

Holcomb, 49, 335
Holcombe, 339
Holden, 16, 42, 97, 223, 225, 455
Hole-in-the-Day, 38
Holgate, 36, 203
Holiday, 158
Holkar, 44, 224
Holladay, 91, 226, 416
Holland, 66, 173, 229, 238, 245, 247, 248, 411, 438, 443
Holland Point, 288
Holley, 10
Holliday, 104, 351, 358, 400
Hollidge, 68, 156
Hollingshead, 231
Hollingsworth, 136
Hollinsworth, 34, 336
Hollis, 430
Hollohan, 68
Holly, 293, 390
Hollywood Cemetery, 281
Holman, 55
Holmead, 16, 175, 197, 275, 362
Holmes, 69, 140, 154, 174, 273, 293, 315, 349, 457, 467
Holroyd, 202
Holston, 376
Holt, 16, 172, 250, 252, 255, 285, 291, 306, 347, 379, 381, 382, 462, 463
Holtzclau, 69
Holtzclaw, 69
Holtzman, 64, 230
Homans, 68, 433
Homberger, 204
Hone, 96
Honenloe, 375
Honey, 235
Hood, 170, 433, 465
Hooe, 90, 426, 441
Hooff, 78, 338
Hoofnagel, 202
Hook, 40, 70, 131, 209, 231
Hooker, 42
<u>hoop skirts</u>, 404
Hooper, 4, 53, 94, 266, 461

Hoover, 37, 68, 69, 105, 117, 231, 246, 299, 305, 401, 473
Hoovey, 246
Hope, 98, 196, 370, 462
Hopewell, 208
Hopkins, 18, 40, 46, 47, 94, 139, 230, 233, 237, 294, 315, 388, 395, 419, 460, 477
Hopper, 28, 43, 63, 134, 165, 173
Horne, 288, 289
Horner, 107, 195, 236, 343
Horseman, 68
Horton, 350
Horwitz, 394
Hoschel, 370
Hoschlet, 375
Hosford, 208
Hoskins, 413, 427
Hoskinson, 77
Hosmer, 123
Hotchkiss, 102, 456
Houck, 306
Houdon, 121
Hough, 11, 105, 230, 240, 264
Houghton, 407
Houmas plantation, 57
Housam, 68
House, 33, 43, 157
Houston, 69, 152, 158, 217, 271, 371, 372, 394, 454, 469
Hover, 197
Hovey, 44, 317
Howard, 15, 43, 68, 69, 115, 153, 165, 170, 215, 290, 311, 356, 360, 379, 405, 419, 425, 450
Howe, 82, 150, 160, 201, 283, 426
Howell, 33, 36, 60, 69, 80, 95, 164, 165, 201, 223, 227, 235, 245, 247, 273, 475
Howison, 69
Howitz, 370
Howland, 386
Howle, 54, 259, 359, 437
Hoxton, 297
Hoyt, 258, 349, 369
Hubbard, 45, 68, 78, 85, 126, 283, 293, 410, 416

Hubble, 119
Hubley, 63
Hudgens, 8
Hudgins, 220
Hudry, 51, 61, 214
Hudson, 102, 148, 218, 309, 365, 371, 467
Huertas, 211
Huertes, 44
Huff, 33
Huffacker, 34
Huger, 473
Huges, 255
Hughes, 45, 55, 69, 77, 114, 141, 169, 175, 193, 270, 298, 302, 328, 332, 361, 393, 424, 443, 461
Huhn, 288
Hulbet, 102
Hull, 29, 147, 173, 226, 368, 394
Hulsart, 15
Hulseman, 233
Humber, 286, 288
Humbird, 275
Humboldt, 250
Hume, 231
Humes, 295
Hummel, 86
Humphrey, 343, 379
Humphreys, 202, 205, 437, 445
Humphries, 68, 123, 189
Hunbeck, 349
Hungarian settlers, 181
Hungerford, 22
Hunnicutt, 232
Hunsberger, 127
Hunt, 29, 41, 68, 69, 92, 110, 178, 182, 191, 257, 416, 439
Hunter, 2, 39, 54, 62, 78, 85, 101, 141, 189, 193, 227, 235, 237, 249, 251, 304, 326, 368, 394, 429, 432, 473
Hunter of Ky, 409
Hunting, 34
Huntingdon, 378
Huntington, 186, 378
Huntley, 404
Huntoon, 471

Hurd, 77, 255, 407
Hurdle, 20, 33, 36, 90, 154, 167, 296
Hurdy, 211
Hurlahy, 237
Hurley, 69
Hurlihy, 237
Hurst, 248, 320
Hussey, 77, 427, 470
Huston, 379
Hutchings, 167, 179
Hutchins, 90, 140, 231
Hutchinson, 44, 69, 159, 199, 203, 204, 223, 228, 232, 244, 262, 295, 320
Huthenson, 225
Huthman, 238
Hutimack, 203
Hutton, 69, 101, 208, 341
Hyam, 163, 189
Hyatt, 69, 78, 138, 141, 152, 159
Hyde, 68, 69, 114, 115, 116, 142, 158, 201, 259, 296

I

Iddins, 69
Ihrie, 360, 405, 443
Ilsey, 236
Imboden, 260
Imlay, 247
Inch, 199
Ingalls, 241
Ingersol, 293
Ingersoll, 26, 41, 135, 157, 214, 271, 387
Ingle, 16, 69, 232, 271
Ingraham, 13, 174, 189, 241, 271, 286, 300, 394, 452, 466
Ingram, 69
Inman, 30, 469, 472
Innes, 350
Innis, 149
intermarriage of first cousins, 451
Ireland, 69
Ironsides, 255
Irvin, 139
Irving, 77, 218, 282, 289, 305, 476
Irwin, 69, 76, 163, 210, 230, 232, 374

Iryal, 27
Isaacs, 311
Isfeld, 370
Isham, 5, 140, 221
Isherwood, 341
Israel, 75, 104, 164
Ittig, 94
Ivagnar, 370
Iverson, 147
Ives, 139, 284, 288
Ivey, 282
Ivy, 288, 289
Izard, 221

J

Jacks, 48
Jackson, 18, 30, 42, 69, 79, 81, 101, 127, 128, 169, 211, 245, 266, 267, 286, 299, 352, 394, 398, 417, 427, 447
Jackson Hill, 250, 381
Jacob, 153, 288
Jacobs, 48, 102, 168, 169, 176, 308, 398, 476
Jagel, 370
Jake, 380
Jamar, 379
James, 59, 69, 122, 152, 194, 229, 284, 463
Jameson, 307, 349
Jamesson, 413
Jamison, 408
Janeway, 270
Janney, 134, 329, 361, 412, 418
Janvier, 176
Jarboe, 342, 364
Jardin, 119, 176, 240
Jardine, 307
Jarvis, 21, 29, 211, 472
Jay, 343, 391
Jeffard, 137
Jeffers, 69, 126, 246
Jefferson, 11, 56, 105, 110, 226, 253
Jeffery, 470
Jeffress, 273
Jeffries, 306
Jeho, 27

Jemison, 44
Jenkins, 24, 25, 48, 76, 140, 183, 189, 192, 223, 225, 232, 239, 247, 252, 262, 271, 281, 316, 349, 393, 394, 398, 435
Jennens, 149
Jennings, 19, 350, 357, 443, 477
Jenny, 87
Jensen, 458
Jericho, 310
Jerod, 171
Jessesson, 50
Jesuit, 18, 343
Jesuit College, 308
Jesup, 97, 120, 123, 152, 200, 287, 443
Jeune, 299
Jewell, 69, 189
Jewett, 41, 155, 160, 170, 314, 396
Jillard, 136, 145, 158
Jirdinston, 239
John, 236, 329
Johns, 167, 438
Johnson, 11, 14, 23, 33, 39, 41, 46, 50, 51, 55, 69, 78, 89, 93, 97, 122, 132, 138, 146, 152, 158, 162, 164, 165, 177, 180, 188, 191, 199, 209, 215, 218, 231, 232, 236, 250, 255, 257, 259, 269, 271, 273, 280, 295, 305, 306, 321, 322, 365, 368, 400, 401, 415, 422, 427, 436, 438, 449, 464, 469
Johnston, 30, 40, 48, 58, 76, 91, 110, 157, 164, 178, 202, 252, 271, 285, 330, 341, 412, 416, 425, 429, 435, 472
Johnstone, 430
Joines, 393
Jones, 3, 10, 11, 12, 15, 18, 30, 40, 44, 45, 48, 55, 66, 69, 77, 78, 79, 84, 85, 91, 93, 94, 101, 106, 111, 112, 130, 133, 134, 148, 151, 152, 153, 160, 162, 164, 169, 171, 173, 180, 190, 193, 199, 201, 208, 210, 223, 224, 225, 226, 227, 235, 236, 239, 245, 247, 254, 279, 282, 284, 285, 289, 291, 320, 322, 325, 330, 332, 344, 346, 352, 357, 386, 394, 397, 432,

446, 448, 449, 457, 458, 461, 462, 464, 465
Jordan, 178, 217, 230, 235, 272, 326, 394, 410, 429
Jouett, 394
Jourdan, 412
Joy, 69, 231, 295
Joyce, 231, 292
Joynes, 237, 365, 366, 398
Judge, 11
Judkins, 327
Judson, 219, 235
Jueneman, 437
Julius, 185
Juneau, 338

K

Kagy, 175, 210
Kahler, 135
Kain, 70
Kaiser, 69, 231
Kalar, 201
Kalorama, 89, 90
Kamaikin, 298
Kamiakin, 437
Kane, 15, 37, 70, 80, 167, 211, 275, 361, 444
Kane Expedition, 273
Karrick, 16, 364
Karze, 380
Kavanagh, 291
Kay, 70
Keach, 445
Keally, 70
Kean, 36, 118
Keane, 310
Kearney, 77
Kearns, 291
Kearny, 40, 118, 317
Keating, 69, 291
Kedglie, 70
Keebill, 443
Keef, 26, 157
Keefe, 230
Keefer, 74, 203, 241, 423
Keegan, 289

Keen, 16
Keenan, 289
Keene, 322, 478
Keep, 188, 215, 236, 247
Keese, 231, 269, 352, 417
Keilholtz, 232
Keith, 5, 289, 336
Keithley, 69
Keittner, 373
Keleher, 132, 349
Kell, 394
Kellar, 144
Kelleher, 231
Keller, 24, 50, 76, 118, 223, 230, 247, 269, 316
Kelley, 77, 105, 136, 394, 430, 447
Kellogg, 83, 127, 137, 143, 365, 378, 465
Kellsey, 83
Kelly, 70, 78, 154, 157, 200, 231, 289, 290, 293, 295, 298, 314, 424, 426, 443
Kelsey, 268
Kelso, 289
Kelton, 23
Kemp, 189
Kendall, 113, 141, 142, 143, 182, 273, 423, 477
Kendall Green, 227, 423
Kendle, 205
Kendrick, 52, 69, 203, 204, 210, 214, 246
Kennedy, 13, 49, 54, 61, 69, 70, 79, 92, 118, 121, 126, 129, 185, 213, 254, 256, 281, 289, 290, 341, 356, 400, 443, 454
Kennelly, 70
Kenney, 296
Kennon, 45, 199, 291, 381, 415
Kenny, 281
Kenrick, 181
Kensel, 284
Kent, 17, 100, 130, 159, 181, 195, 417
Keppell, 36
Kerr, 292
Kerse, 424
Kersey, 393

Kershaw, 339
Kesler, 282, 307
Kessecker, 389
Ketcham, 293
Ketchum, 95, 438
Kettlewell, 102
Key, 56, 69, 70, 90, 133, 179, 315, 330, 387
Keyes, 360, 405
Kibbey, 70, 421, 447
Kibble, 69
Kidwell, 53, 65, 70, 90, 143, 233, 295, 300, 462
Kiemann, 443
Kiernan, 69
Kilgour, 408
Killinger, 410
Killmon, 366
Kilmon, 221
Kilty, 469, 473
Kimball, 42, 144, 162, 459
Kimberley, 460
Kimmel, 324, 431, 465
Kimmell, 256, 287
Kincaid, 159, 348
Kincaide, 348
Kinchy, 385
King, 11, 14, 19, 53, 54, 55, 70, 77, 90, 114, 115, 116, 130, 140, 142, 146, 158, 160, 163, 165, 168, 175, 194, 201, 222, 223, 227, 228, 232, 256, 292, 299, 327, 364, 376, 389, 407, 418, 423, 427, 432, 438
King Wm III, 149
Kingland, 76
Kingman, 69
Kingsbury, 3, 224, 297
Kingsury, 189
Kinkel, 423
Kinne, 122
Kinnear, 160
Kinney, 4, 23, 26, 86, 130, 223, 256, 266, 456
Kinny, 247
Kinsley, 79
Kinsolving, 121, 389

Kinzer, 100, 238, 297, 440
Kinzie, 39
Kip, 22, 287, 360, 405
Kipping, 358
Kirby, 22, 157, 164, 321, 391
Kirk, 175, 233, 289, 329
Kirkham, 312, 360, 405
Kirkland, 106, 395
Kirkwood, 289
Kirtland, 386
Kirtz, 295
Kitchen, 162
Kititaff, 369
Kittredge, 1, 100
Klay, 298, 424
Kleindenst, 69, 70
Kline, 172
Klingeman, 452
Klock, 190
Klopfer, 70, 230, 270, 296, 306
Klotz, 108
Knabe, 396
Knap, 113, 138, 213
Knapp, 55, 163
Knapps, 95
Kneeland, 351
Knight, 53, 70, 116, 205, 214, 233, 289, 350, 352, 353, 436, 440
Knot, 124
Knott, 232, 334, 363, 396, 400
Knowles, 49, 90, 107, 156, 167, 236, 265, 270, 467
Knox, 14, 222, 443, 454
Kob, 34
Kohler, 241
Kohn, 33, 370
Kokowski, 461
Konig, 232
Koones, 333
Koszta, 271
Kownslar, 78
Kraft, 295
Kraitsir, 119
Kraus, 391
Krauth, 121
Kreamer, 231

Krebs, 104, 122, 157, 207, 393, 410
Krepple, 86
Kropp, 411
Krouse, 10
Krudener, 103
Kuglo, 105
Kuhland, 259
Kuhn, 224, 237, 370
Kunkel, 355
Kurtz, 70, 341, 418
Kutz, 394
Kyle, 153, 267, 472

L

L'Enfant, 407
La Bille, 472
La Monte, 324
Labonty, 307
Lacey, 70, 236, 390
Lackey, 70, 91, 364, 394
Lacy, 295
Ladd, 262
Ladies of the Mount Vernon Association, 147
Ladies' Mount Vernon Asociation, 145
Ladies' Mount Vernon Association, 28
Lady Andover, 150
Lafayette, 25
Laferty, 124
Lafitte, 27
Laiblin, 48
Laighton, 395
Laird, 392, 395
Lake, 17, 109, 371
Lakemeyer, 391, 397
Lally, 256
Laloire, 397
Lamard, 210
Lamb, 88, 114, 134, 169, 201, 265, 363
Lambell, 70
Lambert, 6, 70, 350, 372, 397
Lambeth, 104
Lamoy, 55
lamp posts, 265
Lamphere, 24

Lampson, 216
Lamson, 379
Lanahan, 2, 70, 105, 154, 421
Lancanshire, 337
Lancaster, 187, 313, 379
Lancetta, 168
Lander, 100, 163
Landis, 188, 210, 215, 236, 247, 307
Landon, 32
Landrick, 70
Landrum, 273, 404
Landry, 26, 91, 159
Landseer, 468
Landstreet, 105
Landy, 233, 309
Lane, 70, 141, 239, 262, 281, 302, 322, 365, 474
Laney, 104
Lang, 289
Langdon, 132, 175, 223, 228, 235, 247
Lange, 104
Langley, 231, 269, 349
Langly, 205, 207
Langmade, 131
Langstreet, 130, 223
Lanier, 30, 167, 199, 413
Lansdale, 231, 343, 350
Lansing, 89, 90
Larcetta, 201
Larcombe, 11, 70, 107
Lare, 70
Larkin, 442, 459
Larkin's Hill, 358
Larnard, 8
Larne, 476
Larner, 90, 154
Lars, 370, 375
Laskey, 23, 35, 39, 106, 146, 340, 371
Lassiter, 77
Latane, 417
Latch, 394
Latham, 32, 102, 130, 138, 223, 246
Latimer, 30
Latta, 34
Lattle, 248
Laub, 292, 442

Lauck, 62
Laughlin, 78
Laurenson, 49, 152
Laurent, 60, 198, 464
Laurie, 62, 231
Lautler, 337
Lautner, 70
Lavallette, 162, 202
Laverty, 124
Law, 18, 70, 400, 419, 434
Lawrence, 27, 57, 70, 89, 95, 113, 157, 216, 246, 320, 395
Lawrenson, 254, 271
Laws, 20
Lawton, 167, 199, 221, 341, 442
Lay, 301, 464
Layman, 60, 140, 213
le Boterf, 413
Le Vert, 271, 387
Lea, 36, 76, 130, 223, 247, 316, 419
Leach, 201, 219
Leadbetter, 283, 287
Leaf, 105
Leake, 244, 310
Lear, 12, 70
Leary, 477
Leatherbury, 104
Leavitt, 13
Leazer, 442
Leber, 105
Lebleu, 384
Leckie, 70
Lecompte, 30, 282, 289, 469, 472
LeConte, 191
Leddy, 374
Ledwith, 101
Lee, 1, 8, 53, 58, 70, 97, 109, 123, 130, 153, 175, 202, 209, 210, 223, 249, 261, 284, 285, 299, 312, 322, 357, 414, 455, 458
Leech, 105
Leef, 26
Leehe, 126
Leehy, 70
Lefeore, 272
Lefevre, 188
LeFevre, 236
Lefturich, 364
Legare, 451
Leggett, 70
Lehmanowsky, 18
Lehr, 63
Leibrecht, 289
Leigh, 237
Leisa, 111, 159
Leit, 423
Leitz, 231
Leland, 22, 240, 340
Lemmon, 101, 231
Lemoine, 149
Lemon, 105
Lemons, 437
Lenhard, 78
Lenman, 197, 399
Lenox, 35, 70, 96, 231
Lenter, 248
Lenthall, 189, 292
Lentwein, 329
Leoder, 400
Leonard, 202, 309
Lephard, 70
LeRoy, 386
Lerpeux, 138
Leschi, 128
Leslie, 5, 70
Lester, 53, 416
Letcher, 308, 362
Letton, 205
Letts, 282
Level estate, 187
Levely, 139
Leves, 11
Levy, 29, 94, 142, 165, 186, 199, 221, 350, 457, 458
Lewenthal, 353
Lewis, 33, 49, 50, 70, 97, 107, 133, 136, 143, 158, 160, 169, 200, 202, 213, 217, 225, 230, 231, 233, 239, 242, 247, 256, 261, 296, 312, 325, 341, 393, 413, 464, 470
Lewis' row, 410
Libbey, 59, 257, 267

Libby, 329
Lickens, 412
Lieberman, 427, 447
Lieure, 2
Liggett, 105
Ligon, 54
Lincoln, 327, 413, 442, 459
Lindensheim, 380
Lindsay, 19, 70, 279, 308, 409
Lindsley, 256
Lindsly, 107, 189
Lineden, 220
Linhoff, 456
Lining, 394
Linkins, 70, 230, 439
Linn, 102
Linthicum, 6, 105, 256, 354, 408
Linton, 195, 337, 341, 384, 447
Lippitt, 60, 159, 337
Lipps, 294
Lipscomb, 104, 105, 262
Lisa, 4
Lisby, 385
Lisharoon, 188
Littell, 105
Little, 16, 28, 70, 91, 221, 361, 380, 381, 387, 399
Little Gleanings, 216
Littlefield, 20
Littlepage, 379
Littles, 171, 276
Liuber, 289
Living, 372
Livingston, 29, 125, 149, 152, 159, 216, 217, 248, 258
Lloyd, 42, 70, 239, 352, 365, 398, 411
Lochrey, 292
Locke, 136, 270, 310
Lockery, 70
Lockett, 297
Lockrey, 288
Lockwood, 29, 368
Locust Grove, 229
Locust Grove Academy, 335
Loeffler, 429
Loefner, 195

Logan, 161, 331
Loisel, 27, 169, 174, 210, 214, 246
Lomax, 233, 279
Lombard, 355
Lomke, 375
Lonergan, 443
Long, 6, 9, 62, 113, 129, 155, 164, 211, 217, 282, 289, 378, 469, 472
Long Bridge, 25
Longdon, 70
Longevity, 301
Longsbough, 52
Longstreet, 17, 24, 247, 465, 466
Longwood, 254
Longworth, 13
Lonic, 370
Loomis, 46, 94, 203, 204, 213, 327, 341, 358
Loop, 399
Lopez, 119
Lord, 49, 59, 78, 113, 245, 455
Lord Beauchamp, 150
Lord Charles, 420
Lorenger, 55
Lorentz, 396
Loring, 191, 254, 359, 385, 424
Losser, 40
Loudon, 318
Loughborough, 185, 256, 281, 414, 448, 452
Loughlin, 369
Loughrey, 247
Loughry, 163, 223, 225, 235
Louis, 57, 234
Louis Philippe, 234, 241, 270
Love, 50
Lovejoy, 231, 270, 319, 442, 477
Lovell, 300, 438
Lovering, 191, 394
Lovett, 89
Low, 30
Lowber, 337
Lowe, 136, 294, 392
Lowndes, 354, 372
Lowns, 144
Lowrey, 165

Lowry, 36, 90, 135, 199, 252
Loyola College, 383
Lozall, 18
Lucas, 98, 103, 152, 198, 286, 288
Luce, 169, 201, 448
Lucelle, 151
Lucero, 409
Lucket, 289
Luckett, 70, 96, 133, 289, 295
Luckhorn, 248
Lucus, 14
Ludick, 321
Ludlan, 163
Ludlow, 464
Luers, 188
Luff, 260
Luklemann, 370
Lull, 18, 199, 419
Lumsden, 105
Lundy, 70, 90, 449
Lunt, 70
Lurcy, 298
Lusby, 81, 232
Lushington, 224
Lutts, 96, 154
Lutz, 42
Lutzohann, 70
Luxen, 232
Lygon, 150
Lyle, 326
Lyles, 396
Lyman, 211, 225
Lynch, 66, 78, 181, 192, 199, 232, 269, 298, 378, 424, 443
Lyndhurst, 248
Lyne, 201
Lynne, 165
Lyon, 280, 360, 405, 436, 449
Lyons, 85, 169, 231, 253, 255, 260, 271, 313, 459, 460

M

Mabee, 282
Macalester, 302
Macaulay, 471
Maccaboy, 169, 213
Maccoun, 160
Macdonald, 13
Maceron, 232
Macfarland, 153
Machenhimer, 332
Macintosh, 26
Mack, 197, 208
Mackall, 71, 401
Mackenzie, 104
Mackey, 71
Maclay, 376
Maclear, 89
Macleod, 328
Maclure, 203
Macnaman, 419
Macnish, 293
Macomb, 70, 460
Macondray, 87
Macrae, 252
Madan, 281
Maddin, 90, 166, 238
Maddox, 71, 248, 372
Maddrix, 76
Mades, 426
Madison, 33, 63, 93, 172, 225, 261, 458
Madonna, 258
Mador, 409
Madrasz, 306
Maerk, 293
Maffit, 30, 213, 314
Magan, 424
Magar, 425
Magaw, 199, 208, 419
Magee, 45, 201, 449
Magiennan, 36
Magill, 71, 94, 223, 245, 247, 436
Magilton, 284, 287
Maglenen, 76, 130, 223, 247, 316
Magnetic Telegraph Co, 431
magnificent elm, 283
Magnum, 308
Magrath, 359
Magraw, 302
Magruder, 18, 71, 120, 233, 259, 267, 281, 287, 295, 322, 323, 453, 466

Maguire, 15, 30, 71, 75, 281, 282, 288, 289, 363, 382
Maher, 133, 136, 392
Mahon, 50, 447
Maiben, 322
Maillard, 4, 6
Main, 164
Maj Bayley, 44
Major, 32, 289, 425
Malbon, 289
Malehorn, 331
Malein, 462
Malines, 94, 203, 204, 210, 214, 246
Mallory, 112, 351
Malmanoff, 450
Malone, 214, 295
Maloney, 210
Malony, 378
Malsberger, 267
Maltby, 183
Malthy, 219
Malvern, 167
Manayette, 306
Mancy, 122
Mandeville, 160
Mandigo, 27
Manegault, 363
Maney, 460
Mangum, 6, 397
Mankin, 71, 167, 210
Manley, 443
Manlove, 343
Mann, 22, 76, 123, 163, 430
Mannaduke, 379
Mannague, 408
Manning, 162, 168, 287, 465
Manny, 293
Mansfield, 97, 103, 123, 233
Marbury, 279, 354, 376, 475
Marcell, 34
Marceron, 232
Marcet, 318
March, 30, 105
Marchand, 368, 394
Marchioness of Westmeath, 57
Marcy, 18, 156, 330, 391, 455

Mardis, 226, 307
Marin, 30, 469, 473
Marini, 429
Marion, 281
Markham, 155
Marks, 19, 156, 243
Markwood, 106
Marlborough, 277
Marlow, 71
Marmaduke, 163, 202, 285
Marnay, 55
Marron, 257
Marsden, 251
Marselas, 84
Marsh, 4, 183, 201, 227, 297, 393, 441, 446
Marshall, 28, 34, 48, 100, 142, 172, 174, 257, 376, 438
Marsh-market, 407
Marston, 327
Martin, 48, 54, 58, 59, 71, 88, 90, 94, 105, 106, 131, 150, 152, 159, 160, 230, 232, 233, 256, 270, 273, 305, 343, 422, 450
Martini, 224
Marvin, 91, 159
Marx, 417
Mary Martha, 279
Mary's Mount, 358
Marye, 122
Maryland Hotel, 257
Maryman, 71, 262, 323
Marzonie, 471
Masi, 90, 334, 449
Mason, 1, 12, 29, 71, 89, 92, 93, 98, 101, 115, 116, 126, 144, 152, 167, 191, 192, 224, 313, 388, 424
Massey, 70, 92, 328
Massie, 352, 447
Massury, 370
Masten, 285, 287
Masters, 416
Mather, 191
Mathers, 40
Mathewman, 293
Mathews, 34, 180

Mathias, 28
Mathieson, 137
Matlock, 231
Matthews, 35, 40, 50, 70, 101, 364, 419
Mattingly, 11, 28, 90, 221, 224, 233, 242, 270, 282, 349, 449, 455
Mattocks, 59
Maud, 272
Mauer, 337
Mauk, 424
Maulsby, 436
Mauro, 385
Maury, 29, 71, 111, 179, 181, 182, 211, 224, 237, 246, 279, 299, 387, 459, 468
Mauvilain, 413
Mavin, 96
Mavrocordato, 395
Maximillian, 182
Maxwell, 24, 27, 71, 76, 95, 113, 121, 241, 246, 316, 357, 394, 419
May, 1, 18, 34, 71, 91, 153, 195, 230, 277, 298, 358, 368, 385, 391, 414, 443, 478
Maybee, 288
Mayer, 260
Maylan, 152
Maynard, 77, 146, 450, 463
Mayo, 10, 43, 48, 228, 372, 394, 473
Mc Ginnity, 71
McAdamize, 415
McAlear, 231
McAleese, 142
McAlister, 86, 179
McAllister, 173
McAlphin, 424
McArann, 469, 473
McAte, 225
McAtee, 52, 203, 204, 235, 317
McAuley, 256
McBlair, 107, 222, 452
McBride, 45
McBrier, 223, 224, 225, 235, 247
McCaeny, 190
McCaffrey, 251
McCall, 17, 211, 243, 247, 315
McCalla, 71

McCallum, 46
McCann, 393
McCanna, 326
McCarthy, 70, 71, 168, 285, 384
McCartney, 138, 372
McCartny, 88
McCarty, 118, 167, 186, 201, 210, 359, 448
McCathhran, 202
McCathran, 136
McCauley, 37, 71, 96, 105, 109, 135, 211, 267, 368
McCerry, 90
McChesney, 6, 44, 292, 408
McClaws, 131
McCleary, 120
McCleery, 394
McClellan, 320, 425
McClelland, 126, 358
McClendon, 97
McCleneary, 348
McClue, 466
McClure, 104, 223, 228, 235, 247, 317
McCollock, 34
McCollum, 71
McComas, 178
McConchie, 385
McConn, 456
McCorkle, 70
McCormick, 92, 147, 189, 213, 244, 254, 425, 444, 461, 471
McCoy, 232, 271, 278, 450
McCrabb, 80, 159
McCralh, 14
McCrary, 188
McCrea, 218, 394
McCreary, 2
McCreesh, 361
McCue, 260
McCullom, 394
McCullough, 207, 241
McCurdy, 26, 323
McCutchen, 242, 452
McCutcheon, 100, 181
McDaniel, 32, 48, 85, 105, 229, 364, 383, 447

McDermote, 379
McDermott, 49, 230, 353, 360
McDonald, 19, 48, 66, 70, 87, 101, 104, 127, 232, 296, 424, 459, 477
McDonnell, 358
McDonogh, 37, 235, 247
McDonough, 183, 223, 227, 393
McDowell, 23, 71, 152, 163, 330, 349, 443
McDuell, 222
McDuffie, 379, 477
McElderry, 55
McEldowney, 357
McElfresh, 77, 233
McElmell, 394
McElroy, 454
McEntee, 450
McEwen, 154
McFalls, 105
McFarlan, 8
McFarland, 58, 114, 195, 232, 297
McFarlin, 376
McFerran, 164
McFerson, 39
McGarr, 349
McGee, 34, 71, 104, 115, 264, 279
McGill, 71, 181, 232
McGilton, 65
McGinness, 70
McGinnie, 275
McGinnis, 71
McGinniss, 111
McGirk, 379
McGiven, 443
McGlue, 70
McGovern, 443
McGran, 146, 158
McGrann, 229
McGraw, 10
McGregor, 441, 449
McGrew, 470
McGuire, 1, 61, 71, 84, 114, 162, 197, 205, 231, 303, 307, 353, 355, 364, 386, 397, 429, 448, 462
McGunigle, 69
McHansen, 443

McHealy, 443
McHenry, 10, 77, 139, 272, 336, 398
McInitre, 453
McIntire, 11, 40, 398, 452
McIntosh, 57, 160, 178, 199, 316
McIntyre, 170, 191
McKane, 400
McKanna, 322
McKay, 87, 279, 324, 333, 340
McKean, 36, 419
McKee, 26, 103, 146, 257, 275, 286, 466
McKelden, 8, 71, 92
Mckendree, 196
McKenna, 28, 269
McKenney, 410
McKenny, 50, 252, 336
McKeon, 71, 321
McKibben, 240
McKibbin, 258, 357
McKim, 260
McKinley, 199
McKinstry, 109
McKnew, 71, 352
McKnight, 70, 71, 321, 463
McKnitt, 78
McLain, 454
McLaine, 152
McLane, 409, 424
McLaughlin, 30, 42, 71, 98, 138, 199, 231, 232, 281, 361, 443, 446
McLean, 11, 64, 71, 223, 243, 252, 303, 349, 385, 430, 455
McLeese, 10
McLellan, 328
McLeod, 71, 155, 433
McMahon, 34, 274
McMechen, 165, 180
McMeehan, 71
McMicken, 264
McMullen, 28
Mcmullin, 48
McMullin, 105, 364
McMurtha, 322
McNab, 122, 411
McNally, 60
McNamara, 295, 425, 429

McNamee, 70, 232
McNeil, 38, 313
McNeill, 284, 293
McNeir, 11, 291
McNemar, 105
McNerhany, 11, 108, 146, 158, 202, 231
McNew, 299
McNulty, 161, 193
McNutt, 78, 285
McPalmer, 272
McPherson, 9, 11, 99, 230, 231, 289
McPiers, 71
McQuade, 87
McRae, 71, 261
McRea, 61
McShane, 281
McSherry, 35
McVey, 41
McVicker, 331
McWeston, 38
McWilliams, 236, 289, 379
McWillie, 271, 387
Meachan, 433
Mead, 18, 28, 82, 232, 242
Meade, 22, 30, 49, 71, 90, 135, 138, 154, 167, 238, 465, 469, 473
Meads, 86, 306, 321
Means, 97, 455
Mears, 400
Mearus, 217
Mechlin, 75, 81, 230
Medade, 375
Medary, 437, 457
Medes, 435
Medley, 231
Meehan, 318
Meek, 35
Meeks, 140
Meem, 289, 326
Megahey, 256
Meigs, 70, 220, 315, 453
Meihaelis, 370
Meister, 71, 441
Meixsel, 334
Melcher, 231, 292
Mellen, 90

Mellville, 101
Melvin, 71, 102
Memott, 454
Mendell, 448
Mercer, 186, 277, 371, 458, 473
Merchant, 8, 42, 48, 80, 151, 159, 342
Meredith, 376, 460
Mereman, 458
Merenus, 355
Merhant, 42
Meridian Hill, 99, 255
Meriwether, 113
Merman, 71
Meroney, 157
Merrett, 59
Merrick, 166
Merrihew, 204, 461
Merrill, 19, 50, 198, 214, 241, 245, 297, 369
Merritt, 80, 122, 186
Merriweather, 132
Merriwether, 328, 378
Merryman, 243, 348, 398
Mervine, 299, 337
Messenger, 410
Messer, 409
Metcalf, 167, 345
Metcalfe, 33
Metchu, 298
Metropolis View, 34
Mewherter, 423
Meyenberg, 401
Meyer, 350
Michaux, 75
Michel, 437
Michler, 386
Michlin, 70
Mickens, 168
Mickle, 151
Mickum, 71, 230, 271
Micon, 424
Middleton, 17, 31, 34, 41, 92, 102, 109, 155, 156, 190, 201, 231, 267, 275, 277, 310, 361, 386, 412, 448, 452, 458, 475
Middlton, 162

Midshipmen, 18, 199, 378, 419, 473
Mike, 171
Milburn, 70, 275
Milchett, 379
Miles, 11, 49, 66, 231, 232, 256, 269, 409, 423, 424, 475
Milhan, 438
Milia, 213
Military Asylum, 274
Mill, 156
Millandon, 26
Millard, 20, 111
Millaudon, 76, 130, 223, 247
Millburn, 162
Mille, 332
Miller, 5, 9, 33, 42, 47, 55, 70, 75, 90, 91, 107, 111, 124, 125, 136, 157, 196, 199, 204, 213, 214, 223, 228, 232, 235, 236, 239, 247, 256, 269, 275, 284, 286, 287, 296, 298, 303, 329, 332, 382, 431, 432, 437, 449, 455, 460, 475
Milligan, 307
Mills, 153, 167, 183, 211, 212, 233, 415, 454, 460
Milnes, 265
Milo, 384
Milslow, 375
Milstead, 62, 70, 71
Milsted, 239
Milward, 150
Minard, 111, 223, 227, 235
Miner, 245, 394
Minis, 157, 223, 228
Minnigerode, 237
Minon, 69
Minor, 32, 45, 132, 249, 282, 303, 351, 447
Minsicu, 370
Mirick, 139, 335
Misco_, 298
Missimer, 71
Mister, 71, 233, 320
Mitchel, 254

Mitchell, 70, 71, 97, 102, 138, 145, 188, 232, 272, 274, 279, 288, 293, 298, 348, 358, 365, 381, 405, 424, 447, 448
Mitts, 248
Mix, 70, 248, 254, 397
Mobley, 363
Mockabee, 71, 233
Moffatt, 131
Moffett, 132
Mohan, 168
Mohun, 35, 45, 71, 98, 119, 136, 145, 158, 239, 256, 271, 274
Moncrieff, 319
Moncure, 153
Monell, 15
Moner, 51
Money, 235
Monmouth, 300
Monoghan, 362
Monroe, 104, 178, 215, 217, 237, 253, 263, 264, 281, 303
Montague, 34, 424
Montazile, 304
Monteban, 87
Montevue, 475
Montferret, 302
Montgomery, 38, 98, 99, 106, 163, 203, 225, 235, 287, 349, 423, 471, 476
Montony, 352, 402
Montoya, 299
Montrevill, 424
Montreville, 298
Moody, 130, 379
Moon, 379
Mooney, 215, 232, 374, 402
Moor, 20, 461
Moore, 1, 2, 11, 20, 71, 78, 135, 142, 193, 194, 197, 199, 202, 216, 239, 257, 281, 289, 325, 326, 328, 332, 343, 362, 364, 400, 408, 435, 439, 463
Moorehead, 127
Moores, 191
Moorhead, 185
Moors, 177
Moran, 55, 160, 187
Morcoe, 11, 251

Mordecai, 204
Moreland, 138, 449
Moreno, 112, 122
Morey, 196
Morfit, 15, 405
Morfitt, 70
Morgan, 14, 30, 42, 53, 54, 71, 73, 94, 104, 105, 127, 189, 208, 214, 230, 232, 271, 284, 295, 359, 360, 385, 405, 447, 450
Moriarty, 302
Morley, 358
Mormon, 15
Morphy, 353, 358
Morrill, 4, 23
Morris, 29, 34, 48, 54, 61, 71, 76, 89, 93, 117, 163, 189, 193, 208, 230, 263, 337, 359, 372, 387, 416, 424, 431, 433, 463, 465
Morrison, 28, 82, 163, 178, 182, 195
Morroles, 205
Morrow, 46, 71, 222, 355
Morse, 21, 155, 158, 164, 282, 289, 387, 471
Morsell, 7, 69, 71, 222, 304, 343, 367, 384, 406, 474
Morson, 415
Mortimer, 109
Morton, 54, 71, 167, 211, 288, 377, 386
Moseley, 14, 71, 211, 342
Mosely, 89
Moses, 21, 128, 154, 415, 467
Mosher, 70, 71, 375, 383
Mosier, 34
Mosley, 81
Moss, 6, 43, 56, 94, 232, 335, 467
mother-in-law, 216
Motley, 144, 217
Mott, 215, 241
Motzer, 419
Moulden, 475
Moulton, 185, 477
Moultrie, 6
Mount De Sales Academy, 308
Mount Holyoke Seminary, 291
Mount Pleasant, 250, 357, 381, 391

Mount Vernon, 56, 105, 129, 145, 148, 169, 184, 455, 476
Mount Vernon Arsenal, 158
Mount Vernon Association, 56, 414
Mount Vernon Ladies Association, 387
Mount Vernon Ladies' Association, 129, 184, 455
Mount Wellington, 149
Mountz, 71
Mowry, 465, 466
Moxley, 289, 355, 439
Moxon, 265
Mozine, 462
Mudd, 70, 78, 303, 444, 446
Mudge, 371
Mujica, 408
Mullan, 405
Mullany, 97, 365, 473
Mullen, 232, 360, 375
Muller, 247, 370, 383, 446
Mullett, 359
Mulligan, 382
Mulliken, 398
Mullikin, 110, 422, 446
Mullin, 325, 443
Mullins, 283
Mullowny, 404
Mulloy, 71, 145, 158, 218, 232, 239, 296, 309, 448
Mulroe, 444
Muncaster, 206
Munck, 88, 139
Muncy, 443
Mundar, 180
Munday, 147
Mundee, 47, 48
Munder, 108
Mundy, 8
Munford, 417
Munro, 419
Munroe, 182, 322, 362, 378, 454
Munson, 254
Muntz, 429, 431
Murat, 387
Murdaugh, 368, 393
Murdle, 289

Murdoch, 239, 338
Murdock, 48
Murphey, 20, 405
Murphy, 4, 11, 20, 22, 32, 71, 77, 105, 155, 206, 231, 233, 282, 286, 288, 295, 315, 394, 403, 405, 443
Murray, 1, 28, 30, 56, 96, 122, 237, 258, 296, 304, 358, 359, 372, 375, 391, 449
Murry, 406
Murtage, 146
Muse, 271
Musy, 55
mutineers, 42
Mutty, 265
Myer, 134, 230, 235, 359, 368, 370
Myerle, 45, 160, 219, 241, 431
Myers, 6, 70, 104, 108, 136, 168, 230, 259, 326, 347, 354, 364, 381, 394, 402
Myrick, 319

N

N Y Bay Cemetery, 440
N Y C Marble Cemetery, 263
Nabers, 250
Nadal, 105, 406
Nadeau, 160
Nagle, 388
Nailor, 19, 71, 197, 392, 399
Nairn, 71, 256, 274
Nalle, 415
Nally, 71, 220, 432
Napier, 286, 459
Napoleon, 39, 86, 100, 254, 412
Napoleon III, 307
Napoleon's Vale, 254
Napon, 201
Nash, 156, 159, 161, 242, 427, 450, 457
Nason, 59, 113, 130
Nater, 232
Nathl Greene, 469
National Theatre, 399
Nauset Light, 258
Naylor, 71, 167, 185, 210, 307, 425, 461
Neal, 22, 231
Neale, 7, 71, 72, 152, 256, 289, 295, 353
Neander, 383

Necharles, 375
Negro, 424
Negro contest, 412
Nehastic, 347
Neill, 280
Neilson, 129, 315, 380
Neitzy, 233
Nelson, 34, 71, 117, 129, 147, 159, 232, 267, 273, 297, 354, 365, 415, 416, 445, 473
Nesbitt, 168
Nesmith, 302
Nettles, 280
Nettman, 369
Neuman, 181
Nevins, 61
Nevitt, 449
Newall, 289
Newberry, 413
Newbold, 355
Newcomb, 242
Newell, 30, 34, 169, 213, 372, 394
Newhall, 463
Newman, 18, 48, 106, 209, 231, 289, 388, 393, 447
Newton, 34, 63, 68, 71, 169, 170, 229, 231, 358, 391, 400, 452
Nexsen, 25
Niblack, 314
Nicholas, 29, 71
Nicholls, 255, 378
Nichols, 71, 122, 240, 248, 343, 353, 378, 385, 449, 456
Nicholson, 11, 76, 122, 137, 215, 258, 405, 433
Nickerson, 427
Nicodemus, 287
Nigers, 409
Nighingale, 217
Niles, 136, 159, 440
Nivert, 413
Nixon, 105, 381
Noble, 18, 41, 55, 163, 260, 404, 454
Noe, 50
Noell, 328
Nolan, 308

Noland, 283
Noonan, 122
Norfleet, 71
Norfolk Herald, 334
Norman, 216
Normant, 107
Norment, 374
Norris, 71, 179, 272, 291, 306
North, 52
North Bend, 311, 341
North Carolina, 111
Northey, 362
Norton, 31, 88, 90, 151, 152, 193, 229, 232, 355, 404, 419, 426
Norwood, 193, 230, 295, 442, 478
Noteware, 47
Nott, 164, 223, 247
Nottersen, 375
Nourse, 29, 71, 116, 185, 207, 230, 241, 477
Nout, 311
Nowlan, 358
Noyes, 71, 90, 206, 231, 232, 406
Nugen, 285, 288
Nugent, 168, 263, 409, 422
null & void, 42
Nutall, 219
Nye, 52, 94, 137, 268, 432, 449

O

O'Brien, 36, 38, 76, 90, 130, 157, 168, 169, 223, 231, 238, 247, 248, 316, 335, 347, 379, 419, 447
O'Bryon, 314
O'Connell, 87, 138, 241, 279, 333
O'Connor, 466
O'Day, 452
O'Donnel, 460
O'Donnoghue, 30, 72, 289, 376
O'Driscoll, 339, 462
O'Dwyer, 210
O'Flynn, 281
O'Hara, 358
O'Hare, 239
O'Keefe, 224
O'Keefee, 46

O'Leary, 342, 353
O'Neal, 14, 231, 401
O'Neill, 315, 424
O'Rooke, 297
O'Toole, 36, 96, 98, 260, 342, 349
Oak Hill Cemetery, 195, 222, 423
Oakland Farm, 392
Oakland Place, 427
Oakwood, 319
Ober, 239
Occoquan Mills, 418
Oden, 34, 139, 155, 170
Offley, 336
Offutt, 102, 202, 232, 256, 289, 318
Ogden, 20, 29, 118, 204, 214, 263, 387
Ogle, 25, 53, 62, 172, 179
Oglesby, 420
Ogston, 251
Ohio, 149
Ohr, 397
Old Gas Works, 112
old Presbyterian Church, 125
Oldaker, 412
oldest woman, 234
Oldfield, 39, 123
Olgner, 130
Oliver, 226, 383
Olmstead, 24
Omstead, 371
Onderdonk, 449
One Hundred Years, 409
Ord, 287, 360, 405
Order of the Holy Cross, 98
Orme, 11, 81, 220, 239, 256, 271, 281, 296, 341, 397, 448
Orndorf, 163, 227, 235, 246
Orndorff, 223
Orr, 131, 321, 344, 359, 471
Orsini, 134
Osbar, 370, 375
Osborn, 354
Osbourn, 312
Osgodby, 72, 262, 271
Osollo, 301
Ostrom, 376
Otey, 274

Otinger, 18
Otis, 376
Ott, 256, 446
Otterback, 46, 100, 335
Ottinger, 23, 76, 118, 188, 223
Otto, 104
Ould, 25, 167, 215, 289, 306
Ouseley, 170, 302, 462
Outten, 100
Overmeyer, 457
Owen, 96, 97, 105, 137, 139, 250, 257, 267, 285, 323, 360, 386, 389, 390, 405, 412, 442
Owen, 225
Owens, 34, 71, 180, 208, 273, 289, 295, 436
Owins, 199
Owner, 90, 269
Oyster, 71, 146, 158, 296
ozone, 422

P

Pacha, 32
Packer, 24
packet **Flying Cloud**, 321
packet **Galen**, 21
Padgett, 202, 232
Paez, 408, 429
Paff, 55, 94
Page, 3, 44, 55, 63, 157, 163, 167, 226, 246, 311, 323, 346, 350, 357, 361, 393, 395, 416, 421
Paillet, 238
Paine, 122, 230, 280, 286, 297, 441, 469, 472
Pairo, 10, 72, 112, 176, 185, 477
Palfrey, 97, 283, 285, 287
Palizzi, 294
Palmer, 28, 29, 55, 153, 159, 174, 176, 177, 185, 189, 203, 204, 213, 221, 239, 271, 272, 313, 337, 365, 386, 400, 459
Palmerston, 79
Palms, 97
Pancoast, 72
Pangburn, 164

Panmure, 471
Pannell, 102
Papprenitza, 223
Pappreniza, 238
Papreniza, 130
Parish, 60
Park, 42
Parke, 318
Parker, 18, 30, 33, 37, 51, 72, 101, 121, 129, 135, 144, 149, 151, 153, 189, 205, 236, 237, 239, 242, 256, 293, 318, 355, 356, 394, 400, 417, 447, 469, 473
Parkes, 273
Parkhill, 51, 424
Parkison, 105
Parks, 101
Parlin, 13
Parr, 361
Parris, 452
Parrott, 28, 93
Parry, 174, 177, 241
Parsons, 34, 232, 297, 384, 396, 397
Partington, 443
Partridge, 76, 103, 422
Passmore, 132
Pasture & Gleanings, 216
Patch, 380
Paterson, 101
Patrick, 412
Patterson, 10, 13, 72, 101, 126, 132, 162, 232, 237, 256, 279, 325, 326, 338, 345, 396, 458, 463
Patti, 456
Patton, 18, 153, 410
Paul, 72, 144, 255, 292
Paulding, 17, 29, 30, 44, 88, 94, 185, 242, 394
Paxon, 462
Paxton, 415
Payne, 79, 155, 167, 210, 227, 244, 261, 322, 330, 366, 379, 417, 463
Paypers, 370
Peabody, 162, 232, 447
Peach, 86
Peacock, 134, 416

Peader, 443
Peake, 210
Peale, 121, 173, 213
Pearce, 30, 285, 287, 448, 471
Pearson, 1, 29, 53, 164, 223, 239, 343, 383
Pearsons, 366
Pease, 26
Peaslee, 13
Peay, 76
Pecard, 356
Peck, 72, 108, 126, 136, 231, 258, 285, 313, 395, 466
Peckard, 110
Peckham, 471
Peden, 102
Peebles, 449
Peel, 104
Peet, 376
Pegg, 26, 43, 134, 165, 177, 243
Pegram, 368, 369, 394
Peippert, 221
Peirce, 94
Pellet, 271, 387, 455
Pember, 27
Pena, 37
Pender, 360, 465
Pendergast, 165, 211, 213
Pendergrast, 43, 93, 220, 241, 394
Pendler, 405
Pendleton, 385, 387, 403, 406, 410
Penman, 11
Pennegar, 55
Pennington, 396, 436
Pennock, 132, 368, 394
Penny, 172, 326
Percival, 273
Percivall, 350
Perins, 361
Perkins, 41, 90, 104, 140, 154, 203, 214, 224, 247, 316, 355, 393, 394, 415, 458
Perrie, 175
Perry, 13, 29, 48, 55, 57, 90, 93, 95, 96, 98, 100, 104, 164, 210, 223, 283, 293, 317, 393, 404, 441, 447, 455, 457, 461, 469, 473

Persifer, 97, 123, 209, 449
Persifor, 225, 287, 331, 374
Persley, 297
Peter, 72, 250, 335, 381, 392
Peterkin, 436
Peters, 72, 99, 109, 139, 237, 289, 344
Petersen, 21
Peterson, 157, 374, 375
Petery, 89
Petit, 109, 123, 289
Petry, 391
Pett, 384
Pettibone, 231, 233, 256
Pettingall, 94
Pettit, 1, 72, 164, 170, 326, 398, 402
Peugh, 72, 375
Peuguet, 240
Peyton, 196, 472
Pfeiffer, 435
Phagin, 138
Phelps, 50, 54, 61, 72, 105, 106, 178, 189, 196, 211, 238, 328, 372, 394, 429, 432, 472
Phenix, 33, 44, 157, 160, 224, 247, 317
Phifer, 425
Philbrick, 345
Philip, 115
Philippe, 177
Philipps, 202
Philips, 55, 72, 282, 289
Phillip, 72
Phillips, 59, 72, 136, 138, 149, 213, 216, 222, 227, 232, 257, 267, 269, 309, 363, 378, 477
Philp, 104, 123, 171, 229, 274
Phinney, 240
Phoenix, 38
Phythian, 395
Pickard, 55
Pickell, 63, 177
Pickens, 20, 315
Pickett, 28, 377
Pickrell, 90, 196, 214, 260, 305, 326
Pidgeon, 412
Pierce, 38, 61, 79, 90, 156, 166, 180, 185, 213, 248, 356, 411, 426, 455

Pierri, 134
Pike, 188, 220
Pilan, 248
Pilcher, 336
Pillar, 255
Pilling, 136
Pillow, 457
Pillsbury, 463
Pinckney, 118, 376, 379
Pine Grove, 421
Pine Tree Vein, 336
Piney Branch, 338, 383
Piney Point, 126
Pinkin, 452
Pinkney, 160, 262, 319
Piper, 139
Pipsico, 109
Pise, 448
Pitcher, 52, 72, 465, 466
Pitman, 447
Pittman, 76, 183, 223, 247
Pitts, 103, 152
Pitzer, 170
Pizzini, 282, 288
Plain Dealing, 250
Plate, 370, 375
Plater, 291
Platt, 30, 72, 220
Pleasant Plains, 325
Pleasanton, 23
Pleasants, 40, 92, 110, 241, 250
Pleasonton, 72
Pless, 380
Pletke, 375
Plinta, 471
Plonk, 293
Plowden, 288
Plumber, 151
Plummer, 26, 27, 225, 285, 295
Plumsill, 72
Plunkett, 394, 429
Plympton, 97, 123
Poage, 142
Pocock, 174
Pocosin, 277
Poe, 50

Poindexter, 29, 186
Poinsett, 341
Poisal, 106
Poisell, 424
Poitevin, 360
Pole, 375
Polekrusen, 375
Polidore, 429
Polikeruski, 370
Polk, 72, 289, 303, 354, 359, 448
Polkinhorn, 11, 358
Poll, 370
Pollack, 214, 370
Pollard, 53, 72, 266, 447
Pollen, 156
Pollock, 181, 395, 415
Polly, 34, 94
Pomares, 210, 238
Pomeroy, 101, 176
Pons, 72, 91, 183
Poole, 230
Poor, 295
Poore, 11
Pope, 45
Porcher, 18, 181, 419
Porteous, 20
Porter, 8, 15, 18, 30, 72, 84, 107, 122, 130, 132, 147, 163, 174, 213, 223, 241, 252, 297, 304, 376, 392, 395, 425, 469, 471, 473
Porterfield, 118, 213
Portland Manor, 195
Portman, 183, 196, 214
Posey, 72, 155, 203, 424
Post, 42, 371, 448
Potentini, 16
Potter, 58, 182, 282, 286, 289, 394, 449
Potts, 5, 267, 305, 335, 353
Pouder, 102
Poultney, 102
Poulton, 88, 114
Powell, 72, 106, 199, 230, 239, 274, 309, 390, 468
Power, 42
Powers, 10, 72, 96, 154, 372, 411, 464
Pragey, 119

Prather, 127, 452
Prathers, 72
Pratt, 72, 110, 416, 434
Pray, 115, 144
Preinhart, 72
Prentis, 442
Prentiss, 432, 473
Pres' Message, 333
Prescott, 426
Preston, 48, 57, 127, 461
Preswick, 36
Pretty Prospect, 250
Prettyman, 104, 322, 324
Price, 58, 146, 153, 158, 160, 174, 232, 237, 238, 324, 423, 427, 449
Prickett, 163
Prickner, 312
Priest, 168
Prime, 337
Prince Royal of Sicily, 292
Prindle, 72
Pritchard, 289
Pritchett, 352
Proby, 90, 154
Proctor, 337
Prolific, 414
propeller **General Taylor**, 446
propeller **Globe**, 378
propeller **Petrel**, 417
Prospect Hill, 132, 310, 332
Prospect Hill Cemetery, 371
Prosperi, 11
Prout, 72, 238, 256
Provest, 46, 131
Provost, 263
Prudhomme, 289
Pryor, 232
Puckett, 55
Pugh, 72, 355
Pullen, 156, 312
Pumphrey, 72, 90, 136, 242, 357, 371, 378, 381
Purceel, 373
Purcell, 72, 175, 188, 233, 305, 340, 447
Purdy, 33, 36, 72, 199, 232, 256, 296, 305, 332, 448, 461

Purkins, 34
Purse, 394, 429
Pursell, 244, 296, 449
Purviance, 29
Purvis, 108, 144
Putnam, 39, 359
Pye, 301
Pyfer, 245, 356
Pyles, 97, 232
Pyne, 451
Pywell, 89, 132

Q

Quackenbush, 294, 446
Quantrill, 134
Quantrille, 49
Quattlebaum, 285
Queen, 28, 160, 180, 190, 210, 257, 270, 301, 310, 340, 341, 366, 374, 386, 408, 429, 450
Queen Hortense, 307
Queen of Oude, 84
Queen Victoria, 218, 273
Queen's message, 334
Queen's Message, 333
Quenan, 281
Quick, 168
Quigley, 3, 21, 161, 167, 210, 318
Quinby, 476
Quincy, 419
Quinlan, 323
Quinn, 272, 392
Quitman, 300, 303, 387
Quitmen, 297
Quito, 168
Quynn, 102

R

Rabbit, 295
Rachel, 32
Radcliffe, 179
Radetzky, 32, 51
Radford, 81
Radiminski, 340
Radziminski, 461, 465, 466

Ragan, 19, 23, 72, 77, 233, 461
Rainbow, 176
Rainey, 108, 231, 451
Rainy, 289
Raleigh, 109
Ralston, 307
Ramalie, 364
Rambo, 410
Rampono, 169
Ramsay, 138, 176, 327, 471, 472
Ramsburg, 276
Ramsey, 52, 243, 267, 469
Ran, 300
Randall, 17, 46, 56, 155, 159, 243, 255, 274, 276, 317, 358, 362
Randolph, 24, 60, 73, 95, 110, 153, 164, 210, 245, 247, 350, 391, 402, 405, 415, 416, 458
Random, 230
Rankin, 477
Ransom, 360, 405
Ranson, 34
Rappaljee, 376
Rappetti, 72
Ratclif, 114
Ratcliff, 230, 349
Ratcliffe, 72, 137, 306, 341, 454
Rathbun, 59, 164, 223
Ratrie, 72, 83, 181, 187
Raub, 361, 380
Rauch, 1
Raustead, 80
Rawden, 111
Rawle, 329, 432
Rawlings, 21, 72, 77, 117, 230, 305
Ray, 34, 72, 301, 361, 448
Raymert, 191
Rea, 59
Read, 30, 44, 135, 160, 199, 203, 204, 235, 236, 247, 301, 309, 378, 379, 443, 473
Reade, 339
Reading, 299
Reagan, 452
Reaherd, 156
Ream, 150

Reaping Machine, 254
Reardon, 72, 168, 187, 190, 443
Redden, 187
Redfern, 72, 98
Redfield, 252
Redhead, 471
Redin, 63, 72, 83, 109, 251, 305, 412, 436
Redman, 94, 191, 203, 204, 225, 235, 246, 317, 388
Redwine, 420
Reed, 22, 72, 122, 159, 202, 227, 251, 256, 286, 294, 304, 394, 400, 407, 422, 425, 430, 443, 458, 465
Reeder, 231
Reeler, 44
Reese, 86, 145, 158, 231, 297
Reeside, 291
Reeves, 164, 202, 289, 332, 451
Regester, 72
Register, 105, 165
Reid, 34, 56, 171, 248, 278, 318, 321, 469, 474
Reiley, 90
Reill, 469
Reilly, 15, 24, 181, 209, 232, 269
Reily, 16
Reinlanmer, 370
Reiss, 328
Reitz, 91
Remington, 121, 139, 171
Remlander, 375
Remuck, 408
Renahan, 108
Renaud, 373, 413
Rencher, 28
Render, 375
Rendsburg, 370
Reniff, 94
Renner, 126
Reno, 188, 465
Renois, 52, 164
Renon, 308
Renshaw, 368, 395
Repentigny, 155
Repetti, 248

Retke, 370
Reul, 104
Revir, 427
Reyloff, 443
Reynes, 8
Reynolds, 4, 31, 36, 53, 118, 131, 135, 144, 159, 178, 182, 206, 223, 232, 286, 395
Rezin, 53, 220, 366
Rheem, 230
Rhett, 147, 239, 259, 285, 465, 466
Rhind, 469, 473
Rhoades, 449
Rhodes, 90, 108, 167, 342
Ricar, 72
Rice, 183, 198, 294, 471
Rich, 11, 72, 111, 236, 238, 358
Richard, 384, 400
Richards, 25, 45, 50, 73, 136, 150, 329, 427, 444
Richardson, 34, 40, 55, 72, 102, 111, 151, 202, 221, 291, 461
Richey, 105, 175, 229
Richmond, 26, 113, 210, 214, 247, 302, 435
Richter, 370, 375
Richwood Tract, 360
Rickard, 136
Ricker, 72, 93, 221, 235
Rickman, 163
Riddick, 44
Riddle, 122, 465
Ridenour, 11
Rider, 20, 99
Ridgate, 141
Ridge, 140
Ridgeley, 60, 256, 270
Ridgely, 60, 72, 114, 128, 132, 368, 398
Ridgeway, 72, 216
Ridgley, 394
Riedt, 169
Riehle, 49, 436
Riell, 473
Rielly, 15
Riely, 391
Rieper, 380

Riever, 34
Riffle, 62
Rigdon, 414
Riggles, 90, 154, 167
Riggs, 72, 185, 271, 355, 387, 388, 448, 455
Right Angle Triangle, 358
Riley, 73, 91, 102, 154, 214, 256, 310, 311, 394, 409
Rill, 370, 375
Rind, 220, 394, 423
Ring, 43, 99, 223, 247
Ringgold, 29, 421
Rink, 126
Ripley, 163, 317, 330
Rippetoe, 105
Risque, 72, 289
Ritchie, 29, 72, 270, 271, 387, 451
Rithmuller, 72
Ritley, 354
Ritmeir, 473
Rittenhouse, 190, 194, 197, 410
Ritter, 72, 341
Rives, 11, 101, 152, 319, 411, 417
Roach, 148, 220, 223, 232, 289, 292, 294, 322, 354, 357, 478
Roath, 43
Robaldo, 203
Robb, 29, 159, 244
Robbins, 94, 307, 380
Robert, 228
Roberts, 9, 28, 42, 44, 53, 55, 87, 122, 196, 224, 270, 325, 381, 394, 431, 448
Robertson, 12, 83, 111, 153, 165, 166, 231, 246, 301, 316, 366, 414, 431
Robey, 190, 408
Robie, 172, 365
Robins, 240, 471
Robinson, 11, 13, 17, 19, 24, 32, 36, 47, 49, 50, 63, 73, 84, 85, 93, 94, 102, 160, 193, 194, 230, 232, 251, 266, 281, 287, 288, 289, 298, 336, 372, 379, 411, 415, 431, 441
Roble, 168
Roby, 378
Rochampton Lodge, 291

Roche, 259, 278
Rochelle, 218, 394
Rochester, 78, 85
Rock, 11
Rock Creek Church, 90
Rock Spring Farm, 385
Rockland, 89
Rockley, 348
Rockwell, 8, 59
Roddan, 451
Roddy, 177
Rodger, 218
Rodgers, 13, 105, 220, 248, 253, 386, 426
Rodier, 72
Rodrigue, 424
Roe, 347, 471
Rogers, 3, 13, 55, 95, 115, 119, 162, 163, 167, 189, 203, 214, 223, 227, 235, 247, 265, 317, 365, 389, 395, 424, 438
Rohm, 337
Rohmondt, 380
Rohrer, 90
Rojas, 408
Rokohl, 421
Roland, 229
Rolando, 469, 473
Rollings, 306, 312
Rollins, 49
Roman, 348, 463
Roman Catholics, 182
Romero, 224
Romp, 137
Ronckendorff, 394
Roney, 232
Rooke, 33
Rooker, 137, 184, 213, 325
Rooney, 395, 443
Root, 34
Roots, 359
Roper, 94, 224, 246, 435
Rose, 15, 144, 194, 232
Rose Hill, 442
Rosen, 374
Rosendamm, 375

Rosenthal, 255, 370
Rosin, 370, 375
Ross, 15, 32, 34, 48, 72, 122, 190, 231, 289, 355, 423, 425
Rossburg, 348
Rosson, 252
Rost, 397
Roszel, 105
Rothrock, 312
Rothschild, 415
Rothwell, 72, 231
Roulhac, 18, 278
Rouse, 274
Rovendamon, 370
Rowan, 196, 214, 224, 228, 246, 247
Rowland, 14, 72, 156, 159, 247, 316
Rowles, 188, 231
Roye, 460
Rudasel, 178
Rudd, 19, 29, 210, 279, 281
Rudder, 102
Rudenstein, 162
Rudio, 134
Rudler, 459
Ruff, 72
Ruffin, 457
Ruffner, 456
Rugby Institute, 374
Rugg, 104
Ruggles, 72, 299, 379
Ruler, 72
Rumpff, 176
Rumph, 223, 228, 235, 246, 317
Runey, 260
Runnalls, 48
Runnels, 1, 472
Runyon, 193
Rupp, 38, 269, 436
Rupple, 10
Rush, 12, 27, 278
Rushville, 105
Rusk, 26, 89, 144
Russ, 418
Russel, 126
Russell, 26, 27, 58, 163, 223, 239, 242, 294, 380, 430

Rust, 89, 438
Rutger, 246
Ruth, 76
Rutherford, 153, 339, 416
Rutledge, 271, 341, 387
Ryan, 23, 72, 191, 240, 284, 287, 318, 387
Rye, 72, 230
Ryland, 105, 390
Ryler, 405
Ryther, 72

S

Sabin, 325
Sackers, 248
Sadlier, 313
Sage, 73, 275, 349
Salamon, 93
Sales, 351
Saloman, 89
Salomon, 458
Salter, 458
Saltonstall, 32
Samory, 228
Sample, 125
Samson, 87, 254, 273, 275, 315, 345, 355, 377, 382, 439, 454, 472
Sanborn, 242, 396
Sander, 393
Sanders, 78, 85, 174, 288, 313, 342, 427, 451, 465, 466
Sanderson, 335, 416, 449
Sandford, 430
Sandidge, 302
Sandiford, 73
Sands, 73, 101, 160, 176, 187, 242, 467
Sandy, 110
Sandys, 109
Saner, 73
Sanford, 101, 139, 359
Sanger, 202
Sangster, 447
Santa Anna, 26
Santhara, 159
Sardo, 8
Sargant, 259
Sargent, 97, 105, 183, 294
Sarger, 73
Sarmiento, 53
Sartiges, 302
Sartorri, 29
Sasscer, 349
Saucher, 163
Saul, 107, 115, 123, 361, 389
Saunders, 14, 34, 126, 222, 286, 296, 297, 326, 332, 335, 466
Saur, 73
Savage, 108, 118, 155, 230, 231
Sawtelle, 438
Sawyer, 6, 151, 156, 214, 220, 224, 236, 238, 247, 396
Saxton, 191
Sayre, 3, 94, 189, 237, 239
Scaggs, 230, 249, 421, 461
Scaife, 93, 159
Scala, 73
Scanlon, 25
Scarborough, 401
Scarbrough, 115
Scarf, 231
Scarff, 295
Schad, 409, 426, 435
Schafer, 295
Schaffeld, 288
Schaffer, 207
Scharff, 302
Schaubb, 73
Scheck, 375
Scheel, 89
Scheerer, 243
Scheffer, 270
Schell, 11, 12, 252, 302
Schenck, 29, 466
Schio, 441
Schlegal, 73
Schley, 80, 435
Schmidt, 124, 185
Schnackenberger, 344
Schneiwind, 357
schnr **E Atwood**, 396
schnr **Francis French**, 290
schnr **George Franklin**, 274

schnr **Keziah**, 258
schnr **Prairie Flower**, 242
schnr **Revenge**, 95
schnr **Shark**, 95
schnr **Sheppard A Mount**, 245
schnr **Speedwell**, 317
schnr **Susan**, 459
schnr **Traveler**, 213
Schoeffler, 240
Schoenbien, 422
Scholfield, 73
Schoolcraft, 194, 238
Schouler, 185
Schroeder, 164, 223, 227, 235
Schultz, 301
Schunk, 50
Schureman, 73
Schussler, 478
Schuyler, 28, 57
Schwabe, 314
Schwartz, 73, 125, 152, 242
Schwarze, 73
Schwitzer, 451
Scotch girls, 353
Scott, 23, 43, 60, 73, 117, 141, 167, 188,
    209, 232, 251, 256, 258, 269, 330,
    339, 369, 373, 454
Scott, 73, 117, 141, 164, 167, 305, 313,
    346, 459, 460
Scripture, 294
Scrivener, 73, 269, 329, 468
Scrivner, 165
Scullen, 443
Seabrook, 22, 59, 83, 246
Seabrooke, 44
Seaman, 341
Searle, 55
Searles, 397
Sears, 73, 121, 233, 357
Seaton, 11, 49, 152, 254, 256, 281, 357
Seavers, 50
Seay, 110
Secretan, 450
Sedgwick, 280
Segar, 175
Seibel, 73

Seidler, 124
Selby, 72, 122
Selden, 91, 133, 252, 256, 394, 405, 423,
    447
Seldon, 372
Selhausen, 73
Sellman, 76, 398
Semken, 239
Semmes, 4, 30, 73, 90, 117, 122, 179,
    232, 254, 267, 282, 289, 296, 383
Semple, 341
Sener, 166, 183
Sengstack, 62, 73, 230
Senstack, 340
Serena, 26, 27, 203, 204, 219, 246
Sergeant, 471
Sergent, 446
Serrin, 73, 198
Sessford, 167, 210, 231, 281, 355
Settle, 73
Seuftleben, 73
Sevart, 469
Sevier, 192
Sewall, 104, 289, 412
Seward, 48, 194, 449
Sewell, 13, 251, 401, 473
Sexton, 220
Seymour, 43, 96, 289
Seys, 410
Shaaf, 339
Shackelford, 5, 78, 410, 450
Shackley, 52
Shaeffer, 141
Shafer, 55
Shaff, 122
Shaffer, 231
Shaffner, 15, 204
Shaler, 465, 471
Shananhan, 411
Shands, 102
Shaner, 432
Shangles, 193
Shanks, 256
Shann, 50
Shannon, 36, 124, 332
Shannondale Farm, 132

Shanon, 168
Sharke, 78
Sharon, 226
Sharp, 89, 164, 281
Sharpe, 78, 85, 101, 197, 299
Sharretts, 73, 74, 305
Shaughnessy, 423
Shaw, 51, 61, 108, 136, 146, 166, 211, 217, 223, 256, 358, 393, 467, 469, 472
Shea, 300
Sheahy, 263, 409, 422
Shealy, 332, 335
Shearer, 42
Shears, 269
Sheck, 370
Sheckel, 136
Sheckell, 195, 256
Sheckels, 271
Sheckles, 231
Shedd, 73
Sheets, 233, 416
Sheffey, 196, 416
Shehan, 231
Sheid, 382
Shekell, 28
Shekells, 40, 43, 269
Shelby, 134
Shelden, 17
Sheldon, 42, 77, 272
Shelling, 369
Shelton, 151
Shepard, 237, 320, 406
Shephard, 23, 73
Shepherd, 3, 19, 116, 273
Shepperd, 266, 306
Sherlock, 247, 252
Sherman, 42, 43, 73, 99, 198, 214, 230, 247, 290, 314, 332, 394, 467
Sherrard, 362, 393, 448
Sherwood, 55, 157
Shields, 73, 156, 464, 469
Shiinn, 220
Shillinglaw, 192
Shillington, 207
ship **Alleghany**, 189
ship **America**, 27

ship **Arago**, 331
ship **Arctic**, 248
ship **Artic**, 375
ship **Carl**, 211
ship **Cartell**, 172
ship **Catarina**, 380
ship **Chesapeake**, 57, 226
ship **Constitution**, 147
ship **Cyane**, 95, 316
ship **Dale**, 222
ship **Eastern City**, 430
ship **Empress**, 376
ship **Europa**, 443
ship **Fanny Fosdick**, 422
ship **Fashion**, 21
ship **Fredonia**, 178
ship **Herefordshire**, 157
ship **Howard**, 83
ship **Illinois**, 443
ship **Independence**, 88
ship **Isaac Bell**, 412
ship **J J Hawthorne**, 366
ship **John Adams**, 455
ship **John Elliott Thayer**, 423
ship **John Gilpin**, 157
ship **John Milton**, 85
ship **Kate Hooper**, 42, 79
ship **Lawrence**, 55
ship **Leopard**, 226
ship **Lotus**, 370
ship **Margaret Tyson**, 474
ship **Marion**, 172
ship **Mary Caroline Stevens**, 404, 410
ship **Maurice**, 413
ship **Merchantman**, 430
ship **Mersey**, 430
ship **Nathan Hanan**, 426
ship **North Carolina**, 95
ship **Ohio 74**, 55
ship **Ostervald**, 211
ship **Pelican State**, 383
ship **Pennsylvania**, 345
ship **Plymouth**, 218
ship **Portsmouth**, 77
ship **Preble**, 215, 249
ship **Prince Albert**, 370, 374

ship **Roanoke**, 478
ship **Saratoga**, 5, 6
ship **Savannah**, 478
ship **Saxonia**, 401
ship **Sparkling Wave**, 326
ship **Sunny South**, 157
ship **Ticonderoga**, 88
ship **Ultonia**, 365
ship **Vandalia**, 61, 420
ship **Waverley**, 47
ship **Wild Wave**, 420
ships **Cyane & Levant**, 147
Shirley, 247, 291, 341
Shirley Female Seminary, 43
Shoals, 94
Shock, 199
Shoemaker, 73, 92, 210, 250, 256, 296, 379, 413
Sholes, 223, 227, 235, 246
Shorech, 332
Shork, 393
Shorock, 335
Short, 232
Shotwell, 154
Showalter, 104
Shrewsbury, 122, 423
Shryock, 73, 395
Shubrick, 368, 393
Shultz, 392
Shumate, 341
Shunk, 106
Shurbrick, 118
Shurman, 224
Shuster, 73, 303, 444, 446, 475, 477
Shutt, 369
Shyne, 276, 291
Sibbett, 34
Sibley, 17, 73, 113, 230, 436
Sibrey, 145, 158
Sicard, 419
Sichlman, 375
Sichs, 375
Sickles, 291
Sicks, 370
Siddons, 347
Siebel, 391

Sierra, 101
Siffrin, 50
Sigourney, 439
Sigur, 373
Silliers, 50
Silliman, 328
Silsbee, 207
Simcock, 265
Simington, 231
Simkins, 151
Simmons, 73, 146, 166, 232, 465
Simms, 25, 41, 49, 52, 73, 74, 119, 145, 158, 231, 256, 281, 341, 377, 378, 403, 421, 447
Simon, 367
Simonds, 127, 158, 221
Simons, 24, 215, 466
Simonson, 256
Simonton, 410
Simpkins, 242
Simple, 18
Simpson, 125, 168, 186, 201, 275, 292, 365, 396
Sims, 42, 189, 416
Sinclair, 218, 219, 235, 248, 355, 420, 465
Singer, 12
Singleton, 477
Sipes, 105
Sirian, 18
Sismondi, 123
Sister Mary Eleanor, 455
Sister of Charity, 478
Sister Williamanna, 478
Sisters of Mercy, 331
Sitzer, 185
Sixeas, 105
Skeeles, 304
Skelly, 471
Skidmore, 398
Skinner, 49, 254, 281, 341
Slack, 155, 314
Slade, 73, 360, 462
Slane, 258, 259
Slassel, 237
Slater, 73, 90, 375

Slatford, 33, 36
Slatter, 21
Slaughter, 153, 267
slaver **Echo**, 378, 476
Sledman, 246
Slemmer, 62
Slemons, 133
Slidell, 186
Sloan, 148, 297
Sloo, 220, 243
sloop **Exchange**, 388
sloop **Falmouth**, 368, 395
sloop of war **Cyane**, 372
sloop of war **Saratoga**, 238
sloop **Preble**, 394
sloop **St Mary's**, 314
sloop-of-war **Cyane**, 10, 368
sloop-of-war **Erie**, 147
sloop-of-war **Germantown**, 316
sloop-of-war **Portsmouth**, 235, 243, 251
sloop-of-war **St Louis**, 339, 344, 413
sloop-of-war **Water-witch**, 368
Small, 231
Smalley, 331, 404
Smallwood, 73, 352, 419, 438, 455
Smead, 46
Smedley, 233
Smets, 252
Smick, 139
Smiles, 171
Smiley, 242
Smith, 2, 4, 9, 18, 20, 23, 25, 27, 28, 29, 30, 32, 36, 37, 41, 43, 53, 71, 73, 74, 76, 84, 87, 89, 90, 91, 92, 93, 95, 96, 97, 101, 105, 106, 110, 115, 116, 122, 123, 127, 130, 131, 137, 139, 141, 142, 149, 154, 157, 158, 159, 162, 164, 167, 169, 174, 178, 182, 183, 189, 196, 197, 202, 203, 209, 211, 213, 214, 220, 221, 223, 224, 225, 226, 227, 230, 231, 232, 238, 242, 245, 246, 247, 249, 250, 256, 257, 267, 269, 271, 272, 274, 281, 282, 283, 285, 286, 287, 288, 289, 294, 296, 297, 300, 302, 316, 318, 319, 327, 331, 335, 337, 344, 349, 361, 363, 365, 370, 372, 374, 375, 376, 378, 386, 388, 394, 395, 398, 400, 401, 410, 417, 420, 427, 430, 431, 432, 436, 438, 440, 446, 447, 449, 450, 451, 454, 456, 457, 458, 459, 460, 463, 469, 471, 472, 474
Smithers, 95, 173, 213, 246
Smithes, 113
Smithson, 362
Smitson, 73
Smoot, 132, 135, 256, 341, 345, 442
Smyser, 267
Snead, 248
Sneckster, 424
Snelling, 87
Snow, 329
Snowden, 18, 427
Snyder, 11, 12, 62, 105, 134, 179, 337, 386
Society of Friends, 454
Solin, 375
Solomon, 189
Solyman, 353
Somervell, 306, 311, 339
Somervill, 239
Somerville, 156
Sommer, 73
Sommers, 73
Sondheim, 369
Sontag, 348
Sorber, 311
Sorin, 98
Sothoron, 194, 304, 305, 348, 398, 413
Souberbielle, 326
Soulard, 288
Soule, 10, 196, 294
South, 247
Southard, 263
Southcomb, 246
Southgate, 89, 243, 321
Southwell, 18
Soutter, 237
Soyer, 339
Spa Spring, 220
Spaet, 73

Spalding, 90, 167, 188, 209, 212, 230, 231, 259, 349
Spangler, 9
Spargo, 201
Sparklin, 280
Sparks, 218
Speake, 105
Spear, 221, 351
Spedden, 394
Speed, 15
Speiden, 418
Speight, 188, 471
Spence, 35, 73, 361
Spencer, 20, 90, 167, 231, 234, 271, 371, 475, 477
Spicely, 28
Spies, 146
Spilman, 167
Spinney, 137, 259
Spiqual, 73
Spitzlen, 59
Spooner, 341
Spotswood, 253
Spotts, 372
Sprewell, 124
Spring Vale, 337
Springer, 55, 102
Springland, 280, 283
Springman, 50, 73
Sprinkel, 267
Spruance, 253
Spurgin, 122
Squier, 185
St Amand, 19
St Armant, 8
St Augustine, 207
St Basil, 207
St John's College, 45, 322
St Patrick's Church, 124
St Vincent, 248
St Zig, 370
Stabner, 370, 375
Stace, 294
Stachel, 208, 370
Stafford, 116, 118, 119, 134, 163, 223, 225, 235, 247, 262, 295

Stake, 136
Stalker, 93, 159
Stallings, 359
Stambaugh, 11
Stamm, 365
Stancliff, 294
Stanford, 63
Stanhope, 136
Stanley, 121, 183, 187, 223, 347
Stanly, 30, 155, 247, 368, 394
Stanton, 262, 394
Stapp, 240
Star newspaper, 418
Stark, 395, 402
Starke, 101
Starmunt, 370
Starr, 153, 283, 342
Start, 105
Statcup, 353, 366, 374
Staufen, 294
Stauz, 370
Steadman, 95, 225, 394
Stealey, 159, 217, 235
steamboat **Aurora**, 355
steamboat **Daniel Boone**, 450
steamboat **Telegraph**, 273
steamboat **West Point**, 137
steam-cutter **Harriet Lane**, 302
steamer **A B Chambers**, 272
steamer **Albert**, 375
steamer **America**, 100
steamer **Arctic**, 218, 423
steamer **Atalanta**, 368
steamer **Austria**, 370, 373, 374, 375, 413
steamer **Ben Loder**, 290
steamer **Caledonia**, 368, 394
steamer **Calhoun**, 440
steamer **Canada**, 42
steamer **Central America**, 174, 316
steamer **City of Baltimore**, 222
steamer **Col Crossma**, 82
steamer **Colonel Harney**, 455
steamer **Eliza Battle**, 106
steamer **Empire State**, 117, 388
steamer **Engineer**, 126

steamer **Falls City**, 158
steamer **Fanny Fern**, 40
steamer **Florida**, 242
steamer **Fulton**, 368, 372, 394, 427
steamer **Fulton City**, 435
steamer **George Page**, 131
steamer **Gorgon**, 324
steamer **Harriet Lane**, 368
steamer **Kent**, 320
steamer **M W Chapin**, 394
steamer **Magnolia**, 62
steamer **Memphis**, 368, 394
steamer **Metacomet**, 423
steamer **Minnehaha**, 225
steamer **Niagara**, 324, 358
steamer **North Star**, 257
steamer **Ocean Spray**, 183, 201
steamer **Pacific**, 198
steamer **Pennsylvania**, 248
steamer **Perry**, 171
steamer **Persia**, 260, 263
steamer **Planter**, 211
steamer **Porcupine**, 324
steamer **President**, 222
steamer **San Jacinto**, 77, 341
steamer **Savannah**, 115
steamer **Southern Star**, 368, 394
steamer **Star of the West**, 258
steamer **Sultan**, 142
steamer **Water Witch**, 173, 218, 220
steamer **Water-witch**, 368
steamer **Water-Witch**, 394
steamer **Western Port**, 368
steamer **Westernport**, 394, 429
steamship **Agamemnon**, 321, 324
steamship Alps, 369
steamship **Ariel**, 464
steamship Austria, 369, 380, 401
steamship **Central America**, 111, 375
steamship **Hammonia**, 383
steamship **Indian Empire**, 443
steamship **James Adger**, 181
steamship **Oregon**, 357
steamship **Persia**, 218
steamship **Saladin**, 201
steamship **Susquehanna**, 194

Stearns, 423
Stebbins, 33
Stedman, 62, 94, 203, 204, 225, 235, 317
Steedman, 368
Steele, 30, 73, 111, 114, 173, 213, 231, 273, 393
Steen, 285
Steers, 73
Steger, 153
Steiger, 73
Steinbeck, 183
Stepel, 380
Stephens, 12, 176, 252, 402, 454
Stephenson, 51, 171, 427
Steptoe, 298, 405, 443
Sterett, 29
Sterling, 73
Sterrell, 78
Stettinius, 73, 232, 269
Steuart, 39, 159, 446
Stevens, 6, 12, 30, 48, 87, 93, 99, 130, 155, 159, 199, 220, 223, 241, 257, 395, 408, 424, 471
Stevenson, 26, 95, 113, 189, 246, 286, 316, 416, 417
Stewart, 5, 10, 34, 52, 55, 73, 101, 108, 121, 128, 136, 141, 145, 147, 148, 155, 196, 209, 217, 230, 231, 233, 272, 291, 323, 325, 338, 372, 394, 415, 421, 439
Stiles, 344
Stillude, 18
Stillwagon, 448
Stillwell, 372
Stimers, 218
Stimpson, 395
Stinchcomb, 73
Stinman, 201
Stirling, 281
Stith, 110
Stizig, 375
Stockbridge, 458
Stockett, 358
Stockton, 21, 27, 58, 164, 250
Stoddard, 164, 311, 352, 467
Stofer, 272

Stokely, 130
Stoll, 469
Stone, 19, 73, 90, 106, 117, 122, 136, 231, 243, 265, 271, 295, 305, 410, 448, 468
Stoneham, 19
Stonestreet, 73, 192, 291, 343
Stoops, 305, 306
Stoppel, 473
Storer, 271
storeship **Fredonia**, 135
storeship **Release**, 394
store-ship **Release**, 258
storeship **Supply**, 368, 394
Storrow, 136
Story, 164
Stott, 330, 447
Stoughton, 158
Stourton, 98
Stout, 171, 399
Stovall, 160
Stover, 145, 158, 230
Stovin, 244
Stow, 473
Stowell, 262
Stowes, 329
Strader, 85, 95
Strain, 462
Straining, 374
Strange, 73
Strassoldo, 51
Stratton, 85, 141, 172
Street, 73, 280, 477
Streng, 376
Stribling, 364, 382
Stribling Springs, 256
Stribling Springs School, 456
Strider, 37, 119, 126, 173, 276, 277
Stringer, 105
Stroacher, 424
Stromberger, 280
Strong, 78, 85, 414, 421, 430, 467
Stroop, 15, 39, 52, 60, 159
Strother, 252
Stroughton, 255
Stuart, 93, 101, 109, 153, 292, 355, 457

Stubb, 424
Stubbs, 180
Stuck, 90
Stuckey, 223, 227, 235, 247, 317
Stuckley, 163
Sturgeon, 379
Stuyvesant Pear Tree, 155
Styles, 1
Suddards, 37, 43, 60
Sudley, 179
Suit, 279, 306
Sullivan, 8, 32, 52, 73, 132, 157, 168, 169, 218, 237, 245, 257, 267, 350, 399, 400
Sully, 261
Sumby, 73
Summer Hill, 100
Summers, 178, 196, 367, 454
Summerscale, 73
Summerville, 475
Summy, 210
Sumner, 16, 97, 109, 116, 120, 178, 182, 298, 379
Sunderland, 153, 272, 297, 430
Sunster, 173
Surgenson, 375
Surgerizen, 370
Surratt, 349
Suter, 73, 103, 126, 201, 442
Suter's Fancy, 126
Sutherland, 208, 337
Sutter, 155
Sutton, 95, 142, 189, 223, 295, 422
Svensen, 380
Swain, 134, 274
Swan, 108
Swann, 23, 73, 238, 242, 297, 366, 416
Swansey, 3
Swanson, 13
Swanston, 13, 426
Swartwout, 473
Swartz, 229
Swasser, 230
Sweeney, 73, 424
Sweeny, 73, 75, 98, 127, 197, 231, 270, 288, 320, 397, 409

Sweeter, 214
Sweetser, 207
Swentzel, 122, 319, 468
Swentzell, 137, 146, 347
Swenzel, 379
Swertzeck, 380
Swett, 404
Swift, 208, 249, 394
Sylvester, 73, 310
Symmes, 311

T

Tabb, 123, 467
Tabler, 423
Taft, 294
Taggart, 68, 74
Tait, 11, 74
Talbert, 74, 275, 291, 361
Talbot, 18, 149, 216, 395
Talbott, 22
Talburtt, 358, 433
Talcott, 22, 102, 111, 129, 395, 454
Talfourd, 32
Taliaferro, 199, 207, 300, 345
Talks, 156
Tallian, 454
Tally-ho Razors, 449
Taltavuol, 248
Taney, 80
Tannatt, 286
Tanner, 438
Tansill, 393
Tappan, 97
Tardy, 297
Tarr, 471
Tarvin, 28, 224, 228, 246, 318
Tasistro, 200
Tasse, 375
Tasz, 370
Tate, 92, 212, 232, 307, 460
Tatnall, 18, 404
Tatsapaugh, 233
Tattnall, 472
Tatum, 420
Tayleure, 355
Tayloe, 68, 74, 302, 438

Taylor, 4, 11, 26, 27, 35, 43, 44, 45, 55, 57, 60, 70, 74, 78, 82, 85, 86, 91, 93, 97, 107, 111, 114, 115, 153, 168, 180, 181, 190, 201, 209, 210, 213, 219, 225, 228, 231, 233, 238, 241, 253, 271, 294, 297, 298, 311, 325, 342, 355, 374, 379, 394, 397, 400, 401, 406, 416, 424, 425, 426, 437, 440, 444, 445, 465, 466, 468
Taylor's Choice, 358
Taylor's Triangle, 358
Teachem, 177
Teasdale, 279, 368
Tebbs, 105, 309
Tebeau, 131
Teel, 437, 440
Telfair, 379
Temple, 4, 44, 203, 204, 247
Templeman, 92
Templeton, 122
Ten Broeck, 176, 236
Ten Eyck, 341, 394, 452, 453
Tenbrook, 59
Tenney, 74, 97
Tenny, 424
Tennyson, 265
Tepton, 93
Terbell, 240
Terrett, 249, 252, 411
Terrill, 19, 22
Terry, 378
Tetley, 114
Thanksgiving Day, 436
Thatcher, 473
Thaxter, 381
Thayer, 435
the **Mount Vernon Ladies Association**, 271
Thefeldt, 380
Theine, 255
Thiller, 375
Thillier, 370
Thistle, 55
Thocker, 289
Thom, 221

Thomas, 50, 55, 67, 74, 76, 83, 101, 105, 108, 118, 123, 138, 146, 153, 154, 156, 177, 218, 221, 231, 272, 287, 292, 295, 331, 374, 378, 381, 395, 425, 475
Thome, 61
Thompson, 22, 36, 46, 47, 65, 74, 95, 102, 118, 130, 131, 132, 135, 136, 143, 148, 160, 161, 168, 186, 195, 203, 204, 213, 221, 232, 236, 253, 261, 275, 280, 290, 330, 332, 358, 374, 375, 394, 395, 419, 427, 435
Thompsons, 358
Thoms, 471
Thomson, 20
Thorbecke, 369, 370
Thorburn, 29, 76, 238, 258
Thorn, 11, 74, 113, 190
Thornas, 463
Thornbury, 18
Thorndike, 109
Thorne, 55
Thornton, 30, 151, 202, 232, 295, 464
Thorwaldsen, 1
Thrall, 33
Threalkil, 377
Thrift, 23
Throckmorton, 19, 74
Thrush, 104
Thruston, 74, 390
Thumlert, 74
Thurlow, 134
Thurston, 34, 366
Thynne, 456
Thyson, 246, 386
Tiber creek, 25
Tice, 248
Ticknor, 250, 384
Tiemann, 194, 323, 443
Tiers, 33
Tighe, 257
Tilford, 465
Tilghman, 19, 74, 76, 101, 368, 395, 398
Tilley, 152, 218
Tillinghast, 426
Tillman, 161
Tillotson, 151, 263
Tilton, 237, 254
Timmons, 282, 307
Tinkler, 230
Tinokel, 370
Tippet, 170
Tippett, 26
Titus, 47
Tobin, 74
Tochman, 100
Todd, 25, 61, 74, 135, 158, 174, 195, 218, 219, 261, 314, 351, 400, 405, 449
Todsen, 74
Todstchinder, 347
Tol, 477
Toll, 74
Tollman, 34
Tollock, 375
Tolman, 326
Tomer, 371
Tomlinson, 139
Tompkins, 191, 296, 391
Toner, 270
Tongue, 105
Tonndorf, 160
Toole, 59, 96
Toombs, 166
Toomey, 174
Topham, 146
Torbert, 472
Torre, 198
Torrence, 78, 85, 280
Torrey, 34
Torryson, 105
Totten, 408
Toucey, 222, 309, 328, 438
Toulmin, 351
Tower, 162
Towers, 11, 74, 170, 365
Towle, 42, 74, 220
Towles, 167, 231, 267, 448
Town, 380
Towne, 373
Towner, 314
Towns, 78

Townsend, 14, 37, 43, 51, 150, 213, 266, 288, 300, 305, 359, 378, 392, 398, 476
Townshend, 178, 275
Towson, 144, 217, 225, 243
Tracey, 357, 380
Tracy, 48
Tranquillity, 31
transatlantic telegraph, 119
Tras, 370, 375
Trautwein, 423
Travers, 74, 356, 406
Treadway, 268
Tree, 239, 439
Treidhard, 444
Tremble, 52, 83, 164
Trenchard, 30
Trenholm, 11, 380, 426
Tretler, 89, 237
Trevitt, 20
Triay, 326
Trimble, 181
Trinchard, 436
Tripp, 308, 322
triumph complete, 333
Trome, 105
Trook, 74, 361
Trother, 130
Trott, 370
Trotter, 14, 23, 223, 247, 316
Troup, 278
True Delta, 272
Truesdale, 206
Truman's Point, 211
Trumbull, 263
Trumbulls, 121
Trunnel, 62, 154
Trunnell, 90, 179, 449
Trurentine, 399
Truxton, 253, 395
Tschiffely, 195
Tubman, 474
Tuck-A-Lix-Tah, 133
Tucker, 20, 33, 50, 74, 95, 128, 131, 136, 175, 190, 202, 232, 233, 273, 310, 356, 386, 454, 471, 473, 475
Tuckerman, 41, 180

Tudor, 104
Tufts, 360
Tunnell, 52
Turley, 373
Turnbull, 41, 137, 183, 196, 225, 282, 283, 287, 288, 469
Turnburke, 230
Turner, 20, 30, 41, 49, 74, 76, 78, 104, 105, 106, 129, 144, 163, 179, 181, 185, 223, 230, 247, 279, 287, 301, 302, 316, 338, 365, 416
Turpin, 420
Turton, 90, 239, 361, 429, 449
Turvin, 223, 235
Tustin, 106, 202, 419, 436, 439
Tuttle, 187
Twiggs, 123, 200, 399
Twomey, 231
Tyler, 38, 42, 43, 74, 88, 91, 153, 274, 306, 341, 360, 379, 403, 405, 406, 432, 446, 478
Tyng, 207, 447
Tyson, 62, 266
Tyzack, 35

U

Uber, 25
Ubes, 220
Ujehazy, 119
Ujhazy, 306
Ulmer, 339
Underhill, 421
Underwood, 8, 59, 202
Union Lands, 158
Uniontown, 140, 190
Upham, 365
Upperman, 273, 418
Upshur, 372, 421
Upton, 19, 441
Urriga, 130
Uttermohler, 74
Uttermuhle, 62, 127

V

Vadenhoff, 281

Vagner, 370
Vail, 53, 371
Vallandigham, 125
Valley Female Institute, 324
Valley View, 206
Valliere, 168, 238
Van Bibber, 117, 243
Van Bikelen, 287
Van Bol_elen, 285
Van Buren, 103, 124, 156, 377, 391, 477
Van Buskirk, 52, 77, 94, 140, 224, 243
Van Bussum, 409
Van Camp, 17, 242, 390, 424, 465, 466
Van Dean, 140
Van Der Roecke, 456
Van Dorn, 424, 425
Van Dyke, 167
Van Gilder, 302
Van Hensler, 313
Van Hook, 67, 190
Van Horn, 465
Van Horne, 284, 286, 288
Van Limburg, 342
Van Marum, 422
Van Ness, 12, 74
Van Norman, 246
Van Patten, 16, 74
Van Patton, 477
Van Reswick, 74, 202, 239, 449
Van Riswick, 289, 429
Van Sickell, 76, 188
Van Vliet, 286
Van Wert, 242
Van Winkle, 55
Van Zandt, 376
Vance, 198, 211, 310
Vanderken, 146
Vanderwerken, 391, 429, 464
Vanie, 122
Vansant, 394
Vantine, 94
Vanzandt, 394
Varick, 263
Varnell, 136
Varney, 467
Varnum, 143

Vase, 119
Vass, 74, 416
Vaucluse, 98
Vaughan, 221
Vaughn, 91, 416
Vaule, 368
Vaux, 185
Vedder, 145, 158, 199, 231
Veihmeyer, 74
Veitch, 105
Velle, 370
Venable, 20, 74, 210
Verbiski, 461
Verin, 370
Vermillion, 305
Vernon, 61, 361, 422
Verot, 181
vessel **Callao**, 427
vessel **Casual**, 427
vessel **Harraseeket**, 427
vessel **James McIndoe**, 89, 461
vessel **John Bryant**, 427
vessel **Lawrence Brown**, 427
vessel **Rapid**, 427
vessel **Shakspeare**, 427
vessel **Susan Fitzgerald**, 427
Vevan, 381
Vezin, 369, 375
Vickers, 441
Victor, 341
Vierbuchen, 441
Viers, 120
Vierstein, 20
Vilette, 234
Villa Estate, 7
Villa Lots, 190
Villarubia, 38, 203
Villeneuve, 263
Villere, 168
Villiger, 192
Vincent, 223, 230, 235, 247, 315, 471
Vincenti, 382
Vinson, 74, 230
Vinton, 96, 98, 304
Viti, 112
Volcker, 4, 25

Volger, 20
Vollerson, 370
Vollum, 198, 214
Von Humboldt, 80
Von Mengershausen, 369
Von Weber, 327
Voorhees, 87, 469, 472
Vorhees, 169
Voss, 231, 297, 344, 441

W

Waddell, 249, 289, 341
Wade, 58, 112, 154, 294, 471
Wadsworth, 252, 395
Wagner, 75, 78, 129, 151, 297, 375
Wagoner, 432
Wagstaff, 443
Wahl, 322
Wailes, 63
Wainright, 126
Wainwright, 84, 325, 473
Waire, 457
Waite, 178
Waits, 170
Wakefield, 183, 223, 225, 235, 317
Wakefield estate, 184
Wakelin, 161
Walbach, 4, 243, 473
Walback, 469
Walbridge, 381
Walcup, 340
Waldo, 396
Waldron, 56, 91, 126, 203, 205, 292
Waldrup, 85
Walker, 5, 6, 8, 9, 11, 17, 18, 19, 21, 29, 34, 41, 44, 53, 54, 74, 75, 112, 126, 136, 138, 140, 156, 185, 222, 223, 225, 230, 250, 264, 271, 284, 285, 288, 289, 294, 299, 314, 346, 361, 394, 397, 400, 420, 443, 455, 456, 459, 471
Wall, 12, 51, 84, 230, 261, 275, 357, 454
Wallace, 75, 87, 181, 193, 239, 269, 305, 357, 395, 416, 423, 443, 450, 457, 464

Wallach, 11, 67, 74, 97, 143, 197, 216, 237, 280, 283, 357, 399, 429, 431
Waller, 74, 415
Walling, 275
Wallingsford, 75, 154, 233
Walls, 71, 418
Walmsley, 13
Walnut Branch Farm, 312
Walnut Grove, 282
Walron, 119
Walsh, 36, 53, 75, 96, 117, 202, 271, 294, 329, 335, 361, 410, 431, 443
Walshe, 342
Walter, 83, 187, 204, 252, 280, 303, 454
Walters, 25, 74, 75, 146, 245, 307, 394
Waltham, 45
Walton, 109, 142, 170, 271, 387, 413, 444
Walworth, 75
Wankowiz, 149, 216
Wann, 252
Wannall, 145, 158
War of 1812, 254
Ward, 14, 20, 35, 36, 53, 59, 75, 98, 105, 111, 115, 119, 143, 230, 231, 235, 236, 281, 284, 285, 289, 302, 325, 388, 420, 425, 439, 449, 458, 461
Warde, 443
Warder, 174
Ware, 294, 398
Warfield, 35, 278
Waring, 91, 289, 327, 438
Warner, 110, 166, 248, 385, 472
Warren, 220, 252, 288, 294, 349, 421
Warriner, 6, 336
Warring, 75
Warrington, 372, 394
Warrock, 98
Warwick, 392
Washburn, 2
Washburnes, 353
Washington, 6, 12, 28, 75, 81, 82, 88, 102, 121, 122, 129, 143, 145, 147, 148, 169, 176, 184, 195, 206, 211, 218, 235, 253, 261, 266, 278, 294, 357, 360, 377, 387, 407, 455

Washington Cemetery, 212
Washington Theatre, 355
Wasson, 105, 168
Waterbury, 238
Waterhouse, 110
Waterloo, 32, 141
Waterman, 155
Waters, 11, 40, 62, 74, 75, 91, 179, 193, 220, 231, 271, 288, 289, 336, 370, 376, 388, 391
Watkins, 54, 78, 94, 206, 449
Watkinson, 3
Watmough, 75
Watner, 375
Watrous, 99
Watson, 74, 104, 115, 127, 164, 199, 205, 223, 401, 415, 424, 469, 473
Watt, 6, 361
Watterston, 74, 75, 339
Watts, 52, 109, 183, 263, 275
Waugh, 54, 92, 104, 105, 113, 196, 231
Wayne, 268, 275
Weakley, 282
Weaver, 75, 93, 148, 467
Webb, 25, 53, 54, 62, 74, 75, 77, 95, 99, 109, 114, 122, 141, 142, 158, 168, 172, 179, 202, 223, 232, 235, 245, 246, 394, 399, 416, 436
Weber, 384
Webster, 63, 156, 212, 215, 243, 254, 261, 302, 344, 376, 411
Wector, 272
Wedding Presents, 297
Weed, 75, 94
Weeden, 27
Weekley, 289
Weeks, 43, 125, 152, 205
Weems, 27, 95, 113, 130, 140, 159, 211, 246, 360
Wegler, 417
Wehr, 446
Weichel, 91
Weightman, 11, 49, 160, 269, 278
Weisker, 370
Weiskirch, 255
Weisner, 282

Weiss, 139
Weissenborn, 369
Welban, 227
Welbourn Hall, 348
Welch, 4, 74, 435, 464
Welder, 168
Wellbeloved, 379
Welles, 440
Wellesley, 420
Wellingsford, 90
Wells, 136, 157, 220, 231, 309, 344, 420, 471
Welsh, 2, 35, 65, 75, 101, 220, 232, 328, 393, 410
Welty, 106
Wemple, 378
Wendel, 375
Wendell, 11, 19, 219, 232, 370
Wenkheim, 51
Wentworth, 43, 236, 376, 472
Wepfer, 370
Wepper, 375
Werckmuller, 398
Werner, 328, 475
Wertz, 350
Wesley, 104, 441
West, 30, 37, 53, 61, 74, 75, 122, 132, 144, 173, 183, 207, 219, 241, 276, 294, 318, 382, 427, 442, 456, 459
West Point Academy, 297
Westcott, 76
Westerfield, 20
Weston, 45, 59, 147, 165, 210, 342
Westphalia Tract, 260
Westwood, 105
Wetherall, 53
Wetherell, 113
Wetmore, 122
Weummer, 181
Wever, 164
Whalen, 74, 295
Whaley, 11
Whaling, 232
Whalton, 299
Wharton, 3, 102, 122, 220, 250, 394, 444
Wheat, 103, 237, 240, 451

Wheatley, 75, 97, 250, 345, 401
Wheaton, 387, 428, 460
Wheeler, 74, 75, 105, 111, 130, 173, 185, 220, 233, 238, 298, 394, 452, 476
Wheelock, 168, 299, 336
Wheelright, 152
Whelan, 74, 128, 180, 181, 265
Whipple, 243, 409
White, 11, 15, 75, 85, 86, 87, 101, 105, 107, 109, 111, 124, 130, 139, 144, 146, 159, 161, 185, 193, 194, 261, 285, 286, 288, 297, 314, 321, 323, 327, 360, 369, 386, 410, 427, 449, 459, 471
White Haven, 326
Whitehead, 26, 27, 203, 204, 219
Whiteley, 133
Whiteness, 59
Whitfield, 153, 241
Whiting, 30, 126, 183, 197, 215, 308, 336
Whitlock, 59, 152
Whitman, 311, 463
Whitmore, 340
Whitney, 53, 75, 76, 83, 103, 154
Whittier, 164
Whittington, 11
Whittle, 29, 472
Whittlesey, 9, 149, 294, 444
Whitwell, 38
Wiber, 136
Wickham, 416
Wickliff, 295
Widdicombe, 395
Widsentz, 380
Wiebly, 34
Wiedmann, 370
Wiedmayer, 337
Wiest, 78
Wigg, 459
Wiggins, 332
Wight, 477
Wightman, 207
Wiglesworth, 305
Wigton, 36
Wiland, 427

Wilcox, 74, 87, 93, 189, 237, 241, 287, 304, 371
Wild, 154
Wildniss, 370
Wildrick, 284, 295
Wiley, 23, 39
Wilkerson, 74
Wilkes, 74, 203
Wilkins, 17, 99, 113, 279, 398
Wilkinson, 27, 30, 44, 174, 213, 214, 341, 394
Willard, 229, 401, 409
Willcomb, 241
Willcox, 284, 415, 416
Willett, 130, 243, 270, 408
Willey, 344
Williams, 15, 22, 28, 30, 34, 49, 53, 55, 66, 71, 74, 75, 79, 81, 83, 86, 95, 98, 105, 110, 117, 118, 130, 135, 141, 149, 159, 161, 163, 165, 172, 177, 195, 199, 205, 213, 218, 221, 224, 232, 242, 250, 254, 256, 261, 271, 280, 281, 286, 296, 298, 300, 303, 319, 327, 331, 340, 348, 349, 372, 379, 394, 415, 421, 424, 427, 437, 442, 459, 478
Williamsborough, 102
Williamson, 230, 273, 296, 310, 312, 330, 341, 363, 469, 473
Willian, 373, 400, 401
Willing, 216
Willink, 75
Willis, 28, 33, 98, 101, 106, 166, 343
Williss, 228
Willits, 240
Willmuth, 18
Willner, 242
Wills, 76
Wilmuth, 279
Wilson, 7, 13, 21, 34, 47, 48, 74, 75, 90, 104, 105, 122, 131, 147, 149, 163, 164, 179, 184, 190, 227, 230, 239, 242, 254, 265, 268, 271, 272, 279, 307, 311, 322, 349, 374, 386, 388, 393, 394, 427, 428, 458, 476
Wiltberger, 74, 310, 386

Wimsatt, 75, 201, 271
Winch, 213
Winchester, 366
Winder, 66, 74, 75, 107, 112, 113, 197, 298, 360, 399, 405
Windsor, 251, 304
Wineberger, 107
Winfield, 232
Wingard, 157, 230
Wingen, 235
Wingerd, 80, 106
Wingman, 105
Winn, 3, 41, 102
Winne, 321
Winner, 240
Winslow, 94, 379
Winter, 454
Wirt, 2, 25, 75
Wise, 19, 38, 75, 117, 136, 153, 184, 233, 264, 270, 279, 281, 283, 321, 362, 472
Wiseman, 328
Wisenborne, 231
Witherell, 17, 132, 134, 424
Withers, 405, 447
Witte, 309, 370, 375
Wittenauer, 68
Wlodecki, 95, 113, 157, 246
Wm & Mary College, 195
Woff, 375
Wogan, 13, 157
Wolcott, 124
Woldecki, 27
Wolf, 105, 232
Wolfe, 166
Wolff, 105
Wolfk, 370
Wollard, 61
Wollaston's manor, 187
Wollaston's Manor, 379
Wolle, 294
Wolsten, 376
Womrath, 139
Wood, 13, 62, 74, 75, 107, 138, 157, 162, 167, 171, 189, 207, 210, 212, 232, 262, 284, 287, 292, 301, 313, 366, 393, 402, 411, 465
Woodbourne, 174
Woodbridge, 390
Woodbury, 35, 426
Woodcock, 152
Woodford, 248
Woodhull, 393, 454
Wooding, 388
Woodland, 340
Woodlands, 133, 136
Woodruff, 15
Woods, 13, 24, 75, 244, 312, 447
Woodside, 208
Woodson, 241, 328
Woodward, 11, 31, 40, 60, 75, 94, 97, 108, 113, 202, 244, 250, 256, 262, 303, 323, 405, 439, 444, 446, 456, 457, 471
Woodworth, 234
Wool, 97, 123
Woolard, 289
Woolfolk, 142
Woolley, 160, 470
Woolman, 34
Woolsey, 473
Wooster, 174, 225
Wootton, 281
Worden, 104
Worth, 313, 379
Wortham, 415
Worthington, 134, 187, 243, 348, 353, 398, 477
Wortman, 193
Wozencraft, 227
Wretholm, 477
Wright, 6, 11, 19, 23, 62, 74, 101, 108, 111, 130, 176, 194, 223, 227, 229, 232, 236, 250, 284, 288, 294, 322, 326, 405, 417, 435, 437, 455, 461, 477
Wroe, 45, 71, 75, 269
Wulf, 370
Wunnschmann, 370
Wunschmann, 375
Wurst, 78
Wyatt, 39, 93, 248

Wyers, 354
Wylie, 33, 260
Wyman, 20, 158
Wynkoop, 42
Wyse, 360
Wysham, 395
Wysong, 105

Y

yacht **Charter Oak**, 202
yacht **Surprise**, 236
Yah-hah-Toxica, 31
Yale College, 42, 80, 107, 304, 320, 328
Yancey, 250, 335
Yancy, 82, 377
Yandes, 104
Yarboro, 338
Yates, 191, 294
Yazoo plantation, 343
Yeatman, 341, 354, 359
yellow fever, 335, 363
Yellow fever, 357
Yelton, 34
Yerby, 75
Yerger, 301
Yobi, 194
Yonley, 99
York, 46, 324
Young, 26, 45, 49, 54, 75, 76, 95, 104, 105, 111, 117, 121, 129, 157, 167, 169, 181, 205, 210, 221, 224, 227, 232, 249, 253, 254, 262, 271, 295, 319, 329, 338, 359, 362, 363, 388, 394, 429, 436, 449, 454
Younger, 75
Yules, 283

Z

Zaliousky, 443
Zantzinger, 199
Zappone, 451
Zarver, 33
Zeilin, 176
Zell, 210
Zellers, 75
Zimmerman, 34, 379
Zitz, 375
Zoar, 419
Zollicoffer, 348

Other Heritage Books by Joan M. Dixon:

National Intelligencer *Newspaper Abstracts Special Edition: The Civil War Years Volume 1: January 1, 1861-June 30, 1863*
National Intelligencer *Newspaper Abstracts Special Edition: The Civil War Years Volume 2: July 1, 1863-December 31, 1865*
National Intelligencer *Newspaper Abstracts 1858*
National Intelligencer *Newspaper Abstracts 1857*
National Intelligencer *Newspaper Abstracts 1856*
National Intelligencer *Newspaper Abstracts 1855*
National Intelligencer *Newspaper Abstracts 1854*
National Intelligencer *Newspaper Abstracts 1853*
National Intelligencer *Newspaper Abstracts 1852*
National Intelligencer *Newspaper Abstracts 1851*
National Intelligencer *Newspaper Abstracts 1850*
National Intelligencer *Newspaper Abstracts 1849*
National Intelligencer *Newspaper Abstracts 1848*
National Intelligencer *Newspaper Abstracts 1847*
National Intelligencer *Newspaper Abstracts 1846*
National Intelligencer *Newspaper Abstracts 1845*
National Intelligencer *Newspaper Abstracts 1844*
National Intelligencer *Newspaper Abstracts 1843*
National Intelligencer *Newspaper Abstracts 1842*
National Intelligencer *Newspaper Abstracts 1841*
National Intelligencer *Newspaper Abstracts 1840*
National Intelligencer *Newspaper Abstracts, 1838-1839*
National Intelligencer *Newspaper Abstracts, 1836-1837*
National Intelligencer *Newspaper Abstracts, 1834-1835*
National Intelligencer *Newspaper Abstracts, 1832-1833*
National Intelligencer *Newspaper Abstracts, 1830-1831*
National Intelligencer *Newspaper Abstracts, 1827-1829*
National Intelligencer *Newspaper Abstracts, 1824-1826*
National Intelligencer *Newspaper Abstracts, 1821-1823*
National Intelligencer *Newspaper Abstracts, 1818-1820*
National Intelligencer *Newspaper Abstracts, 1814-1817*
National Intelligencer *Newspaper Abstracts, 1811-1813*
National Intelligencer *Newspaper Abstracts, 1806-1810*
National Intelligencer *Newspaper Abstracts, 1800-1805*

www.ingramcontent.com/pod-product-compliance
Lightning Source LLC
Chambersburg PA
CBHW060908300426
44112CB00011B/1382